DATE DUE

NOV 2 3 2004		
NOV 1 9 2007		

Movements and
Issues in
World Religions

MOVEMENTS AND ISSUES IN WORLD RELIGIONS

A Sourcebook and Analysis of Developments Since 1945

RELIGION, IDEOLOGY, AND POLITICS

EDITED BY
Charles Wei-hsun Fu AND Gerhard E. Spiegler

GREENWOOD PRESS

NEW YORK • WESTPORT, CONNECTICUT • LONDON

Library of Congress Cataloging-in-Publication Data

Movements and issues in world religions.

Bibliography: p.
Includes index.
Contents: v. 1. Religion, ideology, and politics.
1. Religion—History—20th century.   I. Fu, Charles
Wei-hsun.   II. Spiegler, Gerhard E.
BL98.M68   1987   291.1'7'0904   86-4634
ISBN 0-313-23238-5 (lib. bdg. : v. 1 : alk. paper)

Library of Congress Catalog Card Number: 86-4634
ISBN 0-313-23238-5

First published in 1987

Greenwood Press, Inc.
88 Post Road West, Westport, Connecticut 06881

Printed in the United States of America

The paper used in this book complies with the Permanent Paper Standard
issued by the National Information Standards Organization (Z39.48-1984).

10 9 8 7 6 5 4 3 2 1

Copyright Acknowledgments

The authors and publisher gratefully acknowledge permission to reproduce excerpts from
the following copyrighted materials:

Donald Eugene Smith, *India As a Secular State*. Copyright © 1963 by Princeton University
Press. Excerpts, pp. 455, 456, 460, 462, 468, and 471-72 reprinted with permission of
Princeton University Press.

*Dharma and Development: Religion As Resource in the Sarvodaya Movement, Revised
Edition* by Joanna Macy. Copyright © 1985 by Kumarian Press. Reprinted by
permission of Kumarian Press, Inc.

Paul Mojzes, *Christian-Marxist Dialogue in Eastern Europe*, pp. 222-29. Copyright © 1981
Augsberg Publishing House. Reprinted with permission of Augsberg Publishing House.

Paul Mojzes, "The Current Status of the Christian-Marxist Dialogue and Suggested
Guidelines for Conducting the Dialogue," in *Journal of Ecumenical Studies* Vol. 15, no.
1 (Winter, 1978): 4-9. Reprinted by permission of the *Journal of Ecumenical Studies*.

Contents

III. Religion and Politics in Developed Nations

IV. Marxism, Religion, and Politics

V. The Holocaust: Christian/Jewish Reflections

Preface

The forty years since the end of the Second World War in 1945 have been marked by constant, rapid, and sometimes profound changes in the political and religious landscape. East and West have become more distant as they have grown closer together. The dominance of the "developed nations" continues politically and economically but is now checked by the assertiveness of the "developing nations." Religion, rather than receding in prominence, has manifested its staying power and, as in the case of Islam, has become the lever for social and political change. In the "developed" and "developing" nations, religion is being reexamined and recognized as a powerful socio-political force, one that must be taken into account even in the ideological world of Marxism.

The year 1945 did not bring peace to a world shaken by the horror of the Holocaust; it did not bring even an absence of war. Conflict, political and religious, has become a constant feature of the political landscape as evidenced in Northern Ireland, the Middle East, Latin America, and Southeast Asia. Religion, in sometimes subtle and sometimes blatant ways, continues to be a partner in this conflict even as it struggles to reassert itself as a force for peace and human understanding.

Christian-Jewish relations have been permanently altered by the Holocaust, an experience not yet digested as the chapters by Nora Levin and Clark Williamson make quite clear. The world of Islam in turn is caught in the struggle with tradition and modernity while Roman Catholicism grapples with a new understanding of itself as a religious and social force in modern society. There is no doubt that religion permeates the socio-political life of modern societies at all levels. Evidence for this can be found in the United States and in Latin America, in Lebanon and in Northern Ireland, in Pakistan and India, and in Japan and even in the USSR.

The religious world of the last forty years is characterized by diversity and pluralism. Western and Eastern religions, traditional and new religions, are interactive social-political forces that cannot be ignored if one is to understand the development of contemporary social forces. It has become increasingly clear that politics has religious dimensions, religion has political dimensions, and both have ideological components.

The chapters in this volume are analytical and descriptive in character, offering critical insights into diverse political, religious, and ideological traditions and their interaction in diverse regions of the world. The attached selected bibliographies should guide the reader in the attempt to form an independent judgment on the various topics covered, providing an opportunity to discover alternative positions and greater detail. All chapters provide in-depth introductions leading to further study. They are meant to circumscribe and to define but not to be definitive.

We are very grateful to Greenwood Press for their valuable advice, assistance, understanding, patience, and suggestions from beginning to end. We wish to express our full appreciation to Jerome Carter, research assistant in the Department of Religion, Temple University, for his editorial help at the final stage. Last but not least, the contributors of this volume all deserve our high praise for their cooperation and scholarly work.

C.W.F. and G.E.S.

Abbreviations

ABPO	All-Burma Peasants' Organization
ABTUC	All-Burma Trade Union Congress
ACBC	All-Ceylon Buddhist Congress
AFPFL	Anti-Fascist People's Freedom League
APRA	Alianza Popular Revolucionaria Americana
BRA	Bureau of Religious Affairs
BSSP	Bolshevik Samma Samaja Party
CBA	Chinese Buddhist Association
CCC	China Christian Council
CP	Communist Party
EBP	Eksath Bhikkhu Peramuna
FP	Tamil Federal Party
GCBA	General Council of Burmese Associations
GNP	gross national product
IRA	Irish Republican Army
IRB	Irish Republican Brotherhood
JCP	Japan Communist Party
JEC	Juventude Estudiantil Católica
JUC	Juventude Universitária Católica
JVP	Jatika Vimukti Peramuna
LEBM	Lanka Eksath Bhikkhu Mandalaya

LSSP	Lanak Samma Samaja Party
MEB	Movimento de Educação
MEP	Mahajana Eksath Peramuna
NCCC	National Council of Christian Churches
NOW	National Organization of Women
NSF	National Science Foundation
OPEC	Organization of Petroleum Exporting Countries
PDRY	People's Democratic Republic of Yemen
PLO	Palestinian Liberation Organization
PQLI	physical quality of life index
RSS	Rashitriya Swayamsevak Sangh (National Volunteer Organization)
SLFP	Sri Lanka Freedom Party
TFP	Tradição, Família, e Propiedade
TM	Transcendental Meditation
TULF	Tamil United Liberation Front
UF	United Front
UNP	United National Party
UR	United Research
UVF	Ulster Volunteer Force
WCIW	World Community of Islam in the West
YMBA	Young Men's Buddhist Association

I

INTERRELIGIOUS CONFLICTS

1

The Arab-Israeli Conflict

TAMARA SONN

> I consider the Jewish question neither a social nor a religious one, even
> though it sometimes takes these and other forms. It is a national question.[1]

With that, Theodor Herzl at once focused the direction of the movement that
would eventually lead to the establishment of the state of Israel, and highlighted
the irony of what would be one of the most protracted and tragic wars in modern
history. Jews, persecuted for centuries for religious differences, established a *why?*
state in order to preserve the integrity of their community. But in so doing they
denied the rights of the indigenous inhabitants of that state. Those inhabitants,
followers of still a different religion, felt it their sacred duty to protect their own
community. Having exhausted moral and political appeals for justice, they continue to find strength only in their religious conviction. Islam, therefore, has
become the rallying cry of a war against the Israelis, who defend themselves in
the name of Judaism. Aside from the blatant incongruity of fighting in the name
of the single, all-merciful and loving creator, God, in whom both sides profess
ultimate faith, there are two further levels of irony in this war. First, it is
essentially a political war which finds both its justification and strategic strength
in religion. Second, and even more striking, no two religions are closer in ethical
structure than Judaism and Islam.

JEWISH AND ISLAMIC ETHICS

Both Judaism and Islam distinguish themselves from Christianity on the basis
of ethics. There are, of course, theological differences among the three Abra-

---

Note: Select terms used in this chapter are defined in the end-of-chapter glossary.

hamic religions. But in the case of Judaism and Islam, the benchmark of such differences is in ethics. Both religions hold ethics to be of primary importance, contending that Christianity, by contrast, considers theology above and beyond ethics. This is not to say that Judaism and Islam place ethics before theology. In both cases ethics is part of theology, whereas in Christianity theology is distinct from ethics. In the Christian context, theology deals with the individual's relationship to God, whereas ethics concerns man's relationship to another. In Judaism and Islam, ethics is an explication of the individual's proper response to God. This is so much the case that until the modern period there has been little in the way of philosophical or historical explications of Jewish or Islamic ethics. Rather, the recommendations and conclusions of speculation on man's response to God have been embedded in religious law. Hence, the primacy of Halakhah (Jewish law) and Sharī'a (Islamic law), relative to canon or Christian law. In a description of Islamic law which could equally apply to Jewish law, Fazlur Rahman says:

. . . [it] is not strictly speaking law, since much of it embodies moral and quasi-moral precepts not enforceable in any court. Further, Islamic law, though a certain part of it came to be enforced almost uniformly throughout the Muslim world . . . is on closer examination a body of legal opinions or, as Santillana put it, "an endless discussion of the duties of a Muslim," rather than a neatly formulated code or codes.[2]

Perhaps the difference between the Jewish and Islamic model and that of Christianity can be traced to the influence of Greek philosophical categories on Christian doctrine. Greek philosophy is generally divided into the theoretical sciences and the practical sciences. Theology is among the theoretical, whereas ethics is among the practical. Christian thinkers, following this scheme, developed a sizable body of literature dealing with ethics, albeit in a theocentric context. Since the Middle Ages, these works have been at the heart of Christian doctrine. In Judaism and Islam, however, theological and philosophical speculation holds a different place in the body of belief. Although it is possible to find philosophical treatises on ethics among their writings, such writings are not central to religious doctrine. In fact, the failure of Islamic speculative philosophy to deal with the fundamental issues facing Islamic society in the Middle Ages led to its being virtually expunged from Islamic curricula at the time. Similar sentiment has been expressed about Jewish speculative philosophy. Samuel David Luzzatto, the nineteenth-century scholar of Italian Jewry, refused to consider medieval Jewish philosophers as representative of genuine Jewish morality. They had substituted intellectualism for moral value, encouraged a kind of strict asceticism unsuitable for the common person, and, in their intolerance of non-Jews, deviated from Jewish universalism.[3]

The Greek/Christian schema has remained dominant, however, just as Christian society has maintained political ascendancy since the Middle Ages. And perhaps not surprisingly, parallel to overall trends of Western society, the autonomy of ethics has led to the utter secularization of ethics. Because the West considers itself a pluralistic society, ethics is seen as the province of no single religious tradition but rather something that can be dealt with outside religion. Both Islam and Judaism have reacted against this secularization. In their effort to maintain the virtue of their respective communities, each has criticized secularism and set out, as a result, to extricate from religious law those principles that deal specifically with human social relations.

In the case of Judaism, ethics became a conscious question toward the end of the nineteenth century. After centuries of statelessness, through periods of greater and less persecution, Jews faced essentially three alternatives. They could attempt either to be assimilated entirely into the culture of the countries in which they lived, eradicating obvious social, cultural, or religious distinctions among them; they could remain aloof within those countries, maintaining and practicing Jewish values on a limited, communal scale; or they could look toward the establishment of a Jewish state. Each of the three alternatives brought up the same question: What is it to live a truly Jewish life? There was a felt need to distinguish Jewish morality from the prevailing, Christian-dominated trends. Is Jewish morality significantly different from Christian or secular morality? If so, what are its implications? In Islam, the case was slightly different. Islam had had state organization since its inception. However, since the sixteenth century, the Ottomans had dominated the Islamic world and were not always perceived as exemplary Islamic leaders. What was more, their domain had been subject to inroads by Western nations since at least the nineteenth century. With the developments of the twentieth century and the Ottoman's inevitable demise, Muslims found themselves with the unique responsibility to recreate an Islamic world. It was assumed all the while that Islamic morality was indeed different from Christian morality, and that the present decline of the Islamic world was due to lax religious practice. Believing a return to true Islamic practice would result in a society strong enough to resist foreign domination, the question was therefore, "What is true Islamic practice?"

The first comprehensive and systematic ethics of Judaism appeared in 1898, *Die Ethik des Judenthums,* by Moritz Lazarus (d. 1903). Jewish morality, according to Lazarus, is based on an ideal of piety expressed through moral perfection. Internal religious conviction must express itself in moral behavior. Moral behavior consists in the submission of personal desires to divinely inspired moral law. Therefore, Jewish law is referred to as "the way" to moral perfection, in the same way Islamic law is called *sharī'a,* which means "the way." It is the way to infuse the material world with spiritual values and thus sanctify human life. The way contains virtues, duties, and the social institutions needed to sustain them. In each age, the rabbis had studied, interpreted, and refined the classical sources of Jewish law in contemporary terms, and that process must continue even in the modern age. The tradition was, therefore, not a set of strictly defined rules but a set of principles. It is "to guide conscience, not fetter it; to whet the mind, not blunt it."[4]

This process may lead to occasional contradictions and aberrant points of view, but there remains a *Gesamtgeist,* a common spirit of Jewish morality transmitted from age to age. And its major characteristic is social. Jewish ethics, Lazarus says, is social ethics. The moral ideal is an ideal of a moral society. Only God is truly holy. Individual human beings can only hope to aspire to goodness by contributing to social welfare. For this reason, Jewish law is full of social legislation and institutions to relieve the plight of the poor and suffering. The harmony and well-being of the community is the goal of Jewish ethics. Every individual is responsible of this task, and the goal is, accordingly, universal social justice.

This social justice ethic is not merely the following of an externally imposed law. It is the inevitable response to personal conviction, the only possible response to God truly recognized. Lazarus cites Genesis 3:22 in this context. "See, man is unique, of himself knowing good and evil."[5] Once an individual truly confronts God, his response will be worship; and worship will be expressed in social virtue. God, therefore, is the ultimate source of Jewish ethics. God is "the source and archetype of the moral idea. He is morality personified and realized or rather the moral idea itself."[6] Still, the ideal is not achievement of a goal as such, not a static end state of eternal bliss, as in Christianity. Rather, as in Islam, the ideal is a dynamic, a process, a proper way of behavior in response to recognition of the ultimate oneness and goodness of God.

Hermann Cohen (1842–1918), a contemporary of Lazarus, criticized certain aspects of Lazarus's work. Yet his fundamental ethical value reflected that of Lazarus: The universality of ethical or social virtues as a necessary consequence of belief in the one, supreme God: "Only the idea of God gives me the confidence that morality will become reality on earth. And because I cannot live without this confidence, I cannot live without God."[7] This universal ideal is nothing less than the Kingdom of God on earth. It is the victory of good over evil in human relations, both individual and collective, that is, on a national level. On the question of establishing a Jewish state, Cohen was openly critical. The goal of Jewish social ethics, he said, is not a nationalistic one. "The Jewish question is not limited to a geographically or socio-politically isolated people."[8] On the contrary, the goal revealed by the prophets requires the independence of religion. Religion, its values and morals, cannot be dominated by the state. It is not merely an instrument of social control. True ethical behavior is a personal response to inner conviction. As such, religion must remain independent of the state; its independence allows for unprejudiced moral criticism of society. The political value of religion is that it transcends individual states. It "directs thought beyond all laws, statutes and political states of present reality. This is the meaning of the Kingdom of God as the ideal of world history."[9]

Therefore, true ethics is a process. There is no ideal of a past to which we should aspire. Rather, the ideal of social ethics derives significance from the moral struggle. It is the tension between what should be and what is that drives human history. What is sought is not so much perfection as responsibility to strive for social justice. And here Cohen distinguishes Jewish from Christian ethics. The focus of ethics in Christianity is the individual. Jesus came to redeem each individual soul. In Judaism, on the other hand, the emphasis is on striving to create a social order based on individual equality.

More recently, Emil Fackenheim has taken up the theme of social striving in Judaism.[10] He begins with an affirmation of Jewish ethics as social ethics:

If there is a single religious affirmation which, first coming with Judaism into the world, has remained basic to Jewish belief until today, it is that God on high loves widows and orphans below; and that He commands men, from on high, to do His will in the social order below. Elsewhere, too, men have had an awareness of the Divine, and a sense of responsibility in the social realm. It was the distinctive contribution of the Hebrew prophets to proclaim that the two cannot be rent apart; that men ought to treat each other as created in the image of a God who challenges them to this task.[11]

Man's task is to close the gap between the "religious and the social," or secular. It is this which comprises the "prophetic imperative." The religious world is divine, however, and the social world human. The ultimate question regarding the prophetic imperative, then, concerns the nature of their relationship. The social realm is the arena for realization of the prophetic imperative. But it is fraught with complexities that render the mere statement of the prophetic imperative useless. It must be made practically applicable.

Here Fackenheim points out what he considers the most important implication of the prophetic imperative. It requires social organization, and all social organization involves power. But power in and of itself is amoral. Therefore, we are confronted with a dilemma. Either we must maintain a distance from this amoral realm of power, in order to maintain moral purity, but at the same time removing ourselves from that very realm where lie our responsibilities, or we must seek power and compromise moral purity. There is only one solution to this dilemma, he claims. We must face up to the need for power in order to establish social justice, yet resist all the while the temptation to use power as a coercive means. That is, power must not be used to force cooperation in any social order; piety consists only in voluntary submission to moral law. Yet it is necessary to implement social measures required to alleviate suffering and realize social justice. Religion must meet this challenge:

A religion which confines itself to general principles condemns itself to ineffectiveness and innocuousness. The Hebrew prophets, in contrast, were neither innocuous nor ineffective. And this was because they asserted the will of God, not in terms of abstract general principles but in and for the here and now.[12]

Fackenheim stops short of specific directives regarding such a use of power. Rather, he claims that the "positive and concrete" link between the spiritual and the social orders is to be found, "not in rules and principles but in a believing attitude."[13] "The believing attitude must . . . stubbornly insist that the will of

God is to be done in the social world of man, and that we are responsible for our share in it.'' The implication is that no individual can escape moral decisions. In fact, as Fackenheim puts it, ''There is no situation which is morally and religiously neutral.'' Every individual in every act is responsible for contributing to the Kingdom of God on earth.

Again, the message is universal. Human responsibility will not cease until social justice extends to every individual. That is the task of Jewish ethics, the prophetic imperative. ''This believing attitude can never forget that so long as the divine image is violated even in one single human being, the Kingdom of God on earth is incomplete.''[14] The utter lack of practical advice on how to implement this prophetic imperative does not detract from its accuracy as a reflection of Jewish ethics. It is an effort to make explicit the expectations of human behavior in society resulting from Jewish faith.

The great Jewish scholar, Eliezar Berkovits, in this context calls for intense study of sacred law. But that scholarship must be couched in an understanding of the ''purpose and functioning of the *halakhah*,'' and the scholars themselves must be fully familiar with the community within which the law is to be applied. ''There is no *halakhah* of the ivory tower. The attitude toward human needs is decisive.''[15]

Is it really so that, because of the unfortunate transformation of the Oral Torah into a stubborn text, nothing can be done until we have succeeded in reversing the process from the text to the living word? There are vast possibilities still present in the *halakhah* to come to grips with problems arising from the contemporary situation.[16]

The ''attitude toward human needs'' is again a reference to the overall social vision central to Judaism. Thus, whether discussing the application of religious law in general, the virtues of religious society as opposed to secular society, the need to establish a state in order to implement religious values or the threat national organization might pose to those religious values, the point on which there is no disagreement is that the principles involved are those that are supposed to guide human behavior to a just social order.

This same theme, the continuing moral struggle to establish a just society on earth, is paramount in Islamic ethical literature. So-called Islamic modernist literature, in fact, is no more than an attempt to revive, explicate, and implement this spirit as the antidote to Islamic decline. The first representatives of this movement were Jamal al-Din al-Afghani (1838–1897) and his disciple Muhammad Abduh (1849–1905). More activist than intellectual, Afghani wrote mainly analyses of the policies of the Great Powers in the Muslim world, along with an exposition of the inner weaknesses of Islam and a call to all Muslims to cure them. He was concerned with spiritual unity, the spirit of cooperation. Each member of the community should feel responsible for the welfare of the whole. Each should desire to live and work together for the common welfare. Yet even this spirit of cooperation could be perverted if it were not guided by Islamic principles. And Islamic guidance directed cooperation to all mankind. Religious solidarity, that is, does not prevent links with communities of other faiths. He said, "There should be good relations and harmony in what pertains to national interest between you and your compatriots and neighbors who adhere to diverse religions."[17]

Still, the strongest bond lay in Islam. And certainly for Muslims, no natural solidarity (language, for example) could replace the bond of Islam. Without it society dissolves, and that is exactly what has led Muslims to their present pitiful state, Afghani claimed. Islamic unity is the unity of hearts and deeds. Islam is the one true, complete, and perfect religion, which satisfies all the desires of the human spirit. And the barometer of this faith? Action. Islam means activity, Afghani said. The true attitude of Muslims is not one of passive resignation to whatever might come, as the will of God. Man is responsible to God for all his acts. He is responsible for the welfare of society. His success or failure is his own. This is what the Qur'an teaches: "God changes not what is in a people until they change what is in themselves."

A far more systematic thinker and prolific writer was Muhammad Abduh. Like Afghani, he began with the problem of inner decay in Islam and the need for revival. Because the message of Islam is unique, Abduh believed the decay in question was peculiar to Islamic society. The Prophet Muhammad had set out to found a virtuous society. The problem was how to bridge the gap between what should be and what was. And the first problem was that of secularization. Abduh expressed this theory in a series of articles on Islamic law. He said all things were created with natural laws. If a being goes beyond its natural law (or form), it is in danger of destruction. For societies, those laws are "the moral laws which limit human behavior . . . They are set down by men of knowledge and wisdom in books of ethics and human education, after they have found expression in divine commandments."[18] But "laws vary as the conditions of nations vary." To be effective they must have some relation to the circumstances of the country to which they apply. Therefore, the simple importation of European laws to Islamic nations could not work. It was this adoption of European laws and European education, in the place of Islamic law and Islamic education, that was destroying the moral base of Islamic society.

But unlike Afghani, Abduh said the solution did not lay in returning to the norm of the past. Rather, the solution lay in accepting the need for change, but linking it to Islamic principles. In fact, he wanted to show that changes were not only permitted in Islam, but were actually necessary implications of Islam when rightly understood. Islam is both a principle of change and a guide or control over it. It contains within itself all the potentialities of rational religion: both social science and moral code. Truly understood and practiced, then, Islam is true civilization. It is based on a simple doctrinal structure consisting of certain beliefs about the greatest questions of human life and principles of human conduct. Those bases, the Qur'an and the Sunna, however, contain only general principles. The true Muslim must use his reason in the affairs of the world, applying religious principles to specific circumstances. That is the spirit of Islamic law; individuals must recognize their social responsibility and act on Islamic principles accordingly. The individual's participation in this process on earth assures happiness in heaven. In this sense, Islam, Abduh says, is a true sociology. It is the science of individual and social happiness in this world and the next. When Islamic law is fully understood and applied, society/civilization flourish.

Hasan al-Banna' (1906–1949), the founder of the Muslim Brotherhood (1928), is representative of the next generation of Islamic thinkers struggling with the question of Islamic responsibility in a non-Islamic world. Deeply inspired by the work of Afghani and Abduh, he took their principles one step further. The Brotherhood was one of the largest and best organized political parties in Egypt and, although outlawed in countries such as Egypt and Syria, it has now become a strong force throughout the Islamic world. The frustration of the continued domination of the Islamic world by non-Islamic forces is reflected in increased emphasis on activity. In his essay, "The New Renaissance," al-Banna' echoes the thought of his predecessors by "proclaiming the necessity for a return to the principal teachings and ways of Islam." A growing belief that Islam is the *only* solution to moral decay is announced in his characterization of this return as initiating the reconciliation of modern life with these principles, and as such a prelude to final "Islamization."

Al-Banna', in fact, explicitly states that the need for Islamization arises from the failure of the West, or as he puts it, "the failure of the social principles on which the civilization of the western nations has been built":

The world has long been ruled by democratic systems, and man has everywhere glorified and honored the conquests of democracy . . . Victory at the end of World War I reinforced these thoughts, but men were not slow to realize that their collective liberty had not come intact out of the chaos . . . Quite the contrary, vice and violence led to the breaking loose of nations and peoples, to the overthrow of collective organization and family structure, and to the setting up of dictatorial regimes.[19]

He then describes the rise of Nazism and Fascism out of this abyss and concludes that not until the end of World War II did the world realize their failure. After similarly decrying the failure of Soviet socialism, al-Banna' characterizes all these systems as based on nothing but secularism and materialism. The people meanwhile are left with an insatiable need of spiritual comfort: "Man's hunger grows from day to day. He wants to free his spirit, to destroy this materialistic prison and find space to breathe the air of faith and consolation."[20]

The cure for this malaise is the Islamic one, which consists of the best elements of both the communist and the democratic regimes: "The greatest virtue of the communist regime . . . is the reinforcement of the notion of equality, the condemnation of class distinction, and the struggle against the claim to property, the source of these differences"[21]—all values deeply ingrained in the Islamic ideal. The merits of democracy are reflected in the fact that religious leaders in

Islam are limited by religious law, and it is the responsibility of Islamic society to correct the leader if he falters. True social justice, therefore, is to be found in Islamic principles of social organization, which al-Banna' enumerates as follows: brotherly love, peace, liberty, happiness, family, work and profit, knowledge, organization and determination of duties, and piety.

Sayyid Qutb (1906–1966), also influenced by Afghani and Abduh, was called "the martyr" *(al-shahid)* of the Muslim Brotherhood after his execution by Nasser in 1966. Like Hasan al-Banna', he believed Islam to be the comprehensive moral system capable of creating a just society. But it is not just a synthesis of the best of other systems; he spoke instead of the "Islamic alternative" to communism, capitalism, nationalism, liberalism, and secularism. It is the unique, divinely revealed ideal of human behavior.

The Islamic social system would provide everything other systems provide and would, in addition, "free us from economic and social disparity, realizing a balanced society while sustaining us spiritually."[22] This is because Islam is a total ideology, guaranteed by its divine origin. Grounding society in God "provides the individual with a goal greater than himself; the goal becomes the welfare of the society in which he lives and the humanity of which he is a member."[23]

Thus, Islam is not just an ideology. It is a call to action:

Islam is not a theological system that is realized when appropriated as an ideology . . . and then its mission ceases. Islam is a pragmatic activist system of life. It withstands other systems which are based on power but is supported by material power. For Islam to establish its divine system, it is inevitable that these material powers be destroyed and the powers that administer the systems that resist the divine way be annihilated.[24]

Thus, *Jihad,* Islamic "holy war." While no specific Islamic state is required, the Islamic system must be established. This is nothing other than bringing about God's kingdom on earth, the realization of the just society, and therefore a liberating force. Nor is it coercive. Qutb claims that it has never been the aim of Islam to coerce people into belief; anyone who understands the religion will naturally and freely choose it. It is only their oppression by unjust and secular forces that keeps them from being able to make that choice. Muslims therefore have a duty to use whatever means necessary to alleviate oppression and allow all people to freely choose. Simply put, Islam is a revolution for "peace in all its aspects: the peace of conscience, peace in the home and peace in society . . . finally, the peace of all humanity."

Similarly, Ali Shariati (1933–1977) saw Islam as a socially committed ideology. He saw the need for commitment on the part of the populace, the youth in particular, as the essential foundation for a just society. He therefore dedicated his life to reawakening in the Iranian youth the Islamic social conscience. Yet he believed it was the intelligentsia who were uniquely capable of understanding the inner conflicts, the alienation of an educated but uncommitted population. Enlightened religious leadership was required to interpret Islamic principles in terms of current social circumstances. These leaders must make Islamic principles applicable on a day-to-day basis, thus curing the spiritual malaise of society. The result will be a society in keeping with the original aims of Islam: a just and progressive social order.

Again, the emphasis is on man's role as God's *khalifa* (vice–regent) on earth and his responsibility to represent God's will in the social order. Shariati, therefore, characteristically stresses the indivisibility of the spiritual and secular spheres of human action. His recurrent theme is the analysis of Islam as a practical culture: piety signified by nothing if not social virtue. No religion could claim legitimacy and no individual could claim religiosity except in practical action. The only legitimate response to recognition of God's unity and supremacy is the reflection of man's equality before God on earth, in the social order.

Shariati expressed this conviction in terms of *tawhid:* the unicity and supremacy of God as the foundation of individual and social virtue. "All human activities and relationships, whether political, economic, literary or artistic, ought to be firmly founded on *tawhid*. It provides one single direction and it guarantees a unified spirit for its adherents."[25] God is the foundation and guarantee of human equality; response to God is necessarily a reflection of that equality in society, in social virtue. The social order based on *tawhid* Shariati described as *nizam-i tawhid*. This was the order established by the Prophet during his lifetime, and this was the responsibility left to man to continue. Constant reference to or remembrance of God, of *tawhid,* is essential in such a society. For *tawhid* "perfects the ethical conscience in man."[26] Even the fundamental duties of a Muslim to bear witness to God (*shahada*) and perform the *salat* (pray five times daily) are therefore components of this ethical system. They are the means by which man frees himself from selfishness and greed, and liberates his spirit so that he can behave virtuously in society. Failure to acknowledge God in this way results in fear and alienation, the roots of social disease.

Not only is Islam universal in its principles, but social justice is the heritage of all mankind, for God is the sole creator of an equal race. Islam is, in addition, the only religion that perfectly reflects the dual dimension of man: his responsibility to God is the same as his responsibility toward man. Spiritual welfare is indistinguishable from social virtue. The special relationship of man to God in Islam, Shariati contends, implies individual as well as social responsibility to create a just social order. *Nizam-i tawhid* is the explicit challenge of Islamic revelation; the creation of a just order is the inevitable outcome of proper recognition of God.

The theme is clear: Islam sees its mission as the call for social justice. Ethical norms are so much a part of religious teaching that they remained undifferentiated during the ascendancy of Islam as a world power and throughout the period of Islamic political unity. Yet, toward the decrepit end of that political unity—a result of lax religious practice, in the Islamic view—and on the verge of political reorganization of whatever sort, the question of the exact nature of Islamic ethical values became conscious. Just as in Judaism, there was no question regarding the ultimate importance of social values or ethics; the question was only what was the most direct, efficient, and appropriate way to effect them in society. And the similarity is striking. In both Judaism and Islam, people's responsibilities to one another are considered a response to the perception of God, and have therefore generally been dealt with in theological discussions and expressed in religious law. Hence, the need for modern explicative efforts, spurred by the fresh opportunity and felt responsibility to organize religious states. Thus, also the unique thrust of the emerging discussion: A decided antisecularism and pronounced emphasis on man's sacred duty in society. Properly organized society is society ordered on divine prerogative. To reiterate, Judaism and Islam each see morality as a response to God, proper response to God as implementing His revealed will, and His will as the creation of a virtuous society on earth. There- fore, personal virtue is seen as participation in the creation of a just society and ethical action as that which is truly conducive to it. Both consider this divine imperative to be inevitably universal. God is the sole creator, and each of His creatures is equally heir to His Kingdom on Earth. And finally, each sees its own community—Jews and Muslims, respectively—as ultimately responsible for this task. They are to be the leaven from which will rise and spread the universally virtuous society.

It would be inaccurate, or at least overly simplistic, however, to trace the roots of the Arab-Israeli war to competition over which community will be ultimately responsible for establishing a just society on earth. Perhaps the greatest tragedy of this war is that the similarity between Jewish and Islamic ethics has very little influence on the political realities involved. The Arab-Israeli war is not a religious war. It is grounded in far more practical and complex matters than religious or ethical distinctions. The complexities are comprehensible only in the context of one of the most persistent and insidious social malaises of the Western world: anti-Semitism.

ANTI-SEMITISM AND ZIONISM

The roots of the Arab-Israeli war lie squarely in anti-Semitism and its response, political Zionism. It is essential at the outset, however, to recognize that anti- Semitism is an entirely European phenomenon. It has nothing to do with either Arabs or Islam. In fact, Arabs are themselves Semites. The term "semitic" refers primarily to the language group which includes Hebrew, Arabic, Assyrian, and the Babylonian and Phoenician tongues.[27] Religiously, "semitic" denotes those who trace their ancestry to Shem, the son of Noah.

Among Shem's descendants was Abraham, to whose two sons, Isaac and Ishmael, the Jews and Muslims trace their ancestry. According to Islamic belief, when Abraham's wife Sarah gave birth to Isaac, she no longer had need of Abraham's other wife, Hagar, and their son, Ishmael. Hagar and Ishmael were therefore sent to Arabia, while Abraham, Sarah, and Isaac settled in Palestine. The religion of Abraham and Isaac is the true religion , the religion of submission

(*Islām*) to God's will. It is the same religion which Jesus, the greatest prophet, was sent to revive and reorient. And it is the same religion as that of the descendants of Ishmael, the Arabs. The Prophet Muhammad was also sent to revive this religion, for the Jews and Christians had allowed their religion to lapse:

And they say, "None shall enter Paradise except that they be Jews or Christians." Such are their fancies. Say: "Produce your proof, if you speak truly." Nay, but whosoever submits his will to God, being a good-doer, his wage is with his Lord, and no fear shall be on them, neither shall they sorrow. (Qur'an 2:105–106)

Who therefore shrinks from the religion of Abraham, except he be foolish-minded? (2:124) And they say, "Be Jews or Christians and you shall be guided." Say thou: "Nay, rather the creed of Abraham, a man of pure faith, he was no idolator." Say you: "We believe in God, and in that which has been sent down on us and sent down on Abraham, Ishmael, Isaac and Jacob, and the Tribes, and that which was given to Moses and Jesus and the Prophets, of their Lord; we make no division between any of them, and to Him we surrender." And if they believe in the like of what you believe in, then they are truly guided, but if they turn away, then they are clearly in schism; God will suffice you for them; He is the All-hearing, the All-knowing; the baptism of God, and who is there that baptizes fairer than God? Him we are serving. (2:129–133)

Islam therefore accepts Judaism completely as an integral part of the development of Islam, just as it does Christianity. From the Islamic point of view, the rejection of the Islamic message on the part of the Jews and Christians is proof that they are turning from the true message of Abraham. If they properly understood their sacred texts, they would recognize the truth of Muhammad's teaching. Yet, this is a criticism of the communities calling themselves Jewish or Christian, not the religions themselves. On the religious level, therefore, just as on the linguistic or racial, there is no anti-Semitism in Islam.

Anti-Semitism is, in fact, of European origin. Its roots lay in Roman law. When Rome was rebuilt under Constantine in the fourth century, its basis of unity was Christianity. As a result, Jews, who maintained their unique religious identity, were considered a threat to both state and ecclesiastical authority. Roman law therefore developed a pervasive tradition of segregating Jews and curtailing their right of self-determination. Along with other aspects of Roman law, this tradition survived into the modern age. But this prejudice was largely political in nature. Fantastic allegations of barbaric practices and treacherous morals were leveled against the Jews to justify the prejudice, just as had been the case with Christians under the pagan Roman government. Still, there was no hint of the theories of racial inferiority which characterize modern anti-Semitism. That abhorrent phenomenon went far beyond the Roman tradition. It can only be understood in the context of modern politico-economic developments.

At the beginning of the eighteenth century there were some two million Jews in the world, 90 percent of whom were in Europe. Since many sections of towns had been off-limits to Jews, trade and craft guilds closed to them, and agricultural land generally unavailable for purchase, many Jews had resorted to the lower trades and money-lending to make a living. The eighteenth century, however, ushered in the Enlightenment and the political upheavals it fostered throughout Europe. Under reforms inspired by the French Revolution in particular, European society opened up to Jews. Schools began to accept Jews, and they took full advantage. For instance, in Germany at this time, the great majority of students in the secondary schools were Jewish. As a result, Jews were able for the first time to make tremendous contributions to the sciences and professions. Some became well-known and respected physicians, bankers, and industrialists, not to mention such scientific geniuses as Paul Ehrlich, Sigmund Freud, and Albert Einstein. As Jewish historian Walter Laqueur points out, "The history of the Jews in central and western Europe during the second third of the nineteenth century was thus one of continuous political and social progress."[28]

One of the most significant aspects of the Enlightenment was its influence on nationalism. States began consolidating into political structures based on geographic contiguity and common interest. Citizenship was no longer to be based on class, ideological, or other such supra-national distinctions, but rather on place of birth. In such a context liberal political thought blossomed and with it the principle of equality before the law.

Among the leaders of the struggle for equality were, not surprisingly, the Jewish politicians. While some Jews remained conservative and others gravitated toward the emerging socialist parties, the majority found success among the liberals. There were high-ranking Jews in the French Republican government of 1848, as well as that of Louis Napoleon. Disraeli, in Britain, rose to the position of prime minister and paved the way for numerous Jews to reach cabinet–level positions. This pattern was paralleled in Holland and Italy. And in Germany, it was the Jewish politician, Heinrich von Simson, who led the delegation offering the German crown to the king of Prussia in 1871.

The prominent position of Jews in government indeed represented progress. The German novelist, Berthold Auerbach, wrote in the 1870s, "Freidenthal is a Prussian minister. Who would have anticipated a generation earlier that a man of Jewish origin would become a minister?"[29] Yet, with the economic decline and ultimate financial crisis of the last quarter of the century came a severe backlash against Jews, particularly in Germany. Individual Jewish speculators and industrialists were held personally responsible for the depression. More damaging still, their liberal politics were targeted as the cause of the crisis. All the old lingering prejudices, temporarily eclipsed in a period of economic prosperity and liberal euphoria, returned with a vengeance as Jews became the most convenient scapegoats for the depression. Thus was made possible the systematic campaign against Jews to which Wilhelm Marr gave the name "anti-Semitism."

Marr argued in his infamous *Der Sieg des Judenthums über das Germanenthum* (*The Victory of Judaism Over Germanism*) that the Jews had taken control of Germany in their drive to create a new empire.[30] As often happens in history, the more devastating the crisis and complex its causes, the more enthusiastically the populace embraces a facile explanation, however far-fetched. Within a short time Marr's theories became immensely popular. By 1880 an anti-Semitic league was founded in Berlin and Dresden. Leadership of the movement was taken over by Adolf Stöcker, a court cleric and conservative member of the Prussian government. Under his leadership petitions were submitted to bar Jews from national schools and universities, and from holding public office. "Jew-baiting," boycotting and insulting, became a common feature of German life.

Simultaneously, the condition of Russian Jews was worsening. In Russia, medieval anti-Jewish paranoia had scarcely abated. Despite the emancipation of serfs, Jews were still confined to "the Pale," a region of western Russia. The condition of peasants in Russia during the nineteenth century was desperate. The misadventures of an insatiable royalty and their increasingly burdensome taxation, combined with years of agricultural failure, created a scene of unparalleled misery for the populace. Among the victims of such conditions, it was not surprising to find ready acceptance of the anti-Semitic lore emanating from Western Europe. Additional fuel was supplied by extreme nationalism espoused by the Slavophile party, which gained prominence in the government. Its basis was in the Orthodoxy and racial unity of the Russian people, automatically excluding Jews. Anti-Jewish sentiment boiled and awaited only an excuse to break forth. That was provided in a tavern brawl between a Jew and a Christian in 1881. The scuffle grew into a riot which spread throughout the town. Similar riots broke out throughout all of western Russia, resulting in the murder of hundreds of Jews and massive destruction of their homes and villages. Official endorsement from the government culminated in years of heinous pogroms against Jews. The only escape was emigration, largely to Western Europe. The situation, much the same in Hungary and Romania, played into the hands of German anti-Semites: the German economy was crumbling under its own weight. Increasing Jewish emigration only burdened it further.

The early German anti-Semitic groups eventually discredited themselves, however. Under the inspiration of Eugen Duhring, their attacks were extended to include Christianity. They claimed it was an offshoot of Judaism, displaying a "semitic" ethos subversive to the German spirit. The anti-Semitic Christian socialists, of course, rejected the argument. Moreover, unlike the Romanovs in Russia, the German royal family (along with many other social elites) publicly denounced anti-Semitism as a disgrace to Germany. And perhaps most importantly, the German economy regained its equilibrium by the turn of the century. Anti-Semitism thus slipped into a period of decline. From a record sixteen members elected to the Reichstag on anti-Semitic platforms in 1893, by 1903 only nine returned. By 1918 all forms of legal anti-Semitism were removed from the German government's books.

The ideology did not die out, however. It survived in what would prove to be an even more insidious form than the religious or politico-economic prejudice of the previous years: pseudo-scientific racial theories. Among the most famous were those of Duhring, Houston Stewart Chamberlain (*Die Grundlagen des neunzehnten Jahrhunderts [Foundations of the 19th Century,* 1899]), Count J. A. de Gobineau, and Paul de Lagarde. Anthropological bases were developed by Ludwig Woltman, Ludwig Schemann, and H. F. I. von Gunther. In general, these thinkers—drawing on currently fashionable theories of human evolution—placed the so-called aryan, white people of Indo-European origin, at the top of the evolutionary scale. All others were inferior. Semites, in particular, were inferior not only physically, but also intellectually, culturally, socially, and morally. It took only the return of political and economic turmoil, combined with the staggering defeat of Germany in World War I, for anti-Semitism to return in its most virulent form yet under the leadership of Adolf Hitler. For the sake of society's continued progress, he argued, these reprobates had to be eliminated.

It was long before the German Holocaust, however, that Jews began to formulate a response to modern anti-Semitism in the form of political Zionism. Simon Dubnow, the great Jewish historian, calls the Jewish reaction to the wave of anti-Semitism which swept Germany and Eastern Europe in the last quarter of the nineteenth century the "second reaction."[31] Its exponents, Dubnow says, "out of disappointment in their hope of civil emancipation, proclaimed the slogan: 'We are strangers everywhere; we must return home!' "[32] The tolerance engendered by the Enlightenment had produced among Western European Jews a distinct assimilationist tendency. Under the influence of such thinkers as Moses Mendelssohn (1729–86), the universality of Judaism was emphasized and the uniqueness of Jewish tradition was downplayed. Jews were encouraged to participate fully in Western secular culture, the essence of Judaism being spiritual and therefore personal anyway. The goal of this movement, called in Hebrew *Haskala* ("enlightenment"), was to take full advantage of the newfound civil and intellectual freedom which characterized European life at the time. And many European Jews eagerly embraced the moment. The assimilationist movement was, however, one of the first victims of the return of anti-Semitism at the close of the century.

Probably the first systematic expression of political Zionism by a Jewish writer was that of the German socialist, Moses Hess (1812–1875). In his short book, *Rome and Jerusalem* (1862; English translation 1918), Hess claimed that anti-Semitism was not dead and never would be. Jews would always be homeless in European society. Jews are "a race, a brotherhood, a nation" and must return to their homeland. An ardent socialist, Hess combined extreme nationalism and religious conservatism, claiming that Jews could only carry out their ethical prerogatives in their own, socialist state. Although he believed that a moral and spiritual regeneration of Jews was necessary to prepare the way for the return to Palestine, he believed the return was imminent. He even appealed to France to protect the new state. France, newly enlightened by nineteenth–century humanism, would certainly cherish the idea of a friendly state in the Middle East.

Yet, Hess's book received virtually no attention when it first appeared. It was written in an ineffective style, was open to serious scholarly objections, and advocated a highly impractical approach to achieving a Jewish state. What was more, optimism about the eventual liberation of all European society was at its peak at the time he wrote. But by the 1880s things had changed.

With the return of rampant anti-Semitism, political Zionism began to find popular acceptance. The Russian physician, Leo Pinsker, published his *Auto-Emancipation* in 1882 (English translation, 1891), appealing to Western European Jews to save world Jewry from oppression and dispersion. Like Hess, Pinsker combined nineteenth–century European nationalism with a belief in the inevitable persistence of Judaeophobia (which he considered an hereditary psychic affliction) and came up with the necessity of Jews establishing a state of their own. But unlike Hess's, Pinsker's style was moving and eloquent. And it coincided with the increased persecution of Jews, which precipitated the end of assimilationist optimism. As a result, his work was well received among Jewish writers in Russia. He was able to attract a small group of followers who took the name *Hovevei Zion* ("Lovers of Zion," or "Palestinophiles" in contradistinction of the "Slavophiles" of Russian nationalism) to promote the settlement of Jewish farmers and artisans in Palestine.

Pinsker's Zionism was not religious but national. He had been an assimilationist before the pogroms beginning in 1881. But the renewed and intensified oppression convinced him that Jews of Russia and Rumania in particular would never be free of persecution and that they therefore needed their own homeland. However, he said, it would not be possible to restore the Jewish kingdom: "We cannot dream about restoring ancient Judea. It would no longer be possible for us to begin anew there where once our political life was brutally interrupted and destroyed . . . The goal of our efforts must not be the Holy Land, but a Land of our own."[33] Pinsker did not even believe the Jewish homeland had to be in Palestine:

All we need is a large territory for our ill-fated brothers, a territory that remains our own property and from which no foreign master can chase us . . . It is even possible that the Holy Land will again become our country. So much the better. But the most important thing is to determine quite simply which country is open to us.[34]

It was therefore not piety which motivated the Lovers of Zion, but practical necessity. Even so, such efforts were severely limited. For one thing, America was offering ready assimilation to newcomers of all religions in addition to unmatched economic opportunities. It was attracting tens of thousands of Europe's oppressed Jews annually. The few hundred a year who did go to Palestine, mainly from Russia, found the only opportunities for survival in a very difficult agricultural life for which they were totally unprepared. What was more, the native orthodox Jews of Jerusalem were very inhospitable. Aside from practical concerns of overcrowding and the added burden on already limited funds, the Orthodox disapproved of the newcomers on religious grounds. At the root of their objections lay the Jewish prohibition of carrying out divine plans by temporal means alone. The return to Zion was to be carried out by God in return for perfect fulfillment of the law by Jews. To covet worldly power was in direct conflict with Jewish law. In addition, the Jerusalem rabbis considered these Europeans utterly irreligious. They did not keep kosher laws, young men and women mixed openly, and people in general flouted Halakhah. "It would be preferable that the land of our forefathers should be again an abode of jackals than become a den of iniquity," was their ultimate appraisal of the "Russian anarchists."[35] Even with the help of the Christians, Lord Shaftesbury and Sir Lawrence Oliphant, and the rich European Jewish financiers, Baron Edmond de Rothschild and Baron Maurice de Hirsch, there were only some 4,500 Jewish immigrants in Palestine by the end of the century.

More successful than political Zionism in Western Europe was spiritual Zionism. It was, in fact, the earliest expression of Zionism. It was, in fact, the earliest expression of Zionism to become popular in Europe. Russian expatriate Asher Ginzberg (1856–1927), writing under the name of Ahad Ha'am ("One of the People"), criticized the Hovevei Zion, pointing out the most serious flaw in their plan: Palestine was not an uninhabited land but on the contrary had a large native population.[36] Therefore, he believed that Palestine should become the Jewish cultural center. The majority of Jews would remain in diaspora, but Palestine would be a place for spiritual regeneration from which Jews would return to their various homelands inspired by a "love of Zion." Zion meant to him all the basic components of Jewish culture, its language, literature, and education. The love of Zion meant the diffusion of Jewish knowledge throughout the world.

Spiritual Zionism became very popular in Europe but was destined to be outstripped by political Zionism. It only took the horrors of renewed anti-Semitism to prepare the ground for the popular acceptance of political Zionism. And there was no one better suited to popularizing and organizing the movement than the Austrian journalist, Theodor Herzl (1869–1904). Another converted assimilationist, Herzl believed that it was European anti-Semitism that had forced Jews, against their own wishes, to form a nation of their own. Like Pinsker, he was not concerned with the rebirth of a religious state in Palestine. In his famous *Der Judenstaat (The Jewish State)* published in 1892, he says:

Two territories are under consideration: Palestine and Argentina. Experiments in Jewish colonization worth noting have taken place on these two points . . . Should preference be given to Palestine or Argentina? The Society [the "Society of Jews" which Herzl proposed be founded to represent all Jews who supported the idea of a Jewish state] will take what it is offered, taking into account indications of Jewish public opinion regarding it. Argentina is one of the richest countries of the world in natural resources, colossal in size and with a small population and a temperate climate. It would be of great interest to the Argentine Republic to grant us a piece of its territory.[37]

Strategically, however, he believed Palestine to be the most feasible: "Palestine is our unforgettable historical homeland. Its name alone would be a powerfully stirring rallying cry for our people."[38]

Nor did Herzl believe that the state to be established would be a model of Jewish life. In his novel *Altneuland* (1902) he portrayed the kind of life he foresaw for Jews in their new state. It was one of secular sophistication such as they had known in their European homelands. What was more, in the novel he espoused closest cooperation with the Palestinian natives in what would be their common homeland. There was no hint of a state exclusively Jewish in religious terms. His main concern was for the survival and welfare of world Jewry.

Herzl's genius lay in his organizing skills. From his original headquarters in Vienna, he published the official Zionist weekly, *Die Welt* ("The World"), which was instrumental in rallying European Jews to his cause. In August 1897 he convened the first worldwide Zionist congress in Basel, Switzerland. The participants drew up a constitution for the movement which came to be called the "Basel program." Its stated purpose was to colonize Palestine with Jewish rural and industrial workers, to organize all Jews through appropriate local and international institutions in keeping with the laws of each country, and to promote Jewish national sentiment for the establishment of a home in Palestine for all Jews, secured by public law. The Zionist congress met every year until 1901, and thereafter every two years.

Most significantly, Herzl realized that the Zionist plan would not work without the support of world governments. He therefore set about trying to convince various powers of the benefit the Zionist state could provide them. He first approached the Ottoman Turkish government, which then controlled Palestine. He described the potential benefits to the Ottomans in his *Judenstaat:*

If His Majesty the Sultan were to give us Palestine, we could undertake to regulate Turkey's finances. For Europe, we would constitute a bulwark against Asia down there, we would be the advance post of civilization against barbarism. As a neutral state, we would remain in constant touch with all of Europe, which would guarantee our existence.[39]

He even sought and received the backing of anti-Semites in Russia. He stated in 1896, "My warmest adherent so far is the Pressburg anti-Semite, Ivan von Simonyi."[40] Russia's motivation in cooperating with the Zionists was clearly expressed by the Czar's finance minister: "I used to say to Alexander III: 'If it were possible, Your Majesty, to drown the six or seven million Jews in the Black Sea, I should be perfectly satisfied. But that is not possible, so we must let them live.' "[41] The minister later added, "But we give the Jews encouragement to emigrate—a good kicking, for example." Herzl realized this cooperation with the anti-Semites would be unpopular. He said it would be tantamount to acknowledging that the anti-Semites were right: "They will hold it against me, with all the reason in the world, that I am serving the anti-Semites' purpose by declaring that we are a people, one people."[42] Still, he believed it was necessary for the essential task of world Zionism: "But let us not be jealous, for we, too, will be happy."[43]

In 1904 Herzl died. At that time he had still achieved only limited support among governments for his goals, and there remained a good deal of Jewish opposition to political Zionism. The Orthodox still condemned the Zionists as irreligious, assimilationism had not been altogether abandoned, and there were still those who believed the Jews could live a separate and uniquely Jewish life in diaspora. Chief among the last group were the Bundists, members of the anti-Zionist general Jewish Workers' Union of Lithuania, Poland and Russia, founded in 1897. There was also dissension within the Zionist movement. In 1902 the Mizrachi party was founded among Russian Zionists who insisted on strict application of Jewish religious laws in the new homeland. The majority of Zionists, however, remained secularists, and the organization officially declared itself neutral in matters of religion.

It was the outbreak of World War I that changed the fortunes of political Zionism. Turkey, in the name of the Ottoman Empire, allied with Germany against Britain, France, and Russia. This presented an opportunity for Zionism to offer its services to Britain on a strategic basis. At this point, the headquarters of the movement was moved from Germany (where it had gone after Herzl's death) to London, and leadership passed to Jews of Russian descent living in London, most notably Chaim Weizmann. Weizmann approached the British government to support his plans for a Zionist state, carefully wording his argument to appeal to British national and imperial interests: "In submitting our resolution we entrusted OUR NATIONAL AND ZIONIST DESTINY TO THE FOREIGN OFFICE AND THE IMPERIAL WAR CABINET in the hope that the problem would be considered in the light of imperial interests and the principles for which the Entente stands."[44]

There was a great deal of dissent in the British government concerning this Zionist proposal. Among its most serious opponents were British Jews, particularly the Jewish ministers Edwin Montagu and Claude Montefiore. Montagu, in fact, had warned Weizmann that he would fight the proposition in the Cabinet. Besides the fact that he believed Judaism to be a religion rather than a race or nationality, he astutely recognized that establishment of a Jewish state would threaten all the gains made toward assimilation of Jews into European society. If there were a Jewish state, what justification would Jews in other countries have for not living there? Would they not be reduced to the status of resident aliens in their home countries? More importantly, if that state were established at the expense of another people, would not anti-Semites have a new weapon to use against Judaism? Overriding such objections, however, Britain did eventually elect to support the project.

On November 2, 1917, the British government charged Foreign Secretary Lord Balfour with informing Lord Rothschild that:

His Majesty's Government view with favor the establishment in Palestine of a national home for the Jewish people, and will use their best endeavors to facilitate the achievement of this object, it being clearly understood that nothing shall be done which may prejudice the civil and religious rights of existing non-Jewish communities in Palestine, or the rights and political status enjoyed by Jews in any other country.

This letter, known as the Balfour Declaration, was the essential factor—support of a world power—required by the Zionists to accomplish their goal.

There has been a good deal of discussion concerning the real reasons Britain went along with the Zionists in 1917, their proposals having been rejected by every other government, and even by the British government previously. The most far-fetched rationale offered was that it was a reward to Weizmann for having invented a powerful explosive which Britain could use in the war. Also unlikely is the popular story that it was primarily in return for the efforts of American Jews to draw the United States into the war. Some have also said that it was to encourage British Jews to buy war bonds. Weizmann himself offers the romantic notion that the Balfour Declaration was "a unique act of the world conscience."[45]

Far more important to Britain at the time, however, was staking a claim in the imminent liquidation of the Ottoman Empire.[46] It is true that Britain was concerned with fostering support among Russian Jews to support the allied cause at a time when Austro-Hungarian and German Jews had been won to the opposite side (largely because it involved fighting Czarist Russia). But more significant was the fact that the Middle East was the gateway to the jewel of Britain's imperial crown, India. As early as 1906 the Imperial Defense Committee had begun to consider possibilities of expanding British holdings in the Middle East in order to secure the Suez Canal. The French, with longstanding interests throughout greater Syria, felt threatened. So suspicious were the three great empires—Britain, France, and Russia—of each other's motives in the Middle East that in September of 1914 they signed an alliance prohibiting any of them from making a separate peace with their enemies, soon to include Turkey. In March of 1915, France had submitted its proposals for desired property. Britain responded in June of 1915, setting up a committee to work out its proposal. The committee's conclusion: "Zones of interest are preferable to partition."[47] It suggested that the Ottoman lands in Syria, particularly Palestine, remain under some kind of international jurisdiction, if for no other reason than to keep them from France. Palestine was, after all, a part of greater Syria, and Britain hoped ultimately to control it.

To this end, Britain proceeded on two simultaneous, yet mutually conflicting, strategic courses from mid–1915 to mid–1916: The McMahon-Hussein Correspondence and the Sykes-Picot agreement. The McMahon-Hussein Correspondence comprised the negotiations between British High Commissioner for Egypt and the Sudan Sir Henry McMahon, and Sherif Hussein of Mecca, head of the noblest of all Arab families (and traditional protector of the Arab holy cities of Mecca and Medine), the Hashemites. The discussions centered around Britain's desire to bring the Arabs into the war against Turkey and concerned the type of commitments Britain was willing to make in exchange for Arab assistance in the war. The Arabs had long been restive under the Ottoman suzerainty. As the Ottoman Empire had gone from world-power in the sixteenth and seventeenth centuries to the "sick man of Europe" in the nineteenth and twentieth centuries, its concern had increasingly focused on its Turkishness. The Arabs suffered in the bargain and responded with their own nationalist aspirations, growing since the nineteenth century. This fact was well known to Britain. Since Britain could not presume the neutrality of the Arabs in the Great War, it used the Arabs to ensure they would join forces against, rather than with, the Turks. The result was the McMahon Pledge. The Arabs' understanding of it, based on assurances from the British government, was that Britain would support the establishment of an Arab kingdom under Hussein in the Arab lands liberated by the Anglo-Arab effort. In McMahon's words:

The districts of Mersin and Alexandretta and portions of Syria lying to the west of the districts of Damascus, Homs, Hama and Aleppo, cannot be said to be purely Arab, and just on that account be excepted from the proposed delimitation . . . Subject to the modifications stated above, Great Britain is prepared to recognize and uphold the independence of the Arabs in all regions lying within the frontiers proposed by the Sherif of Mecca.[48]

The region excepted constituted an area lying essentially north of Damascus and Beirut. The McMahon Pledge, therefore, undoubtedly included Syria and Palestine in the planned Arab state.

This pledge was clearly in conflict with the Balfour Declaration to be made less than a year later. But it also was directly contradicted by the secret Sykes-Picot Agreement between Britain and France made at the same time as the McMahon Pledge. (Russia was also a party to this agreement, but its claims need not concern us here.) Having promised to support the establishment of an Arab state in Syria, Britain went right on to agree with France to partition all formerly Ottoman Arab lands into French and British protectorates. The French would maintain their claim on Syria and Britain would get Transjordan and Iraq, ceding Palestine to some kind of international control. It is no wonder the agreement was kept secret.

On July 24, 1922, the League of Nations gave official international approval to French control of Syria. Britain was granted a mandate over all of Palestine, and the area of international control was reduced to the City of Jerusalem only. The Balfour Declaration was included in the mandate approval.

Not surprisingly, the Arabs were shocked. Winston Churchill, by then colonial secretary, felt the need to clarify Britain's position. He said the Balfour Declaration did not mean

the imposition of a Jewish nationality upon the inhabitants of Palestine as a whole, but the further development of the existing Jewish community, with the assistance of Jews of other parts of the world, in order that it may become a center in which the Jewish people as a whole may take, on grounds of religion and race, an interest and a pride.[49]

It did not mean "the disappearance or the subordination of the Arabic population, language or culture in Palestine."

By Britain's own admission, then, it had no intention of offering the Zionists a sovereign state in Palestine. Britain clearly meant only to strengthen its own control over the region, by championing both Arab and Zionist causes in the region. In fact, it had no intention of giving complete control to either group. It was just this sort of dealing which President Wilson at the time referred to as "the whole disgusting scramble" for the remains of the Ottoman Empire.[50]

The Balfour Declaration was therefore a strictly political move on the part of Britain. Yet it served the ends of the political Zionists perfectly. The Zionists vastly preferred a British protectorate over a French one and used all their influence to assure one. For in the inevitable conflict over independent statehood, Britain was viewed as a more reliable partner. As Golda Meyerson—then a young Zionist socialist from Milwaukee, who later shortened her name to Meir— observed in a letter from Palestine in 1921: "If we dig in here, England will come to our aid ... It is not the Arabs whom the English will pick to have colonize Palestine; it is we."[51] And with that the Zionist set about the next practical steps toward establishment of their state: intense colonization from around the globe. Protected by a politically expedient alliance with Britain, Zionists could carry out their nationalist goals. But what about the nationalist aspirations of the native inhabitants of the region?

ARAB NATIONALISM AND THE ISRAELI STATE

The promulgation of the Balfour Declaration, followed by the League of Nations' mandate, understandably caused a great deal of Arab consternation, which often erupted into violence. For the next several years, the Arab leaders sought clarification from the British, who continued to proclaim their support of Arab nationalist aspirations. In 1918, for example, just after Sherif Hussein learned of the existence of the Balfour Declaration, he approached Commander David George Hogarth of the Arab Bureau in Cairo on the issue. Hogarth responded, not mentioning the Declaration itself, but assuring Hussein: "Jewish settlement in Palestine would only be allowed insofar as would be consistent with the political and economic freedom of the Arab population."[52] Although his followers were growing increasingly skeptical, Hussein was satisfied with the assurances. Like the Zionists, he felt more secure dealing with the British for as much territory as he could get. The alternative in his view was fighting French claims on his own. He therefore reminded the Arabs of their duties of hospitality to the newcomers.

The entry of Jews into Palestine was not in itself troublesome to the Arabs. At the time of the Balfour Declaration, roughly 8 percent of the population was Jewish. Some had lived in the region for centuries (the "oriental" Jews or Sephardim), and some had recently immigrated to escape suffering in Europe (the "western" Jews or Ashkenazim). The Arabs' concern was over control of the region. And the massive influx of Jews from around the world was calling that into question. By 1922 the Jewish population in Palestine had risen to 11 percent of the total. In May 1925 it was officially estimated at 108,000; by the end of 1935 it was around 300,000. By the end of 1936, Jews made up 28 percent of Palestine's population. The amount of land owned by Jews was 177 square miles in 1914. By 1935 it had risen to some 500 square miles. Most of this land was purchased with funds supplied from outside Palestine and in the name of the National Fund (*Keren Kayemeth*) as the perpetual and inalienable property of the Jewish people. The Arabs had no such outside funds or sophisticated legal institutions. Urban growth was even more dramatic. Tel Aviv was founded in 1909 as a suburb of Jaffa. By 1935 its population exceeded 100,000. It had become a center of industrial development, again made possible by the influx of foreign capital.

During this period Zionists made some efforts to reach an accommodation with the Arabs. It was in Britain's best interests to have the Arabs and the Zionists in accord. After all, their goal was to set up a series of buffer states under British control to protect the Suez, to counter France's influence in the area, and to keep a close watch on possible expansionist moves from Turkey and the Soviet Union. The commander-in-chief of British troops, General Edmund Allenby, therefore advised Weizmann to approach Emir Feisal, Sherif Hussein's son and commander of the Arab troops, as early as June 1918. Weizmann consciously followed Herzl's policy of "present[ing] the entire affair in as inoffensive a way as possible."[53] No mention was made of plans for ultimate sovereignty of a Zionist state in Palestine. As far as Feisal knew, the Arabs were only being asked to allow several thousand Jewish colonists to settle next to a vast Arab state already diverse in religious and ethnic population. The settlers would have a high level of technical skill and would therefore be able to provide needed assistance to the new Arab state. At no time did Weizmann mention anything more specific than a "national Jewish home."[54] Feisal, who seemed to like Weizmann, therefore accepted Jewish colonization in Palestine and pledged Arab support. However, recognizing potential Arab hostility to the plan stemming from their growing suspicion of British and Zionist goals, Feisal appended a stipulation making the entire agreement dependent on the granting of Arab independence.

The Zionist leaders also suppressed their nationalist goals for the for the moment Britain in order to maintain Britain's support for increased Jewish colonization. They asked only for settlement facilities and the lifting of immigration quotas. They also expressed full support for British mandatory government, to the extent that they opposed the creation of any representative body of government. The Arabs were still in the majority, and a representative assembly would not have been in their interest yet. It was only British support which could allow the sort of immigration required to establish the population basis sufficient for statehood demands.[55]

The Arabs were becoming more and more aware of their precarious position.

By the time of the Mandate, it was quite clear that they had been deliberately misled and sorely ill advised. Instead of the great united and independent Arab state they had been promised, Arab territory had been divided into protectorates controlled by European powers, in which even their right to determine their own affairs was severely restricted. And a significant portion of their territiory had been given away to another group, whose rights were being put ahead of their own. The Arab populace was losing faith completely in its leaders, who had been placed by the mandatory powers in nominal positions in kingship (Sherif Hussein's sons, Feisal and Abdullah, were given titles in Iraq and Transjordan, respectively), a notion foreign to Islamic tradition. Arab frustration grew and burst forth in major uprisings against the Zionists in 1929, 1936, and 1939.

British policy, meanwhile, was changing. By 1939 the terror of the Holocaust in Europe was generating Jewish immigration into Palestine which far outstripped the earlier growth. Jews now constituted nearly a third of the population. Their demands for statehood began to surface, and the Arabs were organizing in opposition. The British government had no desire to see an independent Jewish state in Palestine, since that would mean total loss of British control there. As a result, Britain shifted its sympathies and issued the now famous May 17, 1939, White Paper. It proposed the setting up of an independent Palestinian state within ten years in which Jews would constitute no more than one-third of the population. With that in mind, the British mandatory government then set limitations on immigration and the sale of land to Jews.

Such limitations were absolutely intolerable in light of Hitlerism. In addition, the *Yishuv,* as the Jewish community in Palestine called itself, had reached a size which made demands for independence feasible in terms of population and military capacity. The new British policy therefore gave the Zionist Revisionist party, which had long advocated military conquest of Palestine, its chance. And the enemy had clearly shown itself to be Britain. There were still Zionist leaders in the mid–1930s who advocated an agreement with the Arabs. Arthur Ruppin, for instance, criticized the Revisionists for their extremist political goals. He reminded both Jews and Arabs of the 1922 Churchill Memorandum and that it had been accepted by the Zionist Organization. The true goal of Zionism, he said, was a national Jewish home which neither Jews nor Arabs would dominate. "It must be a state in which Jews and Arabs can live side by side as two nationalities with equal rights."[56] But by the 1940s world events had changed. The Polish Jew, Vladimir Jabotinsky, had founded the Revisionist party in the early 1930s, demanding the creation of a Jewish state on both sides of the Jordan River as soon as possible. He also called for the formation of a Jewish legion to achieve this goal militarily. He rejected the gradual diplomatic approach followed by Weizmann, which made use of Britain's and the Arabs' cooperation. Instead, he wanted to declare openly their goal and fight whomever necessary to achieve it. With the massacre of Jews in Europe and Britain's attempted imposition of immigration restrictions despite it, the Revisionists' program finally achieved broad popular appeal.

It was therefore against Britain that the Zionist revolt was first aimed. And it was fought by the only means available to such a small group against the overwhelming military power of Britain—terrorism. The two main groups involved in the terrorist attacks were the Irgun (or *Etzel*) and the Stern group (or *Lehi*). The leader of the second group was Abraham Stern. The most extreme of terrorists, he even advocated a Zionist alliance with all of Great Britain's enemies, including the USSR and Nazi Germany.[57] The majority of less extreme Zionists themselves organized into an army, the *Haganah*.

The rising consciousness of the horrors of Nazism, the inhumanity of immigration restrictions in the face of it, and British repression of terrorist activity in Palestine soon spread sympathy for the Zionist cause worldwide. On May 11, 1942, the American Zionist Organization, in a meeting at the Biltmore Hotel in New York, adopted a program presented by David Ben–Gurion, president of the Executive Committee of the Jewish Agency and destined to be the first prime minister of Israel. Called the Biltmore Program and ratified on November 10, 1942, this was the first official and public declaration from the Zionist Organization of its demand for a Jewish state to be established throughout all of Palestine. The program was a complete rejection of the Balfour Declaration, the Churchill Memorandum, and the 1939 White Paper. It was a complete rejection of British imperial control of Palestine.

A few lucid thinkers at the time did recognize that the most important factor in the Palestine equation would be the one Britain and the Zionists were now ignoring: Palestine's native inhabitants. The great Jewish philosopher, Martin Buber, for example, a dedicated Zionist, was convinced Zionism could be successful only if justice were done to the Arabs. He criticized the Biltmore Program for ignoring the Arabs and exacerbating the already growing conflict. He felt Arab suspicions of real Zionist intentions were fully justified in light of such unilateral pronouncements.[58] Others recognized further that current Zionist policy would lead inevitably to war. In 1947 Judah L. Magnes, president of the Hebrew University of Jerusalem, wrote:

A Jewish state can only be obtained, if it ever is, through war . . . You can talk to an Arab about anything, but you cannot talk to him about a Jewish state. And that is because, by definition, a Jewish state means that the Jews will govern other people, other people who live in this Jewish state . . . Jabotinsky knew that long ago. He was the prophet of the Jewish state. Jabotinsky was ostracized, condemned, excommunicated. But we see now that almost the entire Zionist movement has adopted his point of view . . . In his early writings he said: "Has a people ever been known to give up its territory of its own volition? Likewise, the Arabs in Palestine will not renounce their sovereignty without violence." . . . All these things have now been adopted by those who excommunicated him.[59]

By 1948 terrorist activity finally convinced the British to v íthdraw their troops and leave the Jews and Arabs face to face. The United I tions had voted on November 29, 1947, to partition the territory betweeen Jev ; and Arabs, a resolution the Arabs had no reason to accept. They had already seen that European powers and Zionist organizations were not trustworthy. Assurances from Presidents Roosevelt and Truman that no decision would be made concerning Palestine without previous consultation and presumed agreement between the Jews and Arabs had proven worthless.[60] Every agreement and assurance they had accepted had been contradicted. The Zionists had openly stated that their goal was an independent and wholly Jewish state throughout all Palestine. And Zionist terrorism had turned against the Arabs as well as the British. The Arabs' feeble attempts at reprisals were more than matched by the Zionists. As strongly as the Jews felt the need to establish an independent state, therefore, the Arabs felt the need to fight for their homeland. The idea of allowing a body of foreign and hostile powers to parcel out their land was preposterous. The Arab Higher Committee of Palestine therefore responded to the Biltmore Program and the Partition Plan: ''Any attempt by the Jews or any other power or group of powers to set up a Jewish state on Arab territory is an act of oppression that will be resisted by force on the grounds of legitimate defense.''[61] The day after the Partition Plan was announced, the Palestinian Arab guerrilla war began.

Like the early Jewish terrorists, the Palestinian commandos had no military alternative to terrorist attack. They began with sniper attacks and the dynamiting of buildings, the same tactics Irgun and the Stern gang had used against the British and Palestinian resisters. The attacks and reprisals escalated. As Zionist writers Jon and David Kimche point out, ''In the sequence of events, it quickly became difficult to say which were the attacks and which were the reprisals.''[62]

This situation persists to the present day.

The Arab armies did not come to the aid of the guerillas until May 15, 1948 when Israel declared itself a state after the British pull-out. With that, the Transjordanian Arab Legion (still commanded by a British major, Glubb Pasha) led the Arab armies into the West Bank. The Arabs were quickly defeated. They were only 40,000 against 60,000 Jewish soldiers; they had little military experience, and they were suffering under an arms embargo declared by the United Nations while Jewish soldiers were well supplied by Europe and America. As a result, Israel significantly increased its territory (from that provided in the 1947 Partition Plan).

In 1956 and again in 1967, Israel occupied the Sinai Peninsula. In the 1956 instance, diplomatic pressure forced their withdrawal. The Camp David Accords eventually led to their most recent withdrawal from that region. The West Bank of the Jordan River, however, at the heart of Palestine, is a different story. After the 1948 war, King Abdullah of Transjordan occupied the West Bank, ostensibly in the name of the Palestinians. In the 1967 war, Israel occupied that territory as well, plus the Gaza Strip and the Golan Heights. Israel has now annexed the Golan Heights, and maintains its military occupation of the West Bank and Gaza to this day, despite United Nations calls for withdrawal and the Arabs' ill-fated attempt in 1973 to regain control. The Palestinians, natives of present-day Israel, the West Bank, and the Gaza Strip, therefore, remain stateless. And it is their plight which now lies at the heart of the Arab-Israeli conflict.

THE PALESTINIAN QUESTION

Palestinians remaining in their homeland, whether living under Jordanian or Israeli domination, are far from satisfied. Many of those who were able to emigrate to Europe and America have done so. Of the 3.5 to 4 million Palestinian Arabs now scattered throughout the world, perhaps a million live in Jordan, and some have assimilated into Jordanian society. Hundreds of thousands, however, remain refugees, living in camps set up by the United Nations in Lebanon and Jordan. Those Palestinians who remained within the Israeli state (now some 650,000, with another 1 million on the West Bank and in Gaza) were understandably viewed by the Israelis as a potential threat. As a result their rights were, and continue to be, severely limited. As early as 1946, Golda Meir expressed the rationale behind this policy. She was asked "If the Jews as a minority had the same privileges as those you are promising the Arabs as a minority, would you be satisfied?" "No, Sir," she said. "For there must be one place in the world where Jews are not a minority."[63] According to Zionist logic, if the Arabs were given their full rights, they would soon become a majority in Palestine with the power to regain their lands and expel the Jews. There is nothing in this logic, however, to compel Palestinian Arabs to cease their irredentist efforts. In fact, it is Israeli intransigence on this issue which motivates the ongoing Palestinian struggle.

The PLO

In 1964 the Arab League was established under the influence of Gamal Abdul Nasser, then president of Egypt. Nasser appealed to the lingering sentiment within the Middle East for the creation of a unified Arab state. He was a new breed of Arab leader, bitterly opposed to Western domination of the Arab world and boldly revolutionary. It was Western imperialism that had fragmented the Arab world, and Nasser condemned those leaders who cooperated in any way with the West. Chief among the culprits were those, like the leaders of Saudi Arabia and Jordan, who did nothing to implement the erstwhile dream of Arab unity. Choosing rather to maintain the security of their own thrones, these leaders, Nasser believed, betrayed the Arab world and Islamic principles at the same time. He wanted the Arab world to organize and cooperate, independent of Western power, and the Arab League was to be its forum.

Under the auspices of the Arab League, the Palestinian Liberation Organization (PLO) was set up in 1965 as a kind of government in exile for the Palestinians. However, the 1967 loss of the West Bank devastated Palestinian faith in the Arab leaders' desire or ability to regain their land. It was then that the PLO declared itself independent of Arab states. It set for itself the task of regaining its land and establishing a Palestinian state by any means necessary.

Since that time the PLO has continued to evolve. The PLO itself is an umbrella organization with elected representatives, both Muslim and Christian, of virtually every political persuasion: from capitalist to communist, from militant extremist to moderate accommodationist, from pan-Arabist to nationalist. The original charter of the PLO included a call for regaining all territory seized by the Zionists and the establishment of a Palestinian state. The charter was amended in 1974 to call for the establishment of a Palestinian state on any part of formerly Palestinian lands vacated by Israel. The PLO is led by Yasser Arafat and his moderate faction known as Fateh (an acronym for *"harakat tahrir al-filistin,"* "movement to liberate Palestine"). Some groups within the PLO call for the establishment of a socialist state or a religious state. However, just as Herzl's Zionists declared themselves officially neutral in matters of religion, the official position of the PLO is for the establishment of a secular state in which Jews, Christians, and Muslims would have equal rights. The PLO operates hospitals, schools, day-care centers, research centers, and diplomatic and administrative offices. Its main activity since 1967, however, has been commando warfare against the Israeli state.

Israeli Occupation of Lebanon

This type of warfare has been systematically countered by the Israeli forces. Prior to 1971, the majority of PLO attacks against Israel were launched from Jordan. Israeli reprisals were not welcome in Jordan, nor were the Palestinians' condemnation of King Hussein for collusion with imperialist powers and calls for his ouster. Jordan, therefore, attacked the Palestinian forces in Jordan. The result was at least 10,000 Palestinian casualties, many within refugee camps themselves, and the removal of PLO headquarters from Jordan to Lebanon. Continued Palestinian attacks from Lebanon, combined with Israel's longstanding plan to include South Lebanon within her borders, led to the Israeli occupation of that area in 1982 and further dispersal of Palestinian forces.

The Israeli occupation of Lebanon, however, had mixed results. Lebanon had already been involved in its own civil war since 1975. The intrusion of Israeli brutality into the already bloody arena only extended the conflict. Although the Palestinians were indeed once again dispersed, Israel's storming of Beirut in September spurred the organization of Lebanese national resistance. On September 16, the Lebanese National Front was proclaimed and immediately began its attacks on the city's occupiers. Soon other groups formerly at odds with one another within Lebanon (such as various Christian militias, Sunni Muslim groups, and the Shi'ite Muslim Amal movement in the South) joined in the resistance against the Israeli invaders.

Even the religious groups, however, remained committed to nationalist goals. Nabih Berri, leader of Amal, said of his group's goals: "No one in Lebanon is demanding an Islamic republic."[64] And their persistence is proving successful. Their incessant attacks have recently forced Israel to retreat from Lebanon, a lesson not lost on the beleagured Palestinians. Since the beginning of the Israeli evacuation of Lebanon, there has been a marked increase of resistance among Palestinians on the West Bank. Pictures of Lebanese civilians killed by the Israeli forces are being displayed as martyrs by Palestinians in the occupied territories. As one Palestinian said, Lebanese resistance is "affecting everything. The idea that using force may force Israel to withdraw is a concept that now is logical to many Palestinians."[65]

Recent Developments

Meanwhile, the PLO itself has embarked on its most daring peace initiative to date. Arafat has been able to obtain authorization even from more militant Palestinian factions suspicious of U.S., Israeli, and Jordanian motives, to enter into negotiations with the United States for eventual establishment of a Palestinian state on the West Bank and Gaza in confederation with Jordan. Among the stipulations of the Camp David Accords of 1979 was that Israel cease colonization activities on the West Bank in preparation for its eventual autonomy. Settlement activity continued apace, however, and Israel has often reiterated since Camp David its opposton to an independent Palestinian state on its borders. For that reason, the PLO has agreed to confederate with Jordan. The outcome of this plan will be pivotal in the Middle East conflict. Skeptics among the Palestinians predict that Israel will never give up the West Bank voluntarily and believe this "Jordanian option," like previous peaceful attempts at settlement of the issue (U.N. resolutions 338 and 442 and Camp David, for example), will fail. Israel's recent rejection of the list of names of Palestinians to be included in the Jordanian-Palestinian delegation to meet with the United States does not bode well for a more optimistic view. Should this attempt indeed fail, it could well mark the end of moderate Palestinian leadership and a vindication of extremist calls for dismantling the Israeli state through violence.

CONCLUDING REMARKS

Although the Arab-Israeli conflict holds few benefits to either side, Israel does have at least one advantage over the Arabs. Israel is a unified, democratic state with popular consensus at least on the form of government to be employed. The Arab world cannot even boast that. The natural process of state formation following liberation was cut short by the British and French mandates, and then by the declaration of Israeli statehood and Israel's successive waves of occupation. The tendency was for whatever forces that happened to be in control at these various crisis points to become entrenched in the face of external threats, often quite unconcerned with internal popular support. The Arab world therefore displays a staggering array of forms of government, ranging from the traditional

Islamic emirates of the Gulf states and Saudi Arabia, to the more European-style monarchies of Morocco and Jordan, military dictatorships such as in Libya and Iraq, and modified parliamentary forms such as in Algeria and Egypt. This discontinuity is further exacerbated by the vast disparity in wealth caused by the discovery and exploitation of oil in some states, and the ever-widening gap in levels of educational and technological sophistication which oil wealth makes possible.

Yet, Nasser's dream of Arab cooperation (if not unity) remains close to the hearts of Arabs. And the Palestinian question has become its benchmark. Despite the continued infighting among the Arab states, there is general agreement that as long as Palestinians remain refugees, Arab leadership will have failed. And conversely: only through concerted, unified Arab leadership will justice be done to the Palestinians.

Palestine is therefore an extremely emotional issue throughout the Arab world. The depth of feeling involved is directly related to the intensity of appeal of the central Islamic notion of "community" (*ummah*). Islamic belief above all professes the equality of all true believers before God. As above, those who truly submit to the will of God ("*muslims*") will inevitably form a just and cohesive society impervious to the inroads of idolators. The lack of such unity is nothing short of the most glaring indictment of dereliction of religious duty. It is a constant reminder that they are falling short of their most cherished goal. The Palestinian struggle, then, while oriented toward nationalist political goals, finds continued inspiration in religious ideals.

Perhaps the most telling evidence of this is the growing popularity of the Muslim Brotherhood. Established in Egypt in 1928 and living under virtually constant repression by Arab regimes since then, the Brotherhood is now probably the single most universally popular group in the Arab Islamic world. Its popularity is no doubt a reflection of the simplicity of its message: Islamic society must free itself from both Eastern and Western influences to express its truly unique character. The true *ummah* will be marked by solidarity, concrete brotherly allegiance, faith, and piety. The continued inability of the existing leadership in the Islamic world to bring about such peace gives credence to the Brotherhood's call for dismantling the state of Israel and the overthrow of the effete leadership which has allowed it to continue this far. The longer the Arab-Israeli conflict remains unsolved, the more appealing the Brotherhood's message becomes.

It was noted above that it was political Zionism which formulated the practical plan for establishing the state of Israel, yet its essential popular support lay in the spiritual Zionism of Ahad Ha'am and Martin Buber. In the same way, the goal of Palestinian statehood which lies at the heart of the Arab-Israeli conflict finds its popular support in the Islamic ideal of true community. It was also noted that the ultimate goal of spiritual Zionism and that of Islamic *ummah* are virtually identical: the creation of a just society on earth. The tragic irony of a war waged in the name of such a lofty ideal is perhaps the greatest testament to the difficulty of this task.

NOTES

1. Herzl, *Der Judenstaat,* quoted from trans. in Herzberg, *Zionist Idea,* p. 209.

2. Rahman, *Islam and Modernity,* p. 32.

3. Cited from Luzzatto, "Israelitische Moral-Theologie," in Silver, ed., *Judaism and Ethics,* p. 117.

4. Lazarus, *Ethics of Judaism,* trans. Szold, p. 71.

5. Ibid., pp.130–131.

6. Ibid.

7. Cohen, *Reason and Hope,* trans. Jospe, frontispiece.

8. Cohen, "A Reply to Dr. Martin Buber's Open Letter to Hermann Cohen," in *Reason and Hope,* trans. Jospe, p. 164.

9. Quoted from "Das Gottesreich," *Jüdische Schriften* 3: 174, by Meyer, "Problematics of Jewish Ethics," in Silver, ed., *Judaism and Ethics,* p. 127.

10. Fackenheim, "Religious Responsibility for the Social Order," in Silver, ed., *Judaism and Ethics,* pp. 241–248.

11. Ibid., p. 244.

12. Ibid., p. 247.

13. Ibid.

14. Ibid.

15. Berkowits, "The Status of Woman," in Kellner, ed., *Contemporary Jewish Ethics,* p. 355.

16. Ibid.

17. al-Afghani and Abduh, *al-Urwa al-Wuthqa,* i, p. 151ff.

18. Rida, *Ta'rikh al-Ustadh al-Imam al-Shaykh Muhammad Abduh,* ii, p. 97.

19. For quotes of al-Banna' see Karpat, ed., *Political and Social Thought,* pp. 118–122.

20. Ibid.

21. Ibid.

22. Qutb, *Maarakat al-Islam wa'l-Rasmaliyya,* p. 38. All translations of Sayyid Qutb's works are taken from Yvonne Y. Haddad, "Sayyid Qutb: Ideologue of Islamic Revival," in *Voices of Resurgent Islam,* Esposito, ed. (New York: Oxford University Press, 1983), pp. 67–98.

23. Ibid., pp. 50–51.

24. Qutb, *Fi Zilal al-Qur'an,* p. 1544.

25. Shariati, *Islam Shinasi,* pp. 75–76. Trans. Sachedina, "Ali Shariati," *Voices of Resurgent Islam,* p. 200.

26. Ibid., pp. 83–87, trans. p. 201.

27. A prominent Jewish scholar, Arthur Koestler, has argued that most European Jews, those who established the state of Israel, were themselves not Semitic at all. See Koestler, *Thirteenth Tribe.* They are the descendants of the Khazars, a central Asian group which converted to Judaism in the Middle Ages. During the Mongol migrations, these people were pushed westward and became the Russian and Eastern European Jewish community.

28. Laqueur, *History of Zionism,* p. 26.

29. Ibid., p. 28.

30. Wilhelm Marr, *Der Sieg des Judenthums über das Germanenthum (The Victory*

of Judaism Over Germanism) (Hamburg, 1873). Many conflicting allegations have been made concerning Marr's work. For best account, see Mosche Zimmerman, "Gabriel Reisser und Wilhelm Marr im Meinungstreit," *Zeitschrift des Vereins für Hamburgische Geschichte,* 61 (1975):59–84. It is, however, widely accepted that Marr indeed coined the phrase "anti-Semitism." See, e.g., Maxime Rodinson, *Cult, Ghetto, and State: The Persistence of the Jewish Question* (London: Al Saqi Books, 1983), p. 172.

31. Dubnow, *Die neueste Geschichte,* vol. 3.
32. Ibid., p. 327, quoted by Rodinson, *Israel,* p. 39.
33. Pinsker, *Auto-Emancipation,* French trans. by Schulsinger, pp. 69ff, cited by Rodinson, *Israel,* p. 40.
34. Ibid.
35. Quoted by Laqueur, *History of Zionism,* p. 76.
36. Perlmann, "Chapters of Arab-Jewish Diplomacy," pp. 123–124, cited by Rodinson, *Israel,* p. 39.
37. Herzl, *Der Judenstaat, [L'Etat Juif,* French trans.] pp. 92ff. cited by Rodinson, *Israel,* p. 42.
38. Ibid.
39. Ibid., p. 95.
40. Chouraqui, *A Man Alone,* p. 106, cited by Rodinson, *Israel,* p. 102.
41. Ibid., pp. 235ff.
42. Ibid., p. 167.
43. Weizmann, *Trial and Error,* p. 200, cited by Rodinson, *Israel,* p. 47. Emphasis in the original.
44. Ibid.
45. Cf. Monroe, *Britain's Moment,* pp. 39ff.
46. Nevakivi, *Britain, France and the Arab Middle East,* p. 19.
47. Antonius, *Arab Awakening,* p. 419.
48. "Zionism," *Encyclopedia Britannica* 23, p. 977.
49. Rodinson, *Israel,* p.51.
50. Weizmann, *Trial and Error,* p. 188.
51. Syrkin, *Golda Meir,* French trans., p. 63, cited by Rodinson, *Israel,* p. 106.
52. Antonius, *Arab Awakening,* p. 267.
53. Chouraqui, *A Man Alone,* p. 256. As Alexandre Bein put it:

The goal [of Zionism] has remained unchanged since Herzl—the transformation of Palestine into a Jewish homeland, the creation of a Jewish state. For tactical political reasons, this goal has not always been clearly stated. But the evolution of Palestine and of the Jewish problem in general has reached such a point that clarity had become necessary.

See his *Introduction au Sionisme* p. 139, cited by Rodinson, *Israel,* pp. 58–59.
54. Weizmann, *Trial and Error,* pp. 236ff.
55. Weinstock, "Israel," No. 18, pp. 57–63, and No. 20, pp. 20–32, cited by Rodinson, *Israel,* p. 56.
56. Ruppin, *Les Juifs dans le monde moderne,* French trans., pp. 380–382, cited by Rodinson, *Israel,* p. 59.
57. Rodinson, *Israel,* p. 65.
58. Martin Buber, "The Bi-National Approach to Zionism," in Buber, Magnes, and Simon, eds., *Towards Union in Palestine,* p. 11.
59. Magnes, "Solution Through Force?" in Buber, Magnes, and Simon, eds., *To-*

wards Union in Palestine, pp. 14–21. As Professor Rodinson points out, Dr. Magnes felt so strongly on this issue that he left his post and returned to the United States.

60. Letters to Saudi leader Ibn Saud on April 5, 1945, and October 28, 1946, in Lenczowski, *Middle East in World Affairs,* p. 553n.9, cited by Rodinson, *Israel,* p. 70.

61. Ibid., p. 396.

62. Rodinson, *Israel,* p. 72.

63. Syrkin, *Golda Meir,* p. 133.

64. *Al-Safir,* March 3, 1985.

65. Curtius, "West Bank Violence Stirs Debate," International Section, p. 9.

GLOSSARY

Ashkenazim: "Western" or European Jews.

Diaspora: "Dispersal"; the body of Jews living outside Palestine.

Halakha: Jewish law; lit. "the way."

Haskala: "Enlightenment"; the trend among European Jews in the nineteenth century to assimilate to European society.

Hovevei Zion: "Lovers of Zion"; early political Zionist organization in Russia led by Leo Pinsker.

Islām: "Submission" to the will of God.

Jihad: So-called Islamic "holy war"; lit. "extreme effort" in the cause of God.

Khalifa: "Successor" or "vice–regent"; in Islam, one who is entrusted with the task of carrying out God's will on earth.

Muslim: "One who submits" to the will of God.

Nizam-i tawhid: "Political or social order based on the principle of the unicity and supremacy of God"; a concept advanced by Iranian modernist Ali Shariati for Islamic social reform.

Qur'an: Sacred scripture of Islam revealed by God to the Prophet Muhammad.

Salat: "Prayer"; performed by Muslims five times daily.

Sephardim: "Oriental or eastern" Jews.

Shahada: "Bearing witness" to the unicity and supremacy of God; first duty of a Muslim.

Sharī'a: Islamic law; lit. "the way."

Shi'a: "Party or supporters" of Ali, the Prophet Muhammad's son-in-law and cousin; faction of Islamic religion differing from the Sunni majority in theories of leadership of the Muslim community and certain minor points of Islamic law.

Sunna: Customary practice sanctified by tradition; specifically, practice of the Prophet Muhammad which has been accepted as normative. Along with Qur'an, a major source of Islamic law.

Sunni: Majority of Muslims, those who accept the theory of leadership of the Muslim community popularly agreed as that followed by the Prophet Muhammad.

Tawhid: "Oneness or unicity" of God; primary concept in Islam, emphasized especially by the Shi'a.

Torah: Jewish sacred scripture; essentially the five books of Moses, but also referring to the entire religious literature of Judaism.

Ummah: Muslim "community"; all those who follow or submit to the will of God, whether Jewish, Christian, or Muslim.

Yishuv: Name adopted by the early Jewish community in Palestine.

BIBLIOGRAPHY

al-Afghani, Jamal al-Din, and Muhammad Abduh. *al-Urwa al-Wuthqa*. Beirut, 1329/1910.

al-Banna, Hasan. *Muddhakkarat al-Dawah wa'l-Daiyyah [Memoirs of the Call and the Caller]*. Beirut: al-Maktab al-Islami, 1979.

Antonius, George. *The Arab Awakening*. New York: Capricorn Books, 1965.

Arberry, A. J., ed. *Religion in the Middle East*. Cambridge: Cambridge University Press, 1969.

Ayoob, Mohammed, ed. *The Politics of Islamic Reassertion*. London: St. Martin's Press, 1981.

Bein, Alexandre. *Introduction au Sionisme*. Jerusalem: Rubin Mass, 1946.

Berkowits, Eliezar. "The Status of Woman Within Judaism." In Menachem Mark Kellner, ed. *Contemporary Jewish Ethics*. New York: Sanhedrin Press, 1979.

Buber, M., J. L. Magnes, and E. Simon, eds. *Towards Union in Palestine: Essays on Zionism and Jewish-Arab Cooperation*. Jerusalem: Ihud Association, 1947.

Chamberlain, Houston Stewart. *Die Grundlagen des neunzehnten Jahrhunderts*. Munchen: F. Bruckmann, 1901. *[Foundations of the Nineteenth Century*. Translated by John Lees. New York: John Lane Co., 1914.]

Chouraqui., A. *Introduction au Sianisme*. Jerusalem: Keter Books, 1946.

———. *A Man Alone, the Life of Theodor Herzl*. Jerusalem: Keter Books, 1970.

Cohen, Hermann. *Reason and Hope*. Translated by Eva Jospe. New York: Norton Books, 1971.

Cudsi, S. Alexander, and A. E. H. Dessouki, eds. *Islam and Power*. Baltimore: Johns Hopkins University Press, 1981.

Curtius, Mary. "West Bank Violence Stirs Debate." *Christian Science Monitor* International Section (February 12, 1985):9.

Dessouki, Ali E. Hillal, ed. *Islamic Resurgence in the Arab World*. New York: Praeger, 1982.

Donohue, John, and J. L. Esposito, eds. *Islam in Transition: Religion and Sociopolitical Change*. New York: Oxford University Press, 1982.

Dubnow, S. M. *Die neueste Geschichte des judischen Volkes (1798–1914) [The Most Recent History of the Jewish People (1798–1914]*. Berlin: Judischer Verlag, 1920–1923.

Encyclopaedia of Islam. Leiden: E. J. Brill, 1971.

Esposito, John L., ed. *Islam and Development: Religion and Sociopolitical Change*. Syracuse, N.Y.: Syracuse University Press, 1980.

———. *Voices of Resurgent Islam*. New York: Oxford University Press, 1983.

Fackenheim, Emil. "Religious Responsibility for the Social Order: A Jewish View." In Daniel Jeremy Silver, ed. *Judaism and Ethics*. New York: KTAV Publishers, 1970.

Gellner, Ernest. *Muslim Society*. Cambridge: Cambridge University Press, 1981.

Gibb, Hamilton A. R. *Modern Trends in Islam*. Chicago: University of Chicago Press, 1947.

———. *Studies on the Civilization of Islam*. Boston: Beacon Press, 1962.

Haddad, Yvonne Yazbeck. *Contemporary Islam and the Challenge of History*. Albany, N.Y.: SUNY Press, 1982.

Hertzberg, Arthur. *The Zionist Idea*. New York: Harper and Row, 1959.

Herzl, Theodor. *Der Judenstaat [L'Etat Juif*, French translation.] Paris: Lipschutz, 1926.

———. *Old-New Land*. Translated by Letta Levensohn. New York: Bloch Publishing Co., 1941.

Hess, Moses. *Rum und Jerusalem, die letzte nationalitatenfrage*. Tel Aviv: H. Ivrith, 1935 [*Rome and Jerusalem: A Study in Jewish Nationalism*. Translated by Meyer Waxman. New York: Bloch Publishing Co., 1935.]

Hodgson, Marshall. *The Venture of Islam*. Chicago: University of Chicago Press, 1977.

Hourani, Albert. *Arabic Thought in the Liberal Age, 1798–1939*. London: Oxford University Press, 1970.

Hudson, Michael C. *Arab Politics: The Search for Legitimacy*. New Haven, Conn.: Yale University Press, 1979.

Jansen, G. H. *Militant Islam*. New York: Harper and Row, 1980.

Karpat, Kemal H., ed. *Political and Social Thought in the Contemporary Middle East*. New York: Praeger, 1968.

Kellner, Menachem Marc, ed. *Contemporary Jewish Ethics*. New York: Sanhedrin Press, 1979.

Koestler, Arthur. *The Thirteenth Tribe*. New York: Popular Library, 1976.

Laqueur, Walter. *A History of Zionism*. New York: Holt, Rinehart and Winston, 1972.

Lazarus, Moritz. *Ethics of Judaism*. Translated by Henrietta Szold. Philadelphia: n.p., 1900.

Lenczowski, G. *The Middle East in World Affairs*. 3d ed. Ithaca, N.Y.: Cornell University Press, 1962.

Luzzato, Samuel David. "Israelitische Moral-Theologie." In Daniel Jeremy Silver, ed. *Judaism and Ethics*. New York: KTAV Publishing House, 1970.

Marr, Wilhelm. *Der Sieg des Judenthums über das Germanenthum (The Victory of Judaism Over Germanism)*. Hamburg, 1873.

Meyer, Michael A. "Problematics of Jewish Ethics." In Daniel Jeremy Silver, ed. *Judaism and Ethics*. KTAV Publishing House, 1970.

Monroe, E. *Britain's Moment in the Middle East, 1914–56*. Baltimore: Johns Hopkins University Press, 1963.

Nevakivi, Jukka. *Britain, France and the Arab Middle East 1914–1920*. London: Athlone Press, 1969.

Perlmann, M. "Chapters of Arab–Jewish Diplomacy, 1918–1922." *Jewish Social Studies* 6, No. 2 (April 1944): 123–124.

Pinsker, Leon. *Auto-Emancipation*. Translated by J. Schulsinger. Cairo-Alexandria: 1944. (Collection "Les ecrits juifs.")

Qutb, Sayyid. *Al-'adala al-Ijtima'iyyah fi'l-Islam* [Social Justice in Islam]. Cairo: Maktubat Misr, n.d.

———. *Fi Zilal Al-Qur'an* [Under the Shadows of the Qur'an]. Vol. 4, 12–18. Beirut: Dar al-Shuruq, 1974.

———. *Fi Zilal al-Qur'an* [Under the Shadows of the Qur'an]. Vol. 4, 10 N.P., 1966.

———. *Maarakat al-Islam wa'l-Rasmaliyya*. Beirut, 1975. Translated by Yvonne Haddad. *Voices of Islamic Resurgence*.

———. *Social Justice in Islam*. Washington, D.C.: American Council of Learned Societies, 1953.

———. *This Religion of Islam*. Kuwait: New Era Publishers, 1977.

Rahman, Fazlur. *Islam*. Chicago: University of Chicago Press, 1979.

———. *Islam and Modernity*. Chicago: University of Chicago Press, 1982.

Rida, Muhammad Rashid, *Ta'ripkh al-Ustadh al-Imam al-Shaykh Muhammad Abduh*. Cairo, 1344/1925–1926.

Rodinson, Maxime. *Israel: A Colonial-Settler State?* New York: Monad Press, 1973.

———. *Mohammed*. New York: Vintage Books, 1974.

Ruppin, Arthur. *Les Juifs dans le monde moderne*. French translation. Paris: Payot, 1934.

Shariati, Ali. *Intizar . . . Madhabi Itiraz* [Awaiting . . . The Religion of Protest]. Tehran; n.p., 1971.

———. *Islam Shinasi*. Meshad: n.p., 1347/1978. Translated by Abdulaziz Sachedina. "Ali Shariati: Ideologue of the Iranian Revolution." *Voices of Islamic Resurgence*.

Silver, Daniel Jeremy, ed. *Judaism and Ethics*. New York: KTAV Publishing House, 1970.

Smith, Wilfred Cantwell. *Islam in Modern History*. Princeton, N.J.: Princeton University Press, 1957.

Syrkin, Marie. *Golda Meir*. French translation. Paris: Gallimard, 1966.

Weinstook, Nathan. "Israel le sionisme et la lutte des classes." *Partisans*, No. 18 (December 1964/January 1965): 57–63; no. 20 (April-May 1965): 20–32.

Weizmann, Chaim. *Trial and Error*. New York: Harper and Bros., 1949.

2

The Catholic-Protestant Conflict in Northern Ireland

GERARD S. SLOYAN

Northern Ireland is the political entity that came into being in 1920 as a result of the Government of Ireland Act of the British Parliament and became a part of the United Kingdom (with England, Scotland, and Wales) in 1922. It is made up of six counties of Ireland's traditional thirty-two: Antrim (where Belfast, the capital, is located), Down, Armagh, Fermanagh, Tyrone, and Londonderry (formerly Derry and before 1608 Coleraine). The other three counties in the north-eastern province of Ulster, one of Ireland's four provinces, are Monaghan, Cavan, and Donegal. They are in the twenty-six county Republic of Ireland which in its roots emerged from the civil war of 1922–1923. The Republic was declared to be such on April 18, 1949. It had been called the Irish Free State in 1922–1949 (by the External Relations Act) and Southern Ireland, with a separate parliament and government from Northern Ireland, during 1920–1922. The problem of a divided Ireland can be seen to be, at base, the problem of a divided Ulster. Northern Ireland had a separate provincial parliament from its beginnings in 1920, which passed laws pertaining only to the province (as it is popularly called) until March 24, 1972. On that date the parliament which met at Stormont in Belfast was dissolved, and direct English rule was imposed. This means that the six counties of the province are ruled immediately by the parliament at Westminster in London, up to the present writing.

What caused the division into two countries of an island and a people which always considered itself to be one despite—indeed, in virtue of—foreign domination over a period of seven hundred years? Is religious difference the root cause, as is commonly said, of the political differences between the Irish of the north and south? Does it lie at the heart of the violent struggle between the two factions in Northern Ireland, as is usually alleged? This chapter seeks to answer that question, although as an old saying has it, "Whoever thinks he understands Northern Ireland proves he does not."

The short answer to the question posed above seems to be that an active colonialism of four-hundred years' standing is at the core of Ireland's "English problem." Religious difference is a visible and convenient way to describe a profound difference over civil and human rights. The struggle over these rights is rooted in the politics of privilege, standard of living, and economics far more than in religion. Northern Ireland is a land of relative middle-class comfort and grinding poverty that cut across religious lines, much more than it is a country of warring Protestants and Catholics.

There are 35,595 square miles in Ireland, which means it is roughly the size of Maine. It lies opposite Labrador but has a much milder climate (winter average 42°F, summer average 59°F) because of the Gulf Stream. There were 4,497,888 Irish in the census of 1971: 2,978,248 in the Republic (66 percent of the total) and 1,519,640 in Northern Ireland (34 percent of the total). In that same year 93.9 percent in the Republic declared themselves Catholics, 3.3 percent members of the Church of Ireland (the Anglican Communion), 0.5 percent Presbyterians, 0.2 percent each Methodists and Baptists, and 0.08 percent Jews. Those who did not reply and "others" constituted 2 percent. There has been an important decline in religious practice in the Republic since 1971, but the 1986 figures would probably yield only a small increase in those inclined not to reply to the question or declare themselves anything but Catholics.

The religious statistics for Northern Ireland of the same date are as follows: Catholics 31.4 percent, Presbyterians 26.7 percent, Church of Ireland members 22.0 percent, Methodists 4.7 percent, Baptists 1.1 percent, Jews 0.06 percent, and "others" including "no reply" 14 percent. The overall figures would, if broken down, show a large majority of Catholics in the relatively lightly populated counties of Armagh, Fermanagh, and Tyrone and a proportionately higher number of Protestants in Antrim, Down, and Londonderry. The 54.5 percent of Protestants (to whom the unclassified 14 percent should probably be added if sympathies are reckoned) and the 31.4 percent of Catholics is the socio-cultural rather than isolated religious fact that most needs to be taken into account.

Unemployment in Northern Ireland—always the highest in Great Britain— reached a total of 112,978 or 19.7 percent in May 1982: male 24.2 percent, female 13.7 percent. A breakdown of this figure by religion is unavailable and relatively unimportant, for although Catholics in certain areas are familiar with being "last hired, first fired," the overall economic situation is more telling than any figures on religious distinctions among the jobless. Cumulative fatalities in the continuing civil strife in Northern Ireland between 1969 and 1982 rose from 13 to 2,265, with 1972 the peak year; 1,594 of them were civilian deaths and 663 occurred among the police or army (either Ulster or English forces). Those who resist the government may consider themselves an "army" but are in fact civilians.

The immediate situation of conflict goes back to 1967 and 1968 when an integrated civil rights movement with a nonviolent strategy was inaugurated. The Social Democratic and Labour Party, made up largely of Catholics with some Protestants, was formed in 1970. It stands for the eventual reunification of Ireland, or at least a close association of the thirty-two counties. The paramilitary group known as the Irish Republican Army (founded in 1919) was split into the "Officials" and the "Provisionals" in December 1969, and one month later the political party known as Sinn Féin ("we ourselves"), which continues in the Republic from the days of Irish independence under that name but quite separately, saw the Provisional Sinn Féin walk out of the annual convention. The most influential political group is the Official Unionist Party, successor to the Unionist Party, the controlling power in Ulster politics from 1921 to 1972. Since the early 1970s many splinter parties have come into existence: the Reverend Ian Paisley's Democratic Unionist Party (1971), the United Ulster Unionist Party (1977), and the Ulster Loyalist Democratic Party (1978). All favor political ties with Great Britain and a settlement of the region's problems by a majority vote of the present citizens. The last-named party stands for devolution: the return of decision-making powers from Great Britain to Northern Ireland levels of government.

A perfect stalemate seems to exist, and for two reasons: the majority community is aligned with Great Britain and the minority community with the Republic of Ireland, a division reflected along religious lines; and most English governments have been adamant that Northern Ireland not depart from integral union with Great Britain. This is true even though the Sunningdale Agreement of 1977 stated that if a majority of voters wished the (present) north to be a part of the Irish Republic after a border poll, Great Britain would not resist it. Such a poll, testing opinion on the legitimacy of Northern Ireland's border, was subsequently taken. It resulted in 57 percent of those polled in the north opting to stay in the United Kingdom. This figure, in light of the relative strengths of the two religious populations (31.4 percent Catholics, 68.6 percent not so declared), indicates that the difference is more properly a split between "unionists" and "nationalists" than between Protestants and Catholics.

It is often asked why the British government disfavors the self-determination of a neighboring island by way of the ordinary political processes, starting with the withdrawal of "peace-keeping" troops which are not neutral but on one side in the conflict. The usual answers given include the protection of the civil rights of loyal British subjects, the inherent instability of the Northern Ireland situation, and the bloodbath that would follow a "pullout." In fact, the British have probably never forgiven the Irish for displaying the initiative that led to the break-up of the empire, for Ireland precedes India and the many other countries that declared their independence of England, with or without retaining Commonwealth status.

It would be quite wrong to maintain that religious differences have nothing to do with the desires of the two major populations of Ireland to be separately self-governed, whether or not with a tie to Great Britain. Although factors such as the economic and the civil rights issues are much more influential than the religious symbolism in continuing the breach, the religious factor prevails in the popular Irish mind. It makes "Protestant" and "Catholic" code words for the enfranchised and the disenfranchised, the Anglo-Scottish and the Gaelic, the haves and the have nots, even though the reality is in many cases at odds with the categorization. Popular perception prevails and finds its expression in two religious modes of being which are in fact broadly cultural more than narrowly religious.

Some time between 10,000 and 6,000 B.C., after the end of the Ice Age (ca. 15,000), Ireland was cut off from Britain which in turn had been separated from the continental land mass. About 6,000 B.C. the first people came to modern Ulster from Scandinavia by way of Britain. These Middle Stone Age people, hunters and fishers, left only the most primitive tools and weapons behind them. By the year 3,000 neolithic colonizers from the Middle East reached France, the Low Countries, Great Britain, and Ireland. The last-named population became tillers of the soil and fashioners of axes and pottery, in which they seem to have developed a modest trade. They raised massive stone monuments to their dead, with access to the burial chambers through low passages. This was chiefly in the northern part of the island. Dolmens are common throughout Ireland: stone tripods capped by still another stone. The mining and working of copper dates to about 2,000 B.C. and with it the fashioning of objects in bronze. Notable among these is the crescent necklet called the *lunula* which, along with objects wrought in amber, was exported to Europe. Presumably for religious ceremonies, the people created great circles of stones near which fragments of vessels for food and drink have been found. Around 1200 B.C. short heavy swords appeared and with them armory of bronze and leather. Iron came into common use in pre-Christian Europe by the year 600 and, concurrent with it, the expansion westward of a warrior people from Gaul whom the Greeks called *Keltoi*. These were well settled in Ireland by 150 B.C., both in the west (from the continent?) and in the northeast from northern Britain.

Irish history, properly speaking, begins in the fifth century A.D., by which time the whole language and culture of the island was Celtic. The people were primarily farmers; there were no towns or villages. There were petty kings— actually chieftains—around whom sagas gathered, but the heroic age thus celebrated was undoubtedly brief. The social unit was the joint family, much as in Hindu culture, while the political unit was the petty kingdom. The two were not interconnected. There were slaves, laborers, and artisans, as well as land-owning freemen and nobles. Judges and bards comprised the learned class governing this society.

However Christianity reached Ireland (from Roman Britain? from Gaul?), a bishop was appointed by Rome for the Irish Christians in 431. Saint Patrick in his rudely composed Latin autobiography calls himself a native of Britain and says he spent the years from sixteen to twenty-two as a captive of Irish raiders, tending sheep "in the woods and on the mountain." Returned to Britain in safety, he somewhere acquired ecclesiastical learning—perhaps in Gaul—and returned to Ireland, as he tells it, in response to a vision. In this vision a certain

Victoricus handed him a letter which had as its opening words, "The voice of the Irish." It read: "We beg you, lad, come and walk among us once again."

Patrick probably entered Ireland (432 or 456, living until 461 or 490) somewhere in the County Down, where he is also legendarily buried (Downpatrick). His missionary work was, by his own account, highly successful and fraught with peril from resistant pagans. It was probably carried on north of an imaginary line drawn between Galway and Wexford. Patrick introduced bishops into Ireland, as the record of a synod in his lifetime testifies. But he also introduced monastic life which came to outstrip by far in influence diocesan organization. The abbots of the great monasteries like Cormac of Armagh came to be men in bishop's orders as well. Saints Enda, Finian, Columcille, Kieran, Brendan, Kevin, Jarlath, and Finnbar are the best known of the monastic founders. Saint Brigid founded a double monastery of men and women in sixth century Kildare. Irish foundations were made in Scotland, Britain, and Gaul, like that of Columbanus in Luxeuil who then moved on to Bobbio in northern Italy before his death (613). His disciple Gall went on to found a monastery of that name in Switzerland. Irish monasticism peaked in the seventh and eighth centuries and found itself under siege of the Vikings in the ninth and tenth. The dominance of the Norse was broken under Brian Boru of Munster, who operated out of Cashel toward 1000. Many a treasure of Irish craft had ended up in Oslo or Trondheim over the previous two centuries, books and treasures of another sort going to European monasteries and courts for safe-keeping. The poet Sedulius and the philosopher Joannes Eriugena (whose face is on the Irish five pound note) are two whose learning graced the Carolingian court. The Irish love of learning and the bookmaker's art is legendary.

In 1155 Henry II, the Angevin (i.e., Norman French) king of England, seems to have asked Pope Adrian IV—Nicholas Breakspear, that bishopric's only English incumbent—for permission to enter Ireland to achieve its religious reform. The papal bull *Laudabiliter* allowed it, but there was no royal invading action until 1171. The way for this action was paved by Dermot MacMurrough of Leinster, who, driven out of Ireland by his enemy Tiernán O'Rourke, sought the English king's help. A preliminary invasion was mounted with the aid of numerous Norman-Welsh and Flemish knights armed with cross-bows. After numerous bloody engagements, the Normans were victorious over the Norsemen of Dublin and Wexford and the Gaelic Irish. When Henry II landed at Waterford, he progressed triumphantly to Cashel where Normans, Irish, and Norse, as well as all the bishops, submitted to his rule. He ruled through Irish barons of both Gaelic and Norman stock. One of the Normans, John de Courcy, having conquered northeast Ulster early, gave that province twenty-seven peaceful years. Within the next eight decades the Normans were victorious throughout the land except in Connacht, the northwestern province.

The thirteenth century saw considerable order established and an end to the warring of Gaelic families. This was achieved by both careful administrative procedures and intermarriage. The Gaelic Irish settled in the countryside; the

Normans were concentrated in the towns that sprang up everywhere around their fortresses. The Anglo-Irish suffered a defeat at the hands of the Gaelic Irish in 1270, following which the Gaelic Irish increasingly turned to foreign powers for help. Already in 1300, the Irish and English were locked in the question of who would have control in Ireland. The settlers from England and Wales of the twelfth and thirteenth centuries gave Ireland its parliament, its local govenments, and its fiscal accounting system. There was no "religious question," but there was a large one of a foreign colonizing power, which imposed the feudal order of England on a seemingly peaceful Ireland. Great sums of money were drawn from Ireland by Henry II (d. 1272) and earlier by the sainted Edward I, "the Confessor" (d. 1066). The spirit of revival by the Gaelic Irish never entirely died, even though the old high kingship of Tara was not restored. Edward Bruce, a Scot (and brother to Robert), came closest to doing it in 1315. But Ireland's status as a colony continued. Its one outstanding characteristic was the assimilation of the conquerors to the language and customs of the conquered. Becoming "more Irish than the Irish" was not a catchword but has always been a reality of Irish history.

The English government, alarmed at the assimilation process, called a parliament at Kilkenny in 1366 to bring the Anglo-Irish settlers to heel. England devoted much of the fourteenth century to curbing the Gaelic revival. Richard II lost the throne to Henry of Lancaster in 1399, a victim of the Irish wars. Gradually, the colony shrank to the size of the Pale, a four-county area around Dublin surrounded in Henry VII's reign by an earthwork six feet high. Ireland supported York against Lancaster in the War of the Roses and came to be a real thorn in Lancastrian Tudor England's side. Its threat to the stability of the English throne caused England to turn seriously to its repression. The English colonists in despair appealed at one point to Henry VI to ask the Pope to sanction a crusade against their Irish enemies.

The Gaelic Irish had a champion in Thomas, Earl of Desmond, from his victory of Lancastrian forces near Carrick-on-Suir in 1462 until his beheading at Drogheda in 1468. With the eclipse of that house and the Butlers of Ormond, there came to the fore in 1478 Garret More Fitzgerald of Maynooth in Kildare, the "great earl." He attracted the loyalty of both Gaelic Irish and Anglo-Irish, channeling his power to the Yorkist cause. When the Tudor Henry VII was seven years on the throne, he decided to eliminate Ireland as a Yorkist base by reducing it to complete submission. In a parliament of 1494–1495 he resurrected the statutes of Kilkenny of 1366 and forbade the use of Irish customs in law, dress, and hairstyle. This king ruled Ireland fairly peacefully through Sir Edward Poynings, but his son Henry VIII chose to enter into Irish affairs more directly in 1519 by sending the Earl of Surrey across the channel with conquest in view.

Henry was not successful until 1541 when, as part of Tudor imperial expansion, he declared himself king (rather than lord) of Ireland, the first English monarch to bear the title. The Irish wars turned serious under Henry, who then employed a policy of methodically bringing the chief Gaelic and Anglo-Irish lords into camp. By the time of his death in 1547 it had largely succeeded. The notable exception was the introduction of the new state religion into Ireland, for despite the dissolution of the monasteries by the time of the king's death the efforts of the friars in city, town, and countryside kept the old Catholic faith largely alive. Queen Elizabeth had little better success at enforced conversion. The Irish parliament of 1560 tried to make Ireland Protestant by law but the populace resisted, understanding the reformed religion to be an arm of a foreign government. Anglo-Irish and Gaelic Irish alike retained the ancient faith, which showed itself a force for Irish unity against the English oppressor.

Throughout the Middle Ages the province of Ulster, ruled by the O'Neills of Tyrone and the O'Donnells of Tyrconnell, remained largely Gaelic, traditional, and outside the province of English law. "Red Hugh" O'Donnell came home from London as a Renaissance statesman in the late sixteenth century, ready to do the bidding of the Tudor Queen Elizabeth. But after achieving the defeat of the Earl of Desmond he felt uncomfortable in the role of imposer of an alien culture and turned to rebellion against the crown. After nine years of bloody war he confessed himself defeated and, in 1607, took flight with O'Donnell to Spain and Italy. The "flight of the earls" brought the underdeveloped rural population of Ulster close to despair. Early in the century that followed, Tudor policy dictated the "plantation" of lowland Scots in great numbers in Ulster to achieve the domination that force of arms could not. Previous settlement of the English on the land had not been successful (Spenser and Raleigh settled in Munster, for example, on the model of the Virginia plantation), but the efforts of commercial enterprises like the Irish Company of London in the county of Coleraine were. In these schemes the Catholic, Irish–speaking natives were left on their own land which they worked and for which they paid a high rent. Others carried on a guerrilla warfare from the woods and hills.

The Scots made far better colonists than the English, farming more successfully than the herdsmen Irish had ever done. The province of Ulster was thus populated by Catholics, Anglicans, and Presbyterian Scots and in the early seventeenth century lived amid tension much like that of the American frontier with its "pioneers" and native Indians. The "old English" from the Middle Ages meanwhile, remained Catholics and were at odds with the other three populations. Toward the middle of the century, Charles I's lord deputy, Sir Thomas Wentworth, enforced the government's ecclesiastical policy against Catholics and Presbyterians alike. The Presbyterians made common cause with the Scots against the crown in England's parliamentary wars. A native Ulster uprising led by Sir Phelim O'Neill and a "Catholic Army" came to little besides a Catholic parliament in Kilkenny in 1642. The "Roundheads" achieved the execution of the king in 1649, and Oliver Cromwell came to Ireland by way of Wexford as representative of the parliament, for the suppression of an Irish revolt. To this day its bloody character has not been forgotten.

A new landlord scheme ensued outside Ulster, where the landed Irish or old English had until then held the populace in thrall. In Ulster, fierce reprisals were mounted against the planters; this savage treatment likewise lives long in memory. The net effect of the rising of 1641 by the dispossessed natives against their exploiters, the planters, was that a struggle for power and property gave the appearance of being a war of religion. The impression was strengthened when lands were confiscated on the grand scale and distributed to Cromwell's army veterans and "adventurers," creating a Protestant land-owning and ruling class.

In Ulster, however, a certain prosperity ensued among the industrious farmers, weavers, and linen-makers who, being Protestants, were not exploited as elsewhere in Ireland. They provided stiff economic competition to the English by their productivity, which the English attempted to ward off by legislation. Ulster remained a strange cultural and religious patchwork through all this, with the Gaelic Irish retaining the cultural ascendancy that had always marked the province in the midst of political defeat. James II, a Catholic, succeeded his brother Charles in 1685 and two years later brought apprehension to Protestant hearts and hope to Catholics by his appointment of Richard Talbot, Duke of Tyrconnell, a Catholic, as lord lieutenant. When William of Orange deprived James of the throne in 1688, Tyrconnell held Ireland briefly for the English. King James came to Ireland, only to have Protestant Enniskillen and Derry successfully resist him. This weakened the king as he moved north from Dublin to engage the Williamite army at the River Boyne on July 1, 1690 (July 12, new style). The resounding defeat of the Stuart cause at that site lives in Protestant mythology. It was followed by further setbacks in Aughrim, County Galway, and the town of Limerick, making the crushing of Stuart power final. By 1700 nearly all the land of Ireland was in the hands of new owners. The old English and native Irish aristocracy, Catholics all, were thoroughly stripped of ownership and power. The Protestant ascendancy was in full control from then on, enforcing a penal code on the Catholics which was not religious in intent but was meant to deprive them corporately of all property and influence. The net result, however, was to identify by religion the two classes set against each other. The Protestants had the parish churches, the Catholics the tiny chapels. A visual parable was thereby provided of the economic and social reality.

The land–owners of the eighteenth century tended to be adherents to the Church of Ireland left over from the previous century's settlements of Cromwell or William of Orange. Some Catholic land–owners also survived. This was a ruling class of landed and sometimes merchant proprietors whose title was money, not nobility or breeding. Only in Ulster was there any sizable Protestant population among the lower classes. There was sporadic Gaelic Irish support of the Stuart cause (1715, 1745) in unsuccessful uprisings. Quakers, Huguenots, and Presbyterians suffered discrimination at the hands of the established church ascendancy, if not nearly in the same measure as Catholics. The Presbyterians of Ulster solved their problem in good part by emigration to America, leaving a preponderant Irish-speaking population in the province through much of the eighteenth century. Those who remained lost their character as Scots and became Irish of a new kind—Ulstermen, popularly "Scotch Irish." They organized as secret societies to resist the exactions of land–owners and the established church alike—the "Oakboys" in Ulster, the "Whiteboys" (from their hooded heads) in Munster. At the same time these burnings and lootings went on, the ascendancy was resisting the restraints of trade imposed on them by the English. The American Revolution provided Ulster with some relief. After those hostilities the Irish colonists were granted a Dublin parliament freed from that of Westminster and certain liberties of Irish trade.

In Ulster, the landlords began to drive the Presbyterians with their good living-standard off the land, often into exile, and to replace them with the Catholic peasantry, which worked at intolerable rents in direst poverty. Protestant volunteers under arms in Dublin and Belfast in the mid–1780s took the part of Catholics (who under the penal code could not possess arms) against the government. Catholics under arms were greatly feared, however, chiefly for the economic threat they posed. Some Presbyterian violence against Catholics was countered by a movement called the Defenders founded by a dissenting clergyman, but the Catholic capitulation to the exorbitant rents made them a genuine economic competitor. The governor of Armagh, Lord Charlemont, attempted to replace the Protestant raiders of Catholic homes (known as the Peep O'Day Boys) with a legitimate police force to restore order, to which the Williamite or Orange forces responded with provocative, emblematic displays in Catholic Defender areas.

The anti-landlord movement grew as an agrarian secret society from 1787 to 1793, when the crown disbanded and replaced it with a Catholic militia and the franchise for Catholics. This British move—to reduce Irish opposition to ascendancy—brought in its wake Protestant fears and reprisals. James Wilson, a County Tyrone farmer, organized the Orange Boys at Benburb in 1793 against the looting Defenders. A pitched battle at Loughgall, County Armagh, resulted in the definitive formation of the Orange movement by James Sloan, the keeper of a hostelry in the place. It has survived in vigor to the present day. Meantime, Theobald Wolfe Tone, of Protestant stock, founded the United Irishmen at Dublin in 1791, a movement designed to resist English domination, with equality for Catholics as a part of its larger political goals. The movement featured the Gaelic past but also took on a French Jacobin character, pressing for "the rights of man," and became revolutionary in intent. As the United Irishmen and the Defender interests came closer, the Orangemen began to gain the support of the Williamite ascendancy, despite the fact that numerous Presbyterians of the upper class were attracted by the goals of the United Irishmen. The support of the violent Orangemen was accepted by the ruling class, for preservation of their lives and property should armed conflict occur. The English response was to try to drive a wedge between the United Irishmen and the Orange order, disarming Ulster the while. The result was the breaking of the spirit of rebellion in the province, with Catholic supporters of the government set against Presbyterian defenders of the Catholic cause. Sir William Pitt achieved some half-measures of Catholic relief in 1793, but the British moderates largely failed, leaving

Ulster's fate in the hands of Protestants as to support for the Orange or Catholic blocs.

Elsewhere in Ireland the British military struck hard blows in 1798, while the ascendancy went from a policy of repudiating both Defenders and Orangemen to first tolerating and then joining the Orange lodges. The plans of a French landing under Bonaparte in support of Tone's United Irishmen were thwarted in 1797. The rising throughout Ireland of Presbyterian republicanism lost its Catholic support at various key places, but an Irish republic was declared north and south in May and June of 1798 even as reports of a Catholic pogrom of Protestants in Wexford reached the republican centers. The French landed an ineffective force in Killala Bay, County Mayo, that summer (Bonaparte had been deployed to Egypt), Tone was taken prisoner on the French flagship, and the rising was bloodily put down. At that point Pitt united England and Ireland in a single parliament at Westminster.

Two large matters came of the rising: a host of bitter memories and the beginnings of modern Irish nationalism. The Presbyterian republican spirit, admitting the Catholics to full participation, was crushed. It was neutralized by the rapid growth of Orangeism. And the British once more divided to conquer.

Nineteenth–century Irish history took its rise from the Act of Union of 1801. The Dublin parliament of commons was suppressed. The lords began to take up residence in England, while not deserting their Irish landholdings. The Orange lodges remained politically neutral, though in sentiment they opposed the union. While Dublin faded as a political capital, Belfast grew in prosperity and size, becoming Ireland's second largest city (119,000 by 1861). Tanning, brewing, distilling, and the weaving of cotton and linen gave it prestige and power. This industrial development caused new tensions between the Protestant worker class and the Catholics who flooded Belfast and offered themselves as far cheaper labor. The union made all Irishmen the victims of colonial exploitation, the English governing Ireland at a distance through absentee landlords and the control of Ulster markets. Colonial settlers and natives were set against each other more forcefully than ever before. The deep cultural and religious differences of the two parties were underscored by the political and economic division, and vice versa. The chief distinguishing characteristic of Ulster was that it alone had a Protestant worker class, fully Irish, which in the industrial towns was exploited along with the Catholics. The sole comfort which the Protestant laborer had was that the Catholic laborer or peasant farmer was in a still more desperate condition than he.

One major effect of the nineteenth–century colonial pattern was that the Irish language faded and yielded to the English. The Catholic faith and its Latin liturgy did not. The bishops were not especially responsible for this fidelity, as they most often sided with the oppressive government in order to maintain the free practice of religion and education. The village priest—*soggarth aroon*—was literally the preserver of the ancient faith.

Early in the century a man of an old Catholic family of landlords, Daniel

O'Connell, led the movement called "Catholic emancipation." It eventuated in a bill for emancipation in 1829 intended for the middle class. It also won the adherence of the Catholic masses. The country's population grew from five million to eight million in the first forty years of the century, thence to be sharply reduced by the famine caused by three successive failures of the potato crop (1845–1847) and a consequent emigration. By this time O'Connell, who had become a unionist, had lost widespread Catholic support. The Orange order, meanwhile, fell into temporary decline after 1798, even through Robert Emmet's failed insurgency in 1803. It found new vigor in response to O'Connell's successful struggle for emancipation, in particular among the Anglican settlers of Armagh and Monaghan. Tory unionists joined it, despite its violent tactics, as a means to resist perceived attacks on the constitution. Uniformed soldiery and veterans, regular and irregular, marched in each other's strongholds to strike symbolic terror in opposing hearts, sometimes striking each other dead in hand-to-hand clashes.

Union with England was not a primary goal of Orangeism, which did not forget its republican past, but it was seen as a practical goal ensuring protection against engulfment by the Gaelic Catholic Irish. The establishment was riding a tiger but feared the consequences of changing the mode of transport. From 1830 onward, Orangeism with its potent myths (much like those of the American frontiersmen or later Afrikaans trekkers) became a Presbyterian phenomenon and William III the authentic hero at the Boyne over Catholic rather than Stuart pretensions. Belfast liberalism and toleration were casualties of the realignment of forces.

Outside Ulster, a Protestant-inspired movement of romantic nationalists who called themselves "Young Irelanders" sprang up in mid-century under the leadership of Thomas Davis. It appealed to Irish pride by creating a sort of mythical past and centered its energies on the abolition of the landlord system. O'Connell's constitutionalism was repudiated in favor of various resorts to force through secret organizations. The best known of these was a group that originated in 1858 whose watchword, "Fenians, Awake!" lives longer in memory via James Joyce's play on it, *Finnegan's Wake*. The Fenians, properly entitled the Irish Republican Brotherhood, were nationalist and democratic and made their strongest gains among the Irish laboring classes. Michael Davitt's Irish National Land League (which he founded in October 1879, in conjunction with Charles Stewart Parnell) represented his departure from Fenian ranks, for his part in which he had served seven years in English prisons. He turned his attention from politics to economics as he organized the Irish farmers faced by bankruptcy and eviction in the agricultural crisis of 1879. Parnell, a Protestant land–owner, was acceptable to all segments of Irish nationalist society and became the League's first president. In 1880 he led the Irish party in the British parliament.

That same year, in the midst of the Irish "land war" (1879–1882), Thomas Gladstone succeeded Disraeli's conservative government. In that three-year long skirmish tenants successfully stood up against their evictors for the first time.

Gladstone's government at first repressed the League, but in the third government he formed, at age seventy-seven, Gladstone forged a home-rule bill which failed of passage in Commons (1896) by only thirty votes. Lord Randolph Churchill was among its impassioned opponents. Gladstone never gave up fighting for home rule in his eight remaining years in public life. Parnell fell from power in a domestic scandal in 1890, damaging the Irish cause in Britain, but by this time the self-perception of the Irish as politically capable of handling their own affairs was irreversibly fixed. Parnell brought home to the English in a unique way the case for, if not the actuality of, Irish self-government. The situation could never again revert to that of Angevin, Tudor, or eighteenth–century days.

Back in the late 1840s and 1850s an Ulster Tenant Right association had merged with one centered in Dublin to become the League of North and South. In its northern origins it was an attempt to keep alive the distinctive "Ulster custom." This dated to the seventeenth century when, as an inducement to immigrant tenants, leases tended to be long and the deep interest of the tenant in his land recognized. He was not penalized as elsewhere in the country for increased productivity or the improvement of his acres. This, coupled with security of tenure and relative freedom from harassment of farmers who went into crafts (like linen-weaving), resulted in an Ulster prosperity unknown in the rest of Ireland. When in mid-century the "Ulster custom" was threatened along with tenant rights in the other three provinces, the Protestants of Ulster made common cause with the Catholics everywhere. In their efforts they used priests from the south to address tenant meetings in the north and Protestant clergy to do the same in Catholic strongholds. This collaboration continued intermittently on the land question despite Protestant suspicions of the politics of Catholics. The Land League tried to resurrect this earlier solidarity in 1880 but failed in the attempt. To cite the best known example, labor was withheld on the estate of a Captain Charles Boycott of Mayo in that year, but the "boycott" was broken by a workforce of Orangemen who came from Cavan and Monaghan to harvest his fields in September.

In 1886 the Land League mounted a plan to withhold rents from unreasonable landlords, but Ulster did not cooperate fully except in the Catholic areas. Lord Salisbury, the English prime minister, oversaw a new concessionary act in 1887, legislated in good part to dampen Ulster interest in home rule. The revolutionary movement on the countryside, geared to achieve the latter end, was channeled by middle-class Catholics and their Protestant leadership (men like Parnell) toward displacing the Protestant ascendancy. Davitt and Parnell split over this issue, Davitt going in the direction of achieving nationhood for Ireland and Parnell holding fast to the League's earlier aim of tenant relief. When the Catholic bishops were won over to a qualified support of the nationalist cause, the worst of Ulster Protestant suspicions were aroused.

From the defeat of the home rule bill (June 8, 1886) onward, violence in Ulster, especially Belfast, increased. The Royal Irish Constabulary was brought to the fore, its largely Catholic members from outside the city being called in to quell the dockside riots. The Orange order experienced a new birth as it marched to pipes and drums through Belfast streets accoutered in "the sash me father wore." Unionist clubs sprang up everywhere, and unionism, once the battle cry of the Tory ascendancy, became the watchword of the Presbyterian proletariat. "Croppies lie down!" (from the cropped heads of republican sympathizers in the rising of 1798) was a cry heard everywhere. By 1900 the laboring class in Ulster was deeply divided on every issue. The landed descendants of the seventeenth–century settlers took full advantage of this situation to maintain themselves in power.

James Connolly, an Edinburgh-born son of emigrant parents, returned to Belfast in 1917 to organize the Irish Transport and General Workers Union. He stayed to press the cause of the Irish Socialist Republican Party (founded 1911). He stood for the distribution of the private property of the rich as the necessary condition of home rule. The Gaelic League was founded in 1893 by Douglas Hyde and Eoin Mac Neill to foster Irish language, culture, folklore, and sports. It at first had no avowed political purpose. Its rapid growth, however (600 branches in ten years), was a nationalist statement that could not be disregarded. Men like D. P. Moran, Eoghan O'Growney, and the young poet Padraic Pearse worked hard for what Hyde called the de-anglicization of Ireland. The League's renewal of Irish life at every level could not escape the notice even of unionists. It gave its coloration to a political party called Sinn Féin inspired by Arthur Griffith, an unreconstructed Parnellite, which was organized around 1900. Sinn Féin's platform was simplicity itself: the act of union of 1800 was illegitimate; hence every seating of parliament which included Ireland since that time was the same. His separatist movement was marked by passive resistance, and that of the Irish Republican Brotherhood (IRB) (Fenians) by armed aggression. The two inevitably drew closer together and awaited England's entanglement in a foreign war. In these years an expatriate returned from New York, Tom Clarke, and Seán MacDermott rejuvenated the IRB. Pearse and the intellectuals of the Gaelic revival joined them, as did the socialists Connolly and Jim Larkin. The stage was being set for the Easter rising of 1916, notably by Pearse's speech at Wolfe Tone's funeral in 1913 and that of Jermiah O'Donovan Rossa of Skibbereen, County Cork, a Fenian who went back to 1848. A home rule bill of 1914 was kept from passage by violent agitation in Ulster, where the Ulster Volunteers were arming themselves by guns shipped from Germany to take over Ulster on the day home rule became law. Sinn Féin, meanwhile, and Irish nationalists generally, opposed home rule, but they were losing out to the quieter parliamentary tactics of Lord Asquith and Ireland's John Redmond. The coming of the war rendered the question moot.

The Easter Monday rebellion of 1916 in Dublin was only a fragment of what had been planned. It came when James Connolly's Citizen Army was joined to a force founded in Dublin as the Irish Volunteers (a counterpart to those in Ulster). After a heavy week of fighting, seven signers proclaimed Ireland a republic on April 24: Clarke, Pearse, Connolly, Seán MacDermott, Eamonn

Ceannt, and two other poets, Thomas MacDonagh and Joseph Mary Plunkett. Fifteen of the ninety rebels condemned were executed between May 3 and 12, including the leaders. In the next year and a half, everything went in Sinn Féin's direction, so that when an election was called in December 1918 it won seventy–three seats, the unionists twenty–six and John Redmond's parliamentary party six. Sinn Féin constituted itself the Dáil (Assembly) Éirann with Eamonn de Valera, a mathematics professor born of expatriate parents in Rochester, New York, at its head and Arthur Griffith his deputy; Michael Collins was the organizer of the IRB. War with England lasted from early 1919 to July 1921—a bitter, brutal struggle. A compromise peace treaty was signed in December 1921. England gave dominion status to twenty-six counties and withheld it from the others. Although the bulk of the nation was not granted the status of a republic but a chance to achieve liberty, the unionists of Ulster, who had resisted home rule vigorously, received a measure of it in 1920 in the Government of Ireland Act under Lloyd George. Once the treaty was signed in 1921, the "free state" began its laborious march to becoming the Republic of Ireland. Six counties of the province of Ulster remained in the United Kingdom, after Sir Edward Carson's failed attempt at Buckingham Palace in 1914 to except the whole province from any home rule.

The partition of Ireland was done in London by men who had no special stake in Ulster. They drew the border where they did to include non-unionist Tyrone and Fermanagh as a means of carving off the largest territory possible while keeping a two-to-one voting majority for the Union. The name Northern Ireland was, of course, a misnomer, since parts of County Donegal in the "south" are the most northerly in Ireland. The new unionist government, once in place, did little to placate the nationalist minority. From the start and continuously throughout, the Protestant and Catholic laboring poor had a wedge driven between them by a Protestant middle class in the best (or worst) tradition of the preceding century. The Government of Ireland Act of 1920 had envisioned two parliaments, a northern and a southern, "with a view to the eventual establishment of a Parliament for the whole of Ireland." Given the outcome of the civil war that shortly followed, that united parliament never came to pass. A *pro tempore* parliament, however, remained the constitutional basis on which Northern Ireland operated for the next fifty years. Many fiscal and legislative powers were reserved to the English parliament by this act, although Irish constituencies continued to be represented at Westminster.

Within a month of the signing of the treaty, the unionists of Belfast voted to continue to operate under the 1920 Government of Ireland Act, as the articles of the treaty specified they could. The twenty-six counties ratified the articles and thereby became the "Irish Free State" (with commonwealth status like that of Canada under the crown). Republican elements opposed to the settlement launched a year-long civil war against the De Valera government, 1922–1923, which it put down with implacable force. The prospect of political power in Dublin—with or without allegiance to England, for such was the issue in the civil war—drove the question of partition out of the popular southern mind. Northern Ireland as a part of the United Kingdom came into existence, therefore, almost by default. But not without violence.

The Ulster Volunteer Force (UVF) had first been formed as a volunteer army opposed to the home rule bill. In concept it was unarmed, but in 1920 its armed members set about a sustained attack on the Catholic population. The English government stepped in on November 1, 1920 (pre-partition) to recruit for the Ulster Special Constabulary. It established this police force in three classes: one for those on full–time duty to be posted anywhere in Northern Ireland; a second for those on part–time duty in their own localities; and a third for reservists willing to be called up in time of emergency. The chief makeup of this official police force was Orange order men, many of them members of the UVF. They continued to perpetrate violence in uniform as they had done without it. Retaliation came in the form of Irish Republican Army (IRA) violence. The practical result was a separate civil war in the north. The repressive deeds of the special constabulary in 1921–1922 were long remembered, serving as a justification for continued guerrilla warfare over a fifty-year period. The Royal Ulster Constabulary was set up as an armed force on June 1, 1922, to succeed the all but defunct Royal Irish Constabulary. In that same year the Civil Authorities Act (better known as "Special Powers Act") was passed, which allowed the Minister of Home Affairs to arrest people without a warrant on suspicion of "acting, having acted, or being about to act in a manner contrary to the peace," and to detain them indefinitely without specific charge.

Sectarian strife erupted again in the north in the early 1930s during the prime ministership of Lord Craigavon (1921–1940), whose successors were in turn J. M. Andrews (1940–1943), Lord Brookborough (1943–1963), and Captain Terence O'Neill (1963–1969). The Unionist Party continued in power throughout, usually holding 67 to 75 percent of the seats in the parliament at Stormont and eleven of the thirteen seats in Westminster. The Westminster members consistently voted with the British Conservative Party. The 1930s were hard times in the north, with unemployment rising at their beginning to 28 percent and dropping to 20 percent by dint of much emigration a decade later. The Second World War did not bring prosperity but only considerable bitterness in Ulster at the neutrality of the south. The Ireland Act of the British parliament in 1949 promised that Northern Ireland would not cease to be part of the United Kingdom without the consent of its parliament. Throughout the years 1956–1962 the IRA stepped up its campaign of violence to force the British out of Ireland. An apparent sign of peace came with the Anglo-Irish trade agreement (1965) signed at Stormont by the two heads of government. But there was no peace.

Discrimination in hiring was the chief reason for unrest alleged by the one-third minority in the six counties. The O'Neill government in Stormont was pursuing a policy of moderation, but popular Unionist sentiment flourished in opposition to it. The Reverend Ian Paisley of the Free Presbyterian Church proved an effective leader of extremist forces which made their influence felt in Stormont. The IRA was little heard from in the years 1965–1967. The Nationalist Party was small and gerrymandered to death whenever it showed any concentrated strength. The police and the B-specials were keeping order; the Unionists were convinced that they were dealing as fairly with the minority as it deserved. That minority experienced itself as second-class citizens in the centuries-old land of its birth. Belfast's poor were divided into distinct neighborhoods along ethnic and religious lines which were actually two cultures. The profession and practice of religion did not seem to do anything to diminish hostility, only heighten identity. The situation has been described as one of "wary mutual ignorance." People and clergy in the cities had little acquaintance of those in the other camp at first hand except formally in the workplace.

The years 1967 and 1968 saw the beginning of an integrated civil rights movement which, unlike the U.S. experience, brought violence but no political relief. In 1972, the peak year, came Bloody Sunday, Bloody Friday, and the imposition of direct rule from Westminster. A British attempt to encourage power sharing in government (1973–1975) came to nothing. The Sunningdale Agreement referred to above reiterated the 1949 position that departure from the United Kingdom lay entirely with the total electorate.

Permanent violence has led to permanent fear and suspicion. The last bomb or bullet has been the last word for two decades now. Is there any end in sight? Peace initiatives (ecumenical activities, marches, proposals like substituting judicial procedures for the Emergency Powers Act) seem to have been totally unavailing. The churches appear impotent in face of the deep-seated hatreds of small numbers of antagonists on both sides.

What hope is there for the great majority of unionist and nationalist Northern Ireland that longs for peace?

It may come when a British parliament, economically reduced much further than now, realizes that England cannot afford the continuing drain represented by its colonial policy in Ireland. It may come with the acknowledgment by the poor of Northern Ireland across cultural lines that their victimization by the middle and upper classes is their common problem, one which only jobs and food can solve, not guns. It may come with the increased secularization of the Republic, proceeding at a rapid rate, which will reduce Protestant fears of minority status in a thirty-two county Ireland.

Seán MacBride, the Nobel laureate and former U.N. official who was influential in the formation of Amnesty International, has proposed a practical political solution which will not wait for any of the uncertain eventualities above. It is a cantonal government along Swiss lines which will allow complete freedom in all cultural and religious matters to self-determining regions (not necessarily the present border or even the counties), along with government by an all-Ireland parliament. Oversight of both the initial steps and early observance of political agreements will have to be in the hands of some neutral authority which has moral and military force. MacBride does not discount the United Nations.

Does anyone know when the hostilities between warring religious factions will come to an end in Northern Ireland? That is an easier question to answer than the one of internecine, undeclared civil war. These hostilities *as* religious wars came to an end some two centuries ago, leaving only a lively set of symbols to stand for rights of franchise, property, and labor that are not in any true sense religiously based.

BIBLIOGRAPHY

Darby, John. *Conflict in Northern Ireland: The Development of a Polarized Community.* New York: Barnes and Noble, 1976.

Deutsche, Richard, and Vivien Magowan. *Northern Ireland, 1968–73: A Chronology of Events.* 3 vols. Belfast: Blackstaff, 1973, 1974, 1975.

Moody, T. W. and T. W. Martin, eds. *The Course of Irish History.* Cork: Mercier, 1978 (eleventh printing).

Paor, Liam de. *Divided Ulster.* 2d ed.; Harmondsworth: Penguin Pelican, 1971.

Shivers, Lynne, and David Bowman. *More than the Troubles. A Comon Sense View of the Northern Ireland Conflict.* Philadelphia: New Society Publishers, 1985.

Violence in Ireland: A Report to the Churches. Belfast: Christian Journals, 1976.

3

The Indo-Pakistani Conflict

ARVIND SHARMA

I

The role of religion in political conflict is clearly identifiable in the case of the division of the Indian subcontinent into India and Pakistan and the subsequent Indo-Pakistani conflicts. But while its role is easy to identify it is difficult to assess. The assessment of its role is complicated by the following consideration. (1) The division took place under the British who have been accused of following a policy of divide and rule in relation to the Hindus and the Muslims.[1] (2) The history of Muslim rule over India is a long one. Some scholars see the roots of the division reaching far back in history; others see it rooted in the developments that took place during the eighteenth century and after.[2] (3) Awareness of a separate identity on the part of the Muslims is of long standing, but the emergence of Pakistan was rather sudden.[3] "Before 1930 the word Pakistan had not been heard of . . . in 1947 it appeared as a new state."[4] (4) Even after the partition of the country, a sizable number of Muslims continued to live in India and Hindus in East Bengal. To this day India continues to reject the two-nation theory on which Pakistan was founded, namely, that the Muslims do not represent an Indian minority but a separate nation, a Muslim nation as distinct from a Hindu nation.

II

An attempt will now be made, keeping these complications in mind, to analyze the role of religion in the emergence of Pakistan. One must begin with the fundamental realization that the role of religion in the emergence of Pakistan was mediated through other spheres of life—social, economic, political, psychological, linguistic, and so on, and was not always direct. Such a realization enables one to see its influence at a subtler level.

Until the first decade of the eighteenth century Islam was politically dominant in India. The last great Emperor of the Moghul Dynasty, Aurangzeb, died in 1707, and thereafter the Mughal Empire declined rapidly.[5] Political power passed on to the British in Bengal in 1757;[6] by 1818 they were well on their way to gaining political control of India after defeating their main rivals—the Marathas.[7] The establishment of British rule in India thus provides the basic historical context in which the interaction between the Hindus and the Muslims was played out.[8] Geographically, the context is provided by Bengal where the British first successfully established themselves and where the two communities—the Hindus and the Muslims—were well represented, though otherwise unevenly distributed over the subcontinent.[9]

The British supplanted Muslim rule in Bengal. This was welcomed by some Hindus who felt that they would get a fairer deal under the new rulers.[10] They also welcomed the introduction of western education,[11] whereas the "Muslims with one voice spurned western education and in sullen dejection remained aloof from modern schools,"[12] which ultimately resulted in the Hindus coming out "at least seventy-five years ahead of Muslims in western education."[13] This factor complicated Hindu-Muslim relations later as it fed Muslim fears of dominance by the Hindus.

Western education through English was introduced in 1835. Another event occurred in 1857 which caused further difficulties for the Muslims. In 1857 there was a rebellion against the British presence in India, as represented by the East India Company, which was successfuly suppressed by 1859. Although both Hindus and Muslims had participated in this rebellion, "the heavy hand of the British fell more on the Muslims than on the Hindus."[14]

But the Muslims were too numerous and too vigorous to be absorbed or permanently reduced to insignificance. The first movements of revival came from within and may be described as those of internal renewal or purification. These were amongst the body of the people. Then came a movement among the leaders in tardy response to western influences. It was the Pakistan movement which finally welded these two together into a national movement comparable to that of the Indian Congress.[15]

III

The pivotal figure in the indigenous regeneration of Islam was Shah Wali-Ullah (1702–1762) who was inspired to "attempt a revitalization of Islamic values and the Muslim nation in India."[16] during the eighteenth century, "a time of stress for the country." The major foci of his endeavors were, first, the propagation of the Qur'an and, second, insistence on the Sharī'a (Islamic law). To secure the first he translated the Qur'an into Persian against orthodox opinion; it was subsequently also translated into Urdu by his sons.[17] To secure the second he integrated Islamic values through the doctrine of taṭbīq (synthesis) and interpreted Islam not in terms of just one of the four schools of Islamic law or *madhāhib* but as a whole.[18] His insistence on following the Sharī'a is significant because he would not "permit the intrusion of 'Ajamī customs and the habits of the Hindus."[19]

The movement initiated by Shah Wali-Ullah was further promoted by his son Shah Abdul Aziz, who declared that India was *dar-ul-harb* (land of war) as it was under non-Muslim rule.[20] The movement turned militant under Aziz's disciple Sayyid Ahmad of Bareilly and his followers. The struggle was directed, however, first against the Sikhs and later against the British during the period 1826–1868[21] but collapsed thereafter.

The next forward impulse came under the impact of the west—but it evoked a cooperative and educational rather than a confrontational and militant response. The representative figure in this context is that of Sir Saiyad Ahmad Khan (1817–1898). He advocated a rapprochement with the English on the part of the Muslims and succeeded in achieving it. In brief, whereas the Muslims in the pre–1857 period had regarded India under the British as *dar-ul-harb*, Sir Saiyad Ahmad Khan "considered that the tolerance and security of the British régime entitled it to be included in the *dar-ul-Islam*, or region of peace. The British régime having been accepted as the providence of God, Muslims should win British approval by active loyalty. Otherwise they would be out-distanced in the race for governmental favors by the Hindus."[22] Sir Saiyad Ahmad Khan on the one hand defended Islam against its European critics, but on the other also tried to free it from the grip of the conservatives by the successful advocacy of the adoption of Western learning among the Muslims, symbolized by the founding of the Anglo-Oriental College at Aligarh in 1875.

The problems that were to bedevil Hindu-Muslim relations, however, began to make their appearance during this period in the following ways. In 1867 Saiyad Ahmad Khan proposed the establishment of a university with Urdu as the medium of instruction. This was opposed by the Hindus who identified Urdu with the Muslims. The Hindu agitation actually succeeded in getting Urdu replaced by a variety of Hindi as the official language of the province of Bihar. Saiyad Ahmad Khan was upset by the anti-Urdu agitation, and "this movement convinced Syed [Saiyad] Ahmad that the Hindus and Muslims could never 'join whole-heartedly together and the difference between them would immensely increase in future'."[23] In 1885 the Indian National Congress was established. Saiyad Ahmad discouraged Muslims from joining out of the fear that (1) because the organization was critical of the government, it would arouse British ire against the Muslims,[24] and (2) because it was democratically conceived and the Muslims were a minority, they would be at the mercy of the majority.[25] In 1887 he expressed similar fears with regard to the legislative councils, and on the question of filling administrative positions by competitive examinations he pointed out the handicap the Muslims would be under in such an arrangement.[26] In the meantime the extremist elements in the Congress, represented by Bal Gangadhar Tilak, tried to give a distinctly Hindu character to the agitation against the British so that "Saiyad Ahmad Khan's separatist policy was intensified during the later years of his life,"[27] although at one time he had maintained that "India was a bride, whose two beautiful eyes were Hindus and Muslims."[28]

In the meantime the British, watching the growth of nationalism in India with increasing alarm,[29] developed a policy of using one community as a countervailing force against the other—baldly known as the "divide and rule" policy.[30] It resulted in the partition of Bengal under Lord Curzon along religious lines in 1905, though the ostensible grounds for carrying it out were said to be administrative.[31] Although there was considerable agitation against partition, the Muslims of Bengal tended to view it with favor.[32] Out of this ferment emerged the Muslim League, which was founded in Dacca in 1906 by the Muslims to "safeguard their national interests"[33] and "became the centre of organized opposition on the part of the Muslims to the Hindus," when the Muslims felt that their interests were being compromised.[34]

IV

The next phase in Hindu-Muslim relations was marked by a series of events that gave reasons for optimism. In 1916 the Indian National Congress and the Muslim League concluded what is now known as the Lucknow Pact under which they agreed on the distribution of posts among the Hindus and the Muslims which were opened up by the Minto-Morley reforms introduced by the British government in response to the agitation for self-government in 1909.[35] In 1911 the partition of Bengal was rescinded, which aroused anti-British feelings among the Muslims as this was done "contrary to the pledges given to the Moslems."[36] In 1913 the Muslim League also adopted self-rule as its goal for India. "As far as the political aims were concerned, no difference remained between the National Congress and the Muslim League."[37] Then in 1914 the First World War broke out. Turkey and Britain fought as enemies, and a call to fight on behalf of Turkey was issued to all Muslims.[38] The part played by Britain in the dismemberment of Turkey "offended the religious and historical sentiments of the Muslims." They responded favorably to a mass movement organized by Muhammad Ali and Shaukat Ali, who were brothers, and Maulana Abul Kalam Azad. This agitation, known as the Khilafat Movement, was backed by Mahatma Gandhi who was just entering the political arena in India after his success in South Africa.[39] "The Muslims therefore joined forces with the Hindus in a national joint movement before the incredulous eyes of the British."[40]

The alliance, however, turned out to be short-lived. In 1922 the Grand National Assembly of Turkey abolished the Caliphate, and by 1923 Muhammad Ali was himself reflecting on the fact that "Hindu-Muslim relations today are not precisely those that they were two years ago."[41] The deterioration continued, caused by a series of communal clashes over issues such as "music before the mosque, cutting down the branches of the peepal tree, held sacred by the Hindus, which obstructed the very long pole carried in the Muslim Tajiya procession, killing of cows in public places during Id ceremony, and things of this sort."[42] This led to each community organizing and consolidating itself in opposition to the other, as represented by the *Tanzeem* (propagation) and *Tabligh* (organization) movements among the Muslims and *Śuddhi* (reconversion to Hinduism) and *Sangathan* (consolidation) movements among the Hindus.[43] It was also alleged that the British government encouraged or connived the communal flare-ups.[44]

The end of the war in 1918 was marked by the introduction of the Montagu-Chelmsford reforms by the British government in 1919. In 1920 Mahatma Gandhi had started the non-cooperation movement which joined hands with the Khilafat Movement. It was suspended in 1922, however, and "on the withdrawal of the non-co-operation movement, there was an outbreak of communal riots in several places."[45] It has been suggested that "the spirit of frustration caused by the suspension of the mass movement adversely affected the relations between Hindus and Muslims. There was no common programme to bring them together."[46] Whatever the truth of this claim, there is little doubt that after 1922 the Hindu and Muslim communities started drifting apart.

V

The period from 1922–1935 reflected this drift, though it was by no means clear that the breach was irreparable. Historians differ on the interpretation of these events. According to some, for instance, the appointment of the Simon Commission to explore the possibility of further devolution of power to the Indians "increased Muslim fears";[47] according to others, the shared rejection of the Commission, which included a section of the Muslim League,[48] "provided a great opportunity for the restoration of amity."[49] It is an interesting fact, however, that by 1935 the leaders of the Muslim community had more or less given up hope of Hindu-Muslim unity. Muhammad Ali Jinnah, who from 1906 to 1921 was a member of the Indian National Congress and stood for separate electorates, had left the Congress in 1921 when Mahatma Gandhi, whom he considered a "Hindu revivalist," assumed its leadership. After a period of obscurity, he reorganized the Muslim League in 1934, and this "ambassador of Hindu-Muslim unity" finally became a protagonist of Pakistan. Similarly, the great poet Muhammad Iqbal (1873–1938), who at one stage in his life wrote remarkably nationalistic poetry, gave up on Hindu–Muslim unity toward the end of his life. His poetry exercised a powerful influence on the self-consciousness of Indian Muslims.

The next installment of self-government which India received from the British in 1935 led to a widening of the breach. Under the Government of India Act of 1935 elections were held in 1937. The Congress acquitted itself quite well, but the Muslim League fared badly.

The dealings between the Congress and the League during 1937 are generally regarded as a watershed in Hindu-Muslim relations and need to be examined closely. The "Congress emerged as the largest party in seven provinces out of eleven" and proceeded to form governments.[50] This caused problems with the

League. Accounts of what actually happened differ, as often happens with critical events, but the failure of the Congress to form coalitions with the League (or vice versa) is generally believed to be a turning-point in Hindu-Muslim relations.[51] Perhaps the following account of what ensued is as balanced as any.

The Muslims desired to form a Coalition Ministry with the Congress in each Province, but the Congress refused to admit into the Ministry any one who did not subscribe to its creed. This decision widened the cleavage between the Congress and the Muslim League, and Mr. Jinnah, who had hitherto been favourably disposed towards the Congress, and had once vehemently protested against the view that India was not a nation, publicly declared that the "Muslims can expect neither justice nor fair play under Congress Government." This sentiment was now shared by the majority of Muslims. Mr. Jinnah became the unquestioned leader of the Muslim community, and was elected each year as President of the League, which soon rallied round it the great bulk of Muslims all over India.[52]

The fears generated at the provincial level were transferred to what might happen at the federal level in the event of British withdrawal.[53]

After the negotiations for Congress-League coalition ministries broke down, its leader Muhammad Ali Jinnah began appealing directly to Muslim religious sentiments. The breakdown of the negotiations had had a traumatic effect on him. The cry of "Islam in danger" was raised, complaints of ill-treatment of Muslims proliferated, and the resignation of the Congress ministries was celebrated as deliverance day. "These tactics of the League paid rich dividends— it came to be regarded more and more as the representative Muslim organization and Mr. Jinnah, its undisputed leader. In 61 by-elections of Muslim seats between 1937 and 1942, the Muslim League captured as many as 47 against only four secured by the Congress."[54]

VI

Finally, in 1940 the Muslim League adopted a resolution calling for sovereign statehood for the Muslims of India.[55] This represented a crucial development in Hindu-Muslim relations, as the Muslims had decided in effect to separate politically from the Hindus. It was based on the two–nation theory—that Hindus and Muslims constituted two separate nations. That the idea had the solid backing of the Muslim community is clear from the fact that when "after the end of World War II fresh elections were held, the League secured no less than 446 out of a total of 495 Muslim seats."[56]

This new state was to be called Pakistan, a name originally suggested in 1933 by Cahudhary Rahmat Ali, who "derived the name from the first letters of the provinces to be included in Pakistan; P standing for the Punjab, A for Afghāniā, K for Kashmir, S for Sindh, and tān for Baluchistan. The name Pakistan can also be translated as the land of the pure (pāk i.e., pure; stān, land)."[57] Attempts have been made to trace the basic concepts in the writings of Sir Muhammad

Iqbal and even Sir Saiyad Ahmad Khan. There are also differing views on the evolution of the idea, but its adoption by the Muslim League under Jinnah's leadership gave a new turn to Indian politics. For the so-called Indo-Pakistani conflict had now begun with the proclamation of this demand. Prior to this demand there was a negotiable element in Hindu-Muslim relations, and although negotiations continued even after the adoption of the resolution a new and potentially explosive ingredient had been added to the Indian political brew. From the point of view of Hindu-Muslim relations, from 1940 onwards "all attempts at reconciliation between the Congress and the League foundered on this issue of Pakistan."[58] From the point of view of British-Congress relations, "the Government could also now plausibly refuse the Congress demand for national government on the grounds that the Muslims were opposed to it."[59]

In 1945, however, the British government changed its policy toward India and instead of trying to prolong its rule decided to transfer power to the Indians.[60] Now the very Hindu-Muslim antagonism which the British had at times abetted became a problem.[61] From the maze of events that followed this decision two must be selected for special mention—one which almost averted partition and the other which precipitated it.

The British, when they decided to quit, offered the Cabinet Mission Plan in 1946, a plan that evolved from a British cabinet mission which had come to India for the purpose of reconciling Hindu-Muslim differences.[62] It basically recommended a loose federation of the then British India.[63] Remarkably, both the Muslim League and the Indian National Congress accepted the plan. "At this stage Nehru and Gandhi played a decisive role, changing the course of events beyond recognition."[64] Nehru, speaking at a press conference, made the acceptance of the plan provisional, and Gandhi's response, though positive at first, became more tentative.[65] When the Congress acceptance of the plan appeared doubtful, the League also withdrew its acceptance. Many historians feel that this turn of events marked the loss of the last opportunity for a united India.

The Congress, however, had not withdrawn its acceptance, although "sharp differences between the Muslim League and the Congress over the interpretation of the cabinet Mission's Plan" has arisen.[66] The Viceroy therefore proceeded to reconstitute the Executive Council for an interim national government as provided for by the plan. "This complete triumph of the Congress provoked a violent reaction among separatist Muslims, and the Muslim League fixed on August 16, 1946, as the day for 'Direct Action'."[67]

This resulted in the so-called Calcutta riots, which led to unprecedented violence between the Hindus and the Muslims and paved the way for the partition of the country. Leonard Mosley writes:

Between dawn on the morning of 16 August, and dusk three days later, the people of Calcutta hacked, battered, burned, stabbed or shot 6,000 of each other to death, and raped and maimed another 20,000. This may not seem to be a considerable figure to students of India's recent history. Three million people died of starvation during the great famine of 1943 in Bengal alone. Close to three–quarters of a million Punjabis massacred each other during the first days of Indian independence in 1947.

But the filthy and dreadful slaughter which turned Calcutta into a charnel house for seventy-two hours in August 1946 is important because it did more than murder innocent people. It murdered hopes too. It changed the shape of India and the course of history. The corpses of men, women and children lay stinking in the gutters of Chowringhee Square until the only reliable garbage collectors of India, the vultures, picked them clean; and with every mouthful, they picked away the fabric of a unitary India, which Britain had painstakingly built up over more than a century and a half, and finally tore it in two.[68]

VII

The *origin* of the Indo-Pakistani conflict is now clear, although the state of Pakistan had not yet come into being. It lies in the separate statehood claimed by the Muslims of India—not by *all* Muslims to be sure, but by most.[69] The events of the succeeding years make this abundantly clear.

The Cabinet Mission Plan continued to pose problems when the sections dealing with the formation of a constituent assembly were sought to be implemented.[70] Finally, the British government declared its intention to quit India by June 1948 and appointed Lord Mountbatten to carry out the transfer of power to Indians. Lord Mountbatten drew up a scheme that envisaged the division of the country into India and Pakistan.[71] It was reluctantly accepted by both the Indian National Congress and the Muslim League. Thus, finally, August 14, 1947, saw the birth of Pakistan, and August 15 that of India.

One of the factors that had led to the acceptance of the idea of partition was the continuous friction between the Hindus and the Muslims, with the Muslims reacting strongly to any opposition to the idea of Pakistan on the part of the British or the Congress. It would, therefore, seem reasonable to assume that with the acceptance of the demand for Pakistan, Hindu-Muslim disturbances would abate, if not cease. Such did seem to be the case initially.[72] But it ended in a bloodbath which no one expected.[73] Why?

To find the reason one has to go back to the Muslims' demand for separate statehood. Although the Muslims were in a majority in the areas that constituted Pakistan—a geographical fact without which Pakistan could not have come into being—Muslims were also distributed as a minority over the rest of India. Some of them began migrating to Pakistan, while the Hindus and the Sikhs, feeling insecure under the new state of Pakistan, started to migrate out of Pakistan. This event, euphemistically known as transfer of population, was one of the largest mass migrations in history.[74] It was Pakistani insistence on Islamic nationhood which required this, whereas in an undivided India no such migration would have been necessary. So far as India and Pakistan are concerned, "Instead of an era of goodwill, the independence ushered in one of communal hatred and cruelty of which there is no parallel in recorded history of India since the invasion of Tamerlane . . . It will suffice to state that India had to pay a very heavy price for freedom. According to an estimate, not probably much exaggerated, '600,000 Indians died and 14,000,000 lost their homes'."[75] What is even more important is that "the transfer of population was not complete. Some thirty-five million Moslems remained in India and some thirteen million Hindus remained in Pakistan, almost exclusively in East Pakistan."[76]

In the post-Partition era, one must recognize the importance of the fact that— despite the two-nation theory and the two states of India and Pakistan—nationhood did not coincide with statehood. There were Hindus in East Bengal and Muslims in India. It was actually the forced migration of these Hindus along with disaffected Muslims into India which precipitated the war with Pakistan in 1971. But earlier, it was the presence of the Muslims in India which led to war over Kashmir in 1948. It should be borne in mind here that, while Pakistan was a Muslim state, India did not become a Hindu state but rather remained a secular state. So when on October 26, 1948, the Hindu ruler of Kashmir acceded to India, India accepted the accession, although the people of Kashmir, according to the 1941 census, were 77.11 percent Muslim. At the time, the government of India, "while accepting this accession as a provisional step, expressed the view that the future of Kāshmīr should be decided in accordance with the popular will ascertained by means of plebiscite or referendum."[77] Since then the Indian government has in effect gone back on the promise on the ground that India is a secular state and therefore Muslims are full–fledged citizens of India whether in Kashmir or elsewhere.[78]

This issue is really an old one, with the Muslim League denying that the Muslims participate in an Indian nationhood and the Indian National Congress insisting that they do.[79] The fact of partition proved that the Muslim League may have been right, but not totally as a sizable number of Muslims continued to live in India. Thus, the Indian National Congress wasn't entirely wrong either.

The next event which sheds light on the role of religion in the Indo-Pakistani conflict, apart from another war between India and Pakistan over Kashmir in 1965, is the civil war in Pakistan which ended in the formation of Bangladesh.[80] The real issue here, however, was not one of Hindu-Muslim relations but of relations among the Muslims constituting Pakistan itself. When Pakistan was formed, it consisted of two wings which came to be known as Eastern and Western Pakistan. The formation of Pakistan itself was actually made possible by the fact that the Muslims, although dispersed all over India, constituted a majority in these two areas. Had they been evenly dispersed as a minority all over India the emergence of even the idea of Pakistan, much less its establishment, would have been highly unlikely.

It has often been argued that major cultural differences between the Hindus and the Muslims were ultimately responsible for the division of India.[81] The division of Pakistan itself can be traced to such cultural differences between the Muslims of East and West Pakistan. And just as the basic problem of Indian nationalism was one of bridging the gap between the Hindus and Muslims, the basic problem of Pakistani nationalism was to bridge the gap between the East Pakistanis and West Pakistanis. Both failed in their respective efforts.

The major factors that gave East Pakistan a sense of separate identity were its history, geography, and language. Historically, the West Pakistani claims to antiquity grated the East Pakistanis.[82] Geographically, the separation of East and West Pakistan by a thousand miles of Indian territory and the fact that East Pakistan was surrounded on three sides by India left it more vulnerable to India militarily. Linguistically, the attachment of East Pakistan to Bengali as opposed to Urdu was a major factor in giving it a sense of separate identity.

These factors culminated in a civil war in 1970–1971 when national elections were held in Pakistan. A predominantly East Pakistani party—the Awami League—won a majority, but the authorities in West Pakistan did not allow it to form the government. West Pakistan unleashed a policy of repression in East Pakistan. Then India intervened militarily and thus assisted in the formation of a separate Bangladesh.[83]

VIII

Religion has thus been a major, if not the sole, factor in the Indo-Pakistani conflict. Once this is granted, two further nuances in this role must be recognized: (1) as much at issue in the conflict is that of a secular and a theocratic state as the issue of Hindu-Muslim relations, though it is possible that each of the religions is more congenial to the nature of the state which emerged respectively;[84] (2) equally an issue in the Indo–Pakistani conflict has been conflict *within* Pakistan leading to conflict with India. Thus, the Indo-Pakistani conflict reflects problems in the relationships not only between Hindus and Muslims but also among Muslims themselves. It also reflects the problems which a religion-oriented state and a secular state have in dealing with each other.

NOTES

1. de Riencourt, *The Soul of India* p. 304.
2. S. M. Ikram, *Muslim Civilization in India,* Ainslie T. Embree, ed., pp. 290 ff.
3. Sachau, *Alberuni's India,* Ch. 1.
4. Spear, ed., *Oxford History of India,* p. 799.
5. Majumbar, Raychaudhuri, and Datta, *An Advanced History of India,* p. 520.
6. Ibid., p. 657.
7. Ibid., p. 702.
8. French and Sharma, *Religious Ferment in Modern India,* Part Two.
9. Spate and Learmonth, *India and Pakistan,* p. 151.
10. de Bary, ed., *Sources of Indian Tradition,* pp. 578–579.
11. Ibid., pp. 587–595.
12. Malik, *Moslem Nationalism,* p. 193.
13. Ibid., p. 211.
14. Malik, *Moslem Nationalism,* p. 207.

15. Spear, ed. *Oxford History of India*, p. 802.
16. Malik, *Moslem Nationalism*, p. 123. See ch. 5.
17. Mujeeb, *Indian Muslims*, p. 277.
18. Malik, *Moslem Nationalism*, p. 126.
19. Mujeeb, *Indian Muslims*, p. 282.
20. Malik, *Moslem Nationalism*, pp. 151–153.
21. Ibid., Ch. 6.
22. Spear, ed, *Oxford History of India*, p. 803.
23. Majumdar, ed., *British Paramountcy*, Part II, p. 318.
24. Malik, *Moslem Nationalism*, p. 212.
25. Majumdar, ed., *British Paramountcy*, Part II, pp. 315–316.
26. Malik, *Moslem Nationalism*, p. 211.
27. Ibid., p. 222.
28. Ibid., p. 209.
29. See Chirol, *Indian Unrest*.
30. Gopal, *British Policy in India*, pp. 193ff.
31. Majumdar, ed., *Struggle for Freedom*, Ch. 1.
32. Ibid., pp. 53–54. Also see Malik, *Moslem Nationalism*, p. 225.
33. Ibid., p. 225.
34. Majumdar, ed., *Struggle for Freedom*, p. 54.
35. Malik, *Moslem Nationalism*, pp. 225–226.
36. Ibid.
37. Ibid., p. 229.
38. Ibid., p. 228.
39. Majumdar et al., *Advanced History of India*, p. 981.
40. Spear, ed., *Oxford History of India*, p. 784. Also see Malik, *Moslem Nationalism*, p. 237.
41. See Majumdar, ed., *Struggle for Freedom*, p. 425.
42. Ibid., p. 425.
43. Ibid., Ch. 15.
44. Ibid., p. 432.
45. Dodwell, ed., *Cambridge History of India*, Vol. 6, p. 619.
46. Majumdar et al., *Advanced History of India*, p. 982.
47. Spear, ed., *Oxford History of India*, p. 807.
48. Dodwell, ed., *Cambridge History of India*, p. 619.
49. Majumdar et al., *Advanced History of India*, p. 983.
50. Philips and Wainwright, eds., *Partition of India*, p. 417.
51. See Misra, *Indian Political Parties*, Ch. 6; Philips and Wainwright, eds., *Partition of India*, pp. 157 ff., 192 ff., 252 ff., 341, 385 ff.,417ff.; and Spear, ed., *Oxford History of India*, 817–819.
52. Majumdar et al., *Advanced History of India*, p. 985.
53. Philips and Wainwright, *Partition of India*, 83–84.
54. Dodwell, ed., *Cambridge History of India*, p. 620.
55. Philips with Singh and Pandey, *Evolution of India and Pakistan*, pp. 354–355.
56. Dodwell, ed., *Cambridge History of India*, p. 621.
57. Malik, *Moslem Nationalism*, p. 245.
58. Majumdar et al., *Advanced History of India*, p. 987.
59. Ibid., p. 987.

60. Philips and Wainwright, eds., *Partition of India*, pp. 474, 552.

61. Sastri and Srinivasachari, *Advanced History of India*, pp. 746, 751.

62. See Majumdar, ed., *Struggle for Freedom*, Ch. 32, II.

63. For a summary of the scheme, see Majumdar et al., *Advanced History of India*, p. 989; for details, see Philips et al., *Evolution of India and Pakistan*, pp. 378–382.

64. Malik, *Moslem Nationalism*, p. 258.

65. Ibid.

66. Majumdar et al., *Advanced History of India*, p. 990.

67. Ibid. Jinnah

drew up a resolution—which was, of course, passed without dissent—in which he called upon the Muslim League to renounce all the titles they held from the British Government and to set aside 16 August 1946 as "Direct Action Day," when the Muslims of India would demonstrate their determination to achieve a partition of India and a Pakistan of their own.

"What we have done today," he declared, afterwards, "is the most historic act in our history. Never have we in the whole history of the League done anything except by constitutional methods and by constitutionalism. But now we are obliged and forced into this position. This day we bid good-bye to constitutional methods . . . Today we have also forged a pistol and are in a position to use it." (Mosley, *Last Days of the British Raj*, p. 29).

68. Ibid., p. 11.

69. See Majumdar, ed., *Struggle for Freedom*, pp. 1069–1073.

70. Majumdar et al., *Advanced History of India*, pp. 988–989.

71. For a summary of the scheme, see Majumdar et al., *Advanced History of India*, pp. 991–992; for details, see Philips et al., *Evolution of India*, pp. 397–403.

72. Majumdar, ed., *Struggle for Freedom*, p. 779.

73. Mosley, *Last Days of the British Raj*.

74. Malik, *Moslem Nationalism*, p. 260. Gopal, *Indian Muslims*, p. 327.

75. Majumdar, ed., *Struggle for Freedom*, p. 792.

76. Malik, *Moslem Nationalism*, p. 260.

77. Majumdar et al., *Advanced History of India*, p. 999.

78. Brines, *Indo-Pakistani Conflict*, p. 7. Kashmir, however, has a special constitutional status; see Noorani, *India's Constitution and Politics*, pp. 547 ff.

79. Majumdar, ed., *Struggle for Freedom*, p. 607.

80. Majumdar et al., *Advanced History of India*, pp. 1014–1015.

81. Philips and Wainwright, eds., *Partition of India*, pp. 325–326.

82. Malik, *Moslem Nationalism*, p. 267.

83. For details, see Brown, *United States and India, Pakistan, Bangladesh*, Ch 11.

84. Gupta, *Indo-Pakistani Relations*, p. 212.

BIBLIOGRAPHY

The bibliography is divided into different sections for convenience. Section A lists books of a general nature; Section B lists books that take a rather Hindu nationalist view of Hindu-Muslim relations; Section C lists books that are somewhat Muslim nationalist in character; and Section D lists books on Bangladesh.

Section A

Azad, Mavlana Abdul Kalam. *India Wins Freedom*. New York: Longmans, Green and Co., 1960.

Banerjee, Anil Chandra. *The Constitutional History of India*. Vol 3: 1919–1977. Delhi: Macmillan Co., 1978.

Bhatia, Krishna. *The Ordeal of Nationhood. A Social Study of India Since Independence, 1947–1970*. New York: Antheneum, 1971.

Bolitho, Hector. *Jinnah Creator of Pakistan*. London: J. Murray, 1954.

Brass, Paul R. *Language, Religion and Politics in North India*. Cambridge: Cambridge University Press, 1974.

Brines, Russell. *The Indo-Pakistani Conflict*. London: Pall Mall Press, 1968.

Brown, W. Norman. *The United States and India, Pakistan, Bangladesh*. Cambridge, Mass: Harvard University Press, 1972.

Campbell-Johnson, Alan. *Mission with Mountbatten*. London: Robert Hale Limited, 1951.

Chirol, Valentine. *Indian Unrest*. London: Macmillan, 1910.

Collins, Larry. *Freedom at Midnight*. New York: Simon and Schuster, 1975.

Das, Durga. *India from Curzon to Nehru and After*. New York: John Day Co., 1970.

Davis, Kingley. *The Population of India and Pakistan*. Princeton, N.J.: Princeton University Press, 1951.

de Bary, Wm. Theodore, ed. *Sources of Indian Tradition*. New York: Columbia University Press, 1958.

de Riencourt, Amaury. *The Soul of India*. New York: Harper and Brothers, 1960.

Dodwell, H. H. ed., *The Cambridge History of India*. Vol. 6. New Delhi: S. Chand and Co., 1964.

Edwardes, Michael. *The Last Days of British India*. London: Cassell, 1963.

French, Hal W., and Arvind Sharma. *Religious Ferment in Modern India*. New Delhi: Heritage Publishers, 1981.

Gopal, S. *British Policy in India 1858–1905*. Cambridge: Cambridge University Press, 1965.

Gupta, Jyoti Bhusan Das. *Indo-Pakistan Relations 1947–1955*. Bombay, India: Jaico Publishing House, 1959.

Hasan, Mushirul. *Nationalism and Communal Politics in India*. New Delhi: Manohar, 1979.

Hodson, H. V. *The Great Divide*. London: Hutchinson, 1969.

Ikram, S. M. *Modern Muslim India and the Birth of Pakistan, 1858–1951*. Lahore: Sh. Muhammed Ashraf, 1970.

Kaura, Uma. *Muslims and Indian Nationalism*. New Delhi: Manohar, 1977.

Low, Donald Anthony, ed., *Soundings in Modern South Asian History*. Berkeley: University of California Press, 1968.

McDonough, Sheila. *Mohammad Ali Jinnah*. Lexington, Mass.: D. C. Heath and Co., 1970.

Majumdar, R. C., H. C. Raychaudhuri, and Kalikinkar Datta. *An Advanced History of India*. New York: St. Martin's Press, 1967.

Misra, B. B. *The Indian Political Parties*. Delhi: Oxford University Press, 1976.

Moon, Penderel. *Divide and Quit*. Berkeley and Los Angeles: University of California Press, 1962.

————. *Gandhi and Modern India*. New York: W. W. Norton and Co., 1969.

Moraes, Frank. *Witness to an Era*. New York: Holt, Rinehart and Winston, 1973.

Mosley, Leonard. *The Last Days of the British Raj*. New York: Harcourt, Brace and World, 1961.

Mujeeb, M. *The Indian Muslims*. London: George Allen and Unwin, 1969.

Nanda, B. R. ed. *Essays in Modern Indian History*. Delhi: Oxford University Press, 1980.

Nehru, Jawaharlal. *The Discovery of India*. New York: John Day Co., 1946.

Noorani, A. G. *India's Constitution and Politics*. Bombay: Jaico Publishing House, 1970.

O'Malley, L. S. S., ed. *Modern India and the West*. London: Oxford University Press, 1941.

Padmasha. *Indian National Congress and the Muslims 1928–1947*. New Delhi: Rajesh Publications, 1980.

Philips, C. H., and Mary Doreen Wainwright, eds. *The Partition of India: Policies and Perspectives 1935–1947*. Cambridge, Mass.: MIT Press, 1970.

————, with H. L. Singh and B. N. Pandey. *The Evolution of India and Pakistan 1858 to 1947: Select Documents*. London: Oxford University Press, 1962.

Prasad, Beni. *India's Hindu-Muslim Questions*. London: George Allen and Unwin , 1946.

Rahman, Hossainur. *Hindu-Muslim Relations in Bengal 1905–1947: Study in Cultural Confrontation*. Bombay: Nachiketa Publications, 1974.

Sachau, Edward C. *Alberuni's India*. London: Keegan Paul, 1910.

Singhal, Damodar P. *Pakistan*. Englewood Cliffs, N.J.: Prentice–Hall, 1972.

Smith, Percival. *Modern India*. New York: Frederick A. Praeger, 1962.

Smith, Wilfred Cantwell. *Modern Islam in India: A Social Analysis*. London: Victor Gollancz, 1946.

Spate, O. H. K., and A. T. A. Learmonth. *India and Pakistan: A General and Regional Geography*. New York: Methuen and Co., 1967.

Spear, Percival, ed. *The Oxford History of India*. Oxford: Clarendon Press, 1958.

Thursday, G. *Hindu-Muslim Relations in British India: A Study of Controversy, Conflict and Communal Movements in Northern India: 1923–1928*. Leiden: E. J. Brill, 1975.

Tinker, Hugh. *Experiment with Freedom*. London: Oxford University Press, 1967.

Wallbank, T. Walter. *The Partition of India*. Boston: D. C. Heath and Co., 1966.

Wolpert, Stanley A. *Morley and India 1906–1910*. Chapter 8. Berkeley and Los Angeles: University of California Press, 1967.

Section B

Gopal, Ram. *Indian Muslims: A Political History (1858–1947)*. New Delhi: Asia Publishing House, 1959.

Majumdar, R. C., ed *British Paramountcy and Indian Renaissance*. Part II. Bombay: Bharatiya Vidya Bhavan, 1965.

————. *Struggle for Freedom*. Bombay: Bharatiya Vidya Bhavan, 1969.

Prakasa, Sri. *Pakistan: Birth and Early Days*. Delhi: Meenakshi Prakashan.

Sastri, K. A. Nilakanta, and G. Srinivasachari. *Advanced History of India*. New Delhi: Allied Publishers, 1971.

Weeks, Richard V. *Pakistan: Birth and Growth of a Muslim Nation*. Princeton, N.J.: D. Van Nostrand Co., 1964.

Section C

Ahmad, Jamil-ud-din. *Historic Documents of the Muslim Freedom Movement*. Lahore: Publishers United Ltd., 1970.

Allana, G. ed. *Pakistan Movement: Historic Documents*. Lahore: Islamic Book Service, 1977.

Ambedkar, B. R. *Pakistan or Partition of India*. Bombay: Thacker and Co., 1945.

Aziz, K. K. *Britain and Muslim India*. London: Heinemann, 1963.

Aziz, M. A. *A History of Pakistan*. Lahore: Sang-e-Meel Publications, 1979.

Bourke-White, Margaret. *Halfway to Freedom*. New York: Simon and Schuster, 1949.

Choudhury, G. W. *Pakistan's Relations with India 1947–1966*. New York: Frederick A. Praeger, 1968.

Ikram, S. M. *Muslim Civilization in India*. Ainslie T. Embree, ed. New York: Columbia University Press, 1964.

Iqbal, Javid. *The Legacy of Quaid-i-Azam*. Karachi: Ferozsons Ltd., 1967.

Khaliquzzaman, Choudhry. *Pathway to Pakistan*. Lahore: Longman's Pakistan Branch, 1961.

Khan, Mohammad Ayub. *Friends Not Masters*. New York: Oxford University Press, 1967.

Lambert, Richard David. "Hindu-Muslim Riots." Ph.D. Thesis, University of Pennsylvania, 1951.

Malik, Hafeez. *Moslem Nationalism in India and Pakistan*. Washington, D.C.: Public Affairs Press, 1963.

Masani, R. P. *Britain in India*. New York: Oxford University Press, 1960.

Nadwi, S. Abul Hasan Ali. *Muslims in India*. Lucknow: Academy of Islamic Research and Publications, 1960.

Rajput, A. B. *Muslim League Yesterday and Today*. Lahore: Muhammad Ashraf, 1948.

Siddiqui, Kalim. *Conflict, Crisis and War in Pakistan*. London: Macmillan Press Ltd., 1972.

Stephens, Ian. *Pakistan*. New York: Frederick A. Praeger, 1963.

Symonds, Richard. *The Making of Pakistan*. London: Faber and Faber, 1950.

Section D

Bhattacharjee, G. P. *Renaissance and Freedom Movement in Bangladesh*. India: Minerva Associates, 1973.

Bhattacharyya, Buddhadeva, ed. *A Nation Is Born*. Calcutta: Calcutta University, Bangladesh Sahayak Samiti, 1974.

Gill, Stephen M. *The Discovery of Bangladesh*. Melksham: Colin Venton, 1975.

Gupta, Jyoti Sen. *History of Freedom Movement in Bangladesh*. Calcutta: Naya Prokash, 1974.

Johnson, B. L. C. *Bangladesh*. Chapter 1. New York: Barnes and Noble Books, 1975.

Satyaprakash, ed. *Bangladesh: A Select Bibliography*. New Delhi: Indian Documentation Service, 1976.

II

RELIGION AND POLITICS IN DEVELOPING NATIONS

4

Tradition versus Modernization: Methodological Issues Exemplified from African Religions

LEONARD BARRETT

It is reported that Sir James Frazer, when asked if he had ever seen any of the primitive people about whose customs he had written so many volumes, tersely replied, "God forbid!" It is so easy to forget that cultural anthropology from E. G. Tylor to the actual fieldwork by B. Malinowski was an intellectual enterprise attempting to prove that European civilization had evolved to the enviable zenith of the cultural ladder, while other cultures like those of Africa remained at the bottom rung. Evolutionary theorists had little interest in the social relations of those studied. Anthropology was essentially a historical inquiry, and ethnographic information about "primitive" peoples was used to illustrate historical or pseudo-historical hypotheses already formulated in the minds of scholars such as Tylor and Frazer.

One of the serious flaws of nineteenth-century anthropologists was the lack of a first-hand knowledege of the people about whom they so profusely wrote. It had not yet occurred to most early writers that the unfamiliar primitive cultures from which they drew their illustrations might be worth investigation in their own right. It was from these anthropologists that modern writers inherited such chauvinistic concepts as "primitives," "savages," "pagans," and other words which today one should like to forget. Most anthropologists of our modern period find it necessary to explain their use of such words when writing about contemporary traditional peoples. E. Evans-Pritchard wrote: "Some people today find it embarassing to hear people described as primitives or as natives, and even more to hear them spoken of as savages."[1] He, however, found it impossible to divorce himself from such usages. He concluded: "But I am sometimes obliged to use the designations of my authors, who wrote in the robust language of a time when offence to peoples they wrote about could scarcely be given, the good time of Victorian prosperity and progress, and, one may add, smugness, our pomp of yesterday."[2]

Evans-Pritchard also used the language of his predecessors in a "value-free sense," which was thus "etymologically unobjectionable." Unfortunately, such words as "primitive" and "savage" are still used today by good scholars, not in a value-free sense but in a logical and chronological sense. Despite the evolutionists' errors, modern cultural anthropologists owe much to the nineteenth-century scholars, but modern social scientists, unlike their predecessors, are concerned with discovering and recording regularities in human behavior. They are also interested in comparative approaches to cultures by pointing out similarities between the cultural and social institutions of different societies. Although modern, they do not ask the same questions their ancestors did; nonetheless, some of their ideas and insights still influence cultural anthropology today.

The problem of understanding traditional religious thinking on the part of Western scholars, who until recently were the only actors in the field of social science research, stemmed from many factors. First, most recent students of social science have been unfamiliar with theoretical thinking in their own cultures; thus, they have been denied the vital keys to understanding other peoples' methods of thinking. One vital key to understanding traditional cultures is the awareness of religious components that make up the basic patterns of thought in these cultures. Modern anthropology had purposely avoided ethico-mystical thinking, with some exceptions. This trend is not new. Evans-Pritchard, in the illuminating book already quoted above, analyzed the background of the early anthropologists who have influenced modern anthropology:

If one is to understand the interpretations of primitive mentality they [the arm-chair anthropologists] put forward, one has to know their own mentality, broadly where they stood; . . . As far as religion goes, they all had, as far as I know, a religious background in one form or another. To mention some names which are likely to be familiar to you: Tylor had been brought up Quaker, Frazer a Presbyterian, Marett in the Church of England, Malinowski a Catholic, while Durkheim, Levy-Bruhl and Freud had Jewish background; but with one or two exceptions, whatever the background may have been, the persons whose writings have been most influential have at the time they wrote been agnostics or atheists.[3]

Thus, the misunderstanding of this vital key to traditional thinking has "effectively" shut off most anthropologists from seeing traditional thought as equivalent to Western thought.

Second, most anthropologists are blinded by the difference of what Robin Horton called "the idiom of language" and are in the habit of viewing any language different from their own as no language at all. This puzzlement over the idiom of language has resulted in an exhaustive body of anthropological writings which attempts to enumerate differences between Western thought, which is universally called "scientific" or modern, over against traditional thinking, which is universally called pre-logical or mystical. Modern anthropology had had a vested interest in emphasizing the dialectical differences between the Western and non-Western terms as intellectual versus emotional, rational versus mystical, reality-oriented versus fantasy-oriented, causally oriented versus supernaturally oriented, empirical versus non-empirical, abstract versus concrete, and analytical versus non-analytical. At a deeper level of research all these terms are inappropriate when applied to traditional thinking.

Today, scholars who are broadly trained in the vital keys of theoretical understanding suggest that, before attempting to enumerate differences between worlds, one should engage in an exhaustive exploration of features in traditional thought common to those found in modern Western scientific thinking. This is not to say that there is no difference between traditional and scientific thinking; indeed, there is a salient difference between the two. However, differences in idioms are not always differences in substances, and, furthermore, traditional peoples never created the problems surrounding our query—clearly the problem is a Western one. Most writers in the social sciences are products of "developed" societies in which scientific thinking is the major emphasis in everyday life. Although the majority of Western people are still traditional in thinking, they share in the complex technological system; thus, writers from the West, when confronted by traditional situations, tend to misinterpret the thinking of traditional people by presenting traditional thought as a species of science. Consequently, comparisons between traditional and Western thought appear ridiculous. This is so because they fail to compare apples with apples and prefer to compare apples with oranges. Anthropology has persisted in this childish play for over a century. Why? The answer is conjectural. First, it appears that anthropology as a method of study is unable to break with the errors created by its ancestors. Modern anthropologists seldom fail to quote the findings of their predecessors, even though such findings have been refuted years ago (examples are too numerous to mention). Second, most researchers do not have time to engage in a thorough exploration of their field of study, and most lack the vital keys of theoretical knowledge necessary to understand the idioms of the people they study. The result is that preconceived structures and ideas that confuse new issues with old concepts foreign to the people under study are brought into play. Third, Western chauvinism generally prevents the field researcher from an empathetic penetration of the social and institutional structures of other cultures. Finally, few of those who have the time and the vital keys of knowledge are broad enough to present their findings to the public, for fear that their findings may not agree with the sociology of knowledge acceptable to their peers. Thus, one may say that errors in the social sciences die hard.

COMMON SENSE VERSUS THEORETICAL THINKING

Since the days of ancient Greece, theoretical thinking has always been thought to be the sole preserve of European civilization; that is, scientific thinking originated in Europe, and all other cultures have existed in a state of pre-scientific thought. As a matter of fact, to the Greeks, all other cultures were barbaric when compared with themselves. As Europe emerged from the Middle Ages through the discovery of Plato and Aristotle, the same attitude was adopted vis-à-vis the Africans who, according to Europeans, made little or no contribution to thought. Whatever the thinking process, it was considered pre–logical, mystical, and non-empirical.

The thesis of this chapter is that all cultures are individual entities; each has its own life-world or world-view, its institutions, and its social relations. Culture in this sense may be defined as the organic accumulation of behaviors prede-termined by the attitudes manifested toward the instruments of civilization where teleological content is composed of values and symbols of the group. Culture is the composition of life–styles which are manifested in the works of those who transform the physical environment of the human world into the world of culture.[4]

Living society is constantly on the quest for unity underlying apparent diver-sity, for simplicity underlying apparent complexity, for order underlying apparent disorder, and for regularity underlying anomaly. Each society deals with this quest differently. In modern Western societies, the long history of scientific method of recording precise measurements, calculations, and observational data has been preserved for centuries. This written record of trial and error available to Western scientific research gives the West a great advantage over what is now called the underdeveloped Third World. For this reason, Third World thinking is still believed to be in the pre–scientific mode, because scientific thinking cannot advance where there is no recording of scientific activities. But having said this, one must admit that modern scientific activities as opposed to traditional activities, despite the advantage of the one over the other, are only relative. In the scientific world, explanations of observed happenings are often reduced to abstract entities and forces that operate behind and within the world. Explanatory theories of this kind include the kinetic theory of gases, the planetary-atom theory of matter, the wave theory of light, and the cell theory of living organisms. Over against these imposing theories, traditional thought explains its world by the activities of gods, spirits, and ancestors, and through the theories of witchcraft and sorcery. To most Westerners, even those who exist on the same level as their traditional counterparts, it does appear that scientific thinking is simpler and more elegant than traditional thinking. When one considers the number of spirits and powers that inhabit the cosmologies of Nigeria (to name only one system in Africa), the whole pattern seems rather confusing. But, upon reflection, the Westerner should be convinced that the cosmologies in the West are no less complex. For every unitary common-sense object, there is a myriad of molecules. On this point traditional and scientific thought occupy the same ground. The aim of a theory is not to deal with the myriad but with a limited number of kinds of entities or processes underlying the diversity of experience, so as to make sense of one's own world.

Recent research in African cosmologies has begun to cut through the "puz-zlement" of older writers by an empathetic study of the idioms of African people.[5] As a result that which was seen as "primitive mentality" is now understood to be rational observations based on millennia of common-sense thinking. Each category of beings has its appointed functions in relation to the world of observable happenings. The mode of thought common to traditional peoples, as Marcel Griaule discovered in his conversation with Ogotomelli of Mali, is not sentiment but deep discursive thinking based on rational observations.[6] Professor J. E. Wiredu of the Philosophy Department of the University of Ghana has observed:

The principle of rational evidence is not entirely inoperative in the thinking of traditional Africans. Indeed, no society could survive for any length of time without conducting a large part of their daily activities by the principle of belief according to evidence. You cannot farm without some rationally based knowledge of soils and of seed and meteorology; and no society can achieve any reasonable degree of harmony in human relations without a *basic* tendency to assess claims and allegations by the method of objective investigation. The truth, then, is that rational knowledge is not the preserve of the modern West nor is superstition a peculiarity of African people.[7]

Each culture, whether it be Western or traditional, possesses its own "ethico-mythical consensus," or what Emile Durkheim called "collective representation." This body of ethico-mythical consensus in traditional thinking has been rendered sacred; on the contrary, Western tradition from the Greeks to the present had developed a parallel secular tradition outside of the sacred tradition. This controversy between the sacred amid the secular has never been resolved; an example of this is today's controversy between evolution and creation.

To summarize this section on common-sense versus theoretical thinking, one can conclude that—despite the fact that traditional thinking may sometimes appear capricious and puzzling to the Western thinkers trained in secular knowledge—the ethico-mythical experts of pre-scientific cultures, charged with the diagnosis of spiritual agencies which are believed to be at work behind observable events, are able to perceive a modicum of regularity in their world *mutatis mutandis*. To the Westerner, such successes are termed magic. Incidentally, Claude Levi-Strauss, who writes extensively on primitive thought, made this rebuttal:

One deprives oneself of all means of understanding magical thought if one tries to reduce it to a moment or stage in technical and scientific evolution... Magical thought is not to be regarded as a beginning, a rudiment, a sketch, a part of a whole which has not yet materialized. [Magic] forms a well-articulated system, and is in this respect independent of that other system which constitutes science... It is therefore better, instead of contrasting magic and science, to compare them as two parallel modes of acquiring knowledge.[8]

What are the differences between these parallel modes of knowledge? In the first place, theoretical thinking attempts to place things in a causal context wider than that provided by common sense. It also provides a causal context for apparently wild events. Common-sense thinking does put things in causal context but not on all levels. Its principal role is inductive thinking—that is, putting two and two together. In this respect the common-sense thinker shares company with the positivists who see theory as fictional and common sense as the only real method of thought. Generally, the application of common-sense thinking is rather accurate when the antecedent of an event is near; if the event is distant, common sense is deficient. In the second place, the function of theoretical thinking is to help the mind transcend the limitation of the eye. It is in this context that the Westerner boasts that modern thought overcomes traditional thought. One of the obvious achievements of modern scientific theory is the revelation of a whole array of causal connections which the eye cannot detect by itself. Examples of these are the theory of molecules and the theory of viruses and other micro-organisms. Despite these obvious differences and despite the successes of theoretical thinking in the field of technology and medicine, the question remains: Are Western societies more humane, more secure, and spiritually more advanced than their traditional counterpart?

The idea of progress has become a fetish of the "modern" scientific West, and all non-Western peoples have been historically weighed in its balance. Thus, the perjorative concepts of magical, pre-logical, savage, and crude are the West-ern designations of people whose ethico-mythical traditions have constrained them to approach their world quite differently. By this I mean that traditional people see their world not in the abstract, but in the concrete. In Africa, for example, theories take their departure from the world of things and people and ultimately return us to it. A good theory does not reduce something to something else. The basic category of thought revolves about the person, the family, the clan, and the tribe. To the traditionalists, scientific thinking—the fetish of modern people—is merely one facet of the human mind. It is an attitude stressed in the West to the neglect of other attitudes. Professor Weridu, and most other social scientists confirm that all people think scientifically; but to the traditional peoples, scientific thinking is secondary to the wider aspects of life in which science plays only a small part. Western science deals with the measurability of things—things that can be quantatitively assessed. It does not deal with the quality of life; it eschews human values such as love, beauty, and devotion, and there is little or no emphasis on concepts such as God, spirits, and ancestors.

The noted scientist, Max Planck, expressed the nature of science as human knowledge which was ever progressing toward de-anthropomorphization; that is, the extricating of one's mind from the subject under study. Herein lies the difference between scientific thinking and traditional thinking. The scientific is abstract whereas the traditional is concrete. I must repeat that I am not denying that science has made enormous progress from the time of Newton to the present and has made enormous contributions to our technological age, but science, as such, can contribute only a limited statement to culture/history, or the dynamic quality of human life. Scientific progress is not a term applicable to religious life; it is relevant to technology but not to phenomenology. The extrication of the self from reality has created a disturbing psychological and spiritual condition in Western society which has left humanity in a condition of spiritual impotence, estranged in a world of forces, and unable to relate to any of them.

A moment's meditation on technological progress, based on the propositions of measurability and de-anthropomorphization, will show that Westerners have become victims with an overwhelming sense of personal impotence in the face of the all-powerful and self-perpetuating forces of technology, which lack the moral and political institutions to humanize itself. This all-powerful technology has corrupted political life, co-opted our religious institutions, and made beggars of our social checks and balances.[9] Modern science has created this all-powerful madness which has devastated the forests, polluted the rivers and streams, clogged our highways and airways, and destroyed the air we breathe. It has produced an overabundance of edible garbage which slowly poisons the system, produced medicines that do not cure, and supports media that mesmerize us into believing every new falsehood from their scientific Olympuses and Sinais. All this adds up to a breakdown in human existence. Modern technology can correct a malfunction in a ten million dollar aircraft and repair an orbiting space station thousands of miles in space, but it can hardly produce a workable spare part for a gas stove on earth. Our Western system glorifies youth and ignores age; it glorifies riches and condemns the poor; it glorifies success at any cost but damns even honest failure.[10] Such is the quality of our Western scientific progress. Octavio Paz in a brilliant introduction to Claude Levi-Strauss had this to say about progress:

The best and worst to be said about progress is that it has changed the world. The sentence can be turned around: The best to be said about primitive societies is that they have hardly changed the world at all. Both variants need an amendment: we have not changed it as much as we think, nor the primitives as little. The people who raise the banner of progress changed the social balance more than the natural one, although the latter is now beginning to be affected. The modifications have been internal and external. Internally, technical acceleration produced disturbances, revolutions, and wars; now it is threatening the psychic and biological integrity of the population. Externally, progressive society has destroyed innumerable societies and enslaved, humbled, and mutilated the survivors.[11]

AFRICAN THOUGHT AND WESTERN SCIENCE

As already observed, theoretical thinking is not the sole preserve of the modern West. African traditional societies also deal in theoretical thinking. Professor Robin Horton of the University of Ife states: "In evolving a theoretical scheme, the human mind seems constrained to draw inspiration from analogy between the puzzling observations to be explained and certain already familiar phenomena."[12] From this proposition he proceeds to show that this truth is amply demonstrated both in the West and in African traditional thought. Whether one looks at atoms, electrons, and waves, as in the West, or at gods, spirits, or entelechies, as in traditional societies, theoretical notions nearly always have their roots in relatively homely, everyday experiences—the familiar things. In the West, however, the process of electicism has so obscured the everyday experiences from which theoretical notions are derived that explanations in the West are now couched in impersonal idioms. In complex, rapidly changing industrial societies, the human scene is always in flux. Order, predictability, regularity, and simplicity all seem to be lamentably absent. These qualities can be found only in inanimate things. Western peoples can envision themselves at home with things but not with people. In traditional societies, the situation is reversed: Explanations tend to be couched in personal idiom; the human scene is the *locus par excellence* of order, predictability, and regularity. Thus, in traditional societies the mind turns to people and their relationships.

What I have attempted to show to this point is that thinking in traditional societies is not qualitatively different from that in the modern Western world. There are abundant evidences that Western people and the so-called traditional people use their brains in similar fashion when seeking to solve puzzling problems within their own societies. The differences are not in the quality of thinking but in the quantity. In traditional societies there is no awareness of alternatives to the established body of theoretical tenets, whereas, in the scientifically oriented societies such awareness is highly developed. Anyone who reads the history of science from the time of the Greeks to the present is familiar with the controversy between traditionalists and modernists.

Robin Horton in his analysis of modern versus traditional thinking used the terms "open" and "closed."[13] An open predicament is characterized by the awareness of alternatives, a disregard for the sacredness of beliefs, an utter disregard for the magical, and a disbelief that cosmic ruin will result from any deviation from established tenets. The closed predicament is the absence of an awareness of alternatives, which makes for an absolute acceptance of established tenets that cannot be questioned in that this is the idiom of belief—one cannot argue outside this pattern. These are compelling forces; they are sacred, and any challenge is a threat of chaos and therefore evokes intense anxiety. Horton informed us that traditional thought is not merely supernatural forces appealing to gods, spirits, and ancestors. There are elements of scientific thinking within the religious framework. Bronislaw Malinowski was perhaps the first anthropologist to understand this fact. He observed: "It is a mistake to assume that, at an early stage of development, man lived in a confused world, where the real and the unreal formed a medley, where mysticism and reason were interchangeable as forged and real coin in a disorganized country. To us the most essential point about magic and religious ritual is that it steps in only where knowledge fails."[14]

It should be clear from the above analysis that traditional people, contrary to the Western descriptions of pre-logical, mystical, sentimental, and communal, are not devoid of theoretical thinking. Most of what has been written about traditional peoples now appears to be merely anthropological, sociological, and metaphysical constructions rather than realities.

MAGIC

"Closed" as opposed to "open" societies, as we have seen, are not devoid of thinking. The quantity of thinking on the level of common sense is probably the same as in the West. African thought, for example, is still viewed by the Westerner as magico-religious. The closed ethico-mythical nucleus is still influenced by religion, art, and, to a great extent, technology. In modern anthropology this relationship was emphasized by Sir James Frazer. Although they still pretend that Frazer's ideas are outdated, his influence reigns supreme in the classrooms in today's universities. According to Frazer, there was no sharp boundary separating the magical from modes of scientific thought. Magic, however imaginary and fantastic, is scientific in aim. Theoretically speaking, magic is a science, although an elusive one. Frazer finally opted for the word "pseudo-science." Magic argues and acts on the presupposition that in nature one event necessarily and invariably follows another without the intervention of any spiritual or personal agency. According to Frazer, the primitives believed "that the course of nature is determined not by the passions or caprice of personal beings—but by the operation of immutable laws acting mechanically."[15] Magic, then, is implicit or explicit faith, real and firm in the order and uniformity of nature. Frazer was the first to develop a theory of magic in which he stated that like things always influenced each other and things that have once been in contact are continually affecting each other. The first he called homeopathic magic; the second, contagious magic. Although this theory of magic has influenced most anthropologists to the present day, it must be remembered that Frazer had no first-hand experiences with primitive people. Like all other arm-chair anthropologists of his period, he arrived at this theory imaginatively, placing himself with his scientific orientation and intellectual background in the primitive's place. It was from this lofty position that he conjectured what kinds of theories about nature would be possible for traditional folk.

I have already quoted Levi-Strauss, who suggested that one deprives oneself of all means of understanding magical thought if one tries to reduce it to a moment or stage in technical and scientific evolution. John Beattie, who carried out numerous researches in Africa, rejected Frazer's theory of magic. He wrote:

Magic is not thought (by primitive people) to take place by itself, as Frazer's theory implies. It is only when men make magic, that is, when they perform rites, that results are expected. Magic is the acting out of a situation, the expression of a desire in symbolic terms; it is not the application of empirically acquired knowledge about property and substance . . . For the intelligent magician and his subjects it is the whole procedure, the rite, that is thought to be effective, not just the substances by themselves.[16]

Beattie further suggested that magical acts are not scientific behaviors but ritual behaviors. Frazer's theory has misled the West by not explaining what people do in magical activities. He states that magic is both the acting out of a situation and the expression of a desire in symbolic terms. These terms are the keys to understanding traditional peoples. Ritual behaviors are not the reserve of only traditional peoples. Both Western and traditional peoples resort to ritual acts in times of potential danger and misfortune. Where there is no body of empirical knowledge to turn to for help, or where such knowledge is plainly inadequate, ritual procedures provide an acceptable alternative. In traditional societies, this form of behavior is the only alternative based on their collective representations. It is a mistake, however, to believe that traditional people are solely governed by things ritual, or that they base all their day-to-day happenings on acts of gods, spirits, and ancestors.

In Africa and in the Caribbean the cause of sickness is viewed on different levels. An ordinary disease is treated in an ordinary way. Most people have a storehouse of knowledge about herbs for every kind of illness. Most therapy never goes beyond this level. Sometimes, people do visit a European–trained doctor to ascertain, if possible, the ramifications of an illness. Upon receiving the diagnosis and prognosis, many return to the traditional specialists who will effect the cure from their wide knowledge of herbal remedies. In addition, should the disease be resistant to the wide range of ordinary medicine available on the common–sense level, the disease must be diagnosed by another traditional specialist. In Africa and the Caribbean they are known as Diviners. After a period of deep consultation, they are more likely to attribute the sickness to the gods or other spiritual agencies. To the Western clinical specialist, this statement is but a ''copout''—a case of magical manipulation by the traditional specialists; however, this is not always the case. The Diviner must reveal some acceptable account of what moved the spirit to act. This account must also correspond with some event in the tangible world of the patient. The specialist does not deal with viruses or a specific disease in a vacuum, but rather deals with the whole person.

Attributing the disease to the workings of God and other spiritual agencies is a ''cultural short-cut'' which explains to the sick that the present ''human disruption'' is the working of a variety of forces against him. Western medical practice focuses on the individual patient without understanding the social context of his or her illness. African traditional specialists are more concerned about psychosomatic causes like human hatred, jealousy, and elements of witchcraft which do not appear in medical textbooks. In a closed society a breach of kinship relations, misdeeds, and other immoral acts, which might appear harmless to the Westerner, are stress-bearing incidents, because they are viewed as causing the wrath of the ancestors. Any disturbed social relationship is associated with disease and misfortune. Approaches to therapy within these cultural communities are scientific in themselves. Are such theories mere fantasy? There is, at present, a great interest in the expertise of traditional healers. Medical anthropologists and practitioners of Western medicine have come to the realization that a person's social life can, in fact, contribute to a whole series of illnesses, ranging from mental to somatic disease. The techniques of traditional specialists and their skills in treating the whole patient without knowledge of the "germ-theory" of the West are highly sought after. Our modern psychoanalytic theorists and practitioners can learn a great deal from their African counterparts.

RETREAT FROM MODERNISM

Modern technology, with all its benefits to the developed communities of the modern world, is under great pressure to justify itself. The mystification of progress so readily attributed to modern development is achieved at a high cost of dehumanization of the human spirit. It brings with it a callous disregard for the individual, the neighbor, the community, the world, and the so-called underdeveloped others at the periphery of modernism. The cult of modernism is now highly organized with ideological membership cards of a highly political nature which mark East from West. Membership in each "club" is allowed to those who agree with the ideology of each. Traditional societies are systematically excluded from these clubs' secrets by political arrangements, with a view to prolonging their dependence on the technologically developed giants. Today, traditional societies receive the political appellation "Third World" in order to show their marginality vis-á-vis the technologically developed East and West. Incidentally, it is the so-called Third World with its abundance of raw materials which has fueled the mills of the developed countries, without which neither side could continue its dominance and competition; but, at the same time, it is to the Third World that all the amenities of technology and economic development are denied.

With the awareness of their political dilemma—club membership in either camp—most Third World nations consent to opt out from either and choose instead the road of non-alignment. This path, needless to say, leads to greater difficulty both politically and socially, not to mention economically. This stance carries with it severe political sanctions which have resulted in devalued currency, loss of foreign exchange, and slow development. Thus, their future has been rendered precarious, but the principle on which they stand is obvious. In the first place, Third World nations attempt to avoid the shared nuclear holocaust—the obvious Armageddon of the two technological giants. The Third World is conscious of the old maxim, "What shall it profit a man, if he gain the whole world and lose his own soul?" The never-ending pursuit of a newer and better "mouse trap," the never-ending pursuit of bigger and better weapons of destruction, and the disregard for human life point to the fact that the West has lost its soul. In the second place, life in the present-day developed countries has become a miserable and burdensome existence. T. S. Eliot characterized Westerners as papers thrown by winds, "distracted from distraction by distraction." Yet, traditional societies, with all their apparent lack of "progress," can offer much to their citizens. They may lack a better mouse trap, but they are happier with the simple life; they lack the glitter of modern societies, but they are closer to nature; they need not worry about pollution, the side-effects of ineffective medicines, and clogged roadways; nor need they worry about the high death rate due to faster, more expensive cars, which are not better because of their worth but because of staggering competitive commercialism.

In conclusion, the magic of Westernization is creeping into the last reserves of our traditional societies with a missionary zeal. With the never-ending need for raw materials, multinational corporations extend their tentacles to devour the lush virgin forests, the wells, and the mines of traditional societies. Along with this devastation comes the hand-maiden of Western society—Christianity—and, on its heels, commerce, and exploitation. All this inevitably leads to control. This has been the pattern for centuries, and, with this continued fervor for development, traditional societies will constantly be caught up in an endless struggle for their continued existence. Though all things will be changed, yet all things remain the same.

NOTES

1. Evans-Pritchard, *Theories of Primitive Religion*, p. 18.
2. Ibid.
3. Ibid. p. 15.
4. Dussel, *History of the Church in Latin America*, p. 24.
5. Wright, ed., *African Philosophy*, pp. 133–147; Shorter, *African Culture and the Christian Church; African Christian Theology*; Wilson, ed. *Rationality* pp. 131–171.
6. Griaule, *Conversation with Ogotemmeli*, pp. xi-xvii, 1–3.
7. Wiredu, "How Not to Compare African Thought with Western Thought," in Wright, ed., *African Philosophy*, pp. 113–147.
8. Levi-Strauss, *The Savage Mind*, p. 13.
9. Shaughnessy, ed., *The Roots of Rituals*, p. 37.
10. Ibid, p. 37.
11. Paz, *Claude Levi-Strauss*, p. 99.
12. Robin Horton, in Wilson, ed., *Rationality*, p. 146.
13. Ibid.
14. Quoted in Cassirer, *An Essay on Man*, p. 80.
15. Ibid.
16. Beattie, *Other Cultures* p. 206–207.

BIBLIOGRAPHY

Beattie, John. *Other Cultures: Aims, Methods, and Achievements in Social Anthropology.* New York: Free Press, 1968.

Cassirer, Ernest. *An Essay on Man: An Introduction to a Philosophy of Human Culture.* New Haven, Conn.: Yale University Press, 1962.

Dussel, Enrique. *A History of the Church in Latin America: Colonialism to Liberation. 1492–1979.* Grand Rapids, Mich. 1981.

Evans-Pritchard, E. E. *Theories of Primitive Religion.* New York: Oxford University Press, 1965.

————. *Witchcraft, Oracles and Magic Among the Azande*. New York: Oxford University Press, 1936.

Forde, Daryll, ed. *African Worlds*. New York: Oxford University Press, 1968.

Griaule, Marcel. *Conversation with Ogotemmelli: An Introduction to Dogom Ideas*. New York: Oxford University Press 1965.

Idowu, E. B. *African Traditional Religion: A Definition*. Maryknoll, N.Y.: Orbis Books, 1973.

Levi–Strauss, Claude. *The Savage Mind*. Chicago: University of Chicago Press, 1969.

Lloyd, C. E. R. *Early Greek Science: Thales to Aristotle*. New York: Harper Torchbooks, 1970.

Paz, Octavio. *Claude Levi-Strauss: An Introduction*. 2d ed. New York: Delta Books, 1978.

Shaughnessy, James, ed. *The Roots of Rituals*. Grand Rapids, Mich. 1973.

Shorter, Aylward, *African Christian Theology: Adaptation or Incarnation*. Maryknoll, N.Y.: Orbis Press, 1977.

Weridu, J. E. "How Not to Compare African Thought with Western Thought." In Wright, ed., *African Philosophy*, pp. 113–147.

Wilson, Bryan, ed. *Rationality: Key Concepts in Social Science*. New York: Harper and Row, 1970.

Wright, Richard, ed. *African Culture and the Christian Faith: An Introduction to Social and Pastoral Anthropology*. London, 1973.

————. *African Philosophy: An Introduction*. Washington, D.C.: University Press of America, 1979.

5

Tradition and Modernization in Islam

JOHN L. ESPOSITO

The Muslim world stretches from North Africa to Southeast Asia, encompassing more than forty–three Muslim nations. Islam, which is the second largest of the world's religions and includes some 800 million followers, has had a long and glorious history. From its seventh–century beginnings in Arabia until colonial dominance in the eighteenth century, Muslim empires dominated the Middle East, South and Southeast Asia. The Islamic tradition provided the framework of meaning for individual and corporate community life, for to be a Muslim was not only to pray and worship but also to belong to a religio-political community (*ummah*) governed by Islamic law.

The role of the Islamic tradition in modernization, while an important question throughout the twentieth century, has taken on special significance during the past decade. Oil wealth has resulted in a push for rapid modernization in many Muslim countries: Iran, Saudi Arabia, and the Gulf States. At the same time, many parts of the Muslim world have experienced a religious revival which has included a more critical attitude toward the pace, character, and effects of Western-oriented development polities.

This chapter will review the sources and significance of tradition in Islam, analyze Muslim responses to the challenge of modernization, and examine the underlying issues that affect Islamic modernization today.

In order to understand the issues surrounding the process of modernization in Islam, some appreciation of the classical Islamic world–view and the central place of tradition within it is necessary. For Muslims, submission (*islam*) or realization of God's will in history constitutes the Quranically revealed mandate for all believers. This mandate is universal. The ideal to be realized is an Islamic community (*ummah*) in which religion is integral to state and society. This belief is more clearly affirmed in the Muslim doctrine of *tawhid* (unity of God) and is articulated in Islamic law (the *Sharī'a*). *Tawhid* is the affirmation that "there is

Note: Select terms used in this chapter are defined in the end-of-chapter glossary.

no god but the God (Allah)'' and that this one, true, almighty God is lord and ruler of the universe. His governance touches every corner of the world and every area of life. Reflecting this belief, Islamic law provided the ideal blueprint or pattern for Muslim society—encompassing every area of life: prayer and pilgrimage, politics and society.

Many traditional societies (Hindu, Buddhist, Judaeo-Christian) have viewed their way of life as sacred. This is especially so for Muslims because the Islamic world–view or tradition is so deeply rooted in revelation.

In Arabian tribal society, tradition was the accumulated wisdom or practice of tribal ancestors—their ''beaten or trodden path'' (sunna)—beliefs, attitudes, practices passed down from generation to generation, the oral law of society. In Islam, the meaning of tradition was transformed. Social identity based on tribal affiliation and solidarity was replaced by a trans-tribal community of believers, bound together by their common faith commitment. In time tradition in Islam was formulated and expressed in a comprehensive fashion in a written law—Islamic law.

The primary sources of the Islamic tradition are the Qur'an: the eternal, literal, revealed word of God and the Example (sunnah or model behavior) of the Prophet Muhammad, the final messenger from God. Traditions or accounts (hadith) about Muhammad's teachings and deeds were preserved in six authoritative collections which, along with the Qur'an, provided guidelines for the community; however, these traditions of the Prophet came to comprise more than what the Prophet himself actually advocated. Tradition also came to incorporate the accepted practices or way of life for the early Muslim community. Therefore, over time both prophetic tradition and community practice were given a very sacred, authoritative status.

Tradition in Islam is not simply restricted to its revealed sources—the Qur'an and Example of the Prophet Muhammad. Since Muslims claim a divinely revealed vocation to realize God's will in every aspect of life, early in Islamic history attempts were made to discover and set forth in detail the straight path (Shari'a, ''path'') of Muslim life. Thus, Islamic law (the Shari'a) was born. During the early centuries of Islamic history, groups of Muslims sought to delineate the Islamic way of life as fully and completely as possible. If Muslims were to realize God's will, then it was important to know how a good Muslim ''ought'' to act in every area of life. In addition to prescriptions found in the Qur'an and Traditions of the Prophet, they used their reason or independent judgment to develop comprehensive guidelines for Muslim society, laws that encompassed worship as well as criminal and civil law, and family obligations. These regulations were collected and set forth in law books (fiqh). It is important to emphasize that the development of law resulted from the individual, independent judgment or interpretation (ijtihad) of early judges and jurists. However, later generations, in attempting to systematize Islamic law, overlooked the jurists' creative process and instead maintained that the only form of reasoning used in the creation of law was deductive, analogical reasoning (qiyas). Law/tradition

was seen simply as the product of Qur'anic and prophetic prescriptions as well
as laws *deduced by analogy* or derived directly from precedents found in the
Qur'an and *Sunna* of the Prophet and then finally agreed on over time (*ijma*) by
the community. Thus, the creative role of judges' and jurists' interpretations or
opinions and the incorporation of already existing (customary) laws within the
corpus of Islamic law was overlooked or forgotten. This approach tended to
"sacralize" tradition/law and obscure the fact that in addition to revealed texts,
the greater part of the law was the product of human endeavor. The final stage
in the sacralization of tradition occurred in the ninth century. It was generally
accepted that the Muslim way of life had now been adequately and comprehensively stated in the law books produced by Muslim jurists. Continued development of law through individual interpretation or reasoning (*ijtihad*) was
henceforth no longer necessary or permitted; rather, the task of Muslims was
simply to follow or imitate (*taqlid*) God's law as found in the legal manuals.
Any additional interpretation or substantial change was condemned as an unwarranted innovation (*bida*). (Innovation [*bida*], i.e., change or departure from
the revealed law or practice of the community, was viewed as seriously as heresy
[failure to accept sacred doctrines] in Christianity.) Historians refer to this phenomenon as the "closing of the door of *ijtihad*." Tradition became fixed and
sacrosanct. Muslim society had its ideal pattern, comprehensively stated; its task
as well as that of future generations was to follow or conform to this pattern.
The creative expression of tradition as reflected in the work of the law schools
was at an end. Henceforth, courts were never to interpret or develop the law;
they were simply to apply it.

There is a danger of overstating the fixed nature of Islamic law and, thus, of
tradition in Islam. Indeed, change still did occur; yet, there was a sense in which
the norms for society were seen as discovered and established for all time. This
is manifested most clearly in the way in which the law, found in classical legal
manuals (*fiqh*), the product of divinely revealed texts as well as human interpretation (*ijtihad*) and application, was equated simply with the *Sharī'a,* the
divinely revealed principles of law found in the Qur'an and Traditions of the
Prophet. Future generations simply identified the divinely revealed *Sharī'a* with
all of traditional Islamic law, and that became the *corpus* of Islamic laws. The
result is that tradition in Islam, as embodied in law, has enjoyed an especially
sacred status. An idealized sense of history came to obscure the fine line between
revealed material sources—the Qur'an and authentic traditions of the Prophet—
and those areas of the Islamic tradition which were the result of human endeavor,
interpretation, and application. Fabricated traditions of the Prophet and individual
legal regulations which simply reflected the interpretations of a generation's
religious scholars or their acceptance of tribal/regional practices enjoyed an
enhanced status. Practices such as the veiling and seclusion of women, which
have no firm basis in revelation but were historically and socially conditioned
interpretations of the Qur'anic requirement of modesty, came to be seen by many
as integral to Islam.

MODERNIZATION: TRADITION AND CHANGE

Amidst the changing political fortunes and turmoil of Islamic history, whether during the Caliphate period (632–1258) or the subsequent great medieval Muslim empires (Ottoman in the Middle East, Safavid in Persia, and Mughal in India), Islamic law remained the stated ideal of the state. Religious scholars (ulama) were the custodians or guardians of the Islamic traditions and, as such, served as teachers, judges, legal specialists, and advisors to the government. However, in the eighteenth century, the Islamic world experienced a dramatic turn of events with the advent of colonialism. Although Islam and Christendom had long been contenders—during the seventh–century Islamic conquests, in the Crusades, and during the advance of the Ottoman Empire in the fifteenth century—the colonial period represented the Islamic community's first decisive defeat by the Christian West. Militarily, economically, and politically, Muslim areas stretching from North Africa to Southeast Asia fell under British, French, and Dutch colonial rule. For the first sustained period of time, most Muslims no longer lived in an Islamic society governed by their own law and traditions. Rather, they were the subjects of modern non-Muslim, European governments. Their colonial masters attributed their rule not simply to military and political superiority, but also to the truth and vitality of the Western Christian heritage which they claimed had inspired the modern industrialized West. Missionaries often freely criticized the backwardness of the Islamic tradition, characterizing it as antithetical to modernity. For Muslims, this period constituted a major identity crisis—What had gone wrong in Islam; why had Islam lost its power and vitality?[1] The thrust of this self-questioning was not unlike that of the Jews during the Babylonian exile as found in the biblical Books of Ezra and Nehemiah.

The decline and backwardness in Muslim society had, in fact, been recognized prior to the colonial period. During the eighteenth century, both Muhammad ibn Abd al-Wahhab (1703–1792) in the Arabian Peninsula and Shah Wali Allah (1702–1762) in the Indian subcontinent had been critics of Muslim society who sought to reform their communities. Renewal (tajdid) of the community has always been integral to Islam. Both Abd al-Wahhab and Wali Allah sought to "purify" Islam of "un-Islamic" beliefs and practices, unwarranted historical accretions or innovations (bida) which had become part of tradition. Both called for a return to a more pristine Islamic way of life. They repudiated blind imitation (taqlid) of tradition, of those norms and traditions embodied in the classical legal manuals; they called for a return to the Qur'an and authentic traditions of the Prophet and claimed the right to reinterpret (ijtihad) their tradition.[2] Similar movements occurred in other parts of the Muslim world. Thus, even prior to the onslaught of colonialism and the challenge of modernity, Muslims had recognized a weakening or decay of the community and the need for renewal and reform. However, their approach was one of purification through the rejection of "un-Islamic" innovations and a return or restoration to an earlier, more pristine form of Islam. Modernization, which is characterized by rapid and substantive change, would raise different questions requiring a more profound reinterpretation of tradition amidst widespread political, social, and economic change.

The primary impetus for modern Islamic reform movements in the late nineteenth and twentieth centuries was the West. European colonial presence and rule stood as a challenge to Muslim identity and tradition. The industrialized West with its modern armies and weapons was able to dominate the bulk of the Muslim world from North Africa to Southeast Asia politically and economically. How were Muslims to respond? Three principal Muslim responses came from the religious leaders (*ulama*), secular modernists, and Islamic reformers. Initially, the majority of the religious leadership rejected the West and all that it represented politically and culturally. Viewing Western presence as a direct assault on Islam, the leadership had several possible traditional Islamic options: declaring a holy war (*jihad*) against their non-Muslim occupier-rulers; emigrating (*hijra*) from their now non-Islamic territories to Muslim–ruled lands; or for most, pursuing a policy of withdrawal and nonparticipation. A second group, secular modernists, simply accepted the progressive secularization of law, education, and society that accompanied colonial rule. The third, Muslim modernists or Islamic reformers, sought to formulate an Islamic response to modernity's apparent challenge to Islam. If modernity and progress meant reason, science, technology, and the virtues associated with the Protestant work ethic, then the Islamic tradition could be shown to embody the best ideals and values of modernization.[3] The polemics and denunciation of the conservatives were offset by the apologetics of Islamic modernists who were not only defending Islam against its non-Muslim critics, but also justifying the need for change and reinterpretation in Islam to their more traditional fellow Muslims. To buttress their position, modernists could and did point to the pre-modern revivalist movements, such as those led by Muhammad ibn Abd al-Wahhab and Shah Wali Allah, that had rejected medieval authorities (laws/traditions) whose practices were deemed "un-Islamic" and had affirmed the right to their own interpretation or reinterpretation (*ijtihad*). Several prominent figures demonstrate the concerns and approach of Islamic modernists as they struggled with the relationship of tradition to modernization. Jamal al-Din al-Afghani and Sayyid Ahmad Khan in the nineteenth century and Muhammad Abduh and Muhammad Iqbal in the twentieth century were among the principal Islamic reformers in the Middle East and South Asia.

Jamal al-Din al-Afghani (1838–1897), philosopher, orator, journalist, and political activist, traveled extensively across the Muslim world from India to Egypt and also visited France and England. He served as the catalyst for the reform movement in Islam, articulating many of the themes and attitudes that were to characterize Islamic reform in the twentieth century.[4] Afghani called on Muslims to unite against imperialism—rejecting European political hegemony but not the sources of its strength—science and philosophy (reason). He stressed that science and knowledge—civilization—transcended any particular community and had moved back and forth from east to west. Had not the glories of Islamic civilization preceded and informed Western Christendom as it emerged from the Dark Ages to its modern renaissance? Afghani characterized Islam as the religion of progress, science, and reason: "the closest of religions to science and knowledge," emphasizing that "there is no incompatibility between science and knowledge and the foundation of the Islamic faith."[5] Therefore, Muslims should neither fear nor reject modernization as antithetical to Islam.

There is no necessary contradiction between tradition and modernization. Sir Sayyid Ahmad Khan, like Afghani, called on the Muslims of India to stir themselves from their centuries–long slumber and once more reclaim the glories of their Islamic tradition. However, unlike Afghani, he believed they should accept British rule as inevitable. Ahmad Khan rejected mere imitation of following (*taqlid*) of the past and insisted that Muslims were obligated to renew and reform their tradition through reinterpretation and reform (*ijtihad*): "If people do not shun blind adherence, if they do not seek that Light which can be found in the Qur'an and the independent Hadith, and do not adjust religion and science to the science of today, Islam will be extinct in India."[6]

Although Afghani and Khan served as the initiators and catalysts for change during the latter half of the nineteenth century, Muhammad Abduh (1849–1905) and Muhammad Iqbal (1876–1935), the "Fathers of Islamic Modernism" in the Middle East and South Asia, sought to bridge the gap between tradition and modernity. Demonstrating the need for and acceptability of change in Islam, they claimed the right to modernize through reinterpretation, distinguishing between the essentials of Islam and the historically conditioned intrepretations that were subject to further change. Islamic principles, they claimed, can provide the criteria for distinguishing between acceptable and unacceptable change. While affirming the centrality of Islamic law in guiding the model Muslim society, each rejected the notion of *taqlid* and the finality of laws encased in the medieval law books. Both urged Muslims to remember that the Qur'an itself is not a legal code. One must distinguish between general *Sharī'a* principles and values, divinely revealed in the Qur'an and exemplified in the Traditions of the Prophet, and those laws that were created by man's application of the *Sharī'a* to concrete historical situations and that were therefore open to change. Abduh, following the classical division of Islamic law into duties to God (worship, fasting, pilgrimage) and duties to one's fellow man (social transactions including civil, criminal, and family laws) maintained that only the duties to God were immutable. Thus, a broad spectrum of political and social changes was possible. Advocating a similar position, Muhammad Iqbal had concluded: "Equipped with penetrative thought and fresh experience, the world of Islam should courageously proceed to the work of reconstruction before them."[7] Such a reconstruction of Islamic thought would overcome the slavish following of tradition and enable the true dynamic character of Islam to respond to the political, social, and legal demands of modernity. Change was indeed not only possible, but through the concept of *ijtihad*, integral to Islam. This, then was the legacy of Islamic reformers to the process of modernization.

ISLAM AND CHANGE: THE FLEXIBILITY OF A TRADITION

Although varying attitudes toward modernization continue to exist, the reality of change in the Muslim world has been accepted. Radio, television, oil technology, and computers are part and parcel of Muslim life. Even conservative fundamentalist religious leaders freely accept and use loudspeakers to call the faithful to prayer; radio, television, and cassette recordings for religious education or agitational politics; and printing presses to provide a steady supply of religious literature. However, the key questions are: What change, and how much change, is possible? What is the Islamic rationale for change? Whose interpretation of Islam should prevail?

The study of modernization in Islam has too often been fraught with unwarranted dichotomies: tradition versus modernization, fundamentalism versus modernism, stagnancy versus progress and change. Although such categories may be valid and useful in some contexts, they do not reflect or do justice to a far more complex reality of modernizatioin in the Muslim world. For change has occurred and continues to occur both within modern and so-called fundamentalist contexts. Two examples of modern sociopolitical change demonstrate this complex reality. The first, Muslim family law reform, represents the primary arena for modernization in Islam in the twentieth century. The second, political development in Saudi Arabia, a "fundamentalist" Islamic state, provides a contrasting example of reliance on tradition to render and legitimate change.

Changes in law occurred in many parts of the Muslim world during the later half of the nineteenth century. In the Ottoman Empire in the Middle East and the Mughal Empire in the Indian subcontinent, most areas of Islamic law (*Sharī'a*) were replaced by modern European codes. Secular courts were established to handle civil and criminal law, and as a result, the jurisdiction of the religious (*Sharī'a*) courts was severely restricted. In the midst of this approach to modernization, the one area of Islamic law that remained untouched and in force was Muslim family law—the law governing marriage, divorce, and inheritance. This reflected the centrality of the family in traditional Islamic society and, therefore, of family law within the *corpus* of Islamic law. However, in the twentieth century, this important and sensitive area of tradition has also been subjected to change. Although the modernization of law, in general, was originally accomplished by simply replacing traditional Islamic law with new Western–derived legal codes, change in Muslim family law has been rendered through a process of reinterpretation which sought to provide an Islamic rationale for reforming tradition. Selective changes have been introduced to modify traditional law in order to improve the status of women and strengthen the rights of the nuclear family. Each of these reforms represents a response to the process of modernization and to those changes that accompany a shift in emphasis from the traditional (patriarchal) extended family to the more nuclear family.[8]

To justify their departure from tradition, legal reformers sought to establish the Islamic character of their reforms and, thus, to demonstrate a continuity between modernization and tradition. Wherever possible, Muslim states employed Islamic legal doctrines and methods. Although each Muslim country officially follows one of the four major schools of law (Hanafi, Hanbali, Maliki, and Shafii), modernizers claimed the right to utilize regulations selected from one of the other schools.[9] For example, this technique, known as *takhayyur,* has been used in Middle Eastern (e.g., Egypt, Syria, and Jordan) and South Asian (India and Pakistan) countries governed by Hanafi law. The grounds for divorce were substantially increased by adopting additional provisions such as cruelty, failure to maintain, and desertion (from Maliki law).

Finally, where traditional authorities could not be marshalled to justify reform, modernization occurred through the reinterpretation of tradition. Especially useful in justifying reform was an appeal to a subsidiary source of law recognized by the Maliki school—public interest or social welfare (*maslaha*). Islamic reformers like Muhammad Abduh and Sayyid Ahmad Khan had laid the groundwork for this approach in calling for opening the door of reinterpretation (*ijtihad*). For example, both had been critical of polygamy and its potentially harmful effects on modern family life. Their reformist critique of polygamy was based on interpreting the Qur'an in light of social welfare. They maintained that polygamy had been permitted in the Prophet's time as a concession to social circumstances: the many widows and orphans in need of male protection. Both argued that the Qur'anic legislation, "Marry women of your choice, two, three, or four. But if ye fear ye shall not be able to deal justly (with them) then only one" (4:3), was further circumscribed by a later verse, Qur'an 4:129. This verse stipulates that a husband in a polygamous marriage must be able to treat each of his wives with equal justice and impartiality. Because such equal treatment reflects a practical impossibility, reformers stressed that the Qur'anic ideal was actually monogamy. Based on this interpretation, modern legislation restricted a husband's right of polygamy by requiring judicial review and permission for such marriages.

The significant and powerful role that tradition played throughout the process of legal modernization is demonstrated in two important ways: first, while displaying Islamic law with reform, legislation may seem to be quite radical; this move was, in fact, preferred by conservative religious leaders opposed to tampering directly with the *Shari'a.* Displacement of the laws allowed for the possibility that traditional law, the ideal blueprint for Muslim society, could some day be restored—when Islam had regained its power and proper place. Thus, in Iran, Pakistan, Egypt, and other countries today, fundamentalists call for such a return. Second, the selective modern reforms in Muslim family law which remained in force were still influenced by the power of tradition because failure to comply with these new regulations rendered an act illicit, but *not* invalid. Therefore, if a Muslim ignored reform legislation and contracted a polygamous marriage or divorced his wife according to traditional law, the marriage or divorce was still valid, though illegal and subject to legal penalties (fines and/or imprisonment).

A major problem with this approach to modernizing Islamic law is that its prime movers have been Western–educated, political elites, a minority that has legislated change for the more tradition–oriented majority. Moreover, law has traditionally been the province of the religious scholars (*ulama* or *fuqaha*) who are its guardians and interpreters. Although modernizing elites have often skillfully appealed to traditional Islamic jurisprudence for their methodology and, hence, justification, in fact their approach has often been superficial, piecemeal, and *ad hoc*.[10] Lacking rigor and consistency, reforms sponsored by elites have been open to the charge of distortion and manipulation as well as exploitation of the tradition. Legal reformers have assiduously avoided the crucial question of *substantive* reinterpretation and reform (*ijtihad*) in Islamic law. Although Islamic reformers have, for some time, called for reinterpretation and affirmed their right of *ijtihad,* in practice the systematic review and assessment of Islamic law has not occurred. The significance of these unresolved questions and the continued hold of tradition may be seen in those Muslim countries where the Islamic resurgence has led to the repeal of family law reform in Iran or calls for repeal in Pakistan, Egypt, and others.

Family law reform demonstrates the principal way in which Muslim governments have attempted to reinterpret tradition in order to modernize. In contrast, Saudi Arabia's use of Islam in its development shows the flexibility and adaptability of the Islamic tradition itself, as the House of Saud has skillfully appealed to tradition for legitimate change.[11]

Saudi Arabia provides a striking example of the use of tradition by a conservative Islamic state in rendering change. The Saudis proudly proclaim their Islamic heritage and traditions. It is the original birthplace of Muhammad and the homeland of Islam. The Saudis remain the keepers of the Holy cities of Mecca and Medina. Moreover, Saudi history and practice seem to confirm their Islamic character. Modern Saudi Arabia is a product of an alliance struck between the Islamic revivalists, Muhammad ibn Abd al-Wahhab and Prince Muhammad ibn Saud, in Central Arabia which produced a thriving religio-political movement based on a return to a purified Islam; that is, an Islam cleansed of historical innovations that had compromised the original message of the Qur'an and the example of Muhammad. The union of religion and politics is vividly symbolized in the Saudi flag which combines the Muslim profession of faith (*shahada*)—there is no God but God, and Muhammad is His messenger—with the crossed swords of the House of Saud.

From its beginnings, the kindom has appealed directly to Islam as its *raison d'etre*. Islam is the ideological basis for Saudi rule and legitimacy and has continued to be utilized by Saudi rulers in validating their programs and policies. The Qur'an is its constitution, and the *Sharī'a* provides the fundamental structure of the state, its law and judiciary. The use of the Qur'an instead of a formal constitution has allowed the royal family great leeway in most areas that are not covered by scripture. Similarly, while Saudi Arabia's law is derived from the Hanbali School, the strictest and most rigid of the classical Islamic law schools, yet where its law is silent, change is possible. Most importantly, Saudi Arabia's leadership has shrewdly utilized the vast resources of the Islamic tradition to provide a rationale for rendering change. The Qur'an and Traditions of the Prophet have been utilized to introduce such innovations as photography, radio, and television. Although the stronghold of tradition may be seen in the continued enforcement of veiling and the seclusion of women, an Islamic rationale was cited by King Faysal in introducing women's education in 1960.[12]

Although the sensitive area of family law has remained unchanged, modernization has occurred in other areas of Islamic law, such as civil and commercial law. In addition, although the *Shari'a* is a revealed law, and thus, human legislation is proscribed, Muslim governments have long had the power to enact rules and regulations (*nizam*) in areas that were not covered by the *Shari'a*. Islamic jurisprudence accepts a ruler's ability to enact administrative decrees in order to better assure *Shari'a* governance (*siyasa shariyya*). With this justification, the Saudi government has been able to promulgate codes regulating modern institutions such as the Social Insurance Law (1970) and the Civil Service Law (1971) and to expand the judiciary. Thus, even in a state that is ostensibly fundamentalist rather than reformist, tradition has been flexible enough to permit, even legitimate, the development of a modern state.

Despite Saudi Arabia's apparent success in appealing to tradition to legitimate modernization, problems remain. The success of the Saudis has been due in great part to the persuasive skills of its kings and their close working relationship with the *ulama* based on established marital ties between the royal family and leading *ulama* families rather than widespread acceptance of change (a change in outlook and attitudes) due to a process of religious and educational reform. As the pace of change increases, the religious tensions accompanying modernization, and its perceived assault on tradition, mount. Although individual reforms may be possible, the acceptance of more rapid and widespread change requires an orientation or attitude of mind that will not see such change as unwarranted innovation (*bida*) or departure from sacrosanct traditions.

THE ISLAMIC REVIVAL: TRADITION AND MODERNIZATION IN CONTEMPORARY ISLAM

Since the mid–1970s, a religious revival has been observed in many parts of the Muslim world. Whereas the Iranian revolution is its most publicized manifestation, the causes, extent, and character of the Islamic revival or Islamic resurgence are far more diverse and complex than the Iranian experience. A central question that emerges is: "Are Muslims rejecting modernization?"

Rather than viewing the revival of Islam today as the reassertion of tradition against the incursions of modernization, it is more useful to see the current period as a reaction and response to the unresolved conflicts and issues that have been inherent in an *ad hoc,* fragmented process of modernization. In most Muslim countries, modernization has been characterized by the uncritical adoption rather than adaptation of Western models of political, social, legal, and economic change. These models, the products of several centuries of Western history and experience, were simply transplanted onto an alien soil, and as with transplants or grafts, such foreign substances tend to be rejected. Examples of this uncritical process abound: the progressive secularization of the state; adoption of Western-based constitutions containing but a few Islamic provisions, such as the requirement that the head of state be a Muslim; the acceptance of Western law. Thus, Muslim governments failed to produce a new synthesis that provided some continuity between modern changes and long-established traditions.

The uncritical reliance on the West and the failure to more indigenously root the identity of modern Muslim societies eventually produced an identity crisis reflected in Muslim literature in the Arab world and South Asia from the mid–1960s onwards.[13] An increasingly recurrent set of themes concerned with authenticity and identity appeared in Muslim societies. This was reflected in secular as well as religious literature—in books, periodicals, and newspapers. There was a growing disenchantment with the West, for despite modernization policies based on imitation of the West, profound political and socioeconomic inequities continued to grip the Muslim world. Liberal nationalism as well as Arab nationalism and socialism were judged to be failures. Political systems were erratic and authoritarian. Sovereignty and legitimacy were based on power and force. Poverty and illiteracy continued to be a pervasive economic reality. The United States' support for Israel and the Shah's Iran were seen from a Muslim perspective as incomprehensible examples of neocolonialism and a rejection of Muslim "friends." Urbanization and changing family patterns with their social dislocation and problems were deplored as the products of a Western secular–oriented modernization program devoid of traditional Islamic principles and values and responsible for a spiritual malaise and widespread corruption.

Two events in the 1970s contributed to a new surge of Muslim pride. First, the 1973 Arab-Israeli War became a source of new-found pride as the dismal, decisive Arab defeat of 1967 was reversed in Arab eyes by a war interpreted through faith and belief as an Islamic victory.[14] Islamic symbolism and meaning permeated the experience: the October War was the Ramadan War, named after the holy month of Islam; its battle cry was the traditional Islamic cry Allahu Akbar (God is great); its code name was Badr, Muhammad's first military victory; and reports by generals and soldiers of the sighting of angels seemed to confirm divine guidance. Second, the 1973 Arab oil embargo and the consequent sense that for the first time since the dawning of colonialism Muslim countries constituted a power with which the West must reckon also contributed to a new–found sense of pride and purpose. These events gave strong positive reinforcement to the belief that once more, as throughout early Islamic history, God was protecting and guiding His community. Moreover, oil wealth has enabled countries like Libya and Saudi Arabia to export and support Islamic revivalism in other countries. Recognition of the need to reaffirm the Islamic heritage has contributed to calls for the renewal (*tajdid*) of Muslim society to bring about a new renaissance (*nahda*). An increase in religious observances (prayers, mosque attendance, religious dress, fasting during Ramadan) has been quite evident in many parts of the Muslim world. This revival has seen the reemergence of Islam not only in the personal but also in political life. Muslims have reasserted the traditional Islamic belief that the true Islamic state is based on *tawhid* and is actualized through governance by Islamic law, a society in which religion is an integral part of public life: politics, law, and society. This reaffirmation has meant increased calls for a more authentic, indigenously based society. While all might advocate modern Muslim societies that are more clearly informed by the principles and values of their ancient heritage, the meaning of these principles and values varies markedly, depending on their orientation to tradition. Is one to look to the spirit or the letter? Is the task to replicate the past, that is, the life of the early Islamic community, or to renovate in light of the past? Traditionist and Islamic reformers, with their differing approaches to the past and future, clash over such fundamental questions.

The key to resolving the problem of tradition and change is education. Traditionally, education and religious scholarship had been the province of the *ulama*. In the past religious schools trained the leaders of society; however, during the nineteenth and twentieth centuries, many Muslim countries introduced secular education which came to exist alongside the traditional religious education provided by the *ulama*. The existence of two parallel systems has actually caused a bifurcation of Muslim society. Despite some curriculum reform, the traditional system remained relatively isolated from the mainstream. Funding priority has been given to secular schools which provide the training and academic degrees for prestige positions in a modern society (engineering, medicine, law, journalism). Graduates of religious schools, with predominantly traditional educations, continue to serve as religious leaders or teachers. However, they are often ill prepared to understand and respond to the demands of modernity. Most are unable to provide creative reinterpretation of traditional values, the religious leadership required in modern society.

On the other hand, modern elites trained in Western–oriented secular schools are well versed in modern disciplines but are often lacking in the true awareness of their tradition necessary to make changes that are sensitive to the history and values of their cultural milieu. As a result, Western models and presuppositions have been facilely adopted by modern elites. Opportunities to render change reflecting some continuity with the past have gone unrecognized as well as unrealized. Thus, both traditional and modern elites have failed to provide a new synthesis that clearly provides some continuity between tradition and modernity.

Too often the Muslim world has seen, on the one hand, an elite minority convinced that they must forge ahead regardless of the obscurantist opposition of religious leaders and, on the other, a religious leadership suspicious of and resistant to an alien process—modernization—characterized as Western, secularist, materialist, and godless. Thus, to date, the religious leadership is seen as an obstacle to change, while the Western secular elite and their governments are conveniently blamed for the social and spiritual ills of society.

The bifurcation of education and the consequent training of two separate mindsets or outlooks (traditional and modern) is clearly illustrated in the contemporary Islamic revival. The demand for more Islamically oriented states requires a reexamination of political, social, legal, and economic institutions as well as of the principles and values that inform them. If secularists have denied the necessity, let alone feasibility, of undertaking such a task, the religious leadership has generally proven incapable of it. More conservative religious leaders tend to be fixated on the past. They view tradition not so much as a source of direction and inspiration, but rather as the very map to be followed in all its details. This idealized blueprint for Muslim society, contained in the Islamic law of medieval legal manuals, is not seen as a response to a specific socio-historical period—a conditioned product hammered out by jurists in light of Islamic principles and values. Conservatives fail to distinguish between revealed, immutable principles and historically conditioned laws and institutions that were the product of the early jurists' human reason. Moreover, the hold of tradition is to be found in a more hidden form among those who advocate reinterpretation (*ijtihad*) and change in principle but who, when pressed on specific changes, often reflect a "*taqlid* mentality," that is, a tendency to reflexively follow past practice.

The significance and depth of tradition's hold on Muslim society may be seen in the fact that few systematic attempts at reinterpretation and reform have occurred, let alone penetrated Muslim society. Many Muslim countries have found it easier to continue along the parallel paths of religion and secularity as has been seen in the fields of law and education. The systematic reconstruction advocated by earlier reformers such as Abduh and Iqbal has not occurred. Instead of producing Islamic models for development, of discussing the "what" and "how" of a modern Islamic society, secular leaders have been content to mandate or legislate change; and the majority of religious leaders have prefered to bide their time until a "restoration" of Islam might take place. Thus, when religious forces gain power (Iran) or influence (Pakistan) or become more vocal in calling for the Islamization of society (Egypt), the Islam which many advocate and/or introduce is that of the past not simply in its revealed principles, but often in its derivative prescriptions and forms.

The contemporary revival has also seen an attempt (by a new generation of Islamic reformers) to overcome the dichotomy between the traditional–and the secular–educated. Western–educated but Islamically committed and oriented, they emphasize the importance of "Islamic modernization." Islamic modernization does not reject the West; it wishes to learn from the West but not to Westernize Muslim society. They make a distinction between rejection of change (modernization) and uncritical, indiscriminate change, a blind imitation of the

West, variously referred to as Westomania, Westoxification, or Weststruckness. Modern Islamic reformers distinguish between the acceptance of Western science/ technology and the assimilation of Western culture/mores. They stress the need to renew Islam both in the individual and political life of the community. They advocate Islamization, a process of reinterpretation and reform based on a return to the primary sources of Islam—the Qur'an and Sunna (example of the Prophet). Contemporary reinterpreters see themselves as continuing a dynamic process that is as old as Islam itself. Early Muslims interpreted and applied Islamic principles and values to their time and, thus, produced Islamic law: the blueprint for Muslim society. They borrowed freely from the cultures they conquered—adopting and adapting political, legal, and economic practices as long as they were not contrary to Islam. So, today, in light of the Qur'an and sunna of the Prophet, Muslims must once more meet the changing needs of their societies. They must again address fundamental questions such as: "What is the good and how can it best be realized today?" However, this raises inescapable issues such as: "Whose Islam guides us? What change and how much change is needed?" In the past, the traditional religious leadership (*ulama*) claimed the prerogative to interpret Islam. During the twentieth century, Muslim governments and individual heads of state, like Egypt's Gamal Abdul Nasser and Anwar Sadat, Iran's Ayatullah Khomeini, Libya's Colonel Muammar Qaddafi, and Pakistan's General Zia ul-Haq, have themselves interpreted Islam in order to legitimate their programs and policies. At the same time, these self-proclaimed Muslim leaders have been opposed by others in the name of Islam. Since Sunni Islam, which comprises 80 percent of the world's Muslims, lacks a centralized teaching authority or organized hierarchy, "Whose Islam?" How does one distinguish between what is and what is not normative Islam?

One can see this problem quite vividly in post-revolutionary Iran as Muslim persecutes Muslim in the name of Islam. Fundamentalist clergy routed not only the Shah, but also fellow Islamic revolutionaries such as the first prime minister of the Islamic Republic of Iran, Mahdi Bazargan, and its first president, Abul-Hasan Bani Sadr. Although questions of power precipitated the clashes, underlying the confrontation are distinctively different fundamentalist and modernist visions. Similarly in Pakistan, while General Zia ul-Haq's *coup de etat* in 1977 and pledge to introduce an Islamic system of government (*Nizam-i-Islam*) were generally welcomed, many now decry his "negative Islam": exemplified in postponement of democratic elections, banning of political parties, enforcement of traditional Islamic punishments (amputation for theft, whipping for alcohol consumption, stoning of adulterers), and introduction of Islamic wealth and agricultural taxes—all justified in the name of Islam.

Although the *ulama* continue to assert that they alone are the guardians and interpreters of Islam, many contemporary Islamic reformers—most of whom are lay rather than clerical—point out that there is no clergy in Islam and that an *alim* ("learned one," plu. *ulama*) simply means an expert. The development of a clerical class with its special status, dress, and so on, has no religious justification but is due to socio-historical circumstances. In addition, Islamic reformers argue that the needs of contemporary Muslim societies require a broader group of experts. Experts in modern fields—economics, sociology, psychology, and law—as well as in the traditional disciplines, will be required to develop modern Islamically oriented societies. In doing so, whose Islam will they follow?

The second and related question is, "What change and how much change is needed?" Muslims must determine the relationship of tradition to modernization. Does a "return to Islam" mean the reclamation and implementation of the traditional, detailed blueprint for Muslim society, or does it mean a return to the sources of Islam, to those principles and values on which new forms of state and society may be established? In classical terms, is the process simply a following or imitating of the past (*taqlid*) or the reinterpretation (*ijtihad*) and reform of tradition? Is there one classical Islamic model or many possible models for political, social, and economic development? If a new synthesis that provides some continuity with the past is to be achieved, how will this be accomplished? Who will fomulate: the head of state, the *ulama*, "lay experts"? How will new forms be implemented?

In many parts of the Islamic world, Muslims stand at a crossroad. Although independent states for several decades, the political and socioeconomic character and institutions of Muslim states are far from established. To the extent that incumbent governments fail to satisfy the political and economic needs of their societies and to pursue a path of modernization which is sensitive to their Islamic heritage, they will remain in a precarious position in which stability is based more often than not on authoritarian rule and force. If Muslim governments strive to achieve a new synthesis providing some continuity between the demands of modernity and their Islamic tradition, then a broad range of possibilities stretch out before them—from the fundamentalist to the reformist state and society. The possibilities are many. Although the outcome is impossible to predict and indeed will vary from country to country depending on political, social, and economic variables, the process itself is inevitable because it involves national identity as well as religious understanding and commitment.

NOTES

1. Smith, *Islam in Modern History* ch. 1–3.
2. See Rahman, *Islam,* ch. 12, for a brief discussion of pre-modernist reform movements.
3. See Donohue and Esposito, eds., *Islam in Transition,* ch. 1.
4. See Hourani, *Arabic Thought in the Liberal Age,* ch. 5; and Keddie, *Islamic Response to Imperialism* and *Sayyid Jamal al-Din al-Afghani.*
5. Donohue and Esposito, eds. *Islam in Transition,* p. 19.
6. As quoted in Rahman, *Islam,* p. 267.
7. Iqbal, *Reconstruction of Religious Thought in Islam,* pp. 178–179.
8. For a more extended discussion of Muslim family law reforms, see Coulson,

History of Islamic Law, ch. 12–14; Anderson, *Law Reform in the Muslim World;* and Esposito, *Women in Muslim Family Law Reform.*

9. This discussion of family law reform is restricted to Sunni Islam which comprises 80 percent of the world's Muslims and generally does not include Shi'a Islam.

10. Esposito, *Women in Muslim Family Law,* pp. 94ff. Cf. Layish "On Contribution of the Modernists to the Secularization of Islamic Law," 264–274.

11. Piscatori, "Roles of Islam in Saudi Arabia's Political Development," in Esposito, ed., *Islam and Development,* ch. 7.

12. Ibid., p. 129.

13. Donohue, "Islam and the Quest for Identity in the Arab World," in Esposito, ed., *Voices of a Resurgent Islam,* ch. 3; Merad, "Ideologisation of Islam," in Cudsi and Dessouki, eds., *Islam and Power,* ch. 3; and Waheed-uz-Zamaan, ed. *Quest for Identity.*

14. Haddad, *Contemporary Islam and the Challenge of History,* pp. 42–43.

GLOSSARY

ummah: the community of believers, a religio-political community or state.

tawhid: "unity or oneness" of God; Islam's radical monotheism.

Shariah: The revealed law of Islam.

sunnah: "trodden path," example or model behavior of the Prophet Muhammad.

hadith: a report or recorded tradition about the words/deeds of the Prophet Muhammad.

fiqh: "understanding," the science of jurisprudence which elucidated the Shariah.

ytihad: the use of independent reasoning or judgment in interpreting Islamic law.

giyas: the use of analogical reasoning in law.

ijma: consensus or agreement as a source of law.

taqlid: to follow or imitate religious authority (tradition or law).

bida: "innovation," practices which deviate from tradition.

tajdid: "renewal."

ulama: (plural of alim) "learned," religious scholars.

jihad: "struggle or strive in God's way," its military manifestation is a holy war.

hijra: migration of Muhammad and his followers from Mecca to Medina in 622 A.D. This is the beginning of the Islamic community/state and the first year of the Islamic calendar.

fuqaha: (plural of faqih) a legal expert, jurist.

shahada: "testimony," the confession of faith in Islam: "There is no God but God and Muhammad is his Messenger."

siyasa shariyya: "shariah governance," the right of the ruler to issue administrative regulations (*nizam*) to assure Islamic rule.

nahda: "renaissance."

Nizam-i-Islam: an Islamic system of government.

maslaha: public interest or general welfare.

nizam: rule or ordinance promulgated by an Islamic ruler to supplement Shariah law.

BIBLIOGRAPHY

Anderson, J. N.D. *Law Reform in the Muslim World.* London: Athlone Press, 1976.

Coulson, N. J. *A History of Islamic Law.* Edinburgh: Edinburgh University Press, 1964.

Donohue, John J. "Islam and the Quest for Identity in the Arab World." In John L. Esposito, ed. *Voices of a Resurgent Islam*. New York: Oxford University Press, forthcoming.

Donohue, John J. and John L. Esposito, eds. *Islam in Transition: Muslim Perspectives*. New York: Oxford University Press, 1981.

Esposito, John L. *Women in Muslim Family Law Reform*. Syracuse, N.Y.: Syracuse University Press, 1982.

Haddad, Yvonne Y. *Contemporary Islam and the Challenge of History*. Albany, N.Y.: State University of New York Press, 1982.

Hourani, Albert. *Arabic Thought in the Liberal Age*. Oxford: Oxford University Press, 1970.

Iqbal, Muhammad. *The Reconstruction of Religious Thought in Islam*. Lahore: M. Ashraf, reprint, 1968.

Keddie, Nikki R. *An Islamic Response to Imperialism*. Berkeley: University of California Press, 1968.

————. *Sayyid Jamal al-Din al-Afghani: A Political Biography*. Berkeley: University of California Press, 1972.

Layish, A. "One Contribution of the Modernists to the Secularization of Islamic Law." *Middle East Studies* 14 (October 1978): 264–274.

Merad, Ali. "The Ideologisation of Islam in the Contemporary Muslim World." In A. Cudsi and A. Dessouki, eds. *Islam and Power*. Baltimore, Md.: Johns Hopkins University Press, 1981.

Piscatori, James P. "The Roles of Islam in Saudi Arabia's Political Development." In John L. Esposito, ed. *Islam and Development: Religion and Sociopolitical Change*. Syracuse, N.Y.: Syracuse University Press, 1980.

Rahman, F. *Islam*. New York: Anchor Doubleday, 1966.

Smith, W. C. *Islam in Modern History*. Princeton, N.J.: Princeton University Press, 1977.

Waheed-uz-Zamaan, ed. *The Quest for Identity*. Islamabad: Islamabad University Press, 1973.

6

Catholicism and Politics in Latin America

GUSTAVO BENAVIDES

I

As the recent political developments in Latin America show, the relationship between politics and religion—in this case mainly Roman Catholicism—is so intricate that it hardly seems justified to talk about religion *and* politics, because such a formulation implies that these two phenomena can be approached independently.[1] On the contrary, the history of Latin America, from the days of the Spanish conquest to the contemporary civil wars in Central America, shows the constant and active presence of the Catholic Church. From the encounter between Father Vicente Valverde and Atahualpa in Cajamarca in the third decade of the sixteenth century to the Theology of Liberation, the Church has had to play an ambiguous and, not seldom, a contradictory role in the political life of the continent. Most clearly, the first role expected from the Church in the early years of the colonial period was the one of legitimator, while the humanitarian role was perforce only a secondary one. Indeed, both Valverde and Bartolomé de Las Casas are paradigmatic figures.[2] Valverde, by accompanying Pizarro, and blessing, in the spirit of the *Reconquista*,[3] his attack on the armies of the Inca, moved Pizarro's enterprise from a secular to a sacred realm,[4] whereas Bartolomé, by trying to make the whole enterprise more humane (without, however, going as far as condemning it), helped legitimate Spanish power.

The Church's contradictory role in Latin America may be said to arise from the fundamental tension between, on the one hand, "Christianity," understood as a set of moral values—charity, love, brotherhood, and so on—and, on the other, the ideology of Christendom: another set of values whose role was the defense of the medieval world order against the external threats represented by the Muslims, and the internal ones, constituted by Jews and heretics. In the case of Spain, the ideology of Christendom was further intensified by the peculiar historical situation of a country that for centuries had fought against the Muslim kingdoms in the south of the peninsula, and that, not long before the conquest of America, had succeeded in defeating Islam and expelling the Jews.[5] It is not difficult, therefore, to imagine the ideology of Christendom supporting the colonial enterprise, while, at the same time, attempting to ameliorate its brutal character. These brief remarks should serve to give some perspective to the Church's present situation in the countries that were created out of the breakup of the Spanish and Portuguese empires.

In the new republics, the role of the Church continued to be an ideological one. This does not mean, however, that the relationship between the Church and the new governments was without problems. The institution of patronage (*real patronato de las indias*),[6] that is, the right exercised by the king of Spain to nominate or present a cleric for installation in a vacant office, was inherited by the new republics, becoming a source of continued struggle between sacred and secular power.[7] Nevertheless, this difference of opinion regarding the ultimate source of religious power supports, rather than undermines, the view that the values shared by the Church and the new Latin American states were basically similar. At no point did the Church, *qua* Church, question the legitimacy of the economic and social order, that is, the legitimacy of the state itself. At most, as in the days of the *conquista* in the sixteenth century, the Church tried to soften the conditions in which most of the population lived. The most bitter conflicts, on the other hand, took place when the Church had to defend its own interests against the intrusions of the secular powers. These conflicts, which varied from country to country, had to do mostly with the problem of the *patronato* and with related matters, such as taxation of the vast properties of the religious orders; the state's attitude toward other religions (generally Protestant groups); religious versus secular education; and so on.[8] In any event, the conflicts that arose in the republican period had to do less with moral values than with the issue of power: the ideology of Christendom was—and to a great extent is still—very much alive.

II

This is not the place to examine in detail the relationship between Church and state in Latin America in the nineteenth and early twentieth centuries.[9] It is instructive, however, to review some of the instances in which this special relationship was strained, particularly during the wars of independence, since an examination of the contradictory attitudes assumed by the priests, the local hierarchies, and the Vatican may help us understand the contradictory choices which these same groups face at the present time. Today, however, the problem is no longer one of political independence, but one of economic independence from the powers that inherited the position once held by Spain and Portugal.

As late as January 30, 1816, Pius VII issued the encyclical *Etsi longissimo*, in which he told the bishops of America:

You can easily accomplish the suppression of disorders and sedition if each one of you is willing to expose zealously the dangers and grave evils of defections, and expound the noble and exceptional qualities and virtues of our dear son, your king, Ferdinand, Catholic king of Spain, to whom nothing is more important than religion and the happiness of his subjects; and finally, if you cite the illustrious example, which should never perish, of the Spanish people who did not hesitate to sacrifice goods and life in showing their adherence to religion and fidelity to the king.[10]

Later, on September 24, 1824 (less than three months before the battle of Ayacucho, which consolidated the independence of South America), Leo XII issued another encyclical in which he asked the bishops of America to support the cause of "our very dear son, Ferdinand, Catholic King of Spain, whose sublime and solid virtues cause him to place before the splendor of his greatness the luster of religion and the happiness of his subjects."[11] It was not until August 1831 that Gregory XVI, in the bull *Sollicitudo Ecclesiarum*, declared his intention to establish relations with the new governments, while still refusing to recognize the *patronato*.[12]

Regarding the attitude of the local clergy, we find that in many instances the priests supported the struggle for independence. Thus, in Argentina, figures such as Ignacio Cela and Gregorio Funes worked actively for independence. The same can be said of Mexico, where the names of Morelos and Hidalgo represented just two of the many priests who participated in the process. The attitude of the hierarchy, on the other hand, was less than sympathetic to the idea of independence. In Mexico, for example, curate Hidalgo was excommunicated by bishop-elect Manuel Abad y Queipo, who declared that Hidalgo, "a pastor of souls, a priest of Jesus Christ, a minister of the God of Peace, had raised a standard of rebellion and seduced a number of innocent people."[13] The natural alliance between secular and religious powers necessitated the intervention of the Inquisition. Thus, on October 10, 1810, a report by the Holy Office stated, rather inconsistently, that "Hidalgo was a partisan of French liberty, a libertine, a formal heretic, a Judaiser, a Lutheran, a Calvinist, a rebel, a schismatic, and a suspected atheist."[14] The same procedure was used against Morelos, who was declared to be "heretic, propagator of heresy, pursuer and disturber of the ecclesiastical hierarchy, profaner of the holy sacraments, schismatic, lascivious, hypocrite, irreconcilable enemy of Christianity, and traitor to God, king, and pope."[15] Again, in 1812, the metropolitan chapter of Mexico exhorted the curates to "abstain from mixing in questions foreign to their profession,"[16] an exhortation not unlike the ones heard during the visit John Paul II made to Central America in March 1983. A brief review of the situation in other Latin American countries reveals similar attitudes, although nowhere do we find a more colorful political use of natural events as in Venezuela, where the earthquake of March 26, 1812, was interpreted by Archbishop Coll y Prat as "punishment of God irritated against the upstarts who had refused to recognize the most virtuous of monarchs, Ferdinand VII, the annointed of the Lord."[17]

Once political independence was finally achieved and consolidated, the Church turned its energies to securing its privileged position by supporting the new order. At this point, one of the most important issues was the maintenance of Roman Catholicism as the religion of the state. This was not particularly difficult to accomplish, for most of those who had fought against Spain were fervent Catholics, as in the cases of Hidalgo and José María Morelos in Mexico, and of Mariano Moreno, José de San Martín, and Belgrano in Argentina. Consequently, the early constitutions of Latin America grant a privileged place to Roman Catholicism. Such special position is found in the *Estatuto Provisional* of 1815 and the *Reglamento* of 1817 in Argentina; the *Estatuto Provisorio*, promulgated by San Martín in Peru; the constitutions of Chile from 1811 to 1818; the proclamation of independence of Mexico on November 6, 1813; and the declaration of independence of Venezuela on July 5, 1811,[18]

In all the cases mentioned above, the Church transferred its allegiance from the Spanish Crown to the new republican order. It should be kept in mind, however, that the newly achieved independence did not bring about a fundamental change in the economic and social organization of the continent. The struggle for independence had been carried on mostly by a segment of the creoles (*criollos*), who wanted to assert their rights against the Spanish-born (*godos*, *peninsulares*, *gachupines*) inhabitants of the colonies and the economic restrictions imposed by the Madrid government. The mass of people, on the other hand, had little to expect from the new political order, because in a predominantly rural economy in which mining and agriculture were the principal sources of revenue, independence did not change in any significant way the system of land tenure (not to mention other institutions such as slavery). Furthermore, after independence, the new nations engaged in endless rearrangements of frontiers, short-lived confederations, and civil wars, resulting in the consolidation of the phenomenon of military *caudillismo* which has continued to this day. Besides the local oligarchies, the institutions that provided the necessary continuity during these chaotic times were the army and the Church. Both, army and Church, constituted the ideological and instrumental backbone of the structure of domination. Despite the continuous changes of government (or of heads of state), the army was the deciding force, whereas the oligarchy was the ultimate beneficiary of the social order defended by the army. In this context, the Catholic Church provided the ideological justification for this state of affairs. Christian virtues—faith, humility, obedience, respect for authority, glorification of poverty, and so on—helped to maintain the population in a state that made any radical change impossible.

The role of the Church was, then, as in the times of the *conquista* and *colonia*, one of legitimizer of the status quo (albeit it occasionally attempted to mitigate some extreme forms of institutional violence). The authority exercised by the state was perceived as emanating from the supernatural sphere, and the president, or the *caudillo*, was regarded as a figure whose power was inscribed in the natural—hierarchical—order of things.[19] Within this world-view, the Church was condemned to serve as the institution that ultimately validated the authority of those in power. Such a role is evident from the early years of the *conquista* in the sixteenth century to 1973, when the Chilean hierarchy welcomed the coup against the socialist government of Salvador Allende.[20] As mentioned earlier, the medieval fusion of religious and political interests was particularly strong in Spain and Portugal, as a result mostly of the unavoidable confluence of religious, political, and military goals during the wars of the *reconquista* against Islam. Later, the ideology of Christendom was reinforced when the Pope gave the Portuguese Crown the right and the duty to propagate the Christian faith in the territories that were either discovered or regained from the infidels.[21] Therefore, it is not difficult to see how the ideology of Christendom was at the core of the colonial enterprise, and how it has continued to be a central component of the self-understanding of the ruling elites of Latin American societies. In this context, the military titles conferred on religious figures such as the *Virgen de las Mercedes* can be perceived in their full ideological implications and cease to be seen as mere colorful aspects of Latin American religiosity. *Nuestra Señora de las Mercedes* as *generala* or *mariscala* plays a role that is not very different from the one once played by the patron of Spain, Santiago, whose name served as the battle cry of the Spanish armies, both in Europe and in America.

In this historical context, to be a Christian means not so much a purely "religious" fact—if there even is such a thing—but a political one. The sense of identity provided by Christianity inscribes the person thus defined in a world in which "Christianity" is not only a set of moral values, but also a highly charged articulation of political choices. On the other hand, if it is true that the elites used the ideology of Christendom to justify their position, it is also true that the all-encompassing nature of this ideology lent itself to be used by economically and politically deprived groups, this time as the source of utopian movements.[22] In Karl Mannheim's terminology, it could be said that Christendom presented itself both as ideology and utopia: as means of articulating the defense of the status quo, as well as of radical change.[23] In the case of Latin America, however, we should also take into account the role played by non-Christian religious ideologies which in syncretistic fashion collaborated with Christianity in the development of messianic movements.[24] This phenomenon is significant in countries with large Indian populations, where, despite centuries of "hispanization," cultural elements going back to pre-Hispanic times still exist. This is also true of countries in which there was a considerable influx of African slaves (particularly Brazil and the Caribbean area). In both cases, Indian and African religious conceptions have contributed to a general millenarist atmosphere in which European elements were also significant. The influence of the millenarist visions of Joachim of Fiore on the Franciscan and Jesuit missionaries in America remains to be studied, but as Marjorie Reeves has pointed out, the ideas of Joachim may have influenced Columbus himself, who collected many prophecies, including those of Joachim, in his *Libro de las profecías*.[25]

III

An examination of the ideological role of the Church in Latin America in the twentieth century reveals a consistent pattern of identification with the ruling groups of society, especially as these groups identify themselves as the defenders of the traditional values of family, property, and God. It is only around the time of the second Vatican Council (1962–1965) that the attitudes of the Latin American hierarchies seem to start changing and begin to be concerned with the economic problems affecting the continent. After the Vatican Council, Latin American bishops and theologians participated in a series of encounters (*encuentros*) which culminated in the encounter of Medellín, Colombia, in 1968.[26] The Medellín encounter was significant because there, for the first time, the Latin American Church faced the structural problems that had afflicted the continent for centuries. Before Medellín, the Church had reacted to the concrete problems of malnutrition, exploitation, and institutionalized violence of all types either by ignoring them or by preaching the traditional Christian values of faith, hope, and charity, which, in fact, helped perpetuate the system.

Central America. Given the current political situation in Central America, it is important to place the contemporary developments in their historical context. Neither the Sandinista government in Nicaragua, nor the civil war in El Salvador, nor the role played by Protestant groups in Guatemala can be understood merely as aspects of a vast struggle between East and West, or between freedom and democracy on the one hand, and Communist totalitarianism on the other.[27] The reason for these developments lies rather in the economic situation prevalent in these countries and in the extreme poverty in which most of their populations live. With regard to the role of the Church in the maintenance of this order, it can be said that relationships between the local hierarchies and the governments have been generally friendly. In the case of the Dominican Republic, for example, if it is true that at the end of the rule of Rafael Leonidas Trujillo (assassinated in 1961), the Church had made attempts to distance itself from the regime,[28] it is also true that in the previous years the hierarchy had maintained friendly relations with the dictator, partly as a result of Trujillo's encouragement of religious activity during his thirty years in power.[29] After the fall of Trujillo, the Church welcomed the return to democracy but opposed the leftist government of President Juan Bosch, who was deposed by the military in 1963. As is well known, when Francisco Camaño attempted to return Bosch to power in 1965, the United States sent troops to protect the country from communism.[30] The Dominican Republic under Trujillo offers a clear example of an "authoritarian" government which, under the pretext of being a bulwark against Communist "totalitarianism," imposes a regime of repression, with the support of the Church and the government of the United States.[31]

The situation of Nicaragua is, if anything, even more extreme. Since the nineteenth century, Nicaragua has suffered the hegemonic policies of the United States, including several invasions and occupations of its territory.[32] Such invasions were rendered unnecessary when Anastasio Somoza García became commander of the National Guard on November 15, 1932.[33] As commander of the *Guardia Nacional*, Somoza had the power, either directly as president or indirectly through his appointees, to control the country. After his assassination in September 1956, he was succeeded as president by his son, Luis Somoza Debayle, who was succeeded in 1963 by Anastasio Somoza Debayle (called popularly Tachito Somoza). Growing popular opposition against the Somoza dynasty caused the final victory of the Sandinista guerrillas in 1979, forcing Somoza to flee the country and seek asylum in the United States. The position of the Church during the Somoza regimes more or less follows the classic pattern of, first, support of the government, then, distancing from the regime, and, finally, support of the victorious rebel forces.

In the case of Nicaragua, however, the position assumed by the hierarchy is worth examining in certain detail, given the changing attitudes of the hierarchy toward the Sandinista government and given the conflict that has developed between certain priests who are members of the government and the official Church. The case of Nicaragua is also important in view of the efforts by the government of the United States to overthrow the Sandinista government by supporting guerrilla groups trained in Florida and operating in Honduras. Finally, the recent visit of John Paul II to Central America has made clear the tension that exists between priests committed to the political process in progress in Nicaragua, and the traditional attitude of the Vatican and the hierarchy.

Between 1934 and 1970 there is no evidence of any opposition by the Church to the Somoza regime. It is only after 1970—almost forty years after the first Somoza took power—that the Church tried to keep some distance from the regime, especially after Miguel Obando y Bravo became the archbishop of Managua.[34] In March 1972 the Episcopal Conference of Nicaragua issued a pastoral letter in which it was stated that a new order was required for the country. Similar documents were issued in 1974 and in 1977, when the Episcopal Conference condemned the violations of human rights perpetrated by the government. Finally, on June 3, 1979—one month and a half before Somoza was forced to leave the country—the Bishops Conference declared justified the popular insurrection against the government. After the triumph of the revolution, the Church published several documents in support of the new government (July 31, August 19, November 17). In 1980, however, the attitude of the hierarchy began to change, and soon the government was criticized for its policies. A further deterioration took place on June 1, 1981, when the Bishops Conference asked the priests who were members of the government to resign their posts. At the same time, the Vatican opposed the creation of a "Popular Church" and pressured the already mentioned priests to give up their political activities and return to their purely religious functions.

This was the political atmosphere in the country when the Pope, John Paul II, visited Central America in March 1983. While in Nicaragua, the Pope publicly asked priests not to engage in "political activities"—an admonition which, as mentioned earlier, is the same one heard during the days of the wars of independence. Similarly, the Pope condemned "foreign ideologies," especially when supported by the rebel priests. John Paul's visit and the subsequent tensions—which were particularly obvious during the religious ceremonies in which the Pope participated—served to make even more visible the tensions between the ideology of Christendom, represented by the Pope and the hierarchy, and the utopian use of Christianity by those who considered themselves both Christians and revolutionaries. By asking the politically committed priests to devote themselves exclusively to their religious duties, the Pope and the hierarchy clearly implied that the previous Church support, or at least non-opposition, to the Somoza regime was an apolitical activity. This understanding of what belongs to the realm of the political is typical of any institution or group that identifies itself with the status quo. The equation of a given social order with "reality" becomes even more apparent in the Pope's condemnation of "foreign ideologies," because this obviously implies that the prevalent ideology is not such, but rather the way things ought to be: the natural order of things. That these condemnations already imply a political choice should be quite clear and requires no further elaboration. In any event, the selective condemnation of one type of political activity clearly betrays the conservative nature of the Church, not only in Nicaragua, but throughout Central America as well.

The Church's political attitude in El Salvador became evident when, during his visit, Pope John Paul II condemned the social injustice prevalent in the country, while at the same time condemning the military activities of the guerrillas. This position contradicted the stand taken by certain members of the local Church, particularly that of Archbishop Oscar Romero, who was assassinated during the mass on March 24, 1980, by a right-wing group. Romero had energetically condemned the slaughter of civilians perpetrated by the army and by paramilitary groups connected with the government. He did this not in the vague fashion usually employed by the hierarchy, but in a way that left little doubt about his sympathies. Archbishop Romero went so far as to justify the use of violence in the confrontation between the people of El Salvador and the repressive military regime. Significantly, he also was against the participation of the Christian Democratic Party (*Democracia Cristiana*) in the government, for he believed that such participation helped to legitimize the actions of the government. The role of the Christian Democrats in El Salvador suffers from the same fundamental ambiguity that has characterized this party in other Latin American countries. In El Salvador, a Christian Democrat, José Napoleón Duarte, served as president, until elections for a Constituent Assembly were held on May 28, 1982. As a result of the elections, the combined forces of the right defeated the Christian Democrat Duarte and installed as president of the Assembly Roberto D'Aubuisson, a right-wing terrorist, who according to many sources was involved in the assassination of Archbishop Romero.[35] The participation of the Christian Democrats in the elections, and their subsequent defeat by the right, is a typical example of Christian Democratic political opportunism and ineffectiveness, and in this case—as in Chile—outright complicity with a representative government.

Romero's successor, Archbishop Arturo Rivera y Damas, has taken a more conciliatory attitude toward the government, as a result of which no further murders of priests and nuns have taken place since his appointment. (The murder of civilians has continued, despite the efforts made by the U.S. government to give the impression that improvements have been made.) On the other hand, some priests have joined the guerrillas, one of the reasons given for these defections being the disbanding of the so-called Church of the poor ordered by the new archbishop. At the present time it is difficult to predict the outcome of the civil war, but it would be safe to say that if a victory of the leftist forces takes place, the Church would be split, with the hierarchy becoming more and more conservative and some of the priests probably supporting the new government.[36] The events in Nicaragua seem to indicate that such a division is unavoidable.

The history of Guatemala since the regime of Jacobo Arbenz presents the usual succession of military coups, repressions, indiscriminate killings, and the continuation of a militant anti-communism, shared by the government and the Church. During the Arbenz regime, the program of agrarian reform had affected not only the local oligarchy but also the interests of the United Fruit Company. These measures led to the condemnation of Arbenz by the Organization of American States, and to his subsequent overthrow, organized by the Central Intelligence Agency and carried out by a group of exiles under the command of Carlos Castillo Armas.[37] The attitude of the Church against Arbenz had been extremely negative; Mariano Rossell y Arellano, Archbishop of Guatemala from 1939 to 1964, led the opposition against the pretended communism of Arbenz,[38] warning the people of Guatemala against "the barbarity of Moscow and the culture of Genghis Khan."[39] It also seems that Archbishop Rossell played an important role in the coup against Arbenz, praising and blessing those who "rejected the mercenary sale of Guatemala to International Communism."[40] As a typical exponent of the ideology of Christendom, Rossell did all he could to equate the given social order with "Christianity," supporting the newly created *Partido Anticomunista Demócrata Cristiano* and organizing the national pilgrimage of the Cristo de Esquipulas as one of the main events of the *Cruzada contra el Comunismo*.

After the fall of Arbenz the hierarchy continued its campaign, supporting a coup against President Miguel Idígoras Fuentes (1963–1966), who had started a program of moderate reforms and had granted some political freedom to the parties of the left.[41] During all these years, the Church continued supporting the status quo, including the publication, in February 1962, of a pastoral letter warning the people against the Communist menace.[42] It was only after Carlos Arana Osorio became president in 1970 that the repression carried out by the government forced the Church to issue a pastoral letter (February 5, 1971), condemning all types of violence. Later, the regime of General Romeo Lucas

García intensified the repression, particularly in the rural areas. The main massacres committed during the García regime took place in Panzós (May 29, 1978); Uspantán (August-September 1979); the Spanish embassy (January 31, 1980); Chimaltenango (February-April 1981); El Quiché (April-May 1981); Coya (July 19, 1981); and Las Verapaces (September 1981).[43]

In the face of this systematic slaughter of the population, several religious groups issued letters of protest, but it was not until 1981 that the hierarchy published pastoral letters condemning the government's methods. Thus, the *Carta Pastoral de la conferencia episcopal de Guatemala* (April 8, 1981) defends "the basic dignity of man," condemns discrimination, and, after mentioning the "numerous social problems, inequality and unjust participation in the economic production, irrational violence,"[44] denounces all types of violence, maintaining that neither subversive, institutional, nor repressive violence is a solution for social conflicts.[45] Three months later, a *Comunicado de la conferencia episcopal de Guatemala* (July 15, 1981) protested against the murder of several priests. A new *Comunicado* (August 6, 1981) reiterated the Church's opposition to violence and communism,[46] responding thus to the accusations that priests had been participating in guerrilla activities. The Church also excommunicated those involved in activities *against priests*.[47] These documents reveal that the Church, as an institution, generally waits until the political situation becomes truly intolerable to become involved in the protest against what may euphemistically be called "violations of human rights." It is also instructive to notice that, for the Church, the gravity of the political situation sometimes coincides with the beginnings of acts of violence against priests.

As noted earlier, the government of Guatemala—and its protector, the government of the United States—maintain that there has been a significant improvement regarding the violence directed against the civilian population, but published reports indicate that, while the situation may have improved slightly in the cities, it has worsened in the rural areas.[48]

The Ríos Montt regime differs substantially from the other military regimes in Central America, in that General Ríos Montt is an evangelical Christian, a member of a particularly active Protestant Church, the Pentecostal Christian Church of the Word (known in Guatemala as *Iglesia Verbo*). Ríos Montt's religious affiliation, as well as his anti-communism, has helped him gain full support from the Reagan administration, which is also committed to a worldwide crusade in defense of Christian values and the free enterprise system. The relationship between Guatemala and the United States has been further intensified by the presence of missionaries, mostly North American fundamentalists, among the Church's elders, who are also advisers to the Ríos Montt government.

It would be unfair to criticize the Protestant churches for being involved in political activities, for that is precisely what the Catholic Church has done in Latin America for more than four centuries. On the contrary, it should be emphasized that the intimate connection between the political and religious goals of the Ríos Montt regime is simply another example of the use of religion to legitimize political aims. What makes the case of Guatemala especially important in the Latin American context is the way in which the traditional legitimizer, the Catholic Church, is being replaced by a new, colonial Church, which stresses the "spiritual," or "spiritualistic" aspects of religion. It is significant that these new developments are taking place now, when the Catholic Church, willingly or unwillingly, has started to play a role, however ambiguous, in the current social and political struggles. The conscious anti-Catholic stance taken by the Ríos Montt government was made explicit during the visit of the Pope, when the government executed several alleged rebels the day before the Pope's arrival, despite John Paul's efforts to prevent the executions. Such a clear rejection of the Pope's request would have been unthinkable in other Latin American countries, in which the repression would have continued as usual after the Pope's visit but in which well-publicized acts of clemency would have taken place during the visit itself. In brief, Guatemala offers an example of a realignment of religious factions, some of which have been forced to adopt a reformist stance, while others gain strength as legitimizers of the new—that is, old—Christian order.

Turning our attention to Cuba, we must say at the outset that, because of its close identification with Spain during the war of independence, the Cuban Church lost a great deal of its influence on the social and political life of the country.[49] In fact, some of the laws directed against the Church had to be annulled by General Leonard Wood, the military governor-general of Cuba during the occupation of the country by the United States.[50] In the years previous to the revolution of 1959, the Church had supported Batista's authoritarian regime.[51] The Church identified with Batista, as well as with previous dictatorships, partly because most of the priests working in Cuba were Spaniards, used to the authoritarian regime of Franco. An example of the hierarchy's identification with the status quo, and of their fervent anti-communism, can be seen in their reluctance to publish the encyclical *Pacem in terris*, issued by John XXIII, because they considered the Pope to be semi-Communist.[52] Therefore, it is not surprising that, after Fidel Castro came to power in 1959, tensions developed between the Church and the revolutionary government. When the Cuban government established diplomatic relations with the Soviet Union in May 1960, Archbishop Pérez Serrantes issued a pastoral letter with the title "For God and Cuba" (May 22, 1960), in which he referred to the encyclical *Divini redemptoris* of Pius XI (1937) and condemned communism as the greatest enemy of Christianity. A similar message appeared in a pastoral letter from the bishops of Cuba (August 7, 1960), where it was stated that the Church was on the side of the poor but could never be on the side of communism. On August 11, 1960, Fidel Castro responded to the hierarchy, saying that he would have welcomed a letter from them denouncing the aggressions of imperialism.[53] After this exchange, the situation deteriorated; on December 4, 1960, the bishops demanded that Castro formally renounce communism, and on December 16 Castro declared that the government had no obligation to comply with the bishops' request.

The confrontation between the government and the Church reached its climax around the time of the bombing of Havana on April 15, 1961, and the failed invasion of the Bay of Pigs on April 17, in which the exiled Cubans who participated in the invasion were accompanied by three Spanish priests and presented themselves as part of a Christian Crusade against communism. As a result, Castro expelled some foreign priests and nationalized the Catholic schools and the Catholic University. Four months later, on September 10, the procession of Nuestra Señora de la Caridad became an anti-Communist demonstration, which caused the government to take further measures against the Church, including the deportation of the auxiliary bishop of Havana, Boza Masdival. When Castro declared the Cuban revolution to be Marxist-Leninist on December 1, 1961, the activities of the Church were severely curtailed. The relationship between Church and state, which had now reached its lowest point, started improving only after John XXIII sent Cesare Zacchi as chargé d'affaires. With Zacchi the situation has achieved a degree of "normalization," and it can be said that during recent years the Church has found it possible to coexist with the Marxist regime. The possibility of such coexistence is further exemplified by a letter from the Cuban bishops (April 10, 1969) in which they urge Cubans to collaborate in the development of their society and in which they condemn the blockade imposed by the United States.[54]

After almost a quarter of a century in power, the Marxist regime of Cuba seems to have finally managed to establish a working relationship with the Cuban Church. This situation, which would have appeared unthinkable only two decades ago, is another proof of the Church's admirable capacities for political compromise.

IV

South America. Until recently, the views on social, political, and economic matters held by the hierarchies of South America have not been substantially different from those of the Central American churches. In general, the main concern of the South American bishops has been the lack of religious vocations, the disproportion between population and number of priests, the problem of birth control, the survival of the family, and similar "moral" issues. Deeper, that is to say, "structural" problems, have become a central concern only after the already mentioned encounter of Medellín in 1968.

In Venezuela, for example, the Catholic Church, which had at first welcomed the military coup of 1948 and supported the dictatorship of Marcos Pérez Jiménez (1948–1958), soon began to suffer the repressive measures of the government, which included the arrest of priests accused of subversive activities.[55] Finally, in May 1957 the archbishop of Caracas, Rafael Arias Blanco, attacked the Pérez Jiménez regime in a pastoral letter, denouncing its "lack of concern for social justice and human welfare."[56] Since the fall of Pérez Jiménez, the Church has continued to play a political role in the life of the country, although this time—

since violence from the right has been averted—the Church has taken a more conservative position in order to stop possible violence from the left.[57] This more or less conservative position of the hierarchy resulted in a series of confrontations between the Archbishop of Caracas, José Humberto Quintero (1960– 1972), and certain priests, mostly foreigners, who wanted to become more involved in the political and social struggles of the left. The difference of opinions between the conservative hierarchy and the politically engaged priests meant that, until 1972, more than a dozen foreign priests were not allowed to return to Venezuela after having left the country in order to visit their own.[58]

Unlike Venezuela, Colombia is a country in which the Catholic Church has had a pervasive influence in all aspects of life. In the political sphere, the old alliance between the Church and the Conservative Party involved the Church in the struggle between Liberals and Conservatives which caused the so-called *Violencia*, "The Violence," in which it is estimated that around 300,000 people lost their lives.[59] During the famous "Bogotazo" of April 9, 1948, a wave of anticlericalism—similar to the bloody violence directed against the members of religious orders during the Spanish Civil War—resulted in the burning of churches and convents, and the killing of priests, all over the country.[60] The immediate cause for the violence was the assassination of the Liberal leader Jorge Eliécer Gaitán, but the real causes were rooted in the opposition between the forces of the Conservatives—particularly the most extreme faction under the "fanatical proclerical Laureano Gomez"[61]—and the more popular Liberals. During the struggle between these two groups, and despite the efforts of the Archbishop of Bogota, Ismael Perdomo, who on April 1, 1949, issued a pastoral letter asking the hierarchy to avoid denouncing Liberalism, many members of the Church continued condemning the Liberals and threatening to excommunicate those who voted for them.[62] In his study of the Church in Venezuela and Colombia, Daniel H. Levine cites the case of the Bishop of Santa Rosa de Osos, Miguel Angel Builes, who delivered the following Lenten message on the occasion of the 1949 elections: "In the manner of generals of armies that give speeches to enlighten and fire their soldiers with passion, I who by the will of God am now before a portion of the soldiers of the Church militant, direct my call to you for the next electoral battle, which is the battle for the Church in our country."[63]

After the fall of the dictator Gustavo Rojas Pinilla in 1957, fear of a resurgence of the violence led the two main political parties to establish a *Frente Nacional*, which was incorporated into the Constitution after a plebiscite that took place in December 1957. According to the principles of the National Front, both parties would share the government, and the office of the presidency would be held for a period of four years by a member of each party. This compromise was supported by the Church, which saw in it the only alternative to the violence; besides, by supporting the National Front, the Church placed itself above party politics. Yet, as Hans-Jürgen Prien has noted, the National Front was less a movement in which the majority of the population participated than a compromise between the leaders of the two parties.[64] A proof of the indifference of the general population is the low level of participation in the general elections—30 percent in 1976, for example. Such indifference indicates that the National Front represented the interests of the upper classes in a still hierarchically organized society, while the non-partisan—or supra-partisan—position of the Church can be seen as a political support for the status quo. It is this alliance between the Church and the old social order which constitutes the background for the career of Camilo Torres Restrepo, the priest who, after returning to Colombia from the University of Louvain in 1958, became involved in radical politics and founded the *Frente Unido* (United Front) in 1965.[65] Torres has become a symbol for those Christians who are not only unwilling to give up their religious beliefs for the sake of political involvement, but who, on the contrary, see radical politics as the logical outcome of their religious commitment. Torres's rejection of the temporizing attitude of the hierarchy, as well as his increasing political activities, were condemned by the Church, forcing him to return to lay status in June 1965. Four months later he joined a guerrilla group and was killed early in 1966.

Since the death of Camilo Torres not much has changed. Despite the encounter of Medellín in 1968 and the existence of certain groups of priests interested in radical social change—such as the Golconda group[66]—the hierarchy has resisted these attempts, choosing rather to concentrate its efforts on liturgical changes and the general improvement of morals.[67] More recently, in what appears to be an act of support for a generally conservative attitude, the Pope has elevated to the rank of Cardinal the Archbishop of Medellín, Alfonso López Trujillo, who, as it is well known, is one of the principal critics of the Theology of Liberation.[68] In any event, it seems unlikely that the Colombian Church will be able to assume a radical political attitude, particularly now, when the fundamental ambiguity of the Latin American Church has its counterpart in the conservative policies of John Paul II, who has openly supported extremely conservative organizations such as the Opus Dei, while condemning the participation of priests in politics. The conservative stance of the Pope—accompanied, it is true, by calls for peace and justice—and his support for the politically active Opus Dei provide one more example of the ambiguous policy of the Vatican, which seems to be carefully trying out various policies of accommodation with regimes at the extremes of the political spectrum, in order to secure its own survival.

In Ecuador, the traditional alliance between the landowners and the Church—which owns large amounts of land—has only recently begun to change. For example, as late as 1960 the Archbishop of Cuenca threatened to excommunicate those who voted for the allegedly Marxist and atheist Galo Plaza.[69] Similarly, in 1961 the Archbishop of Quito, Carlos María de la Torre, warned in a pastoral letter against the general invasion of Latin America (by communist forces) which, he predicted, would take place during 1961.[70] Around 1971, however, the attitude of certain priests and even bishops started to change. In that year the *Convención de sacerdotes* of Riobamba took place in which the participating priests—including the Bishop of Riobamba, Leonidas Proaño, and the Auxiliary Bishop of Quito, Antonio González—denounced the economic and political situation of Ecuador, and, what is more important, the silence of the Ecuadorean Church regarding the exploitation of national resources by foreign companies.[71] Earlier, in 1970, the *Primera convención de presbíteros* had discussed the structures of power and domination in the country and had defended the right of priests to participate in the political life of the nation.[72]

Since the Spanish conquest, the Peruvian Church, together with the army, has constituted the backbone of the entire structure of domination. The process, started symbolically by Father Vicente Valverde, continued during the *Colonia*, and after managing to survive the process of independence (which took place in Peru later than in most South American countries) survived at least until 1960, when a new social consciousness began to develop. During the early decades of this century, the Peruvian Church supported the mostly dictatorial governments, concerning itself solely with the maintenance of its prestige and power. A significant example of the use of religious symbols for the purpose of legitimizing a given political order is the consecration of the country to the Sacred Heart of Jesus, ordered by the dictator Augusto B. Leguía in 1923.[73] This consecration was opposed by the young radical leader Víctor Raúl Haya de la Torre, founder of the *Alianza Popular Revolucionaria Americana* (APRA).[74] It would not be an exaggeration to say that Haya de la Torre's opposition to this blatant—but by no means unusual—manipulation of religion by government has continued to be perceived by many pious Peruvians as proof of the APRA's extremism, anti-religious bias, and communism, even when, after 1945, the party had lost all of its early radicalism. Significantly, the other main adversary of the APRA and Haya de la Torre was the army, which, as in the rest of Latin America, sees itself as the only institution capable of saving the country from social chaos.

Army and Church were the main supporters of the status quo until the elections of 1963, which brought to power the reformist—and vaguely populist—Fernando Belaúnde Terry. Both army and Church supported the reforms effected during the first months of Belaúnde's term. Soon after, however, the combined forces of APRA and Unión Nacional Odriísta (UNO), which had a majority in parliament, made further reforms impossible. By 1968, ten months before the official end of Belaúnde's term, the political and economic situation had so deteriorated that the majority of the people welcomed the October coup. As already mentioned, during these years the Church had actively supported the government-sponsored reforms. Already in 1963, on the occasion of the presidential elections, the Church issued a pastoral letter entitled *Política, deber social* (Politics, social duty), a letter which constituted another example of the Church's political involvement—albeit, in this case, in the service of a progressive cause. During the Belaúnde regime, a series of documents and speeches by priests and members of the hierarchy urged the government to go ahead with the land reform and with other structural changes. In a speech given at the University of Notre Dame, Cardinal Juan Landázuri Ricketts, Archbishop of Lima, declared that the Latin

American Church identified itself with the "social revolution in progress."[75] On March 9, 1968, seven months before the military coup against Belaúnde, a group of priests issued a declaration concerning the socioeconomic structures of the country (*Declaración sobre las estructuras socio-económicas del país*), in which they denounced the inequalities in the distribution of Peru's gross national product (GNP), the system of land tenure, unjust taxation methods, and lack of adequate education, and ended by asking for a "general mobilization of consciences" and for a "state of war against misery."[76]

After the military coup, many of the measures advocated by the Church (and by APRA in the 1930s) began to be put into practice, including the nationalization of certain banks and newspapers and educational reform.[77] Nevertheless, some confrontations between the Church and the government took place during the military regime. One of the most publicized involved the Auxiliary Bishop of Lima, Luis Bambarén, who together with another bishop and four priests had celebrated mass among the invaders of a tract of land just outside Lima.[78] As the result of this active support for the invaders, Bambarén was detained by orders of the Minister of the Interior, although soon after the President ordered his release, forcing the minister to resign. Cardinal Landázuri remarked in an official communiqué that this invasion "reflected an acute and complex social problem, and is a consequence of a situation of deep injustice."[79] More significantly, on the subject of the political role of the Church, the letter states clearly that "every human act has an unavoidable socio-political dimension."[80]

As we have already mentioned, during the first years of military rule the "reformist" attitude of the military resulted in the implementation of certain reforms, which were supported by the Church. At the same time, however, the authoritarian character of the government and its irresponsible fiscal policies (aggravated by large increases in military expenses) resulted in popular discontent and the eventual replacement of General Velasco (whom the upper and middle classes considered a Communist or worse) by the moderate General Morales Bermúdez. Under Morales Bermúdez, some of the reforms initiated during the first phase (*primera fase*) were reversed, while the economic situation grew worse, until finally the military, unable to cope with the high inflation, unemployment, and general economic chaos, was forced to call for elections.

In the face of the country's social and economic crisis from the mid-1960s to the present, the Peruvian Church has become one of the most progressive of the continent.[81] It is also one of the centers of the so-called Theology of Liberation, a movement that owes a great deal to the work of Gustavo Gutiérrez, a Peruvian priest who maintains cordial relations with the hierarchy.[82] The progressiveness of the Peruvian Church will continue to be tested by the continuous deterioration of the economy, which, as usual, is suffered mostly by the poor. The presence of a guerrilla movement and urban terrorism has made the situation even more tense.[83] It would be difficult to predict what the future attitude of the hierachy will be, but it is safe to assume that, unless the violence becomes more widespread, the Church will continue to demand further reforms.

More than any other Latin American Church, the Chilean has gone, almost in a paradigmatic fashion, through the various stages of legitimation of the status quo, support of mild reformist governments, collaboration with a socialist regime, and, finally, accommodation with a highly repressive—what the U.S. geopoliticians call authoritarian—military government.[84] After the period of the traditional alliance[85] between the Church and conservative forces, the Chilean Church began to become involved in the process of reform in the mid–1930s.[86] In 1938 a group of Catholic intellectuals formed the Falange Party, which, after merging with some other small parties, became the Christian Democratic Party (*Partido Demócrata Cristiano*—PDC) in 1957. Relations between the Falange and the bishops were not without problems. For example, the establishment of diplomatic relations with the Soviet Union was favored by the Falange but condemned by one of the bishops.[87]

Recognizing the urgent need for certain reforms, the Church supported the candidacy of the Christian Democrat Eduardo Frei in the elections of 1964. Although this support was not official, it was clear that the Church, by endorsing reformism while condemning Marxism, was behind the centrist option represented by the PDC. The Church's shift from the old conservative position to a centrist one was in fact inevitable, given the urgent need for reform and the hierarchy's perception that the legitimacy of the Church itself could become endangered if they continued to be identified with the forces that—at least at the time of the 1964 elections—seemed to have lost much of their power. At the same time, groups of upper- and middle-class Catholics, who felt threatened by the new developments, turned to the most conservative elements within the Church, and in the spirit of traditional Christendom ideology, joined the Opus Dei and founded groups such as the Chilean Society in Defense of Tradition, Family, and Property, an organization with close ties to similar movements in Brazil and Argentina.[88] During the 1970 elections, when Allende's victory seemed unavoidable, the hierarchy did not actively oppose the *Unidad Popular* (Popular Unity). When Allende—despite the efforts of the extreme right and the U.S. government[89]—was elected president, the Church endorsed many of the reforms and acknowledged the possibility of supporting a socialist government.[90]

The Church's support for the *Unidad Popular* government and its acceptance, in principle, of the possibility of a dialogue with Marxists and socialists had its limits, however. These limits became obvious in 1972, when the group Christians for Socialism (*Cristianos por el socialism*), comprising lay people as well as 300 priests, demanded a deeper Church commitment to the revolutionary process taking place in Chile. Such a demand was clearly an attempt to move the Church from an attitude of benevolent support to one of wholehearted political engagement. However, the hierarchy was not prepared to take such steps or to give in to the demands of the so-called Group of 80, whose members had endorsed specific measures taken by the government.[91] In any event, the radical position of these groups made clear that the radicalism of the Church—and even more so of the Christian Democratic Party—could not go beyond certain limits.[92]

Significantly, the official Church rejection of the socialist option proposed by the *Cristianos por el socialismo*, decided in April 1973, was made public on October 26, 1973, that is, more than one month after the bloody coup that brought Pinochet to power, and therefore in the midst of the torture and murder conducted by the military.

The attitude of the hierarchy during and after the coup further reveals the accommodating character of the Church, able to survive under conservative, socialist, and fascist regimes.[93] Despite the atrocities perpetrated by the military, the Church openly welcomed the coup (as did the PDC) and offered its help in the task of "reconstruction." Many of the bishops openly thanked the military for having saved the country from the clutches of communism, precisely at the time when thousands of Chileans were being tortured and murdered by the army. (The number of dead is estimated at between 10,000 and 20,000.) As Brian H. Smith has shown, the attitude of the hierarchy during the first three years of military rule was rather positive, despite the already mentioned atrocities. It was only after 1976, when the Church itself was threatened, that the hierachy chose to distance itself from the Pinochet regime, and in so doing, the Church was consistent with its behavior regarding its relations with previous governments. It would be interesting to follow the changing behavior of the Church now that popular discontent is becoming more widespread in Chile, as a result of the collapse of the economic program implemented by the government—the monetarist policies recommended by the so-called "Chicago boys."[94] As in similar cases, the Chilean Church will likely throw its weight behind the dissenting groups once the position of the Pinochet dictatorship becomes intolerable.

In Chile's neighboring Argentina, the Church had rallied around Juan Domingo Perón, when the dictator made religious instruction compulsory in the state schools in 1943, and had otherwise mentioned the social teachings of the Church—particularly the encyclicals *Rerum novarum* and *Quadragesimo anno*— as being the models he was planning to follow.[95] After the elections of 1946, in which the Church supported him, Perón continued to court the hierarchy until some of his programs, especially the rivalry in the field of social welfare, led to an open confrontation with the Church, which ultimately contributed to his downfall.[96] Ever since the fall of Perón, the military governments have made blatant use of the legitimizing values of Christianity. Thus, the military regimes claim to defend Western and Christian civilization (*la civilización occidental y cristiana*), even if this requires the murder—called "disappearance" in Argentina—of around 15,000 people. The most transparent example of the use of religious symbols for the legitimization of a regime was the consecration of the country to the Virgen of Luján during the presidency of Juan Carlos Onganía.[97] (During the coup that brought Onganía to power in 1966, the hierarchy, citing the separation between Church and state, refrained from making any comments.[98])

In subsequent years, groups of priests,[99] and even a bishop,[100] have been involved in certain protests regarding the issue of human rights, but in general the reaction of the hierarchy has been remarkably calm, especially when one realizes the extent to which the most elementary human rights have been violated in that country.[101] Institutionalized terror increased after the 1976 coup, but still there has not been any major Church reaction.

Like Argentina, Brazil has had a military regime since the coup of 1964 against João Goulart. Before Goulart, the Brazilian Church has tried to keep the old Christendom ideology alive, lending its legimitizing support to Getúlio Vargas, and then trying to maintain its influence during the regimes of Juscelino Kubitschek and Jânio Quadros. At the same time, in the 1950s the Church apparently became aware of the social and economic problems afflicting the country. The Church's attitude shifted from benevolent neglect to concern because it realized that, if the situation continued to deteriorate, it would not be able to maintain its influence.[102] As in other Latin American countries, the Brazilian Church did not initiate the movement of social awareness but rather joined in the protest when the situation became unbearable. Again, as in the other countries, the participation of the hierarchy was by no means unanimous; there were cases of bishops who refused to participate in the protests, even in those that were almost perfunctory.[103] Refusal to participate was usually grounded in the almost visceral anti-communism that characterized the Catholic Church until the time of the Second Vatican Council. On the other hand, once the process of social awareness began, the Brazilian Church became involved in a series of projects, with the aim of improving the material conditions of the people, while also trying to involve them in the process of *conscientização* (conscientization, awareness; *toma de conciencia, concientización*, in Spanish). One of the instruments for the *concientização* was the *Movimento de Educação de base* (MEB).[104]

There were differences in the degree of radicalization of the hierarchy and lay groups such as those that constituted the *Açao Católica Brasileira*, the *Juventude Estudiantil Católica* (JEC), and the *Juventude Universitária Católica* (JUC), among others. Eventually, members of the JUC founded the *Ação Popular*, whose aims went far beyond the more traditional ones of the hierarchy.[105] As is well known, a military coup against Goulart took place on April 1, 1964.[106] The Church's reaction was not different from the one the Chilean Church would have nine years later:

In response to the widespread and anxious expectations of the Brazilian people, which saw the quickening pace of communism's rise to power, the armed forces came to the rescue in time to avoid the implantation of a bolshevik regime in our country. . . . In offering our thanks to God, who heeded the prayers of millions of Brazilians and delivered us from the communist peril, we thank the military that, with grave risk to their lives [sic], rose up in the name of the supreme interests of the nation, and grateful are we to them for cooperating to liberate the nation from the imminent abyss.[107]

After the coup, the Church's position remained ambiguous, on the one hand, welcoming the "liberating" military action and on the other, asking for reforms.

For example, the Brazilian bishops decided to dismember their own council (which had been instrumental in bringing about certain reformist actions), while at the same time approving a five-year plan with the aim of adjusting the Brazilian Church to the teachings of the Second Vatican Council.[108]

Not surprisingly, this attitude resulted in isolated and contradictory actions that could not affect the national security ideology of the generals. The Brazilian generals were engaged in transforming their large country into an industrial and military power, without any regard for the human costs involved in such enterprise. The widespread use of torture and murder was meant to pacify the population, with the aim of creating a docile labor force that could be exploited by national and foreign corporations. In order to achieve these goals, the military presented itself as the defender of Western-Christian civilization against the Communist menace. For this crusade they needed the cooperation of the Church, a cooperation which, as we have seen, was available during the first two years after the coup. Later, when the bishops realized that the generals' plans benefited only a very small minority of the population, they were forced to rethink their position, with the result that a series of confrontations took place between several bishops—the most famous being Helder Câmara, archbishop of Olinda-Recife— and the military commanders. The conflicts between the Church and the military continued during 1968 and 1969, a period in which members of the clergy were no longer immune to torture. Around this time, relations between the Church and the military became so tense that even the previously non-politically involved Cardinal Agnelo Rossi, Archbishop of São Paulo, refused to meet with President Artur Costa e Silva when the president visited Santiago, although later, as Thomas C. Bruneau points out, Rossi "went out of his way to improve relations with the government."[109]

After 1974, the number of conflicts between Church and state diminished considerably, although a conflict of sorts took place when the military passed a law allowing divorce.[110] Bruneau maintains that this law infuriated the conservative bishops, who had not otherwise protested against the regime's economic measures.[111] The continuation of the repressive measures taken by the military government in order to curb subversion forced the Church to respond with a series of statements, including one from the bishops of the state of São Paulo[112] and another from a group of bishops protesting the extermination of Indians in the Amazonian region.[113] In 1977 the National Conference of Brazilian Bishops issued a document on the problem of human rights in which they went beyond the usual general statements, proposing instead concrete measures, such as the right to education, just salaries, freedom, and physical integrity as against "excessive repression" [sic].[114] The bishops had already denounced the situation of the poor, as well as the impunity with which the police acted, in a document approved on October 25, 1976,[115] as well as in a declaration entitled *Exigências cristãs de uma orden política* (Christian Requirements of a Political Order), in which they went against the ideology of national security which constituted the foundation of the military regime.[116]

All these documents, pastoral letters, and so on, do not seem to have greatly affected the behavior of the military government. The recent process of political liberalization (*abertura*) seems rather to have been caused by the total failure of the government's economic policies. The collapse of the Brazilian model, both political and economic, has alienated not only the working class, who had to pay for the general's delusions of grandeur, but also the middle and upper classes who have come to the realization that the country is virtually bankrupt. If the upper and middle classes were once willing to overlook the government's policies for the sake of ever increasing economic returns, now, in the face of economic collapse and of a foreign debt amounting to one-hundred billion dollars, they are no longer willing to go along with repressive policies that produce no benefits. (A similar situation is developing in Chile, where the monetarist policies of the Pinochet regime have also led to the collapse of the country's economy, causing widespread unrest, especially among the middle classes, which had earlier welcomed the coup and the bloody repression that followed.)

All of these economic developments have to be considered when trying to explain the changes in the attitude of the Brazilian Church. It would seem that it was not so much the repressive measures that led to the Church's protests as much as the ineffectiveness of the government's economic policies. After all, as mentioned earlier, the Brazilian Church, like the Chilean, welcomed the military coup, and it was only after the bishops realized the failure of the military's program, and the dangers involved in cooperating with such a regime, that the hierarchy raised its voice of protest. This does not mean that the Church was interested only in preserving its influence, but, rather, it would seem that what the Church was protecting was its own survival as an institution, a survival that would have been threatened in the event of a violent revolution.

In the space allowed here, it is impossible to deal with other developments in Latin America. Thus, we will not be able to examine the Church's position on military terrorism in Uruguay; the totalitarian regime of Alfredo Stroessner in Paraguay;[117] or the history of Bolivia's coups and repression.[118] Next, we turn our attention to the most important theological development that has taken place in Latin America, and indeed, in contemporary Catholic theology, during the last two decades.

V

No examination of the issue of religion and politics—or religion-politics—in Latin America would be complete without a discussion of the Theology of Liberation. This movement can be considered the most important contribution of Latin America to Christian theology, and indeed one of the most important developments within Christianity in the last twenty years.[119] The Theology of Liberation (*Teología de la liberación*) is the creation of a group of priests— Gustavo Gutiérrez, Juan Luis Segundo, Hugo Assmann, among others—who have proposed, and successfully carried out, a political reading of the Old and

New Testaments, convinced that the radical dichotomy between a spiritual and a worldly salvation is an ideological construction rather than a constitutive element of Christianity. The liberation theologians argue that the distinction between spiritual realities and, accordingly, between spiritual and material—social, political—liberation responds not to the teachings of the Bible, but to the interests of those concerned with preserving the status quo. It is clear that a radical distinction between the here and now of history, economic conflict, and political struggle, on the one hand, and the supernatural realm where salvation takes place, on the other, results in the legitimation of any given political order. According to the Theology of Liberation, such a spiritualized view of salvation would certainly deserve the attacks by those philosophies, such as Marxism, whose aim is the realization of salvation not beyond but in the world.

There are many points of contact between Liberation Theology and Marxism, notably, the recognition of the importance of economic factors; the notion of alienation; a reevaluation of utopian thinking; and a conception of the individual as involved, through work, in the creation of history. In general, it could be said that the Theology of Liberation arose as a response within Christianity to the challenge represented by Marxism. One aspect of Gustavo Gutiérrez's work in which the Marxist challenge is most clear is in Gutiérrez's discussion of economic problems, particularly his discussion of the theories of economic development and dependence.[120] Going beyond the usual pious lamentations about the poverty in which most of the world population lives, the injustice inherent in such a situation, and so on, Gutiérrez discusses at length the opposed views advanced by developmental theories (*desarrollistas*) and those that advocate structural—or revolutionary—changes. The same is true of his discussion of Latin American dependence, both economic and cultural.

The contribution of Marxism to the analyses performed by Gutiérrez and other theologians of similar views has been the main target of attacks by conservative and moderate members of the Church. For instance, the use of the Marxist concept of class struggle (*lucha de clases*) has been the cause of endless attacks, both by conservatives, for whom anything related to Marxism is anathema, and by the proponents of reformist measures (*desarrollistas*), who must necessarily reject the concept. The notion of class struggle undermines the *desarrollistas'* basic developmental ideology which seeks to convince people, especially the working classes, of the need to cooperate in the creation of a national wealth in which the entire population will share. These developmental models—both those of a merely populist character, as in Peru, and those of a fascist nature, as in Brazil and Argentina—are interested in creating an almost mystical conception of the country—or rather, motherland (*patria*). The aim of this conception is to render invisible the great disparities in the present distribution of wealth, while also promoting the illusion that the sacrifices imposed on the working classes will be ultimately enjoyed by the motherland as a whole. Against this populist or fascist utopia, (which, of course, does not take into account the wealth taken from these countries by foreign and transnational corporations), the advocates of the Theology of Liberation propose an economic model based on the radical change of the present economic structures, including land reform, nationalization of key industries, reform of the educational system, independent foreign policy, end of discrimination against "native" ethnic groups—in short, true participation of the entire population in the political, cultural, and economic life of the country, and in the benefits derived from the economic growth. What makes this liberation a theological liberation is the liberation theologians' insistence on basing this process in the teachings of Christianity. Gutiérrez, for example, undertakes a political reading of the Old Testament, particularly of Exodus, and comes to the conclusion that the liberation of the Israelites from Egypt was both a spiritual and a political liberation.[121] Similarly, he examines the notion of poverty, which has justified economic injustice for centuries, and not only in Latin America. He analyzes the various meanings of the Hebrew terms for poverty in the Old Testament (*rash, ebyôn, dal, ani, anaw*), as well as the Greek translation (*ptojós*), and shows that these terms are not primarily spiritual but rather refer to the concrete facts of need, exploitation, and misery against which the prophets raised their voices.[122]

The Theology of Liberation, then, is an attempt to demystify a Christianity which, through centuries of alliances with the groups in power, has been all too willing to spiritualize suffering and misery, promising in return a paradise where everlasting bliss will be the prize for those who have suffered on earth. This distinction between two histories (a profane one—the realm of ideology, better left to sociologists, economists, and the like—and a sacred one—the concern of theology) has been rejected by Gutiérrez, who maintains that there is only one history, "one human becoming irreversibly assumed by Christ, Lord of history."[123] The conception of "one History," which underlies the entire discourse of the Theology of Liberation, forces the believer to assume in their full religious implications his or her social, economic, and, ultimately, political activities. The *homo religiosus*—that unjustifiable abstraction—is fundamentally a historical man, and, as such, is responsible, religiously, for all his actions. Liberation, then, is not just religious or spiritual, but a comprehensive liberation in which it is no longer possible to distinguish between its sacred and its profane components. The revolutionary—truly utopian—character of such a view of the process of liberation is obvious. Christianity is freed from its endemic subservience to the established order and is transformed into—or rediscovered as—the force that will eventually transform this unjust, alienated society into a truly Christian one.

This conception of liberation has been widely attacked by those who still cling to a dualistic conception of history which has proved so helpful in maintaining and legitimizing the status quo. The attacks have come mostly from conservative Catholic groups, including members of the hierarchy; proponents of a popular, or populist Christianity; and reactionary groups such as the Opus Dei. One of the most vocal opponents of the Theology of Liberation is the Colombian archbishop Alfonso López Trujillo, recently appointed Cardinal by John Paul II.

López Trujillo is one of the main advocates of a diluted, "spiritualized" liberation, emphasizing the positive, universalistic, that is, non-conflictive aspects of Christianity.[124] Another opponent, Bonaventure Kloppenburg, stresses the contemplative aspects of Christianity to which the Theology of Liberation does not pay enough attention.[125] In general, the discussion between the representatives of the allegedly non-ideological Christianity (those who equate the present state of affairs with reality *tout court*) and ideological Christianity (those who acknowledge the ideological functions of religion), exemplifies the tension and the interplay between utopian and ideological thinking.[126] As we have already seen, the role of Christianity in the New World was fundamentally an ideological one, whose function was to maintain and articulate a structure of domination that has continued to this day. The insistence of dictatorial regimes on defending "Christian and Western values" (*el mundo occidental y cristiano*) is fully consonant with the attitudes of the early missionaries and the civil and military authorities. In this context, the apparent break represented by the Theology of Liberation seems to be less a revolutionary change than the latest attempt by Christianity to maintain itself as the guiding force—as the ultimate source of legitimation— of any future social order. This Theology of Liberation is, after all, a Christian reinterpretation of a closed corpus—the Bible—working under the assumption that Latin America is, and must remain, Christian.[127]

Given Latin America's uncertain future, the Christian solution offered by the Theology of Liberation seems to be, in the larger context of history, an attempt to secure the position of Christianity, and therefore of the Church, under any regime, however non-religious or anti-religious. This does not mean that the Theology of Liberation is part of a conscious attempt made by the Church to secure its survival; on the contrary, given the struggles among different groups within the Church, the Theology of Liberation may be regarded as one of the options which the Church is almost unconsciously exploring at present. That all these options are both religious *and* political should surprise only those who still cling to the politically determined view that certain areas of human action are beyond the realm of the political.

NOTES

1. On the origin of the term "Latin America," see Prien, *Die Geschichte des Christentums* pp. 23ff., and 279n.280, where Prien discusses the ideological implications of the concept.

2. On Bartolomé de las Casas, see Dussel, *Historia de la iglesia*, pp. 95ff.; and Friede, *Bartolomé de las Casas*.

3. On the *Reconquista*, see Prien, *Die Geschichte*, pp. 59ff.; Konetzke, "Christentum und Conquista," pp. 59–73.

4. On the distinction between sacred and profane actions, and the legitimizing function of sacred actions, see Eliade, *Le sacré et le profane*, p. 30:

Les "conquistadores" espagnols et portugais prenaient possession, au nom de Jésus-Christ, des territoires qu'ils avaient découverts et conquis. L'érection de la Croix consacrait la contrée, équivalait en quelque sorte à une 'nouvelle naissance': par le Christ "les choses vieilles son passées; voici que toutes choses sont devenues nouvelles" (II Corinthiens, v. 17). Le pays nouvellement découvert etait "renouvelé," "recréé" par la Croix.

The Sacred and the Profane, New York, Harcourt, 1959, p. 32:

The Spanish and Portuguese conquistadores, discovering and conquering territories, took possession of them in the name of Jesus Christ. The raising of the cross was equivalent to consecrating the country, hence in some sort to a "new birth." For through Christ "old things are passed away; behold, all things are become new" (II Corinthians; 5, 17). The newly discovered country was "renewed," "recreated" by the cross.

Eliade, of course, does not consider the fate of those who inhabited the lands of "chaos." It would seem that the inhabitants of the Aztec or Inca empires had been glad to participate in the successful unfolding of a process of "cosmization." On the ideological background of Eliade's "archaic" visions, see Jesi, *Cultura di destra*.

5. On "Christendom," see Prien, *Die Geschichte*, p. 22; Gutiérrez, *Teología de la liberación*, pp. 71ff.; and Bruneau, *Political Transformation of the Brazilian Catholic Church*, pp. 11ff.

6. On the *patronato*, see Mecham, *Church and State in Latin America*, pp. 3ff.; Prien, *Die Geschichte*, pp. 128ff.

7. Mecham, *Church and State*. p. 4.

8. For the history of Church and state in Latin America, see Dussel, *Historia de la iglesia*; Prien, *Die Geschichte*; Mecham, *Church and State*.

9. This relationship is examined in detail by Mecham, *Church and State*.

10. Mecham, *Church and State*, p. 64, referring to Legon, *Doctrina y ejercicio del patronato nacional*, pp. 249–250; and Leturia, *La acción diplomática de Bolívar*, pp. 281–282.

11. Mecham, *Church and State*, p. 77, referring to Ayarragaray, *La iglesia en américa*, pp. 185, 234–235.

12. Mecham, *Church and State*, p. 85.

13. Ibid., p. 52.

14. Ibid., p. 54.

15. Ibid., p. 55.

16. As Mecham comments (p. 53), the members of the archiepiscopal chapter were "exhibiting a refreshing disregard for their own extra-ecclesiastical interference." The same can be said of the pronouncements of John Paul II in Central America, particularly in Nicaragua, on the one hand, and in Poland (June 1983), on the other.

17. Mecham, *Church and State*, p. 58; see also Prien, *Die Geschichte*, p. 392.

18. Mecham, *Church and State*, pp. 44–47.

19. For a critical study of the political functions of religious symbolism, see Topitsch, *Vom Ursprung und Ende*; see also Berger, *Sacred Canopy*. The following collections of articles deal with the ideology of power: *Le Pouvoir et le Sacré*; Kloft, ed., *Ideologie und Herrschaft*; and Kerner, ed., *Ideologie und Herrschaft*.

20. Smith, *Church and Politics in Chile*, pp. 287ff. For some strange reason, Smith uses the word "prophetic" in dealing with the attitude of the Chilean Church toward the military regime. In the context of the coup and the bloody repression that followed, the word "prophetic" applied to the pronouncements of the Church is ludicrous.

21. See Dussel, *Historia de la iglesia*, pp. 80–81; Prien, *Die Geschichte*, pp. 204ff.; Bruneau, *Political Transformation*, pp. 13–18; Bruneau, *Church in Brazil*, pp. 11–14.

22. On the dialectical interaction between ideology and utopia, see Jameson, *Political Unconscious*, pp. 281–299; Jameson, *Marxism and Form*, pp. 117–118, 157–158.

23. Mannheim, *Ideology and Utopia*, pp. 192ff.

24. On messianic movements in Latin America, see Prien, *Die Geschichte*, pp. 319–326, 844–856.

25. Reeves, *Joachim of Fiore and the Prophetic Future*, pp. 128–129; see also Prien, *Die Geschichte*, 143ff.

26. On Medellín, see, for example, Oliveros, *Liberación y teología*, pp. 113–129; Prien, *Die Geschichte*, pp. 893–906; Levine, *Religion and Politics in Latin America*, pp. 38–41.

27. Although, as the case of Cuba demonstrates, the insistence on considering the current events in Central America as part of the confrontation between the United States and USSR will definitely result in the fulfillment of the prophecy. Nicaragua, for example, currently attacked by forces supplied by the United States, will be forced to seek support from friendly countries such as Cuba and the Soviet Union. The problem of the self-fulfilling prophecy is discussed in Merton, *Social Theory and Social Structure*, pp. 475–490.

28. Mecham, *Church and State*, pp. 295–297.

29. Turner, *Catholicism and Political Development in Latin America*, pp. 109–110, 243–244; Prien, *Die Geschichte*, pp. 1085–1086.

30. Prien, *Die Geschichte*, p. 1028.

31. The fanciful distinction between authoritarian and totalitarian governments has been popularized recently by Jeane Kirkpatrick, the specialist in Latin American affairs; see "Dictatorships and Double Standards."

32. On Nicaragua, see Chomsky and Herman, *Political Economy of Human Rights*, Vol. 1, pp. 283ff.; Prien, *Die Geschichte*, p. 701.

33. *Nicaragua, Combate de un pueblo*, pp. 21–27. esp. 25.

34. Cf. *Nicaragua: la hora de los desafíos*, p. 60; for a chronology, see pp. 59–67.

35. Archbishop Romero was assassinated on March 24, 1980; on D'Aubuisson's involvement see the testimony of Robert White, Hearings before the Committee on Foreign Relations, U.S. Senate, April 9, 1981. For a collection of speeches by, and about, Romero, see *El Salvador, Un pueblo perseguido, II, de octubre 79 a junio 80*.

36. At the time this is being written, June 1983, the military situation in El Salvador has not changed significantly. The only new element is the increased presence of military advisers from the United States, one of whom has been killed by the guerrillas.

37. Prien, *Die Geschichte*, p. 712.

38. Mecham, *Church and State*, p. 320, speaks of the "pro-Communist government of Jacobo Arbenz"; the same is repeated by Turner, *Catholicism and Political Developments*, p. 112. Both Mecham and Turner repeat uncritically the propaganda disseminated by the CIA. On the CIA sections against Arbenz, see Immerman, *CIA in Guatemala*, Chomsky and Herman, *Political Economy of Human Rights*, Vol. 1, pp. 276–278; and Chomsky, *Towards a New Cold War*, pp. 200–201. For a chronology of political events after the fall of Arbenz, see *Morir y despertar en Guatemala*, pp. 14–19 and p. 53 (on Rossell).

39. Turner, *Catholicism and Political Development*, p. 131.

40. Ibid., p. 133.

41. Prien, *Die Geschichte*, p. 714.

42. *Morir y despertar en Guatemala*, pp. 53–54.

43. For the history of the massacres, see *Morir y despertar en Guatemala*, pp. 25–49; Chomsky and Herman, *Political Economy of Human Rights*, Vol. 1, pp. 279–283. See also "Extermination in Guatemala," pp. 13–16; Nairn "Guns of Guatemala," pp. 17–21.

44. *Carta pastoral de la conferencia episcopal de Guatemala*, in *Morir y despertar en Guatemala*, pp. 92–108.

45. Ibid., p. 100.

Frente a esta situación, la Iglesia mantiene su voz de denuncia al repetir que la violencia, tanto la institucionalizada como la subversiva y represiva, no es solución para los conflictos sociales. Una vez más repetimos que la violencia, salvo el caso de legítima defensa, es anticristiana.

It could be argued, of course, that subversive violence is in legitimate self-defense.

Regarding this situation, the Church continues its denunciations and repeats that violence, both institutionalized as well as subversive and repressive, is not a solution for social conflicts. We repeat once more that violence, except in the case of legitimate defense, is anti-Christian.

46. *Comunicado de la conferencia episcopal de Guatemala*, in *Morir y despertar en Guatemala*, pp. 114–118:

Como Obispos, lamentamos profundamente que personas, en una u otra forma ligadas a la actividad pastoral de la Iglesia, hayan optado por el camino de la lucha armada para resolver los ingentes problemas sociales, económicos y políticos que aquejan a nuestra patria. Cualquier acción terrorista merece nuestra condena y nosotros jamás podríamos avalar con nuestro apoyo moral a quienes la cometen, como tampoco podemos propiciar acciones que conduzcan a la implantación del comunismo en nuestra Batria. (p. 116).

As bishops, we deeply regret that persons who are in one way or another involved in the pastoral activity of the Church, have chosen the way of armed struggle in order to solve the grave social, economic, and political problems of our country. Any terrorist action deserves our condemnation, and we could never endorse with our moral support those who commit those actions; nor can we favor actions which may lead to the establishment of communism in our country.

47. Ibid., p. 117: "Recordamos a este respecto que los que atentan contra los ministros de la iglesia quedan *excomulgados*." ["We stress that those who act against the ministers of the Church are *excommunicated*."]

48. See note 43 above, particularly Nairn and "Extermination in Guatemala."

49. See Mecham, *Church and State*, p. 299; Prien, *Die Geschichte*, p. 999.

50. Mecham, *Church and State*, p. 300.

51. Prien, *Die Geschichte*, p. 1000.

52. Mecham, *Church and State*, p. 303; Prien, *Die Geschichte*, p. 1011.

53. Ibid., p. 1013.

54. Ibid., pp. 1021–1022.

55. Levine, *Religion and Politics*, p. 68.

56. Ibid., p. 68; see also Prien, *Die Geschichte*, pp. 688–689.

57. Levine, *Religion and Politics*, pp. 68–69.

58. Cf. Prien, *Die Geschichte*, pp. 692–693.

59. On the *violencia*, see Mecham, *Church and State*, p. 134; Prien, *Die Geschichte*, pp. 664ff.; Turner, *Catholicism and Political Development*, p. 27; Levine, *Religion and Politics*, pp. 62ff., 191ff.

60. Mecham, *Church and State*, p. 134, calls the Bogotazo "probably communist inspired." There is no evidence to support such a claim.

61. Ibid.
62. Mecham, *Church and State*, p. 134.
63. Levine, *Religion and Politics*, p. 64, quoting Nieto Rojas, *La batalla contra el comunismo en Colombia*, p. 285
64. Prien, *Die Geschichte*, pp. 672–673.
65. See Gervassi, ed., *Revolutionary Priest*; on Torres, see Prien, *Die Geschichte*, p. 673; Levine, *Religion and Politics*, pp. 41–42; Dussel, *Historia de la iglesia*, pp. 260–264; see also Shaull, "The Church and Revolutionary Change," in Landsberger, ed., *Church and Social Change in Latin America*, pp. 135–153; on Torres, see p. 146; Turner, *Catholicism and Political Development*, pp. 140–145, in the section entitled "The Acceptance of Violent Revolution." On the problem of violence and religion, see M. McFaden, ed., *Liberation, Revolution, and Freedom*; Davies, *Christians, Politics and Violent Revolution*; Brown, *Theology in a New Key*, p. 113, on *"the present reality of violence"* against which Torres reacted by joining the guerrilla group (italics in the original).
66. On the Golconda group, see Dussel, *Historia de la iglesia*, pp. 307–309; Levine, *Religion and Politics*, p. 247; Prien, *Die Geschichte*, p. 674.
67. Levine, *Religion and Politics*, p. 119.
68. On López Trujillo, see Levine, *Religion and Politics*, p. 182; Oliveros, *Liberación y teología*, pp. 317–329; "La espiritualización de la teología de la liberación;" Brown, *Theology in a New Key*, pp. 124–127, and, in general, pp. 101–131, where he discusses critiques of the Theology of Liberation.
69. Mecham, *Church and State*, p. 158.
70. Prien, *Die Geschichte*, p. 646, referring to Albornoz, *Historia de la acción clerical en Ecuador*, pp. 286f.
71. See Prien, *Die Geschichte*, p. 648; Dussel, *Historia de la iglesia*, p. 316.
72. See the text reproduced in *Signos de liberación. Testimonios de la iglesia en américa latina 1969–1973*, pp. 140–144.
73. The incident is discussed in Mecham, *Church and State*, p. 175; Prien, *Die Geschichte*, p. 630; for a history of the relations between Church and state in Peru, see Klaiber, *Religion and Revolution in Peru*.
74. Founded by Haya de la Torre as a radical political movement, in the 1940s the Partido Aprista Peruano became a populist movement with no clear political ideology, and prone to compromises with the forces of the extreme right. Nevertheless, the APRA is—perhaps because of its vague political program, and its revolutionary past—the most significant political force in Peru.
75. The speech is reproduced in *Signos de renovación*, pp. 79–82: "Estamos vitalmente concientes de la revolución social que está en progreso. Nos identificamos con ella" (p. 80). ["We are vitally aware of the social revolution in progress. We identify ourselves with it."]
76. *Declaración de sacerdotes peruanos sobre las estructuras socio-económicas del país*, in *Signos de renovación*, pp. 95–101:

Nosotros entendemos este llamamiento como una movilización general de las conciencias para que, considerándonos en un verdadero estado de guerra contra la miseria, nos pongamos a dar la batalla contra la opresión explotadora" (p. 101). Earlier, the priests acknowledge their previous apathy and silence: "Sólo después de esta confesión de nuestra apatía y silencio anterior podemos pedir a los demás que tomen las actitudes valientes que exige una conciencia cristiana anta la situación actual" (pp. 100–101).

[We understand this call as a general mobilization of consciences in order to fight, in a true state of war against misery, against oppression'' (p. 101); It is only after confessing our previous apathy and silence that we can ask others to adopt the brave attitudes that Christian conscience demands in our current situation.]

77. *Movimiento sacerdotal ONIS, Declaración sobre la reforma agraria*, in *Signos de liberación*, pp. 98–101.

78. Prien, *Die Geschichte*, p. 1050; the incident is discussed at length by Klaiber, *Religion and Revolution*.

79. *Comunicado del Arzobispado de Lima*, in *Signos de liberación*, pp. 113–115: "(las ocupaciones) reflejan un agudísimo y muy complejo problema social y son consecuencias de una situación de injusticias más profunda'' (p. 115).

80. Ibid., p. 114: "Frente a las acusaciones hechas a la Iglesia de 'intromisión en cuestiones políticas,' debemos manifestar que toda acción humana tiene una dimensión socio-política insoslayable.''

81. Fernando Belaúnde Terry, ousted by the military in 1968, was elected president in 1980. The civilian government has not been able to reduce inflation, unemployment, and the virtual economic chaos which the country faces. At present Peru's external debt amounts to fourteen billion dollars.

82. On Gutiérrez, see Brown, *Gustavo Gutiérrez*, in the series "Makers of Contemporary Theology''; the Theology of Liberation is discussed later in this chapter.

83. The guerrilla group *Sendero luminoso* (Shining Path), about which very little is known, seems to have a strong messianic component, in which pre-Hispanic elements play an important role. On messianic movements in Peru, see Ossio, ed., *La ideología mesiánica del mundo andino*; see also Ortiz Rescaniere, *De Adaneva a Inkarrí*. For a general discussion of Andean and European thought and their interaction from the sixteenth century to the present, see Galindo, *Europa y el país de los Incas*.

84. For a general orientation, see Mecham, *Church and State*, pp. 201–224; and Prien, *Die Geschichte*, pp. 1057–1062. We now have a comprehensive study. See Smith, *Church and Politics in Chile*.

85. Smith, *Church and Politics in Chile*, pp. 67–85.

86. While at the same time strongly condemning Marxism; see Smith, *Church and Politics in Chile*, p. 94n.12, where he refers to Bishop Alfredo Silva Santiago, *Estudio sobre la manera práctica de combatir el comunismo en Chile*; and Episcopado chileno, "Firmes en la fe; la masonería, el protestantismo y el comunismo, enemigos de los católicos.''

87. Smith, *Church and Politics in Chile*, pp. 96–97.

88. On the *Sociedad chilena de defensa de la tradición, familia y propiedad*, see Prien, *Die Geschichte*, pp. 1060–1061; Smith, *Church and Politics in Chile*, pp. 136–137, 140, 148 (where Smith discusses the links between the Chilean group and its Brazilian counterpart), pp. 256n.58, 338–339. The Brazilian *Tradição, Família, e Propiedade* (TFP) is discussed in Bruneau, *Political Transformation*, pp. 184, 226–228.

89. On the U.S. efforts to prevent the election of Allende, see Smith, *Church and Politics in Chile*, pp. 183, 202–203; Chomksy, *Towards a New Cold War*, pp. 182–183.

90. Smith, *Church and Politics in Chile*, p. 177.

91. On the *Cristianos por el socialism*, see Smith, *Church and Politics in Chile*, pp. 232ff.; Prien, *Die Geschichte*, pp. 1060ff. The *Conclusiones del encuentro latinoamericano de cristianos por el socialismo* can be found in *Signos de liberación*, pp. 238–243; the document ends with a quote from Ernesto Guevara.

92. Typically, the Christian Democrats turned to the right and announced an alliance with the Partido Nacional for the 1973 elections; see Smith, *Church and Politics in Chile*, pp. 193ff.

93. On the publication of the document rejecting the socialist option, see Smith *Church and Politics in Chile*, pp. 253–254; Prien, *Die Geschichte*, p. 1061; Brown, *Theology in a New Key*, p. 57; Segundo, *Liberation of Theology*, p. 152n:

But it is sad and almost embarrassing to find that the last document . . . was finally approved by the Chilean episcopate on September 13, 1973, *two days after* the military coup and Allende's own death. When their partisans were being persecuted and sometimes killed in the streets, the Chilean bishops were meeting to make some final observations on the "christians for Socialism" movement and to condemn them." (Italics in the original.)

As mentioned earlier (see note 20 above), Smith entitles Part IV of his book "The Prophetic Role of the Church under Authoritarianism" (p. 281), although the word "prophetic," even when qualified by the adjective "ambiguous" (p. 287: "Ambiguous Prophetic Role of the Hierarchy"), is at best inappropriate. See also p. 311, where Smith calls the bishops' tolerance for the junta "apparently surprising." Clearly, no one with even the slightest acquaintance with the history of the Latin American Church would find anything "surprising" in the Church's attitude toward the military coup. On that subject, see Smith, *Church and Politics in Chile*, pp. 287ff.

94. At the time this is being written, June 1983, popular discontent is growing in Chile. In the face of inflation, 30 percent unemployment, and a foreign debt of eighteen billion dollars, the military government has lost the support of the middle classes and is facing a strike by the mine workers.

95. Mecham, *Church and State*, p. 247; Turner, *Catholicism and Political Development*, p. 113.

96. Mecham, *Church and State*; Prien, *Die Geschichte*, p. 588; see also Pike, "South America's Multifaceted Catholicism," in Landsberger, ed., *Church and Social Change*, pp. 53–75, esp. 58ff.

97. See the *Declaración de los sacerdotes del tercer mundo con motivo de la consagración del país a la Virgen*, in *Signos de liberación*, pp. 116–118. The last paragraph is worth quoting: "Esperamos que el pueblo no acuda a una cita en la que lo religioso amenaza ser usado como estupefaciente de las inquietudes del mismo pueblo" (p. 118). ["We hope that the people will not attend a meeting in which religion may be used as a narcotic to dull their anxiety."]

98. Turner, *Catholicism and Political Development*, pp. 89, 237.

99. See the *Comunicado del grupo local del Movimiento de Sacerdotes del Tercer Mundo*, June 25, 1969, in *Signos de liberación*, pp. 39–40.

100. See *El obispo y los sacerdotes de Neuquen frente a los actos oficiales*, August 17, 1971, in *Signos de liberación*, pp 119–120.

101. There is a document dealing with human rights, but it is an "ecumenical" rather than a Catholic one; see *Documento de fundación del movimiento ecuménico de los derechos humanos* (February 27, 1976), in *Signos de lucha y esperanza, Testimonios de la Iglesia en América Latina 1973–1978*, pp. 144–147.

102. On the history of the Brazilian Church, see Mecham, *Church and State*, pp. 261–

283; Prien, *Die Geschichte*, pp. 541–573; Dussel, *Historia de la iglesia*, pp. 234–243; Bruneau, *Political Transformation*, esp. pp. 71–72; Bruneau, *Church in Brazil*, esp. pp. 50–51.

103. Turner, *Catholicism and Political Development*, pp. 124–125.

104. On the MEB, see Bruneau, *Political Transformation*, pp. 79ff.; Bruneau, *Church in Brazil*, pp. 49–50.

105. Bruneau, *Political Transformation*, p. 99.

106. Bruneau, (*Church in Brazil*, p. 56, and *Political Transformation*, p. 119) puts all the blame on Goulart's "political incompetence and the various attempts at structural change," and does not mention the role played by the United States. On that subject, see Chomsky, *Towards a New Cold War*, pp. 24, 205.

107. Bruneau, *Political Transformation*, pp. 120–121. Notice the reference to the "supreme interests of the nation," which, in fact, is not very different from the Brazilian ideology of national security. This is another indication of the "totalitarian" tendencies of the Catholic Church.

108. Bruneau, *Political Transformation*, p. 139.

109. Ibid., pp. 213n.104 and 200–201.

110. See Bruneau, *Church in Brazil*, pp. 70ff.

111. Ibid., p. 74.

112. *Não oprimas teu irmão*; Spanish translation, *No oprimas a tu hermano*, in *Signos de lucha y esperanza*, pp. 75–77.

113. Published on December 25, 1973; Spanish translation in *Signos de lucha y esperanza*, pp. 93–98; see also ibid., pp. 99–109, and Chomsky and Herman, *Political Economy of Human Rights*, Vol. 1, pp. 258ff.

114. See *Signos de lucha y esperanza*, pp. 148–154.

115. Ibid., pp. 206–215.

116. Bruneau, *Church in Brazil*, pp. 77–78; Spanish translation in *Signos de lucha y esperanza*, pp. 216–223.

117. See, however, Turner, *Catholicism and Political Development*, pp. 97, 116–121 (on the Church's support for Stroessner); Prien, *Die Geschichte*, pp. 598–604; Mecham, *Church and State*, pp. 191–200, esp. 199, where Mecham writes that "In April, 1962, the Archbishop commended Stroessner for his collaboration with the Church in its work for 'the moral and spiritual elevation of the people.' "

118. See the compilation of texts *Tierra de dolor y esperanza. Testimonios: Bolivia 1976–1981*, and the chapters in Mecham, *Church and State*, pp. 179–190; Prien, *Die Geschichte*, 618–624, 973–994.

119. The main texts of the Theology of Liberation are Gutiérrez, *Teología de la liberación*, (English trans. *A Theology of Liberation*); Gutiérrez, *La fuerza histórica de los pobres*; Segundo, *Liberación de la teología*, (English trans., *Liberation of Theology*); Assmann, *Teología desde la praxis de la liberación*; Dussel, *Teología de la liberación e historia*, (English trans., *History and the Theology of Liberation*); Seladoc, *Panorama de la teología latinoamericana* (contains articles by Gutiérrez, Boff, Bonino, Dussel, Comblin, Assmann, etc.); *La nuova frontiera della teologia in America Latina* (English trans., *Frontiers of Theology in Latin America*, ed. by Rosino Gibellini); Geffré and Gutiérrez, eds., *Mystical and Political Dimensions of the Christian Faith*; *Espiritualidad de la liberación*. On the Theology of Liberation, see Oliveros, *Liberación y teología*; Blatezky, *Sprache des Glaubens in Lateinamerika*. For studies and "responses" mainly by North American theologians, see Mahan and Richesin, eds., *Challenge of Liberation*

Theology; Míguez Bonino, *Revolutionary Theology Comes of Age*; Brown, *Theology in a New Key*; Novak, ed., *Liberation South, Liberation North*; see further Metz and Jossua, eds., *Christianity and Socialism*; Eagleson, ed., *Christians and Socialism*; Lehmann, *The Transfiguration of Politics*; McFadden, ed., *Liberation, Revolution, and Freedom*; Davies, *Christians, Politics, and Violent Revolution*.

120. See Gutiérrez, *Teología de la liberación*, pp. 35ff.; Sergio Molina and Sebastían Piñera, "Extreme Poverty in Latin America," in Novak, ed., *Liberation South, Liberation North*, pp. 82–88, and the articles by Joseph Ramos, ibid., pp. 50–81. (Roger Fontaine's article, "Conclusion: The Quest for Liberation," pp. 89–95, is merely a plea for democratic capitalism); Blatezky, *Sprache des Glaubens*, pp. 209–228.

121. Gutiérrez, *Teología de la liberación*, pp. 191–196; see also Brown, *Theology in a New Key*, pp. 88–97.

122. Gutiérrez, *Teología*, pp. 351–373.

123. Ibid., p. 189: "no hay dos historias, una profana y otra sagrada 'yuxtapuestas' o 'estrechamente ligadas,' sino un solo devenir humano asumido por Cristo, Señor de la historia." ["there are not two histories, one profane and the other sacred, 'juxtaposed' or 'tightly bound,' but a single human becoming, assumed by Christ, Lord of history."]

124. Cf. Oliveros, *Liberación y teología*, pp. 317–329; Brown, *Theology in a New Key*, pp. 124–127; Shaull, "Church and Revolutionary Change," in Landsberger, ed., *Church and Social Change*, pp. 135–153, esp. p. 149 on Roger Vekeman's "metaphorical revolution"; on Vekeman, see Blatezky, *Sprache des Glaubens*, pp. 155n.35, and Prien, *Die Geschichte*, p. 1061.

125. On Kloppenburg, see Oliveros, *Liberación y teología*, pp. 329–333.

126. The conservative equation of "reality" and prevalent ideology is discussed by Segundo; see *Liberation of Theology*, p. 132. On this problem, see Mannheim, *Ideology and Utopia*, p. 203, and Merton, *Social Theory and Social Structure*, pp. 549–550. On the dialectical interplay between ideology and utopia, see Jameson, *Political Unconscious*, pp. 281–299, and *Marxism and Form*, pp. 117–118, 157–158.

127. For a critique of the Theology of Liberation, see Benavides, "The Discourse of 'Liberation Theology' in Perspective," in Bryant, ed., *Many Faces of Religion and Society*.

BIBLIOGRAPHY

History

Ayarragaray, Lucas. *La iglesia en América y la dominación española*. Buenos Aires, 1920.

Chomsky, Noam. *Towards a New Cold War*. New York, 1982.

Chomsky, Noam, and Edward S. Herman. *The Political Economy of Human Rights*, Volume 1, Boston, 1979.

Dussel, Enrique. *Historia de la iglesia en américa latina. Coloniaje y liberación*. Barcelona: Nova terra, 1974.

Fried, J. *Bartolomé de las Casas*. Mexico, 1974.

Immerman, Richard H. *The CIA in Guatemala*. Austin, Tex., 1982.

Kirkpatrick, Jeane. "Dictatorship and Double Standards." *Commentary*. November 1979.

Konetzke, Richard. "Christendom and Conquista im Spanishchen Amerika." *Saeculum* 23 (1972): 59–73.

Legon, Faustino J. *Doctrina y ejercicio del patronato nacional.* Buenos Aires, 1920.

Leturia, Pedro P. *La acción diplomática de Bolívar ante Pío VIII, 1820–1823.* Madrid, 1925.

Mecham, J. Lloyd. *Church and State in Latin America.* Chapel Hill: University of North Carolina Press, 1966 (rev. ed.).

Merton, Robert K. *Social Theory and Social Structure.* New York, 1968.

Poblete, Renato. "The Church in Latin America: A Historical Survey." In Landsberger, ed., *The Church and Social Change in Latin America,* pp. 39–52.

Prien, Hans-Jürgen. *Die Geschichte des Christentums in Lateinamerika.* Göttingen: Vandenhoeck and Ruprecht, 1978.

Reeves, Marjorie. *Joachim of Fiore and the Prophetic Future.* New York, 1977.

The Church and Political Change

Berger, Peter L. *The Sacred Canopy.* New York, 1976.

D'Antonio, William, and Frederick Pike, eds., *Religion, Revolution, and Reform. New Forces for Change in Latin America.* New York: Praeger, 1964.

Davies, J. G. *Christians, Politics, and Violent Revolution.* Maryknoll, N.Y.: Orbis, 1976.

Dewart, Leslie. *Christianity and Revolution: The Lesson of Cuba.* New York: Herder 1963.

Eagelson, John, ed., *Christians and Socialism: Documentation of the Christians for Socialism Movement in Latin America.* Maryknoll, N.Y.: Orbis, 1975.

Houtart, François "The Roman Catholic Church and Social Change in Latin America." In Landsberger, ed., *The Church and Social Change,* pp. 113–133.

———, and Emile Pin. *The Church and the Latin American Revolution.* New York: Sheed and Ward, 1965.

———, and André Rousseau. *The Church and Revolution.* Maryknoll, N.Y.: Orbis, 1971.

Kerner, Max, ed. *Ideologie und Herrschaft im Mittelalter.* Darmstadt, 1979.

Kloft, Hans, ed. *Ideologie und Herrschaft in der Antike.* Darmstadt, 1978.

Landsberger, Henry A., ed. *The Church and Social Change in Latin America.* Notre Dame, Ind.: University of Notre Dame Press, 1970.

Lehmann, Paul Louis. *The Transfiguration of Politics.* New York: Harper and Row, 1975.

Lesbaupin, Ivo. "The Latin American Bishops and Socialism." In Metz and Jossua, eds. *Christianity and Socialism,* pp. 113–123.

Levine, Daniel H., ed. *Churches and Politics in Latin America.* Beverly Hills, Calif.: Sage, 1980.

McGrath, Mark G. "Church Doctrine in Latin America After the Council." In Landsberger, ed. *The Church and Social Change,* pp. 97–112.

Metz, Johann-Baptist, and Jean-Pierre Jossua, eds. *Christianity and Socialism.* New York: Seabury, 1977.

Ossio, Juan, ed. *La ideología mesiánica del mundo andino.* Lima, 1973.

Poblete, Renato, "Secularización en América Latina." *Mensaje* 21 (1972) 521–530. In Seladoc, ed., *Panorama de la teología latinoamericana,* pp. 43–63.

Le Pouvoir et le Sacré. Bruxelles: Université Libre de Bruxelles, 1962.

Shaull, Richard. "The Church and Revolutionary Change: Contrasting Perspectives." In Landsberger, ed. *The Church and Social Change*, pp. 135–153.

Topitsch, Ernst. *Vom Ursprung und Ende der Metaphysik*. Vienna, 1958.

Turner, Frederick C. *Catholicism and Political Development in Latin America*. Chapel Hill: University of North Carolina Press, 1971.

Vallier, Ivan. *Catholicism, Social Control, and Modernization in Latin America*. Englewood Cliffs, N.J.: Prentice-Hall, 1970.

Church and State in Individual Countries

Bruneau, Thomas C. *The Church in Brazil: The Politics of Religion*. Austin: University of Texas Press, 1982.

————. *The Political Transformation of the Brazilian Catholic Church*. London: Cambridge University Press, 1974.

Castillo, Fernando. "Christians for Socialism in Chile." In Metz and Jossua, eds. *Christianity and Socialism*, pp. 106–112.

de Kadt, Emanuel, "JUC and AP: The Rise of Catholic Radicalism in Brazil." In Landsberger, ed. *The Church and Social Change*, pp. 191–219.

"Extermination in Guatemala." *The New York Review of Books*. June 2, 1983.

Gervassi, John, ed. *Revolutionary Priest: The Complete Writings and Messages of Camilo Torres*. New York, 1971.

Klaiber, Jeffrey L. *Religion and Revolution in Peru, 1824–1976*. Notre Dame, Ind.: University of Notre Dame Press, 1977.

Landsberger, Henry A. "Time, Persons, Doctrine: The Modernization of the Church in Chile." In Landsberger, ed. *The Church and Social Change*, pp. 77–94.

Levine, Daniel H. *Religion and Politics in Latin America: The Catholic Church in Venezuela and Colombia*. Princeton, N.J.: Princeton University Press, 1981.

Nairn, Allan. "The Guns of Guatemala," *The New Republic*. April 11, 1983.

Nieto Rojas, Jose María. *La batalla contra el comunismo en Columbia*. Bogotá, 1956.

Ortiz Rescaniere, Alejandro. *De Adaneva a Inkarrí. Una visión indígena del Perú*. Lima, 1973.

Pike, Frederick. "South America's Multifaceted Catholicism: Glimpses of Twentieth-Century Argentina, Chile, and Peru." In Landsberger, ed. *The Church and Social Change*, pp. 53–75.

Romero de Iguiñiz, Catalina. "Cambios en la relación iglesia-sociedad en el Perú: 1958–1978." *Debates en Sociología* 7 (1982): 115–141.

Schmidt, Karl M., ed. *The Roman Catholic Church in Modern Latin America*. New York: Alfred A. Knopf, 1972.

Smith, Brian H. *The Church and Politics in Chile. Challenges to Modern Catholicism*. Princeton, N.J.: Princeton University Press, 1982.

Sources

Signos de renovación. Recopilación de documentos post-conciliares de la iglesia en américa latina. Lima: Centro de estudios y publicaciones (CEP), 1969.

Signos de liberación. Testimonios de la iglesia en américa latina 1969–1973. Lima: CEP, 1973.

Signos de lucha y esperanza. Testiminios de la iglesia en américa latina 1973–1978. Lima: CEP, 1978.

Tierra de dolor y esperanza. Testimonios: Bolivia 1976–1981. Lima: CEP, 1981.

El Salvador, un pueblo oprimido. Testimonio de cristianos. Lima: CEP, 1980.

El Salvador, un pueblo perseguido. Testimonio de cristianos; II, de octubre 79 a junio 80. Lima: CEP, 1980.

Morir y despertar en Guatemala. Lima: CEP, 1981.

Nicaragua. Combate de un pueblo. Presencia de los cristianos. Lima: CEP, 1980.

Nicaragua: la hora de los desafíos. Lima: CEP, 1981.

The Theology of Liberation

Antes, Peter. "Aspekte der südamerikanischen Befreiungstheologie." In Gunther Stephenson, ed. *Der Religionswandel unserer Zeit im Spiegel der Religionswissenschaft.* Darmstadt, 1980, pp. 54–66.

Assmann, Hugo. *Teología desde la praxis de la liberación.* Salamanca: Sígueme, 1976.

Benavides, Gustavo. "The Discourse of 'Liberation Theology' in Perspective." In M. Darrol Bryant, ed. *The Many Faces of Religion and Society.* Forthcoming.

Blatezky, Arturo. *Sprache des Glaubens in Lateinamerika. Eine Studie zu Selbstverständnis und Methode der "Theologie der Befreiung."* Frankfurt: Peter Lang, 1978.

Brown, Robert McAfee. *Gustavo Gutiérrez.* Atlanta: John Knox Press, 1980.

———. *Theology in a New Key.* Philadelphia: Westminster, 1978.

Comblin, Joseph. "El tema de la 'liberación' en el pensamiento cristiano latinoamericano." In Seladoc, ed., *Panorama de la teología latinoamericano,* pp. 229–245.

Croatto, Severino. *Liberación y libertad. Pautas hermenéuticas.* Lima: CEP, 1982.

Dussel, Enrique. *Teologia de la liberación e historía.* Buenos Aires: 1975. (English translation: *History and the Theology of Liberation.* New York, 1976.)

Eliade, Mircea. *Le sacré et le profane.* Paris: Gallimard, 1965.

Geffré, Claude, and Gustavo Gutiérrez, eds. *The Mystical and Political Dimension of the Christian Faith.* New York: Herder, 1974.

Gibellini, Rosino, ed. *Frontiers of Theology in Latin America.* Maryknoll, N.Y.: Orbis, 1979.

Gutiérrez, Gustavo. *La fuerza histórica de los pobres.* Lima: CEP, 1980.

———. *Teología de la liberación.* Lima: CEP, 1971. (English translation: *A Theology of Liberation.* New York: Orbis, 1971.)

Jesi, Furio. *Cultura di destra.* Bari, 1979.

McCann, Dennis. *Christian Realism and Liberation Theology.* Maryknoll, N.Y.: Orbis, 1981.

McFadden, Thomas, ed. *Liberation, Revolution, and Freedom: Theological Perspectives.* New York: Seabury, 1975.

Mahan, Brian, and L. Dale Richesin, eds. *The Challenge of Liberation Theology: A First World Response.* Maryknoll, N.Y.: Orbis, 1981.

Míguez Bonino, Jose. *Revolutionary Theology Comes of Age.* London: SPCK, 1975.

———. "Unidad cristiana y reconciliación social: coincidencia y tensión." In Seladoc, ed. *Panorama de la teología latinoamericana,* pp. 151–64.

Muñoz, Ronaldo. "Lucha de clases y evengelio." In Seladoc, ed., *Panorama de la teología latinoamericana,* pp. 288–299.

Novak, Michael, ed. *Liberation South, Liberation North*. Washington, D.C.: American Enterprise Institute, 1981.

Oliveros, Roberto. *Liberación y teología. Génesis y crecimiento de una reflexión*. Lima: CEP, 1977, reprinted 1980.

Scannone, Juan Carlos. "Ontología del proceso auténticamente liberador." In Seladoc, ed. *Panorama de la teología latinoamericana*, pp. 246–287.

Segundo, Juan Luis. *Liberación de la teología*. Buenos Aires: Lohlé, 1975. (English translation: *Liberation Theology*. Maryknoll, N.Y.: Orbis, 1976).

Seladoc, Equipo, ed. *Panorama de la teología latinoamericana*. Salamanca: Sígueme, 1975.

Ideology and Utopia

Jameson, Frederic. *Marxism and Form*. Princeton, N.J.: Princeton University Press, 1971.

Jameson, Frederic. *The Political Unconscious: Narrative As a Socially Symbolic Act*. Ithaca: Cornell University Press, 1981.

Mannheim, Karl. *Ideology and Utopia: An Introduction to the Sociology of Knowledge*. New York: Harcourt, Brace, Jovanovich, 1955.

7

Hinduism and Politics in India

ARVIND SHARMA

The discussion of Hinduism and politics in India may be launched by asking the following question: which are the Hindu political parties in India? The complexity of the question becomes apparent when it is recognized that the Indian National Congress regarded itself as a national and not a Hindu or communal party.[1] (A communal party is one that caters to the interests of a particular community rather than the whole nation.)[2] However, the Muslim League—which pressed for the formation of Pakistan as a homeland for the Muslims of India—regarded it as a "Hindu" and therefore communal party.[3] At the other end of the spectrum an organization known as the RSS (Rashitriya Swayamsevak Sangh, or National Volunteer Organization) is an avowedly non-political body, but its existence has definite political implications.[4] In the treatment of Hinduism and politics in India in this chapter both the Indian National Congress and the RSS are included. Nepal, although a Hindu state, is excluded from the discussion, which is confined to India.[5]

For the sake of convenience the role of Hinduism in Indian politics is discussed in terms of the following organizations: (1) the All-India National Congress or the Indian National Congress; (2) the Hindu Mahasabha; (3) the Rashtriya Swayamsevak Sangh; (4) the Jana Sangh; and (5) the Ram Rajya Parishad.[6] The Indian National Congress is treated at the very end, although it historically precedes them all, for reasons that will become apparent.

The rest of the parties mentioned above are generally described by the umbrella term "Hindu communalism."[7] It will be useful, therefore, to begin by exploring the origins of Hindu communalism. As Donald Eugene Smith has noted, the "difference between Indian nationalism and Hindu communalism is not always clear" as "India is the only home of the Hindus, and whatever patriotic demands were made in the name of the majority would naturally appear to be expressions of Indian nationalism."[8] The demand for political independence, as is well known, was preceded by a Hindu resurgence spearheaded by men like Swami Dayananda (1824–1883) and Swami Vivekananda (1863–1902).[9] In other words, one must distinguish between Hindu nationalism and Hindu communalism.[10] The divergence between the two arose in the context of the rise of Muslim communalism in India.

THE HINDU MAHASABHA

According to R. C. Majumdar, the "genesis and early history" of the Hindu Mahasabha is "somewhat obscure."[11] The search for an all-India organization for the Hindus has been afoot since 1900 when various Hindu bodies in some form or other had been meeting at more or less regular intervals. The decision to form such a body seems to have been made in 1910,[12] although the meeting of the Akhil Bharatiya Hindu Conference in 1918 at Delhi "may be regarded as the beginning of the Hindu Mahasabha proper."[13] The formation of the Muslim League, "founded in 1906, significantly, during the period of extremist ascendancy in the Congress,"[14] and the rise of Muslim communalism contributed to its growth. (It has also been alleged that Hindu communalism in the Indian National Congress led to the formation of the Muslim League itself.)[15]

R. C. Majumdar maintains that "There is no doubt that like the other Hindu conferences," the Hindu Mahasabha "was established as a counterpoise to the Muslim League in order to resist the undue concessions made to the Muslims by the Indian National Congress."[16] These concessions included the Lucknow Pact of 1916 by which the Congress acceded to the Muslim demands for separate electorates, Congress's support for the Khilafat Movement, and its allegedly soft attitude toward the fate of the Hindus in the communal disturbances in Malabar, Multan, and Kohat.[17] This policy of appeasement of the Muslims did not go down well with the Mahasabha.

An important session of the Mahasabha was held in 1923 at Banaras and was presided over by Pandit Madan Mohan Malaviya. Some differences of opinion exist, however, regarding the significance of this session. For example, Majumdar draws attention to its communal aspect, calling it the first "representative gathering of almost all the religious sects of India except the Muslims and the Christians," at which the Suddhi movement for reconverting ex-Hindus to Hinduism was "formally sanctioned." He maintains that during the "whole of this period the Hindu Mahasabha really constituted a political organisation to fight for the interest of the Hindus to which the Congress leaders were indifferent and even hostile."[18] But Donald Smith points out that in 1924 the Mahasabha met in Belgium when the Congress session was being held there:

A number of prominent Congress leaders attended the Mahasabha meeting, including the Ali brothers, Dr. Mahmood, M. Hasrat Mohani, Maulana Abul Kalam Azad and other Muslims. Pandit Madan Mohan Malaviya, who presided, declared that every Hindu should support the Congress. The aim of the Mahasabha was to supplement and strengthen the

Congress by dealing with those non-political questions—social, cultural, and religious—which were outside its area of concern."[19]

By 1933, however, this understanding had evaporated and the Hindu Mahasabha began to challenge the Congress.[20] It is clear that it did not succeed in challenging it effectively in the political sphere[21] and seems to have been regarded by the Muslim League as a Hindu body at least until 1937 after which the same came to be said of the Congress.[22] Although the Mahasabha never quite vanished from the political scene,[23] it was "more of a social than political organization."[24] There were two phases in modern Indian political history, however, when it gained some prominence or notoriety.

The first phase came in the mid–1930s. It was during this period that Hindu-Muslim relations took a turn for the worse from which they never recovered. Both the Muslims and the Congress have blamed this deterioration, at least in part, on the aggressively Hindu policies of the Mahasabha represented by the movements of Suddhi and Sangathan.[25] The truth of this charge is not easily determined, but already in 1937 Y. D. Savarkar, who remained the president of the Mahasabha until 1942, declared that in India "there are two nations in the main; the Hindus and the Muslims." As Smith has remarked: "M. A. Jinnah could have constructed his two-nation theory, which led to the demand for Pakistan, on the basis of Savarkar's speech!"[26] It is equally interesting that the demand for Pakistan can be seen in its germinal form in the suggestion "made some time before April, 1925," when "Lālā Lājpat Rai suggested the creation of Muslim provinces in the north-east and north-west of India to set at rest the ceaseless Hindu-Muslim bickering and jealousies in some provinces."[27]

The second phase encompasses the period around Partition when the Hindu Mahasabha fiercely opposed what it regarded as Mahatma Gandhi's pro-Muslim policies. The assassin of Mahatma Gandhi also had past association with the Mahasabha and the RSS.[28] The Mahasabha suspended political activity after January 30, 1948, when Mahatma Gandhi was assassinated but resumed it on May 28, 1949.[29] According to Smith, during the pre-Partition period

Hindu communal leaders regarded the Congress as singularly inept in its handling of the "Muslim problem." Merely because Hindu members of the Congress found it easy to forget their Hindu background and merge with others in a common Indian nationality, they imagined that Muslims would do likewise. This was the basic error. Despite innumerable compromises and special concessions to the Muslim League, the Congress had not been able to secure its cooperation in the nationalist cause. Rather, each new concession was interpreted as a further sign of weakness, and the Muslims demanded more and more. The demand for Pakistan came in 1940, and in the years following the Hindu Mahasabha leveled a steady stream of fire at the Congress for its weakness in dealing with this "fantastic proposal to vivisect the Motherland." Popular support for the Mahasabha increased considerably, although the Congress again swamped the Mahasabha in the elections of 1946."[30]

Although the interaction between Mahatma Gandhi and Quaid-i-Azam Jinnah has received considerable attention,[31] the literature has generally ignored the interaction between Mahatma Gandhi and Vir Savarkar, the Mahasabha leader. This is understandable, for the Gandhi-Jinnah relationship has, of course, been far more consequential. Nonetheless the Gandhi-Savarkar relationship is of some interest.[32] In a sense Gandhi stole a march on Savarkar's Hindu leadership, as well as Ambedkar's leadership of the Untouchables but could not ultimately prevail over Jinnah's leadership of the Muslims. Robert Payne argues that Savarkar represents a

little-known aspect of the Indian struggle for freedom and independence. Although at one time he possessed a vast following running into the millions, his determination to wrest power from the British by force of arms was blunted by the growing power of the Congress Party, dominated by Gandhi and dedicated to peaceful change. He had it in his power, if the proper occasion arose, to let loose thunderbolts. An intense, tight-lipped, fanatical man, commanding many secret stores of weapons and a devoted army of conspirators, he led the Hindu Mahasabha without ever daring to throw it into battle. Long before he died, he knew that he had been like a man waiting in the wings for the call to occupy the center of the stage, but the call never came.[33]

The role of the Mahasabha in the post-Independence period—from 1947 to date—may now be examined. Judged by its performance in the elections at the national level, it has fared poorly. In a house of over 500 members it secured 4 seats in the elections of 1951–1952, 2 in those of 1957, and 1 in those of 1962. Its performance in the elections at the state level was better but hardly impressive.[34]

The ideology of the Mahasabha in the post–1947 phase, and its important policy implications, are as follows:

1. The rejection of Partition: it aims to unite India and Pakistan by all constitutional and, if need be, even violent means.

2. The ideal of a Hindu state which involves a rejection of the concept of a secular state. The policy of a Hindu state toward non-Hindus is variously described, but the basic variable seems to be the degree of commitment to India. "Hindus alone are the nationals of India, and non-Hindus can be classified only as Indian citizens. The non-Hindus shall be entitled to equal rights and privileges under normal conditions; in the event of war or other emergency, however, the government would have powers to distinguish between Hindu and non-Hindu citizens."[35]

3. Rejection of conversion from Hinduism and promotion of conversion to Hinduism. A policy implication of rejection of conversion is a ban on the activities of Christian missionaries in India and of promotion of conversion, the promotion of the Suddhi (or reconversion to Hinduism of ex-Hindus).

4. The cultivation of a Hindu socialism whose content is not easily identified, except that it is based on caste-harmony (*varna*) instead of class conflict.

Finally, Smith has noted that the Mahasabha platform also includes:

a total ban on cow slaughter, the repeal of the Hindu Marriage Act and other "anti-Hindu legislation," the complete integration of *all* of Kashmir within the Indian Republic, a stern policy toward Pakistan, India's withdrawal from the Commonwealth, and an intensive program of compulsory military training. The principle of the militarization of the Hindu nation has long been an important part of the Hindu communalist tradition ("Hinduize all politics" and "militarize Hindudom").[36]

THE RASHTRIYA SWAYAMSEVAK SANGH

The RSS has never functioned as a political party,[37] and in 1949 when the Indian government lifted the ban on it for its alleged implication in the assassination of Mahatma Gandhi, it was on the condition that it would not participate in politics.[38] Feared as a potentially fascist organization partly because it had no constitution, it was required to have a written constitution which it now possesses.[39] Nevertheless, the RSS has not been without political impact as will be seen later.[40]

The RSS was founded in 1925 in Nagpur by Dr. Keshav Hedgewar amid periodic Hindu-Muslim riots.[41] He was also a member of the Mahasabha and remained so until 1929. This fact reflects the close, though informal, ties between the two organizations at that time.[42] With the Mahasabha's increasing political involvement in the 1930s, the two organizations parted company, with the RSS restricting itself to the cultural sphere and to training a cadre of workers.

As the events culminating in India's Independence and Partition began to unfold, the RSS started taking a greater interest in politics without becoming a political body. It "unofficially supported the '42 movement," in which Ghandi led an effort to remove the British from India; it opposed Partition; and in December 1947 it claimed the support of 5 million Hindus.[43] However, the assassination of Mahatma Gandhi and the temporary banning of its activity produced some results. First, the RSS realized the need for political clout to safeguard itself. Second, it wanted to distance itself from the Mahasabha which in the public view was tainted by a possible association with Mahatma Gandhi's murder and wasn't considered an effective body.[44] This led to the formation of a new party—the Jana Sangh.

Before the Jana Sangh is discussed, some concluding observations on the RSS are in order. First, it is "non-political only in one sense: it does not take part in elections nor is it organized for electoral purposes."[45] It is political in the sense that its members are free to join any political party not advocating violence. Second, its links with the new party, the Jana Sangh, have been a subject of debate and controversy.[46] Third, it advocates the assimilation of all non-Hindus into Hindu culture without insisting on the abandonment of non-Hindu religious affiliations.[47] Fourth, it is not opposed to the secular state, though it sees it as an expression of Hindu catholicity rather than as a Western concept.[48] But as Donald Eugene Smith points out, "it is impossible to say how the RSS would respond if political power ever came within reach, either directly or through the Jana Sangh. The implementation of certain aspects of its ideology (the policy toward Muslims and other minorities, for example) presupposes extensive use of the machinery of the state."[49]

THE JANA SANGH

The Jana Sangh was formed in 1951 as a political party under the leadership of Shyama Prasas Mookerjee (1901–1953) who was unhappy with the Mahasabha's decision restricting its membership to Hindus. In its bid to emphasize the Hindu national as opposed to the Hindu communal point of view, the Jana Sangh's membership was open to all, and by contrast with the Hindu Rashtra ideal of the Mahasabha it advocated a *Bharatiya Rashtra* [Indian Nation].[50] The Jana Sangh had close connections with the RSS but because of its common ground with the Mahasabha attempts were made to merge the two.[51] These efforts failed largely because the Jana Sangh insisted on retaining its distinguishing features and wanting the Mahasabha to merge with it.[52]

The Jana Sangh made its political mark quite successfully. At the national level, out of nearly 500 parliamentary seats its scores in the various elections were as follows: 1952 (3); 1957 (4); 1962 (14); 1967 (35);[53] 1971 (22).[54] Following Indira Gandhi's imposition of Emergency the party suffered considerably, but in the following elections in 1975 it secured the maximum number of seats in the Janata Coalition.[55] The lack of ideological cohesion in the Janata Party along with other factors led to its fall in 1980 after which the Jana Sangh rechristened itself the Bharatiya Janata.

In discussing the ideology of the Jana Sangh, it is helpful to distinguish between the pre- and post-Janata period, but generally its ideology contains the following primary features: (1) It is against linking religion and politics; it thus accepts as members people belonging to any religion and upholds the idea of the secular state. (2) Its "Hindu" nationalism assumes the following forms: (a) a call for non-Hindus to nationalize themselves; (b) opposition to alleged "Muslim appeasement in the name of secularism" and (c) similarity with the Mahasabha on several issues:

legislation banning cow slaughter, repeal of the Hindu Marriage Act and other "anti-Hindu" measures, implementation of the Niyogi report calling for a ban on foreign missionaries, Akhand Bharat (undivided India), total integration of Kashmir in the Indian Republic, compulsory military training, and a tough policy toward Pakistan. But the party has given no support to the *shuddhi* movement, and it has gone on record as being strongly opposed not only to untouchability but to "casteism."[56]

This naturally raises the question: to what extent is the Jana Sangh a communal party like the Mahasabha? Although a clear-cut answer is not possible, it may be said that the Jana Sangh is a party with a Hindu complexion.[57]

Major historical developments were involved in the Jana Sangh's change of name to the Bharatiya Janata Party. Following the period of Emergency imposed by Mrs. Gandhi on June 26, 1975,[58] and the parliamentary elections of 1977, the various opposition parties, including the Jana Sangh, decided to merge into the Janata Party, which had won a majority, and proceeded to form the government.[59] These parties, however, were not able to stay united, and so Mrs. Gandhi's Congress defeated them at the polls in 1980. These parties now reverted to their original allegiances, sometimes with altered names. Even though the Jana Sangh agreed to merge in the Janata Party, the RSS, with whose cadre it had been closely associated, "refused to give up its separate identity."[60] The current president of the Bharatiya Janata, Atal Bihari Bajpayee, was also closely associated[61] with the Jana Sangh.[62] Although the old Jana Sangh perhaps benefited from the experience of "coalition" and of holding office, the continuity between the Jana Sangh and the Bharatiya Janata is too obvious to be ignored.

THE RAM RAJYA PARISHAD

The Ram Rajya Parishad was founded in 1948.[63] According to Horst Hart-mann, it was formed with the recognition that "the days of slavery were not our days. We were under foreign domination. We should write off those days from our Calendar. So far as our fresh activities are concerned, we should bridge over the gulf of the foreign domination and thus link our glorious past with the budding present."[64] The glorious past was represented by the concept of Rā-marājya or the "blessed days of Lord Rama's reign" when everyone "was contented, happy, gifted with learning, and religious-minded. . . . All were truthful. None was close-fisted; none was rude; none lacked prudence; and above all, none was atheist. All followed the path of religion."[65] On specific policy issues "confiscation of land without compensation is opposed, the barter system is preferred over the use of legal tender, a ban on cow slaughter is advocated, and the traditional Ayurvedic system of medicine is supported. Much of the manifesto is concerned with a description of the days of Lord Rama."[66]

This political party is said to oppose any reform of caste-ridden society.[67] This characterization is substantially correct. Indeed,

The orthodox orientation of the Parishad is indicated by its treatment of the caste system. While the Hindu Mahasabha, the RSS, and the Jana Sangh reject caste in varying degrees, and untouchability strongly, the Parishad is concerned with helping the untouchables to maintain their heredity occupations, although under improved conditions. "They shall be given high posts in the management of the sanitary departments and the leather and hides trade shall be mostly placed in their hands." In this way fullest attention will be given to their "economic prosperity and spiritual salvation." However, "any responsible post in the government will be open to them on the strength of individual merit.[68]

The Ram Rajya Parishad advocates the creation of a State Department of Religious Affairs, which will "administer justice which shall be based on the recognized religious books, and in consultation with the religious heads with full impartiality, and keeping in view the interests of the Nation and the Society."[69]

The Ram Rajya Parishad is essentially a regional party; such strength as it possesses lies in the Madhya Pradesh and Rajasthan region.[70] Although it did secure two seats at the national level in 1962, it is generally believed to have far less actual strength and potential appeal than the Mahasabha and the Jana Sangh.

The name of the party is historically of some interest. Part of Mahatma Gandhi's charisma for the masses stemmed from his appeal to ideas they could relate to, such as that of Ram Rajya, the "Golden Age."[71] The Ram Rajya Parishad seems to have been less successful, however. It is of further interest that Mahatma Gandhi regarded as an interpolation one major incident in the Rama story in which Rama is shown as upholding caste discrimination.[72]

INDIAN NATIONAL CONGRESS

The Muslim League often accused the India National Congress of being communal, especially after the mid–1930s.[73] Although it is difficult to pass judgment on so complex an issue, the accusation does not appear to be wholly justified.[74] It is even alleged that there was little difference between the Congress and the Mahasabha.[75] The confusion arises from the fact that since the majority of Indians are Hindus, any popular body is bound to have large numbers of Hindu members. But this does not make the body communal. Donald Smith has offered a balanced assessment of this question:

After 1916, Gandhi assumed a major leadership role. While he constantly emphasized Hindu-Muslim unity and read from the Qur'an and New Testament as well as the Gita in his daily prayer meetings, Gandhi's political style was undeniably religious. And his basic technique of *satyagraha* drew heavily on Hindu sources. Throughout its long history the Congress was predominantly secular, but the influence of Hinduism was significant enough to give credence to some of the charges of communal bias made by the Muslim League.[76]

This does not mean, however, that the Indian National Congress and its successor bodies have not been communal in some ways. The communalism within the avowedly non-communal and even anti-communal Congress can take the following forms: (1)"Hindu-minded elements within the organization."[77] Thus, people like Purushottama Das Tandon have been "outspoken advocates of Hindu causes."[78] (2) Electoral alliances with communal parties, including a flirtation with even the Muslim League.[79] (3) The use of religious groups or caste-groups representing political power for political purposes.[80]

It must be added, however, that the Congress Party generally has acted with the interest of the minority communities in mind, consistent with its political self-interest.[81]

HINDU COMMUNALISM

Myron Weiner believes that a profile of Hindu communalism can be presented on two levels: on the precise level of ideology and on the vaguer level of outlook.

According to Weiner, Hindu communal ideology can be characterized by two distinct elements. (1) Although the content of a Hindu Rashtra has never been defined, "In the minds of many of the supporters of the communal parties, *Hindu Rashtra* means a Hindu-ruled state with non-Hindus holding lesser positions, if any at all."[82] (2) The reunion of India and Pakistan is regarded as the ultimate political ideal.

At the more general level of outlook the following five attitudes may be identified: (1) An anti-West feeling specially directed against Westernized Indians. (2) A hawkish approach to various issues as opposed to a Gandhian one. (In this context Savarkar's slogan is often quoted: "Hinduise all politics and militarize Hindudom.")[83] (3) A lack of interest in the political process as an instrument of policy—until recently. (4) A lack of concern with economic issues—until recently. (5) Although democracy has not been rejected, it does not seem to have been deemed worthy of defense—again until recently.[84]

What then is the relationship between Hinduism and politics in India? Prior to making any such assessment, one must modify Weiner's conclusions presented above. First, there is no Hindu "communal" party, with the possible exception of the Ram Rajya Parishad which does not accept the concept of a secular state. Weiner may be correct when he states that this represents no mere lip service to the concept, but the fact remains that no "Hindu" party is openly questioning the concept.[85] Second, in recent years all of the political parties have more strongly than ever espoused democracy. On the other hand, the fact that the anti-cowslaughter campaign has virtually succeeded in attaining its goals in the states of India with a few exceptions such as Kerala and West Bengal indicates that Hindu ideas and ideals cannot be ignored in a democracy. But Austin B. Creel has asked: "If the United States can organize Sunday to suit the sensibilities of its majority community . . . why can not India, without ceasing to be a secular state, answer the cow slaughter question in a way that suits the sensibilities of its majority community?"[86] It is interesting that the Muslim-majority state of Jammu and Kashmir supported the cowslaughter ban and that its constitutionality was upheld by a bench of the Supreme Court with the Muslim judge voting in its favor. With regard to the political parties tinged with Hinduism, it seems safe to conclude that "although greatly over-shadowed by the Congress party, their appeal to both patriotic and religious sentiment gives them a potentially strong position in Indian politics."[87] But it has only remained a potentiality for

over three decades now. It may also be added that after the 1967 elections the
Hindu Mahasabha and the Ram Rajya Parishad for "all practical purposes"
"have ceased to exist."[88] Thus, the Bharatiya Jana Sangh in its new incarnation
as the Bharatiya Janata Party is virtually the only party left in the field, and what
was once said of the Jana Sangh may still apply to it: "Eighty percent of India's
people are Hindu, and although the Jana Sangh may cautiously phrase its public
appeals in secular terms, Hindu communalism is a potent factor in Indian politics,
and the nostalgia for Bharat (Hindu India) is a dynamic element of the nationalist
feeling readily exploited by the traditional right."[89]

NOTES

1. Majumdar, ed., *Struggle for Freedom*, pp. 606–607.
2. Lamb, *India*, p. 130.
3. Philips and Wainwright, eds., *Partition of India*, p. 163. O'Malley, ed., *Modern India and the West*, pp. 752–755.
4. Curran, *Militant Hinduism in Indian Politics*, Ch. 3.
5. Smith, ed., *Religion and Political Modernization*, p. 33. Also see pp. 102–103, 299, 463.
6. The last three are generally labeled communal. The list does not include "one curious political party" which could be so regarded but which is deemed to be of little significance. (See Brass, *Language, Religion and Politics in North India*, pp. 101–102.)
7. Smith, *India as a Secular State*, p. 454.
8. Ibid., p. 455.
9. See Smith, ed., *Religion, Politics, and Social Change in the Third World*, p. 96.
10. This is not always done; see de Bary, ed., *Sources of Indian Tradition*, p. 880.
11. Majumdar, ed., *Struggle for freedom*, p. 419.
12. Ibid.
13. Ibid., p. 420.
14. Smith, *India as a Secular State*, p. 455.
15. Malik, *Moslem Nationalism in India and Pakistan*, pp. 221–225.
16. Majumdar, ed., *Struggle for freedom.*, p. 987
17. Ibid.
18. Ibid., pp. 988–989.
19. Smith, *India as a Secular State*, p. 456. It has often been noted that the withdrawal of the non-cooperation movement by Mahatma Gandhi was followed by an exacerbation of Hindu-Muslim relations (Dodwell, ed., *Cambridge History of India*, Vol. 6, p. 619; Majumbar, Raychaudhuri, and Datta, *Advanced History of India*, p. 982; etc.). The role of the Mahasabha in this deterioration in the Hindu-Muslim stage is difficult to establish.
20. Weiner, *Party Politics in India*, p. 167.
21. Philips and Wainwright, eds., *Partition of India*, p. 160.
22. Ibid., p. 163.
23. Ibid., pp. 371, 390, 397, 436, 483.
24. Ibid., p. 497.
25. Majumdar, ed., *Struggle for freedom*, pp. 425–426, 981–982, 988.
26. Smith, *India as a Secular State*, pp. 459–460.
27. Majumbar et al., *Advanced History of India*, n. 2.

28. Smith, *India as a Secular State*, p. 473.
29. Ibid., pp. 473, 474.
30. Ibid., p. 460. Weiner (*Party Politics in India*, p. 167) divides the history of the Mahasabha into three periods, depending on the main target of its work: hostility to Western impact, hostility to the Muslim League (after the First World War), and hostility to the Congress (1932–   ).
31. Joshi, *They Must Meet Again*.
32. See Payne, *Life and Death of Mahatma Gandhi*, pp. 202, 204, 205–209, 225.
33. Ibid., p. 209.
34. Weiner, *Party Politics in India*, p. 196.
35. Smith, *India as a Secular State*, p. 462.
36. Ibid., p. 462.
37. Ibid., p. 473.
38. Ibid., p. 474.
39. Ibid.
40. Weiner, *Party Politics in India*, pp. 182–183.
41. Ibid., p. 177. For a full account of the RSS, see Curran, *Militant Hinduism in Indian Politics*.
42. Weiner, *Party Politics in India*, pp. 177–179.
43. Ibid., pp. 182, 183.
44. Ibid., pp. 181–185.
45. Ibid., pp. 182–183, 190.
46. Baxter, *The Jana Sangh*, pp. 181–185.
47. Smith, *India as a Secular State*, p. 467.
48. Ibid., p. 468.
49. Ibid.
50. Weiner, *Party Politics in India*, p. 191.
51. Ibid., pp. 197–198.
52. Ibid., Ch. 10.
53. Hartmann, *Political Parties in India*, pp. 150, 153, 157, 168.
54. Zaidi, *The Great Upheaval*, p. 495.
55. Naik, *The Great Janata Revolution*, p. 44.
56. Smith, *India as a Secular State*, pp. 471–472.
57. Ibid., pp. 472–473.
58. Puri, *Bharatiya Jana Sangh*, p. 233.
59. Ibid., p. 242.
60. Ibid., p. 257.
61. *The Hindu*, September 21, 1982, p. 1.
62. Puri, *Bharatiya Jana Sangh*, pp. 52–55.
63. Hartmann, *Political Parties in India*, p. 112.
64. From the Election Manifesto of the All-India Ramarajya-Parishad quoted by Myron Weiner, *Politics of Scarcity*, p. 174.
65. Ibid.
66. Ibid.
67. Hartmann, *Political Parties in India*, p. 112.
68. Smith, *India as a Secular State*, p. 465.
69. From the Manifesto, as cited in Smith, *India as a Secular State*, p. 464.
70. Weiner, *Party Politics in India*, p. 175.

71. Naravane, *Modern Indian Thought*, p. 184; O'Malley, ed., *Modern India and the West*, p. 98; Varma, *Modern Indian Political Thought*, p. 336; Payne, *Life and Death of Mahatma Gandhi*, p. 509.
72. Kumarappa, ed., *Hindu Dharma*, p. 10.
73. Philips and Wainwright, eds., *Partition of India*, p. 158 ff.; O'Malley, ed., *Modern India and the West*, p. 755.
74. O'Malley, ed., *Modern India and the West*, pp. 748, 752, 755.
75. Philips and Wainwright, eds., *Partition of India*, p. 375 ff.
76. Smith, *India as a Secular State*, pp. 96–97.
77. Ibid., p. 481.
78. Ibid., p. 480.
79. Ibid., p. 482.
80. Ibid., pp. 482–483.
81. Nayar, *Minority Politics in the Punjab*, p. 321.
82. Weiner, *Party Politics in India*, p. 172.
83. Ibid., p. 172. Also see Lamb, *India*, pp. 128, 265.
84. See Weiner, *Party Politics in India*, pp. 171–174.
85. Ibid., p. 171.
86. Creel, "Secularization and the Hindu Tradition," p. 111.
87. de Bary, ed., *Sources of Indian Tradition*, p. 880.
88. Palmer, *The Indian Political System*, p. 226.
89. Hardgrave, Jr., *India: Government and Politics in a Developing Nation*, p. 120.

BIBLIOGRAPHY

Aiyar, S. P., and R. Srinivasan, eds. *Studies in Indian Democracy*, New Delhi: Allied Publishers Private Ltd., 1965.
Baxter, Craig. *The Jana Sangh: A Biography of an Indian Political Party.* Philadelphia: University of Pennsylvania Press, 1969.
Bhaskaran, R. *Sociology of Politics.* New Delhi: Asia Publishing House, 1967.
Brass, Paul R. *Language, Religion and Politics in North India.* London: Cambridge University Press, 1974.
Chatterji, Saral K., ed. *Political Prospects in India: A Post-Election Enquiry.* Madras: Christian Institute for the Study of Religion and Society, 1971.
Creel, Austin B. "Secularization and the Hindu Tradition." *Journal of Religious Studies* 5, No. 1–2 (Spring-Autumn 1974): 103–119.
Curran, J. *Militant Hinduism in Indian Politics: A Study of the R.S.S..* New York: Institute of Pacific Relations, 1951.
de Bary, Wm. Theodore, ed. *Sources of Indian Tradition.* New York: Columbia University Press, 1958.
Dodwell, H. H., ed. *The Cambridge History of India*, Vol. 6. New Delhi: S. Chand and Co., 1974.
Golwalker, M. S. *Bunch of Thoughts.* Bangalore: Vikrama Prakashan, 1966.
Hardgrave, Robert L., Jr., *India: Government and Politics in a Developing Nation.* New York: Harcourt Brace Jovanovich, 1975.
Hartmann, Horst. *Political Parties in India*, New Delhi: Meenakshi Prakashan, 1977.

Joshi, Puran Chandra. *They Must Meet Again.* Bombay: People's Publishing House, 1945.

Kashyap, Subhash, C., ed. *Indian Parties and Politics.* Delhi: Institute of Constitutional and Parliamentary Studies, 1972.

Kothari, Rajni. *Politics in India.* Boston: Little, Brown and Co., 1970.

Kumarappra, Bharatan, ed. *Hindu Dharma.* Ahmedabad: Navajivan Publishing House, 1950.

Lamb, Beatrice Pitney. *India: A World in Transition.* New York: Praeger Publishers, 1975.

Majumdar, R. C., ed. *Struggle for freedom.* Bombay: Bharatiya Vidya Bhavan, 1969.

———, H. C. Raychaudhuri, and Kalikinkar Datta. *An Advanced History of India.* New York: St. Martin's Press, 1967.

Malik, Hafeez. *Moslem Nationalism in India and Pakistan.* Washington, D.C.: Public Affairs Press, 1963.

Misra, B. B. *The Indian Political Parties.* Delhi: Oxford University Press, 1976.

Naik, J. A. *The Great Janata Revolution.* New Delhi: S. Chand and Co. Ltd., 1977.

Naravane, Vishwanath S. *Modern Indian Thought.* New Delhi: Orient Longman, 1978.

Nayar, Balden Raj. *Minority Politics in the Punjab.* Princeton, N.J.: Princeton University Press, 1966.

Noorani, A. G. *India's Constitution and Politics.* Bombay: Jaico Publishing House, 1970.

O'Malley, L.S.S., ed. *Modern India and the West.* London: Oxford University Press, 1941.

Palmer, Norman D. *The Indian Political System.* 2d ed. Boston: Houghton Mifflin Co., 1971.

Park, Richard L., and Irene Tinker, eds. *Leadership and Political Institutions in India.* Princeton, N.J.: Princeton University Press, 1959, Ch. 4.

Payne, Robert. *The Life and Death of Mahatma Gandhi.* New York: E.P. Dutton and Co., 1969.

Philips, C. H., and Mary Doreen Wainwright, eds. *The Partition of India.* Cambridge, Mass.: MIT Press, 1970.

Puri, Geeta. *Bharatiya Jana Sangh Organisation and Ideology Delhi: A Case Study.* New Delhi: Sterling Publishers Put Ltd., 1980.

Seminar 216 (August 1977), 229 (September 1978).

Smith, Donald Eugene. *India as a Secular State.* Princeton, N.J.: Princeton University Press, 1963.

———. *Religion and Political Development.* Boston: Little, Brown and Co., 1970.

———. *Religion and Political Modernization.* New Haven, Conn.: Yale University Press, 1974.

———. *Religion, Politics, and Social Change in the Third World.* New York: Free Press, 1971.

———. *South Asian Politics and Religion.* Princeton, N.J.: Princeton University Press, 1966.

Upadhyaya, Pt. Deendayal, Shree Guruji, and Shri D. B. Thengdi. *The Integral Approach.* New Delhi: Deendayal Research Institute, 1979.

Varma, Vishwanath Prasad. *Modern Indian Political Thought.* Agra: Lakhsmi Narain Agarwal, 1964.

Varshney, Manga Ram. *Jana Sangh-R.S.S. and Balraj Madhok*. Aligarh: Manga Ram Varshney, no year.

Weiner, Myron. *Party Politics in India*. Princeton, N.J.: Princeton University Press, 1957.

———. *The Politics of Scarcity*. Chicago: University of Chicago Press, 1962.

Zaidi, A. Moin. *The Great Upheaval*. New Delhi: Orientalia, 1972.

8

Buddhism and Politics in Sri Lanka and Other Theravāda Nations Since 1945

NATHAN KATZ

The statistics are astounding. With a per capita gross national product (GNP) of $179 per annum, Sri Lanka has achieved a physical quality of life index (PQLI) of 82, a rating entirely unprecedented among low-income countries and one that compares favorably with many countries enjoying a per capita GNP ten to twenty times higher than does Sri Lanka.[1] If one correlates Sri Lanka's PQLI with its per capita GNP, one may conclude that Sri Lanka has done more for its citizens, considering its wealth, than any other country in the world. One goal of this chapter is to account for this unique accomplishment. Certainly, such factors as its vibrant Buddhist tradition and its sustained commitment to democratic, socialist development loom large in this regard.

This chapter employs an approach consonant with contemporary Third World theory, one that focuses on those discourses (in Foucault's sense of the term) which constitute politics. Sri Lanka evidences both parallels and divergences from standard Third World theory, both of which are instructive and which might help to explain the remarkable accomplishment alluded to above. If it is the case that Sri Lanka provides a paradigm of a developing nation which "works," then both its commonality with other developing nations and its uniqueness are necessary themes for this study.

THE DATA

A PQLI rating unprecedented among the world's poorer nations has attracted the attention of development theorists to Sri Lanka. The PQLI, which has superseded per capita GNP as a reliable index of development, measures the physical quality of life by considering such factors as life expectancy, infant

Note: Select terms used in this chapter are defined in the end-of-chapter glossary.

mortality rate, literacy rate, and distribution of wealth, affirming the adage that "money isn't everything."[2] One key to improving a country's PQLI rating is the development of social infrastructure, systems for the equitable distribution of resources. As Morris David observes, "The Sri Lanka data . . . suggest once again that substantial PQLI improvement depends on the presence of a solid social infrastructure and cannot be generated merely by some quick technological or medical innovation."[3] Such infrastructure, which correlates with an amelioration of wealth disparities among Sri Lanka's socio-economic classes, as we will see, is derived largely from the Buddhist principles of social organization which have pervaded this nation for more than two millennia.

Sri Lanka's PQLI of 82 does not tell the whole story. If we take per capita GNP as a measure of a country's total wealth, then the ratio between PQLI and per capita GNP should indicate how well a country has utilized its resources. One would expect countries with high per capita GNPs to attain high PQLIs, and while this is generally true (the United States, for example, with per capita GNP of $7,024 maintains a PQLI of 94), there are notable exceptions. (The United Arab Emirates has the world's highest per capita GNP, $14,368, but a PQLI of only 34.) Similarly, countries that are poorer in terms of per capita GNP would be expected to have lower PQLIs (such as Mali, with $90 and 15, respectively), and it is here that Sri Lanka is exceptional ($179 and 82). The accompanying table taken from Morris's study, is instructive.[4]

Country	PQLI	Per Capita GNP
Sri Lanka	82	$179
Kampuchea	40	$70
Burma	51	$105
Vietnam	54	$189
Thailand	68	$318
Singapore	83	$2,111
Laos	31	$70

The first thing one notices in the table is the extent to which Sri Lanka stands alone in providing its people with a high PQLI despite a low per capita GNP. Other Southeast Asian Buddhist countries have been logged as well, and although there are clear exceptions to the rule (notably Laos, Kampuchea, and Singapore), it should be noted that Sri Lanka is not alone in making democratic use of its resources. One sees that Burma, Thailand, and Vietnam, all to the upper left quadrant of the table, follow Sri Lanka's paradigm, even if they do not match its accomplishment. Laos and Kampuchea suffer from excruciatingly low per capita GNPs (each $70), while Singapore, now considered "developed," provides a high PQLI along with its substantial per capita GNP, the highest in the region by a considerable margin. Yet a pattern emerges, with Sri Lanka leading the way, of Southeast Asian Buddhist nations scoring relatively high PQLIs despite very low per capita GNPs.

Returning to Sri Lanka, we find three factors combine to produce its high PQLI, which is claimed to be an unethnocentric measure that focuses as much on distribution of wealth as on wealth itself (as does the per capita GNP figure). Its literacy rate (percentage of the population over fifteen years old who are literate) was 81 percent in 1975. Current estimates put this number at nearly 90 percent. These numbers compare well with literacy rates among high-income countries (i.e., above $2,000 per year) of 84.1 percent and is unprecedented among low-income countries (per capita GNPs below $300) which average 24.3 percent. Certainly, the traditional valorization of literacy within Buddhism helps to account for this statistic, as Burma (60 percent) and Thailand (79 percent) also score very highly.

Sri Lanka also enjoys a low infant mortality rate. Infant deaths per thousand range from 229 (in Gabon) to seven (in Sweden). Sri Lanka's rate is 45, and no other low-income country scores below one hundred, the average for this group being 149.8. Once again, Sri Lanka scores within the parameters common to high-income countries which average 36.1 infant deaths per thousand.

Similarly, Sri Lanka's life expectancy at age one was 70.2 years in the early 1970s, a number consonant with high-income countries (average: 71.5 years). No other low-income country averages as many as sixty years. All of these statistics, it must be remembered, have been accomplished with a per capita GNP of $179.

As Morris comments, "At the moment, understanding of how and why these favorable aberrations have come about is limited."[5] Although no comprehensive explanation is promised, this issue will be addressed by an examination of the varying "discourses of liberation" which have been employed in Sri Lanka since independence. Reference will be made to analogous elements in political discourse in Burma and Thailand as appropriate, although each of these countries has quite distinctive and unique modern political histories.

THE DISCOURSE

A study of political discourse as related to Sri Lanka must be done in a context. The context selected for this chapter is Third World theory, the study of colonial and post-colonial domination of "low-income countries" by wealthier, more powerful countries which tend to be European (a term meant to include North America), Christian, and of the First or Second Worlds.

Such a theoretical approach reveals two distinct, yet mutually related, discourses. The first of these is termed "discourse of oppression" wherein the colonized (or to-be-colonized) culture is denigrated as passive, reactionary, inert, and "womanish."[6] The colonizing power, inversely, is considered to be progressive, active, and "manly." Such a discourse both mirrors and allows for the colonizer's "penetration" of the cultures, economies, and religions of the colonized. Edward Said recently published a very fine study of the colonizer's discourse about Islamic worlds.[7] Some of the theoretical assumptions underlying this present study can be found there, although the nuances of discourse about Buddhist worlds diverge from those about Islamic worlds, as a result largely of historical factors.

The movement from a colonized status to political independence has usually been foreshadowed by a "discourse of liberation." Although the particularities of this liberative discourse in Sri Lanka (and, to some extent, in Burma and Thailand) is the topic for a later section of this chapter, analogies between the Buddhist worlds and other nations that gained independence since the Second World War will become clear. Liberative discourse in general valorizes traditional (i.e., pre-colonial) patterns of social organization, rulership, religiosity, and economic relations. Some of the clearest examples of this liberative discourse can be found in such tracts as the anonymous *The Revolt in the Temple*[8] and in the report of the Buddhist Commission of Inquiry.[9]

This Buddhist resurgence responded to the structures of oppressive discourse largely by inverting these structures. For example, if the European colonizer-missionary imagines Sri Lankan Buddhism to be "superstitious" as opposed to his "enlightened Christianity," then the liberative discourse construes Buddhism as "scientific" and Christianity as "irrational." Indeed, contemporary Sri Lankans often point to the famous Panadura Debates (1871) as a turning point in the nationalist, anti-imperialist movements. In these debates, a Buddhist monk is reported to have intellectually decimated a Christian missionary precisely by presenting his tradition as progressive, rational, and scientific, as one that attempts to account for the human condition with no recourse to unsupportable hypotheses, such as the God-hypothesis, beyond the immediacy of human experience. What is to be noted in this context is the very crucial role religion has played in the articulation of both oppressive and liberative discourses.

As the liberative discourse inverts the structure of the oppressive discourse, the two remain unhappily wedded. Thus, the discourse of liberation leads, inexorably, to new contradictions. This might become clearer by pointing to an analogy from modern American politics, the discourse of "Black Power" in the 1960s.

Black power discourse arose in response to white racist discourse. White racists reflected and maintained their privilege over blacks by claims to racial superiority. Of course, oppression is never complete until the oppressed come to accept the fundamental correctness, the justice, of his or her oppression.[10] Much as the colonized Sri Lankan came to accept, ultimately under the threat of the gunships, the superiority of all things British, from religion to clothing to cuisine, the black American came to accept white standards of beauty, spirituality, and language. The black power movement, especially as articulated by Elijah Muhammad, turned the racist's tables, proclaiming the moral and cultural superiority of the black.[11] Of course, this discourse was most effective in re-empowering American blacks by regaining a sense of pride and in rejecting the white's characterizations of black culture. Similarly, understanding Buddhism as scientific and, going a step further, seeking solutions to contemporary problems by recourse to classical

Sinhalese culture (and rejecting those of the colonizer) was a dynamic catalyst for the "Buddhist renaissance."

In both cases, however, a contradiction was unearthed. In the case of black power discourse, many blacks rejected the claim to racial superiority. The problem, as analyzed by Stokely Carmichael and Charles V. Hamilton, was oppression per se, and the goal was "to deniggerize the earth," not to replace one group's privilege by another's.[12] Similarly, in proclaiming the superiority of all things Sinhalese, little creative role was left over for other ethnic communities of the island: the Tamils, Burghers (Eurasians), and Moors (Muslims). Indeed, precisely this contradiction has manifested itself in the communal difficulties that continue to plague Sri Lanka, most extremely found in the underground "Tigers of Eelam," a Tamil separatist organization.

One finds creative responses to the problem of communalism in such organizations as the Sarvodaya Shramadana Movement, an indigenous movement for the economic and spiritual development of the individual, the village, the nation, and the world. The genius of Sarvodaya is precisely its ability to overcome communalism. The Sarvodaya Movement indicates a new phase in liberative discourse, one that seeks to unearth and overcome the contradictions inherent in a discourse which responded to oppression by inverting, rather than subverting, its categories. This chapter will also view the Guevarist Jatika Vimukti Peramuna (JVP, "People's Liberation Front"), which nearly toppled the traditional leftist government in 1971 and which drew its support from bhikkhu-cadres, disaffected youth from all communities of Sri Lanka, and traditional Sinhalese nationalists. While the JVP's 1971 insurgency failed, its anti-communalism seems to be a theme adopted by Sarvodaya—although the two movements are, on most ideological points, quite distinct.

By an analysis of these forms of discourse, from oppression to liberation in both phases, one can begin to account for Sri Lanka's remarkable achievements in providing a decent standard of living for its people despite scant rescources.

The Discourse of Oppression

The image of the Buddhist monk as a public leader engaging in social and political activities has been obscured, and deliberately so, by Western colonialists and their accompanying Christian missionaries. By imposing a particular type of Christian monasticism upon the Buddhist clergy, restricting the clergy's activity to individual purification and temple ministries, the colonial administrators dispossessed the bhikkhus of their influence on the public life of their people and actually succeeded in instituting a tradition of Buddhist recluses, to the near exclusion of other types of clergy.

—Edmund F. Perry[13]

The image of Buddhism as an other-worldly religion, unconcerned with and aloof from everyday problems of politics, economics, and society, has been the lynchpin in the discourse of oppression. This image, commonplace in introductory textbooks about world religions, has not been a mere intellectual misapprehension but has been a deliberate mainstay in the colonial administration of Sri Lanka, Burma, and elsewhere. By separating the saṅgha from society, a power vacuum was created and immediately filled by the colonizer. Buddhist society, once it had been conceptually, economically, and militarily divorced from Buddhism, was made amenable to colonial manipulation under the guises of liberal secularism and so-called modernity. Claiming the neutrality of the secularist was the colonizer's erasure of the dismantling of Sri Lankan society and its re-shaping after the economic model of a plantation economy which had been so successful (from the colonizer's perspective) in the West Indies. It is worse than pathetic, it is reactionary and racist, to perpetuate the colonizer's myth (especially as articulated by Max Weber) in contemporary scholarship. Yet, as we learn from Foucault, images, myths, and discourses perpetuate themselves. They become ingrained in perception itself, and we see that perception is a thoroughly political phenomenon.

Even the earliest accounts of Sri Lanka are imaginary in the sense that the image found in the would-be colonizer's text was a classical instance of an illusion (in Freud's sense), a construction conditioned by wishes and desires more than by an innocent perception. Such imagining, according to Albert Memmi, was the first indispensable step toward colonization: "Just as the bourgeoisie proposes an image of the proletariat, the existence of the colonizer requires that an image of the colonized be suggested. These images become excuses without which the presence and conduct of the colonizer, and that of a bourgeois, would seem shocking."[14] Just as early merchant travelers (and therefore foreshadowers of the colonizers) saw Sri Lanka as a gem-ladened treasure chest ripe for plundering, so the early colonizers imagined the land as a backward *version* of their own Europe.[15]

It followed, then, that if Protestant Europe's "progress" required the separation of Church and state, so must Buddhism become divorced from society for Sri Lanka to likewise progress, if by progress we understand its receptivity to the thrust of European technology (meaning a plantation economy) and secular enlightenment (read: Christianization). This process has been ably described by Philip Stevens:

So the colonial situation is founded on an imaginative encounter: one between the (European) Self and the Other; and between the Self and what is seen as its potential, its destiny. Imaginative, but not imaginary or lacking in reality: for the real fact of the first encounters between a technologically ascendent Europe and a technologically retarded non-European world was a situation of European power opposed to the weakness of the Other. A rising European bourgeoisie, already consolidating its new economic system of competitive free enterprise with the formation of a proletariat, a class of those who didn't make it in the dog-eat-dog world of the market, found in the non-European world whole continents full of ready-made failures. As history has shown us, the European powers wasted no time in "proletarianizing" these economic sluggards, setting them firmly in their place vis-a-vis the proven victors in the struggle for fiscal supremacy. The way in which this image of the colonized was made real was fully dependent, in its opening stages, on the military superiority of the western powers. Gradually the need for a constant military reassertion waned, as more and more the colonized came to accept and even perpetuate the image which has been proposed for them by the Europeans.[16]

Although this superiority to which Stevens alludes was, first and foremost, a military question, it was disguised in the colonizer's imagining as a cultural (if not racial) superiority. Thus, the "natives' " backwardness became imagined as their superstitious religions, as their conservative family orientations, and as their "laziness." We have Max Weber to thank for ascribing this backwardness to a religion which "is a specifically unpolitical and anti-political status religion."[17] What Weber is saying is that any religion that is not Protestantism is culpable for backwardness, which itself is an invitation for colonial penetration and manipulation. The discourse of oppression boils down to the claim that "they were asking for it."

The oppressive myth, as has been argued, is not produced in toto prior to the colonial adventure. Nor does it emerge only after the colonizer's status is assured. Rather, the fact of colonization and the discourse of oppression arise interdependently. As traditional education was usurped and replaced by missionary education, as the King of England nominally assumed the traditional, royal role as protector of Buddhism, and as the Buddhist saṅgha was forced to fit itself into Weberian paradigms, the religious studies establishment of the day tripped over itself in haste to provide theoretical justifications for the wholesale dismantling of indigenous culture and society by the colonial administration. Some of these administrative strategies are explored in the companion to this chapter,[18] but they included the isolation of the saṅgha, the reconstruction of a plantation economy after the model of the West Indies, the imposition of missionary educational systems, and the greater and greater removal of Buddhist influence from Sri Lankan polity. Another crucial factor of colonial rule was the exacerbation of communal tensions among Sri Lanka's ethnic groups by a blatant favoritism of all communities except the Sinhalese majority.

As we have seen, the colonizer's penetration and administration of the colony are effective to the degree that the colonized came to accept the justice of their colonized situation as embodied in the discourse of oppression, concretized into an image whereby the colonized becomes Other to him/herself. Liberation, which is a process and not an act, therefore, begins with a counter-myth that is articulated in response to the oppressive myth. We will move, then, to an examination of this discourse of liberation, also known as the "Buddhist renaissance."

The Discourse of Liberation

Following the disempowerment of indigenous cultural forms around 1850 when a plantation economy was established, the Buddhist saṅgha was effectively divorced from social realities, and education was placed in the hands of Christian missionaries, one finds the emergence of early forms of liberative discourse. As early as 1828, a reemergent nationalist consciousness focused on the composition of parodies of Christian missionary writings.[19]

Similarly, as the persecution of Buddhism and the experiences of colonization became identified, a reemergent Buddhism and the anti-colonial struggle also became identified. When Bhikkhu Migvettuwatte Gunananda founded the Society for the Propagation of Buddhism in 1862, its missionary techniques—pamphleting, preaching, and debating—closely resembled those of the Christians. We see here a typical aspect of the discourse of liberation: the inversion of the structures of the discourse of oppression. This inversion led to new and creative forms of Buddhism, almost as an unintended consequence.

For example, to counter the fissure between saṅgha and the state, Burmese Prime Minister U Nu invited meditation masters Ledi Sayadaw and Mahasi Sayadaw, both bhikkhus, and lay meditation teacher U Ba Khin into his government in 1949. The result was the development of the Burmese *sātipaṭṭhāna* method, which has become the most widely practiced meditational technique in the Theravāda world and beyond, one that emphasizes lay participation.[20] New and creative roles for the laity also evolved in Sri Lanka, largely through such lay organizations as the All-Ceylon Buddhist Congress and the Young Men's Buddhist Association. One consequence of the Buddhist revival, then, was a redefinition of the traditional roles of saṅgha and laity within the Buddhist culture.

Other major figures in the anti-imperialist Buddhist revival included the Anagarika Dharmapala, whose *Return to Righteousness* became a manifesto of liberative, nationalist discourse.[21] Similarly, a close association of Dharmapala's, Colonel Henry Steele Olcott, an American who arrived in Sri Lanka in 1880, proceeded to struggle single-mindedly against Christian missionary domination of education. His National Trust Scheme led to the establishment of Buddhist colleges which subverted Christian domination.

Sinhalese Buddhist nationalism entered into various coalitions and dialogues with the anti-imperialist, leftist parties and labor unions during the early part of the century. Saṅgha members took the lead in this Marxist-Buddhist coalition, most especially a group of monks from the prestigious Vidyalankara Pirivena who came to be known as the Vidyalankara Group. One of its members, the eminent Ven. Dr. Walpola Rahula, has provided the theoretical underpinnings for their activism in a most important work, *The Heritage of Bhikkhu*. In this work, he argues that only by reconnecting the saṅgha with society can rational development take place. Politics are understood to encompass all human intercourse, and the Christian monastic paradigm of the socially aloof monk, so tenaciously defended by Weberians, is explicitly rejected. Identifying the interests of the saṅgha and those of the nation, Rahula reads the history of Sri Lanka:

A bhikkhu named Theraputtābhaya, at the time about to become an arahant, aroused and inspired by religious and national ardor, renounced the robes and joined the army [which was fighting to expel Cōḷa invaders]. . . . At the request of Prince Duṭagāmunu, a large number of bhikkhus representing the Order of the Saṅgha accompanied the army. The Prince declared that the sight of bhikkhus was "auspicious" and "a protection." More and more people joined and supported the army when they saw the co-operation of the bhikkhus. Blessed and inspired by the presence of bhikkhus, the warriors fought with great courage and determination. From this time patriotism and the religion of the Sinhalese became inseparably linked.[22]

The dialogue between the leftists and Buddhist monks and laypeople continued to develop a Sinhalese Buddhist ideology, finally coalescing around the 1956 Buddha Jayanti celebrating the 2500th anniversary of the death of Lord Buddha. An anonymous work, *The Revolt in the Temple*, extolled religion, race, and language as the pillars for a revitalized Sinhalese Buddhist society and fervently rejected post-colonial structures of Christianity, Europe, and English.[23] At the same time, the government-appointed Buddhist Commission of Inquiry issued a report, *The Betrayal of Buddhism*, which was scathing in its criticisms of how Portuguese, Dutch, British, and some post-colonial administrators had systematically encroached on Buddhism's rightful place in society. As the report concludes,

For what is the history of Ceylon during the last four hundred years but a long and poignant chronicle of the Buddhist tolerance in the face of oppression and injustice? Who but the Buddhists tolerated harassment by the Roman Catholic Portuguese to give shelter and employment to Muslims? Or endured similar treatment from the Dutch to shelter Roman Catholics? Who but the Buddhists tolerated the rank injustice of the foreign rulers who used the revenue from one of the most sacred places of Buddhist worship, the Dalada Maligawa [i.e., the Temple of the Tooth in Kandy], to pay for the construction of St. Paul's Cathedral? Or the like injustice of destroying a Buddhist Vihara in Kotte to erect in its stead a Christian school? Who but the Buddhists tolerated the extortion from them of four hundred pounds a year for the building of Christian churches?[24]

The report argues for a renewal of Buddhism's traditional role within Sinhalese society, especially in education, and for the revitalization of a saṅgha which had suffered centuries of neglect.

Similarly, the Lanka Bauddha Mandalaya (Buddhist Council of Ceylon) identified Buddhism with Sinhalese national identity. In a report prepared for the Buddha Jayanti celebrations, *An Event of Dual Significance*, the parallels are explicit:

. . . for us in Ceylon, the Buddha Jayanti coincides with another day of national significance, namely the 2500th anniversary of the birth of the nation. . . . The coming of Vijaya is undoubtedly the most significant event in the annals of this island [i.e., in the *Mahāvaṁsa*] for with it began her written history. In the course of 2500 years was built the great edifice of our nation whose mighty bond of fellow feeling, oneness of purpose and unity of effort keep the diverse races of our population together. . . . Therefore it benefits us Ceylonese to celebrate the twenty-fifth centenary of the birth of the nation, which occurs at a time when as a nation we have regained our Independence and are putting forth our best effort for our own economic and cultural amelioration, besides contributing, in whatever small way, towards the peace and well-being of the world.[25]

As though foreshadowing significant political themes of the 1960s through 1980s, the Lanka Bauddha Mandalaya's report expresses the hope that its liberative discourse could at the same time promote Sinhalese nationalism and serve to bind together the various ethnic communities of Sri Lanka in the common endeavor of nation-building. As has been shown by Robert Melson and Howard Wolpe, the expansion of an economic and industrial base has not led to the amelioration of communal fissues in many developing countries.[26] On the contrary, by focusing on the case of Nigeria, Melson and Wolpe conclude "that modernization, far from destroying communalism, in time both reinforces communal conflict and creates the conditions for the formation of entirely new communal groups."[27] This is precisely the contradiction which the discourse of liberation unearths.

Liberative discourse, as a response to colonial oppression, takes recourse to traditional cultural models as a way of empowering formerly colonized people against the cultural and economic domination that pervades both colonized and post-colonial nations. However, by virtue of its recourse to a "pure" society prior to the advent of the colonizers, portions of the population (in the case of Sri Lanka, the Tamils in particular) become mythically disenfranchised from full participation in the modern nation. This "reconquest myth," as it has been called, leads to a second phase of liberative discourse, one that subverts rather than inverts the discourse of oppression by destroying its very structures.[28] No longer on the defensive, segments of the Buddhist, Sinhalese majority population have been most creative in articulating indigenous ideologies that make use of Buddhism's traditional spirit of tolerance, egalitarianism, and cooperation. No better example of the second-phase liberative discourse could be found than in the Sarvodaya Shramadana Movement.

Sarvodaya and the Future

The Sarvodaya Shramadana Movement heralds a new phase in the discourse of liberation, one that does not rely on an inversion of oppressive discourse, but that subverts its structures in the sense that it seeks to expound a non-communalist, Buddhist value orientation for the process of development. Before addressing this movement, however, it is important to consider one of its predecessors, the People's Liberation Front (JVP), a radical, Guevarist movement that engaged in an attempted armed revolution known as the Insurgency (*trastavāda*) in 1971.

Only Joanna Macy has pointed to any affinity between the Insurgency and Sarvodaya workers.[29] She points out that many Sarvodaya organizers had been insurgents in 1971. The affinities between the Insurgency and Sarvodaya, I'd argue, go deeper. Both movements grew out of the Buddhist renaissance discussed above; both are operative outside of the electoral system; both involve large numers of bhikkhus as well as laypeople, and both redefine the relationships between saṅgha and laity; both involve women in all strata of their movements, and both are anti-hierarchical; both are thoroughly revolutionary, the Insurgency employing overt class struggle and the Sarvodaya using village-based development as its chief organizing method; both are criticized for receiving funding from abroad; both groups are lauded for their virtuous conduct (*sīla*) and lifestyle; both emphasize national self-sufficiency as a paramount value; both claim to express a Buddhist radicalism; and both seek to overcome the communal fissures of Sri Lankan society through a direct involvement of minorities in their campaigns. For these reasons and despite widely disparate ideological/philosophical positions, the Insurgency may be regarded as a step toward this second phase of liberative discourse, and the Sarvodaya Movement as, essentially, a refinement of such discourse.

The 1971 Insurgency very nearly toppled the Sri Lanka Freedom Party (SLFP)-led leftist government of Mrs. Sirima Bandaranaike. It drew its support from Sinhala-educated peasants, teachers, physicians, and bhikkhus and advocated a Guevarist sort of Marxian analysis coupled with Buddhist nationalism. The movement also caught the romantic sentiments of much of the nation. Agehananda Bharati, quite unsympathetic to both the Insurgency and the attempted Marxist-Buddhist synthesis, reports on this sentiment:

They were said to be heroic; they were said to have taken vows of extreme, acute austerity—no gambling, no smoking, and no sex in spite of the revolutionary co-presence of young women among the insurgents, a co-presence which made them seem much more accessible than in normal village settings. It was this element, actual or fictitious, that drew a good deal of sympathy. A young monk in a small, but well known *vihāraya* in Payingamuwa, near Matale, said this to an audience of half a dozen men and one woman: "What they (the *trastavādi*) do to the people is bad; but what they do for themselves is good—they have *sīla*; they control themselves; they have the virtues Buddhists are told to create." Courage, singleness of purpose, and the general deferment of pleasure and creaturely comforts in view of a goal were all seen as entirely commendable.[30]

The Insurgency, of course, did not win the day, and several thousand of its activists were imprisoned together. However, while incarcerated, one activist told me, they practiced meditation and refined their political analysis. When these inmates were granted a general amnesty in 1977 by then newly elected Prime Minister J. R. Jayawardene, many reorgnized the JVP as a political party and their leader, Rohan Wijeweera, announced that they would seek their revolution through the electoral process. (It will be interesting to see whether the JVP and the traditional left, especially the SLFP, can effect a reconciliation, as many JVPers recall the severe response to their Insurgency by the SLFP government.) Many others joined the ranks of the Sarvodaya Shramadana Movement.

The Sarvodaya Shramadana Movement traces its origin to 1958 when a high school science teacher, A. T. Ariyaratne, led some of his students from Nalanda College, Colombo, on a work camp during a school recess. The work camp was designed to familiarize the urban, middle-class students with the realities of village life, and was termed "shramadana" from *dāna*, giving, and *shrama*, labor. The students gave their labor to such village projects as road repair, well digging, and the like.

This modest experiment grew so rapidly that the movement is now the largest non-governmental organization in the nation, involving more than 4,000 villages and possessing an organization virtually on a scale with the government. As Macy comments:

As a people's self-help movement, which grew from a handful of young volunteers to be Sri Lanka's largest non-governmental organization with activities in over four thousand villages, Sarvodaya serves as a dramatic and instructive example of the relevance of tradition to development; for it bases both its theory and its practice on a clearly articulated value-system drawn from its culture's religious heritage.[31]

Having studied Gandhian politics under Vinoba Bhave in India, Ariyaratne adopted the Mahātma's term, *sarvodaya* ("for the benefit of all"), adding it to his name for the movement and re-translating it as "for the awakening of all." His notion of "awakening" is operative on four levels: the individual, the village, the nation, and the world. "Awakening" is a clearly Buddhist term, and it is here applied in both its spiritual and social senses. To awaken a village means to restructure and re-empower it. The village, which is the basis of all South Asian society, has become decadent as seen in its poverty, oppression, conflict, and disease. The cause of this decadence is a spirit of competition, possessiveness, and disunity. By the practice of selflessness, love, cooperation, constructive activity, and egalitarianism, this decadence could be overcome. Finally, the transformed or awakened village (*gramodaya*) is characterized by health, unity, organization, cultural and spiritual development, and education. Structurally, it should be obvious, Ariyaratne's analysis of the village parallels the Buddha's analysis of the human condition as presented in the four holy truths, the cornerstone of the Dharma.

The awakening of the individual (*purushodaya*), effected through meditation and cooperative labor, remains the basis of the movement. As Macy notes, "[T]he transformation of the personality—the building of a new person—is presented as the chief aim of the Movement."[32] The basis for individual awakening is the re-empowerment of the individual (*swashakti*) and of the people (*janshakti*), just as powerlessness is understood as the basis for decadence.

Following from individual awakening and village awakening are national awakening (*deshodaya*) and universal awakening (*vishvodaya*). One can only imagine an awakened nation, but it seems that the Sarvodaya Movement, which characterizes itself as non-political in the sense that it rejects party politics, has already gone a long way toward the creation of an alternate social structure and organization (and thus does not simply invert the structures of oppression but creatively builds new ones). It has been noted that if Ariyaratne chose to stand for election, he could easily be elected President of the country—an office to which he does not aspire, because of his philosophical (not ideological, as Sarvodaya understands ideology) view of society and development. Universal awakening remains the movement's long-range goal, and in this context it is intriguing to note that offshoots of Sarvodaya have begun to sprout in other developing nations, such as Thailand and Mali.

The movement also maintains that the spiritual goal of awakening provides the basic value structure under which development projects become subsumed. As Macy comments, "Community development is seen as the means for helping the people realize goals that are essentially religious."[33] She elaborates:

The Movement's use of Buddhist teachings stands in contrast to the Buddhist Marxism articulated by some Sinhalese monks in the 1950s and 1960s, who tended to present the Dharma as a form of dialectical materialism. Sarvodaya's call to social engagement keeps the spiritual factor preeminent—both in adducing the roots of inequality and in defining the goals of development.[34]

Philosopher Padmasiri de Silva, quite sympathetic to Sarvodaya's goals and methods, argues that development could be rationalized only when based on a value orientation.[35] Ariyaratne echoes this theme:

The person himself must awaken to his true needs and true strengths if the society is to prosper without conflict and injustice. From the wisdom embodied in our religious traditions we can cull principles for that kind of personal and collective awakening. That is what Sarvodaya has done—listening to the villagers, who constitute eighty percent of our country, and articulating a challenge in terms of the ideals they still revere and in words that make sense to them.[36]

To clarify his notion of "true needs," Ariyaratne has enumerated ten basic needs that serve "both to guide village projects, giving equal priority to some factors which appear 'non-economic,' and to help Sarvodayans set their other wants into perspective . . . [which] appear as motivated by greed, sloth or ignorance.[37] The ten are: water, food, housing, clothing, health care, communication, fuel, education, a clean, safe and beautiful environment, and a spiritual and cultural life. Indeed, many Sri Lankans, such as de Silva, who have thought through the question of goals for development have concluded that their goal should not be the reduplication of First World living standards, even were that possible, but living by an "ethic of restraint,"[38] so characteristic of what has been termed "Buddhist economics."[39]

The movement subverts communal issues through several methods. As the movement is more action-oriented than theoretical, the actual sharing of work, food, and living arrangements during the work camps has had profound impact on many of its participants. Basing a particular project in a Buddhist temple, a

Christian church, a mosque, or a Hindu kovil (temple) the movement seeks to stimulate a liberality from local religious communities. Each day's work begins with a prayer meeting in which the religion of the smallest minority of workers present is the first represented in the interfaith liturgy. Commenting on this anti-communalist emphasis of the movement, Ariyaratne writes:

... the Sarvodaya Movement, while originally inspired by the Buddhist tradition, is active throughout our multi-ethnic society, working with Hindu, Muslim, and Christian communities and involving scores of Hindu, Muslim, and Christian co-workers. Our message of awakening transcends any effort to categorize it as the teaching of a particular creed. Through the philosophy of Sarvodaya—based on loving-kindness, compassionate action, altruistic joy and equanimity—people of different faiths and ethnic origins are motivated to carve out a way of life and a path of development founded on these ideals. Because these ideals are universal, Sarvodaya has been able to bring harmony into situations of ethnic and religious conflict that exist here in Sri Lanka, and to play a unique role in allaying hostility by enlisting people in common projects.[40]

Much more could be written about the Sarvodaya Shramadana Movement, but the reader is recommended to many of the movement's own publications[41] as well as many recent studies.[42] The Sarvodaya marks a new phase in liberative discourse, a most hopeful one which subverts rather than inverts the structures of oppression.

CONCLUSIONS

Has our consideration of political discourses helped us to account for the remarkable economic and human achievements of Sri Lanka in providing for its people? To some extent, it does. We have seen a remarkable degree of creativity and fluidity in those discourses that have characterized Sri Lankan politics since independence.

For one thing, Sri Lanka's Buddhist tradition has facilitated the construction of a persuasive liberative discourse. As a defense against the introjection of the colonizer's myth, Buddhism's powerful traditions of egalitarianism, democracy, and compassionate activity were able to counter the trivialization of the tradition by colonizers, religious studies scholars, and missionaries. The image of the temple and the rank, mainstays of traditional Sinhalese Buddhist culture's blending of spiritual and economic concerns, forcefully negates the pernicious effects of oppressive discourse. Futhermore, Buddhism's traditional strengths of philosphic acumen and ethical endeavors (theory and praxis) provide the background for national pride, for the re-empowerment of the people.

More than these traditional strengths, however, one finds very vibrant and creative responses to post-colonialism in contemporary Sri Lanka. As the contradictions of communalism became clear, a new phase of liberative discourse, based on Buddhist principles yet encompassing the nation's religious minorities, emerged. One may hope for the extension of the range of this discourse beyond the Sarvodaya Movement into all arenas of Sri Lankan society.

Yet, as this chapter is being written not all of the news from Sri Lanka is good. Local elections have sparked some degree of communal violence. For the first time since independence, wealth disparities among the classes have been increasing, and this after thirty-five years of a sustained narrowing of these gaps. During my visit to Sri Lanka in January 1982, increased missionary activities were evident, activities exploitative of north-south economic disparities.

All of these facts are reported not to condemn Sri Lanka, but to indicate that the post-colonial situation presents commonalities with other nations that gained independence in recent times. The discourse of oppression, while effectively countered by the Buddhist renaissance and by new, creative stages of liberative discourse, has not magically disappeared. The plantation economy and an unhealthy emphasis on tourism as a means of gaining foreign exchange still are found in Sri Lanka as in many nations of the Third World.

At the moment, two significant experiments are being conducted in Sri Lanka, experiments that have attracted the attention of much of the world. The first is President Jayawardene's placing of Sri Lanka thoroughly within the world economy, allowing its currency to float in the international market and inviting foreign investment in the Mahaweli Scheme which, it is hoped, will provide both irrigation and hydroelectric power. Unemployment has been reduced significantly as a direct result of these policies.

The other experiment is the Sarvodaya Movement. Whether it will remain an extra-governmental, rural development movement, or whether it will somehow, in effect, become Sri Lanka's government remains to be seen. However, as Sri Lanka has effectively and creatively met its problems in the past, so it will continue. The vision presented is one of a non-communalist, Buddhist society and economy. The fact that this vision cannot yet be fully realized or definitively articulated should in no way diminish the compelling power of such a vision.

NOTES

1. The data for this discussion are taken from Morris, *Measuring the Condition of the World's Poor*.
2. Ibid., p. 60.
3. Ibid., p. 76.
4. Ibid., p. 65.
5. Ibid., p. 64.
6. Feminist discourse reveals how the male construction of an image of woman has been paradigmatic for the economic and sexual exploitation of women. I would suggest that it is no accident that ''Mother India'' is so termed. The qualities attributed to colonized peoples are virtually identical with those ascribed to women in sexist discourse.
7. Said, *Orientalism*.
8. Anonymous (D. C. Wijewardene), *The Revolt in the Temple*.
9. Buddhist Commission of Inquiry, *The Betrayal of Buddhism*.

10. Lindsay, *The Myth of a Civilizing Mission.*
11. As discussed by Malcolm X and Alex Haley, *Autobiography of Malcolm X.*
12. Carmichael and Hamilton, *Black Power*, p. 39.
13. Perry, "Forward to the English Edition" of Walpola Rahula, *Heritage of the Bhikkhu*, p. xii.
14. Memmi, *Colonizer and the Colonized*, p. 79.
15. Said, *Orientalism*, pp. 58–59.
16. Stevens, "Image-Realization-Text," a senior paper at Williams College, 1983.
17. Weber, *Religions of India*, p. 206.
18. See Nathan Katz and Stephen D. Sowle, "Theravāda Buddhism and Marxism in the Postwar Era," Chapter 19, in this volume.
19. Phadnis, *Religion and Politics in Sri Lanka*, p. 67.
20. Swearer, *Buddhism and Society in Southeast Asia*, p. 62.
21. Dharmapala, *Return to Righteousness*, Guruge, ed.
22. Rahula, *Heritage of the Bhikkhu*, p. 21.
23. Wijewardene, *Revolt in the Temple.*
24. Buddhist Commission of Inquiry, *Betrayal of Buddhism*, p. 123.
25. Mandalaya, *Event of Dual Significance*, pp. 4–5.
26. Melson and Wolpe, "Modernization and the Politics of Communalism," 1112–1130.
27. Ibid., p. 1113.
28. Smith, "Religion, Politics and the Myth of Reconquest," in Fernando and Kearney, eds., *Modern Sri Lanka*, pp. 83–99.
29. Macy, *Dharma and Development*, p. 23.
30. Bharati, "Monastic and Lay Buddhism in the 1971 Sri Lanka Insurgency," in Smith, ed., *Religion and Conflict in South Asia*, p. 109.
31. Macy, *Dharma and Development*, p. 20.
32. Ibid., p. 32.
33. Ibid., p. 33.
34. Ibid., p. 36.
35. de Silva, *Value Orientations and Nation Building.*
36. Ariyaratne, "Introduction" to Macy, *Dharma and Development*, p. 14.
37. Macy, *Dharma and Development*, p. 27.
38. de Silva, "Basic Needs and the Ethic of Restraint."
39. Schumacher, *Small is Beautiful*, pp. 50–58.
40. Ariyaratne, "Introduction," p. 15.
41. For example: Ariyaratne, *Struggle to Awaken*; Ariyaratne, *Collected Works*, 2 vols.; Ariyaratne, *In Search of Development*; and *Dr. A. T. Ariyaratne Felicitation Volume.*
42. For examples: Macy, *Dharma and Development*; Goulet, *Survival with Integrity*; Kantowsky, *Sarvodaya*; Moore, *Paraprofessionals in Village-Level Development in Sri Lanka*; Ratnapala, *Sarvodaya and the Rodiyas*; and Ratnapala, *The Sarvodaya Movement.*

GLOSSARY

Bhikkhu (Pali): A fully-ordained Buddhist monk.
Buddha Jayanti (Sinhala): The 1956 celebrations throughout the Buddhist world com-

memorating the 2500th anniversary of the death of the Buddha and, in Sri Lanka, the 2500th anniversary of the founding of the Sinhalese "race" by Vijaya.

Burgher (Ceylonese English): Eurasian.

Dāna (Pali and Skt.): Generosity, giving; one of the cardinal Buddhist ethical values.

Deshodaya (Sinhala): "The awakening of the nation," a term used within the Sarvodaya Movement.

Eelam (Tamil): The name proposed for an independent Tamil state in northern and eastern Sri Lanka.

Gramodaya (Sinhala): "The awakening of the village" in Sarvodaya discourse.

Janashakti (Sinhala): The empowerment of the people.

JVP ("Jatika Vimukti Peramuna," Sinhala): "People's Liberation Front," a revolutionary group in 1971, now a political party.

Kovil (Tamil and Sinhala): A Hindu temple.

Mahāvaṃsa (Pali): The "great chronicle" of Buddhism in Sri Lanka, a sixth-century CE Pali text.

Moor (Ceylonese English): Muslim.

PQLI: "Physical quality of life index."

Purushodaya (Sinhala): "The awakening of the individual" in Sarvodaya discourse.

Saṅgha (Pali, Skt., and Sinhala): The order of the Buddhist monks and nuns.

Sarvodaya (Sinhala and Hindi): "For the benefit of all"; in Sarvodaya Movement discourse, "the awakening of all."

Sātipaṭṭhāna (Pali): A form of Buddhist meditation called, in English, "mindfulness."

Shrama (Sinhala): labor.

Sīla (Pali and Sinhala): Virtue.

SLFP: Sri Lanka Freedom Party, a leftist party.

Swashakti (Sinhali): The re-empowerment of the individual.

Tamil: The largest ethnic minority in Sri Lanka, Hindus of south Indian origin.

Trastavāda (Sinhala): The 1971 Insurgency.

Trastavādi (Sinhala): An insurgent.

Vidyalankara Group: A group of bhikkhus from the Vidyalankara Pirivena influential in the "Buddhist renaissance" and in the Buddhist-Marxist synthesis.

Viharāya (Sinahal): A Buddhist temple.

Vishvodaya (Sinhala): "The awakening of the world" in Sarvodaya discourse.

BIBLIOGRAPHY

Ariyaratne, A. T. "Introduction" to Macy, *Dharma and Development.*

———. *A Struggle to Awaken.* Moratuwa, Sri Lanka: Sarvodaya Shramadana Movement, 1978.

———. *Collected Works.* 2 vols. Netherlands: Sarvodaya Research Institute, 1979 and 1980.

———. *In Search of Development: Sarvodaya Effort to Harmonize Tradition with Change.* Moratuwa: Sarvodaya Press, 1981.

Dr. A. T. Ariyaratne Felicitation Volume. Ratmalana, Sri Lanka: Sarvodaya Research Institute, 1981.

Bharati, Agehananda. "Monastic and Lay Buddhism in the 1971 Sri Lanka Insurgency." In Bardwell L. Smith, ed., *Religion and Conflict in South Asia.* Leiden: E. J. Brill, 1976, pp. 102–112.

Buddhist Commission of Inquiry. *The Betrayal of Buddhism.* Balangoda, Sri Lanka: Dharmavijaya Press, 1956.

Carmichael, Stokely, and Charles V. Hamilton. *Black Power: The Politics of Liberation in America.* New York: Vintage Books, 1965.

de Silva, Padmasiri. *Value Orientations and Nation Building.* Colombo: Lake House, 1976.

——. "Basic Needs and the Ethic of Restraint." *Ceylon Daily News,* June 23–24, 1982.

Dharmapala, Anagarika. *The Return to Righteousness.* Edited by Ananda Guruge. Colombo: Government Press, 1965.

Goulet, Denis. *Survival with Integrity: Sarvodaya at the Crossroads.* Colombo: Marga Institute, 1981.

Kantowsky, D. *Sarvodaya: The Other Development.* New Delhi: Vikas, 1980.

Lanka Bauddha Mandalaya. *An Event of Dual Significance.* Colombo: Ministry of Home Affairs, 1956.

Lindsay, Louis. *The Myth of a Civilizing Mission: British Colonialism and the Politics of Symbolic Manipulation.* Kingston, Jamaica: Institute of Social and Economic Research, University of the West Indies, Working Paper No. 31, 1975.

Macy, Joanna Rogers. *Dharma and Development: Religion as Resource in the Sarvodaya Self-Help Movement.* West Hartford, Conn.: Kumarian Press, 1983.

Malcolm X and Alex Haley. *The Autobiography of Malcolm X.* New York: Ballantine Books, 1965.

Mandalaya, Lanka Bauddha. *An Event of Dual Significance.* Colombo: Ministry of Home Affairs, 1956.

Melson, Robert, and Howard Wolpe. "Modernization and the Politics of Communalism: A Theoretical Perspective." *American Political Science Review* 64 (1970): 1112–1130.

Memmi, Albert. *The Colonizer and the Colonized.* Boston: Beacon Press, 1967.

Moore, Cynthia. *Paraprofessionals in Village-Level Development in Sri Lanka: The Sarvodaya Shramadana Movement.* Ithaca, N.Y.: Cornell University Press, 1981.

Morris, Morris David. *Measuring the Condition of the World's Poor: The Physical Quality of Life Index.* New York: Pergamon Press, and Washington, D.C.: Overseas Development Council, 1979.

Perry, Edmund F. "Foreword to the English Edition" to Rahula, *The Heritage of the Bhikkhu.*

Phadnis, Urmila. *Religion and Politics in Sri Lanka.* New Delhi: Manohar, 1976.

Rahula, Walpola. *The Heritage of the Bhikkhu.* New York: Grove Press, 1974.

Ratnapala, Nandesena. *The Sarvodaya Movement: Self-Help Rural Development in Sri Lanka.* Essex, Conn.: International Council for Educational Development, 1978.

——. *Sarvodaya and the Rodiyas: The Birth of Sarvodaya.* Ratmalana: Sarvodaya Research Institute, 1979.

Said, Edward. *Orientalism.* New York: Vintage Books, 1979.

Schumacher, E. F. *Small is Beautiful: Economics As If People Mattered.* New York: Harper and Row, 1973.

Smith, Donald E. "Religion, Politics and the Myth of Reconquest." In Tissa Fernando and Robert N. Kearney, eds. *Modern Sri Lanka: A Society in Transition.* Syracuse, N.Y.: Syracuse University Press, 1979, pp. 83–99.

Stevens, Philip. "Image-Realization-Text." Unpublished senior paper, Williams College, 1983.
Swearer, Donald K. *Buddhism and Society in Southeast Asia*. Chambersburg, Pa.: Anima Books, 1981.
Weber, Max. *The Religions of India*. Glencoe, Ill.: Free Press, 1958.
Wijewardene, D. C. *The Revolt in the Temple*. Colombo: Sinha Publications, 1953.

9

Postwar Confucianism and Western Democracy: An Ideological Struggle

CHARLES WEI-HSUN FU

For more than two thousand years, Confucianism as the main philosophical and cultural tradition of China provided the basic pattern of ethical and sociopolitical thought for the Chinese rulers and their subjects in the changing dynasties until the Communist liberation of the nation. This basic pattern is primarily set up in terms of what is traditionally called "the way of inner sagehood and outer kingship," the way that constitutes the Confucian ideal or goal of life.[1] According to Confucianism, the ultimate goal of life consists in the moral perfecting of the individual and society; our attainment of inner sagehood (as a matter of individual morality) and outer kingship (as a matter of sociopolitical morality) soteriologically implies the ultimate identity of human morality and supreme happiness of life. The way of inner sagehood is grounded in Mencius's theory of human nature that the human, as distinguishable from beast, is originally (potentially) good and can attain inner sagehood through constant engagement in personal cultivation and daily moral practice. The way of outer kingship is the Confucian sociopolitical extension or application of the way of inner sagehood: constant moral perfecting of each and every member of the society—especially the rulers and their ministers who must set a moral example for the people—will not only lead to the individual attainment of sagehood but also assure the eventual sociopolitical realization of what is called "the world of grand unity."[2] The traditional Confucianists as moral idealists were optimistically convinced that social harmony and political order could be well maintained if the rulers were able to set a personal, moral example for and exert a politico-moral influence on their subjects.

Unfortunately, this high-minded ethical and sociopolitical program never materialized in imperial China. After the overthrow of the Ch'ing dynasty, modern China witnessed the further shattering of the age-old Confucian political dream, resulting from the enormous challenge and influences of Western democracy and sciences on the one hand and the political victory of Chinese Communism on the other. When the Nationalist government lost its power in mainland China, quite a number of Confucian scholars and thinkers found refuge in Hong Kong, Taiwan, or the United States, and continued to advocate and develop the Confucian Way. The most prominent among them are Professors T'ang Chun-i (1909–1979), Mou Tsung-san (1909–   ), and Hsu Fu-kuan (1903–1982), all of whom have much to do with the creative revitalization of the Confucian tradition, with New Asia College, now belonging to the Chinese University of Hong Kong, as the major academic center. But there were also many Confucianists who chose rather to remain in Mao's China. Understandably, almost all of them have undergone an extremely difficult politico-ideological struggle with Marxism-Leninism-Maoism, and have denounced, voluntarily or not, Confucianism as ideologically reactionary and harmful to China's socialist construction. The repeated anti-Confucian confessions made by the well-known Professor Fung Yu-lan (1895–   ) are a most conspicuous example. There is, however, one interesting exception: the existence of the late Professor Hsiung Shih-li (1885–1968), who alone dared to speak of what may be called "Confucian socialism" as a politico-ideological alternative to Marxism-Leninism-Maoism.[3] The following sections will first introduce Hsiung's Confucian socialism and then discuss the other Confucian attempts made by T'ang Chun-i, Mou Tsung-san, and Professor Liu Shu-hsien, now chairing the Department of Philosophy at the Chinese University of Hong Kong. Finally, I will also mention a modernistic approach taken by Professor Wei Cheng-tung, now in Taipei, and give my own critical reflections on the problems in Confucian ethical and sociopolitical thought.

HSIUNG SHIH-LI'S CONFUCIAN SOCIALISM

Hsiung Shih-li, perhaps the most creative and influential philosopher in contemporary China, made the first attempt at a modern reorientation of the philosophical (metaphysical) foundation of Confucianism. In his magnum opus *A New Philosophy of Ideation-Only*, he tried to integrate Mahāyāna Buddhist philosophy, Yogācāra Idealism in particular, into Confucian metaphysics and moral idealism. But after the Communist liberation of mainland China, he began to rethink his early philosophy and finally abandoned completely what he originally held in the magnum opus. In *On Substance and Function* (1958), he said:

Since this book is now completed, *A New Philosophy of Ideation-Only* in its two versions should be destroyed, for there is no necessity to preserve this [early] work. . . . My own philosophical ground is [the moral metaphysics of the *Great Treatise on Yi-ching*], where the position of the nonduality of substance (*t'i*) and function (*yung*) is taken. . . . My [present] position has nothing in common with that of the [Yogācāra] Buddhist doctrine of ideation-only. [That is why] *A New Philosophy of Ideation-Only* need not be preserved at all.[4]

Hsiung's new philosophy was Confucian through and through, not making the slightest compromise with Buddhism or Taoism. In his latest work *Ch'ien-k'un-yen* (1961), which means "a philosophical derivation of the meaning of the *Yi-ching* theory of Heaven (or the Creative) and Earth (or the Receptive)," he said that he had finally reached a definitive conclusion of his entire philosophy. He also said that it took him nearly fifty years to totally abandon both Buddhism and Taoism and reestablish Confucianism in terms of inner sagehood and outer kingship as the best philosophical expression of the Chinese Way.

Like many other Confucian intellectuals, Hsiung Shih-li learned to focus on the problem of socialist practice in Mao's China. Living quietly in Peking (Beijing) during the 1950s, Hsiung was impelled to critically reflect on the entire traditional way of presenting Confucian sociopolitical thought. He reached a very radical conclusion—without, however, any historical or textual evidence—that Confucius was the first great revolutionary-socialist in ancient China, but that Mencius and nearly all the other subsequent Confucian thinkers turned out to be political conservatives, who designed various forms of pseudo-Confucian sociopolitical programs for the imperial rulers' politico-ideological manipulations in the successive, feudal dynasties. Hsiung's radical but misleading conclusion, that the original Confucian Way (of Confucius himself) was a scientific and revolutionary socialism, shocked his philosophical friends and students, who were living outside of mainland China, with disbelief and displeasure. To introduce his socialist radicalization of the Confucian Way of outer kingship, I have selected some of the most important sayings from his *Ch'ien-k'un-yen* and translated them as follows:

Confucius wrote *Li-yün-ching* (*Classic of the Evolution of li* [as the ancient Chinese religious and sociomoral culture]), in which he advocated the elimination of the individual-managed family system, in order that all people would be able to cooperate with one another and organize a commune. That is why he said, "Each and every member is not to look upon his own father as his sole father, nor is he to treat his own son as his only son." Once the individual-managed family system is abandoned, all men will get used to a communal life. . . . The individual-managed family system is formed because of the existence of the ruling class. (pp. 75–76)

Philosophers of the Smaller Peace school [which was essentially different from the Grand Unity approach of Confucius] like Mencius and Hsün Tzu did develop a theory of political revolution, advocating the overturn of despotism. But their [political] thought was basically intended to preserve the ruling class. (p. 92)

Confucius . . . created the philosophy of the great Way, and advocated revolution. . . . His words, "Each and every member is to treat all fathers as his father and all sons as his son," and the words following these clearly show [that his political theory is a revolutionary] socialism. (p. 141)

Confucius created *Yi-ching* (*Classic of Changes*) and developed the great way of inner sagehood and outer kingship. . . . Confucius's learning of inner sagehood completely wiped out the notion of the heavenly Lord: he changed the meaning of the word *T'ien* (Heaven) [into Nature] and used the word *Yi* (Changes) to express the dynamic reality of the universe. . . . [Confucius's] teaching of outer kingship tried to eliminate the ruling class, and this [revolutionary] idea is grounded upon his teaching of inner sagehood which presupposes no heavenly Lord at all. (pp. 163–171)

Confucius's thought on social revolution involves no utopian idea, nor is it an empty theory at all. His attitude and method is purely scientific and empirical. (p. 426)

Confucius's Yi-ching is great and all-inclusive, and can be generalized in terms of two aspects, namely, inner sagehood and outer kingship. The learning of inner sagehood can be found in detail in the first two hexagrams, Ch'ien (the Creative) and K'un (the Receptive). Although these two hexagrams are different in name, they should be treated as one and the same hexagram. Ch'ien and K'un are originally not two things independent of each other. . . . The learning of inner sagehood resolves the major problems of the world and man, . . . whereas the learning of outer kingship resolves the major politicosocial problems. The distinction between "inner" and "outer" here is rather provisional, for self and other [or man and the world] are originally one and the same reality. . . . Confucius said in the Analects: "There is one thread that runs through my Way." (p. 491)

Hsiung's contentions in the above sayings, that Confucius was the author of Yi-ching and Li-yün-ching, that his teaching of inner sagehood completely wiped out the notion of the heavenly Lord, that his teaching of outer kingship tried to eliminate the ruling class, that his attitude and method were purely scientific and empirical, that the subsequent Confucianists manipulated his teachings, and so forth, can hardly be supported by any existing Confucian texts or historical documents. All these points are no more than Hsiung's personal, unfounded speculations. As to his central thesis, that Confucius was the first Chinese "scientific revolutionary-socialist" advocating the commune system and abolition of the individually managed family system, it is utterly false. But the question is: Why did Hsiung (have to) construct a false image of Confucius as the first "scientific revolutionary-socialist," strikingly resembling Karl Marx and Friedrich Engels, who was the author of Socialism: Utopian and Scientific? Why did he (have to) distort the original sociopolitical thought of Confucius, who never advocated any classless, commune system—the system that is interestingly comparable to the People's Communes nationally organized under Mao's directive during the Great Leap Forward period? Unfortunately, no clue to Hsiung's own answer can be found in his writings. Nonetheless, it seems quite reasonable to say that, based on his personal experience of the exciting socialist construction and the Chinese people's moral zeal in New China, Hsiung began to accept, on the Confucian ground, the Marxist theory of sociopolitical revolution and classless society in the higher phase of communism. In other words, consciously or not, he was impelled to believe that the Marxist egalitarian ideas were in accord with the moral teachings of Confucius in terms of jen (human-kindness) and yi (righteousness or moral oughtness), and that the traditional way of interpreting and practicing Confucius's teachings of inner sagehood and outer kingship in the successive, feudal dynasties did not do justice to what Confucius really meant or intended as an egalitarian. To be more precise, he began to believe that there was a meeting point between Confucianism and Marxism in terms of egalitarian vindication of social justice and human love that can be truly manifested only in a classless society. But, as one of the most creative Confucian metaphysicians himself, Hsiung simply could not accept the dialectic-materialist *Weltanschauung* of Marxism-Leninism, according to which ultimate reality is nothing but matter-in-motion.

If this explanation is accepted, then it can be said that Hsiung's critical reflections on and socialist radicalization of the traditional Confucian way of inner sagehood and outer kingship, through his own historical and philosophical distortion of Confucius and Confucianism, do reflect his painful realization of the traditional Confucian limitations in sociopolitical thinking and practice. But, one may ask: why did he put all the blame on Mencius and the other great Confucianists, and not on Confucius himself? Wasn't Mencius more revolutionary than Confucius according to history? At any rate, Hsiung Shih-li's personal, ideological struggle as the last Confucian representative thinker in Mao's China poignantly reflects the tragic Chinese intellectual conditions today.

T'ANG CHUN-I'S ESSAY "CHINESE CULTURE AND THE WORLD"

Professor T'ang Chun-i was one of the three Chinese scholars who left for Hong Kong and founded the New Asia College in 1949—the year the Communists liberated mainland China—in order to carry on overseas the historical mission of inheriting and developing Chinese thought and culture, as represented by the Confucian Way, in the postwar era. His long essay "Chinese Culture and the World" has been translated into English with a new title, "A Manifesto for a Re-appraisal of Sinology and Reconstruction of Chinese Culture," which appears in the appendix of the second volume of the late Confucian scholar Carsun Chang's English work *The Development of Neo-Confucian Thought* (1962). Chang proposed the writing of this essay in the spring of 1957, after a talk with T'ang about many shortcomings in the methods most of the Western sinologists had been using in their studies of Chinese thought and culture. Chang (in San Francisco) then wrote Professors Mou Tsung-san and Hsu Fu-kuan (both in Taiwan at that time), asking them to participate with him and T'ang in the joint publication of a manifesto, which would express their common view with respect to the essense of Chinese thought and culture. With his three friends' consent, T'ang (in Hong Kong) worked out the first draft of the essay, which he sent to Mou and Hsu for their comments and suggestions. After several revisions, the final version of the essay was completed. The manifesto or treatise is intended primarily as a philosophical guide to those Western intellectuals interested in studies of Chinese—especially Confucian—thought and culture. It can be said that this essay exemplifies T'ang's and his Confucian friends' common attempt at a creative development of the Confucian Way of inner sagehood and outer kingship. The following selections represent some of the essay's most significant statements involving Confucian sociopolitical thought (my translation):

We hope that when people of the world study Chinese culture they will pay special attention to the [Chinese] thought on the unity of Heaven (nature) and man, as well as to the religious belief in the Way (Tao) in the [Chinese] engagement in [everyday] moral practice. This is the first point to which we would like to draw the attention of the [Western] people. . . .

Next, we may turn to the subject of Chinese learning of *hsin/hsing* (mind and human nature). This learning of *hsin/hsing* is another aspect of the traditional Chinese learning of *yi-li* ("moral principle," philosophical inquiry with ethical emphasis); it refers to the [Chinese] inquiry into the primordial source of man's principle of moral oughtness. This learning of *hsin/hsing* is what most Westerners tend to overlook or misunderstand in their studies of Chinese learning and culture. As a matter of fact, this learning of *hsin/hsing* is the central theme of Chinese thought; it is also the true reason for the existence of the theory of moral co-operation between Heaven and man. . . . According to our understanding, it is totally misleading or wrong to treat the Chinese philosophy of *hsin/hsing* as a kind of rationalistic theory of soul in Western psychology or traditional Western philosophy, as a kind of epistemological or metaphysical theory [in the Western substantive sense]. . . . The Chinese learning of *hsin/hsing* from Confucius and Mencius to the Sung and Ming Confucian philosophers must be understood as the human learning that can be deepened and enriched by way of the deepening and enrichment of man's daily engagement in moral practice. . . . It is because this learning of *hsin/hsing* from Confucius and Mencius to the Sung and Ming Neo-Confucian philosophers has the above characteristics that, if one does not engage in moral practice, or if one simply abides by the moral code established by social conventions or the divine Commandments as given in the Bible, one cannot be expected to have a true and intimate understanding [of the learning of *hsin/ hsing*] at all. In other words, this learning [makes us realize that] we must engage in moral practice on the basis of our own [existential-moral] self-awakening, and become more and more humanly awakened on the basis of our [lived-experience of the] practice. *Chih* (knowing, theory) and *hsing* (acting, practice) must co-advance inseparably. . . . It is based on this [inner awakening and determination] that all human engagements become a matter of man's moral self-perfecting. Man's abiding by social conventions or by the divine Commandments, or his accomplishments in moral virtue, social work, and good words, have usually been understood from the external point of view [in the West], but these [human engagements and achievements] are, if seen from the perspective of inner awakening and determination, to be considered a matter of man's utmost exertion of his *hsin/hsing*. . . . Chinese philosophers from Confucius and Mencius to the Sung and Ming Neo-Confucianists have established a clear and consistent common thesis: they all realize that the conduct involved in man's moral practice and the knowledge involved in his self-awakening and self-determination must depend upon each other and co-advance inseparably, that all moral-practical activities in our dealing with the external world must come out of our spontaneous and irresistible self-demand that we exert our inner *hsin/ hsing* to the utmost, and that if man can exert his *hsin/hsing* to the utmost he will reach the stage of the heavenly virtue, the heavenly principle, the heavenly mind, thus attaining a moral [and metaphysical] identity with Heaven and Earth or forming the threefold Ultimate with Heaven and Earth. This is the very tradition of the Chinese learning of *hsin/hsing*. . . . In Western culture, however, metaphysics, philosophy, and sciences all seek knowledge of the objective world [as a matter of intellectual curiosity] separable from moral practice—this originates in the Greek tradition; religion is treated as a subject which must first posit God and his Commandments—this originates in the Hebrew tradition; law, politics, social conventions, ethics and morality are treated as a kind of externalized system of norms imposed upon all members of human society—this originates in the Roman tradition. That is why those scholars in both China and the West who get used to the viewpoint of Western culture and learning, tend to overlook or misunderstand the essential nature of Chinese learning of *hsin/hsing* in their sinological studies. That is why Chinese culture can never be understood if the Chinese learning of *hsin/hsing* is not understood. . . . The Chinese [cultural] ideal should make the Chinese realize himself that he is not only "a subject of moral practice" but also "a political subject" in political affairs, "a cognitive subject" in the realm of nature and knowledge, and "a subject of practical, technological activities." That is to say, China is in need of democracy; it is also in need of sciences and practical technology. Thus, Chinese culture must integrate Western or world cultures. But the reason why China needs to accept Western or world cultures is that the Chinese can realize himself not only as a moral subject but also a political subject, a cognitive subject, and a subject engaged in practical, technological activities. . . . We admit that the modern Western democratic system, sciences, and practical technology has been lacking in Chinese culture and history; that is why China has not yet been truly modernized and industrialized. But we cannot admit that China's cultural ideal contains no potential seed for [the development of] democratic thought and that the inner demand of China's political development is not favorable to the establishment of a democratic system, nor can we admit that Chinese culture is opposed to science and that from the beginning science and technology have been neglected in China. . . . But if we still admit that Chinese culture lacks Western science, it is because we do admit the fact that the basic spirit of Western science transcends a mere practical, technological motivation. The scientific spirit of the West in fact originated in the ancient Greek's seeking knowledge for knowledge's sake. . . . The shortcoming that the Chinese people lack this [Western] scientific spirit basically has to do with the overemphasis placed upon moral practice in traditional Chinese [Confucian] thought, the overemphasis that always prevents the Chinese from reserving temporarily their value judgment on [man's encounter with] the objective world. . . . If the Chinese really want to establish themselves as a moral subject, they must also make a self-demand that they become a cognitive subject at the same time. When this moral subject makes such a self-demand, he must become temporarily forgetful of his being a moral subject [who makes a value judgment], and temporarily step behind the cognitive subject [that takes the position of scientific objectivity or value-neutrality], and thus become the supporter of the cognitive subject.

After the cognitive subject accomplishes his task of obtaining [scientific] knowledge, then and only then the moral subject should pass his value judgment, engage in moral practice, and provide a human guidance for pragmatic activities [such as technological improvement of the living condition]. Man as the moral subject in the highest and truest sense must be the one who can become the master of the moral as well as the intellectual subject within himself in moving forward or backward. This is what may be called man's greatest *jen* (human-kindness or morality), which is combined with cognitive intellect. . . . As to the problem of the democratic construction of the Chinese nation, as we have said before, a modern, Western-style, democratic system has never been established in Chinese culture and history. . . . The shortcoming of Confucian thought in the past is that it failed to establish a legal institution for the smooth and proper transition of the ruling power and for the realization of the genuine wish of the people. . . . However, Confucianism insists that the world does not belong to one single person [Chinese emperor], that in moral practice every man can become a worthy or sage [like legendary sage-kings Yao and Shun], and that [the rulers] must love what the people love and detest what the people detest. We can see that this Confucian insistence harbors the [politico-moral] thought of "the world for all men and equality of all men," and this very thought is the original source or seed for democratic, political thought. The reason why we say that the Confucian thought of "the world belongs to all men" and "all men are equal" in the past must develop into present-day thought of democratic construction of the nation, is that further development of this thought will definitely run into conflict with [absolute] monarchy. . . . From the fact that the establishment of moral subjectivity has been stressed in Chinese history and culture, we can declare that the democratic system in politics must be developed in order to make man truly establish his moral subjectivity. . . . The moral spirit of Chinese culture and [absolute] monarchy basically contradict each other. This contradiction can be resolved only through constitutional democracy, and this constitutional democracy is what the moral spirit of Chinese culture and its development demands.

The Marxist-Leninist ideology of dictatorship cannot serve as the highest guiding principle for Chinese culture and politics for long. The fundamental reasons are: (1) Marxism-Leninism attempts to deny universal human nature and only recognizes class nature. It therefore attempts to wipe out all kinds of religion, philosophy, art, and morality, which are based on universal human nature. . . . (2) The proletarian institution, in accordance with the Marxist-Leninist view of class nature, tries to destroy individuality, liberty, and human rights. . . . (3) Chinese culture in its historical development necessarily demands that the Chinese become a moral subject as well as a political subject, a cognitive subject, and a technological subject. If one wants to become a cognitive subject, then one's thought and reason cannot be controlled by any dogmas [such as the Marxist-Leninist dogma]. . . . (4) The demand that the Chinese people become the political subjects cannot allow the existence of one monarch ruling the people, nor can it allow the dictatorship of one single party. . . . (5) In the totalitarian politics of the Communist Party, the problem of succession to the highest political leadership is . . . eventually resolved in terms of mutual destruction, as evidenced by the cases of Lenin's and Stalin's deaths. . . . The reason why Marxist-Leninist thought cannot last long . . . is that it is not positively grounded upon the demand made in the spiritual life of the Chinese people. . . . We can affirmatively say that the objective, spiritual life of the Chinese people will necessarily turn in the direction of democratic construction of the nation.[5]

In summary T'ang Chun-i states, first of all, that the Chinese theory of *hsin/hsing* (mind/nature) is the essential theme of Chinese thought, and that it is, especially in the Confucian tradition, the foundation of human morality. The Confucian learning of *hsin/hsing* enables the Chinese to become an autonomous moral subject in terms of moral self-awakening and self-determination.

Second, from the Confucian point of view, the individual as an autonomous moral subject must also demand of himself/herself that he or she become a political subject, a cognitive subject, and a subject of technological activities, in order to engage in political affairs, scientific studies, and technological developments. All of these are very necessary for the realization of the (Confucian) goal of life in terms of the moral perfecting of the person and society, world peace, and so on. Unfortunately, China has never developed true democracy, science, and technology of the types found in modern Western societies. China's lack of modern science and technology in the past has much to do with the traditional overemphasis on moral practice in the Confucian manner, at the expense of objective (non-ethically oriented) studies of nature and society. As to the Chinese lack of true democracy, one main reason is that in the past Confucianism failed to promote a legal institution for the appropriate transmission of the political power and for the realization of the general will of the people.

Third, the Confucian overemphasis on moral practice does not imply that the Confucian Way runs into conflict with democracy (or science and technology). On the contrary, the Confucian moral teachings, which harbor the political thought of "the world for all men and equality for all men," can be the original source for a full development of true democracy. Because Confucianism is opposed to absolute monarchy, it must pave a modern way for the democratic construction of the Chinese nation. Democracy in the constitutional form is what the moral spirit of Chinese (Confucian) thought and culture necessarily demands today. Finally, Marxism-Leninism as the political ideology of mainland China today can hardly be accepted by the great majority of the Chinese people who have inherited and value the great moral and cultural legacy of Confucianism, which always promotes human rights and reason. In short, the best political alternative to communism in China today is constitutional democracy which can fully realize the Confucian ideal of life for all Chinese.

FURTHER CONFUCIAN REFLECTIONS ON OUTER KINGSHIP

Professor T'ang Chun-i himself never wrote any single work on the further development of Confucian sociopolitical thought before or after his writing of the essay "Chinese Culture and the World." Some of the sociopolitical ideas in the essay were probably suggested by his long-time friend Professor Mou Tsung-san, who wrote no less than three books dealing with the problem of modern reorientation of the Confucian Way of outer kingship grounded in the way of inner sagehood. These three books are *A Philosophy of History* (1955), *Moral Idealism* (1959), and *The Way of Politics and the Way of Government* (1961). *Moral Idealism* is the most important of the three, for it presents the essentials of Mou's critical reflections on Confucian sociopolitical thought in the post-liberation era, with a view to counter-challenging the political ideology of Marxism-Leninism-Maoism in mainland China.

In *Moral Idealism*, Professor Mou reaffirms his Confucian conviction that, among all the traditional thoughts and learning in China, only the moral philosophy and cultural system of Confucianism can serve as the guiding principle for our social practice. If this principle cannot be given, then Karl Marx will outsmart all of us. Mou states, "The central thought in the Confucian cultural system is . . . moral idealism, that is, the idealism developed out of man's moral, practical reason."[6]

According to Mou, the politico-social practice of Confucianism in the traditional form consists in governing, loving, and taking care of the people—idealistically speaking, the rulers' looking on the subjects as their own children. But traditional Confucianists made no further effort to train the people as politically active citizens, so that they would be able to participate in the political process of electing government officials or expressing their general will. In advocating the way of inner sagehood in terms of moral self-cultivation by the ruler as a sage-king and each subject as a good member of the society, traditional Confucianists failed to provide a workable solution with respect to the limits of the ruler's power and the people's political involvement. Mou particularly mentions Mencius's idea of the "fivefold moral relationship" (*wu-lun*) to illustrate the pros and cons of traditional Confucian sociopolitical thought. Mencius said, "The sage [the legendary sage-king Shun] . . . appointed Hsieh to be the Minister of Education, to teach the people the relations of humanity (*jen-lun*): (1) affection between parent and child; (2) righteousness between sovereign and minister; (3) functional distinction between husband and wife; (4) orderliness between old and young; and (5) fidelity between friends."[7] These human relations constituted the basic sociopolitical order in traditional China. But this fivefold moral relationship alone would not be sufficient to solve the problems of impersonal sociopolitical morality, such as social justice, beyond daily concrete, human relations. Mou critically reflects that no true and objective political and legal system can be set up on the sole basis of this fivefold moral relationship. This helps explain why China's traditional political form turned out to be a kind of monarchical dictatorship.

Mou thinks that the transition from aristocracy in the Chou dynasty to monarchical dictatorship since the Ch'in and Han dynasties represented great political progress, and that the transition from monarchical dictatorship to modern democracy would be another great progress. If we want to attempt a modern explication of the meaning of the Confucian Way of outer kingship, we must reorient it in terms of establishing a modernized state's political and legal system, as can be seen in the Western nations. Mou, therefore, suggests that the Confucian historical mission today is to integrate this modernized political and legal institution, in the form of constitutional democracy, into the Confucian Way of outer kingship. If the modernized political and legal system cannot be built in China, then the way of outer kingship, which all genuine Confucianists have advocated for the promotion of social well-being, cannot be fully realized; and, if the way of outer kingship cannot be fully realized, the moral idealism of Confucianism in terms of *jen-yi* (human-kindness and righteousness), which constitutes the essence of the Confucian Way of inner sagehood, cannot be extensively realized either. In short, we must, Mou says, understand that a full realization of democracy will mean an objective realization of Confucian moral reason. If we really know that moral reason must be extended and objectively manifested, then we must also know that democracy can be well developed out of the Confucian

Way, by integrating modernized political and legal reforms as achieved in the West.

Mou further states that, regardless of whatever method or form we may adopt for China's democratic construction in the future, the concrete contents of democracy, such as freedom of speech, freedom of the press, and religious liberty, as well as the legal system based on the constitution of the state, must be considered a universal and everlasting political truth. This truth must be affirmed in the practice of Confucian moral idealism. If we do not affirm such a political system, then human dignity and the realization of moral value as advocated by Confucianism cannot be preserved at all. And if we want to affirm the universality and constancy of modern democracy, we must reject Marx's theory of human nature and historical materialism. But this does not mean that we must deny the social revolution of the working men and women. On the contrary, Mou suggests democracy can be combined with socialism on the basis of the social practice of Confucian moral idealism. Moral idealism (of the Confucian kind), not historical materialism, makes democracy and socialism complementary. Thus, the social practice of Confucian idealism today must not only take the political form of Western democracy but also integrate socialism. Traditional Confucianists did espouse the teachings of loving the people and making them prosperous, of humane distribution of welfare, of the primacy of agriculture, and so on, but they were concerned mostly with the problem of moral education of the people and did not attempt to deal with the teachings in a politically more realistic manner. Nonetheless, based on these teachings all true Confucianists would certainly affirm socialism as well as democracy. Thus, Mou's conclusion with regard to the Confucian Way of outer kingship is very simple: Confucianism as moral idealism must manifest itself socially and politically in the modernized form of constitutional socialist democracy.

Under the philosophical influence of Mou Tsung-san, Professor Liu Shu-hsien of the Chinese University of Hong Kong also presents his critical reflections on Confucian sociopolitical thought, if rather sketchily, in his recent book *Chinese Philosophy and Modernization* (1980). Some of his important statements in this book, as I have selected and translated them, are as follows:

First of all, we must distinguish the ideal aspect [of Confucius] from its actual aspect. I have consistently upheld the Confucian ideal, but I have never denied the fact that our traditional sociopolitical institution no longer suits the actual needs of the present China; the ultra-conservative attitude held by those second-rate Confucianists today even becomes an obstacle to any [sociopolitical] progress in our modern time. . . . Based on my personal lived-experience, the essence of Confucian learning is none other than man's direct and intimate embodiment of *jen* (humanity) within his own mind-heart. By extending this mind-heart of *jen* one can metaphysically realize the inscrutable Way of Heaven in terms of ever-creative production and reproduction of things. With such a lived-experience, one can naturally feel that one has no regret in living this life and that one's (Confucian) Way is self-sufficient. . . . But we lag far behind [the Western nations] in the implementation of a democratic, political, and legal program. Those who love to keep the Confucian tradition intact take delight in saying that long before, in Mencius, we already had the idea of "the priority of the people over the sovereign." This, of course, is true. But the thought of the priority of the people is not the same as the thought of democracy. The West already has a workable system to realize the democratic ideal, while we are still remaining at the stage of vague or unclear thinking about democracy. . . . Confucianism in the past did not attempt a thorough solution of the problem of how to properly restrain the power of the imperial rulers. It is totally meaningless to nostalgically praise the golden age of [the pre-historic, legendary sage-kings] Yao and Shun. The separation of political affairs and the Tradition [as often manipulated by the imperial rulers and pseudo-Confucianists in the past] is the only proper way to avoid any absolute dictatorship. . . . However, as all anthropologists today have pointed out, any reform totally severed from the tradition can never be successful. In truth, China's spiritual tradition not only contains a valuable legacy, which cannot be destroyed by modern civilization, but harbors a seed for the development of scientific and democratic thought. . . . The highest achievement of contemporary Confucian philosophy [of Hsiung, T'ang, Mou et al.] undoubtedly lies in a creative reinterpretation and deep realization of Confucian metaphysical teachings and enlightenment. In the fields of politics, economy, and social philosophy, however, contemporary Confucianism only gives us a very rough outline, which is utterly insufficient to counter-challenge capitalism and socialism. Thus, we find a very paradoxical phenomenon: the strongest point of traditional Confucianism now becomes the weakest point of contemporary Confucianism at the present time. . . . It is beyond the capacity of one or two [Confucian] men to establish the Confucian ideal [in terms of the way of inner sagehood and outer kingship]; this task requires many people making their respective efforts and attempts in order to find one and the same focal point, thereby creating a consolidated power.[8]

WEI CHENG-TUNG'S ATTEMPT AT A MODERNISTIC BREAKTHROUGH

Professor Wei Cheng-tung, one of the most prolific philosophical writers in Taiwan today, has been highly critical of the contemporary Confucianists' defense of the traditional way of inner sagehood as the basis for the way of outer kingship. According to his understanding, T'ang Chun-i and Mou Tsung-san hold that democracy must be a sociopolitical expression of the inner demand of Chinese culture itself, that the basic pattern of inner sagehood and outer kingship need not be changed, and that democracy as imported from the West constitutes a new (modern) outer kingship on the ground of the way of inner sagehood. In his essay "The Mentality of Contemporary Confucian Philosophers" (1982), Wei presents his modernistic view that the modernization of a nation such as China is not simply a matter of scientific-technological development and politico-institutional changes; it must deeply involve a proper adjustment of the entire traditional value-system. Above all, the modernistic transformation of the traditional moral spirit is the most fundamental and crucial.

Wei is particularly critical of the contemporary Confucianist's insistence that Chinese culture is self-sufficient and contains a good seed for the development of democratic thought, and therefore that democracy is basically what the traditional moral spirit within Chinese culture necessarily demands. If this statement is true, Wei says, then there must be some historical evidence showing that the traditional moral spirit of China did in fact demand democracy. But there has never been any such evidence. Contemporary Confucianists suggest that we do not apply a simple "external criterion" in our reappraisal of the value of Chinese culture. In some sense, their suggestion is right. But, ironically, Western democracy in addition to modern science is what makes up the "external criterion"; as far as this criterion is concerned, the value of Chinese culture is far less than that of Western culture. The fact that modern science and democracy have never been developed in Chinese history is clearly indicative of the limitations or insufficiency of Chinese culture in its original source.

In his critical examination of contemporary Confucianism, Wei also states that the deep-rooted pan-moralistic consciousness that exists in traditional (Confucian) culture helped to fashion China's traditional politics and government into a special type of "political moralization." As a result, Confucian teachings of inner sagehood and outer kingship turned out to be a castle in the air in Chinese history and often became a rationalized basis for the absolute dictatorship of the imperial rulers. Wei himself proposes,

To rectify the traditional pan-moralistic consciousness, the fundamental solution is to constantly promote and strengthen public education about liberty and democracy. In our realization of democracy, politics must be severed from (traditional) morality. . . . Morality should not be politicalized, nor should politics be moralized—I am not, of course, saying that politics has nothing to do with morality. That the government tries to solve the people's daily problems is not a matter of [what traditional Confucianists call] "virtuous government"; it is rather a matter of political duty and accountability.[9]

In his most recent works, *Drastic Changes and Tradition: In Search of the Modern Significance of Traditional Chinese Thought* (1978) and *A Breakthrough in Ethical Thought* (1982), Professor Wei attempts to work out a modern (or post-modern) ethical program for Chinese society—especially Taiwan which is on the way to complete modernization. His program consists of integrating democracy, science, technology, human rights, and freedom as commonly understood and accepted in the industrialized Western nations, and of effecting a modernistic transformation of some traditional Confucian moral ideas, such as *jen*, which still have universal significance in the modern world. Although his modernistic breakthrough in ethical and sociopolitical thought remains to be refined and completed, he has at least demonstrated an unusual sensitivity to the urgent need of a new morality for the Chinese nation which is working toward political democratization and scientific industrialization, without abandoning its ethical legacy.

CONCLUDING REMARKS

As we have learned, contemporary Confucianists like T'ang and Mou still believe that the way of inner sagehood is the moral basis for the way of outer kingship, and that Western democracy (and science) can easily be absorbed into Confucian sociopolitical thought because Confucian moral idealism contains the seed for the development of democracy (and science). Professor Wei Cheng-tung, however, has discovered that this Confucian way of thinking presents some problems, and he has suggested that politics (or the way of outer kingship) should not be moralized in terms of the traditional way of inner sagehood. In these concluding critical remarks, I would like to make a further observation on his thoughts.

That the way of outer kingship is a natural extension or application of the way of inner sagehood is most clearly stated in one of the Confucian Four Books, *The Great Learning*, which presents the Confucian educational, moral, and sociopolitical programs in a nutshell, neatly summed up in terms of the "three fundamentals and eight steps." The "three fundamentals and eight steps" are given in the main text of *The Great Learning* as follows:

The Way of Great Learning [for adult education] consists in enlightening man's (potentially) enlightened character, in loving (or renovating) the people, and in abiding in the highest good. Only after one knows what to abide in can one be determined; only after one is determined can one maintain tranquility; only after one maintains tranquility can one be at ease; only after one is at ease can one begin to deliberate; only after one begins to deliberate can one attain the end [which has already been set from the beginning]. Things have their roots and branches; affairs have their beginnings and ends. To know what is first and what is last will lead one near the Way. The ancients who wished to enlighten the (potentially) enlightened character [of all men] throughout the world first governed their state properly; wishing to govern their state properly, they first regulated their family; wishing to regulate their family, they first cultivated themselves; wishing to cultivate themselves, they first rectified their own mind; wishing to rectify their own mind, they first made their own will sincere; wishing to make their will sincere, they first extended (or acquired) their (moral) knowledge; the extension of (moral) knowledge consists in the investigation of things. When things are investigated, (moral) knowledge will be extended; when knowledge is extended, the will will be made sincere; when the will is made sincere, the mind will be rectified; when the mind is rectified, the person will be cultivated; when the person is cultivated, the family will be regulated; when the family is regulated, the state will be properly governed; when the state is properly governed, the world will be pacified. From the Son of Heaven (the imperial ruler) down to the common people, all must take personal cultivation as the root. It will be preposterous if the root remains in disorder while the branches are well ordered; it will also be preposterous if what should be treated as a matter of priority is slighted while what should be considered less important is treated as a matter of priority.[10]

As this passage shows, the three fundamentals are: to enlighten one's (potentially) enlightened character; to love (or renovate) the people; and to abide in the highest good. The eight steps are: investigation of things; extension of (moral) knowledge; sincerity of the will; rectification of the mind; cultivation of the person; regulation of the family; proper governance of the state; and pacification of the world. The first fundamental, "man's enlightening his own potentially virtuous nature," and the first five steps, from "investigation of things" to "cultivation of the person," refer to the way of inner sagehood, namely, individual morality, whereas the second fundamental, "to love (or renovate) the people," and the sixth to eighth steps—"regulation of the family," "proper governance of the state," and "pacification of the world"—refer to the way of outer kingship, namely, sociopolitical morality. The third fundamental, "to abide in the highest good," can be said to refer to the complete and perfect realization of the Confucian Way of *jen* in terms of both inner sagehood and outer kingship. Thus, the way of outer kingship is grounded in the way of inner sagehood; the way of outer kingship is the branch and the way of inner sagehood is the root. A crucial question here is: can the traditional Confucian moral idealism, that the way of inner sagehood is the moral basis for the way of outer kingship, be justified and suit the sociopolitical need of modern China which is on the way to complete democracy and industrialization? A critical examination of the original teachings of Confucius and Mencius may provide a good clue to the answer.

Confucius was, of course, the originator of the way of inner sagehood and outer kingship, by creating the doctrine of government by *jen* (benevolence) as against that of government by law or by force. His teaching of outer kingship in terms of virtuous government appeared over-idealistic, for he was far less concerned with the actual human conditions, the economic condition in particular, than with the moral condition at that time. Note, for example, the following conversation between Confucius and his disciple Tzu Kung:

Tzu Kung asked about government. The Master said, "Sufficient food, sufficient armament, and sufficient confidence of the people in their ruler." Tzu Kung said, "If it cannot be helped, and one of these three must be dispensed with, which should be foregone first?" The answer: "The armament first." Tzu Kung again asked: "If it cannot be helped, and one of the remaining two must be dispensed with, which of them should be foregone?" The answer: "Give up food. From of old, death has been the lot of all men. But if the people have no confidence in their ruler, the state cannot survive."[11]

Confucius's emphasis on the priority of the confidence of the people in their ruler over sufficient food seems to indicate his lack of understanding of the actual human condition, in which morality (*jen*) cannot be maintained or practiced unless economic survival is guaranteed first. There is, indeed, a great difference between Confucius's moral idealism and the realistic thesis presented in the *Kuan-tzu*, allegedly one of the earliest Legalist classics, that "only after the granaries are full [the people] will know [the importance of] sociomoral norms; only after clothing and food are in full supply [the people] will know [the meaning of] honor and disgrace."

Being overly optimistic, as Confucius was, about outer kingship as a natural extension of inner sagehood, Mencius never really understood the ever-existing tension between individual (person-oriented) morality and sociopolitical (impersonal-oriented) morality in terms of impartiality, justice, equality, fairness, and liberty in our modern, democratic sense. Let us cite two examples from the *Book of Mencius* to illustrate this point. The first example concerns the following hypothetical case:

T'ao Ying asked, "Suppose, when Shun was sovereign and Kao-yao his appointed minister of justice, Ku-sou [Shun's father] murdered a man, what would have happened in such a case?" Mencius said, "[Kao-yao] would simply have apprehended him." "But wouldn't Shun have forbidden such a thing?" "Well, how could Shun have forbidden it? [Kao-yao] was delegated with the judicial authority to do his job." "What would Shun have done, then?" "Shun would have regarded abandoning the kingdom as discarding a worn-out sandal. He would secretly have carried [his father] on his back, fled to the edge of the Sea, and lived there [with his father] happily for the rest of his life, without giving any thought to the kingdom."[12]

In this hypothetical case, Mencius tried to resolve the moral dilemma between filial piety, the first Confucian cardinal virtue, and criminal justice very poorly— even selfishly. It seems, in appearance, that Mencius wanted to support Kao-yao's impartial execution of the penal law on the one hand and vindicate, at the same time, Shun's fulfillment of filial love on the other. But, in actuality, it was impossible to have it both ways. If we read this passage more carefully, we will find that in the final analysis Mencius was defending the moral primacy of filial piety over impersonal justice. But Mencius also said that killing another man's father or brother is, as a matter of moral reciprocity, tantamount to killing one's father or brother.[13] Thus, in giving his support to Shun's fulfillment of filial love, Mencius only created more difficulties for Confucian ethics, which can hardly resolve the tension or dilemma between familial morality and sociopolitical impartiality (in modern, legal terms).

Another example from the *Book of Mencius* concerns the following case:

Wang Chang said, "Hsiang [Shun's brother] devoted himself everyday to plotting against Shun's life. When Shun was made sovereign, how was it that he only banished Hsiang?" Mencius said, "No, he enfeoffed Hsiang, though some called it banishment." Wan Chang said, ". . . . Hsiang was a most wicked man, yet he was enfeoffed in Yu-pi. What crime had the people of Yu-pi committed [in being forced to accept Hsiang as their lord]? Is that the way a man of *jen* [like Shun] should act? In the case of other men, Shun cut them off; in the case of his own brother, he enfeoffed him instead." Mencius said, "A man of *jen* neither harbors anger nor cherishes resentment against his brother, but only regards him with affection and love. Regarding him with affection, he wishes him to be honorable; regarding him with love, he wishes him to be wealthy. To enfeoff Hsiang was to make him wealthy and noble. If Shun, being sovereign himself, had left his brother alone as a commoner, could he be said to have regarded his brother with affection and love?"[14]

In this example, Mencius could hardly escape the ethical criticism that familial morality at the expense of sociopolitical impartiality will eventually lead to nepotism. Following Confucius, Mencius developed the principle of *jen-yi* (*jen* or human-kindness manifested through *yi* or gradational love), as the highest governing principle of human morality, beginning with familial love through friendship and patriotism to love for all humanity. But Mencius never resolved the moral conflict between natural affection, personal love, individual virtue, and so on, on the one hand and sociopolitical rights and obligations, law and order, public virtue, and the like, on the other. In Mencius, as well as in Confucius, we can clearly see the Confucian failure to justify the way of inner sagehood as the practicable moral basis for the way of outer kingship. It is also very surprising that none of the subsequent Confucian thinkers since Mencius, including contemporary Confucianists like T'ang and Mou, has ever attempted to resolve the ethical dilemma between individual morality and sociopolitical morality (in the nonpersonal, democratic sense) within the Confucian Way.

If we can distinguish *minima moralia* and *maxima moralia* as two categories of human morality, then Confucian morality belongs in the second category. Although *minima moralia* only concerns the individual's minimal fulfillment of moral duties or obligations in human society, such as observing law and order, promotion of human rights, moral reciprocity (in Confucius's own words, "Do not do to others what you do not want them to do to you"), social justice, and so on, without emphasizing the constant moral perfecting of man and society, Confucian morality as a typical representative of *maxima moralia* insists on the ethical necessity to realize *jen* as the way of both inner sagehood and outer kingship. But the constitutional democracy which contemporary Confucianists advocate only requires *minima moralia* in the legal form. Thus, without being able to see the distinction between *minima moralia* and *maxima moralia* in their attempts to absorb Western democracy into the Confucian tradition, contemporary Confucianists have not successfully shown us why and how the traditional way of inner sagehood can still serve as the moral basis for constitutional democracy in China today and in the future. Perhaps their attempts will be more successful if they can make a clear (Kantian) distinction between the regulative principle and the constitutive principle, and speak of Confucian *maxima moralia*, in terms of the full realization of *jen* in man and society, only as the regulative principle of China's sociopolitical morality. In any case, there is a long way to go before contemporary Confucianists will be able to accomplish their difficult task of reshaping Confucian moral idealism in the post-modern world of *Realpolitik*.

NOTES

1. The term "the way of inner sagehood and outer kingship" originally appeared in the last chapter (Ch. 33) of the Taoist classic *Chuang-tzu*. It was later adapted as a Confucian term. "Inner sagehood" refers to individual morality (moral perfecting of

each individual), whereas "outer kingship" refers to sociopolitical morality (moral perfecting of the entire human society).

2. We can find a standard account of "the world of grand unity" in the *Li-yün* [Evolution of *li* or Rites], one of the most fascinating chapters in the ancient Confucian text *Book of Rites*, which I translate as follows:

When the Great Tao prevailed, the world was an impartial and just commonwealth: the worthies and talented were elected [for public service] and the people were trustworthy and maintained human solidarity. Thus men did not regard only their parents as parents, nor did they treat only their children as children. The aged were provided with sufficient security for the remaining years; the grown-ups were able to employ their respective talents or skills; the children were reared well. All the old widowers and widows, orphans and childless persons, as well as the crippled and sickly were well cared for. Males had their proper occupations and females their proper homes. The people hated to see goods lying about in waste, but would not hoard them for their own advantage; they hated not to exert their labor power, but would not exert for their own profit. In this way [egoistic] schemings were repressed, and robbers, thieves, and traitors did not appear, and so the outer doors remained unlocked. This can be called "the Grand Unity" (*ta-t'ung*).

3. There was another representative Confucian thinker, Liang Shu-ming (1893–   ), who openly challenged Mao in a political meeting during the early 1950s, but Liang did not develop any sociopolitical thought of his own after the Liberation.

4. See Hsiung Shih-li, *T'i-yung-lun* [On Substance and Function], pp. 5–6.

5. T'ang Chun-i, *Chung-hua jen-wen yü tang-chin shih-chie* [Chinese Humanities and the Presentday World], Vol. 2, pp. 865–929.

6. Mou Tsung-san, *Tao-te te li-hsiang chu-yi* [Moral idealism], p. 22.

7. See Legge, trans., *The Works of Mencius*, pp. 251–252.

8. Liu Shu-hsien, *Chung-kuo che—hsüe yü hsien-tai-hua* [Chinese Philosophy and Modernization], pp. 64–76.

9. See Wei Cheng-tung, *"Tang-tai hsin-ju-chia te hsin-t'ai"* [The Mentality of Contemporary Confucianists], p. 49.

10. My translation. See also Wing-tsit Chan, *A Source Book in Chinese Philosophy*, pp. 86–87.

11. My translation. See also Chan, *Source Book*, p. 39.

12. My translation. See also Legge, trans., *Mencius*, pp. 469–470.

13. My translation. See also Legge, trans., *Mencius*, p. 481.

14. My translation. See also Legge, trans., *Mencius*, pp. 349–350.

BIBLIOGRAPHY

Chan, Wing-tsit, trans. and comp. *A Source Book in Chinese Philosophy*. Princeton, N.J.: Princeton University Press, 1963.

Chang, Carsun. *The Development of Neo-Confucian Thought*. 2 vols. New York: Bookman Associates, 1957 and 1962.

Chow, Tse-tsung. *The May Fourth Movement: Intellectual Revolution in Modern China*. Stanford, Calif.: Stanford University Press, 1960.

Creel, Herrlee C. *Confucius and the Chinese Way*. New York: Harper and Brothers, 1960.

de Bary, Wm. Theodore, ed. *The Unfolding of Neo-Confucianism*. New York: Columbia University Press, 1975.

————, et al., comps. *Sources of Chinese Tradition*. New York: Columbia University Press, 1960.

Fairbank, John K., ed. *Chinese Thought and Institutions*. Chicago: University of Chicago Press, 1957.

Fang, Thomé H. *The Chinese View of Life: The Philosophy of Comprehensive Harmony*. Hong Kong: Union Press, 1957.

————. *Chinese Philosophy: Its Spirit and Its Development*. Taipei: Linking Publishing Co., 1981.

Fu, Charles Wei-hsun. "Confucianism, Marxism-Leninism and Mao: A Critical Study." *Journal of Chinese Philosophy* 1 (1974): 339–372.

————. "Maoism and Chinese Philosophy in the People's Republic of China." In John R. Burr, ed. *Handbook of World Philosophy: Contemporary Developments Since 1945*. Westport, Conn.: Greenwood Press, 1980, pp. 499–522.

Fu, Charles Wei-hsun. *Ts'ung hsi-fang che-hsüe tao ch'an-fo-chiao* [From Western Philosophy to Zen Buddhism]. Taipei: Tungta Publishing Co., 1986.

Fu, Charles Wei-hsun. *P'i-p'an te chi-ch'eng yü ch'uang-tsao te fa-chan* [On the Critical Inheritance and Creative Development of Chinese Thought and Culture]. Taipei: Tungta Publishing Co., 1986.

————, and Wing-tsit Chan. *Guide to Chinese Philosophy*. Boston: G. K. Hall, 1978.

Fung, Yu-lan. *A History of Chinese Philosophy*. 2 vols. Translated by Derk Bodde. Princeton, N.J.: Princeton University Press, 1952–1953.

————, et al. *Selected Articles Criticizing Lin Piao and Confucius*. 2 vols. Peking: Foreign Language Press, 1974–1975.

————. *The Spirit of Chinese Philosophy*. Translated by E. R. Hughes. Boston: Beacon Press, 1962.

Hsiao Kung-chuan. *A History of Chinese Political Thought*. Vol. 1. *From the Beginnings to the Sixth Century A.D.* Translated by F. W. Mote. Princeton, N.J.: Princeton University Press, 1977.

————. *A Modern China and a New World: K'ang Yu-wei, Reformer and Utopian, 1858–1927*. Seattle: University of Washington Press, 1975.

Hsiung Shih-li. *Ch'ien-k'un-yen* [An Explication of the Meaning of the Creative/Receptive in the *Classic of Changes*]. Taipei: Hsüe-sheng Book Co., 1976.

————. *Ming-hsin-p'ien* [An Inquiry into the Nature of the Mind]. Taipei: Hsüe-sheng Book Co., 1976.

————. *T'i-yung-lun* [On Substance and Function]. Taipei: Hsüe-sheng Book Co., 1976.

Hsiung Shih-li. *Yüan-jen* [An Inquiry into Confucianism]. Hong Kong: Lungmen Book Co., 1970.

Hsu Fu-kuan. *Chung-kuo jen-hsing-lun shih* [A History of Chinese Theory of Human Nature]. Taichung, Taiwan: Tunghai University Press, 1963.

————. *Ju-chia cheng-chih ssu-hsiang yü min-chu tzu-yu jen-ch'üan* [Confucian Political Thought and Democracy, Freedom, Human Rights]. Taipei: Pa-shih-nien-tai Press, 1979.

Hu Shih et al. *Hu Shih yü chung-hsi wen-hua* [Hu Shih, Chinese and Western Cultures]. Taipei: Shui-niu Press, 1967.

Legge, James, trans. *The Works of Mencius*. New York: Dover Publications, 1970.

Levenson, Joseph R. *Confucian China and Its Modern Fate: A Trilogy*. Berkeley: University of California Press, 1968.

————. *Liang Ch'i-ch'ao and the Mind of Modern China*. Berkeley: University of California Press, 1959.

Liu Shu-hsien. *Chung-kuo che-hsüe yü hsien-tai-hua* [Chinese Philosophy and Modernization]. Taipei: Shih-pao Publishing Co., 1980.

Moore, Charles A., ed. *The Chinese Mind: Essentials of Chinese Philosophy and Culture*. Honolulu: University Press of Hawaii, 1967.

Mou Tsung-san. *Cheng–tao yü chih-tao* [The Way of Politics and the Way of Government]. Taipei: Kuangwen Book Co., 1961.

————. *Li-shih che-hsüe* [A Philosophy of History]. Taipei: Hsüe-sheng Book Co., 1978.

————. *Tao-te te li-hsiang chu-yi* [Moral Idealism]. Taipei: Hsüe-sheng Book Co., 1978.

Needham, Joseph. *Science and Civilisation in China*. Vol. 2: *History of Scientific Thought*. Cambridge, England: Cambridge University Press, 1956.

Rubin, Vitaly A. *Individual and State in Ancient China: Essays on Four Chinese Philosophers*. New York: Columbia University Press, 1976.

T'ang Chun-i. *Chung-hua jen-wen yü tang-chin shih-chie* [Chinese Humanities and the Presentday World]. 2 vols. Taipei: Hsüe-sheng Book Co., 1975.

————. *Chung-kuo jen-wen ching-shen chih fa-chan* [The Development of Chinese Humanistic Spirit]. Taipei: Hsüe-sheng Book Co., 1978.

————. *Wen-hua yi-shih yü tao-te li-hsing* [Cultural Consciousness and Moral Reason]. Taipei: Hsüe-sheng Book Co., 1978.

Wei Cheng-tung. *Chü-pien yü ch'uan-t'ung* [Drastic Changes and Tradition: In Search of the Modern Significance of Traditional Chinese Thought]. Taipei: Mutung Press, 1978.

————. *Lun-li ssu-hsiang te t'u-p'o* [A Breakthrough in Ethical Thought]. Taipei: Talin Press, 1982.

————. "*Tang-tai hsin-ju-chia te hsin-t'ai*" [The Mentality of Contemporary Confucianists]. *Chungkuo Lunt'an* 15,1 (1982) 44–50.

Yang Hui-chieh. *Chu Hsi lun-li-hsüe* [The Ethical Theory of Chu Hsi]. Taipei: Mutung Press, 1978.

————. *Jen te han-yi yü jen to che-hsüe* [A Study in the Confucian Concept of Jen in Ancient Chinese Texts]. Taipei: Mutung Press, 1975.

III

RELIGION AND POLITICS IN DEVELOPED NATIONS

10

Religious Liberty: The Present Challenge

FRANKLIN H. LITTELL

Religious liberty, we must remember, is a very recent experiment in social adjustment. For as long as the mind of man runneth not to the contrary, rulers have used a priestly caste—along with tax-gatherers, generals, and judges—to keep their peoples under control. In ancient civilizations the function of religion was to make sure that the gods came into action when needed—in an impending war, in the birth of an heir, in a change of dynasty, to avert or moderate natural disasters. Socrates was compelled to die precisely because he questioned that prescribed role of the gods of the Athenian *polis*.

The first break from the ancient pattern came, as Eric Voegelin described it in *Israel and Revelation* (1956), with a "leap in being" when God created a people *to do His will*.[1] Out of the ragtag and bobtail of escaping Hebrew slaves a people was created whose only charter of existence was to be obedient to "the Way" (Torah). Since that time, when persons of conscience have been faithful to their calling, the question of obedience to political authority has always been secondary to obedience to God. The gods have served their purpose and are removed from their pedestals.

Nevertheless, with human nature as refractory as it is, and with the pride of the earth's shakers and movers what it is, there have been recurring regressions to the ancient patterns of control. Ironical as it is, the greatest Christian rulers— from Constantine through Innocent III, from Ferdinand and Isabella through King Frederick William III of Prussia—have often been the greatest persecutors. The Enlightenment brought toleration in some countries, but merely as a pragmatic realization that persecution had become counterproductive. But the vision

Note: Materials first prepared in connection with the Action Conference on Religious Liberty sponsored by the North American Religious Liberty Association, Los Angeles, California, November 19, 1983.

of a unified, monolithic, monochromatic Good Society has persisted—in most nations, and in some parts of Canada and the United States—to the present time.

The first government in history to risk disengaging itself from an effective establishment was Virginia, an independent state under the Articles of Confederation. When the House of Burgesses determined to eliminate the privileged position of the Anglican communion, many wise men in both Europe and America viewed the experiment in separation with horror. Patriots like George Washington and Patrick Henry opposed it, for an official religion had always served as the cement of a society. But Virginia, under the leadership of James Madison and Thomas Jefferson, undertook the risk of separating the civil covenant from the religious covenants.

With the founding of the American republic, the Virginia model became the center of the First Amendment of the Federal Constitution. In due time other state establishments accepted the new pattern of religious liberty, the last being Massachusetts (1834). That pattern was *not* toleration, where persecution is ended and an area of freedom is granted by a wise government—which may very well continue to support some preferred religion. Religious liberty has two poles: the free exercise of religion and the prohibition of establishment or patronage. The concrete expressions of it are voluntary membership and support of religion *and* a secular and limited function for government.

The Founding Fathers were not hostile to organized religion, and the separation they envisioned was quite different in quality and kind from the severance accomplished by anti-clericals in the French and Russian Revolutions. And the Virginia model has nothing in common whatever with the practice of modern totalitarians, where an established ideology functions as an *Ersatzreligion*—and dissenters and non-conformists are persecuted as they were a few generations ago under the established religion of "Christendom."

This is not the occasion to review again the great price which the pioneers of freedom of conscience paid in suffering and in martyrdom from the sixteenth century on.[2] Nor is there time to relate the story of how religious voluntaryism and pluralism achieved success on the American scene. The most important Protestant invention and formative factor was mass evangelism, from the "new methods" of revivalism to radio and TV preaching. The most important invention of American Catholics was the extensive parochial school system. The most important invention of Jews in America were the agencies of mutual aid and philanthropy.[3]

But the reminder of the newness of the experiment is important. Again and again, in times of crisis—and never more than today—some anxious Christian leaders have tried to revert to the old way of doing things, the way learned over a millennium and a half of compulsory and coercive religion in "Christendom." The way of coercion is known: through civil legislation, or perhaps constitutional amendment, to attempt to quiet the confusion of tongues by enforcing a perceived set of religious values.

The exercise of our liberties, risky though they are, affords a higher path to social unity and—ultimately more important—to future concord. And there is Truth at stake, which is the dearest matter of all. As a defender of the integrity of conscience wrote during the middle of the last century, before his sector of Christianity had come to appreciate that the liberty, integrity, and dignity of the human person is a *theological* issue and not merely a matter of politics—

It must be clearly understood how great the gulf is which divides the holders of this principle [liberty of conscience] from those who reject it, both in faith and morals. He who is convinced that right and duty require him to coerce other people into a life of falsehood . . . belongs to an essentially different religion from one who recognizes in the inviolability of conscience a human right guaranteed by religion itself, and he has different notions of God, of man's relation to God, and of man's obligations to his fellows.[4]

Violating the free exercise of religion is not primarily a political affair: it is a profoundly theological matter, cutting to the heart of true religion itself. Our liberties rest on a higher plane than enlightened self-interest or wise political policy.

FROM "HIGHER LAW" TO JUDICIAL ABSOLUTISM

It is often stated that Americans accepted religious liberty and pluralism because with their many "sects" they had no alternative. That is not what was said in the debates in the conventions that ratified the Federal Constitution. What was said was that high religion and good government are both served well when religious cabals are removed from control of government and when politicians are unable to manipulate religion for self-serving ends.

Frequent reference was made to a "higher law" to which both political and religious institutions were answerable and by which they were to be judged. As Gerrit Smith put the matter in 1835, during the sharpening controversy over chattel slavery and the claims of a good conscience:

Our political and constitutional rights, so called, are but the natural and inherent rights of man, asserted, carried out, and secured by modes of human contrivance. To no human charter am I indebted for my rights. They pertain to my original constitution; and I read them in that Book of books, which is the great Charter of man's rights. No, the constitution of my nation and state create none of my rights. They do, at the most, but recognize what is not theirs to give.[5]

The consciousness of a higher law, to which the makers of temporal law were to defer, was strong in the early republic. So, too, was the conviction that the traditions and spirit of English Common Law was being maximized in the institutions of the American Zion. The moral relativism, so evident in the language and substance of recent court decisions, had not yet removed the landmarks fixed by centuries of Biblical preaching and teaching and by generations of struggle to expand the protections guaranteed free men.

There were two fatal turning points in American constitutional law which have brought voluntary, free, sub-political associations—including especially religious communities and university campuses—into serious jeopardy. The first was the Supreme Court decision in the Slaughterhouse Cases, which created a fictional "person" which has become today's anonymous corporation/cartel/multinational.[6] Just three years before the 1876 Electoral College deal which removed the protection of the Fourteenth Amendment from the newly freed slaves, the Supreme Court used the language of the Fourteenth Amendment to create the modern corporation. The guarantee that no person was to be deprived of life, liberty, or property without due process of law meant little to the oppressed blacks for another eighty years. But by means of the fictional "person" thus created, owners and directors of large companies were largely freed of responsibility for the social consequences of their decisions. Indeed, it has become virtually impossible in many cases even to discover who the directors really are.

One of the principal ironies of American history is the fact that the constitutional amendment that was supposed to protect the freedmen did them little good for nearly a century. Instead, it provided anonymous boards of directors, with their skillful lawyers and accommodating government agencies, with a device to allow them to pursue unchallenged their autonomous and increasingly quasi-governmental functions.

Average citizens, subject to powers beyond their control or even understanding, are driven back into the corner of their private familial and club-like relationships. Here, at least, they can assert their potency for a time—at least until outside pressures have so wracked the nuclear family that spreading child abuse indexes the collapse of this circumscribed reservation of freedom also. Some sociologists have argued that the vanishing of the frontier—where survival required cooperation and toleration, if not always amicability—eliminated America's safety valve on religious, ethnic, and cultural tensions. I would argue that at least as fatal to civility, let alone cordiality and understanding, has been the triumph of huge political, military, and economic combines which control major aspects of everyday life and are beyond the reach or even the understanding of ordinary citizens. In such a situation their threshold of toleration is substantially lowered. When—as they see it—a black man invades their club or church, or a pornographer sets up shop near their home, or a "Jew for Jesus" or "Moonie" alienates their sons or daughters, they fight the invasion of their cave with the fury of the desperate defender of a small territory.

The second turning point came with the abandonment of Common Law standards at the federal level. To be sure, a federal common law of procedures has thoroughly matured, and procedural technicalities have become the major menu of law schools and court rooms. But the substance of the Common Law, which had sometimes restrained impatient social reformers and also confused federal and state jurisdictional issues, was finally thrown out in Erie Railroad v. Tompkins (1938).[7] In this case the Supreme Court declared that "there is no federal general common law" and, with Mr. Justice Hugo Black speaking, condemned as an "incongruous excrescence of our constitution" that which those who wrote the charter had believed to be its cornerstone.

The most radical way of defining the shift that occurred is to say that the anchor of constitutional discussions and decisions shifted from the developmental and historical to the abstract and speculative. Traditional liberties increasingly yielded to "human rights." Today, in the most specific sense, the law is what the judges say it is. There is neither higher law nor substantive Common Law to check them. And with the many areas of hurt and injustice where state legislatures and the federal Congress have wretchedly failed to make reasonable public policies, the judiciary has been moved to act as a higher legislative body.

During the Bicentennial Conference on Religious Liberty, held in Philadelphia in 1976, it was noteworthy that the black leaders expressed a quite different slant on the governmental "balance of powers" from that of their white colleagues. They had learned from decades of bitter injustice that they had to look to the federal government—and usually to the courts, and not to the state legislatures—for protection of their liberties as citizens. And they were less interested in preserving traditional lines between church and state than they were in achieving equal opportunity in the marketplace and for their children in the schools. They had learned a bad lesson at the feet of corrupt and ineffective legislatures.

Activist courts, judges with a strong sense of justice derived from the spirit of the times, have thus redeemed our society from some long-standing inequities grown intolerable. In the name of "human rights," basic constitutional liberties have been extended to deprived minority citizens. But there is a trade-off, and it is conspicuous today in the abandonment of judicial restraint toward the internal order and integrity of sub-political associations. Legislatures that do not serve the good of all citizens will be made to answer by aroused and organized bands of those who feel most discriminated against. And law schools that do not teach the history of jurisprudence, that do not study the law of nations, that ignore comparative law, that slight the traditions of the Common Law and treat with scorn any reference to a higher law, are poor schools for training lawyers—on the bench and on the floor—to deal with such delicate issues as the rights of colleges to self-government, the rights of voluntary associations to freedom of interference, the rights of religious denominations to be free of government interference.

None of these latter preserves was in earlier times defined by "rights." Rather they were protected by received, traditional liberties. Today even those received liberties have to be battled for as "rights" against other and newer "rights."

In this development, we are in danger of sliding into a genuinely pre-totalitarian understanding of government authority in all matters of law and order. We are in danger of forgetting that in an open society there are laws, orders, and disciplines which are holy—and which do not derive from government agencies at all.

PROTECTING THE INTEGRITY OF VOLUNTARY ASSOCIATIONS

As the modern nation-state slides toward totalitarianism, the centripetal attraction of a single center of power increases. As a refugee scholar pointed out in the final years of the Third Reich: "The last vestiges of societal freedom precariously preserved through the existence of rival organizations with a wide margin of inter-group friction were definitely annihilated."[8] Working through synchronized labor unions, industrial teams, agricultural combines, professional societies, youth and student groups, and the like, the police state is able to control the life of all sub-political centers of life. Even the nuclear family becomes in theory, though not even in the Third Reich completely in practice, a breeding farm for warriors. The *Lebensborn* program, which was the other face of Nazi eugenics (to destruction of *lebensunwertes Leben*), had to be set up apart from the family. But everywhere else the dictatorship is able to control, and, most importantly, to control the flow of information and to eliminate the open exchange of opinions which is the oxygen supply of free peoples.

In the rise to power of a terrorist movement like the Nazi Party, the assassination of moderates and the bombing of opposition rallies and political headquarters are common practice. The Nazis killed 322 leading critics and opponents in the decade before they came to power and, with the Enabling Act, acquired the formal facade behind which their criminal proclivities could move freely in the name of law.

At the same time, the synchronized groupings became instruments of external aggression as well as internal terror. Through their cartels the Nazis were able in 1939 to compel the destruction of the Jasco acetylene plant in Baton Rouge and, as Joseph Borkin thoroughly documents in *The Crime and Punishment of I. G. Farben*, even after America and Germany were at war to elicit the cooperation of American corporations in actions dangerous to this country's survival.[9]

On the world map, two major factors may inhibit religious liberty. First is the existence of a considerable number of people who have not yet reached the level of civilization to permit even toleration of dissenting minorities: they are still two levels removed from constitutionally protected religious liberty. Second is the expansion of fascist and communist ideologies and dictatorships, modern in the technological sense, that practice as *Ersatzreligionen* the same coercion, repression, and persecution that have characterized the clerical establishments of earlier ages. Of the fascist type, these coercive ideological establishments are usually atavistic; of the communist type, they spring from the failure to master the dialectic of particularism and universalism, and the paradoxical nature of human existence.

THE AMERICAN SCENE

On the American map, the chief threat to religious liberty has become—again—governmental intervention in religious affairs. During the Vietnam War, the only significant centers of resistance to government policy were the campuses and the congregations. Since 1980 there have exploded literally thousands of cases in which the traditional liberty and self-government of colleges and universities and churches has been challenged by some agency of government. Increasingly, these formerly independent centers of discussion and decision are subject to government intervention and control—by federal agencies in the name of "human rights" or equal justice, by state and federal courts in the name of some abstract theories of perfect justice, by state legislatures expressing the hostility of the mob to "cults and sects."

Unhappily, the broad assault by government agencies on unpopular "sects and cults," and the general failure of police agencies to protect adherents from mobs and calculated violence like "de-programming," and the general indifference of the larger religious bodies to attacks on "youth religions," "Asian cults," and so on, has permitted precedents to be established, which if they stand will threaten all of organized religion.

Consider a few of many illustrations of the slide into *Gleichschaltung* in the educational field:

Item: At Princeton University, following normal disciplinary procedures, a student was penalized for blatant plagiarism in a senior thesis. A civil court intervened to supersede the University's authority and dishonor its integrity.

Item: At the University of Georgia, following normal rules of evidence and confidentiality, a department decided against granting tenure to a candidate. A civil court intervened, usurped the authority of the *universitas fidelium*, and the chairman had to spend thirty days in jail rather than betray his professional integrity.

Item: At Temple University, following normal disciplinary procedures, a student was suspended for misbehavior in a drunken brawl which involved damage to property and persons. A civil court intervened to order his reinstatement.

Item: At Georgetown University, a homosexual student organization was denied university hospitality by normal administrative procedures and according to Roman Catholic religious teaching. A civil court ruled in favor of the university. But what business does a meddling civil court have in hearing such complaints at all?

In these items, and dozens more, there is an ominous pre-totalitarian slide endangering the integrity of colleges and universities. Whatever happened to the Common Law tradition of "judicial restraint"? From what abyss emerged the arrogant assumption that a passel of lawyers, on the bench or off, knows more about justice and due process in the republic of learning than the professors themselves?

The point of reference is the truth that vigorous centers of discussion and initiative are the very oxygen from which a free society draws its life. No one has summarized this process better than A. D. Lindsay, at one time Master of Balliol College. In his little essay *The Essentials of Democracy* (1929) he refers to

Lord Acton's doctrine that liberty is possible only in a society where there are centers of organization other than the political. Nothing so much makes possible a public opinion which is real because it is based on free and frank discussion as the existence of independent voluntary organizations with public purposes.
If we reflect upon it, what matters most in the tiny democratic societies which we feel to be thoroughly satisfactory forms of government is what comes out of the free give and take of discussion.
A comparatively large voluntary society, with a membership running into thousands, can keep the real spirit of democracy provided that its primary units of discussion—its branches or lodges—are vigorous and alive.
Good representative government . . . needs not only a strong opposition. It needs also that the opposition should be an alternative government.[10]

Lindsay's essay gives a political-theoretical conceptualization to a process that can be stated equally well in religious or cultural terms. The vitality of the open society depends on the liberty of alternative systems-of-being and life-styles. They represent in both word and practice the higher standard that they hope some day to see generally accepted. In this they excite the jealousy of political bureaucrats, the anxiety of economic lords, and the hostility of culture-religions that have accommodated to the spirit of the times. The inexorable logic of totalitarian societies and dictatorships requires that such alternatives be strangled in their cradles—or, if they antedate the seizure of power, that they be decapitated and their members synchronized.

We have been speaking and writing lately on the development of an Early Warning System to identify potentially genocidal movements before they become strong enough to prove a mortal danger. We also need an Early Warning System to distinguish those signs and stages by which a once free society—a constitutional monarchy, a republic, or a representative democracy—abandons step by step, usually quite unwittingly, the landmarks of liberty and self-government.

ON THE FREE EXERCISE OF RELIGION

Religious liberty stands on two foundations: voluntary membership and support, and secular and limited government. In the First Amendment the concept of liberty is expressed in protection of the free exercise of religion and prohibition of any establishment or preferment.

Unlike toleration, religious liberty does not rest on a grant of government. Failure to perceive this fundamental difference between toleration and religious liberty continues to produce many blunders and false starts—nowhere more than in the effort of anti-clericals to challenge the tax-exempt status of religious bodies and other eleemosynary institutions. The Founding Fathers, in the state conventions that ratified the Federal Constitution, operated within the intellectual framework of the covenant (or compact) theory of government. Religious liberty was one of the fundamental rights which antedated, logically if not chronologically, the entire frame of government. And like the other liberties, it was more precious than any frame of government: governments could be changed or overthrown and formed anew, being mere instruments of human contrivance, but basic liberties were as precious as life itself.

No sound government would seek to abrogate liberty of conscience. Nor did any government create basic rights: they were given by the Author of History Himself.

What the Founding Fathers did, writing in Philadelphia, was to build on an insight that William Penn had uttered just a century before (in 1687):

I ever understand an impartial liberty of conscience to be the natural right of all men, and that he that had a religion without it, his religion was none of his own. For what is not the religion of a man's choice is a religion of him that imposes it: so that liberty of conscience is the first step to have a religion.[11]

Unlike the French Revolutionaries and the Russian Revolutionaries, they were concerned for high religion as well as good government. Any violation of the free exercise of religion is not, therefore, primarily a political affair: it is a profoundly theological matter, cutting to the heart of high religion itself. The demand that whether religious groups—especially despised ''cults and sects''— should be permitted to function must be argued on the basis of political realities is in itself an irreligious and sometimes anti-religious demand.

We see this in the arguments offered by the defenders of kidnapping and de-programming. Whatever the political arguments, we can document the hostility to organized religion which has been regnant in many professional psychiatric associations for two generations. We can also document the special role of psychiatrists in Hitler's euthanasia program, his ''final solution to the Jewish problem,'' and his suppression of ''sects and cults'' in the Third Reich. In America, especially in connection with a ''Christian Family Foundation,'' we can document the associated psychiatrists' presupposition that religious conversion and intense commitment are themselves *ipso facto* signs of a disturbed personality and that heartfelt religion may require a ''medical solution.''

Invoking the spectre of Jonestown, they argue that such disturbed personalities must be protected from themselves and from the rest of us by forceful intervention—legal or illegal. This is totalitarianism in its most blatant form, and it is but a paper boundary between this and the key role of psychiatrists in the euthanasia and eugenics programs of the German Third Reich.

Nazi theoreticians justified their programs (incidentally, often citing articles by British and American anthropologists and eugenicists) by extensive use of medical concepts. And in the killing centers of the Holocaust the facade was maintained. The truck that brought Zyklon B to the gas chambers was driven by men wearing the white cloak, and not infrequently the truck was marked with Red Cross insignia. The officer who stood on the welcoming platform, supervising the *selexia* of those to be killed immediately from those to do slave labor while they lasted, wore the medical epaulet. No wonder Robert J. Lifton calls the role of S.S. doctors and psychiatrists "the medicalization of the Holocaust!"[12]

The slide toward *Gleichschaltung* in matters religious is even more striking than the slide toward synchronizing the institutions of higher education. The arguments are frequently phrased in populist or "majoritarian" language, demanding the conformity of religious minorities to the value-judgments of the dominant society.

Item: A petition drive was launched in Oregon to drive the commune of Bhagwan Shri Rajneesh from the state. The attorney general's office approved the ballot title, thus turning a matter of constitutional liberty over to the organizers of popular prejudice.

Later, the level of outside pressure was raised when, on speculation, the attorney general issued a warrant against one of the commune's leaders who fled. (The Bhagwan, supposedly the prospective victim of an assassination attempt, was himself cornered and bargained his way out by promising to leave the country and not return.)

Item: A court in Santa Ana, California, has levied a killing penalty in damages against the Hare Krishna organization, on a suit brought by a disaffected member.

Item: Reverend Sun Myung Moon was prosecuted by the Internal Revenue Service for failure to pay taxes on moneys he was holding in trust for the Unification Church—a practice common in many larger church bodies, including the Roman Catholic Church. He served a year in prison for a disputed sum of $7,000, at the same time that the IRS, in widely reported cases, was letting politicians and corporation executives escape punishment for deliberately and selfishly plotting non-payment of hundreds of thousands of dollars in taxes.

Item: "The Way," a Protestant order, had its 501-C-3 status revoked in August 1985, retroactive to September 1, 1975. The justification given was that members had been actively engaged in politics in three states and that the organization was guilty of "private inurement." The special kind of mutual aid practiced involved letting some seventy-six members, none of them officers, have temporary interest-free loans.

Maintaining the delicate balance of justice in a republic—whether the issue is religious liberty or another basic preserve of citizens—requires good faith on the part of all branches of government. In the case of black citizens, for generations the shortfall was in the legislatures. In the case of American Indians, since the early years the executive branch has been a frequent offender. In the case of the "new religions," "youth religions," "cults and sects," and so on, the courts have been the major offenders, both failing to protect minorities in their free exercise and meddling in matters where they have no legitimate jurisdiction.

THE IMPORTANCE OF CHURCH DISCIPLINE

Over the centuries of Christendom, government provided the decrees that defined the temporal structures of the church. In 1525 the radical *Taeufer* split from Ulrich Zwingli because he insisted on deferring to the Zurich City Council as to how the Reformation should proceed there. The *Taeufer* were pioneers of the Free Church and said it was none of the City Council's business how the church should be reformed. In 1817 in celebration of the three hundredth anniversary of the Reformation, the King of Prussia began the forceful amalgamation of Calvinist and Lutheran churches over which he functioned as lay bishop. In 1928 the House of Commons refused to legislate a new Book of Common Prayer for the Church of England—even though ecclesiastical commissions and authorities had agreed on it. Even with tolerance, with (temporary) "free exercise", the religious and political realities fall far short of full religious liberty.

In European Christendom, "church" and "sect" are defined by law, and their privileges and limitations are laid out by the civil authorities. The educational standards for the clergy, the circumstances under which a person may be licensed to preach, the political procedures for an individual's appointment to a parish, and even his or her right publicly to use an ecclesiastical title, have all been determined by government as carefully as the terms on which a 20-ton truck may use a residential street. When a child is born, the religious civil servant receives the salary increase enjoyed by all other civil servants; when the child reaches the age to attend the university, there is again an appropriate salary mark-up. The church offices are listed in the yellow pages along with police, fire department, post office, social security, health insurance, and other necessary public facilities.

In America, the logic of the separation of the political from the religious covenants has been—at least until recently—to leave matters of religious decision to the religious authorities. The quality of the clergy is a matter of church discipline, not of civil code. Internal church order—from the primitive *viva voce* democracy of some to the absolute monarchy of others—depends on the *consensus fidelium*, not on the opinions or preferences of government bureaus. In America, synagogues can no longer count on gentile hostility and government supervision to compel communal loyalty. In America, churches can no longer count on civil supervision to maintain doctrinal, moral, ethical, and fiscal probity.

Such, at least, has been in broad outline the situation in the American republic. During the colonial period the churches functioned as extensions of European Christendom. With separation, equally entitled, our churches and synagogues entered a new age in religious history.

This new age of religious liberty, along with its great positive potential, had two built-in dangers. One danger was that government pressures might become so great as to scuttle "judicial restraint" and break into the preserves set aside for religious integrity and independence. The other danger, which is becoming acute in the age of the superstate, was that the failure of the churches to maintain standards and internal discipline would create a vacuum. Both of these dangers have become acute, and precedents are being set—usually in the treatment of smaller and unpopular religious bodies—which will in time rise to destroy all organized religion not subservient to the state.

In matters of ultimate significance, there is no poorer guide than "the spirit of the times." Both church leaders who have accommodated to the prevailing cultural values and judges who apparently know no higher standards than their own opinions need to be reminded of that truth.

Church leaders need to remember the importance of civility in public discourse. As Senator Edward M. Kennedy pointed out in his now famous address under Jerry Falwell's auspices at Liberty Baptist College (October 3, 1983), we must "never lose sight of our own fallibility." "Today's Moral Majority could become tomorrow's persecuted minority." And he went on to warn very vigorously against the loss of civility in public debate. Both on the right and on the left in recent years it has become a facile tendency to stand *in statu confessionis* on innumerable issues of public policy where the wise course is still in doubt. As a center of public discussion, is the "School of Christ" becoming a school of anarchy?

And public officials need to remember the importance of respectful self-restraint in confronting the mysteries of faith. In a famous school case that went to the Supreme Court, Professor John Hostetler put the matter succinctly—and in the language of those peaceful, law-abiding citizens who were being charged as criminals by arrogant bureaucrats. The spokesman for the Board of Public Instruction, in typically authoritarian language, demanded that the children be compelled to be educated along lines that would "make them ready to take their place in the world." Dr. Hostetler, himself a member of the Old Mennonites, quietly responded: *"Which world?"*

Jonestown is the spectre evoked by those who argue that public good requires governmental supervision over "cults and sects." In fact a recent survey revealed that only Pearl Harbor and the assassination of President Kennedy have been more vividly fixed in people's memories than that tragedy. Occurring on November 18, 1978, it has given enormous impulse to anti-cult legislation of the kind religious libertarians consider dangerous. But shouldn't the churches take stock of themselves, of their standards? James Jones was a minister in good standing in a major denomination, admitted after another major denomination had refused him ordination for cause.

The point is this: the failure of the churches to maintain their own integrity creates a vacuum of order into which the press of pre-totalitarian thought and action—like Chief Justice Warren Burger's reference to the "common political conscience" and deference to government purpose in the Bob Jones University Case—will eagerly move. Perhaps the axiom is this: a church that does not use its liberty to fight for human rights as matters of enlightened conscience will in time find the case of these same human rights brought against its traditional, reserved liberties.

A church without standards, a church that has collapsed into the black hole of *Kulturreligion*, a church that does not live in anticipation of and preparation for a brighter time to come but rather simply blesses prevailing values in the dominant society, is a dying church. As Dean M. Kelley has pointed out in his classic *Why Conservative Churches are Growing* (1972), the membership of "mainline churches" is declining because of flaccidity and formlessness, while churches with clear positions, with standards that evoke identification with the groups and may involve real sacrifice, are growing rapidly.[13]

In order to survive, religious liberty, like other liberties, must grow. Liberty that is not expanded to other persons and other issues, that is not in process, declines; a society that does not cultivate liberty does not remain static: *it goes bad*. And the religious issue is like unto it: liberty is not rightly a vacuum, but rather a space for living within which the pursuit of truth may be carried on without fear or favor. The battle for religious liberty is thus for the sake of truth, and is not an end in itself.[14]

In the rise of terrorist movements like the Nazi Party, in the triumph of idolatrous populist creeds and practices, in the loss of individual and minority rights, the failure of the organized church to provide formation and discipline has been as important a factor as the ingrained arrogance of servants of the superstate. A church without formation, without discipline, is a church that invites government intervention.

Totalitarianism is made possible by low-grade religion as well as bad politics. A religion of accommodation and assimilation is a false religion. It is a settler's creed rather than a pilgrim's vision. In the words of Eric Voegelin, "The death of the spirit is the price of progress. Nietzsche revealed this mystery of the Western apocalypse when he announced that God was dead and that he had been murdered. This Gnostic murder is constantly committed by the men who sacrifice God to civilization."[15] For the pilgrim, it is not the blessing of the high places but "the exodus from civilizations"—the movement toward fulfillment in the City of the Future—that shapes the life of faith.

Arrogant, overreaching government is always demanding that religion bless the prevailing values. Low-grade culture-religion is always eager to accommodate and win favor, to help crush dissenters and countercultures. High-grade religion is the faith of those who demand more of themselves than they expect of those who belong to the dying age; it is the commitment of those who have no continuing city, but rather look to the city that has foundations, the City whose Builder and Maker is God. Unquestionably, the bitter hostility of the "mainline" churches to the so-called cults and sects, against whom it is complained that they fundamentally change persons, arises from the social establishment's guilty memories of earlier years of passion and commitment when they too made a difference.

IN CONCLUSION

In Holocaust studies we speak of the victims and the perpetrators, as well as the guilty spectators. There is the classic scene in the Holocaust story: the *razzia* is going on; the victims are being herded toward the *Umschlagplatz* by the evil ones; and the spectator/neighbor is peering from behind the edge of the drawn curtain—watching, avoiding involvement.

Today those who enjoy their own liberties and then peer from behind closed curtains while the rights of fellow citizens are assaulted are not just bad neighbors. They are faithless stewards of a precious heritage. They are allowing wells to silt up and trees and vines to be blighted toward which generations yet to come may have to look back with the agonized longing of slaves whose fathers and mothers were once free.

Let us then look to the internal standards of the free communities in which we have membership. And let us say boldly, in the face of the political aggressors and those who seek a collaborator's privileges by assisting them, "I was born free! And I intend that my children and children's children—and yours—will be born free, too!"

NOTES

1. Voegelin, *Order and History 1: Israel and Revelation*, p. 123.
2. Littell, *Origin of Sectarian Protestantism, passim.*
3. Littell, *From State Church to Pluralism, passim.*
4. von Döllinger, cited in Lindsay, *Essentials of Democracy*, 2d ed., p. 69.
5. Quoted in Dumond, *Antislavery Origins of the Civil War in the United States*, p. 231.
6. 16 Wallace 36 (1873).
7. 304 U.S. 64 (1938).
8. Kirchheimer, "In Quest of Sovereignty," p. 175.
9. Borkin, *Crime and Punishment of I. G. Farben, passim.*
10. Lindsay, *Essentials of Democracy*, 1st ed., pp. 36, 38, 40, 47.
11. Penn, *The Great Case of Liberty of Conscience once more briefly debated, etc.*, 1670.
12. Lifton, "Medicalized Killing in Auschwitz," 283–297.
13. Kelley, *Why Conservative Churches Are Growing.*
14. Forsyth, *Faith, Freedom, and the Future*, p. 200.
15. Voegelin, *New Science of Politics*, p. 131.

BIBLIOGRAPHY

Bainton, Roland H. *The Travail of Religious Liberty*. Philadelphia: Westminster Press, 1951.
Borkin, Joseph. *The Crime and Punishment of I. G. Farben*. New York: Free Press, 1978.
Dumond, Dwight L. *Antislavery Origins of the Civil War in the United States*. Ann Arbor: University of Michigan Press, 1939.
Durnbaugh, Donald F. *The Believers' Church*. New York: Macmillan Co., 1968.
Forsyth, Peter Taylor. *Faith, Freedom, and the Future*. New York: Hodder and Stoughton, n.d.

Hudson, Winthrop S. *The Great Tradition of the American Churches*. New York: Harper and Brothers, 1953.

Kelley, Dean M. *Government Intervention in Religious Affairs*. New York: Pilgrim Press, 1982.

———, ed. "The Uneasy Boundary: Church and State." *Annals of the American Academy of Political and Social Science* 446(1979).

———. *Why Conservative Churches Are Growing*. New York: Harper and Row, 1972.

Kirchheimer, Otto. "In Quest of Sovereignty." *Journal of Politics* 2(1944) :175.

Lifton, Robert J. "Medicalized Killing in Auschwitz." *Psychiatry* 45(1982) :283–297.

Lindsay, A. D. *The Essentials of Democracy*. 1st ed. Philadelphia: University of Pennsylvania Press, 1929; 2d ed. London: Oxford University Press, 1935.

Littell, Franklin H. *The Free Church*. Boston: Beacon Press, 1957.

———. *From State Church to Pluralism*. New York: Macmillan Co., 1971.

———. *The Origin of Sectarian Protestantism*. New York: Macmillan Co., 1973.

———., ed. *Religious Liberty in the Crossfire of Creeds*. Philadelphia: Ecumenical Press, 1978.

Pfeffer, Leo. *Church, State and Freedom*. Boston: Beacon Press, 1953.

Sanders, Thomas G. *Protestant Concepts of Church and State*. New York: Holt, Rinehart and Winston, 1964.

Schaff, Philip. *Church and State in the United States*. New York: G. P. Putnam's Sons, 1888.

Smith, Elwyn A. *Religious Liberty in the United States*. Philadelphia: Fortress Press, 1973.

Voegelin, Eric. *The New Science of Politics*. Chicago: University of Chicago Press, 1952.

———. *Order and History, 1: Israel and Revelation*. Baton Rouge: Louisiana State University Press, 1956.

11

New and Transplanted Religions

JANE HURST AND JOSEPH MURPHY

In the more than forty years that have passed since 1945, the global interaction brought about by World War II seems to have had profound religious results. New religious movements have appeared in all parts of the planet, incorporating both native and imported elements. No traditional society has remained untouched by these currents of change. The Americas and Europe have been influenced by a wave of Eastern ideas. African religions brought to America nearly 300 years ago have shown a resurgence and the development of several new forms. In both cases the centuries-long missionary movement of Christianity and Islam to the East and into Africa has been reversed. Christian groups throughout the world have adapted to a pluralistic world environment. Islam has seen the rise of several vital sects, often in response to cultural contact with the West. In the People's Republic of China and the Soviet Union, the political suppression of religion has not prevented some religious survivals which are adapting to those situations. Perhaps in response to this multiplicity, nondenominational "New Age" religious groups are springing up which propose an essential unity of all inhabitants of the earth as "planetary citizens," and foresee a new age of global unity.

THE HISTORICAL CONTEXT

How are we to understand these cross-currents of religious developments, and, particularly, how are we to understand the new religious movements that have grown out of them? The first impulse has been to focus on the newness of the phenomenon of religious movements in the late twentieth century. It seems to be an unprecedented event. Furthermore, the new religious movements seem a suspicious development, promoting social and cultural dislocation. It has been asked, are these groups not a further erosion of the traditional religions that have promoted civilization? Are they not themselves creating conditions in which "things fall apart"? Are they not an escape from rationality?

Rodney Stark and William Sims Bainbridge deal with these issues in a series of articles on cult formation. Their thesis is that cults (which we are calling new religious movements throughout this chapter) form where traditional, dominant religions are weak and declining. Using statistical data from several locations and historical eras, Stark and Bainbridge have verified their prediction that "cults will flourish where the conventional churches are weakest."[1]

In other words, there seems to be an inability of anything but supernaturalistic religion to provide an understanding of death, an explanation of suffering, and some sense of the meaning of life. The need for these answers is a human constant, though the particular religious forms in which they come are ever-changing. When traditional ways of answering these questions are no longer satisfying, new answers, that is, new religious movements, emerge.

This finding supports Stark and Bainbridge's view that religion is a universal human phenomenon which no amount of rational explanation or political suppression can eliminate. For example, they see the growing secularization of the twentieth century, which many have predicted will spell the end of religion, as providing the very conditions for the formation of new religious movements. They conclude that "secularization is a self-limiting process prompting religious revival and innovation. . . . Secularization of the long-dominant religions is the mainspring behind current religious innovation. Particular religious bodies are withering away, and in consequence human religious energy is pouring into new channels."[2] History has shown that where cultural change is rapid and culture contact is common, new religions arise. The world's major religions began from just such origins: Islam, Christianity, Buddhism, and Judaism. Today's burgeoning new religions do not, however, necessarily foretell the emergence of a new major world religion, since religious movements almost always fail to thrive for more than a generation or two.

Stark and Bainbridge's conclusions are compelling. New religious movements in the late twentieth century seem to be the repetition of a recurring historical process. They are a response to religious and cultural change, a response that we have seen before and will surely see again. That most of these groups are now found in parts of the world in which traditional religion and culture have weakened since World War II—Europe, Asia, Africa, and America—verifies this hypothesis.[3]

This chapter explores the ways in which this religious change is taking place. First, we examine how movements form as a response to religious gaps within a culture. Next, we focus on the content of the movements that have emerged in the modern period. It is not enough to show why and how these movements develop, for it is our contention that what particular religious concerns these movements promote is their most significant feature. We are concerned with the appeal of their religious visions in a way consistent with the outward phenomena of the movements and the inward experiences of the believers themselves. That new religious movements exist in the twentieth century, that they have existed and will continue to exist in human history, is a given. Precisely what form and religious direction they take in their creative expression of the religious impulse is what interests both the historian and futurist of religion.

In the sections entitled Afro-American Religious Movements, Religious Movements of Eastern Origin, and New Age Religious Movements, only a cross-section of these movements is presented, for reasons of brevity. Each of these movements is found throughout the world, although we will look primarily at their manifestation in the United States. Because the number of groups within each of these categories is large, we have selected certain representative new religious movements which show the continuum of religious creativity within each area.

One caveat is in order. Because our focus is on new and transplanted religions, we have had to omit many important developments within religious traditions which existed before the twentieth century, such as the growth of Shi'ite sects in Islam, the Hasidic movement in Judaism, the fundamentalist movement in Christianity, and the resurgence of traditional religion in Africa.

THE FORMATION OF NEW RELIGIOUS MOVEMENTS

The systematic and comparative study of new religious movements owes its theoretical foundation to anthropologist Anthony F. C. Wallace. In his seminal paper "Revitalization Movements," Wallace classifies a wide variety of new and dynamic religious activity as examples of movements of cultural and personal revitalization. They are "deliberate, organized, conscious efforts by members of a society to construct a more satisfying culture."[4] As attempts at revitalization, movements as diverse as the Ghost Dance of the American Plains Indians, Elijah Muhammad's Nation of Islam, or Sun Myung Moon's Unification Church can be seen to have comparable causes, development, organization, and adaptation.

The origins of new religious movements are to be found in conditions of stress, which Wallace describes as "a condition in which some part, or the whole, of the social organism is threatened with more or less serious damage."[5] Like the human organism, society functions to maintain a kind of homeostasis. It presents pathways, which Wallace calls mazeways, to satisfy its members' needs and reduce the stress and frustration that result from its inadequacies. When stress reaches critical levels, the individual is presented with a choice: maintain the present mazeway, grin and bear the heightened stress, or change the mazeway. Wallace emphasizes that this change is a radical step. The mazeway is constructed out of the individual's deepest conviction of proper conduct, the fundamental system through which life's goals and sufferings are given meaning. In Wallace's words, "Changing the mazeway involves changing the total gestalt of his image of self, society, and culture, of nature and body, and of ways of action."[6] From the individual's point of view, changing mazeways is changing reality.

The fundamental nature of the mazeway and the radical quality of the change bring personal transformation into the realm of religious life. Nothing less than an entirely new vision of life's meaning will suffice to reduce the stress of an inadequate and anomic mazeway. Because this change is so difficult and because an alternative mazeway is incongruent with the assumptions of the vast majority of people in a society, individuals undergoing mazeway transformation join groups where the new reality is articulated, maintained, and put into practice. The new reality, like the old, is maintained by social reinforcement.

For Wallace, those who first experience "dreams" or "visions" of mazeway reformulation often interpret them as a call, not only to personal transformation, but also to leadership in the foundation of a new community. They are thus "prophets" whose vision of an open path of action in a strangulated society appeals to other individuals. The individual prophetic vision becomes the model for the mazeway reformulation of others.

In Wallace's prophetic model of revitalization, once the mazeway is reformulated in the mind of the prophet, he or she develops skills in communication. The new vision is encoded in understandable terms, an audience is targeted, and emissaries are empowered to preach the "good word."

If the communication task is performed successfully, converts are made and the movement needs increasingly institutionalized forms of organization. At the earliest stages, Wallace writes, "an embrionic campaign organization develops with three orders of personnel: the prophet; the disciples; and the followers."[7] Wallace describes the prophet as the link between the followers and the new reality of the movement, citing a parallel charismatic relationship: "as God is to the prophet so (almost) is the prophet to the followers."[8] (Although Wallace's view of the role of the prophet is true for those religious movements with strong charismatic leadership, it is the vision of personal transformation, and not the personality or role of the prophet, which is the driving force of new religious movements.)

Once a movement has successfully communicated its vision and organized its personnel, it must face the task of adaptation in response to the inevitable social resistance which a radical new vision of life's purpose will engender. A new mazeway challenges those committed to the old: those who have elected to tolerate the increased individual stress or cultural distortion. The new movement must adopt strategies to convert, overcome, or co-exist with the surrounding society: strategies that may involve "doctrinal modification, political and diplomatic maneuver, and force."[9] The success of these strategies brings the movement into a stage of development which few revitalization movements ever reach: cultural transformation. Here the movement comes to dominate the surrounding society, transforming the social, political, and economic institutions of that society into congruence with its organization and adapted vision.

On the stage of world history only a handful of revitalization movements can claim these successes: world religions such as Buddhism, Islam, or Christianity, and the secular ideologies of Marxist-Leninism. This success creates a new steady state where the social and individual organism can once again fulfill its needs within tolerable limits of stress. And inasmuch as no cultural mazeway can totally eliminate stress, every new steady state contains the seeds of new revitalization movements.

Wallace provides the basic outline for the development of a new religious movement, locating its causes in individual and social stress, its appeal in a new vision that opens the individual and society to effective and meaningful living, its development of leadership and organization to articulate the vision, and its survival and growth in adaptation. In Wallace's terms, then, the way new religious movements develop is a rather straightforward process. Cultures under stress generate ways to reduce that stress, and this can happen through the vehicle of a new religious movement. However, we must not omit the religious dimension of this transformation. In other words, there is an element of mystery in the emergence of new religious movements that cannot be explained away by using models of social and psychological development.

New religious movements form not only in response to specific individual and cultural needs (deprivation theory), but also as an expression of a deeply felt and profoundly experienced creative religious impulse. To those who join new religious movements this religious dimension is primary. It is the key to personal and social transformation. In order to be true to the data gathered on new religious movements, both by the authors and by other researchers in the field, the purely religious dimension must be taken into account.

So, in addition to looking at how new religious movements develop, what their characteristics are, and how they enter the flow of history, we also want to leave some space for an answer to the "why" of religious movements that includes the possibility that the religious realities they posit are genuine. We want to allow conceptual room for the possibility that new religious movements are speaking of something real, that there may be an ultimate dimension to the universe, and that the various religions may be ways of relating various cultural groups to that ultimate.

AFRO-AMERICAN RELIGIOUS MOVEMENTS

In America's rich history of religious innovation, black Americans have produced particularly new and creative religious forms. Once forbidden the devotions of their African homelands and denied access to the mainstream Christian denominations, black Americans forged alternative religious systems to express their longing for a world of meaning and hope. We see in black religious history a continual triumph over the social stresses of enslavement, terror, lynchings, beatings, and the indignities of Jim Crow and white paternalism. In religious devotion, black men and women could get down beneath the racist stigmas that plagued them to celebrate the Soul within. In ecstasy, in the *affirmation* of the spoken words of revelation, they could bask in the life-giving grace of the God who recognized the dignity of all His creatures.

It is very easy to see this ecstasy as compensation for the economic deprivation and social humiliation that black Americans have endured for centuries. Social scientists have taken pride in reducing spiritual sophistication to economic deprivation by maintaining that interest in a spiritual world is directly proportional to deprivation in the "real world" of economics. Religious movements are thus seen as compensations, inferior opiates for the wretched of the earth. The black community is often the test case for this viewpoint as its economic deprivation and religious creativity and fervor are so readily apparent. We agree that deprivation is a factor in the religious life of the deprived—nothing else so clearly brings home the arbitrariness of social reality and the need for alternatives—but we must also assert that deprivation is not the *explanation* for new religious movements. Deprivation theories lack the check of the participants' point of view. Within many religious communities of the economically deprived, the economic hardships they suffer are interpreted as temporary conditions, tests, and signs of the hidden reality of God's plan. From this viewpoint are not the economically advantaged, with their material possessions, compensating for their lack of spiritual communion and center?

Religious movements among American blacks are by no means limited to the postwar period of this century. From the very origins of black communities on the American continent, blacks took creative approaches to their religious life. Although the predominant expressions of black American religious creativity have been Christian, in this chapter we focus on two non-Christian contemporary movements of the black community. Although both movements have roots in black American religious history, each has chosen to locate its spiritual center in Africa or "Afro-Asia." In addition, both movements have developed in the modern environment of global contact and change. They thus fit the limitations of our study to concentrate on those American movements that are either "new," "transplanted," or both. In order to express the range of these movements in America, we have chosen the World Community of Islam in the West, known popularly as the Black Muslims, and the less well-known Orisha movement of devotion to the gods of ancient Nigeria.

The World Community of Islam in the West

Islam first came to America with other African religions in the minds of slaves. Throughout the antebellum South, there were many African-born slaves with Muslim names, practicing Muslim prayers and ablutions, and reading and writing Arabic.[10] But like the other religions brought from Africa, Islam on American soil underwent the fragmentation and reinterpretation that transformed African into Afro-American cultures.

The emergence of black American Islam on a national scale can be credited to the charismatic leadership of Noble Drew Ali, a prophet of Allah born in North Carolina in 1886. The details of Noble Drew Ali's prophetic experiences have not been recorded, but around 1913 he began to preach a way to God that involved a wholehearted and thorough rejection of the values and symbols of white Christian America. "Before you can have a God, you must have a nationality," he explained.[11] He taught that American blacks were in reality "Asiatics," or, more specifically, members of a displaced Moorish nation that preceded the European domination of North America. Though scrupulously observant of American laws, Noble Drew Ali's Moors looked forward to the imminent collapse of the white European domination of America and the recovery by the indigenous Moors of their lost greatness.

The Moors insist that Islam is the original religion of black Americans. A Moorish hymn reworks a familiar black American theme with a refrain which runs, "Moslem's that old time religion."[12] Noble Drew Ali's quest to recover black America's "old time religion" crumbled before internal dissension and external harassment. Though splinter Moorish groups continued to meet (and still meet) in the largest American cities, the mantle of national black American Islamic leadership would fall to the Messenger Elijah Muhammad, born in Georgia in 1897 and called by God in 1930s Detroit.

At that time blacks were reeling from the blows which the Great Depression had dealt to their heightened hopes of progress in the North. Just as they were leaving their Southern homes in large numbers, the economic opportunities that had drawn the first wave of emigrants were disappearing. Although these hardships do not explain the rise of Black Islam, the stresses and mazeway blockages of the period did much to make alternative pathways appealing. For American Black Islam, the vision came from a mysterious source.

Sometime in the late 1920s a dark-skinned seller of silks named W. D. Fard began to instruct sympathetic members of Detroit's impoverished black community in their own mysterious history. Fard taught a "knowledge of self": that the origin of "so-called Negroes" was a glorious "Asiatic" civilization about which white Christian America had conspired to deceive them. The true religion for this sleeping "Nation in the West" was Islam. The noble history of Afro-Asiatic Islam refuted the myths of Negro servility and restored to black America its own superior civilization.

In 1934 Fard disappeared as suddenly as he had arrived, and the strong hand of Elijah Muhammad was immediately felt in a movement estimated at 8,000 members.[13] Elijah Muhammad moved his headquarters to Chicago and began to formulate the basic theology and ideology of a Nation of Islam. In C. Eric Lincoln's words, "Fard became identified with Allah: having been thus deified, he was worshipped with prayer and sacrifice. Muhammad who had served 'Allah', naturally assumed the mantle of 'Prophet' which 'Allah' had worn during his mission in Detroit."[14]

A vigilant disciplinarian, Elijah Muhammad made careful choices in his appointment of ministers and was quick to suspend or expel members guilty of moral laxness or insubordination. The Muslims became famous for their fearlessness, their asceticism and industry, and their utter faith in Allah and Elijah Muhammad. Like the Moors before them, the Nation of Islam was not without its own internal dissension and external harassment. Elijah Muhammad was forced to flee his home several times as a result of inter-Muslim rivalries and police harassment. In 1942 he was arrested for his refusal to submit himself to the Selective Service and was imprisoned for three and a half years for draft evasion. Released in 1946, he emerged with new vigor and resolve to expose the white conspiracy of "tricknology" on the black race and to lead blacks back to God through their original religion, Islam.

The Nation of Islam became a truly national movement in the late 1950s and early 1960s. World War II signalled to many American blacks the final collapse of the colonial philosophy which had created the entire "Negro problem" in the first place. The continued successes of nationalism in Africa during the postwar period inspired new levels of hope and militancy among blacks in America. The greatness prophesied by the black nationalist leader of the 1920s, Marcus Garvey, seemed to be at hand. By 1960 there were at least sixty-nine Islamic temples or missions in twenty-seven states.

Coupled with the successes of the Pan-African movement, the Nation of Islam also benefited from the services of its most charismatic and articulate spokesman, Malcolm X. As his ministry attracted the attention of the media, he dared to express the rage and hope of millions of black Americans, and his fearlessness fueled a huge influx of Muslim converts.

But Malcolm X's high visibility (and the inability of Elijah Muhammad to control these thousands of new Muslims) led to rifts within the movement. Once the most dedicated of Elijah Muhammad's followers, Malcolm X was staggered by revelations of instances of poor judgment and immorality in the behavior of the Prophet himself. More importantly, Malcolm X's travels and wide contacts had opened him to the international Muslim community, where myths of racial segregation and divine incarnation had no place. Many feel that Malcolm X's assassination in 1965 was the result of gangster elements which had crept into the movement and sought to silence a powerful leader about to break with Elijah Muhammad.

Three years later the national secretary of the Nation of Islam, Hamaas Abdul Khaalis, did take the step toward orthodoxy and established the Hanafi Muslim movement with the support of basketball great Kareem Abdul Jabbar. One of Malcolm X's and Khaalis's longtime supporters within the Nation of Islam was none other than the Prophet's son, Wallace D. Muhammad. At his father's death in 1975, he set about transforming the Nation of Islam in the direction indicated by Malcolm X and Khaalis. To reflect the move toward international, orthodox Islam, Wallace Muhammad renamed the movement the World Community of Islam in the West (WCIW). The racial ideology of black superiority and white deviltry was abandoned. The divinity of W. D. Fard as Allah's incarnation was relinquished, and Wallace Muhammad was to be referred to as Imam, "leader," rather than the exclusive title Prophet, reserved by orthodox Muslims for Muhammad, Jesus, and the Biblical prophets of ancient times.

These sweeping moves toward orthodoxy were not without repercussions. Some estimate that as many as 100,000 Muslims left the organization, mainly to set up rival mosques faithful to Elijah Muhammad's original teachings. Wallace Muhammad admits that in his father's final years he could no longer discipline the huge numbers of Muslims and pseudo-Muslims associated with the Nation of Islam. Gangsters had taken cover under the Muslim umbrella, and the Nation had fallen on evil times. Wallace Muhammad's accession thus signalled a purge of these elements as well as a move toward the world community. According to WCIW's own figures, there are 1.5 million members registered and some 250,000 active devotees in the movement today.[15] Others estimated a lower population of 150,000 members in seventy temples in 1977.[16]

The development of the World Community of Islam in the West follows the process of religious revitalization. It has moved from the stresses of mazeway blockage in the deprivation and racism of the 1930s to routinization as the movement joined the world religion of orthodox Islam. The integrity of the movement throughout this process would move most observers to consider it a "success," though dissident members faithful to Elijah Muhammad's vision could hardly see Wallace Muhammad's routinization as successful. Black Islam, routinized or not, still provided an alternative means to sacred experience and demanded personality transformation to realize the vision of an open way. In the words of one of Elijah Muhammad's early followers, "The Messenger taught us knowledge of ourselves."[17]

Orisha

This theme of self-knowledge runs through another non-Christian revitalization movement current among black Americans and among Puerto Ricans and Cuban Americans: the religion Orisha, which means "spirit" in the African language Yoruba. Among Hispanics it is frequently called *santería*, the way of the saints, since the Catholic saints and African spirits are frequently identified with each other. Like Afro-American Islam, the Orisha tradition has a long history disrupted by the vicissitudes of American slavery and revitalized in recent years by international contacts.

The American Orisha tradition is derived from the Yoruba people of what are now the West African nations of Nigeria and Benin. In the late eighteenth and early nineteenth centuries, a crumbling Yoruba empire furnished hundreds of thousands of slaves to work and die in the plantations of the Caribbean, Brazil, and the United States. In a barbarous New World of cruelty and dislocation, many Yoruba slaves clung to their ancestral religious traditions to preserve a spiritual world of balance and succor. Succeeding generations would come to accept the Christianity that underlay the slave system, but many continued to practice the old religion within the symbols of the devotions to the Catholic saints. This tradition endured for centuries misunderstood under such names as "hoodoo" or "voodoo." Beginning in 1959, however, an exodus of nearly one million Cubans to the United States has brought a complete and sophisticated Orisha tradition to the cities of America.

Devotees of the orishas seek communication with the spirits in order to meet the challenges of ordinary life with power and courage. The orishas endow their children with *ashé*, numinous effective power. They receive in turn sacrifice and praise. An intensely personal relationship of mutual dependence and exchange is established between the orishas and human beings.

Out of the hundreds of orishas inhabiting and animating the seas, rivers, plants, and minerals of our world, one particular spirit will reveal himself or herself as a faithful devotee's patron. This relationship is sealed in an initiation ceremony called *kariocha* where the patron Orisha is enthroned inside the devotee's "head." A mystical bond of human and divine consciousness is created whereby the Orisha acts as the devotee's protector, guide, and "true self." The most dramatic manifestation of this relationship is in the phenomenon which observers call "possession." Often in an elaborate ceremony an Orisha will emerge through the personality of a devotee, and will speak and dance with the assembled congregation. The devotee thus acts as a medium to bring the healing personality of the Orisha into the community to cure the sick, prophesy the future, and bring success to all who offer praise.

Thus in dances and songs, divination and sacrifice, the religious traditions of Africa have been preserved for at least 200 years within the framework of Christian, Euro-American society. When this religion arrived in the United States full blown from Cuba, many black Americans and Puerto Ricans found in it resonances of cultural traditions half-remembered, half-forgotten. In the orishas, devotees find knowledge of and communication with their true selves.

The Orisha movement continues to grow in the United States. Without a centralized organization or interest in denominational issues such as creeds or membership, it is very difficult to estimate the size of the movement. One indicator of its size in any one city is the existence of *botanicas*, stores that retail the herbs, candles, and religious articles used in the devotions to the orishas. In Miami today there are over eighty *botanicas*; in New York, at least one hundred.

Although the impetus of the movement came from Cuban exiles, today there are as many black American and Puerto Rican initiates as Cuban ones. One of the most interesting developments in the restoration of African religions in America is the Yoruba movement of Oseijeman Adelaldu Adefunmi. Born of Baptist parents in Detroit, Adefunmi was active in the Pan-African nationalist movements of the 1950s but became dissatisfied with the underlying Western cultural assumptions of these political movements. He felt that only a religious revitalization could transform black Americans into their true selves as Africans on the North American continent. He discovered in the then small Cuban communities of New York the Orisha tradition hidden within the forms of Roman Catholic devotions to the saints. In 1959 he traveled to Cuba to receive his own initiation into the mysteries of the orishas, and he founded his own Yoruba temple in Harlem, devoted to bringing the devotion of the orishas to black Americans. He found the Catholic forms of Cuban Orisha devotions unnecessary in the pluralistic society in America and set about recreating as completely as possible an African lifestyle in the streets of Harlem. The movement grew, and in 1970 Adefunmi moved his community to a rural area of South Carolina where they established a Yoruba village. Here Yoruba culture is painstakingly recreated in architecture, dress, diet, family organization, and, naturally, religion. Although few Orisha initiates and fewer black Americans are willing to undertake the massive resocialization of Adefunmi's movement, the appeal of the religion as a vehicle for black pride is apparent and growing.

The World Community of Islam in the West and the Orisha movements represent attempts to revitalize black Americans by the restoration of alternative cultural and religious values. They are nativistic movements in that they maintain that the key to black America's future lies in returning to the posited ideal values of black civilizations past. We believe that they must be seen as more than political movements against white oppression. Although they create a "consciousness of kind" by defining a common, often caricatured enemy, they are more than reactions to deprivation. This level of analysis feeds on white guilt and robs the movement of its creativity by placing the motivation for the movement in white behavior. Rather, the movements revitalize their participants by providing a "knowledge of self," a social personality of worth. They are new visions of power and beauty that offer the faithful open ways to live meaningful lives.

The creation of new religious movements naturally implies a criticism and rejection of old religious forms. To define itself, every religion must make use of the "errors" which its existence stands to correct. But as maintained in this chapter new religious movements cannot be understood exclusively as protests, but must also be seen as creative visions of meaningful life. The next section of this study, Religious Movements of Eastern Origin, shows that the protests of youth against age account for some of the ideology of these movements, but once again it is the vision of wholeness and mystic awareness which must be understood for the movements to be seen as "new" and "religious."

RELIGIOUS MOVEMENTS OF EASTERN ORIGIN

Asia seems to have always held a fascination for Westerners in search of spiritual wisdom. Successive waves of Eastern religions captivated the young Roman Empire until one of them eventually transformed it. In the Middle Ages, the Arab and Turk were thought to embody a combination of forbidden hedonism and subtle philosophical speculation. By the colonial era, India and China were seen to hold the key to unfathomable riches and secret wisdom.

Romance thrives on distance, and in our own age of interglobal communication and contact, the presence of Eastern ideas has become less mysterious to Westerners and consequently more real. Although Americans had been exposed to Eastern philosophy in the works of such writers as Emerson and Thoreau, only in the beginning of the twentieth century did Asian practitioners of these traditions come to this country to teach.

The most important early figure in the transplantation of Hinduism to America was Swami Vivekananda, a Western-educated disciple of the Bengali saint, Ramakrishna. The Theosophical movement of Madame Blavatsky and Colonel Olcott helped develop an intellectual and upper-class audience for Vivekananda's mission. When Vivekananda addressed the World Parliament of Religions in 1893 at Chicago, the effect of hearing the "perennial philosophy" articulated by an exotic but genteel Indian was sensational. In the wake of his brief career in America (he died in 1902), Vedanta societies were founded in several American cities, devoted to the exposition of non-dualist Hindu philosophy and, sometimes, the practice of yoga. Other Indian swamis would follow Vivekananda by appealing to this same literate and liberal audience.

After World War II the flow of Eastern thought to the United States began to be felt more from the Pacific, in the austere tradition of Japanese Zen Buddhism. Zen found a hearing especially among artists and poets, who in the hard freedom of the tradition found an antidote for the growing materialism of the 1950s. "Beat" poets and "square" seekers desired the experience of religious transcendence without the constrictions of dogma and denominationalism. They considered Zen a breakthrough into a new world of inner experience and a raison d'etre for a mobile, liberated lifestyle.

The first conspicuous expansion of Eastern religions in America beyond these liberal and Bohemian exponents was the *bhakti* movement of His Divine Grace, A. C. Bhaktivedanta Prabhupada. His International Society for Krishna Consciousness, better known as Hare Krishna for its practice of public chanting, brought devotional Hinduism to the poor and to the growing number of rootless teenagers in the American cities of the 1960s. Combining stern discipline with ecstatic worship, Prabhupada presented an entirely new lifestyle to orient American devotees toward God-consciousness.

The most famous Indian teacher in America, however, is surely Maharishi Mahesh Yogi, founder of the Transcendental Meditation (TM) movement and briefly guru to the world's most popular band, the Beatles. Instead of Prabhupada's reculturation of Americans into traditional Hindu cults, Maharishi has streamlined Hindu meditation into a thoroughly Westernized technique for relaxation and the pursuit of the good life. For students of TM, the Maharishi does not represent a religious teacher, but a promoter of systems for reducing stress and fulfilling human mental potential.

Against this background we now focus on two Buddhist groups in America, the Vajrayana Buddhism of Tibet's Chogyam Trungpa and the Japanese movement of Nichiren Shoshu Sokagakkai. Both are coping with the same problems of their Eastern predecessors in presenting a non-Western tradition in a Western idiom. It will remain to be seen if they can make Buddhism as American as Paul of Tarsus and his successors made Christianity Roman.

Trungpa's Tibetan Buddhism

Among the Eastern religions emerging in America in the post-war period, few display the flair of Chogyam Trungpa's Vajrayana Buddhism. Since its American foundation in 1970, it has become the nation's second largest Buddhist group with an estimated 20,000 adherents.[18] It boasts meditation centers in most major American cities, retreat complexes in the mountains of Colorado and Vermont, a university of Buddhist Studies in Boulder, Colorado, a therapeutic institute in New York State, and a solvent foundation devoted to funding Buddhist study projects throughout the country. This organizational success is due to the energy and genius of the movement's founder, Chogyam Trungpa, called Rinpoche or "precious one."

Vajrayana is the "thunderbolt" or "diamond" Buddhist teaching which has been developed in Tibet from the eighth century onward. Its techniques are closely associated with *Tantra*, a mystical discipline that uses innate physical, psychic, and spiritual energies to transform consciousness toward self-transcendence.

Although one of Trungpa's major efforts is to discourage the romanticism which most Americans attach to Eastern mysticism, the drama of his own story is difficult to underplay. Born with miraculous portents in Tibet in 1939, he was recognized as a *tulku* or reincarnation of the highest monastic offices of Tibet. At the age of thirteen months he was ordained as the abbot of the Surmang monasteries and consequently trained to be the spiritual leader of one of Tibet's most venerable Buddhist lineages. But in 1959 Communist upheavals in Tibet forced him to flee his homeland in a daring and dangerous escape recounted in his autobiography, *Born in Tibet* (1971). Winning a scholarship to Oxford, Trungpa began to see his life's work as fulfilling the prophecy of the great Indo-Tibetan guru Padmasambhava who in the eighth century foresaw a Tibetan diaspora and the transmission of Buddhism to the "red men" of the West.

In 1967 Trungpa established Samye-Ling, a revitalized meditation community in Scotland, and in 1970 some of his Scottish students went to the Tail of the Tiger, a similar community in the Green Mountains of Vermont. He began a whirlwind speaking tour of American and Canadian cities which led to the establishment of several *dharmadhatus* or retreat houses in Boston, San Francisco, New York, and other American cities. In 1971 and 1972 he developed the Karma Dzong meditation community in Colorado which gradually became an urban administrative center in Boulder and a retreat community high in the Rockies.

Trungpa's desire to preserve the intellectual as well as the practical essence of his rigorous Buddhist training has made his movement popular among American intellectuals and artists. In 1974 this led to the formation of the Naropa Institute, with a Buddhist studies curriculum that attracted Buddhologists and psychologists from many American universities as well as renowned poets and writers such as Allen Ginsberg and William Burroughs. The glamour of famous artists, the beautiful Rocky Mountain setting, and the insight and energy of Trungpa himself have made the Naropa Institute the most popular of all Trungpa's projects.

Paradoxically, Trungpa explicitly rejects this glamour associated with Eastern spirituality. As he came to accept his mission as a Western Rinpoche, he left behind his Tibetan robes and much of the dramatic ceremonial life of Tibetan Buddhism, to concentrate on a thoroughgoing Westernization of Tibet's ancient Vajrayana tradition. This decision to "unmask" the exoticism of Tibetan Buddhism disappointed his British students in 1969 and continues to disturb many American seekers. The title of one of his many books, *Cutting Through Spiritual Materialism* (1973), expresses both the hope he sees in Western hunger for spirituality and the pitfalls of identifying spirituality with the romantic trappings of Eastern dress, diet, or ceremony. Utilizing the Western language of humanistic psychology, Trungpa explains the problems of the Western spiritual search:

The problem is that ego can convert anything to its own use, even spirituality. Ego is constantly attempting to acquire and apply the teachings of spirituality for its own benefit. The teachings are treated as an external thing, external to "me," a philosophy which we try to imitate. We do not actually want to identify with or become the teachings.[19]

Trungpa thus adapts the tantric practices of Tibet to the mundane world of American life, advising students to transform boring jobs and irritating relationships into tantric exercises for the renunciation of the ego. This attitude is reinforced by daily sessions of sitting meditation and monthly and yearly extended meditations. Serious students also make long, solitary retreats at the various mountain sanctuaries of the community. Only after completing a meditational foundation of 100,000 prostrations, sutra recitations, and symbolic offerings is a student considered to be sufficiently disenchanted with romanticism to begin some of the more advanced traditional practices of Trungpa's homeland.

Trungpa's extraordinary devotion to the Americanization of one of Buddhism's most esoteric traditions has struck a powerful chord among young and intellectually motivated Americans. His no-nonsense interpretation of tantric teachings has rebuffed dilettantes and bonded to him a large and serious following. He has embarked on a great missionary enterprise to bring Buddhism to the West as it was brought to Tibet, China, and Japan; that is, to make it as thoroughly American as it has become Asian. His vision of a completely American Buddhism may hold the key to the future of Eastern religions in America today.

Nichiren Shoshu Sokagakkai

The Nichiren Shoshu Sokagakkai is the layman's organization of a Japanese Buddhist sect founded in the thirteenth century by Nichiren Daishonin. Nichiren's teachings were preserved and Nichiren temples were maintained throughout the following centuries by several priesthoods, each claiming orthodoxy. In 1928 an educator named Tsunesaburo Makiguchi coverted to one of these groups, Nichiren Shoshu, and by 1937 with sixty other people he had founded the Soka Kyoiku Gakkai (later shortened to Soka Gakkai) whose aim was to promote the teachings of Nichiren to laypersons. After a period of wartime persecution for their pacifist beliefs, which resulted in the death of Makiguchi in prison, the

Soka Gakkai re-emerged and blossomed during the religious freedom of the American occupation of Japan.

By the 1960s Soka Gakkai had become the largest of Japan's New Religions and had also become a worldwide movement under the name Nichiren Shoshu Sokagakkai. It sent missionaries—first American servicemen and their Japanese wives and later more formally trained members—to the United States, Canada, Mexico, and several countries in Europe and South America. Under the leadership of the second postwar President, Daisaku Ikeda, Nichiren Shoshu Sokagakkai claimed 7,890,000 member families by 1979, or 22 million members.[20] In the 1980s Nichiren Shoshu Sokagakkai has continued its international interests with the creation of Soka Gakkai International, headed by former President Daisaku Ikeda. (His Presidency of Soka Gakkai was taken over in 1979 by Hiroshi Hojo, when the International Division was created. After President Hojo's death in 1981 the current President, Einosuke Akiya, was appointed.)

Before discussing the various controversies and developments in the course of Nichiren Shoshu Sokagakkai's postwar history, let us examine some of the religious and philosophical ideas that support this movement. The central teaching of Nichiren Daishonin, and hence the movement, is the Lotus Sutra. Its ritual centers around chanting the title of the sutra, *Namu-Myoho-Renge-Kyo*, called *Daimoku*, and selected parts of the sutra (*Gongyo*) to a sacred scroll originally inscribed by Nichiren Daishonin, called the *Gohonzon*, the supreme object of worship. There are three obligations a member must undertake: faith, practice, and study.

Through faith (daily chanting), practice (telling others about Nichiren Shoshu), and study of Nichiren's teachings, the benefits that an individual receives through chanting are inextricably linked to benefit for all mankind. Each person's daily endeavor is part of a greater cause, world peace. General Director George Williams of the American organization urges: "Take pride in the glorious quest of which each of you is a part and with faith, practice, and study, awaken each day your determination for our wonderful and most noble mission."[21] That mission is possible because "a person's environment is simply a mirror of his inner condition of life."[22] As members effect human revolution in themselves, they effect great change in their surroundings.

From this description of the belief system of Nichiren Shoshu Sokagakkai, one can abstract the ethos of this group around three themes: (1) individual power, (2) change, and (3) the mission for world peace. Individuals feel power because their daily chanting ritual attunes them to the universal law of cause and effect, an always personally accessible ultimate. With the help of the Gohonzon, they feel they cannot fail. Change is always possible and desirable in Nichiren Shoshu Buddhism because karma can be altered by chanting. There is nothing that cannot be improved through harmony with the universal law. Finally, Nichiren Shoshu Sokagakkai's teaching of "world peace through individual happiness" connects the process of enlightenment of all other human beings and the bringing of peace to the earth. We are all one in our relation to universal law, and as we ourselves overcome our obstacles, we are part of the destiny of all mankind.

These three themes, individual power, change, and the mission for world peace, have influenced the development of Nichiren Shoshu Sokagakkai during its brief history. Yet no movement exists or thrives in a vacuum, and it is the interaction of the group's own teachings and ethos with the historical context of its development that has finally shaped the Nichiren Shoshu Sokagakkai movement in the twentieth century.

In Japan, where the movement is known as Soka Gakkai, controversy has surrounded the group since its beginning. It began with persecution for refusing to fight for the Emperor in World War II. After the war, this stand was forgiven and in retrospect seemed even admirable. But as Soka Gakkai began to gain a large number of converts and to exercise the power of a newly successful organization, Soka Gakkai was widely criticized.

First, it was attacked as a nascent neo-fascist movement, something greatly feared in postwar Japan. Its public Culture Programs in the 1950s and 1960s, involving thousands of Soka Gakkai youths, seemed all too reminiscent of the Nuremberg rallies.[23] That Soka Gakkai filled the vacuum of valuelessness felt by the Japanese after the defeat of the Empire is clear. The fear that it would do this in the form of a totalistic movement was strongly felt, however.

The second wave of criticism centered on the formation of a Soka Gakkai-supported political party in Japan in 1964 called Komeito. Its anti-establishment outsider status became a political tactic and enabled Komeito to become the third largest political party in Japan by the following year. This was felt to be a serious threat to the economic and political status quo, and Komeito's suppression of a book critical of the party and Soka Gakkai did not allay these fears. (For a complete discussion of this incident, see Hirotatsu Fujiwara's *I Denounce Sokagakkai* [1970].) By 1970 the force of public opinion compelled Soka Gakkai and Komeito to formally separate as religious and political organizations, respectively.

As the Nichiren Shoshu Sokagakkai movement has matured, it has also gradually adapted itself to the status quo. Despite controversy in the past, its religious activities now seem rather mainstream, and the political power of Komeito has not continued to grow. Its situation is rather like that of the Mormon Church in the United States, which began under a cloud of suspicion and persecution and has gradually become as American as apple pie. Like the Mormon Church, and most religious organizations for that matter, leadership is not democratically chosen, and attempts at political influence by Nichiren Shoshu Sokagakkai are not always well received. However, as religious groups age they either adapt or self-destruct, and Nichiren Shoshu Sokagakkai has chosen accommodation.

The controversy surrounding Soka Gakkai in Japan did not generally spread to its worldwide mission, which represents another parallel with the Mormon Church. In the United States, for example, Nichiren Shoshu Sokagakkai maintained a low-key, deliberately nonpolitical profile. In this way it was able to attract 250,000 members at its peak in 1976 and to build Community Centers in most major American cities, while being among the least known of the Eastern movements. There have been some tensions about how much the Japanese leadership should influence the organizations in other countries, and after a few shake-ups a more balanced organizational structure has been achieved.

What is the future for Nichiren Shoshu Sokagakkai? A few years ago it looked rather bleak. After a huge surge of growth, helped by the rebuilding of Japan in the 1950s and 1960s and the deep cultural changes in the United States during the 1960s, by 1975 the membership had stabilized and in some areas declined. Now, after six or seven stagnant years, circumstances have given it new opportunities for growth. After years of teaching world peace and an antinuclear message, Nichiren Shoshu Sokagakkai has finally found a platform in the 1980s as these ideas have developed into an international movement. Its Youth Division has collected and published fifty volumes of experiences of Japanese civilian victims of World War II, published in English as one volume, *Cries for Peace* (1978), as part of its antiwar effort. It has lobbied against nuclear power at the United Nations and with other international groups. It has funded lecture series and conferences on nuclear disarmament, and it sent a delegation to the United Nations General Assembly session on disarmament in June 1982.

Whether Nichiren Shoshu Sokagakkai will be able to attract new members to its spiritual message as a result of the coincidence of its antiwar, antinuclear stance with the mood of the 1980s remains to be seen. Certainly, there is a great hunger for deeper values in many parts of the world today, and Nichiren Shoshu Buddhism has an opportunity to satisfy that hunger. However, the Nichiren Shoshu failure to satisfactorily accommodate the demands of religious pluralism to its view that it does have the right answer to the problems of our era may likewise hinder its growth.

The influence of the philosophical and religious concepts of Eastern religion in the West has not been felt exclusively in the form of exported religious movements. These concepts have also found their way into American-originated movements, especially the New Age religious movements. These movements are our next topic of discussion.

NEW AGE RELIGIOUS MOVEMENTS

There is nothing completely new about the loose conglomeration of groups that recognize one another as New Age. In fact, the foundation of these groups is in the basic mystical principles found cross culturally in the mysticism of all traditional religions: the oneness of human beings and God, the interrelatedness of all life on earth, the balance of male and female, the multi-dimensionality of human beings (including such concepts as soul, the *kundalini* yoga, energy, astral body, and Buddha-nature), and the ultimate reliability of the person's inner self at the point at which it is one with God. What is new about the New Age groups of the last forty years is that they see these principles as applicable in a new wave of consciousness which will transform human history just as such movements as Christianity, Confucianism, or the Industrial Revolution have done in the past.

Three historical streams feed into New Age consciousness. The first is spiritualism which as an American nineteenth-century movement attempted to separate personal inner exploration from religious dogma. The spiritualists thought of themselves as scientists of a sort, along with their later academic allies, the psychical researchers. R. Laurence Moore in his study of spiritualism and psychical research, *In Search of White Crows* (1977), describes how those working in these two areas expected that their activities would verify the existence of spiritual and psychic realms outside of the preconceptions of traditional religious teachings. Their openmindedness to inner experience set a precedent for New Age thought. Furthermore, occultist offshoots of spiritualism, such as Madame Blavatsky's Theosophical Society and the I Am movement, fostered an interest in ancient religious teachings (Gnosticism, Egyptian religion, and the Essenes) as applied to personal experience. This interest continues to flourish in many New Age groups.

The second stream is the consciousness change associated with the Counter Culture of the 1960s. During that turbulent time, people began to pursue experiential activities: hallucinogenic drugs, yoga, meditation, group-generated *conscience collective*, musically induced altered states of consciousness, movement systems, and relationships to nature. Some interesting collective insights came out of these experiments: that the mind-body duality of much of Western thought is a distorted concept, that time and consciousness are not inherently linear, that all human beings on the earth are ecologically interrelated (the moon landing was influential here as it showed us all to be common voyagers on "spaceship earth"), and that reality is relative and not absolute. These ideas are the basis of many New Age concepts, as we will see later in this section.

The third historical stream is Freudian psychoanalysis, which proposes that each person contains the clues and resolution to his or her own mystery. In the New Age, with its expanded concept of what is to be found when one looks within, psychoanalysis gives a warrant to inner awareness on a profound level. Lawrence Kushner describes this transition nicely in his book *The River of Light* (1981) which looks at Judaism in the New Age. Kushner sees a new realization in consciousness:

That the Self and the divine are one and the same. In which case, psychotherapy is the legitimate heir (along with the new biology and the new physics) to the old gnostic traditions, since its promise is not even so much health and happiness, as it is self-knowledge on the deepest levels. It offers only intuitive self-insight, which one may or may not choose to use. This primary gnostic equation of inner self and the Holy One is the touchstone for all spiritual renewal. One idea alone perpetually breaks away the accretions of centuries of piety: we are in the image. Surely this will be the Messiah's teaching.[24]

We learn two things from this quotation. First, we discover the openness of New Age thinkers to adapting what they find useful from other systems. Freud in his totality is not part of the New Age, but certain aspects of his work are. Second, we see that the New Age can be found in many contexts, including the Jewish renewal movement, which seeks to find a new understanding within the tradition. It is not where the New Age is found that is important; what it is saying is the issue.

What distinguishes New Age groups from other new religious movements of this century is their model of how change is accomplished. The traditional Western religious model of change is historical, based on a linear model of time into which God inserts Himself. Change in the traditional mode flows from God to man. Revelation, whether through myth, prophet, or scripture, is God's way of communicating to human beings. Religions are established to preserve this revelation, and a hope for further divine action is found in apocalyptic or messianic expectations. Man, although bearing some special relationship to God and hoping for eventual unity, is for now separated and alienated from God in the traditional view. Waiting for change, man can only watch and pray.

The New Age view sees change as transformation which flows not from God to man, but from the very center of human beings. In the New Age there is no relationship between the human and the divine because the two are one and the same. God is found not "up there" but "in here," clearly visible in the variety and beauty of the physical world and clearly experienced in the glory and energy of the inner world. Change does not come through revelation, but through human actualization of the divine within.

For this reason, the term "New Age religions" is a misnomer. If it is a religion, it is not New Age. If it relies exclusively on a charismatic leader for divine knowledge and a tight organization with clear boundaries as to who is or is not in the group, or on any kind of inflexible moral or ethical code, it is not New Age. So radically individualistic are New Age groups that some do not have dues, membership rolls, or standards for inclusion in the community.

Yet these groups do form and maintain continuity, and they do recognize each other as part of the New Age. There are national publications which network these groups, such as *New Age Magazine* and *Inner Paths Magazine*. There are national organizations which attract a varied constituency such as the Spiritual Frontiers Fellowship and the Association for Humanistic Psychology. On the local level, New Age community resource publications in several cities publicize the activities of various New Age groups and individuals. Examples include *The New Frontier* in Philadelphia, *Pathways* in Washington, D.C., *Rainbow Visions* in Fort Lauderdale, and the *L.A. Light Directory*. In most major cities several New Age educational groups such as Chrysalis in Bucks County, Pennsylvania, or the Washington Network of Light, can also be found.

In 1980 Marilyn Ferguson published a book called *The Aquarian Conspiracy* describing the many groups and individuals which she sees as part of this underground movement taking place around the world. She describes the New Age as a leaderless network of consciousness reform, and this network is the conspiracy. She writes:

The paradigm of the Aquarian Conspiracy sees humankind embedded in nature. It promotes the autonomous individual in a decentralized society. It sees us as stewards of all our resources, inner and outer. It says that we are *not* victims, not pawns, not limited by conditions or conditioning. Heirs to evolutionary riches, we are capable of imagination, invention, and experience we have only glimpsed. Human nature is neither good nor bad but open to continuous transformation and transcendence. It has only to discover itself.[25]

There are two distinguishing features to this New Age unity. One is a dynamic principle as to how transformation and understanding proceed. The New Age view is as follows: if change and knowledge come from an outside source (revelation, teaching, ritual), they are traditional in form; if transformation and understanding come from within (prayer, meditation, contact with the divine center), they are New Age. The second unifying feature is the concept of Light. Every group uses the metaphor of Light to explain something central to the nature of human beings. Light is the energy source which activates the divine-human unity. This Light is not something bestowed on some portions of humanity by God. Light is the natural source of life and love in all humans which they will learn to use in the New Age to transform themselves and the world.

The next subsection presents two examples of groups that are trying to apply New Age principles, one well known and the other less so. These two groups recognize each other as sister "Light Centers" sharing in a common project of planetary transformation, but they are in no way formally connected and their approaches are very different. (There are many such centers throughout the world; one New Age traveler, Alex Langhof, reports that he has visited Light Centers in eighty countries in the last twenty years.)

The Findhorn Foundation

Since its founding as an agricultural community in 1962 by Peter and Eileen Caddy and Dorothy Maclean, the Findhorn Foundation has become known throughout the world as a very special place. It has been visited by seekers, both famous and unknown, who feel that it has a unique energy. According to its members, this energy is the result of cooperation established between the physical dimension of earth and the nonphysical dimensions such as nature spirits and the divine creative flow. This cooperation has meant successful gardens under rather resistant conditions in northern Scotland, and the building of a community and an educational program to work with communication between the realms, especially with regard to nature.

Many features of the New Age are found at Findhorn: a cooperative organization in which the divine within is considered to be the only authority (termed a "theocratic democracy"); a sense of possibility in exploring dimensions of consciousness; work on balancing male and female; no fixed dogma or teaching; and a feeling of unity with the earth and all the beings, seen and unseen, on it. This feeling of planetary oneness influenced David Spangler, a philosopher of the New Age and a chronicler of Findhorn, during his three-year stay there. His writing contains the New Age notion that transformation of person and planet occur at the same time, and he feels we are on the verge of this process:

So what we are asked to engage in is psychological change. The birth of a new planet is basically the personal birth of new individuality. The birth of a new world is the birth of a new image of humanity, collectively and individually; and Findhorn, like many individuals and centres also striving to embody this planetary action, is a womb within which this birth can occur.[26]

This action is propelled by the divine self within individuals and the divine presence in all the earth. These are ultimately one and the same.

Findhorn believes it is in the process of manifesting New Age consciousness on many dimensions. As it does so, it helps bring the New Age to the whole planet by its example. New Age groups do not proselytize; they feel that the example of "being divine" will encourage whoever wishes to follow that same path.

United Research

Our second New Age example, the United Research Prayer Center in Black Mountain, North Carolina, was founded in the early 1970s by Jim and Diana Goure. United Research bases its name on the initials UR from Jesus's saying "You are the light of the world." Much like Findhorn, it has a small stable community of people who live and work in the area and take part in center activities on a regular basis, and a much larger transient community of visitors and regulars who come to Black Mountain. As a nonprofit educational corporation, UR sponsors several workshops and Advances (as opposed to Retreats) throughout the year, as well as twice-weekly lectures.

In keeping with its New Age identity, UR has no fixed dogma or teaching and no organizational hierarchy or initiation, and makes no judgment of anyone's beliefs or experiences. UR seeks to create an environment in which individuals are encouraged to heed the authority of the divine within. In order to become aware of this inner divinity, the Prayer Center provides techniques for its realization, including sitting under colored lights, meditation to inspired music, and a process called the "Seven Steps to Effective Prayer."

Continuous effective (creative) prayer at the Prayer Center for the planet earth is the eventual goal of UR, although at present several hours a day is the most that is possible. The building itself is not considered a sacred place; rather, it is an externalization of the Light Center which is the center of creativity in each person. Every person can radiate Light to create positive conditions in him or herself, in other people, and in the planet earth as a whole. Individuals take on personal "missions," areas that need light and healing such as the economy or nuclear waste. UR has recently undertaken a twelve-year group mission to pray in all the capitals of the nations of the world. It began with Colombia, Mexico, Ireland, England, Egypt, and Israel in 1982.

In the atmosphere of UR, the New Age ideas we have been discussing are again manifest: the unity of the human and the divine, the balance of male and female for each person, the use of Light for understanding and action, and the simultaneous transformation of the individual person and the entire planet. In his book *The Tree of Life* (1981) Jim Goure says:

Being Divine means that you are not passively waiting for the Divine to work through you. You are not that—that's the old way, the old age. The New Age is Being the authority, the authority of the Creator, creating the New Life Energy Force, bringing about the New Heaven and New Earth, which means breaking through all traditional thinking about planet earth. It means we have to think of what heaven and earth combined as one would be like. . . . Think also in terms of the universality of man, of earth, and the rest of the universe joining together, increasing, not just for planet earth, but for everyone.[27]

At UR, there is a sense of excitement about the New Age. The people there feel that we have just begun to discover what fruits New Age consciousness will bear, and they look forward to what is to come. There is optimism and inner peace. UR feels that the New Age is here, and we are all part of it.

New Age consciousness and ideas are manifested in many different areas: the graphic arts, music, dance, film, human relationships, political action, technologies, social awareness, inner exploration, healing, poetry, literature, and, of course, religious movements. The identification of this trend is so recent that its implications are as yet unclear, its breadth unknown, and its future a mystery. It is too soon even for analysis. Here we endeavor simply to establish an awareness of New Age groups in order to suggest how or whether they will survive.

CONCLUSION

America's emergence as a world power following World War II has signalled great changes in the nation's spiritual life. As never before, Americans have been challenged to live in a pluralistic world and to accept the pluralism in America itself. This relativization of white Anglo-Saxon Christian values has allowed room for the consideration of alternative religious systems which may express the special spiritual needs of individuals and groups. This overview of new religious movements shows that they are not new to America, for to a large extent the nation was settled by them. Yet our era of global interdependence and communication has allowed an explosion of new ideas, lifestyles, and experiences in American religious life.

This overview also shows that new religious movements are creative responses to the changes and stresses of the postwar world. They are attempts to revitalize individuals and groups whose sense of purpose and dignity has been blocked and thwarted by articulations of social reality which they have found inflexible and oppressive. A new vision of life's meaning offers new mazeways for individuals to pursue rewards. Black Americans have long been aware of the arbitrariness of mazeways that espouse principles of equality under God, yet practice subtle and not so subtle forms of discrimination. The blocked mazeways of mainstream religious denominations have allowed black Americans to express their religious creativity in hundreds of new religious movements. The gap between assent to faith principles and personal religious experience has prompted millions of Americans to turn Eastward for techniques of spiritual development. The inability of mainstream denominations to present instruction in religious experience has blocked the mazeways of these seekers. In the New Age religions, individuals have sought explanation and confirmation of their "paranormal" experiences which the traditional churches usually treat with disbelief and embarrassment, if not alarm. These individuals, finding their spiritual quest blocked by a social reality which the traditional religions uphold, have chosen to find new movements for mutual exploration and support.

New religious movements are not merely responses to blocked spiritual progress or compensations for social frustration. Rather, they are creative opportunities to explore new ways of being religious. Although historical, social, and economic studies help us to understand the conditions surrounding the origin and development of new religious movements, worthwhile study must take into account the possibility that the religious visions of these movements are genuine and accurate. By allowing this possibility, new religious movements can be seen as more than reactions to change, as more than attempts to fulfill needs; they can be joyful celebrations of change and the variety of human responses to it. New religious movements can be at the edge of historical innovation and creativity.

What, then, is the future of new religious movements? Historically, social, cultural, and economic changes have allowed space for experimentation in religion. As the power of traditional religion to relate the individual to the divine, reduce stress, and make meaningful the lives of its adherents declines, alternate religious forms are created. This process is more complex than it appears to be. Rapid cultural change does not automatically produce new religions. In fact, it sometimes produces a religious reaction that harkens back to whatever that culture perceives as traditional. This reaction produces religious movements, though not necessarily new religions.

For new religious movements to be created, then, there must be cultural change and a weakening of the traditional religious view. However, such change does not always result in new religious movements; it just as often results in reaction and retrenchment. What remains constant is the desire of human beings to form some relationship to what they perceive as the divine. When existing ways of living in this relationship are blocked, new religious movements will develop.

NOTES

1. Stark and Bainbridge, "Secularization and Cult Formation," p. 363.
2. Ibid., p. 362.
3. There has been little published information on new religious movements in Europe, a point which Stark and Bainbridge address: "*Europe is crawling with cult movements.* This fact is little known because European intellectuals and the news media tend to ignore cults—dismissing them as only 'false' religions or dismissing *all* religions as false" (p. 371).
4. Anthony F. C. Wallace, "Revitalization Movements," p. 265.
5. Ibid.
6. Ibid., p. 267.
7. Ibid., p. 273.
8. Ibid., pp. 273–274.
9. Ibid., p. 274.
10. Raboteau, *Slave Religion*, pp. 46–47.
11. Fauset, *Black Gods of the Metropolis*, p. 47.
12. Ibid., p. 49.
13. Lincoln, *Black Muslims in America*, p. 18.
14. Ibid., p. 19.
15. *Philadelphia Inquirer*, July 28, 1978.
16. Melton, *Encyclopedia of American Religions*, p. 372.
17. Lincoln, *Black Muslims*, p. 19.
18. *Washington Post*, July 26, 1982.
19. Trungpa, *Cutting Through Spiritual Materialism*, p. 14.
20. *Japan Times*, May 12, 1979, and *Soka Gakkai News*, June 1982.
21. Williams, "Faith, Practice and Study," p. 63.
22. Williams, "The History of Buddhism," p. 131.
23. McFarland, *Rush Hour of the Gods*, pp. 194–220.
24. Kushner, *River of Light*, p. 81.
25. Ferguson, *Aquarian Conspiracy*, p. 29.
26. Spangler, *Explorations*, p. 87.
27. Goure, *Tree of Life*, p. 12.

BIBLIOGRAPHY

General Works on New Religious Movements

Aberle, David. "A Note on Relative Deprivation Theory as Applied to Millenarian and Other Cult Movements." In William A. Lessa and Evon Z. Vogt, eds. *A Reader in Comparative Religion*. New York: Harper and Row, 1972, pp. 527–531.
Bellah, Robert N. *Beyond Belief*. New York: Harper and Row, 1970.
———. "Christianity and Symbolic Realism." *Journal for the Scientific Study of Religion* 9. No. 2 (Summer 1970) 89–96.

Clark, Elmer T. *The Small Sects in America*. New York: Abingdon Press, 1949.

Ellwood, Robert S. *Alternative Altars*. Chicago: University of Chicago Press, 1979.

———. *Religious and Spiritual Groups in Modern America*. Englewood Cliffs, N. J.: Prentice-Hall, 1973.

Festinger, Leon, Henry W. Riecken, and Stanley Schachter. *When Prophecy Fails*. New York: Harper and Row, 1956.

Gerlach, Luther P., and Virginia H. Hine. *People, Power, Change*. New York: Bobbs-Merrill, 1970.

Glock, Charles Y. "The Role of Deprivation in the Origin and Evolution of Religious Groups." In Robert Lee and Martin E. Marty, eds. *Religion and Social Conflict*. New York: Oxford University Press, 1964, pp. 24–36.

———, and Robert N. Bellah, eds. *The New Religious Consciousness*. Berkeley: University of California Press, 1976.

Lanternari, Vittorio. *The Religions of the Oppressed*. New York: New American Library, 1963.

Linton, Ralph. "Nativistic Movements." *American Anthropologist* 45 (1943): 230–240.

Lofland, John. *Doomsday Cult*. 2d ed. New York: Irvington Publishers, 1977.

Melton, J. Gordon. *The Encyclopedia of American Religions*. Wilmington, N. C.: McGrath Publishing Co., 1978.

Needleman, Jacob. *The New Religions*. New York: Pocket Books, 1970.

———, and George Baker, eds. *Understanding the New Religions*. New York: Seabury Press, 1978.

Robbins, Thomas, and Dick Anthony, eds. *In Gods We Trust*. New Brunswick, N. J.: Transaction Books, 1980.

———, Dick Anthony, and James Richardson. "Theory and Research on Today's 'New Religions'." *Sociological Analysis* 39, no. 2 (Summer 1978): 95–122.

Snook, John B. *Going Further: Life and Death Religion in America*. Englewood Cliffs, N. J.: Prentice-Hall, 1973.

Stark, Rodney, and William Sims Bainbridge. "Secularization and Cult Formation in the Jazz Age." *Journal for the Scientific Study of Religion* 20, no. 4 (December 1981): 360–373.

Wallace, Anthony F. C. "Revitalization Movements." *American Anthropologist* 58 (1956): 264–281.

Wilson, Bryan. *Religion in Sociological Perspective*. Oxford and New York: Oxford University Press, 1982.

———. *Religious Sects*. New York and Toronto: McGraw-Hill, 1970.

Zaretsky, Irving I., and Mark P. Leone, eds. *Religious Movements in Contemporary America*. Princeton, N. J.: Princeton University Press, 1974.

Afro-American Religious Movements

Barrett, Leonard. *Soul Force*. Garden City, N. Y.: Anchor/Doubleday, 1974.

Bastide, Roger. *African Civilizations in the New World*. London: Hurst and Co., 1971.

Benyon, Erdmann Doane. "The Voodoo Cult Among Negro Migrants in Detroit." *American Journal of Sociology* 43, no. 6 (1938): 894–907.

Burkett, Randall M. *Garveyism as a Religious Movement*. Metuchen, N. J.: Scarecrow Press, 1978.

Cronon, Edmund. *Black Moses*. Madison: University of Wisconsin Press, 1948.

Fauset, Arthur Huff. *Black Gods of the Metropolis*. Philadelphia: University of Pennsylvania Press, 1944, 1971.

Herskovits, Melville J. *The Myth of the Negro Past*. 1941. Reprint. Boston: Beacon Press, 1958.

Lincoln, C. Eric. *The Black Muslims in America*. 1961. Reprint. Boston: Beacon Press, 1973.

Malcolm X. *The Autobiography of Malcolm X*. 1964. Reprint. New York: Ballantine Books, 1973.

Murphy, Joseph. "Afro-American Religion and Oracles: Santería in Cuba." *Journal of the Interdenominational Theological Center* 8, no. 1: 83–88.

Raboteau, Albert J. *Slave Religion*. New York: Oxford University Press, 1978.

Simpson, George Eaton. *Black Religion in the New World*. New York: Columbia University Press, 1978.

Washington, Joseph R. *Black Sects and Cults*. Garden City, N. Y.: Doubleday, 1972.

Religious Movements of Eastern Origin

Anesaki, Masaharu. *Nichiren, the Buddhist Prophet*. 1916. Reprint. Gloucester, Mass.: Peter Smith, 1966.

Babbie, Earl R. "The Third Civilization: An Examination of Sokagakkai." In Charles Y. Glock, ed. *Religion in Sociological Perspective*. Belmont, Calif.: Wadsworth, 1973.

Dumoulin, Heinrich, ed. *Buddhism in the Modern World*. New York: Collier-Macmillan, 1976.

Ellwood, Robert S. *The Eagle and the Rising Sun*. Philadelphia: Westminster, 1974.

Fields, Rick, ed. *Loka: A Journal for the Naropa Institute*. Garden City, N. Y.: Anchor, 1975.

Hirotatsu Fujiwara. *I Denounce Sokagakkai*. Tokyo: Nisshin Hodo, 1970.

Ikeda, Daisaku. *The Human Revolution*. 1972. Reprint. New York and Tokyo: Weatherhill, 1976.

Isherwood, Christopher. *Ramakrishna and His Disciples*. New York: Simon and Schuster, 1970.

Kapleau, Philip. *The Three Pillars of Zen*. New York: Weatherhill, 1965.

Kashima, Tetsuden. *Buddhism in America*. Westport, Conn.: Greenwood Press, 1977.

Kornfield, Jack. *Living Buddhist Masters*. San Francisco: Unity Press, 1976.

Layman, Emma McCoy. *Buddhism in America*. Chicago: Nelson-Hall, 1977.

Maharishi Mahesh Yogi. *Transcendental Meditation*. New York: New American Library, 1963.

McFarland, H. Neill. *The Rush Hour of the Gods*. New York: Harper and Row, 1967.

Murata, Kiyoaki. *Japan's New Buddhism*. New York and Tokyo: Walter/Weatherhill, 1969.

Prebish, Charles S. *American Buddhism*. North Scituate, Mass.: Duxbury Press, 1979.

Suzuki, D. T. *Essays in Zen Buddhism*. New York: Grove Press, 1961.

Suzuki, Shinryu. *Zen Mind, Beginner's Mind*. New York: Weatherhill, 1974.

Trungpa, Chogyam. *Born in Tibet*. Baltimore: Penguin, 1971.

———. *Cutting Through Spiritual Materialism*. Berkeley: Shamballa, 1973.

Williams, George M. "Faith, Practice and Study: The Glorious Quest Begins Each Day."
    NSA Quarterly (Winter 1967): 63.
————. "The History of Buddhism." *NSA Quarterly* (Summer 1976): 131.

New Age Religious Movements

Ferguson, Marilyn. *The Aquarian Conspiracy.* Los Angeles: J. P. Tarcher, 1980.
Goure, Jim. *The Tree of Life.* Black Mountain, N. C.: United Research, 1981.
Hawken, Paul. *The Magic of Findhorn.* New York: Harper and Row, 1975.
Kushner, Laurence. *The River of Light.* San Francisco: Harper and Row, 1981.
LeShan, Lawrence. *Alternate Realities.* New York: Ballantine Books, 1976.
Moore, R. Laurence. *In Search of White Crows.* New York: Oxford University Press,
    1977.
Roberts, Jane. *The God of Jane.* Englewood Cliffs, N. J.: Prentice-Hall, 1981.
————. *The Individual and the Nature of Mass Events.* Englewood Cliffs, N. J.: Prentice-
    Hall, 1981.
Schwartz, Jack. *The Path of Action.* New York: E. P. Dutton, 1977.
Spangler, David. *Explorations: Emerging Aspects of the New Culture.* Forres, Scotland:
    Findhorn Publications Lecture Series, 1980.
————. *Revelation: The Birth of a New Age.* Elgin, Ill.: Lorian Press, 1976.
Talbot, Michael. *Mysticism and the New Physics.* New York: Bantam Books, 1980.
Thompson, William Irwin. *Passages About Earth: An Exploration of the New Planetary
    Culture.* New York: Harper and Row, 1974.
Watts, Alan. *The Book: On the Taboo Against Knowing Who You Are.* New York: Random
    House, 1966.

12

Religion and Politics in the United States

PATRICK BURKE

The status of religion in the United States is paradoxical. On the one hand, any official alliance of the state with organized religion is excluded by the Constitution. There is no specifically ecclesiastical law, as there is in, say, England, and the courts treat religious disputes entirely on the same basis as any other dispute. It is true that religious bodies in most states are exempt from taxation, but this is because they are nonprofit organizations.

On the other hand, not only are Americans by and large a particularly religious people in the formal sense of the word, but aspirations of a religious type tend to infuse even their more worldly dreams, so that Sidney Mead could call the United States with some justification "the nation with the soul of a church."[1] The basic conceptions of the Judaeo-Christian tradition—God, creation, judgment, and salvation—provide a common language which anyone who would enjoy the confidence of the people must probably speak, an aspect of the national life which Robert Bellah has dubbed "civil religion." Legislatures open their sessions with prayers, and the armed forces have salaried chaplains. Furthermore, Americans have historically been especially concerned about moral issues and moral concerns, which invariably have religious implications. Religious and moral concerns, intertwined, have played a prominent role in the political life of the country. This chapter will focus on a number of such issues, where moral, religious, and political concerns have overlapped since World War II, and where religious convictions have played a notable part in affecting political developments.

Since World War II those issues have fallen roughly into three areas. One area consists of questions that have to do with the desires of certain groups to obtain a larger measure of social equality, such as the civil rights movement, the women's liberation movement, the growth of the welfare state with its accompanying critique of capitalism, and the problem of reverse discrimination.

The second area consists of questions concerning the family, such as abortion and education, including the problems of prayer in public schools and the teaching of creationism. The third group contains issues of war and peace: communism versus anti-communism, Vietnam, nuclear disarmament, and the economic and social condition of the Third World. Some of these issues overlap; thus, abortion also occurs as a problem of women's rights, and the Third World figures prominently in the debates over socialism and capitalism. Although taken as political issues, none of these has been directly initiated by religious bodies (with the possible exception of prayer in the public schools and creationism). Particular political positions have been widely adopted on each issue and rejected in the name of religious and moral considerations.

Because the terms "liberal" and "conservative" are usually employed to describe these positions, a word should be said about this terminology. In general, a conservative position is one that emphasizes tradition and authority, whereas a liberal one stresses freedom and criticism. The terms are used of both religious and political stances, but the two do not always or exactly coincide. In religion the more conservative positions among Christians typically accept a literal interpretation of the Bible and its absolute inerrancy, while the more liberal positions may go so far as to reject the existence of God and a future life, interpreting Christianity as a purely human movement for the encouragement of certain ideals, and now tending to focus their attention particularly on social issues. One of the most remarkable developments since World War II has been a growing identification of otherwise liberal Christianity, both Protestant and Catholic, with Marxism, which is, of course, the very opposite of liberal.

Judaism in the United States takes four organizational forms distinguished by their degree of religious liberalism or conservatism: Orthodox, which adheres most strictly to rabbinical custom; Conservative, which is less so than the Orthodox and has made numerous adjustments to the demands of modern life; Reform, which has gone still further in that direction; and Reconstructionism, which interprets Judaism naturalistically as an aspect of Jewish culture.

As an account of the variety of political opinions and their relationship to one another, the simple distinction between liberals and conservatives is inadequate. Furthermore, the political use of the terms "liberal" and "conservative" in the United States is confused. Overall, at least four main political positions can be distinguished, and they are related to one another not so much like the points on a line, but rather like the corners of a square:

Conservatives ⌐‾‾‾‾⌐ Classical Liberals

Socialists ⌊____⌋ "Liberals"

In general, political conservatives are nationalistic, and are prepared to use the power of government in order to achieve national ends which they consider desirable. For example, they are typically protectionist in economic matters and socially paternalistic. Classical liberals, on the other hand, believe that people should be free to do what they want to do, without interference by the government, as long as they do no harm to others. They believe in the free market and tend to downplay nationalist considerations. In their view, an action is free when it is voluntary, that is, not coerced by physical force or the threat of it, and because government is always coercive, they wish to see it strictly limited. Those who are now called "liberals" in the United States, however, identify freedom rather with the positive possession of a certain range of choices, and believe that it is both possible and morally justifiable to use the coercive power of government to expand the range of choices particularly of the poor and unfortunate. By contrast in Europe the term "liberal" tends to be reserved for classical liberals, while the positions typical of American "liberals" are usually associated with Social Democratic parties. To avoid this confusion, it is better to use the term "neo-liberal" for what Americans now call liberal in the political sense. Socialists, of whom there are few in the United States, believe typically not merely that government should intervene in the market to increase the range of choices, but that it should own the means of production, distribution, and exchange.

These four positions have various natural alliances with one another. Since the Founding Fathers were for the most part classical liberals, or inclined in that direction, and the Constitution reflects that, to be a conservative in the United States is to defend a tradition that has a strong element of classical liberalism in it, particularly as regards the free market. On the other hand, conservatives, neo-liberals, and socialists all consider it justifiable in principle to use the coercive power of government to achieve particular social ends they view as desirable. Conservatives in religion also tend to be conservative in politics (though there does exist on a small scale a left-wing religious conservatism). People of liberal religious views, however, may be classical liberal, neo-liberal, or socialist in their political views.

In recent years a number of writers who had previously been known as liberals, such as Irving Kristol, Norman Podhoretz, and Michael Novak, have announced their conversion to conservative positions and have been dubbed "neo-conservative."

ISSUES OF SOCIAL EQUALITY

A prominent group of moral-political-religious issues arises out of concern for persons who lack certain advantages and from the desire to use the power of government to improve their situation. These issues are as follows:

1. The civil rights movement, including the questions of affirmative action and reverse discrimination.
2. The women's liberation movement.
3. The welfare state and the critique of capitalism.

In each case we will first briefly review the history of the movement and then survey the principal theoretical issues.

The Civil Rights Movement

History

On May 17, 1954, the Supreme Court under Chief Justice Earl Warren ruled, in the case of Brown v. the Topeka Board of Education, that the earlier doctrine of separate but equal facilities for whites and blacks could not be upheld and that public schools should not be segregated. This decision gave a new impetus to the desire for racial equality and can be considered the effective beginning of the post-World War II civil rights movement.

In December 1955 Reverend Dr. Martin Luther King, a Baptist clergyman, led an attempt to desegregate the city bus service in Montgomery, Alabama. For that effort he was tried and fined, and then tried again, but before he could be penalized a second time the Supreme Court ruled that public transportation must be desegregated. King subsequently became the acknowledged leader of the civil rights movement, through the Southern Christian Leadership Conference which he founded. He consistently advocated a policy of nonviolent resistance.

In 1957 black students were registered at Central High School in Little Rock, Arkansas, under the protection of the U.S. Army, despite opposition from the governor, Orville Faubus. Segregation was eliminated from the U.S. armed forces during the 1950s.

In 1960 sit-ins were conducted in Woolworth's in Greensboro, North Carolina. Yale Divinity School students marched in support of these sit-ins, which were followed by numerous similar demonstrations in other chain stores.

In 1961 the Congress of Racial Equality organized the Freedom Riders, bus-loads of blacks and whites who traveled through the South (Charlotte, North Carolina, Birmingham and Montgomery, Alabama) to protest segregated facilities.

In 1962, James Meredith, a black man, was registered at the University of Mississippi in Oxford through the intervention of the Federal Government.

In August 1963 there took place the March on Washington, a peaceful and well-disciplined demonstration by some 200,000 Americans, including thousands of whites.

In the summer of 1964 the black community turned from nonviolent resistance to violent protest in the Harlem riot. This was the beginning of several years of black riots throughout the country. Congress passed the Civil Rights Act of 1964, prohibiting discrimination in public schools, housing, and employment.

In 1964–1965 in Jackson, Mississippi, when two whites and a black participating in a civil rights demonstration were murdered, a guilty verdict was brought in against the white perpetrators by a white judge and jury. This was apparently the first time in the south, and possibly anywhere in the U.S., that a white person was convicted of the murder of a black.

In March 1965 a march of 54 miles was conducted from Selma to Montgomery, Alabama. In a second march some 300 white clergy took part. Three whites participating were murdered, including a clergyman and a seminarian. Congress passed another civil rights act in 1965, authorizing federal examiners to intervene to protect the voting rights of blacks.

In August 1965 blacks rioted in the Watts area of Los Angeles; 34 people were killed, and almost 4,000 arrested. Approximately $35 million worth of damage was done in the ghetto.

In the summer of 1966 blacks rioted in forty-three cities. At this time several prominent blacks began to advocate separatist policies, rejecting white support, a development known as the Black Power movement.

In the summer of 1967 there were riots by blacks in 114 American cities, in 32 states, leaving some 88 dead, and more than 4,000 other casualties; 12,000 were arrested.

In April 1968 Martin Luther King was shot and killed by James Earl Ray. From that moment the civil rights movement began to disintegrate, with a diffused leadership advocating a diversity of policies with varying degrees of militancy.

Issues

Although it is now widely taken for granted that the civil rights movement was right and necessary, opposition to it was not lacking in compelling arguments. One of these was that according to the Constitution the rights of states take precedence, in internal affairs, over the desires of the federal government; and in general that it is better for local affairs to be settled locally. It was also felt that blacks should take responsibility for their own condition and try to improve it by their own efforts, rather than by securing the intervention of government, that is, that a solution to the racial problem could come only by persuasion and not by force. In general, these were the positions taken by the white Protestant churches in the South.

Those who supported the movement argued that justice as well as compassion demanded that racial discrimination should cease in the public domain, which was conceived as including not only government but also the whole of commercial life and employment. It was felt that it was justifiable to use the power of government to achieve such goals, not only in the facilities owned by government, but also in those owned privately, but open to public use—whereby, however, the distinction then between public and private was necessarily vague. In general, this position was taken by liberal Protestants and Jews, and by the Roman Catholic Church.

Two further issues closely related to these are that of factual versus intentional discrimination, and that of equality of result, or reverse discrimination. In order to have discrimination, is it necessary to act with that intention, or is it sufficient if certain states of affairs develop without anyone's intention? For example, if whites settle in one area and blacks in another, and consequently the schools in the first are all white, while those in the second are all black, is this a case of discrimination or not? In numerous cases law courts have decided that intention is not necessary, and so steps have had to be taken to remedy factual imbalance. This has led to the widespread use of busing to transfer black students to white schools and *vice versa*. In 1982, however, the Supreme Court decided that intent to discriminate must be proved.

Affirmative Action

A considerable portion of civil rights concern has been taken up by the development of affirmative action programs. These were derived from a series of presidential executive orders, especially those issued by President Lyndon B. Johnson in 1965 and 1967, concerning contractual suppliers of goods and services to the federal government. Such employers must ascertain whether there was "underutilization," in any of their job classifications, of blacks, persons with Spanish surnames, persons of oriental ancestry, American Indians, or women. Underutilization was held to occur whenever the proportions of these groups were smaller than in the general population. Discrimination was therefore defined in purely factual terms, without reference to intention. Where underutilization was found, the contractor had to establish goals for each such group, specifying the number of persons to be employed and a timetable to be followed in good faith for their employment.

Affirmative action was conceived in the belief that positive ("affirmative") actions were needed to overcome the effects of past discrimination. This quickly led to the problem of reverse discrimination, for on the other side it was argued that positive actions to overcome discrimination against minorities could be just only if they did not discriminate against whites. For the whites now being discriminated against were not those who were guilty of discrimination in the past.

In practice, this largely comes down to an argument about goals versus quotas. Granted that it is legitimate to have goals, but not quotas, do the procedures in their actual operation result in the conversion of goals into quotas, because they encourage or tolerate the use of minority preference devices to achieve the goals?

The Bakke Case

In March 1973 James Bakke applied for admission to the medical school of the University of California at Davis. The medical school had a policy of reserving 16 out of the 100 places annually available for "economically and/or educationally disadvantaged persons." This reservation was made publicly, and applications for admission under this special program were handled by a special subcommittee consisting of five white and two Asian-American faculty members, and eleven minority students. Under the regular admissions procedures, applicants with a grade point average of less than 2.5 were automatically eliminated, but not under the special program. Although many whites applied for admission under this special program, none were admitted.

Taking both programs together, from 1971 through 1974, minorities comprised about 11 percent of the applicants but received 27 percent of the places, securing 13 percent of the regular places in addition to all those of the special program.

In July 1973 the admission committee informed Bakke that, although he had ranked within the top 10 percent of the applicants and was "remarkably able and well-qualified," his application was rejected because of lack of available spaces. In August Bakke applied for admission again, and in April 1974 he was again rejected. In June he filed suit against the university. The county court judged in his favor but did not require the medical school to admit him.

Both parties appealed to the California Supreme Court, which struck down, 6 to 1, minority preferential admissions as unconstitutional. The University of California at Davis then appealed to the U.S. Supreme Court. A large number of *amicus curiae* briefs were submitted (fifty-seven in all), three-fourths against Bakke, including the federal Department of Justice, many other universities, minority organizations, civil rights groups, and professional groups in law and medicine. On Bakke's side were seven Jewish organizations, as well as some ethnic groups and conservatives, reflecting the growing disenchantment of many Jews with affirmative action.

The Court's decision, delivered on June 28, 1978, was that Bakke was entitled to admission to the Davis medical school but that the university had the right to take race into account as one item in its admissions criteria. Only one judge, however, Justice Lewis F. Powell, Jr., agreed with both findings; the others were equally divided, 4 to 4.

With the election of President Ronald Reagan in 1980, a new mood of conservatism asserted itself across the country. At the present time the chief efforts in the field of race relations are being made in the areas of traditional politics and economics. More blacks are being elected to positions of political power, particularly the mayoralties of large cities, such as Chicago and Philadelphia; and there is more emphasis on the general conditions needed for economic prosperity and on the necessity of self-help in economic matters.

The Women's Liberation Movement

History

In 1963 Betty Friedan published *The Feminine Mystique*, which argued that women in the United States were in a state of great distress, despite many improvements in their living and working conditions, because the culture insisted that their only happiness lay in the home as wives and mothers. This book aroused much interest and is widely considered the beginning of the contemporary women's movement. In the same year a Presidential Commission on the Status of Women, set up by President John F. Kennedy, recommended an increase in child care services, the reform of property laws in regard to women, equal opportunity for women in employment, and a larger role for women in politics. This resulted in the setting up of two official bodies, the Interdepartmental Committee on the Status of Women, whose members were government officials, and the Citizens' Advisory Council on the Status of Women, whose members were private citizens.

The Equal Pay Act of 1963 and the Civil Rights Act of 1964, Title VII, made it illegal to discriminate on the grounds of sex in hiring and promotion.

In 1966 the National Organization of Women (NOW) was founded, with Betty Friedan as its first president. The first item on its agenda was the elimination of sex discrimination in classified advertising. In 1967 NOW drew up a Women's Bill of Rights, which included eight demands: the Equal Rights Amendment to the Constitution, the enforcement of laws against sex discrimination, maternity leave, tax deductions for home and child care expenses, the creation of child care centers, equal and unsegregated education, equal job training opportunities and allowances for women in poverty, and the right of women to control their own reproductive lives. Meanwhile, a somewhat distinct women's rights movement was emerging out of the radical students activity of the Student Non-violent Co-ordinating Committee and the Students for a Democratic Society. Advocates of women's rights within those movements, finding their claims rejected, withdrew and set up their own radical women's movements. Eventually, a number of these (such as The Women's Radical Action Project, Westside Group, Radical Women, and New York Radical Women) were created. They fell into two fairly distinct groups, those of a socialist persuasion (Socialist Feminists) who explained the oppression of women in terms of Marxist economic analysis and class conflict, and others who attributed it to biological factors (Radical Feminists). In 1968 Jo Freeman published the first newsletter of these more radical groups. In September 1968 Radical Women protested the Miss America contest. A subsequent meeting of the group in Chicago that year was attended by some 200 women.

In 1969 a group of women broke away from the New York Radical Women to form the Redstockings, a group intent primarily on "consciousness-raising." Another group, the "Feminists," were particularly concerned to achieve an extremely egalitarian internal organization, devoid of all leadership. In the same year a meeting was called, the Congress to Unite Women, which brought together the radicals and the more moderate sections of the movement, represented especially by NOW. Some 500 women attended.

August 26, 1970, witnessed the Women's Strike for Equality. Also in that year San Diego State University sponsored the first fully fledged college program of women's studies. By that time the women's liberation movement was news. Its membership, however, was essentially white and middle class. A consequence of the movement was the election of more women to Congress, such as Patsy Mink, Shirley Chisholm, and Bella Abzug, who formed the National Women's Political Caucus.

In 1972 Gloria Steinem and others began to publish *Ms* magazine, which proved to be a financial success and has had considerable success in popularizing the goals of the movement.

Other consequences have been the increased acceptance of women in a greater variety of occupations formerly thought reserved to men, an alteration in manners in many sections of society in a direction less protective of women, and pressure for the "desexing" of language (omitting the use of "man," "he" and the like to refer to both genders). At the present time it may be said that the movement has largely achieved its more moderate goals and has perhaps lost some of its original impetus.

The proposed Equal Rights Amendment to the Constitution reads: equality of rights under the law shall not be denied or abridged by the United States or by any state on account of sex. It was passed by Congress on March 22, 1972, but failed to gain the necessary approval of thirty-eight states.

Issues

Those who support the movement argue in general as follows:

1. Women are the victims of oppression by men. This is not so much by individual men, as by society, or the culture, which is male-dominated and works to restrict the freedom of women in numerous ways.
   - It creates an image of women as inferior, dependent, emotional, passive, submissive, indecisive and vacillating, unintelligent, and of weak character; their feelings are easily hurt, and they lack self-confidence. Both males and females are socialized into accepting this view of women, not only as a fact but even as an ideal, so that women who act differently are classified as unfeminine. This view of women is also supported by a legal system that takes special steps to protect women.
   - The male-dominated culture insists—and the majority of women accept the view— that the only proper sphere of activity for women is in the home and the family, as wife and mother, and it is only here that she can find true fulfillment.
   - In consequence, many fields of employment are closed off to women, either by law or custom, by an automatic assumption that they are incapable of satisfactory performance. Hence, women who are capable of satisfactory performance in those positions never have the opportunity to demonstrate it.
   - The fact that women are represented in many professions and occupations in numbers lower than their numbers in society at large is evidence, it is said, that they have been positively excluded from them, rather than that they lack interest in them, or would lack interest in them if they had equality.
   - Not only men but also most women accept a double standard of morality, so that the same action, for example, prostitution, brings down a heavier penalty on the female than on the male.
   - The benefits of society are made available to men much more easily than to women. Thus, education is considered more important for men than for women.
   - Sexual stereotypes are reinforced by ordinary language, in that references to the human race as a whole are made simply by using terms that refer to males, for example, "man" for the human race, "he" for "he or she," and so on.

2. This state of affairs can be remedied only by absolute equality between the sexes, enforced by government and the courts, in particular by passage of the Equal Rights Amendment.

   Those who oppose the women's liberation movement consider in general that it distorts the natural relationship between the sexes and that the views on which it is based are either groundless or mistaken.

   - The theory that women have different or lesser abilities in some areas than men solely because they have been reared to believe that, for example, is unsupported by any solid evidence. On the contrary, there is much evidence that such differences begin too early in life to be merely the product of socialization.
   - The view that women in general in the past have directed their abilities toward the home and family because of societal pressure rather than their own personal interest seems likewise to be without any solid foundation.
   - Absolute equality for the sexes would deprive women of much protection which experience has shown they need and which most of them continue to want.
   - In blaming forces outside themselves for their condition, they are adopting an attitude that is servile and juvenile, and can only increase the sense of helplessness against which they protest.

The Democratic Party's nomination of a woman, Geraldine Ferraro, as its candidate for the Vice-Presidency in the 1984 elections has given considerable encouragement to feminists—tempered, however, by a certain pessimism about the outcome of such elections.

The Welfare State and the Critique of Capitalism

The welfare state and the critique of capitalism have been religious issues in that the appeal to compassion and social justice which has animated them has often been spurred on by religious motives and has aroused the support of many religious persons and organizations. On the other hand, both are now encountering increasing resistance from others equally religious, both liberals and conservatives, also in the name of justice and freedom.

History

In the United States the initial impetus to welfare measures in a contemporary sense was given by the Great Depression. In 1931 Monsignor John A. Ryan published *A Living Wage* which, on the basis of the teachings of Pope Leo XIII, called for a $5 billion public works program. The following year the Federal Council of Churches, the National Catholic Welfare Conference, and the Central Conference of American Rabbis called on government to finance work relief projects, as well as unemployment and old age insurance. Franklin D. Roosevelt secured the passage of a number of bills in Congress to implement such measures, instituting two compulsory systems of income support. One was a contributory insurance program to provide for old age and unemployment. The other was a public assistance program, financed by general revenues, to help special classes of needy: the elderly poor, the blind, and dependent children. The children in question, it was assumed, would be chiefly those who had lost a parent before reaching the age of eligibility for social security. It was expected that the public assistance would die a natural death as insurance programs developed. In fact, however, both kinds of program underwent expansion, at first moderately and then rapidly.

Beginning in 1947, Congress enacted a series of housing bills to provide home finance and to encourage the clearing of slums and urban renewal. In 1949, however, the Wagner-Murray-Dingell bill to introduce compulsory health insurance was opposed by the major Catholic welfare organizations and failed. In 1953 the Department of Health, Education and Welfare was created, and in 1954 and 1956 funds were legislated for the training of social workers.

Under the Kennedy administration plans were laid for an ambitious welfare program, with the advice and help of numerous intellectuals, but Congress showed no enthusiasm for such measures, and little was done.

Meanwhile, the intellectual critique of capitalism was gathering strength. John K. Galbraith published *The Affluent Society* in 1958, and in 1962 Michael Harrington published *The Other America*. Both writers exerted immense influence, especially on liberal clergy and intellectuals, and a radical social criticism soon became current on campus and in the press, as well as in liberal churches and synagogues.

The general theme of this critique was the failure of capitalism to eliminate poverty. In explanation of this failure, it was asserted that unrestrained capitalism destroyed the market freedom that had created it. It resulted in the formation of very large corporations, or of a class of very rich people, who control the market for their own ends. Capitalism was therefore, as Marx had claimed, exploitative: it exploited the poor, the worker and the consumer, the environment, and the poorer nations of the Third World. Thus, the wealth of the rich was not merely an affront to the poor, but the very cause of their poverty, and the intervention of government in the market was needed as a "countervailing power."

Under the presidency of Lyndon Johnson public assistance explosion took place, his "War on Poverty." The original programs were greatly expanded, and many new programs were added. By 1974 federal public assistance programs included: Social Security (to provide income in old age), Medicare (medical treatment for the aged), Unemployment Compensation, Federal Civil Service Retirement, Veterans Compensation Pension, Temporary Employment Assistance, Medicaid (medical treatment for the poor), Aid to Families with Dependent Children, Supplemental Security Income (for aged, blind, or disabled individuals), Food Stamps, Public Housing, Child Nutrition (school lunches for those unable to pay), and manpower policy: MDTA programs—institutional on the job training, job opportunities in the business sector, Job Corps, Neighborhood Youth Corps, Work Incentive Program, and Public Employment Program.

This explosion of public assistance programs produced a budgetary crisis in the federal government, which all subsequent governments have tried to solve, but so far without success. President Richard M. Nixon, in his Family Assistance Plan, proposed to replace the existing programs with a negative income tax, in effect a guaranteed income, but Congress rejected the plan. He then expanded the earlier programs and added a number of new ones, including the Supplemental Security Income program and the Earned Income Tax Credit. President Jimmy Carter likewise tried to reform the mass of public assistance programs, but with equal lack of success. Under President Reagan the growth of the programs has been slowed.

At the present time the effectiveness of these programs, massive though they have been, is also being seriously called into question. For it appears that they have produced little, if any, improvement in the standard of living of the poor. Indeed, the median black family income relative to that of whites has actually declined over the last twenty years. Furthermore, it is increasingly being accepted that the public assistance programs have even done great harm precisely to the sections of society they were intended to help. In particular, they seem to bear a large part of the responsibility for the astonishing decline of the black family: a majority of black children are now born out of wedlock. For the role of the husband and father is in effect abolished by welfare, and his absence from the family is even an explicit requirement of some programs. Yet families without husbands and fathers are statistically the most likely to sink further into poverty. And, in general, it must be acknowledged that welfare programs tend to induce a spirit of dependency and passivity which is the very opposite of the self-reliance and determined striving for independence which alone in the long run can lift the poor to a better life. At the same time capitalism and the idea of a free market, formerly so decried, are increasingly being defended among economists and writers on public policy. The earlier work of Friedrich von Hayek and Ludwig von Mises, both influential in the Chicago school of economics, in that direction has been further developed and popularized by such authors as Milton Friedman, Irving Kristol, Michael Novak, and George Gilder. These writers argue, for example, that free market capitalism maximizes the material welfare of society as a whole, especially of the poor, and that its values are in harmony with those of Western civilization and the Judaeo-Christian tradition.

The Catholic Bishops of the United States meanwhile issued a statement on this subject in 1985 parallel to the one they issued in 1983 on nuclear war (see below). There are signs of mounting opposition by the Catholic laity to such a stance.

ISSUES CONCERNING THE FAMILY

Abortion

On January 22, 1973, the Supreme Court ruled, 7 to 2, that a state may not prevent a woman from obtaining an abortion during the first six months of pregnancy. With this decision a public controversy flared up which is still raging. In the majority opinion, Justice Harry Blackmun denied that the unborn fetus was a person entitled to the due process of law as provided by the Fourteenth Amendment to the Constitution. On the contrary, he agreed, the Fourteenth Amendment guarantees the right of privacy, which implies that it is a woman's own decision what to do with her body.

After three months, the court ruled, a state may intervene to protect the health of the woman, and during the last ten weeks it may proscribe abortion.

On July 15, 1976, the Supreme Court ruled that a woman was not required to obtain her husband's consent to an abortion nor, if under eighteen, to obtain her parents' consent.

These decisions elicited a strong reaction from the Roman Catholic Church as well as from many Protestants, particularly the more conservative. The widespread sentiment against abortion, fueled by religious beliefs, has been reflected in the political parties, in Congress, and in decisions of the lower courts. During the presidential campaign of 1976, the Republican platform protested the Supreme Court's "intrusion into the family structure" and supported a constitutional amendment to protect the life of the unborn child. The Democrats said they recognized the religious and ethical concerns many Americans had about abortion but were not in favor of a constitutional amendment.

In February 1975 Dr. K. C. Edelin was found guilty by a Boston jury of manslaughter in the death of a male fetus, although he estimated it to be not more than twenty-two weeks old.

In June 1977, however, the Supreme Court ruled that states do not have to fund elective abortions, and in August 1977 the Secretary of HEW, Joseph Califano, ordered that no federal funds be provided for non-therapeutic abortions. In December 1977 Congress passed the Hyde Amendment, which bans Medicaid reimbursement for all abortions except those performed to save the mother's life, and in June 1978 the House of Representatives expressly allowed federal funding of abortions when the mother's life was in danger. In August 1978 Congress barred the use of defense budget money for abortions for military personnel and their dependents.

Issues

The principal moral issue is, when does the fetus become a person? The deliberate killing of an innocent person is generally recognized to be murder.

The teaching of the Catholic Church, enunciated at the Second Vatican Council, is that the fetus becomes a person at the moment of conception. This became official Catholic teaching only during the nineteenth century, although the Christian Church had from its beginning condemned abortion, and the early Protestants, such as Martin Luther and John Calvin, did likewise.

In modern Catholic teaching, this view is based on the belief that it is at the moment of conception that the fetus receives its soul from God. (In the Middle Ages belief was not yet so uniform. Aquinas, for example, believed that the fetus received its soul at the time of "quickening," when it first begins to stir in the womb.)

Other arguments have been made of a biological and ethical nature in support of the view that the fetus is a person from the moment of conception. The biological argument is that the fetus has the same biological identity as the subsequent adult, possessing the same unique combination of genes. It is also argued that any dividing line between personhood and non-personhood which is drawn between conception and birth must be arbitrary. In the Catholic view an abortion should not even be performed in order to save the life of the mother, for it is not permissible deliberately to kill one innocent person in order to save the life of another.

Other Christians and many Jews agree that abortion should be generally condemned but make an exception for the case where the pregnancy threatens the life of the mother and no other remedy is available, or when it is the result of rape or incest, and therefore not the responsibility of the mother. Churches that have made liberal statements on abortion include: the American Baptist Convention, the Lutheran Church in America, the Presbyterian Church in the U.S., the United Church of Christ, the United Methodist Church, and the United Presbyterian Church in the U.S.A.

The decision of the Supreme Court, however, goes far beyond therapeutic abortion. Justice Harry Blackmun, explaining the grounds on which the decision rested, asserted that "there is no assurance that the word 'person' as used in the Constitution has any possible prenatal application." That is, it is impossible to prove that the fetus is a person until a relatively advanced stage of pregnancy.

Against that view, opponents of abortion have argued that the mere fact of doubt that something is a person does not justify killing it. In turn, against that rationale it can be argued that the illegitimacy of killing some object rests on the possibility that subsequently it can be identified with certainty as a human being.

Many of those who defend the legalization of abortion are deeply concerned about the social problems associated with it. Abortions have always occurred, they argue, and always will occur whether or not they are forbidden by law. What is at stake then is not whether abortions will happen, but whether they will happen safely. For if abortion is a crime, then it is very often performed under circumstances that make it much more dangerous to the health of the mother. This is a utilitarian approach, however, which cannot satisfy the proponents of a strict morality.

Creationism

The use of tax money to support school systems inevitably subjects education to political pressure. Nowhere has this been experienced more acutely than in regard to courses that conflict with certain religious and moral beliefs. Since the 1960s two states, Arkansas and Louisiana, have passed legislation placing restraints on the content of science courses for religious reasons, and some twenty other states have been considering similar measures.

Science excludes belief in special interventions of the deity in the physical world, for it works on the twofold principle that natural explanations are always to be preferred to supernatural ones and that a natural explanation of a physical event is always possible. The biological sciences tend further to emphasize the continuity and thus the similarity between human beings and animals. Science has no methods for studying the moral or spiritual aspects of human existence. This has led some practitioners of science and many philosophers to conclude that science requires a materialistic understanding of human existence, a view reflected in some public high school science material.

On the other hand, a considerable number of Christians believe not only that human beings are in many respects discontinuous with the animal and material world, but also that the Bible is verbally inspired by God, and so the account which the book of Genesis gives of the creation of the world, of life and of the human race, is literally true, according to which the world and man were created within a week, and at a not very remote date in the past. Of late the claim has further been made that the Genesis account itself can be supported by scientific, that is, geological, paleontological, and biological evidence.

This conflict between a reductionist view of science and a fundamentalist understanding of Christianity is by no means new, nor is its political expression. Between 1921 and 1929 anti-evolution bills were introduced into thirty-seven state legislatures and passed into law in Tennessee, 1925; Mississippi, 1926; Arkansas, 1928; and Texas, 1929. The most famous incident in this movement was the Scopes trial in 1925, in which John Scopes, a biology teacher, was convicted and fined in Dayton, Tennessee, for teaching evolution.

This Tennessee law was not repealed until 1967. In 1968 the U.S. Supreme Court ruled the Arkansas law unconstitutional, with corresponding effect on similar laws in other states. However, this by no means signified the end of the movement to harmonize science courses with religious belief. In 1969 the California Board of Education was persuaded to adopt guidelines for public school biology courses which gave equal time to the Genesis account of creation as to evolutionary theory.

In the mid–1970s a furor erupted over the funding by the National Science Foundation (NSF) of *Man: A Course of Study*. This was a social science course for upper elementary schools devised by a group of scholars headed by Jerome Bruner, emphasizing animal behavior as a key to the understanding of human behavior, and in effect placing sexual and family customs of Eskimos such as infanticide and senilicide on the same moral level as those of civilized societies. When this course was introduced into schools under the aegis of the NSF, a storm of protest erupted across the country. In Kanawha County, West Virginia, at the same time, not unrelated violence broke out over the introduction of English teaching materials considered offensive: there were beatings, shootings, and the firebombing of school buildings. The widespread protest led to congressional investigation of the NSF, which cut off all further funds to MACOSA (*Man, A Course of Study*) and was itself rather thoroughly reorganized, so that its educational programs were largely terminated.

In 1981 Arkansas and Louisiana passed legislation requiring that the creationist account of the origins of the world and life be included in school courses, not as a religious belief but as a scientific theory. Although the Arkansas law was subsequently ruled unconstitutional by a federal judge, some twenty other states have been considering similar legislation.

A public opinion survey conducted by NBC News in 1981 showed that 76 percent of the American people felt that public schools should teach both the scientific theory of evolution and the biblical theory of creation; 8 percent favored teaching only the scientific theory; and 10 percent only the biblical theory.

Prayer in the Public Schools

Despite the constitutional separation of church and state in the United States, it had long been the practice in many public schools to have prayer and Bible-reading. In some states they were even required by law as being necessary for character development and moral training. It was also widely customary to have released time for formal religious instruction by church representatives during regular school hours in the classroom.

In 1948, however, the Supreme Court decided, in the case of McCollum v. the Board of Education of Champaign, Illinois, that such released time for religious instruction during ordinary school hours and in the classroom was unconstitutional. In 1952, however, it declared (Zorach v. Clauson) that released time for religious instruction off the school grounds, even though during regular class hours, was legitimate.

In 1962 the Court heard the case of Engle v. Vitale. The Board of Education of Union Free District No. 9, New Hyde Park, New York, had directed the following prayer to be recited each morning by all the children in the presence of the teacher: "Almighty God, we acknowledge our dependence on Thee, and we beg Thy blessing upon us, our parents, our teachers and our country." This prayer had been composed and published by the New York State Board of Regents. When the parents of ten pupils brought action in a New York State court against the practice, the New York Court of Appeals upheld the right of the state to employ such a prayer as long as no student was compelled against his or her parents' will to participate in it. The parents, however, appealed this decision to the Supreme Court, which ruled it unconstitutional.

In 1963 the Court gave a similar ruling on Bible-reading. In 1959 the Commonwealth of Pennsylvania had passed a law that "at least ten verses from the Holy Bible shall be read, without comment, at the opening of each public school on each school day. Any child shall be excused from such Bible-reading, or attending such Bible-reading, upon the written request of his parent or guardian."

In Abington, Pennsylvania, the Bible-reading was accompanied by recitation of the Lord's Prayer. Suit was brought by Edward L. Schempp, a Unitarian.

In its decision the Supreme Court stated, on the one hand, that education was incomplete without the study of comparative religion, the history of religion, and its relationship to the advancement of civilization, that the Bible was worthy of study for its literary and historic qualities, and that such studies should be conducted objectively as part of a secular educational program. On the other hand, it ruled that the Abington practice was not of that kind but was a religious exercise, and thus unconstitutional.

These last two decisions of the Court have aroused a considerable amount of opposition which has become a significant political force. President Reagan has repeatedly avowed his desire to see prayer and Bible-reading readmitted to the public schools.

ISSUES OF WAR AND PEACE

Communism and Anti-Communism

The violent hostility of communism toward religion impelled many religious people to oppose it strongly from the beginning. This was especially true of Catholics: the popes condemned it in the most severe terms. When the Russian Revolution broke out, intellectuals and liberals widely viewed it as a necessary evil, but the brutal persecution of the Church which followed it made the Catholics' worst fears a reality, and prayers and sermons on the subject became a standard feature of Catholic worship.

Franklin D. Roosevelt's New Deal was in general supported by Catholics, who were mainly Democrats, though some, such as Father Charles Coughlin and the *Brooklyn Tablet*, rejected it as the beginning of a Communist regime. Roosevelt's official recognition of the Soviet Union was a blow to Catholics because it seemed to imply approval or at least tolerance of the persecutions carried out there. In March 1937 Pope Pius XI issued his encyclical *Atheistic Communism*, condemning communism because of its militant atheism. When the Spanish Civil War broke out in July of that year, many in the West sympathized with the Loyalist or government cause (an alliance of anticlericals, socialists, anarchists, and communists), but because of Loyalist persecution of the Church, Catholics in general sided with Franco.

The U.S. alliance with the Soviet Union in World War II made little difference to the anticommunism of U.S. Catholics. As the war ended, however, their hostility to communism increased markedly. The Soviet Union occupied Eastern Europe, including Poland, a Catholic country. In Yugoslavia Archbishop Aloysius Stepinac was condemned on trumped-up charges to sixteen years in prison which prompted, among other protests, a mass demonstration of 40,000 people in Philadelphia. In Hungary in 1948 Joseph Cardinal Mindszenty was arrested, apparently tortured, and condemned to life imprisonment, which Catholics again protested in public rallies. Meanwhile, the Soviet Union refused to demobilize its armed forces, and communism became increasingly a synonym for disloyalty to the United States. In 1949 Alger Hiss, a former high official of the State Department, was accused of espionage for the Soviet Union, and in January 1950, when the statute of limitations precluded that verdict, was convicted of perjury. During the same period Judith Coplon, of the Department of Justice, was arrested in the act of giving secret FBI reports to a Soviet agent, and Julius and Ethel Rosenberg were tried and later executed for giving information about the atomic bomb to the Soviets. It was also at this time that China fell to the Communist armies of Mao Tse-tung and shortly after that the Korean War broke out.

The strong anti-Communist feeling among U.S. Catholics then, based on religious grounds, led to their patriotic alliance with the country at large. Americans in general are averse to communism because of its totalitarianism, its rejection of individual freedom. They entertained not entirely dissimilar opinions about Catholicism, however, and Catholics for their part have not manifested any overriding interest in individual freedoms. On the contrary, the popes have condemned liberalism as well as communism, considering both to be antireligious. The attack on communism, however, was something both Catholics and other Americans could share and in that sense it gave U.S. Catholics a new sense of being American. Two particularly prominent leaders of the anti-Communist crusade were Francis Cardinal Spellman and Bishop Fulton J. Sheen of New York.

This was the situation in 1950 when Senator Joseph McCarthy, a Catholic Republican from Wisconsin, charged that the U.S. State Department had been infiltrated by Communists and Communist sympathizers. This charge marked the beginning of an era in which something approximating hysteria over domestic communism dominated U.S. public life. For some five years Senator McCarthy, through his chairmanship of the Permanent Senate Subcommittee on Investigations, which rendered him immune to libel suits, made wholesale, unproven allegations of treasonous conduct, association, and inclination, plunging the nation into fear. To a considerable extent he paralyzed government. Eventually, in 1954 in the course of two months of televised hearings over accusations he had directed against the Army, it became plain that he had told a considerable number of lies and half-truths, and he was censured by the Senate. He died in 1957, by which time the Korean War was also over, and the issue retreated from the public headlines.

Political commentators have widely assumed that McCarthy enjoyed the solid support of Catholics. It is true that McCarthy helped increase tensions between Catholics and Protestants, especially the liberal Protestant clergy. Liberal Protestants feared him as a representative of intolerant Catholicism, while Catholics thought liberal Protestants were soft on communism. So far as voting support for McCarthy and his supporters went, however, for example in the election of

1952, the idea of a Catholic bloc vote for McCarthy seems to have been a myth. By and large Catholics voted along party lines. Catholic support for McCarthy was strong in Massachusetts and New York, but not elsewhere—particularly not in Chicago, where Bishop Bernard Sheil absolutely rejected him. McCarthy himself never campaigned specially for the Catholic vote, and the truth seems to be that he appealed to a wide cross-section of the population.

Next, we consider two military issues, both of which are also related to the threat of communism, and have further reflected a growing polarization of the religious community in the United States: the war in Vietnam and the movement for nuclear disarmament.

Vietnam

For the United States Vietnam was above all a moral problem. To understand this moral problem, however, some details of its historical background are necessary.

Before the Japanese occupation during the Second World War, the area now known as Vietnam together with Laos and Cambodia (now Kampuchea), had been under French rule, and when the war ended the French attempted to regain their previous sovereignty there. During the war, however, Vietnamese Communists and nationalists had formed a united party, the Viet Minh, led by Ho Chi Minh, which already in 1945 had set up an independent regime in the North. The Vietnamese intelligentsia in particular, it seems, had long accepted the view that socialism was necessary for national liberation. Beginning in 1946 the Viet Minh engaged in war with the French until 1954 when they inflicted the disastrous defeat of Dien Bien Phu on the French, which was followed by the armistice signed at the Geneva Conference.

In the South, Ngo Dinh Diem set up a nominally democratic regime in 1954, which became increasingly authoritarian, losing the support of the people.

In 1955 the United States, which had provided financial support to the French, assumed the training of the South Vietnamese armed forces, with a view to halting the spread of communism. During the late 1950s, sabotage and terrorism increased in the South, and 1959 saw the first American casualties. At first American participation was limited to sending military advisers, whose numbers were considerably increased. The resistance also increased, and a full-scale war developed, with the U.S. forces taking over the chief combat role, supported at home by a selective service draft. By 1969 the United States had some 550,000 troops in South Vietnam, was bombing not only military but also industrial targets in the North, and had suffered tens of thousands of casualties.

This war effort was hotly debated. One issue concerned the methods employed, such as napalm, which many critics considered particularly brutal. But the central issue was the nature and moral status of the insurgent forces. The U.S. government, as well as many ordinary and more conservative citizens, including the more conservative churches, understood these forces as primarily a Communist movement developed and supported by Moscow and Peking for the spread of international communism throughout Southeast Asia. The Communist North had invaded the free South, they thought, and should be repulsed. According to this view, the indigenous resistance in the South (the Viet Cong) was not of special significance. The liberal clergy, however, with large numbers of college students, the liberal intelligentsia, and the journalistic world, believed that the insurgent forces were predominantly a movement of national liberation, which was indigenous, and only incidentally Communist, and which had considerable moral right on its side. As the war continued, this latter point of view became more and more widespread.

When Richard Nixon became president in 1969, he acceded to this view and quickly began to withdraw U.S. forces. In April 1975 the last U.S. troops left Saigon, which immediately fell to the Communist army, which by then consisted mainly of regular troops from the North. By then some 46,000 U.S. soldiers had been killed and some 300,000 wounded.

Perhaps no issue since the Civil War has so deeply divided the American people. The one side considered the war a noble and heroic effort necessary for the defense of freedom, an effort strictly demanded by conscience and a due sense of historical responsibility. The other side saw it as fundamentally misguided, and indeed evil, directed toward imperialistic ends and employing brutal means.

Nine years after the U.S. pullout, the public controversy has ceased, but the deep differences of opinion about the war remain. Some things have become a little plainer. The insurgent movement was not in the first place an arm of Moscow and Peking, but genuinely indigenous, and it has been at pains to stress its independence of both, particularly of China, with which it now exists in a state of armed hostility. On the other hand, it is genuinely Communist, displaying all the more unlovely features of that system, both wretched economic failure and the savage suppression of civil liberties. It has also invaded Kampuchea. In view of these developments, it is perhaps easier now to see the war in a somewhat more nuanced moral light, in which praiseworthy ends were betrayed by regrettable choices of means.

The Nuclear Freeze and Disarmament Debate

The horrors of nuclear war have been clear since 1945, and although both the United States and the USSR have built up large armories of nuclear weapons, during that period they have also engaged in well-publicized talks to control them, so that the level of public anxiety over the likelihood of nuclear war was for the most part not high. In the early 1970s tension between the two powers even relaxed in what was known as *détente*. Since then, however, a number of Soviet actions have cast renewed doubts on their desire for peaceful relations. In 1975 the Soviets equipped and helped to transport a Cuban armed force to Angola to support one side of the civil war there, which had the effect of putting the SALT II talks on ice for a year. In 1978 they again joined with Cuba to intervene militarily in Ethiopia, and in 1979 they invaded Afghanistan. Furthermore, during this time, having achieved a state of rough military parity with the United States in 1970, they engaged in a massive and very expensive buildup of nuclear arms in what seemed to be a clear attempt to attain superiority. In consequence, arms control talks have flagged. Three treaties negotiated with the USSR in 1974, 1976, and 1979, including SALT II, were never even put to the vote for ratification by the Senate.

The effective abandonment of the arms control talks has left many Americans feeling extremely disturbed. In 1979 a grassroots movement began with the aim of securing passage in Congress of a resolution calling for a nuclear freeze. This movement was also spurred on by statements made by President Ronald Reagan reaffirming the United States' determination to resist Communist aggression, which to many appeared to have a tone of unnecessary bellicosity.

By mid–1981 eleven legislatures had adopted a freeze proposal. The elections of 1982 returned an increased number of its supporters to Congress, and in May 1983 the House formally adopted a resolution calling for negotiations to secure a bilateral, verifiable freeze. In the course of 1983 an intense national debate took place on the subject of nuclear weapons, including proposals for nuclear disarmament.

The churches played a prominent part in this debate. Official statements were issued by the Roman Catholic Bishops, the Episcopalian House of Bishops, the Lutheran Church in America, the United Methodist Council of Bishops, the American Baptist Church, and the United Presbyterian Church in the U.S.A. All advocate disarmament, but none unilateral disarmament. The fullest and most noteworthy statement is that of the Catholic Bishops, which takes as its point of departure a version of the traditional Catholic doctrine of the Just War. This allows a country to defend itself against aggression provided that certain conditions are met, such as that only military and not civilian targets are attacked, and there is some proportion between the damage inflicted and the good to be attained. Against this background, the bishops discuss some of the main moral problems raised by nuclear weapons, such as whether it could be moral to initiate the use of nuclear weapons or to threaten to attack civilians. They conclude reluctantly that nuclear deterrence is morally tolerable as long as there is no acceptable alternative, and the intent is to prevent war.

Public pressure for a nuclear freeze and even nuclear disarmament has apparently had some impact on the Reagan administration, leading it to make additional efforts in the direction of arms control negotiations. It is widely expected that this public interest and pressure for a solution will continue.

Looking back over the forty years that have elapsed since the end of World War II, we see that after an initial period in which conservative sentiment predominated, expressing itself, for instance, on the international front in a strong anticommunism, during the two decades from 1960 to 1980 the general trend of feeling in government, legislatures, and the courts moved to what may be called "the left," as embodied in the opposition to the war in Vietnam, *détente* with the Soviet Union, and domestically in the various so-called liberation movements, which resulted in an unprecedented mass of social legislation.

In the last few years, however, a considerable change has become apparent in the opposite direction, manifested in and reinforced by the election of Ronald Reagan to the presidency. Conservative religious opinion, mobilized, for example, under the banner of the Moral Majority, led by the Reverend Jerry Falwell, exerted considerable influence in the elections of 1980, and after a slight decline in 1982 appears at the time of writing (1986) again to be quite strong. The President's stance against abortion and in favor of prayer in the public schools, while criticized by his opponents as transgressing the due boundaries between church and state, seems to enjoy widespread support. Congress has now passed a bill that allows meetings of religious organizations to take place in public schools. Some Catholic opponents of the President, in their turn, such as former Vice-Presidential candidate Geraldine Ferraro and Governor of New York Mario Cuomo, have been publicly criticized by Catholic bishops for vowing not to impose their personal beliefs about abortion on others. Religion then is an issue in political campaigns. To what extent it influences the voters remains to be seen.

NOTE

1. Sidney Mead, *The Lively Experiment* (New York: Harper and Row, 1963).

BIBLIOGRAPHY

Religion and Politics: General

Adams, James L. *On Being Human, Religiously: Selected Essays in Religion and Society.* Edited by Max L. Stackhouse. Boston: Beacon Press, 1976.

Brockman, Norbert C., and Nicholas Piediscalzi, eds. *Contemporary Religion and Social Responsibility.* New York: Alba, 1973.

Childress, James F. *Civil Disobedience and Political Obligation: A Study in Christian Social Ethics.* New Haven, Conn.: Yale University Press, 1972.

Dunn, Charles W. *American Political Theology: Historical Perspectives and Theoretical Analysis.* New York: Praeger Publishers, 1984.

Lazareth, William H. *God's Call to Public Responsibility.* Philadelphia: Fortress Press, 1978.

Hauerwas, Stanley, and Richard Bondi. *Truthfulness and Tragedy: Further Investigations in Christian Ethics.* Notre Dame, Ind.: University of Notre Dame Press, 1977.

Hertz, Karl H. *Politics Is a Way of Helping People.* Augsburg, 1974.

Kelsey, George D. *Social Ethics Among Southern Baptists, 1917–1969.* Atla Monograph Series, No. 2. Metuchen, N. J.: Scarecrow, 1973.

Lee, Robert, and Martin E. Marty. *Religion and Social Conflict.* New York: Oxford University Press, 1969.

Niebuhr, Reinhold. *Christianity and Power Politics*. Hamden, Conn.: Shoe String Press, 1969.

————. *Faith and Politics*. Edited and introduced by Ronald H. Stone. Braziller, *Moral Man and Immoral Society: A Study in Ethics and Politics*. New York: Scribner's, 1932.

Powell, Enoch. *No Easy Answers*. New York: Seabury, 1974.

Ross, J. Eliott. *Christian Ethics*. Greenwich, CT: Devin, 1951.

Runner, E. H. *Scriptural Religion and Political Task*. Richmond, Calif.: Wedge Publishers, 1974.

Sleeper, C. Freeman. *Black Power and Christian Responsibility*. Nashville, Tenn.: Abingdon Press, 1969.

Wilhelmsen, Frederick D. *Christianity and Political Philosophy*. Athens: University of Georgia Press, 1978.

Williamson, Rene D. *Independence and Involvement: A Christian Reorientation in Political Science*. Baton Rouge: Louisiana State University Press, 1964.

Religion and the Civil Rights Movement

Barnett, Gordon and Douglas Barnett. *Sex, Racial Miscegenation and the Churches*. (Ethnic Studies). New York: Gordon Press, 1974.

Berrigan, Philip. *Punishment for Peace*. New York: Macmillan Co., 1969.

Boggs, Marion A. *What Does God Require in Race Relations?* Atlanta, Ga.: John Knox, 1964.

Clark, Henry. *The Church and Residential Desegregation*. College and University Press, 1965.

Cleage, Albert B., Jr. *Black Messiah*. Fairway, Kans.: Sheed Andrews and McMeel, 1969.

Cone, James H. *Black Theology and Black Power*. New York: Seabury, 1969.

Crain, James A. *Development of Social Ideas Among the Disciples of Christ*. St. Louis: Bethany Press, 1969.

Dollen, Charles. *Civil Rights*. (Magister Paperback Series.) Daughters of St. Paul, 1964.

Forell, George W. and William H. Lazareth. *Human Rights: Rhetoric or Reality*. (Justice Books.) Philadelphia: Fortress Press, 1978.

Gleason, Philip. *Conservative Reformers: German-American Catholics and the Social Order*. Notre Dame, Ind.: University of Notre Dame Press, 1968.

Hooft, W. A., and J. H. Oldham. *The Church and Its Function in Society*. (Problems in Modern Christianity Series.) New York: Gordon Press, 1977.

Hughes, Emmet J. *Church and the Liberal Society*. Notre Dame, Ind.: University of Notre Dame Press, 1961.

Institute for Religious and Social Studies (New York). Jewish Theological Seminary of America. *Discrimination and National Welfare: A Series of Addresses and Discussions*. Edited by R. M. MacIver. Port Washington, N. Y.: Kannikat Press, 1969.

Kelly, George A. *The Catholic Church and the American Poor*. Alba, 1976.

Kelsey, George D. *Social Ethics Among Southern Baptists, 1917–1969*. Metuchen, N. J.: Scarecrow Press, 1973.

Konvitz, Milton Ridvas. *Judaism and the American Idea*. Ithaca, N. Y.: Cornell University Press, 1978.

Miller, Allen O., ed. *Christian Declaration of Human Rights*. Grand Rapids, Mich.: Eerdmans, 1977.

Niebuhr, Reinhold. *Christian Realism and Political Problems*. New York: Kelley, 1953.

Reimers, David M. *White Protestantism and the Negro*. New York: Oxford University Press, 1965.

Ruether, Rosemary R. *The Radical Kingdom: The Western Experience of Messianic Hope*. New York: Paulist Press, 1975.

Shockley, Donald G. *Free, White and Christian*. Nashville, Tenn.: Abingdon, 1975.

Sidorsky, Avid, et al., eds. *Human Rights: Contemporary Issues and Jewish Perspectives*. Philadelphia: Jewish Publication Society, 1978.

Tanenbaum, Marc H. *Religious Values in an Age of Violence*. (Pere Marquette Theology Lectures.) Milwaukee: Marqette, 1976.

The Civil Rights Movement

Adams, A. John. *Civil Rights: A Current Guide to the People, Organizations, and Events*. Edited by A. John Adams and Joan Martin Burke. New York: Bowker, 1970.

Blaustein, Albert P. *Civil Rights and the American Negro: A Documentary History*. Edited by Albert P. Blaustein and Robert L. Zangrando. New York: Washington Square Press, 1968.

Lewis, David Levering. *Martin Luther King: A Critical Biography*. London: Allen Lars, 1970.

McCord, John Harrison. *With All Deliberate Speed: Civil Rights Theory and Reality*. Urbana: Illinois University Press, 1969.

Meier, August. *Black Protest in the Sixties*. Edited by August Meier and Elliott Rudwick. Chicago: Quadrangle Books, 1970.

Westin, Alan F. *Freedom Now!: The Civil-Rights Struggle in America*. New York: Basic Books, 1964.

Civil Rights: General

Biddle, Francis Beverly. *The Fear of Freedom*. Introduction by Harold L. Ickes. New York: Da Capo Press, 1971.

Cohen, Marshall, Thomas Naget, and Thomas Scanlon, eds. *Equality and Preferential Treatment*. Princeton, N.J.: Princeton University Press, 1977.

Dorsen, Norman, ed. *The Rights of Americans: What They Are—What They Should Be*. New York: Pantheon Books, 1971.

Falk, Richard A. *Human Rights and State Sovereignty*. New York: Holmes and Meier Publishers, 1980.

Feinberg, Joel. *Rights, Justice, and the Bounds of Liberty: Essays in Social Philosophy*. Princeton, N. J.: Princeton University Press, 1980.

Henkin, Louis. *The Rights of Man Today*. Boulder, Colo.: Westview Press, 1978.

Kiefer, Howard E. and Milton K. Munitz, eds. *Ethics and Social Justice*. Albany: New York State University Press, 1970.

Laqueur, Walter, and Barry Rubin, eds. *The Human Rights Reader*. Philadelphia: Temple University Press, 1979.

Lester, Richard Allen. *Reasoning About Discrimination: Analysis of Professional and*

Executive Work in Federal Antibias Programs. Princeton, N. J.: Princeton University Press, 1980.

Machan, Tibor R. *Human Rights and Human Liberties: A Radical Reconsideration of the American Political Tradition*. Chicago: Nelson Hall, 1975.

Melden, Abraham Irving. *Rights and Persons*. Berkeley: University of California Press, 1977.

————, ed. *Human Rights*. Belmont, Calif.: Wadsworth Publishing Co., 1970.

Newman, Edwin S. *Civil Liberty and Civil Rights*. 6th ed. Dobbs Ferry, N. Y.: Oceana Publications, 1979.

Pole, J. R. *The Pursuit of Equality in American History*. Berkeley: University of California Press, 1978.

Reverse Discrimination

Glazer, Nathan. *Affirmative Discrimination: Ethnic Inequality and Public Policy*. New York: Basic Books, 1975.

Goldman, Alan H. 1945. *Justice and Reverse Discrimination*. Princeton, N. J.: Princeton University Press, 1979.

Gross, Barry R. 1936. *Discrimination in Reverse: Is Turnabout Fair Play?* New York: New York University Press, 1978.

Sindler, Allan P. *Bakke, DeFunis, and Minority Admissions: The Quest for Equal Opportunity*. New York: Longman, 1978.

Women's Liberation Movement

Braxton, Bernard. *Women, Sex and Races: A Realistic View of Sexism and Racism*. Washington, D. C.: Verta Press, 1973.

Carroll, Alexander. *Women of Early Christianity*. New York: Gordon Press.

Channeson, Joan. *Woman Survivor in the Church*. Minneapolis: Winston Press, 1980.

Christ, C. P., and J. Plaskow. *Womanspirit Rising: A Feminist Reader in Religion*. Harper and Row, 1979.

Cohart, Mary, ed. *Unsung Champions of Women*. Albuquerque: New Mexico University Press, 1975.

Cummings, Bernice, and Victoria Schnuck, eds. *Women Organizing: An Anthology*. Metuchen, N. J.: Scarecrow Press, 1979.

Deckard, Barbara S. *The Women's Movement*. New York: Harper and Row, 1975.

Decter, Midge. *The New Chastity and Other Arguments Against Women's Liberation*. New York: Coward, McCann and Geohegan, 1972.

Equal Rights Amendment Project. *Impact ERA: Limitations and Possibilities*. California Commission on the Status of Women. Milibrae, Calif.: Les Femmes Publishing, 1976.

Evans, Sara. *Personal Politics: Roots of Women's Liberation in the Civil Rights Movement and the New Left*. New York: Alfred A. Knopf, 1979.

Freeman, Jo. *The Politics of Women's Liberation: A Case Study of an Emerging Social Movement and Its Relation to the Policy Process*. New York: McKay, 1975.

Fuchs, Cynthia Epstein. *The Other Half: Roads to Women's Equality*. Englewood Cliffs, N. J.: Prentice-Hall, 1971.

Gage, Matilda J. *Woman, Church and State*. New York: Arno Press, 1972.
Harrison, Cynthia E. *Women in American History: A Bibliography*. Santa Barbara: ABC-Clio, 1979.
Haughton, Rosemary. *Feminine Spirituality*. New York: Paulist Press, 1976.
Hole, Judith, and Ellen Levine. *Rebirth of Feminism*. New York: Quadrangle, 1971.
Janeway, Elizabeth. *Between Myth and Morning: Women Awakening*. New York: William Morrow, 1974.
Koedt, Anne. *Radical Feminism*. Edited by Anne Koedt, Ellen Levine [and] Anita Rapone. New York: Quadrangle Books, 1973.
Lynn, Mary C., ed. *Women's Liberation in the 20th Century*. New York: John Wiley, 1975.
McBeth, Leon. *Women in Baptist Life*. Nashville: Broadman, 1979.
Morgan, Robin. *Sisterhood Is Powerful: An Anthology of Writings from the Women's Liberation Movement*. New York: Random House, 1970.
Rabuzzi, Kathryn A. *The Sacred and the Feminine: Towards a Theology of Housework*. New York: Seabury, 1982.
Reed, Evelyn. *Problems of Women's Liberation: A Marxist Approach*. 5th ed. New York: Pathfinder Press, 1970.
Ruether, Rosemary. *Religion and Sexism. Images of Woman in Jewish and Christian Traditions*. New York: Simon and Schuster, 1974.
Rutgers University Center for the American Woman in Politics. *Women and American Politics: Bibliography 1965–1974*. New Brunswick, N. J.: Rutgers University Center 1974.
Safilios-Rothschild, Constantina. *Woman and Social Policy*. Englewood Cliffs, N. J.: Prentice-Hall, 1974.
Salper, Roberta, ed. *Female Liberation: History and Current Politics*. New York: Alfred A. Knopf, 1972.
Schlaffley, Phyllis. *The Power of the Christian Woman*. Salem, N. H.: Standard, 1981.
Showalter, Elaine. *Women's Liberation and Literature*. New York: Harcourt Brace Jovanovich, 1971.
Swidler, A. *Woman in a Man's Church*. Mahwah, N. J.: Paulist Press, 1972.
Turner, Podvey. *Woman and the Priesthood*. Salt Lake City: Deseret Books.
Washburn, Penelope. *Becoming Woman: The Quest for Spiritual Wholeness in Female Experience*. Harper and Row, 1979.
White, William. 1934. *North American Reference Encyclopedia of Women's Liberation*. Philadelphia: North American Publishing Co., 1972.

Women's Liberation Movement in U.S. History

Chamberlin, Hope. *A Minority of Members: Women in the U.S. Congress*. New York: Praeger, 1973.
Evans, Sara. *Personal Politics: The Roots of Women's Liberation in the Civil Rights Movement and the New Left*. New York: Alfred A. Knopf, 1979.
Gurko, Miriam. *The Ladies of Seneca Falls: The Birth of the Woman's Rights Movement*. New York: Macmillan Co., 1974.
A History of the American Women's Movement (sound recording). Baltimore: Great Atlantic Radio Conspiracy (1972?).
Krichmar, Albert, assisted by Barbara Case, Barbara Silver [and] Ann E. Wiederrecht.

The Women's Rights Movement in the United States, 1848–1970: A Bibliography and Sourcebook. Metuchen, N. J.: Scarecrow Press, 1972.
Meider, Keith. *Beginnings of Sisterhood: The American Woman's Rights Movement, 1800–1850*. New York: Schocken Books, 1977.

Women and Religion: Academic

Bloom, Naomi. *Contributions of Women: Religion*. Minneapolis: Dillon, 1978.
Clark, Elizabeth, and Herbert W. Richardson, eds. *Women and Religion: Readings in the Western Tradition from Aeschylus to Mary Daly*. New York: Harper and Row.
Lantero, Erminie H. *Feminine Aspects of Divinity*. Wallingford, Pa.: Pendle Hill, 1973.
Plaskow, Judith, and Joan A. Romero, eds. *Women and Religion: Proceedings*. Rev. ed. American Academy of Religion. Aids for the Study of Religion. Decatur, Ga.: Scholars Press, 1974.

Women in Judaism

Meiselman, M. *Jewish Woman in Jewish Law*. Hoboken, N. J.: KTAV Publishing House.
Priesand, Sally. *Judaism and the New Woman*. New York: Behrman, 1975.
Swidler, Leonard. *Women in Judaism: The Status of Women in Formative Judaism*. Metuchen, N. J.: Scarecrow Press, 1976.

Women in Christianity

Ashe, Geoffrey. *The Virgin*. London: Routledge and Kegan, 1976.
Burghardt, Walter J., ed. *Woman: New Dimensions*. Mahwah, N. J.: Paulist Press, 1977.
Coriden, James A., ed. *Sexism and Church Law: Equal Rights and Affirmative Action*. Mahwah, N. J.: Paulist Press, 1977.
Daly, Mary. *Beyond God the Father: Toward a Philosophy of Women's Liberation*. Boston: Beacon Press, 1973.
———. *The Church and the Second Sex with a New Postchristian Introduction*. Rev. ed. New York: Harper and Row, 1975.
Demarest, Victoria B. *God, Woman, and Ministry*. St. Petersburg, Fla.: Valkyrie Press, 1978.
Durkin, Mary G. *The Suburban Woman: Her Changing Role in the Church*. New York: Seabury, 1975.
Gardiner, Anne M. *Women and Catholic Priesthood: An Expanded Vision*. Mahwah, N. J.: Paulist Press, 1976.
Luder, Hope E. *Women and Quakerism*. Willingford, Del.: Pendle Hill, 1974.
McGrath, Albertus M., Sr. *Women and the Church*. New York: Doubleday, 1976.
Ruether, Rosemary R. *New Woman-New Earth: Sexist Ideologies and Human Liberation*. Seabury, 1978.
Smith, Betsy. *Breakthrough: Women in Religion*. New York: Walker and Co., 1978.
Swidler, Arlene and Leonard Swidler, eds. *Women Priests: A Catholic Commentary on the Vatican Declaration*. Mahwah, N. J.: Paulist Press, 1977.
Tavard, George H. *Woman in Christian Tradition*. Notre Dame, Ind.: University of Notre Dame Press, 1973.
Turner, Rodney. *Woman and the Priesthood*. Salt Lake City: Deseret Books.

Women in Islam

Abdul-Rauf, Muhammad. *The Islamic View of Women and the Family*. New York: Speller, 1977.
Allman, James, ed. *Women's Status and Fertility in the Muslim World*. New York: Praeger, 1978.
Beck, Lois, and Nikki Keddie, eds. *Women in the Muslim World*. Cambridge, Mass.: Harvard University Press, 1978.
Maududi, A. A. *Purdah and the Status of Women in Islam*. Chicago: Kazi Publications.
Siddiqui, M. M. *Women in Islam*. Chicago: Kazi Publications.

Capitalism and the Free Market

Ashton, T. S. *The Standard of Life of the Workers in England, 1780–1830*. In F. Hayek, ed. *Capitalism and the Historians*. Chicago: University of Chicago Press, 1954.
Bauer, P. T. *Dissent on Development*. London: Weiderfels and Nicolson, 1971.
———. *Equality, the Third World and Economic Delusion*. Cambridge, Mass.: Harvard University Press, 1981.
Bell, Daniel. *The Coming of Post-Industrial Society*. New York: Basic Books, 1973.
———. *The Cultural Contradictions of Capitalism*. New York: Basic Books, 1975.
———, and J. Kristol, eds. *Capitalism Today*. New York: Mentor, 1971.
Benne, Robert. *The Ethic of Democratic Capitalism: A Moral Reassessment*. Philadelphia: Fortress Press, 1981.
Brandt, Richard. *Social Justice*. Englewood Cliffs, N. J.: Prentice-Hall, 1962.
Chamberlain, J. *The Roots of Capitalism*. Indianapolis, Ind.: Liberty Press, 1959, reprinted 1976.
de George, Richard, and Joseph Pichler. *Ethics, Free Enterprise and Public Policy*. New York: Oxford University Press, 1978.
———. *Capitalism and Freedom*. Chicago: University of Chicago Press, 1962.
Friedman, Milton. *Free to Choose*. New York: Harcourt, Brace, Jovanovich, 1980.
Galbraith, J. K. *The Affluent Society*. Boston: Houghton Mifflin, 1958.
———. *American Capitalism*. Boston: Houghton Mifflin, 1956.
———. *The New Industrial State*. Boston: Houghton Mifflin, 1967.
Gilder, George. *Wealth and Poverty*. New York: Basic Books, 1981.
Gremillion, Joseph, ed. *The Gospel of Peace and Justice*. Maryknoll, N. Y.: Orbis Books, 1976.
Harrington, Michael. *The Other America*. New York: Saturday Review Press, 1972.
———. *Socialism*. New York: Saturday Review Press, 1972.
Hay, Donald. *A Christian Critique of Capitalism*. Bramcotte, Notts, England: Grove Books, 1977.
Heckel, Roger S. J. *Self-Reliance*. Vatican City: Pontifical Commission on Justice and Peace, 1978.
Hook, Sidney, ed. *Human Values and Economic Policies*. New York: New York University Press, 1967.
Kristol, Irving. *Two Cheers for Capitalism*. New York: Basic Books, 1978.
Leo XIII. *Rerum Novarum*.

Levy, Bernard Henry. *Barbarism with a Human Face*. Translated by George Holoch. New York: Harper and Row, 1979.

Lippman, Walter. *The Good Society*. Boston: Little, Brown and Co., 1943.

Lukacs, John. *The Passing of the Modern Age*. New York: Harper and Row, 1970.

National Council of Churches. "World Poverty and the Demands of Justice." Mimeo., 1968.

Niebuhr, Reinhold. *Moral Man and Immoral Society*. New York: Charles Scribner's Sons, 1932.

————. *The Nature and Destiny of Man*. New York: Charles Scribner's Sons, 1949.

Novak, Michael. *The American Vision: An Essay on the Future of Democratic Capitalism*. Washington, D. C.: American Enterprise Institute for Public Policy Research, 1978.

————. *The Spirit of Democratic Capitalism*. New York: Simon and Schuster, 1982.

Pius X. *Quadragesimo Anno*.

Podhoretz, Norman. *Making It*. New York: Random House, 1969.

Rawls, J. *A Theory of Justice*. Cambridge, Mass.: Harvard University Press, 1971.

Revel, Jean-Francois. *Without Marx or Jesus*. New York: Doubleday, 1970.

Schumpeter, Joseph. *Capitalism, Socialism and Democracy*. New York: Harper and Row, 1975.

Silk, Leonard, and David Fogel. *Ethics and Profits*. New York: Simon and Schuster, 1978.

Tawney, R. H. *Religion and the Rise of Capitalism*. Harcourt and Brace, 1926.

Thurow, L. *Generating Inequality*. New York: Basic Books, 1975.

————. *The Zero Sum Society*. New York: Basic Books, 1980.

Tillich, Paul. *Political Expectation*. Edited by J. L. Adams. New York: Harper and Row, 1971.

————. *Religious Socialism*. New York: Harper and Row, 1978.

————. *The World Situation*. Philadelphia: Fortress Press, 1965.

von Hayek. *The Constitution of Liberty*. Chicago: University of Chicago Press, 1960.

————. *The Road to Serfdom*. Chicago: University of Chicago Press, 1944.

von Mises, Ludwig. *The Anti-Capitalist Mentality*. South Holland, Ill.: Libertarian Press, 1972.

Walzer, Michael. *Radical Principles: Reflections of an Unreconstructed Democrat*. New York: Basic Books, 1980.

————. *Spheres of Justice*. New York: Basic Books, 1983.

Wanniski, J. *The Way the World Works*. New York: Basic Books, 1978.

Weber, M. *The Protestant Ethic and the Spirit of Capitalism*. New York: Charles Scribner's Sons, 1958.

Recent Welfare State

Anderson, Martin. *Welfare*. Stanford, Calif.: Hoover Institution, Stanford University, 1978.

Cheung, Steven. *The Myth of Social Cost: A Critique of Welfare Economics*.

Feldman, A. *Welfare Economics and Social Choice Theory*. Boston: Nijhoff, 1980.

MacKay, A. F. *Arrow's Theorem*. New Haven, Conn.: Yale University Press, 1980.

Mueller, Dennis C. *Public Choice*. Cambridge, Mass.: Cambridge University Press, 1979.

Murray, Charles. *Losing Ground: American Social Policy 1950–1980*. New York: Basic Books, 1984.

Economics

Jackson, Larry R. *Protest by the Poor: Welfare Rights Movement in New York City*. Lexington, Mass.: Lexington, 1974.
Knight, Frank H. *The Ethics of Competition*. Chicago: University of Chicago Press, 1935.
Obenhaus, Victor. *Ethics for an Industrial Age*. Westport, Conn.: Greenwood Press, 1975. Reprint of 1965 ed.
Probert, Belina. *The Political Economy of Protestant Social Formations*. Belfast, Maine: Porter, 1978.
Reed, E. D. *Profit Makes Perfect*. New York: Vantage, 1978.
Rogge, Benjamin A., et al. *The Christian in Business*. Tacoma, Wis.: Lutheran Academy for Scholarship, 1966.
Rose, Tom. *Economics: Principles and Policy from a Christian Perspective*. Milford, Mich.: Mott Media, 1977.
Sanger, Mary B. *Welfare of the Poor*. New York: Academic, 1979.
Sen, Amartya Kumas. *On Economic Inequality*. Oxford: Clarendon, 1973.
Van Oyen, Hendrik. *Affluence and the Christian*. Philadelphia: Fortress, 1966.
Vickers, Douglas. *Economics and Man: Prelude to a Christian Critique*. Phillipsburg, N. J.: Presbyterian and Reformed Publishing Co. 1976.
Weber, Max. *Protestant Ethic and the Spirit of Capitalism*. New York: Scribner's, 1930.

Abortion

Kluge, E. H. W. *The Practice of Death*. New Haven, Conn.: Yale University Press, 1975.
Mohr, James C. *Abortion in America*. New York: Oxford University Press, 1978.
Sass, Lauren R., ed. *Abortion: Freedom of Choice and the Right to Live*. New York: Facts on File, 1978.

Creationism

Godfrey, Lawrence R. *Scientists Confront Creationism*. New York: W. W. Norton, 1983.
LaFollette, Muriel, ed. *Creationism, Science and the Law: The Arkansas Case*. Cambridge, Mass.: MIT Press, 1983.
Nelkin, Dorothy. *The Creation Controversy*. New York: W. W. Norton, 1982.
Thompson, Adell. *Biology, Zoology, and Genetics: Evolution Model vs. Creation Model*. Washington, D.C.: University Press of America, 1983.

Prayer in Public Schools

Beggs, David W., III, and R. B. McQuigg, eds. *America's Schools and Churches: Partners in Conflict*. Bloomington: Indiana University Press, 1966.
Boles, Donald E. *Bible, Religion and the Public Schools*. 3d ed. Ames, Iowa: Iowa State University Press, 1965.

————. *Two Swords: Commentaries and Cases in Religion and Education*. Ames, Iowa: Iowa State University Press, 1967.

Butts, R. Freeman. *The American Tradition in Religion and Education*. Westport, Conn.: Greenwood Press, 1974; reprint of 1950 ed.

Engel, David E., ed. *Religion in Public Education: Readings in Religion and the Public School*. Mahwah, N. J.: Paulist Press, 1974.

Giannella, Donald A., ed. *Religion and the Public Order*. 3 vols. Chicago: University of Chicago Press, 1964–1966.

————. *Religion and the Public Order, Number Five*. Ithaca: Cornell University Press, 1969.

————. *Religion and the Public Order, Number Four: An Annual Review of Church and State, and of Religion, Law, and Society*. Ithaca: Cornell University Press, 1968.

Hook, Sidney. *Religion in a Free Society*. Lincoln, Nebr.: University of Nebraska Press, 1967.

Johnson, Alvin W., and Frank H. Yost. *Separation of Church and State in the United States*. Westport, Conn.: Greenwood Press, 1970; reprint of 1948 ed.

Krinsky, Fred, ed. *Politics of Religion in America*. Encino, Calif.: Glencoe, 1968.

Laubach, John H. *School Prayers*. Washington, D. C.: Public Affairs Press, 1969.

Lowry, Charles W. *To Pray or Not to Pray: A Handbook for Study of Recent Supreme Court Decisions and American Church-State Doctrine*, Seattle: University Press of Washington, 1976.

Muir, William K., Jr. *Prayer in the Public Schools: Law and Attitude Change*. Chicago: University of Chicago Press, 1973.

Murray, Albert V. *The State and the Church in a Free Society*. New York: AMS Press, 1978; reprint of 1958 ed.

Pfeffer, Leo. *Creeds in Competition: A Creative Force in American Culture*. Westport, Conn.: Greenwood Press, 1978; reprint of 1958 ed.

Piediscalzi, Nicholas. *Teaching About Religion in the Public Schools*. Edited by William E. Collie. Allen, Tex.: Argus Communications, 1977.

Rice, Charles E. *Supreme Court and Public Prayer: The Need for Restraint*. New York: Fordham University Press, 1964.

Smith, Elwyn A. *Religious Liberty in the United States: The Development of Church-State Thought Since the Revolutionary Era*. Philadelphia: Fortress, 1972.

Stokes, Anson and Pfeffer, Leo. *Church and State in the United States*, Rev. ed. Westport, Conn.: Greenwood Press, 1975; reprint of 1964 ed.

McCarthy

Adams, John G. *Without Precedent: The Story of the Death of McCarthyism*. New York: W. W. Norton, 1983.

Cook, Fred J. *The Nightmare Decade: The Life and Times of Senator Joe McCarthy*. New York: Random House, 1971.

Crosby, Donald F. *God, Church and Flag: Senator Joseph R. McCarthy and the Catholic Church, 1950–1957*. Chapel Hill, N. C.: University of North Carolina Press, 1978.

Fried, Richard M. *Men Against McCarthy*. New York: Columbia University Press, 1976.

Griffith, Robert. *The Politics of Fear*. Lexington: University Press of Kentucky, 1970.

Latham, Earl, ed. *The Meaning of McCarthyism*. Boston: D. C. Heath, 1965.

Oshinsky, David M. *A Conspiracy So Immense. The World of Joe McCarthy*. New York: Free Press, 1983.

Rogni, Michael P. *The Intellectuals and McCarthy: The Radical Specter*. Cambridge, Mass.: MIT Press, 1967.

Rovere, Richard. *Senator Joe McCarthy*. New York: Harcourt Brace, 1959.

Vietnam

Berdler, Philip D. *American Literature and the Experience of Vietnam*. Athens: University of Georgia Press, 1982.

Bromby, Dorothy D. *Washington and Vietnam: An Examination of the Moral and Political Issues*. Dobbs Ferry, N. Y.: Oceana Publications, 1966.

Chen, John Hsuch-ming. *Vietnam: A Comprehensive Bibliography*. Metuchen, N. J.: Scarecrow Press, 1973.

Cooper, Chester L. *The Lost Crusade: America in Vietnam*. New York: Dodd Mead, 1970.

Cotter, Michael. *Vietnam: A Guide to Reference Sources*. Boston: G. K. Hall, 1977.

Durker, William J. *The Communist Road to Power in Vietnam*. Boulder, Colo.: Westview Press, 1981.

Ellsberg, Daniel. *Papers on the War*. New York: Simon and Schuster, 1972.

Foreign Policy Association. *Vietnam: Vital Issues in the Great Debate*. New York: 1966.

Gelb, Leslie H. *The Irony of Vietnam: The System Worked*. Washington, D.C.: Brookings Institution, 1979.

Halberstam, David. *The Best and the Brightest*. New York: Random House, 1972.

Hamilton, Michael P., ed. *The Vietnam War: Christian Perspectives*. Grand Rapids, Mich.: Eerdmans, 1967.

Herring, George C. *America's Longest War: The U.S. and Vietnam: 1950–1975*. New York: John Wiley, 1979.

Lynd, Alice. *We Won't Go: Personal Acts of War Objectors*. Boston: Beacon Press, 1968.

McCarthy, Mary. *Hanoi*. New York: Harcourt Brace and World, 1968.

———. *Vietnam*. New York: Harcourt Brace and World, 1967.

McGee, Gale W. *The Responsibilities of World Power*. Washington, D. C.: National Press, 1968.

Merklin, Lewis. *They Chose Honor: The Problem of Conscience in Custody*. New York: Harper and Row, 1974.

Mersmann, James F. *Out of the Vietnam Vortex: A Study of Poets and Poetry Against the War*. Lawrence, Kans.: University Press of Kansas, 1974.

Nguyen, Van Canh, and Earle Cooper. *Vietnam Under Communism, 1975–1982*. Stanford, Calif.: Hoover Institute, 1983.

Patti, A.L.A. *Why Vietnam?* Berkeley: University of California Press, 1980.

Pike, Douglas. *History of Vietnam's Communism, 1925–1976*. Stanford, Calif.: Hoover Institute Press, 1978.

Schlesinger, Arthur M. *The Bitter Heritage: Vietnam and American Democracy*. Boston: Houghton Mifflin, 1967.

Shaplen, Robert. *The Lost Revolution: The Story of 20 Years of Neglected Opportunities in Vietnam and America's Failure to Foster Democracy There*. New York: Harper and Row, 1965.

Sugnet, Christopher L., John T. Hickey, with assistance of R. Gaspino. *Vietnam War Bibliography*. Lexington, Mass.: Lexington Books, 1983.

Webb, Kate. *On the Other Side: 23 Days with the Viet Cong*. New York: Quadrangle, 1972.

Zagoria, Donald S. *Vietnam Triangle: Moscow, Peking, and Hanoi*. New York: Pegasus, 1967.

War, Peace, and Nuclear Weapons

Ansberry, William F. *Arms Control and Disarmament: Success or Failure?* Berkeley, Calif.: McCutchan Publishing Corp., 1969.

Burns, Richard Dean. *Arms Control and Disarmament: A Bibliography*. Santa Barbara, Calif.: ABC-Clio, 1977.

Chatfield, Charles, ed. *Peace Movements in America*. New York: Schocken Books, 1973.

Milford, Theodore R. *Christian Decision in the Nuclear Age*. Philadelphia: Fortress Press, 1967.

Potter, Ralph H. *War and Moral Discourse*. Nashville, Tenn.: John Knox, 1969.

Schilling, Warner R., et al. *American Arms and a Changing Europe: Dilemmas of Deterrence and Disarmament*. New York: Columbia University Press, 1973.

Sheerin, John B. *Peace, War and the Young Catholic*. New York: Paulist Press, 1973.

Taylor, William J., Jr. and Paul McCole, *The Nuclear Freeze Debate*. Boulder, Colo.: Westview Press, 1983.

United States Department of the Army. *Disarmament: A Bibliographic Record, 1916–1960*. Prepared for the Office, Special Assistant to the Joint Chiefs of Staff for Disarmament Affairs. Washington, D.C., 1960.

13

Religion and Politics in Japan

CARL BECKER

There have been many politico-religious ideologies in the twentieth century, but none has surpassed that of Japan in its impact on war and politics. Now more than ever, while inflation and internal pressures again turn Japan toward the right wing, and external influences urge Japan to rearm, it is important to reexamine the relationships between Japan's religious ideology and politics.

The politico-religious world-view of Japan embodies a juxtaposition of beliefs and feelings which to Western minds constitutes a unique paradox. On the one hand, the Japanese do not consider themselves a particularly religious people. Most of them neither attend periodic religious services nor contribute financially to any religious organization. Even those who claim "affiliation" with some religious sect hold a relatively unformulated commitment to a group of chosen people, rather than to a body of creedal beliefs. Few Japanese become religious by devoting themselves to the principles of a particular sect; rather, they are born into particular sects just as their fathers were. Thus, the Japanese have often been called "mushukyo"—without religion—but this implies neither an atheism nor a skepticism as much as a lack of concern with doctrinal clarity or conviction.[1]

At the same time, the vast majority of Japanese subscribe to a single common world-view which involves many axiological "leaps of faith." This world-view is not carefully organized into doctrine, but still obtains such a wide religious adherence by the Japanese that it has been christened "Nipponkyo"—"Japan-ism" or the religion of Japan. Basic to this religious view are such ideas as (1) that the Japanese people are unique in all the world and have a central role in Japan's destiny; (2) that the Japanese archipelago is a blessed land, the center of everything holy; (3) that the Japanese people are a special and homogeneous

Note: Select terms used in this chapter are defined in the end-of-chapter glossary.

race, which has developed a language and culture unparalleled in complexity and beauty; and, for many Japanese, (4) that the Japanese race is descended from the gods and the emperor is the living proof of that heritage. Throughout the twentieth century, Japan has paid homage to this creed—sometimes overtly and with tragic consequences as in World War II and sometimes more discreetly, as in postwar politics.

Nipponkyo is not a religion in the Western sense, as it lacks specific deities, services, and scriptures. When Westerners look at Japan, or when Japanese define religion in such purely Western terminology, it is easy for them to conclude that the Japanese are in fact totally irreligious—mushukyo. For the same reason, legislation designed to guarantee "freedom of religion" or to dissociate "religion from the state" seems of little value or necessity to modern Japanese, who almost never martyr themselves for reasons of doctrinal commitment, and have no prayers mixed into their schooling or politics. But it is precisely this vagueness, ambiguity, and non-doctrinal nature of Nipponkyo as a national faith which means that no law can easily identify, much less prohibit, the ideas, speeches, and practices that stem from this larger religious ideology and infiltrate every aspect of public life, especially politics.[2]

There do exist a number of formally constituted religious bodies in Japan, to which many Japanese show at least occasional allegiance. Before studying these religions or observing their influence on politics, however, we should make a few more observations on the nature of Japanese society. Japanese politics and religion have always been intimately interconnected.[3] Even today, sociologists have been able to identify many positive correlations between religious behaviour and political behaviour.[4] The traditional religions of Japan never provided a strong theological grounding, or even a sense of the need for a moral system or ethics by which any individual could determine the propriety of his own actions.[5] Rather, the individual's participation was first and foremost in his social group. The approval or disapproval of the group established the rightness or wrongness of an action, and because the individual never found himself outside of the social group, the question of what to do in their absence never presented itself. (Prior to the twentieth century, Japanese almost never left their home provinces, much less their country. The absence of social-group pressure when they began leaving Japan in large numbers is largely responsible for their apparent total lack of moral sense both in their occupation of China and Korea, and today in their sex tours and business exploitation abroad.) The twentieth century, with its modernization and social mobility, has led to the fracturing of old social groups and their pressure, and an increasing sense of "loss of direction," which an individual choice of religion in a more Western sense may help to provide.[6] But for most Japanese people the importance of organized religion is still not at all apparent or obvious.

Now let us turn to a brief survey of the major religious traditions within Japan, which are more sectarian than the universal commitment to Nipponkyo. Shinto is the oldest of these religions, dating back to Japanese pre-history. Buddhism and Confucianism were introduced together in the sixth century. Christianity was only admitted for a brief period in the late sixteenth century and again late in the nineteenth century, but has made little progress. Finally, there are the "New Religions" (*shinko shukyo*) whose rapid rise after the war deserves special attention.

RELIGIONS IN JAPAN

Shinto

From the earliest days of Japan, rulers and shamans were closely, perhaps indistinguishably, affiliated. Emperors justified their reigns on the divine right theory that they were descended from and in contact with the primal divinities— and neither a Hobbes nor a Locke arose to challenge this notion. When they encountered the Confucian idea that the ruler must be moral in order to retain the mandate of heaven, they turned it on its head and interpreted it to mean that, since the ruler clearly possesses the mandate of heaven hereditarily, whatever he does must be moral by definition, that is, he is above human judgment. When Buddhism reached Japan from China, "they were inclined to utilize it as a means and an instrument to realize a certain socio-political end. They were not converted to Buddhism; they converted Buddhism to their own tribalism."[7]

All the standard histories of Japanese religion make it clear that Shintoism and Buddhism were largely the province of governmental officials and that government was the province of religious leaders; that in each successive era, the government used the religions to justify itself, and the religions tried to make themselves indispensable to the court.[8] When the Tokugawa Shoguns took political power and made the emperor their puppet, they naturally downplayed the role of Shinto, which stood for the divinity and irreplaceability of the emperor. Conversely, the instigators of the Meiji Restoration which overthrew the Shogunate refurbished the Shinto ideology and made the divinity of the imperial line a cornerstone of their revolutionary rationale for restoring the emperor to power.

After Emperor Meiji came to power in 1869, his Ministry of Religion adopted three principles of instruction:

1. "reverence for the gods and love of country,"
2. "Principles of Heaven and the Way of Man," and
3. "exalting the Emperor and obeying the court."[9]

Even from these three points of policy, we can immediately see the utter confusion (or charitably, nondistinction) between political and religious ideology. When the Meiji Constitution was established in 1889, it began with words stemming from Shinto Scriptures, to the effect that the emperor and his rule were divinely authorized. Under foreign pressure, the government agreed to grant religious freedom to all Japanese "insofar as it did not adversely affect the nation." But once again, by defining Shinto to be a part of government rather than a religion, it was assumed that all Japanese would simultaneously follow the imperial Shinto line, with whatever additional religious beliefs they individually chose.[10]

Such a move is only possible, of course, where principles of exclusiveness and noncontradiction are not recognized (as they are not in the Japanese language); where historical analysis and criticism are absent, if not prohibited; and where the majority of the people also fail to see any important distinction between the right to political power and the essence of religious ideology. These preconditions all existed in the past century in Japan and were reinforced by sanctions like those which forced historian Kume Kunitake from his post at Tokyo University when he published his opinion that Shinto was the survival of a primitive religious cult.[11] As Max Weber has appropriately noted, the whole history of religion in Japan demonstrates that the state functioned not as a patron (*Schutzpatronat*) but as a police of religion (*Religionspolizei*).[12] But we must beware of imagining that this ideology was somehow imposed on the Japanese people from above by propaganda alone. Rather, it was possible precisely because the majority of Japanese already subscribed to the tenets of Shintoism, although sometimes without careful formulation.

Curiously, even the Japanese state agreed, at least from the 1870s to the 1940s, that Shinto was not a religion, and many Japanese people still accept this distinction. After all, it has no weekly services, no daily demands, no codified ethical or metaphysical systems, and there is even disagreement about what constitute its Scriptures. The argument runs that Shinto

definitely could not be measured in terms of foreign concepts of religion; that Shrine Shinto was focused upon rites which antedated religion (!) and as such should be considered the original pattern of the national spirit, a pattern that predated such cultural diversification as is represented in the terms "moral," "political," etc.[13]

Thus, at various times in the government of Japan, Shinto has been classified within (and taught as) history, government, politics, morals, patriotism, and even "ritual," a category foreign to Western education. It has alternately found a home within the Ministries of Education and the Ministries of the Interior (or Home Office). The Shinto leaders themselves have often denied their being a religion on the grounds that

1. they lack standardized doctrines of religious import;
2. they have no sect founders or clear hierarchy; and
3. they have no church organization except that of voluntary association.[14]

But it was precisely this disavowal of religious nature which enabled the Japanese people and government to incorporate Shinto teachings throughout their educational system, to grant federal funding to important shrines, and to teach the fundamentally religious texts of Shinto as if they were history books, calling on the state to repress dissidence in these matters.

Shinto, as a state religion officially glorifying the emperor, was disestablished by General Douglas MacArthur during the American occupation of Japan. Shrine Shinto, however, was allowed to continue in keeping with "religious freedom." Shrine Shinto includes the worshipping at local Shinto shrines whenever one has a specific prayer to the gods; the performing of christening and marriage ceremonies at Shinto shrines; and the conducting of occasional mass pilgrimages to the major shrines at New Year's or on other national holidays. There can be no question that Shinto is still essential to Japanese religious consciousness.[15]

Postwar Shinto has seen a number of minor changes, as a result primarily of the changing demographic picture. Postwar Japan saw a massive migration from the countryside to the cities, as mechanized farming reduced the need for hand labor and as the glamour of jobs in trade and industry beckoned. This led to a concomitant drop in shrine attendance in rural areas and to a simultaneous rise in urban shrine attendance. People moving into suburban communities more often commuted to large famous shrines in the central metropolis than patronized their local suburban shrine in which they had no traditional stake.[16] But this movement has further consequences. The major shrines have become far wealthier, both because they attract larger numbers of people and because they can charge more for their services. This in turn enables them to put on a flashier show, which again attracts more devotees.

The other by-product of this move to worship at the larger metropolitan shrines is political. Most rural shrines are dedicated to the spirits of ancient warriors, trees, or animals, in whom the worshippers can feel little personal belief or interest. But most major urban shrines are dedicated to more current figures: late emperors, generals, war heroes, and statesmen. So the net effect is that in the process of worshipping there, the young Japanese gradually reinforce the deification of these modern Japanese heroes and the nationalism with which they are associated. More than one scholar has seen in the recent centralization and numerical increases in Shrine attendance "a nostalgia for pre-war patterns."[17]

Of course, Japanese worship at shrines is not only a holiday ritual, but specifically a request for material benefits: college admission, a better salary, a healthier body, or a husband. Some of the increase in shrine attendance may simply be due to the increasing materialism and desire for social status emerging in a Japan where for the first time social classes have been viewed as more economic than hereditary. In either case, the vast majority of "religious" Japanese may be said to be "religious" in the sense of attending and worshipping at Shinto shrines, and their "theological commitments" are either totally lacking or highly unformulated. What shrine worship does inculcate, particularly in the major urban settings, is loyalty to Japan, admiration of its heroes, and the subtle belief that those who attain high ranks in the military-imperial establishment become fit subjects for adulation after death. The direct connections of Shinto with politics—through the emperor—are discussed in a later section. The following section examines the more doctrinal of Japan's traditional religions—Buddhism.

Buddhism

Buddhism was introduced from Korea to Japan in the sixth century. Wars were fought over its adoption; even today, it is seen as something of a foreign religion, whose scriptures and rituals are unintelligible except to the tiny minority of priests trained in its ancient Sino-Japanese idiolect. For centuries the success of Buddhism was dependent on its affiliation with the proper families and political factions. When wealthy families promoted Buddhism in the eighth century, it flourished so much that Nara became a virtual Vatican, and the emperors were forced to move the capital to Kyoto to remove themselves from the influence of the powerful priesthood. By the thirteenth century, Kyoto itself was dominated by temples and nunneries, sponsored by wealthy families seeking heavenly benefits, and by members of the imperial family who felt it safer to retire into an elegant monastery than to continue their reigns at court. The great religious reformers of the Kamakura period—Nichiren, Shinran, and other disciples of Honen—were ostracized from the capital of Kyoto on politico-religious grounds, and it was their banishment to north, east, and western Japan which initiated some of the first grass-roots movements in Japanese Buddhism.

When the Tokugawa shoguns consolidated their power in the early 1600s, it was only through alternately allying with and crushing in battle the forces of popular Buddhism. It was the Tokugawa Shogunate which co-opted Buddhism and divested it of religious value and commitment by investing it with specifically political and economic roles. The Shogunate, under the guise of sponsoring Buddhism, demanded that powerful families make periodic pilgrimages to distant mountain temples and tombs (such as those on Mount Koya), to help decentralize and economically tax the competitive wealthy families. At the same time, they demanded that all Japanese register their births, deaths, and marriages at their local temples at periodic census times. In effect, they reduced the Buddhist temple to a census-house, school-room, and sometimes a crematorium, and under the rubric of supervision, effectively squelched all but the most ritualized and politically uninteresting religious behaviours of the temples.

It was this state of affairs which obtained when the Meiji restoration took place in 1868. The Meiji reformers continued to oppose Buddhism, both because of the wealth it had lazily accumulated under the patronage of the Shogunate and because Shinto was a better rallying-point for their new focus of interest on the emperor. So for much of its history in Japan, Buddhism was less a living religion than a ritualized salute to Chinese culture and a very foreign (originally Indian) philosophy. Of course, the Japanese tried to Japanize Buddhism, by adapting a Shinto-like pantheon of dieties and by equating their leader (Dainichi or Vairocana) with the sun-god Amaterasu from whom the emperor was descended. They continually used Buddhism for their ends and stressed the superiority of Japanese Buddhism to other forms.[18] But the affiliation of the Japanese people to Buddhist temples was less one of doctrinal commitment than of tradition: their fathers had registered at a local temple, the family's ancestral tablets were all engraved there, and so the children and grandchildren would continue to patronize it.

Although Buddhism is no longer officially subordinated to State Shinto, it has fared little better in recent times. The average man continues to regard it as the rather funerary and classsical resort of old people, part of Japanese cultural history, to be sure, but hardly a source of spiritual renewal. Buddhist temples continue to be thought of as very wealthy institutions causing some social jealousy and occasionally sensational headlines when a temple mismanages its resources. Japanese Buddhism has been traditionally divided between the *jiriki* (self-salvation) schools of Zen, and the *tariki* (salvation by divine power) schools of Nichiren- and Jodo-related sects. Not surprisingly, research has found that Buddhists believing in self-salvation are more likely to be politicaly active than those who believe themselves incapable of their own salvation and trust all to a godlike and benevolent *bodhisattva* (the Buddha-to-be). This may also be due to the fact that Zen had traditionally been the religion of the samurai elite and Jodo of the peasants, or to other demographic factors.[19]

Buddhist temple membership has been declining in the postwar period as temples have found themselves particularly hard-pressed by the so-called New Religions. Some have followed the example of the New Religions by setting up active social programs, like Kodo Kyodan in Yokohama which tries to attract youth to its Tendai Buddhist heritage. Other groups have attempted to elevate the prestige of Buddhism through socially relevant scholarship, like that of the Bukkyo Dendo Kyokai in Tokyo. Many local temples have begun nursery and calligraphy schools simply to survive in the modern economy; other larger temples have established universities or schools for the handicapped. Occasionally, Buddhist groups have undertaken political protests of nuclear armaments at home or at the United Nations. But on the whole, Buddhism has never recovered from its transformation into a political and educational (rather than religious) institution under the Tokugawas, and it continues to lose membership today.

Christianity

Christianity was first introduced to Japan by Francis Xavier in 1549, but less than fifty years later it was banned and persecuted by the Shoguns who feared its rising power and independence. It was re-introduced in the 1860s by American and European missionaries but never had much success in recruiting Japanese converts. The reasons for its failures—and minor successes—are fairly clear. The Japanese worship of their ancestors was an ancient practice, pre-dating the introduction of Confucianism and Buddhism, but much reinforced by them. Christianity, by contrast, emphasized the worship of one jealous god. Christianity was frequently opposed on the grounds that it discouraged appropriate ancestor-worship, so central to East Asian culture.[20] Other would-be converts were appalled at the idea that their (non-Christian) ancestors would necessarily be damned because they had not embraced Christianity. Astute Christian missionaries have recently striven to resolve this apparently insurmountable problem by arguing that the kind of love which the Christian God demands is not at all like the kind of respect addressed to familial ancestors. Therefore, they contend that the respect for ancestors and the reverence for the supreme Being need not come into conflict.[21]

Another common reason for the rejection of Christianity has been the fear that Christianity would oppose the divinity of the emperor of Japan (as it had in Rome), and ultimately the whole imperial system.[22] In fact, many Christians in Japan continue to oppose the imperial system (even after its divestment of divinity), and this factor often alienates them from more traditional Japanese. Moreover, the Bible is replete with images and issues that are very remote from the Japanese way of looking at the world: there are no flocks and pastors, no tents and camels, no exoduses and no messiahs in the Japanese world-view. So even after good translations of the Bible were made available, Biblical metaphors for man's damnation and salvation were not particularly comprehensible, much less attractive, to the Japanese. For reasons such as these Christianity has found adherents in less than 1 percent of Japan's entire population.

Why has Christianity been tolerated at all in Japan? Just as Buddhism was originally adopted because it was thought to heal plagues and protect the country, so Christianity was adopted more for its promises of material benefits than for any spiritual message within it. The Westerners who brought Christianity to Japan were possessed of a material culture which Japan desired to trade for and eventually to emulate. The first Christians were admired more for their guns, glass, and technology than for their Bibles. To the postwar generation, conversion to Christianity is sometimes seen as a sign of being "fashionably modern, foreign, and innovative." But the values of modernity, foreignness, and innovation have never had a deep hold on Japanese culture, and just as Xavier was expelled from Kagoshima when his presence did not bring in new foreign trade, so modern missionaries are often abandoned when they can promise no quick roads to success in international business, language, or study abroad. During the height of Shinto emperor-adulation in the prewar period, Japanese Christianity was virtually dead. Since that time, it has regained a small following—but just what does postwar Christianity look like?

Some scholars feel that Japanese Christianity is more outward show than content—as has also been said of their other religious forms. Never terribly concerned with theory or doctrine, Japanese Christians are sometimes content to establish new social circles based around Christian churches, without really understanding the theology behind conversion.[23] Many Japanese Christians, like the famous author Shusaku Endo, see Christ less as a saviour than as a suffering human, who can serve as a Buddha-like model of patience and humility in the face of oppression—virtues with which the Japanese have long sympathized.[24] Others have found their way into Christianity not by a sense of love, but by a sense of duty toward their creator; it has been argued that the Japanese are much more attuned to feelings of responsibility than to love.[25] Although the formats of Japanese church services are quite similar to the Western liturgies they copied, the content of their faith takes on a much different color. Of course, there are notable exceptions, like philosopher Uchimura Kanzo, and the faith of many Western Christians may be equally vacuous. But Christianity is built into the life and culture of the West, and it remains very foreign to most Japanese.

On the positive side, despite their small numbers, postwar Christian congregations have become quite active in promoting the rights of minority groups (besides themselves), including the much-ignored problems of *eta* and *burakumin* (outcastes) and the much-oppressed Korean populations living in Japan.[26] They have worked vigorously in the fields of women's rights and have fought prostitution first in Japan, and now in the Japanese-owned and patronized hotels throughout Southeast Asia. They have also worked for temperance in a society addicted to alcohol and tobacco—a noble if difficult cause. In their more successful campaigns, however, they are often co-opted and succeeded by larger movements without religious affiliation, wherein their Christian origins become incidental and unimportant to their social goals. In other cases, their movements toward greater equality or morality are "shoved under the rug," and they find that Japanese society turns a particularly deaf ear on pleas for nontraditional behaviours.[27]

In any case, Japanese Christianity has been too small a movement to influence politics, except as an occasional gadfly for more moral policies. Although its doctrines of pacifism, modernism, and egalitarianism appeal to some, it had not found a major political role in Japan's society or government.

New Religions

The term "New Religions" (*shinko shukyo*) includes a wide range of native Japanese religious groups, probably numbering in the hundreds. Typically organized by a lower class but charismatic visionary in response to social problems and the need for physical healing, they so proliferated after the war that the period was aptly termed "The Rush Hour of the Gods."[28] New Religions tend to be of three types. The oldest, Shinto-based new religions such as Konkokyo and Tenrikyo date back more than a century and were licensed as legitimate Shinto sects before the war, in return for a certain amount of government surveillance and supervision. The second group of New Religions such as Soka Gakkai and Rissho-Kosei Kai ground themselves on the Lotus Sutra and the ultra-nationalism of the Japanese Buddhist-prophet, Nichiren. The third group attempts to be "universalist"; in their writings and teachings, we can see the influences of many great world religions and a broadly ecumenical internationalism which led to their persecution, if not abolition, by the prewar government.

Important survivors include such sects as Ōmoto-kyo and Seicho-no-Ie. Although their specific doctrines and platforms vary considerably, it is appropriate to view the rapid postwar rise of the New Religions as a manifestation of the same socio-religious phenomenon. Moreover, as they are more publicized, younger, and more visibly active than any other religions in Japan, they present a fascinating set of case studies in the origins of religions for sociologists and religious historians.

Immediately following the surrender of Japanese forces in 1945, the Japanese people faced a bewildering loss of direction.[29] The dream toward which they had organized their efforts and sacrificed their lives for nearly a decade had ended. The old nationalist and miltarist values were repudiated by the conquering army of occupation and removed from school textbooks. Those accustomed to the absolute obedience to authority which a military state had required suddenly found themselves without leaders who spoke their languages and without a hierarchy in which to identify themselves. And although many vestiges of its influence remained, State Shinto had been officially disbanded, removed from government, and the schools—the "national faith" of Japan—had been destroyed or at least forced into new forms. The New Religions were quick to fill the power vacuum created by this loss of direction, and quick to supply social and hierarchical supports for a culture that depended more on social structures and vertical relationships than on individual initiative for its very functioning.[30] The charismatic leaders of the New Religions, now free from all government supervision, held public rallies and gave demonstrations of healing. They brought relief teams to victims of famine and flood, and set up weekly meeting groups which enabled neighbors to share their problems and difficulties with each other—always under the direction of trained preachers. Their memberships mushroomed, and within a decade after the war, several were building huge edifices in prominent cities and claiming memberships in the millions. Soka Gakkai was the fastest growing and most nationalistic of the New Religions, and it formed the Komeito, or "Clean Government Party," in the 1950s. By 1959 it had placed all fifty-seven of its Tokyo candidates, and the vast majority of its candidates in other prefectures, into the national assembly.

Other New Religions are less political in the sense that they have not publicly sponsored political candidates—but their nationalism is no less evident. Konkokyo still claims that Japan is the origin of the golden light of the sun and gods. Tenrikyo continues to insist that Japan is the origin of life and of the human race, and that all must return to Japan to attain salvation. Reiyukai and its successor Rissho-Kosei Kai stress that Nichiren was the saviour of the world, and his message came expressly to the Japanese. Even the eclectic Taniguchi, founder of Seicho-no-Ie, has taken a passionately nationalist tone in some of his writings, glorifying the fatherland and advocating religious involvement in politics.

In the 1960s the New Religions were helped by the same demographic changes that broke traditional bonds between shrine and devotee, as large numbers migrated to the metropolises of modernizing Japan.[31] Finding themselves lost and uncommitted in the impersonal city, Japanese workers and especially their wives were readily drawn into the friendly social groups on which the New Religions centered their activities. Their followings are especially strong among the lower classes and lower middle classes, and some New Religions strove desperately to attract the wealthy and the intellectuals who continued to spurn them.[32]

By the mid–1970s the dramatic increases of the New Religions were tapering off and reaching a plateau. Many reasons have been adduced to explain this phenomenon.[33] The economic crises of the postwar years were a thing of the past, and people no longer needed to pray for prosperity. The Japanese were again becoming self-assured, both in the crowded streets of their cities and as they ventured into foreign markets; they needed no links to the gods for confidence in the face of defeat. Even more than the elimination of religion from school curricula, the thoroughgoing education in the material sciences was casting unprecedented doubt on the existence of invisible powers which every preceding generation of Japanese had accepted. Not least important, the generation that had most vigorously embraced the New Religions in the decade after the war was now grown and teaching children of its own—but the appeal, the spirit, the urgency of the message which the parents had felt a generation earlier could not always be effectively communicated by word of mouth to an affluent, if not cocky, younger generation.[34] It almost seemed as if the heyday of the gods was over.

Then came the defeat of America in Vietnam. The Japanese had always judged human worth partly by strength in battle; therefore, they have always looked down on the countries they defeated, and respected the conquering United States. But now America was a loser and was pulling its troops out of Southeast Asia, Korea, Taiwan, and Okinawa, at the very moment that Russia was moving more aggressively in northern waters. Again Japan found itself facing a crisis: of values, because the authority figure it had respected had lost its absolute authority, and of nationalism, because it began to appear that if America could not protect Japanese interests, Japan would have to protect its own.

At home, Japan was facing a crisis of values in other areas. A highly competitive collegiate examination system was causing unprecedented numbers of suicides and psychological illnesses. Youngsters convinced that they could not succeed by traditional channels were setting up teen-age protection rackets, and juvenile crime (especially shoplifting and auto theft) was markedly up, for the first time in history. As traditional social patterns further disintegrated, the divorce rate rose dramatically, and with it, problems of women's rights, alcoholism, and drug abuse. Nor could America provide any model solution for these problems of modernity. The New Religions have been quick to step in to try to answer this growing need for values-education and socialization.[35]

On the political front, the New Religions have been quick to support nationalist tendencies, ranging from the singing of patriotic songs to the advertisement that Japan should retake the northern islands from the Soviet Union. However preposterous some of these claims, they have been successful in attracting the attention and often allegiance of the increasingly unsettled Japanese public. On the home front, the New Religions have organized youth groups and "value corps" to inculcate the youth with more traditional Japanese values of fidelity, honesty, filial piety, loyalty, and respect to elders. They are re-translating and re-evaluating many classics of Japanese religious culture to find the resources on which to found movements analogous to America's "moral rearmament" or "Moral Majority." At this moment it is hard to tell whether the New Religions are leading or following the ideological trends of Japanese society, but it is clear from the latest turn of events that they will continue to foster and benefit from Japan's growing nationalism and concern with its own crisis of values.[36]

THE POLITICAL SIDE OF JAPANESE RELIGION

The Emperor and Imperial System

It is hard for a Westerner to conceive of the centrality and importance which the emperor of Japan had—and may still have—for the Japanese people. Although the West has known theorists who defended "the divine right of kings," and although there have been demagogues who would have deified themselves, there has never existed an individual or a population since Rome so convinced that their ruler was descended from, a spokesman for, and indeed their racial link to, the gods themselves. This is precisely what the Japanese had been taught to believe in the first half of this century. In fact, one reason for the Japanese hesitancy to surrender in World War II, which led to America's tragic decision to use atomic bombs, was their fear of losing their imperial system.[37] Considering its disastrous effects on the rest of the world in the war, the Allies had good reason to disband the imperial system altogether. They did not, for MacArthur believed he could control the country better by preserving the existing channels of power than by threatening further chaos by destroying them. But in another sense, it might not have mattered what MacArthur chose to proclaim or disclaim about the imperial system, as Japanese philosophers have pointed out:

There is a mystic quality about the politics of Japan that is inscrutable to the outsider. And I think it cannot be denied that there exists a strong impression that all our extreme nationalism, with its threat to the outside world, is deeply rooted in the concept of unity of worship and (political) administration.[38]

Regardless of the particular forms sanctioned by American administrators, this aspect of Japanese character was bound to continue. So, too, was their reverence for their emperor, as philosopher Testsuro Watsuji noted: the emperor was not important because he happened to be the sovereign; rather, he was important because he was continually revered throughout history, *even in the periods when he had hardly a vestige of sovereignty.*[39] The emperor was the symbol, both of the divinity of the Japanese people and of their manifest destiny. Even if his official status had been drastically changed by the Allied occupation, it would not alter the centuries-old and carefully inculcated reverence of the people toward him.

But the Allies did not even insist on a radical change in his status. Five months after the Japanese defeat, the emperor was asked to make an official statement disavowing his divinity. This he did—but in such ambiguous language that emperor-worship remained an open option to anyone who so desired. His statement announced first that "The ties between Us and Our people have always stood upon trust and affection. They do not depend upon mere legends and myths." This much was identical to the prewar ideology, which held that the emperor's heavenly ancestry was neither legend nor myth but absolute history, that the emperor cared for his people as a father for his children, and that the people in turn owed him absolute obedience and affection. It continued: "Our ties are not predicated on the (mistaken) conception that the emperor is divine and that the Japanese people are superior to other races and are fated to rule the world." In this English translation, it appeared that the emperor was repudiating his divinity and the superiority of the Japanese race. In Japanese, however, the term "mistaken conception" falls after the words "fated to rule the world." It allows Japanese readers to interpret that, although they were not fated to rule the world, the divinity of the emperor and the superiority of the Japanese people may remain—although they are not the reasons for the (continuing) loyalty of subjects to the emperor. Scholars immediately recognized that the emperor's statement was "tantamount to an offer to modernize the *tennoate* (imperial rule) by removing the anachronisms associated with its operations, and by so doing, to enter a bid for its retention."[40]

It is true that the emperor does not direct the affairs of postwar government, but then it could be argued that he never really directed things single-handedly before the war either. He still signs into law every bill approved by the National Assembly. He still lives in a huge palace and owns vast acreage and villas, kept up by an army of servants and reverent volunteers. In addition to a royal budget of millions of dollars per year, he has large private investment holdings directed by the leading banks of Japan. His children and those of the court still attend a special private school. Indeed, the political composition and military background of his court in 1963 was almost identical to that in 1943![41] The emperor's status is still strongly supported by frequent public opinion polls.[42] Some Japanese observers believe that the preservation of his office has made elected officials feel less directly responsible for the fate of their nation, while he has continued as a symbol not only of the Japanese nation, but also of its nationalism and supremacy.[43] Even today, the terms and honorific language used to refer to the emperor of Japan are far loftier than those applied to any foreign ruler—or to any living human for that matter.

The emperor's religious roles have changed in name but hardly in fact. Before the war, the emperor conducted Shinto rites within the palace and made periodic visits to report to the sun-goddess at Ise Shrine, for the sake of the country, using federal funds. Today, he continues to conduct Shinto rites within the palace and to report to the Ise Shrine, but now it is in his capacity as a "private person," using his own "pocket money" (which, of course, the government has provided). It is highly doubtful that the Japanese citizenry makes the fine distinction between his actions as emperor and his actions as private individual that the lawyers do. The emperor continues to worship and practice Shinto, and observers are free to make their own conclusions.[44]

Even more direct evidence of unchanged atitudes and activities is found in the visits of the imperial family to World War II battlefields, and more particularly in their worship at the Yasukuni Shrine. Yasukuni has sometimes mistakenly been called the "Arlington Cemetery of Japan"; in fact, it is not only the place where many war dead are buried, but also the shrine that promised heaven and divinity to all those who gave their lives with the emperor's name on their lips for the increase of the Japanese empire. Worship at Yasukuni is symbolic of, and almost tantamount to, advocating remilitarization, emperor worship, Japanese nationalism, and the imperial cause for which so many Japanese died four decades ago.[45] Although the emperor's picture is no longer hung in every classroom, it is glorified in countless weekly magazines; and although the worship of the emperor is no longer publicly evident, he continues to be viewed as a symbol of Japanese divinity.

Education

Prewar education was esential to the creation of a state that was willing to die for its destiny and emperor; postwar education quickly tried to do away with the more major evidences of nationalistic religion. Scholars rejoiced that governmental restrictions on their publishing were removed at the end of the war. But even in his proclamation of defeat, the emperor affirmed the superiority of Japan, asking his people, "to continue to enhance the glory of the imperial state and keep pace with the progress of the world."[46] The new freedom of education was not total, however; it exchanged one set of governmental requirements for another. Even today, the government still has strict controls on what books can be used as textbooks—and such texts are notably lacking in references to Japanese responsibility for the war, much less to their prewar atrocities in Korea and China. Children in schools today are once again allowed to sing their school songs—frequently prewar anthems glorifying emperor and country.[47] The Kimigayo—a hymn of praise to emperor and country—has been reinstated as the national anthem. Recent concern for the "morality" of schoolchildren has been used as an excuse for distinctly rightist, if not imperialistic, revisions of modern textbooks.[48] At the same time, criticisms of the emperor and of the military, which had begun to appear in the 1960s, were being deleted in more current revisions.[49] The schools continue to seek greater subsidies from their federal government, and as they do, the danger of increasing federal control looms ever greater.[50]

The newspapers continually speak of the growing public demand for a reinstatement of morals courses in the schools, for parents seem unwilling or unable to take on the responsibility, and Christian Sunday Schools are not well attended in most of Japan. Trends in education are therefore moving in the direction of nationalism and emperor-praise, if not emperor-worship. At the present, the forms are more modern, the message more subtle; the object of worship is Japan and not the deified emperor. But the drift toward both political right-ism and reinstatement of a politics of nationalism is quite evident within education as well as in the public view of the emperor. Recent opinion polls have found a majority of Japanese youth either supportive of or resigned to Japan's rearmament in the 1980s.[51]

The Japanese are voracious readers, and the major sources of public information are their leading newspapers, the *Asahi, Mainichi,* and *Yomiuri.* The military leaders of Japan's Self-Defence Forces have recently played up the dangers of Russian or even North Korean military threats. Incredible as these tales may sound to an outsider, the Japanese themselves no longer trust that America will support them in a coming war with Russia.[52] As if to support this contention, America is asking Japan to increase its naval and air defenses (to reduce America's commitment and help balance its budget.)[53] Legislation is not before the Assembly which would grant special power to Japan's military and enable a declaration of military standby or even martial law without congressional approval. Editorialists can find numerous analogies between the situation in the early 1980s and the early 1930s,[54] as increasing Japanese dependence on foriegn oil, markets, and capital leads Japan to contemplate again the dream of an Asian co-prosperity sphere, and the possible need to resort to military force if its vital interests are unacceptably threatened.[55]

Much of this may be purest speculation, for the Japanese love to revel in their own history. The important point is that the channels of popular education, particularly the press, are reinforcing attitudes and conditions conducive to rearmament in the 1980s. The rearmament of Japan may be a two-edged sword. It may provide more jobs for Japan's inflated economy—but it may equally create fears and rivals in Southeast Asia, which still remembers the years of Japanese war and occupation. Japanese newspapers today also report upsurges of New Rightist youth movements and a desire on the part of the Japanese themselves to rearm. The teenagers who were indoctrinated to die for their emperor in the 1940s are now the leaders of their country. Fortunately, there seems to be more freedom of discussion and more international interchange now than half a century ago. But Shinto nationalism is far from dead in 1986.

The Japan Communist Party

In the face of so much movement to the right, let us reconsider the role of the Japan Communist Party (JCP), which we might expect to oppose militarism and nationalism with its own brand of para-religious ideology. In fact, unlike many other Communist parties, the JCP has long held a uniquely independent, pro-Japan and anti-Moscow course.

Japan and the Soviet Union have a long history of rivalry. After beating Russia in the Russo-Japanese War in 1905, Japan was outmaneuvered at the Portsmouth bargaining table and lost most of its military gains. Japan and Russia underwent a long stand-off over a demilitarized zone on Sakhalin Island, rich in coal and timber. Japan kept tens of thousands of troops on Russian soil supporting the White Russian Army against the Bolsheviks for many years after the Russian Revolution. Japan and Russia have never signed an official truce after World War II, and Japan continues to claim at least four of the Kurile Islands which the Soviet Union now occupies. So it is hardly surprising that the JCP should be cool toward Moscow from the outset.

The original bones of contention between Moscow and the JCP were theoretical. The JCP criticised the Soviet interpretations of Marx and Lenin, repudiated the use of the term ''dictatorship of the proletariat,'' insisted on the inalienability of all basic political rights and freedoms of the individual, and eventually deleted all references to Marx and Lenin altogether! After the Japan-China Friendship Alliance the JCP became increasingly anti-Soviet, quarreling not only over differences in Communist theory and dogma, but also over more concrete political problems.

The return of the Kuriles was a perpetual political issue. The JCP had a choice between acknowledging the Soviet claims and losing all hope of voter support at home, and playing the role of negotiator to try to regain the Kuriles for Japan. Of course, they chose the negotiator route to gain public support but their early prognostications of Soviet openness to negotiation were soon contradicted by Soviet intransigence and re-fortification, and the JCP went down yet another notch in public estimation. Further crises emerged when the Soviets demanded absolute sovereignty for a 200-mile maritime fishing zone, which would significantly limit the Japanese catch in northern waters, and also when the Soviets made frequent reconnaissance flights over Hokkaido which the Japanese were powerless to resist. As Japanese opinion increasingly polarized against the Soviets, the JCP had little choice but to disaffiliate itself from Soviet ties and seek to establish its own neo-socialist approaches.[56]

In the meantime, the Soviets vacillated, alternately condemning and declining to recognize the JCP on the one hand, and then again wooing them on the other hand by playing up the undependability of the Americans and the danger of Japanese military build-ups to the security and peace of Northeast Asia. Apparently, the Soviet rhetoric was only half-convincing, for, although the JCP adopted a rather pacifist and occasionally anti-American stance, it never completely agreed to follow Moscow. Indeed, that would probably toll its death knell in an increasingly conservative Japan. Occasional attempts and failures at rapprochement with the Soviets only demonstrated the unworkability of such alliances.[57]

The red-brigade student activists of the early 1970s have left their colleges for the more conservative halls of banking and business, while the few who continue to hijack airplanes or destroy airport towers only crystallize public opinion against them today. Although there are still a few socialist-leaning writers who oppose the centralization, federalization, and monopoly of big business which continues in Japan today,[58] the Japanese Democratic Socialists have been unwilling to ally with the JCP to form a voting bloc, and the JCP suffered severe losses in the elections of 1979 and the early 1980s.[59]

Most of the JCP's losses have been gains for the "Clean Government Party"— the Komeito, representing the nationalist New Religion Soka Gakkai.[60] The Komeito's policies and propaganda appear to be moving increasingly to the right, supporting the more recent moves toward remilitarization.[61] From an historical perspective, this neo-fascist tendency is more traditionally Japanese, stronger, and closer to the Japanese world-view than any egalitarian Communist world-view could ever hope to be.[62] At the same time, a clear correlation between votes for the conservative majority party (the LDP) and religious conservatism has been documented in at least one community.[63] As Japanese of the "baby boom" generation mature further, they may well become more mainstream or conservative in their politics as well as in their religious behaviour. In overview, Communism in Japan has never held the ideological attraction or the capacity of serving as an alternative doctrinal commitment to religion, as it has in Western Europe, Russia, and even China. This may be due to the fundamental un-Japaneseness of the idea of the working class being the most important, or to its potential rejection of the emperor system and Japanese cultural uniqueness, or to the continuing history of Japanese conflicts with the Soviet Union. But no politico-religious ideology of communism has ever possessed the Japanese mind with such an appeal as their own native Shinto mythology—nor is one ever likely to do so.

CONCLUSIONS

This chapter has presented a brief survey, first of the state of the various religions in postwar Japan, and second of the roles of the emperor system, the educational system, and the Communist Party in influencing Japanese religions and political consciousness. If we dare to speculate further based on such sweeping generalizations, we might venture certain broad conclusions. First, Japanese religious consciousness is made up not of sin, Godhead, or salvation, but rather of belonging to a unique race and nation which deserves absolute loyalty. Second, Japanese religious consciousness has always been inextricably intertwined with Japanese politics—partly in the sacred figurehead of the emperor, and partly in that every ruler, shogun, and prime minister has catered to religious authority and sought to use it for his own political ends. Third, Japanese religious interests are inherently conservative and nationalistic; even the new religious movements are an attempt to reinstate traditional values through updated programs and formats. Hence, the Japanese religions will likely continue to support Japanese superiority, right-wing administrators, and probably rearmament. Fourth, Japanese fears of Soviet or Korean aggression (however groundless), together with suspicions that America will not support Japan (based on America's repeated requests that Japan rearm), will likely lead Japan to rearm within the next decade.[64] If history is any guide, Japan's political shift to the right will be coupled with a growing appreciation for Shinto, for Japan's myths of its sacred uniqueness, and possibly even for greater reverence for the emperor and those who die for him. This is *not* to predict another Pearl Harbor. But the intertwining of Japan's politics and religion will remain an important as well as sociologically fascinating theme for decades to come.

NOTES

1. Picken, "Religiosity and Irreligiosity in Japan," pp. 51–67.
2. Kitagawa, *Religion in Japanese History*, pp. 270–278.
3. Miyata, "The Politico-Religion of Japan" pp. 25–30.
4. Shupe, "Conventional Religion and Political Participation."
5. Smit, "Ethics and Religion in Japan," pp. 613–629.
6. Swyngedouw, "A Few Sociological Notes on Sacredness and Japan," pp. 17–38.
7. Nakamura, *Ways of Thinking of Eastern Peoples*, p. 528.
8. For example, Kitagawa.
9. Muraoka, *Studies in Shinto Thought*, p. 234.
10. Holtom, *Modern Japan and Shinto Nationalism*, p. 39.
11. Kitagawa, *Religion in Japanese History*, p. 213.
12. Cited in Nakamura, *Ways of Thinking of Eastern Peoples*.
13. Muraoka, *Studies in Shinto Thought*, p. 237.
14. *Kokugakuin Zasshi*, July 1932, pp. 79–80.
15. Kitagawa, *Religion in Japanese History*, p. 288.
16. Morioka, *Religion in Changing Japanese Society*, p. 71.
17. Shupe, "Conventional Religion and Political Participation," p. 614.
18. Nakamura, *Ways of Thinking of Eastern Peoples*, p. 529.
19. Shupe, "Conventinal Religion and Political Participation," p. 623.
20. Holtom, *Modern Japan and Shinto Nationalism*, p. 207.
21. Offner and Van Straelen, "Continuing Concern for the Departed," pp. 1–16.
22. Tsukada, "Christianity and the Emperor System," pp. 313–323.
23. Picken, "Religious Worship and Christian Spirituality," pp. 38–75.
24. Baynes, "Japanese and the Cross," pp. 146–150.
25. Bellah, *Beyond Belief*.
26. Grier, "Fighting for Human Liberation on the Home Front," pp. 151–159.
27. Morioka, *Religion in Changing Japanese Society*, pp. 132–133.
28. MacFarland, *Rush Hour of the Gods*.
29. Kitagawa, *Religion in Japanese History*, p. 260.
30. Thomsen. *New Religions of Japan*, pp. 18–20.
31. Morioka, *Religion in Changing Japanese Society*, p. 164.
32. Kodera, "Nichiren and His Nationalist Eschatology," pp. 41–53.

33. Hashimoto and MacPherson, "Rise and Decline of *Soka Gakkai*," pp. 82–92.

34. Private communication from Clark Offner, Nojiriko, 1974.

35. Solomon, "Response of Three New Religions to the Crisis in the Japanese Value System," pp. 1–14.

36. Swyngedouw, "Japan at the Beginning of the Eighties," pp. 132–138.

37. Titus, "Making of the Symbol Emperor System," p. 529.

38. Muraoka, *Studies in Shinto Thought*, p. 232.

39. Titus, "Making of the Symbol Emperor System," p. 544.

40. Holtom, *Modern Japan and Shinto Nationalism*, p. 177.

41. Titus, "Making of the Symbol Emperor System," p. 544.

42. Kojima, "Public Opinion Trends in Japan," pp. 206–216.

43. Ishihara et al., "A Nation Without Morality," pp. 276–291.

44. Kitagawa, *Religion in Japanese History*, pp. 274–275, and Holtom, *Modern Japan and Shinto Nationalism*, pp. 48–52.

45. Powles, "Religion and Politics in Contemporary Japan," p. 492.

46. Ballou, *Shinto, the Unconquered Enemy*, p. 195.

47. Bonet, "Priest-Emperor Concept in Japanese Political Thought," pp. 39–49.

48. Yamazumi, "Textbook Revision," pp. 477ff.

49. Powles, "Religion and Politics in Contemporary Japan," p. 502.

50. Kroehler, "Christian Higher Education in Japan," pp. 20–25.

51. Nosaka, "Rising Forces of Militarism" p. 494.

52. *Japan Quarterly*, "Peace and Security in Statistics," p. 197.

53. Nosaka, "Rising Forces of Militarism," p. 491.

54. Ibid., p. 490.

55. Powles, "Religion and Politics in Contemporary Japan," p. 502.

56. Falkenheim, "Eurocommunism in Asia," pp. 64–77.

57. Lewis, "Communist Dream That Failed," pp. 34–35.

58. Kawata, "Japan's Unbalanced Economy," pp. 11–20.

59. Copper, "Japanese Communist Party's Recent Election Defeats," pp. 353–365.

60. Falkenheim, "Eurocommunism in Asia," p. 75.

61. *Japan Quarterly*, "Tilting to the Right?" pp. 13–16.

62. Kamishima, "Mental Structure of the Emperor System," pp. 702–726.

63. Shupe, "Conventional Religion and Political Participation," p. 623.

64. Imazu, "Rising Hawk Mentality," pp. 175–186, and Takahashi, "Japan's Security and Public Opinion," pp. 56–63.

GLOSSARY

Burakumin, eta: Sweepers, garbagemen, and other traditional outcastes in Japanese society, not allowed to intermarry with other classes.

Honen (1133–1212): Founder of the Japanese Jodo Sect of Buddhism, which taught that even sinners could be reborn into a "Pure Land" or heaven at death, if they had adequate faith in the Bodhisattva Amida.

JCP: The Japan Communist Party.

Jiriki: The Buddhist doctrine that a person can gain salvation or enlightenment by his own power.

Jodo: The Pure Land, in which tariki believers expected rebirth at death; also, the name of the sect founded by Honen.

Komeito: The "Clean Government Party," political arm of the Soka Gakkai.
Konkokyo: A New Religious sect of Shinto, founded in Okayama by Bunjiro Kawate in 1859.
Kyoto: Capital city of Japan from the ninth to nineteenth centuries A.D.
Mushukyo: "Without religion," subscribing to no organized religious group, but not necessarily atheistic and irreligious.
Nara: Capital city of Japan in the eighth century A.D.
Nichiren (1222–1282): Self-proclaimed Buddhist saint, prophet, and saviour; advocated sole reliance on Lotus Sutra, against Honen's Jodo teachings; unique in Buddhist history as an aggressive and nationalistic proselytizer.
Nipponkyo: "Japanism," an informal body of para-religious beliefs widely held in Japan.
Rissho-Kosei Kai: A New Religious sect of Nichirenite Buddhism, founded 1938 by Shikazo Niwano in Tokyo.
Shinko Shukyo: "Newly Arisen Religions"; the indigenous religious movements that have sprung up in Japan in the nineteenth and twentieth centuries.
Shinran (1173–1262): Disciple of Honen and founder of the Jodo Shin (True Pure Land) Sect, who taught that not only is salvation based on tariki faith alone, but that even the possession of this faith is a gift from the Bodhisattva Amida, and beyond man's power.
Shinto: The ancient native faith of the Japanese, which traces the emperor's ancestry back to the gods.
Soka Gakkai: A Nichirenite New Religion, begun in 1930 by Tsunesaburo Makiguchi, now the largest and most political of all New Religions.
Tariki: The Japanese Buddhist doctrine that man can attain salvation or enlightenment through the power of deity-like Bodhisattvas.
Tendai: An early and once powerful Buddhist sect, transplanted from China to Mount Hiei near Kyoto in 805 by Saicho. The tariki offshoots of Jodo and Nichiren Buddhism trace their origins to Tendai.
Tennoate (or Tennosei): The emperor system of Japan.
Tenrikyo: A New Religion founded in 1838 by Miki Nakayama, classified as Shinto until 1945, which holds that the gods first created man in Nara.
Yasukuni: The state cemetery in Tokyo which serves as the sacred home for the souls of those who died in war for the Japanese empire.

BIBLIOGRAPHY

Note: This bibliography covers only English sources. For a comprehensive bibliography of Japanese works to 1970, see Kiyomi Morioka, "A Bibliography on the Sociology of Japanese Religions," *Social Compass* 17, no.1 (1970): 171–194.

Anzai, Shin. "Catholicism in an Isolated Village." *Journal of Asian and African Studies.* 3 (1968): 44–53.
Ballou, Robert. *Shinto, the Unconquered Enemy.* New York: Viking Press, 1945.
Baynes, Simon. "The Japanese and the Cross." *Japan Christian Quarterly* 46 (Summer 1980): 146–150.
Beardsley, Richard K., and John W. Hall. *Twelve Doors to Japan.* New York: McGraw-Hill, 1965.
Bellah, Robert N. *Beyond Belief: Essays on Religion in a Post-Traditional World.* New York: Harper and Row, 1970.

Best, Ernest E. *Christian Faith and Cultural Crisis: The Japanese Case*. Leiden: E. J. Brill, 1966.

Blacker, Carmen. "New Religious Cults in Japan." *Hibbert Journal* 60 (1962): 305–313.

Bonet, Vincente M. "The Image of Religion in Japanese Education." *Japanese Religions* 11, no. 1 (1979): 39–49.

Brett, C. "The Priest-Emperor Concept in Japanese Political Thought." *Indian Journal of Political Science* 23, no. 1 (January-March 1962): 17–28.

Buckley, R. "Britain and the Emperor: The Foreign Office and Constitutional Reform in Japan, 1945–1946." *Modern Asian Studies* 12 (October 1978): 553–570.

Cooper, J. F. "The Japanese Communist Party's Recent Election Defeats: Signal of Decline?" *Asian Survey* 19 (April 1979): 353–365.

Dator, James A. *"Soka Gakkai—Komeito* and Its Role in the Sociopolitical Development of Postwar Japan." *Journal of Developing Areas* 6, no.3 (1972): 345–364.

Davies, D. "Return of the Rising Sun." *Far East Economic Review* 107 (March 14, 1980): 18–22.

———. "Shinto Sword Glistens in Its Scabbard." *Economist* 276 (September 13, 1980): 33–34.

Drummond, R. H. "Japan's Political/Economic/Religious Mix." *Christian Century* 95 (April 5, 1978): 365–367.

Dumermuth, Fritz. "Religion in Sociological Perspective." *Contemporary Religions in Japan* 9 (1968): 1–29.

Earhart, H. B. "Toward a Theory of the Formation of the Japanese New Religions." *History of Religions* 20 (August 1980): 175–197.

Earl, David M. *Emperor and Nation in Japan*. Seattle: University of Washington Press, 1964.

Ellwood, Robert S. *The Eagle and the Rising Sun*. Philadelphia: Westminster Press, 1974.

Falkenheim, P. L. "Eurocommunism in Asia: The Communist Party of Japan and the Soviet Union." *Pacific Affairs* 52, no. 1 (1979): 64–77.

Flanagan, S. C. "Value Cleavages, Economic Cleavages, and the Japanese Voter." *American Journal of Political Science* 24 (May 1980): 177–206.

———, E. S. Krauss, and Kurt Steiner, eds. *Political Opposition and Local Politics in Japan*. Princeton, N.J.: Princeton University Press, 1980.

Fridell, Wilbur. "A Fresh Look at State Shinto." *Journal of the American Academy of Religion* 44, no. 3 (1976): 547–561.

Fuse, Toyomasa. "Religion and Socio-Economic Development." *Social Compass* 17, no. 1 (1970): 157–170.

Gordon, B. K. "Loose Cannon on a Rolling Deck? Japan's Changing Security Policies." *Orbis* 22 (Winter 1979): 967–1005.

Grier, L. N. "Fighting for Human Liberation on the Home Front," *Japan Christian Quarterly* 46 (Summer 1980): 151–159.

Hambrick, Charles H. "World Messianity: A Study in Liminality and Communitas." *Religious Studies* 15 (1979): 539–553.

Hashimoto, Hideo, and William MacPhersan. "The Rise and Decline of *Soka Gakkai:* Japan and the United States." *Review of Religious Research* 17, no. 2 (1976): 82–92.

Holtom, Daniel C. *Modern Japan and Shinto Nationalism*. Chicago: University of Chicago Press, 1947.

Ikado, Fujio. "Trends and Problems of New Religions: Religions in Urban Society." *Journal of Asian and African Studies* 3 (1968): 101–117.

Imai, Ryukichi. *Nuclear Energy and Nuclear Proliferation: Japanese and American Views.* Boulder, Colo.: Westview Press, 1980.

Imazu, H. "Rising Hawk Mentality." *Japan Quarterly* 28 (April 1981): 175–186.

Ishida, Tsuyoshi. "Comtemporary Sociology in Japan." *International Journal of Contemporary Sociology* 8, no. 3 (1971): 211–223.

Ishihara, Shintaro, et al. "A Nation Without Morality." *Japan Interpreter* 9, no. 3 (Winter 1975): 276–291.

Japan Quarterly (editorial). "Peace and Security in Statistics." 29, no. 2 (April 1982): 197–199.

————. (editorial). "Tilting to the Right? Sweeping Changes in Komeito Defense Policy." 29, no. 1 (January 1982), 13–16.

Kamishima, Jiro. "The Mental Structure of the Emperor System." *Developing Economies* 5, no. 4 (1967): 702–726.

Kawata, Tadashi. "Japan's Unbalanced Economy." *Japan Christian Quarterly* 43 (Winter 1977): 11–20.

Kimball, Bruce A. "The Problem of Epistemology in Japanese New Religions." *Tenri Journal of Religion* 13 (1979): 72–93.

Kitagawa, Joseph M. *Religion in Japanese History.* New York: Columbia University Press, 1966.

Kiyota, Minoru. "Buddhism in Postwar Japan: A Critical Survey." *Monumenta Nipponica* 24 (1969): 113–136.

Kodera, Takashi. "Nichiren and His Nationalistic Eschatology." *Religious Studies* 15 (March 1979): 41–53.

Kojima, Kazuto. "Public Opinion Trends in Japan." *Public Opinion Quarterly* 42, no. 2 (Summer 1977): 206–216.

Kroehler, W. G. "Christian Higher Education in Japan and the Ministry of Higher Education." *Japanese Christian Quarterly* 46 (Winter 1980): 20–25.

Kurokawa, Minako. "Social Characteristics of Japanese Religion." *Sociologia Internationalis* 8, no. 1 (1970): 97–114.

Langer, Paul F. *Communism in Japan.* Stanford, Calif.: Hoover Institute Press, 1972.

Lebra, Takie Sugiyama. "Religious Conversion as a Breakthrough for Transculturation: A Japanese Sect in Hawaii." *Journal for Scientific Study of Religion* 9, no. 3 (Fall 1970): 181–196.

Lewis, J. "Communist Dream That Failed." *Far Eastern Economic Review* 107 (March 21, 1980): 34–35.

McFarland, H. N. *The Rush Hour of the Gods.* New York: Harper and Row, 1970.

Maki, John M., trans. and ed. *Japan's Commission on the Constitution: The Final Report.* Seattle: University of Washington Press (Asian Law Series no. 7), 1981.

Minear, Richard H. "The Present: Coping with Affluence." In Leon E. Clark, ed. *Through Japanese Eyes*, Vol. 2. New York: Center for International Training and Education, 1981.

Miyabe, Tadashi. "The People Wanted a Change, But." *Japan Christian Quarterly* 43 (Spring 1977): 118–120.

————. "Who Gets the Religious Vote?" *Japan Christian Quarterly* 44 (1978): 118.

Miyata, M. "The Politico-Religion of Japan: Revival of Militarist Mentality." *Bulletin of Peace Proposals* 13, no. 1 (1982): 25–30.

Morioka, Kiyomi. *Religion in Changing Japanese Society*. Tokyo: University of Tokyo Press, 1975.

Murakami, Shigeyoshi. "New Religions in Japan." *East Asian Cultural Studies*. 11 (1972): 17–27.

Muraoka, Tsunetsugu. *Studies in Shinto Thought*. Translated by James T. Araki and Delmer M. Brown. Tokyo: Ministry of Education, 1964.

Nakamura, Hajime. *Ways of Thinking of Eastern Peoples*. Edited by Philip Weiner. Honolulu: East-West Center, 1964.

Nebreda, Alphonso M. "The Japanese University Student Confronts Religion." *Monumenta Nipponica* 23 (1968): 31–65.

Newell, W. H., and K. Morioka, eds. "An Integrated Bibliography." *Journal of Asian and African Studies* 3 (1968): 118–137.

————. *The Sociology of Japanese Religion*. Leiden: E. J. Brill, 1968.

Norbeck, Edward. *Changing Japan*. New York: Holt, Rinehart and Winston, 1976.

————. *Religion and Society in Modern Japan*. Houston: Rice University, 1970.

Nosaka, Akiyuki. "Rising Forces of Militarism." *Japan Quarterly* 28 (1981): 489–495.

Offner, Clark B., and Henry Van Straelen. "Continuing Concern for the Departed." *Japanese Religions* 11, no. 1 (1979): 1–16.

————. *Modern Japanese Religions*. Leiden: E. J. Brill, 1963.

Picken, Stuart D. "Religiosity and Irreligiosity in Japan." *Japanese Religions* 11, 1 (1979): 51–67.

————. "Religious Worship and Christian Spirituality." *North East Asia Journal of Theology* 18 (1977): 38–75.

————, and Edwin O. Reischauer. *Shinto: Japan's Spiritual Roots*. Tokyo: Kodansha, 1980.

Powles, C. "Religion and Politics in Contemporary Japan." *Pacific Affairs* 49, no. 3 (1976): 491–505.

Reischauer, Edwin O., and Albert M. Craig. *Japan: Tradition and Transformation*. Boston: Houghton Mifflin, 1978.

Rieck, Joan. "Fictive Parent-Child Relations in Japanese Religion." *Journal of Comparative Family Studies* 5, no. 2 (1974): 88–97.

Sakurai, Tokutaro. "The Major Features and Characteristics of Japanese Folk Beliefs." *Journal of Asian and African Studies*. 3 (1968): 13–24.

Samejima, Shinsuke. "Can Japan Steer Its Foreign Policy Clear of Militarism?" *Japan Quarterly* 29, no. 2 (1982): 30–38.

Schull, William, et al. "Kuroshima: Impact of Religion on an Island's Genetic Heritage." *Human Biology* 34, no. 4 (December 1962): 271–298.

Shapiro, I. "Risen Sun: Japanese Gaullism," *Foreign Policy* 41 (Winter 1980–1981): 62–81.

Shibata, Chizuo. "Christianity and Japanese Ancestor Worship Considered as a Basic Cultural Form." *North East Asia Journal of Theology* 22 (1979): 62–71.

Shimpo, Mitsuru. "Impact, Congruence, and New Equilibrium." *Journal of Asian and African Studies* 3 (1968): 54–72.

Shupe, Anson D. "Conventional Religion and Political Participation in Postwar Rural Japan." *Social Forces* 55, no. 3 (1977): 613–629.

————. "Towards a Structural Perspective of Modern Religious Movements." *Sociological Focus* 6, no. 3 (Summer 1973): 83–99.

Smit, Harvey A. "Ethics and Religion in Japan: A Study in Contrasts." *Japan Christian Quarterly* 43 (1977): 131–138.

Sokyo, O. "Shinto and Worlds of Life and Death." *East* 12, no. 6 (1976): 26–34.

Solomon, Ted J. "The Response of Three New Religions to the Crisis in the Japanese Value System." *Journal for Scientific Study of Religion* 16, no. 1 (1977): 1–14.

Spae, Joseph J. *Japanese Religiosity*. Tokyo: Oriens Institute, 1971.

———. *Shinto Man*. Tokyo: Oriens Institute, 1972.

Spier, Rik. "Rearmament for Japan?" *Christian Century* 97 (July 30-August 6, 1980): 761–762.

Swyngedouw, Jan. "A Few Sociological Notes on Sacredness and Japan." *Japanese Religions* 11, no. 1 (1979): 17–38.

———. "Japan at the Beginning of the Eighties." *Japan Christian Quarterly* 46 (Summer 1980): 132–138.

Takahashi, S. "Japan's Security and Public Opinion." *Japan Quarterly* 28 (January 1981): 56–63.

Thayer, Nathaniel B. "A New Social Portrait of the Japanese." *Wilson Quarterly* 1, no. 4 (Summer 1977): 61–72.

Thomsen, Harry. *The New Religions of Japan*. Tokyo: Charles E. Tuttle, 1963.

Titus, D. A. "The Making of the Symbol Emperor System in Post-War Japan." *Modern Asian Studies* 14 (1980): 529–578.

Tsukada, O. "Christianity and the Emperor System," *Japan Interpreter* 10, no. 3 (1976): 313–323.

Tsurutani, T. "Japan's Security, Defense Responsibilities, and Capabilities." *Orbis* 25 (Spring 1981): 89–106.

Van Straelen, Henry. *The Religion of Divine Wisdom*. Kyoto: Veritas Shoin, 1957.

Watanabe, Emi. "*Rissho Kosei Kai:* A Sociological Observation of Its Members, Their Conversion and Their Activities." *Contemporary Religions in Japan* 9 (1968): 75–151.

Weisbrod, R. J. R. "Voluntary Organizations: A General Analysis Applied to the Japanese New Religions." *Cornell Journal of Social Relations* 1, no. 2 (1966): 64–83.

Weng, Carolyn. *Religion in the U.S.S.R. and Japan (The Religious Dimensions of World Cultures)*. Dayton: Wright State University, 1976.

Werblowsky, R. J. Z. "Religions New and Not So New." *Numen* 27 (June 1980): 155–166.

Williams, J. "Buddhist Politics" (Review). *Annals of the American Academy of Political and Social Science* (January 1973): 181–183.

Wimberly, Howard. "The Knights of the Golden Lotus." (Seicho-no-Ie). *Ethnology* 11, no. 2 (1972): 173–186.

Yamazumi, Masami. "Textbook Revision: The Swing to the Right." *Japan Quarterly* 28, no. 4 (1981): 472–478.

Yanagawa, Keiichi. "The Family, the Town, and Festivals." *East Asian Cultural Studies* 11 (1972): 125–131.

Yinger, J. M. "A Comparative Study of the Substructure of Religion." *Journal for Scientific Study of Religion* 16, 1 (March 1976): 67–86.

14

Religion and Politics: Cultural Background of Soka Gakkai

T. P. KASULIS

The major religious traditions of Japan have had little direct influence on the sociopolitical scene. There have been important exceptions to this generality including, of course, Shinto's role in the nationalism leading to Japan's entrance in World War II. Since the war's end, however, the fear of religious involvement in political affairs has generally kept the interaction minimal. The most striking counter-example to this trend has been the rise of Soka Gakkai's political party, the Komei. This chapter briefly reviews the historical interactions between religion and sociopolitical change in Japan and then focuses on that postwar phenomenon.

RELIGION IN JAPANESE SOCIETY AND POLITICS—ITS ORIGIN AND NATURE

One of the initial difficulties in dealing with this topic is the definition of the term "religion" as a Japanese social phenomenon. Because of the complexities of its own intellectual and cultural development, Japanese society cannot be neatly divided into segments corresponding to the Western categories of philosophy, religion, politics, social theory, and aesthetic theory. Thus, the analysis of interaction is inherently problematic. Does the continuity indicate interaction among the spheres? Or does it indicate instead no interaction because there are no separate spheres? For the purposes of this brief overview, we need to stipulate a definition for religion that will help us to isolate its influence, if any.

In this analysis we will consider a religious tradition as involving a set of doctrines, a social form of communal participation (such as ritual), and a personal form of spiritual cultivation (a soteriological path or discipline that an individual may pursue). With these three criteria in mind, let us briefly examine the five main candidates for possible qualification as Japanese religions: Confucianism, Taoism, Christianity, Shinto, and Buddhism.

Confucianism and Taoism are, of course, Chinese in origin, and they were already present in Japan by the sixth century. In terms of our criteria, however, neither strictly qualifies as a religion in Japan, although both would qualify as religions in China. Taoism simply did not take hold in Japan except as a folk belief related to alchemy and fortune-telling. The philosophical works of Lao Tzu and Chuang Tzu, for example, have seldom been used creatively by any Japanese thinker. Some Taoist ideas did, of course, filter into Japan through the influence of Chinese Buddhism, medicine, and art, but as a distinct tradition Taoism can be disregarded as a Japanese religion.

The case for Confucianism is much more complex, but in its Japanese forms it seldom involves either communal participation or a spiritual path. Even during the Tokugawa period (1603–1868) when Confucian thought was at its apex in Japan, it functioned more as a paradigm of intellectual rigor and source of moral epithets than a truly religious tradition. This is not to deny that Confucianism influenced "civil religion" in Tokugawa times (as analyzed very well in Robert Bellah's *Tokugawa Religion*, for example), but only to insist that Confucianism has not generally functioned as an independent religious tradition bringing to bear its religious ideals in the secular realms of social and political ideology or action. In short, the vocabulary of Confucianism has often been used to articulate certain social and political ideals, but those ideals usually came from somewhere else. Confucianism did not function as a discrete religious world-view in the Tokugawa period; Japanese intellectuals utilized various ideas (especially ethical principles) where they seemed useful, but other central Confucianist ideas (such as the "mandate of heaven" [*t'ien ming*] or the primacy of "principle" [*li*]) were simply discarded when they seemed unuseful. There was no attempt to keep the Confucianist world-view intact as a possible source of religious ideological inspiration. In conclusion, although the Confucian influence on Japanese social and political thought has been notable, the influence has not been particularly religious, but more terminological or didactic. The situation with the other three traditions is quite different.

Christianity was first introduced into Japan in the sixteenth century, and it immediately gained a significant popular following, particularly in the southern areas such as the island of Kyushu. In the early seventeenth century, however, Christianity was formally banned, and it virtually disappeared except as a very small underground movement in isolated areas until the latter part of the nineteenth century when it was reintroduced. It appealed especially to those of the upper classes who were interested in various other aspects of Western culture as well. Thus, to this day, only about 1 percent of the Japanese population is Christian, but for them Christianity does function as a full-fledged religious tradition. Although the numbers prohibit the possibility of any major practical impact on Japanese social and political action, it should be noted that the overall influence of Christianity on Japanese thought is disproportional to the smallness of the following, probably because of the high number of intellectuals or socially prominent people who are Christian or are at least sympathetic to Christianity through their Japanese or Western Christian associates. In this very diffused way, therefore, Christian ideas of peace and universal brotherhood do filter into the society, but these ideals are seldom distinguished from other Western values and even the Buddhist ideal of universal compassion.

In terms of Shinto's popularity, we have almost the opposite extreme from Christianity. Most Japanese consider themselves to have some connection with Shinto, and it seems that almost all Japanese at some time participate in some Shinto ritual: paying homage to a shrine, a New Year's purification rite, a wedding ceremony, a celebration ritual for a key birthday, and so on. Shinto so permeates Japanese culture that it is often difficult to define the boundaries of what is Shinto and what is simply a secularized tradition with Shinto roots. Besides the obvious communal rituals, the individual path is delineated for those who want to pursue it (sacred pilgrimages, purification rites known as *harae*, reading the ancient classics associated with Shinto such as the *Kojiki* and *Man'yoshu*, etc.). If Shinto falls short of our three criteria, it would be in the area of doctrine. Traditionally, until the past 200 years or so, Shinto has been quite content to leave philosophizing to Buddhism and to be satisfied with instilling certain attitudes among the people: respect for nature, recognition of human failings along with their need for purification, and reverence for the ethnic harmony of Japan as flowing from the *kami* (sacred presences) through the vehicle of the imperial family. In the last two centuries, however, attempts have been made to develop at least the outline of something like a Shinto theology. This movement started with the intellectual tradition known as *kokugaku*, "national studies" or "nativism." Historically speaking, however, Shinto has generally avoided the development of dogma and has lived in harmony with Buddhism. Even today, many Japanese find no problem in saying they are both Shinto and Buddhist. Most weddings, for example, are Shinto whereas most funerals are Buddhist.

The main point for our concerns is to note Shinto's flexible standpoint with regard to doctrine. When its doctrine is developed, Shinto can function as a powerful Japanese religious tradition with deep influence on the larger society. This is exactly what happened in the rise of nationalism during the periods leading up to World War II. That is, Shinto was developed doctrinally in such a way that it would reinforce the sociopolitical aims of the militarists: belief in the ethnic purity of the Japanese "race," emperor worship, subordination of individual welfare to the good of the state, and so on. This was not a case of distorting Shinto teachings (as Christian doctrines may have been distorted by the Nazis or even Confucian doctrines by some Japanese Tokugawa figures). Rather, it was more a matter of *giving* doctrines to Shinto where previously there had been only ambiguity. Shinto is ideologically pliable in just that way.

Obviously, the Shinto of the Japanese jingoists had little to do with rice planting festivals and rituals at New Year; hence, the distinction between "State Shinto"

(Kokka Shinto) and "Shrine Shinto" (Jinja Shinto) became very sharp. With the Japanese defeat in the war, the occupation forces dismantled every semblage of State Shinto they could find. Since 1945, therefore, the sociopolitical impact of Shinto has been virtually nil. The situation could, of course, change. In the past five or ten years, there has been a resurgent interest in defining "Japaneseness." Politicians, businesspersons, and bureaucrats as well as intellectuals often spend their leisure time reading the old classics or at least books about the classics. So far, this seems to be a healthy, nonpolitical interest in exploring the interface of the traditional and the modern, and there have been no signs as yet of any significant connection being made between those interests and traditional Shinto practices and values. As we have just noted, however, the potential is always there as long as Shinto continues to play its usual role in Japanese society.

This leads to our fifth tradition: Buddhism. Buddhism came to Japan via China and Korea in the sixth century and at least from the seventh or eighth century, it has met all three criteria we have stipulated for religion. Most of Japanese Buddhist history reveals Buddhism as adapting itself to the sociopolitical situation rather than being an active force of change within it. Perhaps the populist movement of the medieval Kamakura period is the most obvious exception, but for the most part, Buddhism has worked to stay in the good graces of those in power, rather than serve as a social or political critic.

One Buddhist tendency that does run counter to the general thrust of Shinto is the fact that Buddhist doctrine almost always argues in the direction of universalism and thus does not readily lend itself to being a source of ethnocentrism. It is true that Japanese Buddhism has often assumed a nationalistic tone, but careful observation reveals this almost always to be a protective garb in the face of a dominant (and potentially threatening) social or political movement. Japanese Buddhism has been acutely aware of the fact that it can be considered a "foreign" tradition, and it has often tried to assert its Japaneseness in the face of mounting criticism. Thus, Japanese Buddhist nationalism almost never arises from the Buddhist doctrines themselves, but rather comes to it from outside as a function of self-defense. Preaching from within its own tradition, Buddhism does advocate the ideals of universal compassion and nonviolence, two ideas that have been very prominent in postwar social movements for world peace and international harmony. On the popular level at least, these ideas have been associated with Buddhism, and various Buddhist groups have been active in promoting them.

If there is a single historical exception to the Japanese Buddhist emphasis on universality over ethnocentrism, that exception would have to be the Nichiren sect of Buddhism, a sect named after its thirteenth-century founder. This sect has undergone an interesting and politically important revival in the twentieth-century movement known as Soka Gakkai. Because this group represents the most significant blend of religious ideals and sociopolitical action in present-day Japan, we will give it a more detailed analysis in light of the historical overview developed above.

RELIGIOUS ROOTS OF SOKA GAKKAI

As just mentioned, Soka Gakkai (Society for Value Creation) has its origins in the medieval tradition of Nichiren. Nichiren shared many of the concerns of the other Kamakura period Buddhist reformers (in the Pure Land and Zen traditions) insofar as he recognized his historical time to be one of spiritual decay in need of severe measures. For Nichiren religious practice involved mainly an absolute reverence for, and devotion to, the *Lotus Scripture*. The intensity and exclusiveness of this devotion was a new developoment, although actual reverence for the *Lotus* was a long-standing Japanese tradition, especially within the Tendai sect out of which Nichiren emerged. Other aspects of Nichiren's teachings were not so traditional, however.

First, Nichiren's person itself was considered an integral part of the teaching. Nichiren believed himself the physical incarnation of the highest spiritual principle, the *dharmakaya*, thereby superseding even the historical Buddha of India in importance. Thus, Nichiren Buddhism was Buddhism specifically for Japan, specifically for that critical moment in history. Second, Nichiren believed it necessary to undertake an intensive propagation campaign. Unless Japan was completely converted to revering the *Lotus*, Nichiren warned, it would suffer severe social and natural disasters, including a successful invasion by the Mongol Empire. Two aspects of this missionary zeal have particular relevance to understanding Soka Gakkai. One point is that it is the responsibility of the devotee to convert others. The soteriology is essentially collective rather than individual: one's salvation depends on the conversion of others. The other relevant point is that spiritual benefit (*kudoku*) and material benefits (*riyaku*) are correlated. Many forms of Buddhism have been criticized in Japan as being other-worldly in perspective. The Nichiren sect, however, has traditionally emphasized the material improvement of this world as the direct correlation to its spiritualization. This concern for material welfare became an important component of the Soka Gakkai belief system.

Soka Gakkai was formally organized in 1937. Its first president, Tsunesaburo Makiguchi, set the tone for the movement by emphasizing that the proper goal of life was happiness, especially happiness in *this* world. The three pillars of Soka Gakkai practice, following Nichiren, are the *daimoku* (chanting a formula indicating one's complete devotion to the *Lotus*), the *gohonzon* (meditating on a mandala, a geometric, symbolic representation of spiritual reality as depicted by Nichiren), and the *kaidan* (placing an altar devoted to the *Lotus* in one's home as a place of daily prayer). All three practices are framed within the larger enterprise of promulgating the relgion throughout Japan, and eventually throughout the world.

Since its origin, Soka Gakkai, like most of the other so-called Japanese New Religions developed in the last hundred years, has found most of its support in the lower economic and social classes, usually among those who did not attend college. The possibility of benefits in this world and the prospect of improved social conditions may be an important factor in accounting for this appeal. In recent years, however, the sect has worked to change its anti-intellectual public image and has supported scholarly projects on Buddhism in general, as well as on Nichiren and Soka Gakkai. Much of this work has been fairly high in academic merit, transcending narrow sectarianism in most cases while still displaying a clearly defined religious orientation.

SOKA GAKKAI AND THE KOMEI PARTY

The fruits of Japan's postwar economic growth have not been equally distributed across all sectors of the society. For decades after the war's end, the improvement of the average Japanese family's standard of living was given a lower priority than the reinvestment of capital for long-term development. Furthermore, the benefits of long-term growth, once they were reaped, tended to be distributed from the top of the social ladder down, and many lower class groups felt they were not getting their fair share. Housing costs remain exorbitantly high, for example: it takes the average Japanese family twice as many years of saving before they can afford a house than is the case in any Western industrialized nation. In terms of social welfare programs, the national health service is quite good, but social security for the retired is notoriously poor. Meanwhile, Soka Gakkai has grown to be the largest of the New Religions with a following of about 10 to 17 percent (depending on who is doing the counting and what methodology is used). Given its size, commitment to material as well as spiritual well-being, and its socioeconomic constituency, it is not surprising that the group would try to use politics as one means of achieving its transformation of Japanese society.

It may have been disturbing to the Soka Gakkai leadership that, even though its membership had swollen to significant size as a spiritual force, the *riyaku* (material benefits in this world) did not seem to advance proportionally. The obvious conclusion was that the political structure was so spiritually corrupt that it was blocking the natural accord between spiritual and material well-being. Hence, by the early 1950s Soka Gakkai candidates began to run as independents for office in local assemblies. (In 1955, for example, there were already fifty-three such locally elected representatives.) In 1964 Soka Gakkai decided to form its own national political party, the Komeito (Clean Government Party). The party's platform is clearly aimed at social reform, generally advocating improved social welfare programs. On most issues, therefore, they vote much the same as the centrist Democratic Socialist Party (left of the ruling conservative Liberal Democratic Party, but right of the Japanese Socialist and Japanese Comunist parties).

The main difference between the Komei and other parties is, of course, ideological perspective. The Komei Party rejects the exclusively materialistic outlook of the communist and leftist socialists. The communists, in turn, see the

Komei Party as permeated with a pernicious religious ideology. Thus, there is a deep hostility between the Komei adherents and the Japanese Communist Party that periodically bubbles over into vicious propaganda campaigns. To the right, the Komei Party rejects the ruling party as morally corrupt and self-aggrandizing. In short, even though its practical platform is often indistinguishable from that of a centrist-socialist outlook, the motivation is quite different. In a significant sense, the Komei Party is religiously utopian, trying to bring about a better world through spiritual and political change. The utopian side of the movement is theoretical, and, in practical terms, the party has sometimes worked against its own ends. The most obvious case of this situation was the sequence of events in 1970 that culminated in the formal, legal separation of the Komei Party from Soka Gakki.

In 1970 a much publicized scandal was uncovered involving an alleged attempt of the party to use its political influence to prevent the publication of an anti-Soka Gakkai book. The religious fervor of the Soka Gakkai in its missionary enterprises is universally recognized in Japan, and the religion has often been accused of being intolerant of opposing viewpoints. Thus, the accusation was made that Soka Gakkai was trying to use the Komei Party as a political instrument for its religious fanaticism. The furor in Japan was strong enough that the Komei Party formally disengaged itself from the religious sect. There is little doubt, however, that the Komei Party remains an organ of Soka Gakkai in terms of its membership. Election analyses indicate that Komei candidates receive most of their support from Soka Gakkai members, and Soka Gakkai members tend to strongly support Komei candidates whenever they have the opportunity. In any case, over the past few years, the percentage of the popular vote for Komei candidates has hovered fairly steadily around 10 to 11 percent.

The last five years reveal subtle indications of what may become new trends. First, the Komei Party has occasionally joined with another party (the Democratic Socialists) in mutual support of a candidate in local elections where no Komei candidate was running. Second, as recently as the summer of 1982, one could witness an example of a previously unthinkable alliance: the Komei Party joined with the Japanese Communist Party in proposing a no-confidence motion in opposition to the Diet's passing a constitutional amendment to change the procedure for electing members of the upper house. The amendment had been pushed through mainly with the support of the Liberal Democratic Party and the Democratic Socialist Party. The odd alliance of the opposition came through the mutual recognition that the amendment would tend to strengthen the power of the majority parties by making it virtually impossible for an independent to run for an upper house seat. Interestingly, both the Komei and Communist parties saw the amendment as a sign of moral corruption and tied the move to the tactics used to protect guilty parties in the Lockheed scandal. Thus, the Komei and Japanese Communist parties temporarily put aside their ideological differences and emotional conflicts in order to assert their joint moral outrage and concern for political survival. The alliance was particularly striking because there was no practical expectation of carrying a no-confidence motion, and the gesture was mainly symbolic.

Thus, recent behavior indicates that the Komei Party may be more willing to compromise than it has in the past. Political pragmatism, at least sometimes, may be given priority over religious or ideological idealism. This seems to be a new twist in the development of Soka Gakkai. Perhaps this is a prelude to yet another instance in which Japanese Buddhism has had to adapt itself to socio-political realities, rather than to be a critic of them. On the other hand, the religious fervor and idealism of Soka Gakkai may once again come to the fore in the face of some new national (or international) crisis, thereby following in the tradition of its forefather, Nichiren. It is too early to predict what the future of this movement may be.

CONCLUSION

In some cultures, at some times, a religious tradition will develop a world-view that influences sociopolitical theory and eventually culminates in real social or political change. In the West, for example, the medieval theory of the city of God had an important impact on sociopolitical realities. Similarly, the dem-ocratic revolutions of the eighteenth and nineteenth centuries had religious roots in the Reformation. In general, however, this type of influence of religion on sociopolitical theory has not been typical of the Japanese tradition. There have been a few exceptions, certainly, and it may be the case that we are today witnessing one of those rare exceptions in the emergence of Soka Gakkai and its political party, the Komeito. The factors are complex and the data mixed, however, so it is still far too early to predict exactly what the ultimate interaction between religion and politics will be in this case.

BIBLIOGRAPHY

Bellah, Robert. *Tokugawa Religion.* New York: Free Press, 1957.

Gendaiseijimondaikenkyūkai (Research group on modern political issues), ed. *Shiawase na jimintō* [The fortunate Liberal Democratic Party]. Tokyo: Gendaihyōronsha, 1974.

Izumi, Kaku. *Sokagakkai no rekishi* [History of Sokagakkai]. 2 vols. Tokyo: Seikyo Shinbunsha, 1977.

McFarland, H. N. *The Rush Hour of the Gods.* New York: Harper and Row, 1970.

Passin, Herbert, ed. *A Season of Voting: The Japanese Elections of 1976 and 1977.* Washington, D.C.: American Enterprise Institute for Public Policy Research, 1979.

Watanuki, Joji. *Politics in Postwar Japanese Society.* Tokyo: University of Tokyo Press, 1977.

White, James W. *The Sokagakkai and Mass Society.* Stanford, Calif.: Stanford University Press, 1970.

IV
MARXISM, RELIGION, AND POLITICS

15

Marxism and Religion in the West

PAUL MOJZES

That a secular criticism of religion may function much in the same way as religious doctrines are created and defended may seem odd. Nevertheless, this is the case with the Marxist critique of religion. Marx's own criticism of religion may be viewed as analogous to the inspired prophetic judgment of existing conditions, including religious conditions. But when Marxism became "established" (in the ecclesiastical sense of the word) in communist countries, the Communist Party, in particular its ruling center, analogously to the church authorities of the past, promoted and protected those pronouncements, thereby creating an official orthodoxy. This orthodoxy, or "diamat" in the Marxist-Leninist jargon of the Soviet Union, will be called "dogmatic Marxism" here because it tends to treat certain traditional views regarding religion as unchangeable and set.[1] These views are repeated with ritual frequency with the conviction that the very repetition of the sacred utterances is sufficient to convince, with little or no need for additional contemporary proofs or analyses.

There is another, less popular, but nevertheless vigorous Marxist critique of religion which does not dogmatize Marx's own views but uses them as a methodological approach in the ongoing analysis of religion. To orthodoxy, such efforts are revisionist, which is analogous to "heresy" and is frequently condemned by the dogmatic Marxist as a distortion of and departure from Marxism. Thinkers in this group will be called "humanistic Marxists" in this chapter because they defend their heterodoxy by claiming concern for a Marxist humanistic tradition which expresses concern for concrete human well-being. "Humanistic Marxists" often charge their dogmatic counterparts with causing much human misery and corrupting the original Marxian approach, much in the same way as reformers tend to charge the upholders of orthodoxy with departure from the original inspiration of their religious movement.

This chapter will explore these two contemporary forms of the Marxist critique of religion. It will not aim to analyze and explore Marx's own views about religion, except insofar as it will be unavoidable to point out that certain views of Marx were adopted and upheld by one or the other of these two approaches. Nor will the views of other "classics" of Marxism be presented here (Engels, Lenin, Kautsky, Stalin, etc.). Only contemporary Marxist notions will receive an airing and an evaluation. This will be followed by consideration of the politico-ideological challenge of Marxism to religion and of the religious or "quasi-religious" nature of Marxism, a presentation of the forms of interaction between Marxism and Christianity including the Christian-Marxist dialogue, and a brief mention of the Buddhist-Marxist interaction in Asia.

DOGMATIC MARXIST VIEWS OF RELIGION

The common dogmatic Marxist assumes that Marx, Engels, Kautsky, and Lenin have adequately and scientifically determined the origin, nature, and duration of religion.[2] The "vulgar" Marxist arguments tend to depend on "proof-texting" from some writings of the Marxian canon, feeling that a quote from one of the classic founders clinches the argument. Particularly popular is Marx's statement on religion as the opiate of the people—quoted out of context. Because Christianity is the most advanced religion and the founders proved its untenability, it is not necessary to undertake specific, concrete studies of religion to check whether the conclusions are correct. Those theoretical conclusions were based on the best criticism of religion accomplished in the nineteenth century, culminating in Ludwig Feuerbach and then corrected by Marx. The only task for a contemporary Marxist scholar is to present and explain the views of the founders and to point out how their research supports the complete validity of Marxist-Leninist forecasts. It is also the task of the researcher to point out the continued perfidy and cunning of religion so as to stir up the communist resoluteness to struggle against religion until it is eliminated.[3]

In conventional Marxism some of the insights of the founders of Marxism were taken not merely as important principles but as absolute truths. Instead of using these principles as theoretical assumptions to guide them in research and action, they were taken as sources for deductive conclusions with no necessity of verification in practice.[4] Its basic postulate is that there is a complete incompatibility between Marxism-Leninism and any form of religion. This idea was formulated by Lenin, who said, "Marxism as materialism is absolutely atheistic and resolutely hostile to all religion. We must combat religion."[5] Religion is seen as a mystification of natural and social relations, which appears under the conditions of class society. The ruling classes, with the aid of the clergy, use religion to hold exploited classes in passive subjection. It offers to the suffering an escape into an illusory happiness of an otherworldly salvation, thereby dulling the responses of the exploited classes by lulling them into passivity. Religion is based on superstition and magic. It warps the mind of its adherents, casting them into reactionary political and social positions and cultural backwardness. People with religious convictions can never truly support social progress. It is Marxism's task to actively struggle against religion in order to speed up its inevitable demise. Religion will completely wither in the future communistic society, when all people come to recognize that the highest being for humans is the human being. True happiness can be found only in creative self-fulfillment through useful work for society. Religion is the product of the imagination rather than a gift of supposed supernatural forces. Human beings are not God's creation; on the contrary, God is a human creation. When humans recognize that they have been worshipping their own best characteristics in the form of God, they will shed this unnecessary apparition and come to glorify their own best achievements. Future human beings will be atheist, anti-God, but pro-human.

Out of this composite picture of the conventional Marxist view of religion, we can distinguish three typical responses advocated by Marxists:

First, using the approach of enlightenment and rationalism, the task of Marxism is to show the nonsensical and unscientific character of religious dogmas and superstitions by pointing to how they obstruct human progress.[6] This can be done through atheist education and propaganda. Consequently, great efforts were and are being made, particularly in the USSR and Albania, but also in other countries, to produce a great variety of atheist propaganda in order to combat religion at this level.

Second, the natural-economic approach stipulates that religion as a false social consciousness is caused by adverse natural circumstances and the class system. As soon as people cease to be terrorized by natural disasters and when the last vestiges of class rule disappear under new socialist economic relations, religion will collapse of itself. Human beings are merely the sum total of social conditions. As soon as the social conditions cease to be enslaving, there will be an automatic change in human social consciousness. It will become nonreligious.

Third, religion can be removed by "administrative measures" against religious people, especially the clergy and institutions. "Administrative measures" is an innocuous term that stands for the not so innocous physical and psychological persecution and terror, legal restrictions, administrative harassment, job discrimination, vilification in the press, destruction of church edifices, removal of items necessary for the conduct of worship, as well as other repressive measures for the purpose of weakening and finally eliminating religion. Religion will disappear when the religious person finds no support in society and when the institutional conditions for the expression of religiosity are removed.

Most frequently, a mixture of two or all three approaches is advocated to increase the efficacy of the opposition to religion. These views on religion were developed first in the Soviet Union and have continued, with little deviation, to be most consistently advanced by Soviet Marxists and those Marxists to whom the Soviet interpretation of Marxism is mandatory, if not "sacred."

The conventional Marxist view of Christianity provides no more consolation to a Christian than the Marxist's common view of religion. Marxists generally assume that a successful attack on Christianity, which they regard as the most developed form of religion, is simultaneously an adequate invalidation of all religions. For "vulgar Marxism" Christianity is hopelessly compromised through its close association with reactionary governments. The Bolshevik appraisal of the Russian Orthodox Church was that it had completely and irrevocably enmeshed itself with the old tsarist order. Therefore, as a pillar of that society, it must disappear together with the old order. Only occasionally does someone remember that Engels regarded primitive Christianity and Thomas Münster, a radical reformer of the sixteenth century, as progressive because they sided with the poor. But the Constantinian pattern of church-state relations drastically changed that association. It was unlikely, if not impossible, that the church would ever extricate itself from its preference for the upper classes until socialism forcibly accomplished this by destroying both the privileged classes and the privileges of the churches.

For the Marxist Christianity is based on dogmas that are irrational and must be accepted on blind faith under the threat of eternal damnation. It is a religion that demands meekness and servility. It dangles the hope of afterlife for those who will accept its dogmas and morality. It worships a nonexistent God. Its religion consists of a series of myths, the greatest of which is the myth of an incarnate God, Jesus Christ. The historicity of Jesus is usually denied. The virgin birth is a biological impossibility, as is the resurrection of the dead. Miracles are contrary to nature and have been created along with elaborate rituals to hold the masses in awe, in order to more easily trick them. The churches hold human beings down, denying them any dignity through the doctrines of innate sinfulness, depravity, and corruption. The intense guilt feelings thus created can be forgiven only with the aid of the church, making this a weapon whereby people are kept in perpetual dependence on the church and its clergy. The Bible is a book of myths, legends, and improbable stories, written by a group of people who consciously wanted to deceive the masses.

It is the task of all Marxists to discredit Christianity in order to liberate the people from it. Marxists must fight clericalism, as well as attempts by religious people to poison the minds of the young with the products of their sick imagination. Young people should, instead, be given a scientific, atheist education. If necessary, Marxism should provide substitute rites of passage (name-giving ceremony instead of baptism, *Jugendweihe* instead of confirmation, state weddings and funerals instead of church ceremonies, etc.). Christianity is a moribund religion; the sooner it disappears, the better off humanity will be.

The above views are often officially endorsed and carried out by those Communist parties that have a Leninistic, Stalinistic, or Maoist orientation, though in real life the policies may be tempered by greater toleration in those countries where the churches have maintained a more powerful influence, as, for instance, in Poland, East Germany, Hungary, and Romania. The dogmatic Marxists do not have great, original scholars, but among the noted protagonists of that view one can mention the Soviets V. D. Timofeev, I. G. Ivanov, D. M. Ugrinovich, and A. F. Okulov. I. Slanikov (Bulgaria), I. Loukotka (Czechoslovakia), and

O. Klohr (German Democratic Republic) are Eastern European representatives of this view, while Robert Steigerwald (West Germany) is an example among Western European communists.

The Communist parties in Yugoslavia, Italy, France, and Spain tend to have a much greater appreciation of religion, influenced somewhat by thinkers in the humanistic Marxist tradition as well as by different political realities in their respective countries. The differences between the dogmatic and the humanistic approaches to religion are so startling that it is no exaggeration to speak of two different *forms* of Marxism which are at such odds with one another that it is questionable whether they can be reconciled. Although the dogmatic brand uncritically passes on a received content and accepts Officialdom's decrees on how to interpret the Marxist canon, the humanistic approach is characterized by a Marx-inspired methodology of radically critiquing all social phenomena, including religion.

HUMANISTIC MARXIST CRITICISM OF RELIGION

The dogmatic Marxist criticism of religion can be more concisely summarized because of the near unanimity of its approach which is vested in the nature of all orthodoxies that pressure for unanimity of thought. The humanistic Marxist approach is characterized by diversity inherent in its "heterodox" approach. Therefore, no attempt will be made to summarize the divergent views of the many humanistic Marxist thinkers; rather, a schematic analysis of their approaches to religion will be made.

The humanistic Marxists tend to agree that Marx's own work, especially his analysis of religion and Christianity, was incomplete, fragmentary, and limited. They see his critique as an oversimplification and the result of mostly pragmatic considerations and historical influences. In the meantime, especially since the establishment of socialism, many new issues have arisen in regard to the relationship of Marxism and Christianity which affect the Marxist notion of religion. Especially significant have been strong evidences of religious flexibility and the ability to adjust to changing conditions.[7]

These Marxists, variously labeled by themselves or by their sympathizers as "humanistic," "creative," or "authentic" (but by their dogmatic Marxist opponents as "revisionists"), undertook to restudy Marx's views and elaborate or rectify them. In their revisiting of the classics of Marxism they came to the conculsion that the "vulgar" Marxist view consisted of a one-sided emphasis on a few of the founders' views, usually their most negative judgements, with little attention to their positive assessments. Hence, they started reworking the Marxian theories of religion.

Among the writings of these Marxists we can schematically discern four variants of the Marxist theory of religion.[8]

1. Religion arises out of the specific conditions of class society. It reflects and perpetuates class divisions. The religion of the rulers tries to maintain the given situation. The

religion of the ruled mirrors their suffering and expresses, mostly ineffectively and passively, their revolt against misery.

2. Religion is a form of alienation—an erroneous picture of the world, a social anomaly— that came into existence under specific socioeconomic conditions which caused human estrangement. Religion is the incorrect, illusory attempt to overcome this estrangement.

3. Religion is an attempt to cope with some perennial, unresolved human problems. Although it may be an escapist attempt, nevertheless the problems (fear of death, meaning of life, and personal traumas) persist and may continually give rise to religion.

4. Religion is an ideological social practice which is irreducible to and different from all other social practices. The experience of the "holy" is a real experience. Insofar as concrete forms of this experience contribute to the entrenchment of class divisions, Marxists should fight it. If it contributes to the class struggle on the progressive side, Marxists should cooperate with it. In and of itself religion is neither good nor bad.

The responses to religion by Marxists can also be presented schematically:[9]
1. Three responses are possible within the first variant.

The first response is that religion will expire with the elimination of class society and exploitation. Struggle against religion is nonsense. Marxists should work only to bring about the classless society and leave religion alone. It will take care of itself, withering when its causes have been removed.

The second response is that the struggle against religion is important because it helps the class struggle since people's consciousness can be changed.

The third alternative is to support those forms of religion that help in the class struggle and attack the other. In the long run religion will wither.

2. Three responses are possible within the second variant.

The first response is that religious alienation is in the sphere of consciousness and is secondary to the more fundamental economic alienation. One need not attack religion until the other, more primary, sources of alienation have been eliminated.

The second response is that religion is a part of total alienation. Marxists must fight religion in order to liberate the whole human being and society.

The third response is a compromise between the other two. Religion is, indeed, a secondary type of alienation which makes it difficult to see one's alienation and to accomplish emancipation. The criticism of religion helps people see their shackles and assists them in freeing themselves.

3. The response to the third alternative can be twofold.

The first response is to try to strengthen human personality so that the perennial human problems can be solved more authentically, without recourse to religion. Some people, however, among them the most sensitive and perceptive, may continue to seek religious solutions, even at advanced stages of a classless society. They will be of no danger to that order.

The second response is that Marxism as a world-view can help shift the focus to problems other than personal problems. In preoccupying themselves with social problems, people will not dwell excessively with personal dilemmas, and thus religion will lose ground but perhaps never disappear entirely.

4. The response to the fourth alternative is to explore each concrete religion as a form of inescapable ideological grappling with reality. The relationship toward religion should not be based on differences in the religious and Marxist world-views but only on the evaluation of the religion's role in class struggle. With the role of religion changing, Marxism needs a flexible response. The Marxist attitude toward religion should not depend on the Marxist world-view or on its theories of religion, but rather on the needs of the class struggle, because Marxism is primarily a theory and strategy for changing the existing world.

Individual Marxist thinkers rarely adhere to any of these approaches in a pure form and often follow a combination of several approaches. Among the most significant humanistic Marxist thinkers in regard to religion are Roger Garaudy (France), Ernst Bloch (Germany), Konrad Farner (Switzerland), Lucio Lombardo-Radice and Alceste Santini (Italy), Milan Machovec and Vitêzslár Gardavský (Czechoslovakia), Adam Schaff and Janusz Kuczyński (Poland), József Lukács (Hungary), and a large number of Yugoslav Marxists, including Esad Ćimić, Zdenko Roter, Andrija Krešić, Marko Kerševan, Branko Bošnjak, and Srdjan Vrcan. Among American Marxists one should mention Herbert Aptheker and Howard Parsons.

POLITICO-IDEOLOGICAL AND RELIGIOUS CHALLENGE OF MARXISM TO RELIGION

Practically all Marxists consider themselves atheists; most interpret their atheism as anti-theism, that is, a concerted attack on theists. On the level of practical discussion one should take the claim of atheism seriously. Certainly Marxist atheism has become a challenge and an alternative to the theistic positions that characterize most religions (with the exception of some forms of Buddhism). The confrontation between Marxists and religious people is often interpreted by both as an atheist/theist confrontation. A world-view that bases itself on belief in God and a world-view that interprets reality without God are very different, and this is, indeed a major area of conflict between the two.

Many people, however, claim that Marxism, functionally speaking, manifests many religious or quasireligious aspects. Both common people and students of religious phenomena have made this observation. If one were to take, for instance, a Tillichian approach and define God as one's ultimate concern, then it is obvious that Marxists are also gripped by an ultimate concern, a concern that many religious people may consider idolatrous because it is a concern that should not be ultimate.[10]

Marxist practice, perhaps more than theory, betrays many religious traits. The writings of the founders of Marxism are often given the regard that the staunch fundamentalists give to the Holy Scriptures, using the proof-text method as the final arbiter. The great personages, Marx, Engels, Stalin, Mao, Tito, Castro, and others, are treated with veneration rarely exceeded by the cult of the saints, and deservedly, even in Marxist circles, the term "cult of personality" has been applied to them. For many Marxists there is an "apostolic succession" of Marxist leaders who alone are regarded to have passed down the unblemished truth. Offenders in the worldwide Marxist movement, both individual as well as entire Communist parties, are "excommunicated" with all the pressures and censures which a papal interdict of the past could deliver.

The ritual side is also well represented in Marxism. Huge public parades stir the feelings of the masses. Embalmed bodies of departed leaders are buried in splendourous tombs that are accorded as much reverence and provoke as much emotion as visits to partiarchal tombs or tombs of Imams. Surrogates for religious holidays have been established which resemble holy days in ritual and practice. New Year's is celebrated instead of Christmas with "Grandfather Frost" bringing gifts to children gathered around a decorated pine tree. In East Germany *Jugendweihe* competes strenuously with confirmation practices. Increasingly elaborate wedding ceremonies take place in the "Palace of Weddings" instead of churches. It is evident that Marxists have sensed that their attempts to abolish religion and prohibit religious holidays have deprived the people of the festive and ritual element in life. Attempts are being made to replace these with secular festivals that assume very religious overtones.

Much more subtle is the expression of the religious feeling of dependence which theologians like Friedrich Schleiermacher regarded as a central earmark of religion. Marx criticizes capitalist conditions in which human beings are so dependent and alienated that they create symbols of powers over them to which they acknowledge such dependence. But a few Marxist scholars and many non-Marxist analysts have noted that socialism has created its own conditions of alienation and feeling of dependence and that instead of eradicating religion, socialism not only provides conditions for the continuation of the traditional religions but can also create its own religious manifestations, as, for instance, the cult of Stalinism.[11] The negation of religion starts assuming forms of religion; clericalism is being replaced by a form of anti-clericalism which is expressed in explicitly clerical forms. ("Black clericalism" is being replaced by "red clericalism.") The individual still feels unequal, dependent, passive, lives in inhumane conditions, and seeks to overcome these feelings with a leap of faith. Instead of faith in the theological absolute, now one expresses faith in the anthropological absolute. Instead of the church being the mediator of salvation, it is the Communist Party which mediates it, taking into its hands the decision-making, which, it is claimed, liberates the human being. Thus, it is evident that people under Communism, at least in its present form, are not being liberated from religion but are being converted from one form of religion to another. However, millions in communist societies are not convinced of the truth of the new religion. Although they do tend to lose their original religion, they often find no convincing substitute. They end up apathetic, disinterested, uninvolved, and interested mainly in self-gratification. In this respect communist society has been as much a failure as capitalist society, both producing enormous numbers of people whose highest goal is personal pleasure. The trauma of the process of atheization has not produced liberated and happy people, but people who distinctly resemble those creatures whom Marxists considered to be the product of captialist exploitation, inequality, and oppression.

Many religious institutions have come to regard Marxism as a politico-ideological challenge. This is particularly true in those societies where the churches or religious institutions had a near monopoly on political and ideological life. This model of church-state relations is often referred to as the "Constantinian" model because it was Emperor Constantine the Great who granted Christianity a privileged position in society, which often expressed itself in the desire for exclusive power. Many countries had, and still have, establishment clauses in their laws which grant the church or churches not merely a social prominence, but often dominating roles which oppress all who are not members or who are not like-minded. Marxism advocates the abolishment of such privileges and has thereby been perceived as a threat and foe by religious institutions. Yet, Marxism is often viewed as an ally by others who advocate separation of church and state and the guarantee of freedom of conscience and freedom to believe or not to believe, to belong to a church or not to belong.

If Marxism, when implemented in socialist societies, had meant that the state would not favor any religious group and that people could freely choose their political and ideological preferences, it is possible that many, if not most, religious institutions would have come around and supported such Marxist endeavor. Those religious groups which were discriminated against in pre-socialist times would have welcomed being placed on an equal footing with the formerly established churches. But equality before the law turned out to be equal denial of religious liberties as well as an attempt at complete ideological monopoly and complete concentration of power (euphemistically called "the leading role of the party") by the Communist Party. As Milovan Djilas perceptively analyzed in *The New Class* the new class of communist bureaucrats has increased the tyranny over those who are ruled to include a tyranny over the mind which is more comprehensive than anything attempted since the Inquisition, only on a scale much greater than ever before.[12]

Such comprehensive political and ideological aspirations have drawn opposition not only from those traditional religious groups whose own political and ideological domination is threatened, but even from those religious people who seek democracy and pluralism in political life and the absence of any one monopolizing ideology which is being imposed on all. Thus, the political and ideological claims made by Marxist parties (this is not to say that all Marxists are in agreement with this effort) have inevitably drawn the opposition of religious institutions. Because most of the other potential opposition groups were factually abolished, it is not surprising that many people who oppose this or that Marxist policy often have no other means of expressing it than by associating themselves with the religious institutions, the only alternative left in otherwise monolithic societies. When Communist parties criticize the religious institutions for opposing them, it is often the result of self-fulfilled prophecy. The religious policies of most Marxist parties (the Italian Communist Party and a few like it are notable exceptions) have driven most religious institutions and people into opposition.

The fault does not lie only on the Marxist side, however. Often the religious institutions' unthinking, mechanical opposition to Communism, justifying even the most inhumane conditions only to preserve its privileges, has brought about the negative Marxist response. Which comes first is hard to decide. One thing is clear: clerical domination was not replaced by conditions of freedom under Marxism, but by a changed form of domination by the hierarchies of Marxist parties.

INTERACTION BETWEEN MARXISM AND CHRISTIANITY

The interaction between Christians and Marxists, now over a century old, has ranged from open hostility to adoption of Marxism by some Christians as the system most congruent to God's wishes.[13] Four basic patterns of interaction are discernible.

The Anathematizers. The first and still by far the most pervasive mutual response between Christians and Marxists is rejection and condemnation. The classic founders of Marxism—Karl Marx, Freidrich Engels, and Lenin—as well as their doctrinaire followers had little to say positively about Christianity. To this day the self-identification of the vast number of Marxists includes a militant atheist posture and a desire to eliminate the Christian churches, even though more positive views of religion are being found today in the writings of Marx and Engels.

Conversely, Christians reacted with an abhorrence of Marxist theory and practice. Marxism was rejected not only for its atheism, historical dialectical materialism, and threat to religious freedom, but also for its notion of class warfare, desire to abolish private ownership of the means of production, and revolutionary zeal. Starting with Pope Leo XIII and culminating in Pius XII, who threatened to excommunicate every Roman Catholic who in any way collaborated with communists regardless of the perceived benefit of the cooperation, the Roman Catholic Church saw itself as the bulwark against the spread of Communism.[14] Other churches did likewise. Although such antagonism has its origin in some deeply rooted differences between the two movements, for most Christians and Marxists this rejection is not based on a careful examination and evaluation of the other's views, but rather on a gut-level identification of the other as the demonic or reactionary source of evil.

The Synthesizers. At the other end of the spectrum is a small synthesizing minority. It consists mostly of Christians who remain metaphysically Christian but who absorb the socioeconomic and related theoretical and practical strategy of Marxism. In this group are also some Marxists who hold that Marxist atheism is not an essential element of Marxism; hence, belief in God is not perceived as contradictory to Marxism, and Jesus is viewed as a great human liberator. Such people call themselves Christian-Marxists or perhaps Marxist-Christians and they may or may not have joined a Communist party. Among them are not only lay people but also clergy. Though not limited geographically, more synthesizers are found in certain geopolitical areas, for example, East Germany, Latin America, and the West European Mediterranean countries. Many, though not all, belong in the category of naive acceptance because they have not seriously faced the contradictions and differences between the two interpretations of reality.

The Accommodators. A third, very large group of Christians and Marxists are coming to difficult accommodations. Neither enthusiastic nor trusting of the other, but pressed by historical circumstances, they hesitatingly look for ways to adjust to the new situation. This stance exists mainly in the Soviet Union and Eastern Europe, but is also represented in the Vatican's *Ostpolitik* since Pope John XXIII. Many of these relations fall under the rubric of church-state relations, but, more importantly, this group consists of the millions of Christians who in their day-to-day lives cannot avoid dealings with the Marxists who are giving the tone to the socioeconomic structure of the societes in which they live. The degree of adjustment and cooperation varies from country to country, from church to church, and from one individual to another. But the entire relationship is one of cautious accommodation. Knowledge about the tenets of the other tends to be superficial and, in any case, plays an insignificant role in this type of relationship. The main emphasis is on how to proclaim effectively and practice what one believes in the face of the likely antagonism of the other. The best example at hand may be Poland, where the communist government must reckon with the power of the Roman Catholic Church as it seeks to implement some of its policy goals. Conversely, the Polish Christians must seek to express their faith within the context of a communist milieu.

The Dialoguers. Another minority interacts differently from the above three groups. It consists of Christians and Marxists who take each other seriously. Generally, they concede that both Christianity and Marxism are important factors in the contemporary world, and both are likely to persist in the foreseeable future. These Christians and Marxists are willing to listen to and learn about each other, but not uncritically. They consider it important to maintain their own commitment to integrity. But they often admit that their dialogue partners have significant insights that can be either adopted or used as spurs to encourage their own responses to human problems. This group may be called the dialogically oriented Marxists and Christians. Some perceive the dialogue as a vehicle for cooperation; others see it as a process going on simultaneously with cooperation; still others perceive it as a method of mutual relations, whether or not it issues in short-range practical cooperation.

THE CHRISTIAN-MARXIST DIALOGUE

The approach of dialogue is still largely unfamiliar to most Christians and Marxists. That is one of its greatest limitations at the current stage of relations.

Dialogue has only recently been applied so positively as to have credibility to those who seek to apply it to Christian-Marxist relations. There are sufficient overlapping concerns and interactions in life to warrant it. Common dangers and opportunities call for the exchange of ideas and experiences and for selective cooperation.

Historically, the earliest Christian-Marxist dialogues occurred in Poland, first spontaneously during the 1956 upheavals which marked the end of Stalinism, and later in a more organized form.[15] The unusual feature of the Polish dialogue was that it did draw much international attention until the election of the Polish Pope John Paul II. From 1962 onward there were carefully planned academic dialogues, dialogues in print and in clubs of intelligentsia. Vatican II gave further impetus to the Polish dialogue for which the main inducement was the unusually pervasive role of Roman Catholicism in Poland. Without the church's tacit consent it is hardly possible to rule that country. Although the Catholic hierarchy's encounter with the state and party authorities can be described as one of negotiations rather than dialogue, the precarious balance has made a richly varied dialogical encounter possible. The topics discussed at various university conferences and in publications of Catholic lay organizations or philosophical journals varied from the role of work to the evaluation of the Middle Ages; from peace on earth to settling of difficult domestic problems. The emphasis is on practical issues, though ideological questions were not avoided.[16]

In Czechoslovakia during the period between 1957 and 1962, despite internal opposition, the Marxist professor Milan Machovec held seminars at Charles University in Prague on prominent contemporary Christian thinkers.[17] Among those studied was Professor Josef Hromádka who had taken Marxism seriously and had brought about a serious study of Marxism at the Comenius Theological Faculty in Prague. But actual dialogue took place only in 1964 when Machovec invited a number of Christian theologians to his seminars.[18] In 1967 and 1968 many spontaneous as well as organized dialogues were held throughout Czechoslovakia, where hope was expressed that in dialogue a "socialism with a human face" could be jointly built.

In 1964 a book entitled *Il dialogo alla prova* [The Dialogue Put to Test] was published in Florence, Italy. Five Marxist and five Roman Catholic authors contributed to it. These authors reflected the changing situation in Italy since the convocation of the Second Vatican Council in 1962. Likewise, the historic pronouncements of Palmiro Toggliati, leader of the Italian Communist Party, shortly before his death in 1964, in which he rejected atheist propaganda and encouraged Catholics to join the Communist Party without abandoning their faith, also marked a culmination of a process of the reexamination of relationships pioneered primarily by the Marxist professor Lucio Lombardo-Radice and reciprocated on the Christian side by such people as Mario Gozzini and Giulio Girardi.

The Italian situation appears to be the opposite of Poland's. Whereas Poland has a Marxist government that must reckon with the power of the Roman Catholic

Church, the reign in Italy is in the hands of Roman Catholics who must reckon with a very powerful Communist Party. Under such a circumstance, the Italian Catholics and Marxists are in constant dialogue through "Christians for Socialism," through the communist attempt to work out the "great compromise" with the Christian Democrats, through the communist attempt to woo a Roman Catholic electorate, or through the Catholic intellectual's perception that the Italian communists are a new breed of communists with whom one may work jointly. All these dynamics are going on simultaneously.

In the 1960s the Paulus-Gesellschaft, active primarily in West Germany and Austria, turned its attention to the Christian-Marxist dialogue. In the spring of 1964 at the Muchich meeting of the Paulus-Gesellschaft, Ernst Bloch, the German Marxist professor, took part.[19] In the fall of that year at Cologne, Adam Schaff, the Polish Marxist professor and member of the Central Committee of the Polish United Worker's Party, presented a paper at a symposium entitled "Christianity and Marxism Today."[20] At both symposia only one Marxist appeared among a large number of Christians. But with each succeeding Congress of the Paulus-Gesellschaft (Salzburg, Austria, 1965, with the theme "Christian and Marxist Future";[21] Herren Chiemensee, West Germany, 1966, with the theme "Christian Humanity and Marxist Humanism";[22] Marianske Lazňe, Czechoslovakia, 1967, with the theme "Creativity and Freedom"[23]), the number of Marxist participants increased, peaking, naturally at Marianske Lazňe. Participation was to fall off sharply at the Paulus-Gesellschaft youth congress in Bonn which took place after the Soviet invasion of Czechoslovakia in the fall of 1968.[24] The congresses were discontinued after it was obvious that the Marxist partners in the dialogue, especially the very active Czechoslovakians, were being actively repressed. As an act of solidarity, the Paulus-Gesellschaft suspended its dialogues until 1975. The Paulus-Gesellschaft was later made into a scapegoat, being accused of mixing into Czechoslovakia's internal affairs and fomenting unrest. This was given as the official reason for discontinuing the dialogue by the dogmatic Marxists and by those Eastern European Christians who always publicly endorse official positions, whatever they may be.

By 1974 the Paulus-Gesellschaft decided to resume sponsorship of Christian-Marxist meetings. The major partner for Christians in this dialogue would be the Italian communists, though others were not excluded. In October 1975 a symposium was held in Florence with a primarily Western European participation. (Yugoslav participants were the only ones who came from a socialist country.) A meeting took place in Salzburg, Austria, in September 1977. The only Marxists present were from Spain and Hungary. Another meeting took place at the World Philosophical Congress in Düsseldorf in 1979.

Out of France came the individual who initially made the greatest impact on the worldwide Christian-Marxist dialogue, Roger Garaudy. His book, *De l'Anatheme à Dialogue* [From Anathema to Dialogue] (Paris: Ed. Plon, 1965), describes the change in Christian-Marxist relations.[25] Garaudy, then a member of the Central Committee of the Communist Party of France, was responding to

Vatican II and to Pope John XXIII's *Pacem in Terris*.[26] Garaudy's worldwide involvement in the dialogue made a great contribution to the growth of the dialogue.[27] Since his expulsion from the French Communist Party in 1970, his effectiveness has decreased, though many people still respond to his ideas.[28]

In its first, spontaneous, even exhilarating form, the dialogue did not last very long. It ended abruptly in Czechoslovakia by late 1968 and shortly thereafter in Austria, Germany, and France. Many of those who participated in these dialogues concluded that the form was dead.[29] Some maintain that position to this day. Soviet Marxist scholars delivered sharp attacks on this form of the dialogue, charging that it leads to a convergence that falsifies and weakens the Marxist position.[30] Dogmatic Marxists saw the ideological dialogue as a threat, as did establishment Christians, though to a lesser degree.[31] Others argued that, while the dialogue was dead, Christians and Marxists could cooperate on concrete projects.

This indeed became the case in Latin America. The Latin American motto became liberation, and for the sake of liberation many Christians were willing to cooperate with Marxists in revolutionary endeavors. Marxists, too, sought such cooperation.[32] First, a large number of essays and books were published by Latin American theologians proposing a "liberation theology" which was implicitly or explicitly inspired by some Marxist insights. Later, a whole battery of books specifically on the dialogue was written by such Christian writers as Jose Miguez-Bonino and Jose Miranda. Such theological treatises indicate that some Latin American writers do not reject ideological or theological reflection on issues of Christian Marxist relations. However, public dialogues are rarely, if ever, taking place. This is not surprising in light of the oppression that followed the fall of Allende's regime in Chile or the political situation in Argentina, Brazil, Uruguay, and most other Latin American Countries.

This Latin American self-conscious reflection on Christian-Marxist relations started at just about the time when the formal European dialogues came to a close. But in Europe matters were not uniform by a long shot. In Yugoslavia, Poland, Italy, Spain, and England, fascinating interactions were taking place. The Yugoslav Marxists and Christians who had attended the Paulus-Gesellschaft meetings decided to continue their dialogues at home, and from 1968 to 1972 a very fruitful and active period of dialogue ensued. Marxist philosophers and sociologists such as Branko Bošnjak, Esad Ćimić, Zdenko Roter, Marko Ker-ševan, Andrija Krešić, and Srdjan Vrcan were involved both publicly and in print in dialogues with Christians such as Archbishop Frane Franić, Vjekoslav Bajsić, Tomislav Šagi-Bunić, Drago Simundža, Tomo Vereš, and Jakov Romić. Only an internal purge and tightening of ideological lines by the League of Communists of Yugoslavia brought this dialogue in public virtually to a halt, but it continues to the present in private and to some degree in print.

In Spain the original initiative seems to have been taken by such theologians as Jose Maria Gonzales-Ruiz, an initiative not surprising under the conditions of illegality imposed on Spanish communists during Franco's regime.[33] Spanish communists and Catholics gradually changed their mutual perceptions and sought ways to cooperate against oppression.[34] With the emergence of "Eurocommunism" in which the Spanish and French communists seem to have followed the example of Italian communists, one may expect further impulses for the dialogue.

In England, where there is a longer tradition in Christian socialism and common action between Christians and the labor movement, the dialogue which first emerged in 1966 in the series of published dialogues in *Marxism Today* soon spread to many smaller public dialogues in churches, universities, Communist Party branches, and so forth. The major brunt of the discussion was carried by Protestant churches primarily through the British Council of Churches and the Society of Friends, but Catholics also became involved. Many of the dialogues were published in newspapers, journals, and books.[35]

Showing much more vigor than opponents and some supporters of the dialogue expected, a new phase of the dialogue emerged in the 1970s. It is characterized by much less publicity and seems to be more widely diffused. For its base it has a considerable literature that has emerged from the protagonists in the first phase and from a new group of authors reacting to those writings. It consists of a series of peace symposia, reactivation of the Paulus-Gesellschaft activities, and a new North American involvement.

The writings of both Marxists and Christians produced in the 1960s were published as books only toward the end of the decade and continued to be translated and disseminated in the 1970s. Themes regarding the nature of human beings, transcendence, Christian attitudes toward evolution, Marxist attitudes toward religion and the Bible, as well as those dealing with the question of the relationship between Christians and Marxists were reaching an increasingly wider audience. Some were asking questions as to whether Christians could be socialists; others were wondering if it might not be mandatory that Christians be socialists. Courses dealing with the dialogue appeared at a number of universities and colleges. International travel and conferences kept the interest alive. The policy of *detente* and the Helsinki Agreement provided the atmosphere for continued Marxist-Christian interaction.

The Institut für Friedensforschung of Vienna University (initiated by the Roman Catholic Theological Faculty), under the leadership of Professor Rudolf Weiler, and the International Peace Institute of Vienna jointly organized a series of nine symposia between 1971 and 1981.[36] The first four symposia consisted of participants from Eastern and Western Europe; at the rest of the symposia there was, in addition, a significant North American group. These symposia were carefully prepared, with participation by invitation; each group had both Christian and Marxist participants, though the Eastern groups were predominantly Marxist and the Western predominantly Christian. Usually, only two major papers with two respondents were read; hence, the emphasis was on discussion.[37] A good deal of time was given for informal interpersonal contacts. For this reason the number of participants in each of the symposia was between thirty and sixty. For this dialogue the most significant is the Soviet participation.

Outside of this context no Soviet Marxists and no Russian Orthodox theologians have taken part in dialogue. Very highly placed and competent representatives came to these symposia.

On the national level several dialogues have taken place beginning in the 1970s. In Hungary the normalization of church-state relations and the increasingly liberal policy of the Kádár regime has brought about a dialogue, mostly in journals between Marxists (led by Professor Josef Lukács) and prominent Catholic and Protestant theologians. The Hungarian Reformed Bishop Károly Tóth, the General Secretary of the Christian Peace Conference, constantly stresses that conditions for the Christian-Marxist dialogue are improving. A major impetus for the dialogue came from the East Berlin Conference of European Comunist parties (July 1976), where mention of the dialogue and cooperation with Christians has been included in the final document. Particularly significant is the usage of the word "dialogue" because it has been a problematic one, particularly for the Soviets. It has finally been accepted as official terminology.

In the United States interest in the dialogue was marginal until very recently. Individuals involved themselves in European dialogues or Latin American cooperation. Those involved in Latin America were frequently radicalized by their experiences and were very sympathetic to Archbishop Helder Camara's call for dialogue.[38] "Liberation theology" has made a considerable impact on American theologians and has made many of them receptive to dialogue. Those involved in the European dialogue became convinced that a North American dialogue, suited to American circumstances, was also needed. American Christians are aware that Marxism is relatively marginal in the United States and Canada and that it is badly splintered. Hence, the pattern developed for Christians to initiate such dialogues and to invite diverse Marxist partners to such dialogues. Thus, in addition to the American contribution to the worldwide dialogue and to conferences on the relationship of Christianity to socialism, a series of North American Christian-Marxist dialogues were initiated. The sponsor is the Task Force for the Christian-Marxist Encounter of Christians Associated for Relationships with Eastern Europe. The first meeting took place in Rosemont, Pennsylvania, in 1978, the second in Dayton, Ohio, in 1980, and the third in Washington, D.C. in 1982. The topics were both theoretical and practical, ranging from discussion of the future of the socioeconomic system to dehumanization and its curtailment, and finally to the meaning, organization, and control of work.

Thus, the dialogue between Christians and Marxists reflects the vitality of both movements and the diversity by which they are manifested in various regions of the world. But it likewise betrays weaknesses stemming from its political implications and the world power struggle realities which can either foster or impede the dialogue.

BUDDHIST DIALOGUE WITH MARXISTS

Non-Christian religions have not involved themselves in dialogue with Marxism, with the minor exception of Buddhism. The reason for this is primarily political and ideological. In the Soviet Union, where there are sizable Jewish, Muslim, and Buddhist minorities, the Marxist attitude toward all religion is so intolerant as to preclude dialogue. The Soviet practice has had a harmful effect on other countries. While there are indeed Muslims and Jews with socialist convictions or those influenced by Marxism, political and ideological conditions have not favored the emergence of Jewish-Marxist or Muslim-Marxist dialogue up to this point.

The political situation in Asia also tends to be unfavorable to dialogue. Many Buddhists, including monastics, tend to favor forms of socialism and have been attracted to some aspects of Marxism. As Trevor Ling points out in *Buddha, Marx and God*, many Buddhist students who attended British universities between the two world wars became attracted by Marxism because they saw in it an ally in their anti-imperialistic national striving. However, when some of these students became leaders in such countries as Burma and Sri Lanka, they tended to follow a socialist but non-Marxist or at least non-communist orientation. The religious policies of Maoism prevented the emergence of a dialogue in China; the post-Maoist era has brought a resurgence of religious activities in the People's Republic of China, but there is no evidence as yet that any dialogue has taken place either in China or in Tibet.[39]

A mutual Buddhist-Marxist exploration seems to have taken place in Burma before 1962 during the U Nu regime, but the isolationist military regime of Ne Win did not seem to provide further opportunities.[40] The only other Asian country where conditions exist for dialogue is Sri Lanka. According to John May, there are opportunities for a Buddhist-Marxist-Christian trialogue in Sri Lanka, one not theoretically oriented but rather an action-oriented revolutionary encounter that has more in common with the Latin American liberation encounter than with the European and American dialogues.[41] The common purpose of such dialogue partners appears to be "socialism in freedom." Thus far, the purpose is being carried out by a number of uncoordinated individual and group initiatives. The common concern of the protagonists of such a dialogue is to help the poverty-stricken masses of Asia to liberate themselves from colonialist and neocolonialist oppression, to protect themselves from consumerism, and to provide opportunities for the free development of the human potential. The main obstacle to the Buddhist-Marxist dialogue seems to be that many Buddhist leaders are relatively unconcerned about radical social change, whereas Marxists seem to be concerned about little else.[42] The fact that both Buddhists and Marxists tend to be atheist does not seem to have played any role as yet.

Buddhist dialogue with Marxists is still in the rudimentary stages, and there is little evidence that it may become a significant movement in the near future.

CONCLUSION

The encounter between Marxism and religion is overwhelmingly hostile. Specifically, the overall assessment of religion by Marxism is negative, the concrete policies toward religion in Marxist-dominated countries have led to religious oppression, and most religious institutions have recoiled from the stinging criticism by Marxism and have found many Marxist theories and practices objectionable. The concrete political situation has forced many Marxists and religious people to come to uneasy accommodations. Only a limited number of religious individuals and Marxists have sought a more open, sympathetic mutual exploration which has resulted in dialogues or theological and ecclesiastical movements friendly to Marxism or in Marxist political parties tolerant of religion. These more creative alternatives do not have a guaranteed future because strong forces in both Marxist and religious circles are distrustful of the dialogical approach. Those hoping for the extermination of the other or for short-range practical coexistence retain the upper hand in the decision-making of how Marxism relates to religious people and vice versa.

NOTES

1. Diamat is a bureaucratic Soviet acronym for "dialectical materialism."

2. Most of the material in this section and the section on humanistic Marxist views of religion are taken verbatim (but not necessarily in the order in which it was originally published) from Mojzes, *Christian-Marxist Dialogue in Eastern Europe*, pp. 222–229. Reprinted with permission of Augsburg Publishing House.

3. William C. Fletcher, *Soviet Believers* (Lawrence: Regents Press of Kansas, 1981), pp. 15–20, 45–47.

4. Arif Tanović, "Dogmatism and Contemporary Socialism," *Survey* (Sarajevo) 2, No. 2 (1975): 137.

5. Lenin, "Attitude of the Worker's Party toward Religion," *Selected Works* (New York: International Publishers, 1943), Vol. 2, p. 666.

6. This typology was developed by Esad Ćimić, *Socijalističko društivo i religija* (Sarajevo: Svjetlost, 1966), pp. 13–23. Ćimić surveys these views but rejects them as incorrect Marxist approaches.

7. Zdravko Kučinar, "Marksizam i kritički pojam religije," *Kultura* (Belgrade), Nos. 1e–14 (1971): 45.

8. The schema (Items 1, 2, and 4) is based on Marko Kerševan, "Odnos komunista prema religiji," *Naše teme* (Zagreb), 19, No. 5 (May 1975): 887–891 and Tone Stres, "Religija kot druzbena praksa," *Bogoslovni vestnik* (Ljubljana) 35, No. 3 (July-September 1975): 283, but modified and extended by this author.

9. Kerševan, "Odnos komunista prema religiji," pp. 887–891.

10. Paul Tillich, *Dynamics of Faith* (New York: Harper and Row, 1957), pp. 9–11.

11. For example, Esad Ćimić, *Čovjek na raskršću* (Sarajevo: Svjetlost, 1975), pp. 108–109.

12. Miliran Djilas, *New Class* (New York: Frederick A. Praeger, Publisher, 1957) pp. 37–69 *passim*.

13. This section depends heavily, often verbatim, on Paul Mojzes, "Christian-Marxist Dialogue: Opportunity for Renewal of Christian Life," *Spirituality Today* 31, no. 4 (December 1979): 312–315. Used with permission of the editor of *Spirituality Today*.

14. John Cronin, *Catholic Social Principles* (Milwaukee: Bruce Publishing Co., 1951), p. 580.

15. For comprehensive surveys of the Christian-Marxist dialogue in each Eastern European country, see Mojzes, *Christian-Marxist Dialogue in Eastern Europe*, pp. 35–182.

16. Tadeusz M. Jaroszewski, "Confrontation, Dialogue and Cooperation," in Erich Weingärtner and Giovanni Barberini, eds., *Church Within Socialism* (Rome, IDOC International, 1976).

17. Most of the material that appears here to the end of this section is used, often verbatim, from Mojzes, "The Current Status of the Christian-Marxist Dialogue and Suggested Guidelines for Conducting the Dialogue," *Journal of Ecumenical Studies* 15, No. 1 (Winter 1978): 4–9. Used with permission of the *Journal of Ecumenical Studies*.

18. Milan Opočensky, "Christlich-marxistischer Dialog in Prag," in Bé Ruys and Josef Smolik, eds, *Stimmen aus der Kirche der ČSSR* (München: Chr. Kaiser Verlag, 1968), p. 132.

19. The overall topic of the Munich meeting was "Man, Spirit and Matter." Papers presented by Ernst Bloch, Karl Rahner, and others were published under the title *Der Mensch, Geist und Materie* (München: Paulus-Gesellschaft Selbstverlag, 1965).

20. *Christentum und Marxismus heute* (München: Paulus-Gesellschaft Selbstverlag, 1966) contains, among others, papers by Johann B. Metz, Adam Schaff, and Alfonso Alvarez-Bolado.

21. *Christliche und Marxistische Zukunft* (München: Paulus-Gesellschaft Selbstverlag, 1965).

22. *Christliche Humanität und marxistischer Humanismus* (München: Paulus-Gesellschaft Selbstverlag, 1966).

23. *Schöpfertum und Freiheit* (München: Paulus-Gesellschaft Selbstverlag, 1968).

24. *Evolution oder Revolution der Gesellschaft* (München: Paulus-Gesellschaft Selbstverlag, 1969).

25. Manfred Spieker, *Neomarxismus und Christentum: Zur Problematik des Dialogs* (München, Paderborn, Wien: Verlag Ferdinand Schöningh, 1974), pp. 63ff.

26. In 1970, Garaudy was not only relieved of his high post but was also expelled from the Communist Party of France because of "revisionism."

27. In addition to his participation in the Paulus-Gesellschaft symposia, he carried on a dialogue with many theologians. See, for instance, Garaudy and Lauer, *Christian-Communist Dialogue*; Roger Garaudy, "Christian-Marxist Dialogue," and Johann B. Metz, "The Controversy About the Future of Man: An Answer to Roger Garaudy," *Journal of Ecumenical Studies* 4, No. 2 (Spring 1967).

28. For example, Russell Norris, "Transcendence and the Future: Dialogue with Roger Garaudy," *Journal of Ecumenical Studies* 10, No. 3 (Summer 1973): 498–514; and Russell B. Norris, *God, Marx and the Futrure: Dialogue with Roger Garaudy* (Philadelphia: Fortress Press, 1974).

29. For example, Günther Nenning, "Warum der Dialog starb," *Neues Forum* (Vienna), March, 1972.

30. For example, Lev N. Mitrokhim, "About the 'Dialogue' of Marxists and Christians," *Voprosy filozofii* (Moscow), (July 1971).

31. Most notorious is the removal of Giulio Girardi from the Salesian University in Rome. Eventually he moved to Paris and continued to write on the topic but was expelled

from the Salesian Order in September 1977, apparently for his continued involvement with Marxists. His most important book is *Marxism and Christianity*.

32. Piediscalzi and Thobaben, eds. *From Hope to Liberation*; Eagleson, ed., *Christians and Socialism*.

33. Gonzales-Ruiz, *The New Creation*.

34. Santiaho Alvares, "Towards an Alliance of Communists and Catholics" in Oestreicher, ed., *Christian-Marxist Dialogue*, pp. 68–93.

35. James Klugmann, "The Pattern of Encounter in Britain," in Oestreicher, ed., *Christian-Marxist Dialogue*, pp. 170–188.

36. Rudolph Weiler, "Der Ausbau des Institutes für Friedensforschung in den Jahren 1972 und 1973," *Wiener blätter*, No. 1 (January 1974): 6.

37. The papers and discussion of the first three symposia were published by Rudolph Weiler and Walter Hollitscher, eds., *Christen und Marxisten in Friedengespräch* (Vienna, Freiburg, and Basel: Herder, 1976), Vol. 2 under the same title appearing in 1979. Papers from all symposia have been published in English and German in *Peace and the Sciences* (Vienna: International Institute for Peace).

38. Delivered at the University of Chicago, November, 6, 1974. A special issue on the dialogue in response to this speech was published by *New Catholic World* 220, No. 1317 (May/June 1977).

39. Ling, *Buddha, Marx and God*, pp. 89–119.

40. Ibid, pp. 91–97.

41. John May, "Christian-Buddhist-Marxist Dialogue in Sri Lanka: A Model for Social Change in Asia?," a manuscript accepted for publication in the *Journal of Ecumenical Studies*

42. Ibid, p. 23 of typescript.

BIBLIOGRAPHY

Adler, Elizabeth, ed. *Here for a Reason: Christian Voices in a Communist State*. Translated by Leslie Seiffert. New York: Macmillan Co., 1964.

Aptheker, Herbert, ed. *Marxism and Christianity: A Symposium*. New York: Humanities Press, 1968.

———. *The Urgency of Marxist Christian Dialogue*. New York: Harper and Row, 1964.

Beeson, Trevor. *Discretion and Valour: Religious Conditions in Russia and Eastern Europe*. Glasgow: Fontana Books, 1974. 2d Rev. ed. Philadelphia: Fortress Press, 1982.

Bhattacharya, P. K. *Marxism and Buddhism*. Calcutta: Lipi Enterprise, 1976.

Bociurkiw, Bohdan, and John W. Strong, eds. *Religion and Atheism in the U.S.S.R. and Eastern Europe*. Toronto: University of Toronto Press, 1975.

Bonino, Jose Miguez. *Christians and Marxists: The Mutual Challenge to Revolution*. Grand Rapids, Mich.: William B. Eerdmans Publishing Co., 1976.

Dunn, Dennis J., ed. *Religion and Communist Society*. Berkeley, CA: Berkeley Slavic Specialties, 1983.

Eagleson, John, ed. *Christians and Socialism*. Maryknoll, N.Y.: Orbis Books, 1975.

The Encounter of the Church with Movements of Social Change in Various Cultural Contexts (With Special Reference to Marxism). Geneva: Department of Studies, Lutheran World Federation, 1977.

Garaudy, Roger. *From Anathema to Dialogue*. New York: Herder and Herder, 1966.

————, and Quentin Lauer. *A Christian-Communist Dialogue*. New York: Doubleday and Co., 1968.

Gardavský, Vitézsláv. *God is Not Yet Dead*. Translated by Vivienne Menkes. Harmondsworth, Middlesex: Penguin Books, 1973.

Girardi, Giulio. *Marxism and Christianity*. Translated by Kevin Traynor. New York: Macmillan Co., 1968.

Gonzales-Ruiz, Jose Maria. *The New Creation: Marxist and Christian?* Translated by Matthew J. O'Connell. Maryknoll, N.Y.: Orbis Books. 1976.

Gsovsky, Vladimir. *Church and State Behind the Iron Curtain*. New York: Frederick A. Praeger, 1955.

Hebblethwaite, Peter. *The Christian-Marxist Dialogue: Beginnings, Present Status, and Beyond*. New York: Panlist Press, 1977.

Kertzer, David I. *Comrades and Christians: Religion and Political Struggle in Communist Italy*. Cambridge: Cambridge University Press, 1980.

Ling, Trevor. *Buddha, Marx, and God*. 2d ed. New York: St. Martin's Press, 1979.

————. *Karl Marx and Religion in Europe and India*. New York: Barnes and Noble Books, 1980.

Lochman, Jan Milič. *Church in a Marxist Society*. New York: Harper and Row. 1970.

————. *Encountering Marx: Bonds and Barriers Between Christians and Marxists*. Translated by Edwin H. Robertson. Philadelphia: Fortress Press, 1977.

Machovec, Milan. *A Marxist Looks at Jesus*. Philadelphia: Fortress Press, 1976.

Marx, Karl, and Friedrich Engels. *On Religion*. New York: Schocken Books, 1961.

Miranda, Jose. *Marx and the Bible*. Translated by John Eagleson. Maryknoll, N.Y.: Orbis Books, 1974.

Mojzes, Paul. *Christian-Marxist Dialogue in Eastern Europe*. Minneapolis, Minn.: Augsburg Publishing House, 1981.

————, ed. "Christian-Marxist Encounter: Is Atheism Essential to Marxism." *Journal of Ecumenical Studies* 22 (Summer, 1985): 435–593.

————, ed. *Varieties of Christian-Marxist Dialogue*. Philadelphia: Ecumenical Press, 1978.

Oestreicher, Paul, ed. *The Christian Marxist Dialogue*. New York: Macmillan Co., 1969.

Ogletree, Thomas W., ed. *Openings for Marxist-Christian Dialogue*. New York: Abingdon Press, 1969.

Piediscalzi, Nicholas, and Robert G. Thobaben, eds. *From Hope to Liberation: Towards a New Christian-Marxist Dialogue*. Philadelphia: Fortress Press, 1974.

————, eds. *Three Worlds of Christian-Marxist Encounters*. Philadelphia: Fortress Press, 1985.

Poland: Church Facing Socialism. Rome: IDOC International, 1979.

Simon, Gerhard. *Church, State and Opposition in the U.S.S.R.* Los Angeles: University of California Press, 1974.

Stumme, Wayne. *Christians and the Many Faces of Marxism*. Minneapolis, MN: Augsburg Publishing House, 1984.

Tobias, Robert. *Communist-Christian Encounter in East Europe*. Indianapolis: School of Religion Press, 1956.

Weingärtner, Erich, ed. *Church Within Socialism: Church and State in East European Socialist Republics*. Rome: IDOC Europe Dossiers, 1976.

West, Charles. *Comunism and the Theologians*. London: SCM Press, 1958.

16

Religion and Politics in the USSR and Eastern Europe

HOWARD L. PARSONS

What are the relations between religion and politics in communist states in Eastern Europe? To answer this question we must understand (1) the presocialist history of religions in these societies, (2) the policies of the different socialist states toward religion, and (3) the general tendencies and laws at work in the relations of religion and the socialist state.

PRESOCIALIST AND EARLY SOCIALIST HISTORY

Historically, religions have differed widely from culture to culture and so have had different relations to the economic-social-political orders in which they were situated—dominant, submissive, collaborative, combative, critical, detached, or indifferent. These past relations influence present relations.

Russia

The Slavonic tribe of the Rus in 988 C.E. at Kiev adopted the Christian faith, taking it from the Eastern Church of Byzantium but using the Slavonic vernacular.[1] In 1448 the Russian Orthodox Church broke away from the rule by the Patriarchate at Constantinople and by Greek metropolitans and bishops, a step that coincided with the decline of the Tatar domination and the rise of Muscovite tsardom. Under the Mongols the Church had given spiritual comfort and counsel to landowners and peasants, and its monastic movement, inspired by both meditation and physical labor, generated wealth in monasteries and surrounding villages. All such Christianization provided a base for a reformation movement after liberation. The idealistic, mystical wing was critical of the wealth of the Church, the practical, conservative Josephites argued that the social work of the Church required both the wealth and protection of the state, whereas the heretical Judaizers were critical of icons and Church estates. Agreeing with the Judaizers, Ivan III, circa 1550, confiscated Church lands in the Novgorod region; in the ensuing struggle heretics were burned at the stake, mystics lost influence, and collaborators achieved control of Church administration. From then on the Church worked hand in glove with the tsars. The Church was further weakened by Peter the Great, who, affected by Lutheranism and the doctrine that the king's religion was the state's religion, denied the election of a new Patriarch in 1700 and later abolished the office. It remained so until 1917. During the period of imperial expansion launched by Peter, the tsars confiscated 2,000 churches with their immense properties, much of which they retained until the nationalization of land and monasteries in 1917.

Although the Orthodox Church was a patriotic force until 1650 and although for a short period after that it asserted its independence under the reformer Nikhon (1605–1681) and the nationalistic (and schismatic) Old Believers, after 1700 it sank into lassitude and subservience, and was splintered into small dissenting sects.[2] Old Russia never experienced a continuous and explosive Reformation like that in the West, a movement that was both cause and effect of the bourgeois revolution. Lenin was correct in describing religion as "one of the most corrupt things existing in the world," though he and many Bolsheviks took pains to win over individual believers.[3] At one point he even asserted that priests might be members of the Party.[4]

On December 11, 1917, an ordinance was issued requiring all religious organizations to surrender their schools, seminaries, academies, lower, intermediate, and higher schools and institutions to the People's Commissariat of Education. On January 20, 1918, all monies from the state for the maintenance of churches, clergy, and religious ceremonies were cut off. Affirming the separation of church and state as well as of school and state in a Decree of January 23, 1918, the state upheld "freedom of conscience" and "free performance of religious rites." Ecclesiastical and religious associations were deprived of property and the right to own property, but were permitted the right to make use of religious buildings and objects for worship.

The struggle between church and state in the USSR has passed through several stages: the militant atheism of 1919–1929 (during which time the Patriarch Tikhon first supported the White Army and then Soviet power); restriction of religious activities in connection with Stalin's collectivization of agriculture, beginning in 1929; acceptance of the "progressive role" of the Orthodox Church in history, Russian art, and literature; mutual support during the Great Patriotic War (1941–1945); postwar tolerance of religion; renewed state action against religion under Khruschev (1958–1964)—antireligious propaganda, the closing of seminaries, monasteries, and churches, the initiation of a secular alternative to baptism; and the last two decades of relative peace between religion and state.[5]

Today there are more than 20,000 houses of worship in the Soviet Union, including the large churches of the Russian Orthodox, Roman Catholicism, and Protestantism, prayer-houses of small Protestant sects, Muslim mosques, and

Buddhist monasteries. In the absence of a religious census, estimates of membership can only be approximate. According to William Mandel "there are probably well over 20,000,000 Orthodox Christian believers" and 35,000,000 "of Moslem heritage"; 30 percent of Armenians are Christians (more than 1 million); 50 percent of the people in the Lithuanian Republic, where Roman Catholics are concentrated, are believers—1,750,000; and among persons of Jewish nationality fewer than 5 percent are religious, that is, fewer than 90,000 out of a total of 1.8 million.[6] Protestants (Lutherans, Baptists, Mennonites, Seventh Day Adventists, etc.), Buddhists, Confucianists, and others number several millions.

Because of Poland's partition in the late eighteenth century and the Russian acquisition of southwestern territories, masses of Jews found themselves under the oppressive conditions of medieval tsardom. They could not become citizens, practice most professions, join a merchant or craft guild, or (with exceptions) hold government office or get a public education. Confined to a "pale of settlement" in the rural regions of restricted provinces, they were the victims of anti-Semitism and brutal pogroms organized and funded by the tsar.[7]

The Bolshevik revolution changed all this. Many Jews were prominent in the Communist Party and later in the foreign office.[8] In the Great Patriotic War 500,000 Jews served in the Red Army and other forces, 200,000 died in combat, and 313 became gernerals—"probably more than in all other armies combined, in all history." To save Jewish people from extermination by the Nazis, the Soviets evacuated hundreds of thousands of them from threatened areas like the Ukraine and Poland. Although suspicions of bourgeois nationalism and Zionism (which is considered a reactionary political position) have persisted in Soviet society since Lenin and although for a period Stalin's postwar policies brought some Jews under persecution, their participation in social life has been extensive. In more than twice their proportionate share Jewish students are admitted to higher education, and more than one-quarter of all working Jews are employed in occupations requiring higher education—nuclear physics, engineering, medicine, law, journalism, culture, and the arts.[9] There are no Jewish neighborhoods or ghettos.

A Soviet source reports that in 1979 there were 180 open synagogues and several dozen minyans in the USSR in 1979,[10] though only 92 were functioning as of 1985. "Really devout Jews" in the USSR today number "about 60,000," the most devout being found among the Georgian, Bukhara, and Highland Jews. All are free to practice their customs and rites. Eighty of the 92 synagogues are made available free of charge; the others are rented. Matzos are baked and sold, poultry is slaughtered, kosher meat is sold in shops, books are printed (a calendar, Bible, prayer book), and ritual items like prayer shawls are provided through exchange with fraternal communities in socialist countries.[11]

The largest religious faith in the Soviet Union is that of Islam, most of whose adherents live in the Central Asian Republics, the Caucasus, and the mid-Volga areas. After the liberation of these ethnic regions from colonialism, many continued in the ways of their ethnic tradition, closely interwined with the beliefs and practices of Islam. The majority of the Muslims from dozens of nations and ethnic groups follow the Hanafite school of the Sunni persuasion; but there are Shafiites, Shiites, and Ismailies. From the beginning Soviet political policy has followed Lenin's firm oppostion to national chauvinism, colonialism, racism, and oppression based on religion. The result has been twofold. First, these formerly subjugated people have experienced great material and personal progress, emerging out of poverty, illiteracy, and cultural backwardness into a world of abundance and opportunity for fulfillment. Second, they have been free to maintain or give up their religious beliefs within the society. Like Armenians and Lithuanians, large numbers, out of attachment to their ethnic heritage, have chosen to remain Muslims. In turn they have found and emphasized the humanistic elements in Islam which correspond to the values of socialism—for example, the duty of every Muslim state to guarantee "the six basic requirements" of food, clothing, housing, health, security, and education. In concert with other religious believers and with non-believers in the USSR, Muslims have been active in the cause of peace.

Poland

Polish culture has been deeply shaped by its geographical position between East and West: its people have spoken a Slavic tongue but for nearly a thousand years have been predominantly Roman Catholic. Mieszko I adopted Western Culture to block the Germans who threatened a Poland that served as a buffer of western Slavonic tribes, and in 1000 he secured from the Pope an independent Roman Church freed from German control. During the division of the country from 1138 to 1314, when various principalities as well as local bishops became powerful, Poland included large numbers of Ukrainians of Eastern Orthodox persuasion. In 1596 the Unitate Church was created to allow them to retain their ritual and discipline while recognizing the authority of the Pope in matters of faith—a move that proved to be a source of friction between Polish prelates and Russian Orthodoxy. Then, in the long period following the three partitions at the end of the eighteenth century, Poland, one of the largest states in Europe, suffered a protracted crisis of identity.

After World War I Poland became a republic. But the military dictatorship of Pilsudski and his successors compounded its problems. Under it the Catholic Church acquired freedom to carry out its mission, in return for the support of the state. Church jurisdiction was restricted to Polish prelates only. The Protestant Church was separated from foreign influence. And an autocephalous Orthodox Church was established and accepted by Constantinople.

Through all these centuries of decentralization, partition, occupation, revolts, and struggles for national unity, the prime cohesive agency of Polish culture was the Roman Catholic Church. It owned large amounts of land and other property. The Church carried the symbols and dispensed the practice of a spiritual ideology that sustained its believers amidst the uncertainties and changes of secular life. The Church played this role between the two world wars and after Poland became the Communist People's Republic in 1945. During World War II the Poles lost more than six million people and 38 percent of their prewar permanent assets. The redrawing of the boundaries of Poland shifted it westward, so that it lost Orthodox regions in the east and gained areas in the West vacated by German Protestants. The result has been a Poland whose people today are formally 90 percent Roman Catholic. The saying of the Counter-Reformation applies today: "to be truly Polish is to be Roman Catholic."

In April 1950 the state and church agreed on religious toleration, recognition of the Pope as head of the Church, and the Church's support of the government's foreign policy. After initial refusal the Vatican named bishops in the recovered lands east of the Oder-Neisse line, but it would not recognize the line, as demanded by the government, and in February 1953 the government claimed the right of approval to high Church office. As a result Monsignor Stefan Wyszynski (later Cardinal) was arrested and detained, and bishops and others were forced to take loyalty oaths. When Wladyslaw Gomulka returned to power in 1956, Cardinal Wyszynski was released and restored to his office as head of the Polish church and five bishops and all priests were set free. The government agreed to the appointment of the bishops in the recovered territories, accented the jurisdiction of the Church, with religious publications staying free of politics, and permitted religious instruction once more in the public schools, but only after regular school hours.[12]

From the eighteenth century onward the masses of Jews in the world were concentrated in Eastern Europe, especially in Russia, Poland, and Romania; they had been living in Poland in the thirteenth century, with rights to settle and to have their own schools and religion. Large numbers went over into the control of tsarist Russia during the eighteenth-century partitions. And in spite of the "minority protective clauses" of 1919, anti-Semitism was rampant in Poland, particularly among the peasantry. During World War II the Nazis exploited this hatred; large numbers of the Nazi death camps, with their gas chambers and crematoria, were constructed in Poland—at Oswiecim (Auschwitz), Majdenik, Treblinka, and elsewhere. Nearly all of Poland's 3,351,000 Jews were exterminated.[13] In 1956 there were an estimated 65,000 Jews remaining in Poland.

The German Democratic Republic (GDR)

Charlemagne, crowned king by the Pope in 800, and Otto I, self-crowned in 962, represented attempts to revive the Roman Empire in Germany through the collaboration of secular and spiritual powers. But this Holy Roman Empire was in fact a loose union of hundreds of separate and semi-autonomous states. Although such separatism worked against a nationalist revival under Maximilian (d. 1519), the German princes, unlike their counterparts in France, England,

and Spain, could not unite to curb the power of the Italian Pope; in Germany he reigned supreme.

Corruption also reigned: simony, heavy taxes on the clergy, annates levied on bishops, and the widespread payment of indulgences for the laity to obtain forgiveness of sins. Such flagrant corruption jarred the Germans into action. Economic, nationalistic, and moral sentiments converged to raise up a powerful resistance movement against the Italian Papacy. Enlightened by the intellectual movement of Biblical humanism inspired by Erasmus, the German Reformation found its driving force in the independent and courageous energies of Luther— restive and aroused to put his rugged peasant faith and his knowledge of the Bible against the might of Rome. He robustly maintained that his people would not be "the puppet of the Roman pontiff."

The revolt and victory of the Protestants—simultaneously the victory of the German princes—profoundly molded German culture and history. Civil wars followed the break with Rome, and then the Thirty Years' War; in consequence, the country was exhausted, both economically and politically, until the nineteenth century. Yet the Reformation removed the control of religion from the imperial authority and gave it over to the princes; the Protestant flood swept over central and northern Germany; and at the end the Protestants retained most of the Catholic properties they had seized. In other parts of Europe Protestantism in the form of German Lutheranism was succeeded and promoted by the more democratic, millitant, practical, and Puritanical Calvinism. And despite the Counter-Reformation and the Inquisition, the principle of religious toleration gradually made its way, though at first only under the formula, *cuius regio eius religio* (which means literally whose religion, his religion). It can therefore be understood that the religion of the land is the religion of its ruler.

Most Protestants and Catholics under the Hitler regime were not engaged in the resistance against the Nazis; the German tradition of authoritarian conformity had nearly submerged the critical spirit of the people.[14] But the formation of the new socialist state, the German Democratic Republic, compelled the German Christians to look seriously at the human, social, and political meaning of their faith. (In this way the presence of real socialism, like the Protestant Reformation for the medieval Catholics, was a bracing moral challenge.) Most German Christians were at first hesitant about supporting the new communist government. But gradually clergy and laity came to see that the best way to carry out their beliefs in neighborly love, justice, and peace on earth was to do their civic duty in working for the humanistic goals of the socialist state. Those goals coincided, though not identically, with their own goals.

The result has been that the cooperation between Christians and Marxists in the GDR has been as fruitful a balance of independence and integration as in any other socialist country. Of the five political parties represented in the People's Chamber, the Christian Democratic Union as one party holds 52 seats (in a total of 335), and Christians are otherwise active in the political life of the society. The principle of separation between church and state, written into the constitution, makes worship, preaching, doctrine, education, church statutes, pronouncements, publications, the collection of funds, and other church affairs the exclusive concern of the Church. The Church in turn does not interfere with the state. The Federation of Evangelical Churches in the GDR, formed in 1969, stated: "We want to be a Church neither alongside nor against, but a Church in socialism."[15]

In a population of 17 million, 60 percent of the citizens of the GDR are affiliated with churches or synagogues.[16] The Federation of Evangelical Churches in the GDR—principally Lutheran but also German and French Reform groups—claims more than 9 million members; the Free Churches (other Protestants), 208,000; and the Roman Catholic Church, 1.2 million. There are eight autonomous Jewish congregations with synagogues in as many different cities, three of them built with government funds.

Within this cooperation, the Christian Church has its own independent religious life. Dr. Carl Mau (USA), General Secretary of the Lutheran World Federation, has stated that "the theological work which is being carried out in the land of the Reformation is a constant source of help to us."[17]

Czechoslovakia

In response to the missionary activity of Cryil and Methodius in the ninth century, the Slovaks, the Slavic tribes in Great Moravia, adopted Orthodoxy. Then in 907 the Magyars conquered and destroyed Moravia, and in the eleventh century Slovakia became part of Hungary and remained so until 1918. After the first Magyar king was crowned by Pope Silvester II in 1000, Roman Catholicism became the predominant religion of the Slovaks and Magyars through this long history.

As the Slovaks came under Magyar rule, their close Western kin, the Czechs, founded the kingdom of Bohemia, which lasted for centuries as a powerful state and culture. Charles IV in the fourteenth century strengthened its ties to Rome, and the Prague bishops were elevated to the status of archbishop. At the same time a movement for Church reform boiled over in revolt against the largest landholding Church in Europe, against clerical worldliness and German domination. Inspired by the doctrines of John Wyclif, clergy and laity rose up in protest and revolt. Among the reform preachers was one Jan Hus. Over against the Pope, Hus held up Christ as head of the Church, a Christ whose law is the New Testament, obedience to whom spells necessary poverty for the clergy. Although Hus was put to the stake in 1415 and his many followers were crushed, the Hussite Reformation reverberated throughout Eruope and the thunderous Teutonic Luther a century later amplified that revolutionary rumbling. For a time in the fifteenth century the Hussites ruled parts of the Slovak region. They emerged in the sixteenth century, only to be put down mercilessly in 1547 by the Jesuits. The Counter-Reformation was pressed hard upon the people, Bohemia's population was cut by more than one-fourth, many Protestants fled, and

Bohemian independence was destroyed. In the course of time the Czech culture and language were nearly extinguished.

Although the Edict of Toleration in 1781 permitted two branches of German Protestantism legal status, the old Bohemian Church remained underground. Its cause of freedom became identified with the cause of Czech national independence. Suspension of the political rights of the Czechs and their use of their language in the schools by the imperial Austrian government at the end of the eighteenth century set off a national renaissance, paralleled by a small Slovak revival movement. This renaissance prospered, and both nobility and clergy took up the struggle for national independence.

The new Republic of Czechoslovakia formed in 1918 out of the Austrian provinces of Czech Bohemia and Slovak Bohemia included 3 million Germans (in a total of 14 million) and many Orthodox believers among the 600,000 Ukrainians in Ruthenia, as well as the ancient antagonism between the anticlerical Czechs and the predominantly Catholic Slovaks. The Treaty of Versailles legalized the Evangelical Church of the Czech Brethren, after nearly 500 years of supression. They became the leading Protestant body in the country, engaged in important social and political work.

At the time of the Munich appeasement of September 30, 1938, there were more than 350,000 Jews in Czechoslovakia. Under the Nazi policy of dismemberment of territory, forced labor, and death camps, most of these Jews were exterminated. During the Nazi occupation and the war, the Church's role was divided. The Socialist and Clerical Sudeten Germans stood against the treason and anti-Semitism of the Sudeten German Nazi Party. But the Nazi collaborationist Slovak regime advanced both the "clerical fascism" of President Monsignor Josef Tiso and the open Nazism of Tuka. Yet some Christians fought against fascism, and some of their leaders, like Professor Josef Hromadka, were forced to flee the country. On their return these leaders worked closely with the communists to construct a socialist Czechoslovakia.

But among Christians they were a small minority. Although more than 500,000 Germans emigrated to Germany during the war, nearly 2.5 million (mainly Roman Catholic) were sent back right after the war, and almost 1 million persons in Ruthenia (mainly Orthodox) were taken into the Ukrainian Republic of the USSR late in the war. The Roman Catholics remained by far the largest denomination—having perhaps 75 percent of the population—while the Protestants could not claim more than 10 percent.

In 1948, when the communists came to power, the government backed certain priests who were candidates in the May elections, set up a commission on religious affairs to secure the cooperation of the bishops, passed laws prohibiting religious criticism of the state, and called, unsuccessfully, for a loyalty oath from the bishops. In 1949 it organized the Catholic Action movement designed to move the Church away from its dominance by the Vatican by emphasizing the Slavic history and language of the Church and the enmity of the Vatican. Although such changes were not accepted, the regime did succeed in establishing the July 1949 law for subsidies to the Church, payment of the clergy's salaries, and the creation of a Bureau for Church Affairs. During the period of relaxation of international tensions in the 1960s Archbishop Josef Beran, removed from office in 1951, was released into exile. In response to the growth of interest in religion during the Dubcek regime, the government undertook more systematic work in scientific education, restricted religious education in schools, seminaries, and media, established firmer legal control of clergy (in secular work and travel), and encouraged progressive religious tendencies like those in *Pacem in Terris*, which urged Christians to put faith into social practice.

Hungary

The Magyars, established on the Danube plain of present-day Hungary in the early 900s, took up Christianity when Stephen, their first king, was crowned by Pope Silvester II in 1000 or 1001. Stephen generously granted large estates to the clergy and conferred on it special privileges. This feudal-ecclesiastical system remained in place until the change to socialism in 1945. The system was dominated by a monarchy, a few wealthy landholding families with huge estates, the Roman Catholic Church (the largest landowner), the backward ideology of the Church, and chauvinistic nationalism.

The Reformation made a dramatic impact on Hungary. From the time of the adoption of the Augsburg Confession by an Erdod synod in 1545 the Magyars became virtually all Reformed, in spite of fierce imperial persecution. They came under the protection of the nearby Transylvanians, among whom Unitarianism first took hold in 1568 (about the same time as Socinianism in Poland), and they enjoyed religious liberty for the first half of the seventeenth century. But in the same period most of the nobles were converted to Catholicism, and Leopold I (1657–1705) intensified the persecution of the Protestants, crushed a rebellion, executed many nobles, and sent Protestant ministers into galley slavery. Thus devastated, the Reformed Church of Hungary never recovered its former strength throughout the whole reign of the Hapsburg monarchy (1699–1918) and its powerful clerical class. Yet the Reformed Churches (both Magyar and German branches) acquired considerable land, created a system of schools, and advanced their culture.

Within the immense Austro-Hungarian empire the Reformation had spread to the Romanians, Slovaks, and Yugoslavs. But the dismemberment of the empire by the Treaty of Trianon in 1920 reduced Hungary to 30 percent of its previous size, some 8 million people, and only one-half of its Reform community. The communist regime of 1919 was undermined by peasant and religious opposition and a Romanian invasion supported by British, French, and American governments. In the ensuing White Terror, Jews and communists became special targets of the landlord class. Led by Admiral Miklos Horthy, the regent, and impelled by obsessive nationalism to recover lost territories, this class preserved the power of large estates, viciously suppressed the socialists and communists, censored the press, and collaborated with the Nazis. In this collaboration the feudal Catholic Church in Hungary played a prominent role.

For centuries the Cardinal in Hungary was, next to the king, the most powerful person in the realm. Presiding over the House of Magnates, he served, like all clergy, in the pay of the state. A concordat between Horthy and the Pope ratified the traditional tie between the feudal autocracy and the Church. As late as 1948 nearly 65 percent of all Hungarian schools and most establishments of higher education were Catholic; the rest of the schools were parochial. The much vaunted savior of Hungary, Cardinal Joszef Mindszenty, who represented this system, was a reactionary and counter-revolutionary to the core.[18]

The fascism of prewar Hungary was openly expressed in the anti-Semitism of the minister-president, Gyula Gombos (1932–1936), and in a 1938 law limited the number of Jews in certain occupations. In the winter of 1944, when Nazism was about to be smashed by the Red Army, some 400,000 Hungarian Jews were executed, an action of unparalleled proportion.

After liberation, the new socialist state confiscated the immense landholdings of the Church, compensating the Church where property losses occurred, disestablished religion, and secularized the school system. The resistance to these and other changes in church-state relations was led by Cardinal Mindszenty, who was arrested and imprisoned in 1949 and who went into exile in 1971. In 1977, after fourteen years of negotiation, the Holy See and the Hungarian state agreed on a normalization of relations in which the Church agreed to respect the constitution and support "the constructive plans of the Hungarian people" and the state would respect the autonomy of the churches and guarantee freedom of religion.[19]

Romania

The Christianity of Rome, brought to Dacia, the original land of Romania, was suppressed during the barbarian invasions but reappeared when the Bulgars in the ninth century introduced the Slavonic alphabet and liturgy of Orthodoxy. The Daco-Roman Christians in Transylvania, having adopted the Orthodox rite, became isolated from their neighboring Hungarians and others; hence, during the Great Schism of 1054 they sided with the Eastern Church, whereas the Hungarians gave their allegiance to Rome. Likewise, when Moldavia and Walachia (the two principalities that became Romania) emerged in the fourteenth century they became Orthodox, enemies of the Hungarians. In spite of the efforts of Stephen the Great of Moldavia (1457–1504)—who endowed the monasteries with land, built many churches, and tried to rally Western Christendom against the Muslims—the Turks prevailed and dominated Moldavia and Walachia from the mid-sixteenth century onward. Still the princes protected the monasteries, and as Greek monks flowed into the country the Greek language gradually replaced Romanian in the liturgy. Under the influence of the Transylvanian Reformation the first Gospels in Romanian were printed in 1561, and the first

Romanian Bible apeared in 1688. But in the next century, under the Phanariot regime of the Turks, Greek influence again grew strong. A nationalistic movement of 1848 and the Crimean War treaty produced the union of Walachia and Moldavia in 1859. Four years later the monasteries' lands—more than one-fifth of the area of the new state—were confiscated, and Greek was banned in all monasteries and churches. In 1865 an autonomous Church of Romania was created.

After a full independence in 1877 the Orthodox Church was made autocephalous. Then, in 1925, following the formation of the unitary national state in 1918, the Orthodox Church united many separated groups: the Transylvanian Orthodox (Uniates since 1698), the Bukovina Orthodox previously under Austria, and the Bessarabian Church under the Russian Orthodox. With the decline of the Russian Church after 1917, the Romanian Orthodox of 13 million members became a leading Church in Eastern Orthodoxy.

Between the two world wars the Romanian regime exercised a strong and discriminatory hand in the control of religions. By the 1923 constitution, the Orthodox Church and the Uniate Church of Transylvania were named Romanian churches, the Orthodox Church assuming first place. Jews, Baptists, and others were restricted in their operations.

After 1930, when King Carol came to power, the government and ruling classes moved step by step toward fascism, led first by Codreanu's terrorist Iron Guard—Christian, mystical, racist, chauvinistic, violent, anti-Semitic, and anticommunist. In December 1937 Carol appointed as premier the leader of the anti-Semitic National Christian Party, Octavian Goga. Within a month he sponsored laws that threatened the very existence of the Romanian Jews; by November 1939 more than one-third of the Jews were disenfranchised and barred from jobs—though in 1920 they had been the third largest ethnic group in Romania, numbering 900,000. In 1943 Ion Antonescu extracted $40 million from Romanian Jews as ransom against incarceration in concentration camps.[20] After the war most migrated to Israel and elsewhere. The supporters of the war against the USSR included Churchmen, motivated like many by patriotic aims such as the reoccupation of Bessarabia. But the antifascist resistance movement included in time a great variety of groups, including religious people.[21] In 1943 a broad anti-Nazi patriotic front was formed, a united front of the Communist Party, the Ploughmen's Front, MADOSZ, the Socialist Peasant Party, the Patriot's Union, and local organizations of the Social-Democratic Party.

After the armistice of 1944 the Romanian Orthodox Church resumed relations with its counterpart in the USSR, after a separation since 1918. The land reform law of March 1945 put 1.1 million hectares into the hands of the landless and other poor peasants, eliminating in one stroke the powerful landlord class and depriving the large landholding churches, Orthodox and Roman Catholic, of most of their wealth. The 1948 constitution made all churches equal before the law, ended all Church control of schools, and separated church and state.

Bulgaria

In the ninth century Methodius and Cyril went as missionaries to Thrace and Moesia, the site of the Bulgar Empire, and in 864 converted Tsar Boris to Christianity. They brought a script that facilitated the adoption of the Slavonic or Old Bulgarian language into the church liturgy, heightening the appeal of the new religion. The controversy between Pope Nicholas I of Rome and the Orthodox Patriarch Photius of Constantinople was already far advanced. For his schismatic claim of independence Photius had been excommunicated; Photius in turn anathematized the Pope in 867; then between the Byzantine Empire and Christian Great Moravia, Boris chose Byzantium. Orthodoxy became a decisive force in the formation and survival of Bulgarian culture for a thousand years. After the decline of the Greco-Roman civilization, Bulgaria became the first European culture to make use of the vernacular, and the Orthodox Church was the principal vehicle for disseminating Bulgarian culture. (A parallel and much later development was Luther's translation of the Bible into simple German—though, of course, its effects were more immediate and far-reaching because of the printing press and the popular ferment within feudalism.)

Popular disaffection in the empire in the tenth century gave rise to the Bogomils—a prominent group of heretics who preached the equality and perfectibility of all believers (alongside Christ), a symbolic interpretation of the miracles, "baptism" as adult self-discipline, ordination by the elect congregation, and pacifism. They denied the divine birth of Christ, the efficacy of the sacraments, the necessity of church buildings, and priestly ordination; and they denounced wealth, the luxury and idleness of monks, and landlords. Their doctrines spread to Serbia, Russia, Bosnia, Italy, Hungary, and other parts of Europe; the Roman popes in their crusade against the Albigenses called for their extermination. Contemporary Bulgarians regard the Bogomils highly for their expression of the struggles of landless peasants and the urban poor and for their rationalism and "consumer communism."

With the approval of Constantinople and the Eastern Patriarchs, the Bulgarian Church in 927 became a Patriarchate. Lost after the Byzantine conquest, this status was restored in 1235, only to be usurped by the Church of Constantinople at the very end of the fourteenth century and not to be regained for nearly five centuries under the Turkish domination.

During this long medieval period harmony developed between the state and church, the tsar reigning over Church matters and the Church exercising control and direction over the arts, patterns of thought, education, and other cultural affairs. Unlike Byzantium and some Western countries, the Bulgarian Church possessed "exclusive spiritual supremacy" in all areas of culture and, moreover, maintained close ties with the Constantinople Patriarchate and the Church in Rome. Thus, the early and continuing struggle for national liberation was led by church figures. The most influential figure was the monk Paissi of Hilendar whose *Slav-Bulgarian History* in 1792 voiced a passionate pride in past glory and rallied the people to an independence movement. Furthermore, the Enlightenment fostered the establishment of churches independent of the Patriarchate in Constantinople. As the bourgeois economy grew in the early nineteenth century, pressure mounted to replace the Greek bishops with Bulgarians.

Toward the end of the centuries of the Turkish yoke (1396–1878), a literary revival sparked a national revival against the oppression by the Greek Patriarchate. Its long spiritual domination had damaged Bulgarian nationalism more than the rule of the secular Turks. Thus, the struggle for an autonomous church became vital to national liberation. In 1872, before the Bulgarians attained the status of an autonomous principality (1878), the Bulgarian Orthodox Church was founded, resulting in the excommunication of the first Exarch and his followers by the Patriarchate at Constantinople.

In the period between the two world wars, when Communism and monarchofascism were locked in struggle, the forces inside the Orthodox Church, a state religion, became sharply polarized, A small part of the upper leadership was connected with the fascists; the great majority of laymen were sympathetic to the Russian Orthodox Church, and many priests were openly anti-fascist. One such priest, Father Rusinov, the "red priest," worked in the resistance and was sentenced to 100 years of imprisonment. Large numbers of religious people, including the lower clergy, for years organized into Priests' Union, participated in the struggle against fascism. Led by the communists, that movement brought together the Military movement and the left-wing Agrarians. Similar leadership appeared in the Fatherland Front, formed in 1942, a militant alliance of five parties and other groups who ordered the general insurrection in September of 1944 against the Nazi forces. In his report to the Communist International in 1935, Georgi Dimitrov had already called for a "united front" against fascism "by all sections of the working class, irrespective of the party or organization."[22] This included, of course, religious believers opposed to fascism.

When the coalition came to power, the communists and a considerable number of priests had already agreed on the separation of church and state. The radical priests demanded democratization within the Church. A group of nine lower clergymen and thirteen laymen recommended that priests and laymen participate in administrative affairs, that women vote in church elections, that the Church enter into social policies of the new government, that monasterial lands be organized into collective farms, that priests engage in the collectivization of agriculture, that the theological curricula be revised in the direction of a scientific and social outlook, and that the authoritarian viewpoint be eliminated. But the Synod rejected such recommendations. Moreover, a special *subor* (council) went on to elect Stefan as Exarch—whose recognition by the Ecumenical Patriarchate removed the schism against the Bulgarian Orthodox Church.

In 1945 the state changed religion from a required subject to an elective in the elementary schools of the Bulgarian majority and abolished the teaching of religion in the high schools. The traditionalist conservatives fought these changes, and Dimitrov answered with a call for "a truly people's, republican and progressive church.'' Led by Stefan, the Synod rejected Dimitrov's appeal for a new constitution; it did not want a dissolution of the ''age-long'' relations between church and state. But if separated, Stefan argued, the Church should be an agency of the state, retaining its own internal organization and subsidized by the state. In 1947 the Dimitrov constitution was adopted. Freedom of conscience and religion was guaranteed, church and state were separated, the legal status, financial support, and internal organization and government of the Church were to be regulated by a special future law, and the Church was forbidden to enter into politics or to perform marriages.

In the struggle the Synod forced Stefan to resign. The Synod agreed to let priests participate in the Fatherland Front, to give up religious propaganda among youth, to obey the Constitution, and to expound religious and ethical truths of the Church from the pulpit.

The Bulgarian law, like Soviet law, separates church from state. The Constitution guarantees freedom of conscience to believe or not to believe in God. It permits believers to choose their own religion freely and to perform religious rites, as atheists are free to conduct antireligious propaganda (Article 53, paragraph 1). No privileges or restrictions for citizens based on religion are allowed. At the same time propaganda of hatred or humiliation of any person for his or her religious beliefs is forbidden. The state view in Bulgaria today is similar to that in the USSR, though because of their history the Bulgarians came to it sooner: while religious peoole can believe and paractice their faith within the limits of the law, scientific education is the ultimate means by which religious superstition will be overcome.

Yugoslavia

Because modern Yugoslavia is a federation of several ethnic groups, let us briefly examine their separate histories.

The Croats, after more than 500 years of disorganization, with shifting relations to the Holy Roman Empire, the Franks, Byzantium, Venice, Moravia, the Bulgars, and Magyars, were unified in 924 under Duke Tomislav (recognized by the Roman Pope). Simultaneously, they came under the Byzantium protectorate of Dalmation towns. In 1102 King Koloman of Hungary was crowned king of Croatia and Dalmatia, and for 800 years thereafter Croatia was an autonomous kingdom subject to the sovereignty of St. Stephen and connected to Western Christianity. When Bosnia fell to the Turks in 1463, the nobles halted them at Jacje, but two centuries later the Turks took the northern region, between the Sava and Drava rivers, along with Hungary. Zagreb became the capital, the fortress at the border marking the separation of Western Christendom from Islam.

The struggle for the religious control of Serbia was not as easily settled. The Orthodox Church contended with the Greek emperors, and the kingdoms of Venice and Hungary, both Roman Catholic powers, opposed the Church in Rome. In addition, the Bulgars grew powerful, and from the eighth to the twelfth century most Serbs fell under the suzerainty of either Bulgars (Orthodox) or Greeks. In the first Serbian empire (twelfth-fourteenth centuries) Prince Rastko, son of the first king, became an Orthodox monk and a pioneer in the support of education. Stefan Dushan (fourteenth century) unsuccessfully tried to unite Serbs, Greeks, and Bulgars against the Turks. During the Turkish occupation (1449–1807) "only the Church kept the national spirit alive."[23]

Between eastern (and southern) Serbia, western Croatia, and northern Hungary, Bosnia became an early battleground of Christianity. When the Bogomils arose there in the twelfth century, the Papacy pronounced them heretical. The Pope also wanted to separate Serbia and Bulgaria from Eastern control. In the struggle Bosnia along with Hum (the future Hercegovina) became Roman Catholic. Later, with the exception of the northwest area, it fell under Turkish rule, as did Hercegovina, and Islam in time predominated.

Macedonia, which from the time of Philip II had passed back and forth from Western to Eastern hands, was also conquered by the Turks. Liberated in 1912–1913, Macedonia was divided among Serbia, Greece, and Bulgaria and restored to Serbian authority at the Paris Peace Conference—an integration that it ferociously fought against.

When Montenegro, which had broken off from the Serbian Empire when the latter collapsed in the fourteenth century, was overrun by the Turks, Ivo the Black Crnojević removed his capital to the mountains, founding a monastery and bishopric. There for two centuries the Montenegrins held out against Islamic Turks and Albanians, governed by Orthodox bishops.

In 1917 the three southern Slav (Yugoslav) nations—Serbs, Croats, Slovenes—agreed to a united kingdom and got it on December 1, 1918. It embraced Serbia, Croatia-Slovenia, Bosnia, Montenegro, Dalmatia, and small territories. The new state was torn by national and religious tensions, as well as by political differences ranging from Communism to fascism. An acute conflict raged between Serbian centralism and Croatian federalism. Under the regency of 1935–1941 Italy was regarded with suspicion, and fearful of a restored Hapsburg dynasty in Austria, the ruling class cultivated friendship with Germany and the lesser evil of a German-Austrian *Anschluss*. A government proposal in 1937 for a concordat with the Vatican—sponsored by a Slovene—stung the Serbian Orthodox Church into leading a broad opposition composed of nationalists, democrats, and communists; the policy of a united front began to take effect. But the influence of the Germans and the Nazis grew. A powerful majority of Croats was set against a united Yugoslavia, and during World War II many supported Germany in the hope of gaining an independent Croat nation. These included Roman Catholic priests taking the side of the Croat *ustaše*, whose leader, Ante Pavelić, had connections with Hitler. By contrast, the Orthodox clergy was active in the struggle against the occupiers; more than 370 priests were executed, and few were collaborators.

During the Nazi occupation the League of Communists, under the leadership of Josip Broz (Tito), organized the people, an army, and an extended civil administration of people's committees. They insisted on respect for the rights of national and religious groups, emphasizing above all the unity of the common struggle against fascism. A number of laws enacted and enforced during the Yugoslav revolution of 1941–1945 guaranteed freedom of religious worship and respect for the religious feelings of believers.

The Federal People's Republic of Yugoslavia was formed in 1945 out of six socialist republics—Bosnia-Hercegovina, Croatia, Macedonia, Montenegro, Serbia, and Slovenia—and two socialist autonomous republics as parts of Serbia (Kosovo and Vojvodina). It was also a multiconfessional state, with the Orthodox (the largest group) concentrated in Serbia, the Roman Catholics mainly in Croatia, Slovenia, and Vojvodina, and the Muslims in Bosnia-Hercegovina, Kosovo, and Macedonia. Article 26 of the 1946 Consitution guaranteed freedom of conscience and religion to all, separated church and state, and permitted religious denominations to engage in religious but not political activities for religious ends.

The chief point of friction was economic. The April 1945 currency reform devaluing the old dinar hurt the rich peasants, the town middle class, and those who had saved money during the war. The same groups were hit by laws nationalizing 80 percent of industrial property. Then the Constitution of 1946 called for the abolition of all large private landholdings (Article 19); about 1.6 million hectares of land were expropriated or sequestrated from collaborators and *Volksdeutsche* and distributed to peasants and kept for collective purposes. But nationalization and redistribution of land to peasants on the large estates had long been advocated by the Croatian and Slovenian peasant parties. (There were few large estates in Serbia.) As the Roman Catholic Church was a major landholder in these two republics, its hierarchy became bitterly hostile toward the new land policy of the socialist state. The hostility was deepened by the trial, imprisonment, and execution of priests and Church officials who had collaborated with the Nazis during the war. The symbol of this clash was Archbishop Aloysius Stepinac of Zagreb, who in 1946 was tried and convicted of collaboration with the fascist *ustaše* in Croatia and was sentenced to sixteen years in prison, though released five years later under confinement. The Orthodox Church and the Muslims more easily accepted their position in the new order.

Yugoslavia is the only socialist country that has diplomatic relations with the Vatican. In its protocol of June 25, 1966, the Church was guaranteed the right freely to carry on its religious affairs and conduct religious services, and the state recognized the right of the Holy See to exercise its jurisdiction over the Church in Yugoslavia in all spiritual matters in conformity with civic law.

Albania

When the Roman Empire was divided, Albania became part of Byzantium. But after its conquest by the Goths in the fourth and fifth centuries, it returned to the Romans under Justinian in 535. Then the Serbs invaded it in 640, and the Bulgars, taking southern Albania in 861, defeated the Serbs in the tenth century. In 1014 southern Albania was reconquered by an emperor and was subject to Byzantium until 1204, when it was brought under the rule of the Greek despotate at Epirus. Subsequently the Orsinis, the Sicilian kings, the Serbs, Stefan Dushan, the Norman Balshas, and the Venetians conquered Albania. The scattered Albanian chieftans were driven together by the Turkish occupation, but by 1571 the last Venetian possessions in Albania has surrendered. More than half of the Albanians gave up Christianity to accommodate themselves to the Turks. About 1760 the northern clansmen threw off the Turkish suzerainty, but the power of their leaders was broken in 1831. A similar fate befell a successful independence movement in the south.

But inspired by the nationalistic movements in Greece, Bulgaria, and Serbia, the Albanians' growing revolt achieved autonomy in 1912 for certain vilayets within Turkish rule. Bent on the partition of Albania between them, the Balkan states went to war with Turkey. In the settlement by the Conference of Ambassadors in London, Albania secured its independence as a state on July 29, 1913. World War I brought occupation of the country by the Greeks, Italians, French, Serbs, and Montenegrins—who remained after the armistice. In 1920 a congress appointed a council of regency of Roman Catholics, Greek Orthodox, Sunni Muslims, and Bektashis, who made Tirana their capital and elected a government.

A brief republic followed, and then in 1928, the first king, Zog, was crowned, under whom progress was made in education and economics. Italy took over Albania in 1939, and the German Nazis overran it in 1941. But with the help of British detachments who landed in 1944 the guerrilla movement, led chiefly by General Enver Hoxha, communist commander of the Albanian Army of National Liberation, drove the German and Italian forces from most of the country.

When the communists assumed power in November 1944 and Hoxha was elected prime minister, they took stringent measures against the three religions that had enjoyed autonomy since 1912—the Muslims (70 percent of the population), the Orthodox (20 percent), and the Roman Catholics (10 percent). During the partisan struggle against the fascists for national independence, the communists alleged that "traitorous clergymen" urged the people to oppose the partisans. After the war these reactionary clergymen continued to engage in counter-revolutionary activity, resisting all work of the government such as the land reform law of August 29, 1945, which stripped the religions of nearly all their property. The communists first aimed at complete separation of church and state as well as separation of education from religion. In the period 1945–1950 the state severely restricted religion: its revenues were limited; religious instruction was forbidden (only the state might educate youth); all religious publications and communications were made subject to government approval; the state controlled the election and appointment of all holders of religious positions; and religious charitable institutions were banned.

In these early years the Communist Party waged an energetic war of propaganda against religion on Hoxha's view that "the religious world outlook and the communist World outlook are irreconcilable."[24] Religion, it held, had been introduced into the country by "foreign invaders" and imposed on a people naturally atheistic and pagan. Foreigners had divided the people. For example: before independence from the Turks in 1912, religious services were carried out in three languages, and because the Turks identified nationality with religion, Muslim Albanians were called Turks, Orthodox were called Greeks, and Catholics were called Latins. Religion was therefore a source of division and conflict among Albanians. Furthermore, it was the cause of the ignorance and backwardness of Albanian society with its traditional oppression of women, workless holidays, unhygienic kissing of icons, and circumcision. The Albanian Party of Labor saw the Vatican as an ally of the United States and the USSR, and all as agents of counter-revolution suppressing national liberation movements.

Early in 1966 the Party launched its "ideological and cultural revolution" to block the restoration of capitalism and its bourgeois ideology. A movement that started in February 1967 among high school students led to the closing of all churches and mosques by May. At that time the Church was brought before "popular courts of reason" and was denounced for its sins by old and young, workers and farmers, and others. The people renounced belief in God and the saints, castigated the clergy as exploiters and frauds, and refused to participate in religious worship and holidays.

On November 13, 1967, the People's Assembly of Albania voided the religious statutes of 1949, 1950, and 1951 that had given the three major religions the right to operate. Religion, at least officially, was finished in Albania—though people continued to practice it in various ways, especially in rural regions.

What conditions account for Albania's becoming "the first atheist state in the world"? The long history of violation of its national intregrity by foreign powers; its intense nationalism; its identification of religion with foreign (especially Western), divisive, and antinationalist forces; the role of religion in perpetuating backwardness; the uneducated and reactionary clergy; the weak institutional hold of religion on the people; and the militant zeal of the communist leadership.

POLICIES OF SOCIALIST STATES TOWARD RELIGIONS

By definition every state holds a monopoly of power over the affairs within its borders and chooses to regulate those affairs in one way or another. Thus, the state always regulates religion in some form of mutually determinative relation. The state policy of "freedom" of all religions within the limits of the law prevails in the United States—mainly as the result of the number and diversity of religions existing at the time of the founding of the Republic. But it is by no means the only policy. In the Netherlands Protestant, Catholic, and Jewish religions receive state monies, the Belgian state assists all ministers, and England has an established Church as do Sweden, Spain, Finland and other capitalist countries. The United States, in fact, has an "informal" establishment. Of all states supporting establishments, one-half are republics, while in states without establishments two-thirds are republics.[25]

Like capitalist states, socialist states must decide how to exercise their monopoly of power, both economic and ideological, over religion. On the positive side, they must succeed in their economic productivity and their scientific education and propaganda. As they are Marxist and hence atheistic in philosophy, such states have necessarily sought to limit the power of religion and at the same time to secure the loyalty of religious communities to the laws of society and their cooperation in building socialism. Marxism, beyond that, strives for the ultimate dissolution of religion; this is a long-range strategy which, in the sixty-five-year history of state socialism, has yielded to emphasis on the tactics of achieving some form of containment and diminishment of religion. If the state's power over and limit on religion are too strong, loyalty grows lax and believers revolt in thought and action against the socialist state, disrupting its functioning and undermining its credibility. If the power and restriction are too mild, religion may grow strong and the state proportionately weaker. Taking power in a society that carries over its religious institutions, attitudes, and ideas from a feudal or capitalist order into a socialist one, the socialist state is dialecticized into a unity-of-opposition with religion. Religion is an integral part of the new socialist society, but its presocialist (and present) practices and ideas are antagonistic to those of socialism. What is to be done by the state?

1. Separation of church and state. This is usually first effected in a general legal way and then carried out in particular legal economic, political, and educational forms. (The fact that such separation is not stated in the constitutions of Czechoslovakia, the German Democratic Republic, and Romania does not mean the principle is not in effect there.)[26] The principle of separation affirms that the Church no longer holds primary power in the economy and ideology and that the ruling power is the socialist state. It also affirms that religion while separate from the state has rights; freedom of conscience and worship is stated in all socialist constitutions.[27]

2. The expropriation of properties of religious denominations. The material base of any institution is its property; to limit the power of the institution is to limit its power through property. Rents, interest, and profits must be curtailed, if not eliminated. Not only must the power of religious institutions and all institutions be subordinated to that of the state; the old exploitative system of productive relations must also be abolished. Because most churches had accumulated real property (land, buildings, and hereditaments) under feudal and capitalist systems, making use of their surplus value in exploitative ways, one of the very first steps of socialist states has been to take over most or all of such property for the people. The Soviet Decree on Land in November 1918 nationalized the 42 percent of the country's land and appurtenances held by the tsar's family, other landowners, and the Russian Orthodox Church. And in 1949 and 1950 in Czechoslovakia, Hungary, and Romania all monasteries and convents were closed. Nearly 90 percent of the Catholic Church's vast holdings were

expropriated in March 1945 by the Hungarian state. In Yugoslavia some 1.6 million hectares of land were expropriated or sequestrated and distributed to peasants or kept for collective purposes. Yet under the May 1953 law in Yugoslavia the state dispersed monies to religious communities—Orthodox, Muslim, Roman Catholic—for the repair of church buildings. (Similar assistance has been given to churches by the state in the USSR, Poland, the GDR, and Yugoslavia.) These communities are able to own, construct, reconstruct, and rent their religious edifices. Albania represents the extreme case of government control over religion: in 1971 all places of worship were closed down.

3. Regulation of the structure and activity of religious institutions. From the onset of socialist power, the common procedure has been to stipulate by decree or law the exact position of the religious organization with its rights and restrictions. In some countries, such as Bulgaria, Hungary, and Romania, special statutes were required for each denomination. The law specifies that each religion must register and be recognized by the authorities, that is, either a department or director of religious affairs. Such a department also supervises and enforces other legal regulations—for example, the appointment, election, and transfer of clergy, publications, and budgets (as in Bulgaria and Romania in 1948 and Czechoslovakia in 1949), the education of the youth (in Czechoslovakia), and other matters. The communist state has assumed the primary right to perform the marriage ceremony—a right not persistently challenged, perhaps because most states permit a religious ceremony too. Some states, like the USSR, the GDR, and especially Albania, have created other secular substitutes for traditional religious rituals and symbols like baptism, confirmation, funerals, and holidays honoring a great figure or event of the past. Since the beginning of the socialist revolutions, when reactionary forces in religion were most strong and open and church-state rivalry was most sharp, accommodation and detente between religion and state have progressed, and these regulations have been relaxed.

The separation of church and state signifies that religious faiths are forbidden to engage in political activities under the forms of religion. What this means is: (1) they cannot propagate political ideas and enter into political behavior in indirect and covert ways, using religion as a guise; (2) political ideas and practice must be expressed in explicitly legal and political ways; and (3) disobedience to the law and subversion are prohibited. Can religious people express themselves politically? Of course. In addition to the usual channels for all citizens, the Catholics in Poland are directly represented in parliament; and in the German Democratic Republic the Christians have their own party, the Christian Democratic Union, which has representation in the People's Chamber alongside eight other parties and organizations.

4. Subsidies to religions. Economic subsidies represent a positive reinforcement of certain activity, a form of regulation, and a way of integrating religious organizations into secular society. In the USSR, where there have been long-standing tensions between the Orthodox religion and the state, the state has given no direct subsidies to religion—though, while the state owns all lands and re-

ligious buildings, it repairs and restores at its own cost the churches and other buildings that have special historical or aesthetic value. Likewise in Poland, where 90 percent of the people are Roman Catholic and where the independence of the Church is too massive to be ignored with impunity, the state, which must authorize new church buildings, has subsidized the reconsturction of nearly 900 churches destroyed in World War II. In the German Democratic Republic since 1949, where the new socialist state needed the strength and cooperation of the Evangelical Church and the Church in turn needed the financial support and cooperation of the state, extensive aid has been given to the Church. The churches have retained 200,000 hectares of land, receive 12 million marks every year for clerical stipends and more than 4 million marks annually for the training of theologians at universities, and are allocated public funds (190 million marks a year) for institutions of charity and the maintenance, restoration, and upkeep of valuable historical cathedrals and other religious structures.[28]

The socialist states do not legally bind themselves to such subsidies, and where the "subsidy" is mentioned in the constitutions, it is stated as a possible and not a guaranteed policy. Concrete conditions determine how much subsidy is given and for what ends. In Yugoslavia, where an early constitution noted that the state "may" give financial aid to religious communities, priests and their families have been able to participate in social insurance, church buildings have been repaired, and salaries and church expenses have been paid by the state— though this policy did not become even-handed until the late 1950s because of the postwar recriminations taken against the Nazi collaborationists among Roman Catholics in Croatia.

5. Regulation of education. Material regulation and restriction of the economic power of religions must be supplemented by ideological regulation. The main point of concentration here is the education of the youth, for the thoughts, attitudes, values, and practices of the youth embody the character of the society that is coming to be. Hence, it is necessary that the socialist state enforce its own system of scientific public education and curtail or eliminate the various forms of non-scientific education among the religions.

The first step of the socialist state in this process is to prohibit the continuance or founding of schools of general education by religious denominations. As usual, Soviet policy established the model. On February 5, 1918, the Soviet state prohibited the teaching of religious doctrines in all private and public institutions of education. Does this mean that religious education entirely disappears? No. It does mean that the institutional transmission of religious ideas and values to the young is strictly confined to specified times and places. The strictest confinement is practiced in Albania, Bulgaria, and the USSR, where all formal, institutional religious instruction of youth up to age eighteen is proscribed.

A less strict policy is followed in Poland, Romania, and Yugoslavia: instruction is permitted only on church premises and in special centers. (In all cases private and unregistered instruction is illegal.) In Czechoslovakia, the German Democratic Republic, and Hungary religious instruction is permitted on the premises of the schools but *outside the curriculum.*[29]

In Hungary, Czechoslovakia, and Croatian Yugoslavia, in all of which the Roman Catholic Church, powerful and reactionary, had almost exclusive control over education, the communist state took severe measures. In 1948 in Hungary all religious schools were nationalized—starting with 1,216 elementary schools and ending with 32 teacher training schools. In spite of stiff resistance by the Catholic hierarchy to the socialist state and an intense struggle between church and state, the influence of religion in these countries has declined—though believers in Slovakia now number as high as 70 percent. Decrees on religious instruction in Czechoslovakia in 1971 called for the signatures of both parents on children's applications, teaching by approved personnel, non-payment of clerical teachers, payment of secular teachers by religious organizations, only one hour of instruction per month for classes of less than sixteen students and so on.[30] Today in Yugoslavia the teaching of religion outside the curriculum does not appear to be an issue on either side because of increasing secularization, the association of religion with national identity, the relative success of Roman Catholicism, and the decline of Orthodoxy and Islam.[31]

Most of the socialist states have discouraged the training of religious leaders both at home and abroad, with considerable success in Czechoslovakia, where the enrollment in religious schools fell off precipitously after 1970, and in Hungary, where nearly all the schools—all of which were parochial, almost 65 percent of them Roman Catholic—were nationalized and secularized.[32] However, the German Democratic Republic assists in the education of Protestant theologians, and students studying theology in Yugoslavia receive the same privileges as others in the state system.[33]

6. Regulation of publications. The printed word is a principal instrument of ideological power. Consequently, socialism's coming to power produced a sharp conflict between secular and religious forces. As in the struggle over education, the first stage was marked by firm control and repression of religious publications; in various degrees the religious faiths in different countries resisted, moving eventually into a third (and present) stage in which each side is not fully satisfied but lives more or less peacefully with the other.

In December 1917 the Soviet state not only deprived the Church of land, buildings, subsidies, and schools; it also assumed strict control over the press, so that the main avenue of the Church to its people was the ritual of worship, which was not interfered with. Today religious groups publish fifty different kinds of materials—journals, sermons, theological studies, calendars, prayer books, hymnbooks, Scriptures, and so forth. In Albania religious publications have been abolished. In Poland, at the opposite pole, three Catholic weeklies have a combined circulation of 200,000, in addition to monthlies, quarterlies, and annuals. PAX publishes a daily newspaper with a daily circulation of 95,000 and more than twice that on Sunday. On August 31, 1980, the government guaranteed the broadcast of the Sunday morning mass on radio.[34] In 1949 the

Czechoslovak government confiscated all publishing firms and libraries of the Catholic Church, and similar steps were taken in Yugoslavia as early as 1945. Romanian law of 1948 required state approval of all "pastoral letters and circulars of general interest." In Hungary, where all Church property was confiscated, there are today three Catholic publishers and four others, including the Reformed, Lutheran, and Jewish; one-fourth of the sixty-four works published in 1976 were on religious instruction. Likewise the policy in Yugoslavia has been greatly liberalized: more than 13.5 million copies of religious reviews, magazines, and books were published in 1965, 11 million of them by the Catholic Church.[35]

7. Regulation of foreign contacts. Since the first communist state of 1917, socialist societies have been the targets of subversion and overthrow by capitalist forces and some religious persons and groups have been vehicles for such activity. From the start these states have protected themselves by stringent control over the foreign ties of the religious bodies in the bounds of their states and the potential domination of such bodies by external forces for either religious or secular ends. The Church most affected has been the Roman Catholic Church, for in both conception and practice it is a worldwide body demanding adherence to a single central authority in the Vatican.

In Albania in 1951, the Catholic clergy, which represented not more than 10 percent of the population, were pressured into severing all relations with the Vatican. In Romania today the law allows the Catholic Church contacts with the Vatican through the Ministry of Foreign Affairs.[36] Likewise in Bulgaria all relations of churches with persons and churches abroad have had to be authorized by the Director of Religious Denominations.[37] Hungary adopted a similar practice. Faced with the bloody legacy of the clerical-feudal-fascist Horthy regime, it forced the separation of the Catholic Church from Rome. And after the counter-revolution of 1956 it required governmental approval of all ecclesiastical appointments.[38] However, in 1977, climaxing fourteen years of negotiation, the Holy See and the Hungarian state normalized their relations: the Church agreed to observe the law and support "the constructive plans of the Hungarian people," while the state acknowledged the spiritual-canonical authority of Rome over its institutions in Hungarian society. A like protocol was worked out between the Yugoslav government and the Vatican in 1966, permitting bishops to maintain religious contacts with the Holy See. On this basis, Yugoslavia and the Holy See established diplomatic relations in 1966, the first such agreement for a socialist country.[39] If the foreign contact of a religious person or institution does not threaten or upset the order of the socialist society, or if it indeed strengthens it internally and in its international relations, then the state permits or even encourages it. Thus, since 1970 the provincial churches in the GDR have participated independently in the World Council of Churches, the Lutheran World Federation, and the Conference of European Churches. Catholic bishops there are active in the institutions of the Vatican.[40] The churches of the GDR, as well as of other socialist countries, regularly engage in the work of national and international peace organizations. They were participants in the World Congress of Peace Forces in Moscow in 1973, the Congress of Builders of Peace in Warsaw in 1977, the World Conference of Religious Workers for a Lasting Peace, Disarmament, and Just Relations Among Nations in Moscow in 1977, the Special Session of the World Peace Council in Berlin in 1979, and the World Parliament of the Peoples for Peace in Sofia in 1980.

8. Encouragement of progressive elements in the Church. Historically, the creation of a socialist state has always split every religious group into three parts: those who sympathize and are ready to cooperate with the state; those (usually in preponderant numbers) who are cautious but follow the rule of the state once established; and those who are strongly and perhaps openly and violently opposed to it. The religious persons sympathetic to socialism found common cause with it in the humanistic values of material welfare, justice, equality, mutual aid, cooperation, social responsibility, peace, and the like. Those opposed saw in socialism a secular and totalitarian threat to the individual freedom and spiritual life of religion.

The strategy of the socialist states has been to restrict and isolate its opponents in the various ways described above and to give material and moral support to its sympathizers among religious people and to enlist their cooperation in the building of socialism. Thus, after the disestablishment of the Russian Orthodox Church on February 5, 1918, the confiscation of all its property, and the prohibition of religious education, a very influential group called the "Living Church" (with other Renovationists) sprang up with its own reform administration. It got the support of the Soviet government, which at the same time suppressed the Tikhonites—whose leader in 1922 had urged his people to refuse the Soviet requisitioning of non-liturgical gold and silver to relieve the great famine. In the early years the Baptists were also favored against the Orthodox.

After the death in 1925 of Tikhon, the first Patriarch since 1721 when Peter abolished the office, the Church remained without a permanent Patriarch. Then in September 1943, with the Soviet Union under the siege of the Naxi armies, Metropolitan Sergei was received by Stalin; in recognition of the Church's staunch support of the Great Patriotic War, the government muted its antireligious propaganda, allowed churches to reopen, and agreed to the election of a Patriarch and synod by a newly convoked *Sobor* (Council). Likewise in the postwar period of struggle for peaceful coexistence, *detente*, and disarmament, state and church (chiefly Orthodox and Baptist) have worked closely together.

In Poland as early as November 1945, a small group of progressive priests emerged, upholding the social and economic aims of the communists, and in 1949 another group of "patriotic priests" organized themselves. Some of these were appointed to positions in the Church over the objection of the bishops.[41] Church leaders and laymen appeared in all the Eastern European countries after their socialist revolutions, and the strife between them and their conservative brothers was especially acute in countries with encrusted reactionary traditions—especially Czechoslovakia and Hungary. In Czechoslovakia the principal progressive thrust came from the Protestants, particularly by the theologian Josef

L. Hromadka, who founded the Christian Peace Conference, an important bridge to the West and an effective instrument for demonstrating the compatibility of the Christian faith with the social goals of socialism, especially social justice and peace. The Czechoslovakian Protestants, the Russian Orthodox, the Russian Baptists, and other churchmen in socialist countries have taken an increasingly active role in world organizations like the World Council of Churches, and have consistently struggled for peaceful settlement of international disputes and understanding between peoples and between governments. Those who complain that these religious groups follow their governments' lines do not discuss the merits of the peace position, nor do they take into account the horrors of the Nazi aggression and the collaborationist role of many of the churches during that war. Nor do they ask what the real duty of a Christian or Jew or Muslim is when faced with the choices between socialism and capitalism (or feudalism) and between peace and nuclear omnicide.

GENERALIZATIONS AND CONCLUSIONS

1. Religion endures and has endured in societies because: (a) as ideology and as practice, religion has served the central tendencies of class society; it has provided in whole or in part the world-view, moral values, sanctions, prescriptions, and behavior that perpetuate the institutional life of class societies; (b) as part of the moral dimension of the superstructure, religion has expressed in symbols some of the generic values of humankind—mutual aid, love, justice, truth, integrity—and to a much lesser degree has realized such values in institutional and social practice; (c) the human values expressed in religion in history have been so long and so closely associated with the cultural life of societies that it is difficult, if not impossible, to separate religion from culture in thought or in practice: who can conceive Greek culture without the Parthenon, Russian culture without Byzantine Church and icon, Western European culture without medieval cathedrals, English culture without the King James Bible, India without temples, Arabic culture withous mosques, or Jewish culture without Moses? (d) the accumulation of religious artifacts, of embodied human values in religious-cultural forms, often generates an inertia of custom in thought and social practice that is not easily changed. Lenin appealed to the Bolsheviks to know and transform the entire culture of the past.[42] Thus, we may say that just as the primary accumulation of material wealth under capitalism, while used in exploitative and alienating ways, is the embodiment of human labor and hence human value, and can be turned to humanizing uses, so the accumulation of human spiritual values, while in religious form, may be appreciated and appropriated in their essentially human kernel. The husk of each must be discarded.

2. Religion is a cultural activity, reflecting and influencing other cultural activities. Its practices and ideas mirror the class struggles of society and so either advance or retard the progress of humanity. The complex textures of religions have included both progressive and conservative, radical and reaction-

ary, humanistic and antihumanistic strands, often woven together intricately in the same religion. So it is important in judging and understanding religion to be clear about this distinction and relation. Very early Christianity was a devastating critique of contemporary society, a secession from it, and probably a revolutionary movement of urban slaves and other poor against it.[43] In contrast the Christianity adopted three centuries later by the Roman emperors was tame and conformist and justified a slave society. Likewise, the insurrectionary forces in the Protestant Reformation corresponded to and facilitated the antifeudal revolution then underway; their suppression in Germany, Czechoslovakia, and Hungary by both economic and religious conservative forces set back the development of these countries for centuries. Present-day Latin America evinces a similar class struggle between humanistic, democratic forces (secular and religious) on the one side and antihumanistic forces on the other.

Although the radical force is present in most religions, the predominant tendency has been conservative: religion on the whole has provided the spiritual form and justification for class societies. In all of the societies of Eastern Europe before they turned socialist, religion was fundamentally conservative; it furnished the framework of thought, spiritual direction, and philosophical justification for the existing reactionary class order. Hence, when socialism came to these societies, rigid and sometimes extensive resistance to the new progressive order was raised by some Christians—as in the USSR, Poland, Czechoslovakia, Hungary, and Yugoslavia. But in all countries a minority of Christians cooperated with the new government from the start. And in the GDR, where the Reformation tradition prevailed, large numbers of Christians, realizing that their Protestant past was at many humanistic points compatible with the socialist order, soon came to accept it and to cooperate with it.

3. All enduring religions contain humanistic elements in thought and practice. But in class societies religions have commonly been "the spirit of an unspiritual situation" and hence have been hard put to incarnate those important human values proclaimed and confessed.[44] Yet during times of decisive crisis in society, times of overt class war and upheaval, these humanistic elements have found more complete expression than in settled times, when religions have quietly and smugly confirmed the settled class arrangements. Thus, the religious movement of Jesus and his early followers was an insurgent movement, an outbreak of a troubled, discontented consciousness among the slave classes in the Roman Empire. The radicalism of Western Christianity since the fourteenth-century Peasant Revolt (and earlier) has been a concomitant of the class struggle within feudalism first and then capitalism. Against the economy of large landholding and serfdom, of barons and aristocrats, new capitalists and the poor peasants in revolt expresed the economic side of this struggle; the radical Christians (such as John Ball and John Wyclif), restating the Christian first-century critique of class society, expressed the ideological, moral side. (Reactions were complex: Luther, for example, hated the commercialism of the Roman Church as did the peasants, but sided with the princes against them.) Alongside the brash young

entrepreneurs storming the gates of the old estates and forcibly forging new towns and trade routes, the religious dissidents and recusants were damning high Church crimes from the pulpit in Allstedt, raising rebellion in the fields of Kent, throwing the Hapsburg King's men from a castle window in Prague, and nailing inflammatory theses to the door of the castle church at Wittenberg.

In those countries where Orthodoxy or Roman Catholics held sway—Russia, Poland, Czechoslovakia, Hungary, Romania, Bulgaria, Yugoslavia—and where the capitalist revolution never gathered steam and revolutionized production, Christianity did not play even a liberal role in social change. It was peripheral, passive, harmless; it baptized, married, comforted, and buried people; it lit no incendiary fires and incited no mass risings. But strictly speaking, it cannot be faulted overmuch: it had not been brought to a boil by the economic fires from below. Christianity's position was more an effect than a cause of these stagnant, feudal, merchant-capitalist economies. As cause, it was secondary and super-structural. Christianity sanctioned the ruling class order, but it could not take the lead in transforming it because it did not stand at the base. When the base began to change, when capitalism began to develop on a world scale, and later when the socialist revolution threatened and succeeded, then Christians were forcibly divided into sheep and goats: some rejoiced in the revolution and gave aid and comfort to it; most stood by the old order with its established injustices. Many are called, but few are chosen.

4. In precapitalist societies such as feudalism and slave society, religion was central to the social superstructure and institutional practice. The simple emotions and limited thought that we find in the mentality of old religions correspond to the relatively backward state of development of productive relations. Religion for such economies was a significant force in determining the character and direction of society, providing the principal forms of thought for the productive and political energies. For example, in ancient slave society, religion on the whole sanctioned the submission of slaves to the masters in labor, war, and social relations generally.

5. As capitalist society arose and developed with its secular mode of life, with its application of human thought and power to the exploitation of nature and labor power on a concentrated, centralized, and massive scale, religion gradually became decentralized and yielded to the dominance of secular ideology and practice, though still reflective and facilitative of the economy. (Even in the long struggle of European kings with the Papacy, religion served the purpose of the landholding kings—as in Luther's day—and did not wane in its ideological influence until the capitalist revolution had eroded and replaced the feudal structure.)

For instance, in the Dutch revolution of the 1500s and the English revolution of the 1600s, religious ideology played a central role.[45] But in the French and American revolutions of the late 1700s and in the communist revolutions of the 1900s, secular thought and practice succeeded religion as a leading force.

6. In socialist society, as under matured and decadent capitalism, religion had

been still further weakened by secularization and has been made still more peripheral to the central tendencies of society. In the capitalism of the United States today, the guiding ideology is generated by public relations specialists in the media and advertising, and not by religion.

Secularization is the process by which the persons and institutions of a whole society turn away from the superhuman and supernatural world to the world of human beings and nature and history for their knowledge, reality, and values. The base on which this outlook arises, which accompanies and drives it forward, is the industrial-scientific-technological revolution. Such a revolution was first initiated and carried forward by capitalism and later by socialism. Under pre-capitalist societies the primary carrier of personal meaning in life (philosophy), social order, and culture was religion. As an essential aspect of the social superstructure of class society, religion has engendered feelings, shaped thought, and directed action within the bounds of such a society.

Secularization means that the practices of people are increasingly directed toward the affairs and concerns of this world and that their general ideas reflect this new practice and become more natural and directly humanistic. It means a transformation of the rural, sparse, manorial world of local landlord and serf, of poor parishioner and cleric, of the scattered, static world of family, estate, rank, personal loyalty and obligation, craft, barter, tradition; audacious individual enterprise and calculated self-interest; the growth of capital; cities; centralized, concentrated, large-scale production; specialized, divided, and integrated labor; new skills and knowledge in both labor (artisans, artists) and economic organization; the rise of impersonal relations and the shift from status to contract; restless change and dynamism in invention, science, technology, industry, art, and social patterns and concepts; social mobility; in both practice and thought the breakdown of habitual, customary limits—the destruction of provincial and regional boundaries, the creation of nations, the emergence of the world market and of world perspectives. In this world-shaking transformation wrought by eruptive forces within both feudalism and early commercial capitalism—essentially the forces of venturous, creative, social labor—religion is thrown into the fiery vortex of change along with all other ways of life and modes of thought. It tends to remain unchanged among those people and institutions relatively unaffected by the secularizing processes of modernity—in remote geographical areas not touched by modern industry and technology, in the countryside and villages, among old persons, among uneducated and unspecialized workers, and among women more than men. In short, the degree of religiousness varies with the degree of secularization. (Of course, there are exceptions, and they suggest that for a small minority religious faith is grounded in something other than socioeconomic forces—inner spiritual workings and external realities that transcend transient social conditions and fashions.)

It is reported that in the GDR, where Christianity is relatively vigorous, only "approximately ten to fifteen percent of the poeple have regular contact with the institutional churches" and "about five percent can be considered genuinely active."[46] Likewise in Poland only about 10 percent of the people are traditionally and deeply religious, while more than 30 percent do not accept religious doctrine or church guidance unconditionally. The latter tendency is especially common among youth, people with higher education, and highly specialized workers.[47] Similar tendencies are evident in Yugoslavia and the Soviet Union.[48]

7. In precapitalist class societies, religion arose as an adaptation of thought processes to a world split by exploitation and alienation in particular ways. Through symbol and ritual, it reinforced the personal, hierarchical, authoritarian systems of slave and feudal societies. But when at the end of the medieval period in Europe the feudal system crumbled and a new system supplanted it, the old religious ideology did not serve. It was too elaborate, too filled with the hatred of this life and the fear of hell, too punitive and guilt-inducing, too melancholic, to hold the loyalty of the new person in process of creation by the new town economy.[49] It impeded the fresh, vital energies called forth by that secularizing economy. When in the evolution of society a new base begins to take form, with new forces and relations of production, religious forms must readapt to the new system or die. In the crisis of feudal disintegration, traditional Christian authoritarianism turned in the direction of mysticism, yearning for an imaginary uncorrupted past, Protestant individual faith, orthodox dogma and terror, humanism, revolutionary movements, agnosticism, and eventually atheism.

The ideology of capitalism in its various stages illustrates this shift.[50] Calvin and Luther affirmed the freedom of the individual person from the Catholic Church and the importance of hard work. Adam Smith upheld the free market as the source of good. Today the ideology still revolves around the "free individual" in the "free world," and it is rendered effective by the scientific and highly sophisticated instrument of advertising.

8. As socialist economies develop, the secularization process proceeds quite apart from any positive intervention by the state, though such intervention effectively applied can accelerate the process, while ineffective intervention can arouse a reaction of resistance.

9. The decline of religion under industrial, technological society, whether capitalist or socialist, and its consequent peripheral position in the social scheme bring it under the control of the secular power and within the limitations laid down by its internal order and law. The tendency in all modern bourgeois societies is to move toward tolerance of different religions, some degree of separation of church and state, and even disestablishment and disendowment. The prevailing power is now secular, not only because the working of the economy depends exclusively on scientific understanding and control, but also because the common mentality among people is secular in spirit and approach. Religion is thus reduced to one among many institutions required to subordinate its interests and values insofar as they are social values to the ruling secular order.

People in capitalist countries often criticize socialist societies for imposing legal "restrictions" on religions. But such restrictions are in principle no different from those in capitalist societies. It is true that in the United States, for example, religions are free, if money is at hand, to accumulate property, to organize their own religious schools, and to enter into politics. But even in these spheres the law regulates the religions, and if the politics are radical it will be curbed or punished. In addition, although religion is constitutionally disestablished, an informal establishment prevails, for the ruling political groups presume Christianity to be the national religion, and those who are not Christian, if they are outspoken, may be discriminated against. Every state protects itself by the power and by the law of power behind that. Thus, in both capitalist and socialist societies the great majority of persons and institutions in religion conform to the prevailing mores, laws, values, and reigning ideology of the society. Religious people living under capitalism express surprise and chagrin that religious people living under socialism are not in rebellion against "a slave state." But they do not understand that acceptance of the ruling order is normal and that socialism is perceived as good and not bad by most religious people living within it. If such critics were to become socialists, they would be surprised and chagrined that religious people living under capitalism are not in rebellion against its wage slavery. The general position of religion under capitalism is acceptance of its premises; Hitler's Germany, among other states, illustrates this. Religion in turn is integrated into the society. In the United States, for example, the property of religious institutions is exempt from taxes, religious schools receive government financial aid of various kinds, prayers are common on public occasions, and a religious confession, "In God we trust," is printed on currency. If one believes the state should be separate from religion, then one should object to this integration of the two. But if one believes that capitalism is better than socialism and is compatible with a particular religion, one should make a case for such a belief.

10. Because of the endurance of religion, communist political economies have been forced to accept its presence and to accommodate to it in one form or another. Since 1917 the methods of accommodation have ranged from militant attacks on the ideas and material property of religions to tolerance toward them and even cooperation with them. At present writing, all socialist states in Eastern Europe, except Albania, appear to have effected a stable *modus vivendi* with religious people in which the religions are free to carry on their religious activities and in turn conform to the secular law. In some countries, like the German Democratic Republic, the Church has its own political party with representation in the parliament.

Religious ideology on the whole is at variance with communist ideology. Because Communism is in power and restricts the dissemination of religious ideas, some critics argue that the ideological struggle between the two is not fair. But essentially the same relation of forces holds under capitalism. Generally, religions in the United States do not have access to public funds or public schools. Moreover, every modern secular state, capitalist or socialist, requires a secular education of its future citizens if it is to reproduce itself and progress. (Some small sects, of course, do not accept the premise of "progress.") Even in the

United States, where people have easy access to religious ideas in parochial schools and the public media, interest in such ideas is not widespread and, apart from periodic but temporary "revivals," is declining.

Accommodation means separation of state and church: the place and powers of each are so defined that each is able to pursue its own interests and responsibilities, and neither interferes with the other. Each may wish for more power to extend its influence and propagate its viewpoint. But for the sake of civil peace boundaries mutually agreed on must be drawn somewhere, and in each socialist society today the two sides, through experience, have found boundaries that are more or less tolerable. Perhaps Albania is the one exception.

The accommodations achieved between socialism and religion in these socialist countries, while evolving arrangements with a certain satisfaction on both sides, have not been achieved without hostility, injury, and acrimony on both sides. A certain amount of these results could be expected. But the positive fact is that each side appears able to live with the accommodation created, and no destruction of the magnitude of the Crusades, the Inquisition, the Thirty Years' War, or the burning of witches has occurred. One reason for (and result of) the accommodation is that for more than forty years Europe has experienced no war on its soil and the spirit of peaceful opposition has prevailed between religion and state within nations and between nations of different social systems. This general spirit as well as the memory of the horror and toll of World War II have no doubt produced a favorable atmosphere for the peaceful coexistence of religion and socialism within the communist countries. Religious people recognize this fact by increasingly devoting their energies to the causes of world peace and disarmament.

11. Over time a single religion like Christianity evolves into variants under the selective pressures of various cultural environments. We have tried to demonstrate this notion by tracing the history of Christianity in different countries. To understand events today in church-state relations in the socialist countries of Eastern Europe, we must understand the history of the various church-state relations in these countries.

For example, the spirit of separation and independence from the state, radical criticism of it, and revolt against it, has marked Western Christian history much more than Eastern. (In this regard, Hussite Czechoslovakia must be classified with the West.) Eastern Christianity had generally been assimilated to the secular power, and although there were peasant revolts in Russia in the 1600s and 1700s, they were not primarily religious in ideology—as, say, the Peasant Revolt of Wat Tyler and John Ball in England. Nor were they grounded in any fundamental economic transformation of the kind we find in the Dutch and English revolutions. In Czechoslovakia the Reformation was virutally wiped out, and in Hungary it was effectively contained by a ruthless and reactionary Roman Catholic Church. Orthodox countries and the heavily Roman Catholic country of Poland—whose Church, for geographical and national reasons, played a role similar to the Orthodox—had no Reformation. They did not because their churches did not claim and celebrate their radical roots in Biblical Christianity, and because those countries did not experience a structural crisis in their chiefly agrarian economies until the impact of the world industrial economy in the nineteenth century. When the time for revolt arrived, some form of secular liberalism or socialism, based on modern conditions and accompanied by nationalism, was prepared to provide leadership, not a Church fixed in prefeudal liturgy and thought. In fact, the political movements among the peasants in the nineteenth century in Italy, Spain, France, and elsewhere sometimes were militantly anti-Christian.[51] In short, when men revolt they lay hold of the ideology that is most handy and usable: from the fourteenth through the seventeenth centuries in Western Europe, that was radical and Biblical Christianity; in the eighteenth century, it was the liberalism of the Enlightenment; in the twentieth century it is Marxism. And so far as Christianity has been a revolutionary ideology in protest against the ruling order, it has been accompanied by and fused with a deeper economic protest. (This is occurring in a peculiar way now in Latin America.)

This historical-religious difference between East and West explains some of the differences today between state-church relations in Eastern socialist countries and Western countries. When France, Italy, and England become socialist or communist, we will see new patterns emerging.

12. In sum, the policies of socialist states toward religions have been shaped by the demands and aims of socialism and by the specific historically conditioned circumstances of society and of the religions confronted by the governments after the revolution. The policies, while common, have been applied differently, and have been modified by the responses of the religions. Three different general patterns of state-church relations have evolved in the socialist nations of Eastern Europe.

Where the predominant church has been Orthodox, closely associated with the state through history, economically dependent on it, and identified with the spirit of the ethnic culture, church-state relations have tended to become non-antagonistic and eventually cooperative. Such are the church-state relations today in the USSR, Romania, Bulgaria, and the Orthodox regions (chiefly Serbia) of Yugoslavia. In part, because of the value it places on liturgy, contemplation, and mysticism, the Orthodox Church generally has not distanced itself from the state in any radical or revolutionary way. As the bearer of certain cultural values, it has tended to maintain and conserve the forms of national tradition during crises or breaks in that tradition—as the Orthodox Church in Russia during the Mongol occupation, and in Romania, Bulgaria, and Serbia during Turkish rule, and in the nineteenth-century movements for national independence. Such a Church, regardless of its other values, would find it relatively easy to adjust to the demands of a socialist state that did not seriously threaten its existence.

In the countries where Roman Catholicism has been strongly established—Poland, Hungary, and Czechoslovakia (and in Croatia and Slovenia in Yugoslavia)—much greater hostility has developed between church and state. One reason is that since its beginning the Roman Catholic Church has stood aloof from national states and has struggled against them not only to assert its own independence but also to influence them by that independent economic and ideological power. In Poland, Hungary, and Czechoslovakia, the Catholic Church was never entirely a handmaiden to the state; in its own way it ruled economy and politics alongside the state, maintaining its separate identity and drawing strength from its relations with Rome. It never became a distinctly national church, entirely absorbed in the national tradition. If, as in Poland, it was a bearer of ethnic-cultural tradition, it kept its autonomy within the state and its leverage in the Holy See. The Catholic Church never forgot its international position and its aspiration to a one-world Church. Hence when these countries became socialist, the Catholic Church within them could not easily attach itself to the methods and goals of the new state. More importantly, the Catholic Church in those countries had an investment in the land and other wealth of the previous social order; it belonged to the ruling class, and its ideology and practice were for the most part conservative or reactionary under feudalism, capitalism, and Nazi occupation. Hence, the clash between the Church and the socialist state was unavoidable. Any accommodation between church and state under such circumstances had to be worked out over a long period of struggle, not yet complete.

Where the Church had been to some degree distanced from the state, either in historical practice or in thought, but was in possession of a humanistic theology of social concern, then insofar as it had no external pressures to maintain its material investments in the economy (pressures to which the Catholic Church in various nations is always subject) the Church would be able to make common cause with the socialist state in creating a better society. Such was the situation of the Protestant Church in the GDR, which constituted a large majority there, and of the Hussite Church in Czechoslovakia.

Where the Church has been weak, backward, and divided, it may be easily abolished by the state. Such may have been the situation in Albania. But it is problematical whether legal abolition can effectively annihilate religion there or in any other country. Both socialist states and religion in its various forms will go on into the indefinite future, and as long as they do, the tension between science and faith will continue and will be dealt with in a variety of ways. Right now, however, under the mounting nuclear menace, the important thing for everyone is survival, peace, and the coexistence of conflicting social systems. The ideological struggle between socialism and religion, while continuing, is secondary to the struggle for a peaceful world order and for life, which must continue if anything else human is to do so.

NOTES

1. Many of the facts in the following are taken from relevant articles in the *Encyclopedia Britannica* (Chicago: William Benton, 1959).

2. Sumner, *Short History of Russia*, p. 164.

3. Lenin, *Religion*, pp. 37–38.

4. Ibid., p. 17.

5. Estimates of the number of churches closed during Khrushchev's tenure range from one-half of those previously operating to 10,000. See Marshall, ed., *Aspects of Religion in the Soviet Union*, p. 153.

6. Mandel, *Soviet But Not Russian* pp. 23, 24, 264, 307.

7. Marcus and Epstein, "Jews, III. Modern Period," p. 59

8. Werth, *Russia*, Ch. 17.

9. For documentation of these statistics, see Mandel, *Soviet But Not Russian*, pp. 320, 323.

10. Kuroyedov, *Church and Religion in the USSR*, p. 37.

11. Rukhadze, *Jews in the USSR*, p. 54–58.

12. Smogorzewski, "Poland. The People's Republic," *Encyclopedia Britannica*, Vol. 18, p. 152.

13. Ibid., p. 153.

14. Passant et al., *Short History of Germany*.

15. *Christians and Churches in the GDR*, p. 36.

16. Ibid., pp. 38–40. Max L. Stackhouse estimates this to be 40 percent in "Religious Situation in the German Democratic Republic," *Occasional Papers on Religion in Eastern Europe*, p. 2.

17. *Christians and Churches in the GDR*, p. 37.

18. Aptheker, *The Truth About Hungary*, chs. 2, 4.

19. *Policy of the Hungarian People's Republic Toward the Churches*, pp. 45–52.

20. Snow, *Pattern of Soviet Power*, p. 37.

21. Otetea, ed., *History of the Romanian People*, p. 555.

22. Dimitrov, *Selected Works*, vol. 2, p. 28.

23. Seton-Watson, "Serbia," *Encyclopedia Britannica*, vol. 20, p. 343.

24. *Report on the Role and Tasks of the Democratic Front for the Complete Triumph of Socialism in Albania*, cited in Bociurkiw and Strong, eds., *Religion and Atheism in the U.S.S.R and Eastern Europe*, p. 393.

25. Collins and Fawkes, "Establishment," Vol. 8, p. 727.

26. *Religion and Atheism in the U.S.S.R. and Eastern Europe*, p. 194.

27. Citing examples of the violation of such rights in socialist societies in itself proves nothing; the same goes for violations in capitalist and "democratic" societies. To get a proper estimate of what is happening, one must look at the whole society in its history, its principles, values, and goals, and its achievements and failures.

28. *Christians and Churches in the GDR*, p. 47.

29. *Religion and Atheism in the U.S.S.R. and Eastern Europe*, p. 199.

30. Ibid., pp. 286, 289.

31. Ibid., pp. 378–379.

32. Aptheker, *The Truth About Hungary*, p. 62.

33. *Religion and Atheism in the U.S.S.R. and Eastern Europe*, p. 363.

34. Will, "Church and Contemporary Social Dynamics in Poland," *Occasional Papers on Religion in Eastern Europe*, pp. 7–8.

35. *Religion and Atheism in the U.S.S.R.*, p. 363.

36. Ibid., p. 397.

37. Ibid., p. 339.

38. Ibid., p. 292.

39. Samardžić, *Religious Communities in Yugoslavia*, pp. 45–46.
40. *Christians and Churches in the GDR*, p. 49.
41. *Religion and Atheism in the U.S.S.R. and Eastern Europe*, p. 205.
42. Lenin, *Collected Works*, Vol. 31, p. 287.
43. Brandon, *Jesus and the Zealots*.
44. Marx, "Contribution to the Critique of Hegel's Philosophy of Right," in Marx and Engels, *On Religion*, p. 42.
45. George, *Revolution*.
46. Stackhouse, "Religious Situation in the German Democratic Republic," p. 2.
47. Will, "Church and Contemporary Social Dynamics in Poland," p. 5.
48. *Religion and Atheism in the U.S.S.R. and Eastern Europe*, pp. 144–145, 366, 377, 383.
49. Huizinga, *Waning of the Middle Ages*.
50. Tawney, *Religion and the Rise of Capitalism*.
51. Hobsbawn, *Age of Capital*, p. 225.

BIBLIOGRAPHY

Aptheker, Herbert. *The Truth About Hungary*. New York: Mainstream, 1957. Detailed study of the historical background and complexity of immediate causes of the 1956 uprising. A Marxist defense and critique of Hungary's socialism, bringing out the counter-revolutionary role of the Roman Catholic Church.

Babakhan, Ziyauddin Khan Ibn Ishan. *Islam and the Muslims in the Land of the Soviets*. Moscow: Progress Publishers, 1980. The author, a member of the Supreme Islamic Council for Mosques at Mecca, is Chairman of the Muslim Religious Board of Central Asia and Kazakhstan.

Beeson, Trevor. *Discretion and Valour: Religious Conditions in Russia and Eastern Europe*. Rev. ed. Philadelphia: Fortress Press, 1982.

Bokov, G. *Modern Bulgaria*. Sofia: Sofia Press, 1981. History, politics, economy, culture.

Bociurkiw, Bohdan R., and John W. Strong, eds. *Religion and Atheism in the U.S.S.R. and Eastern Europe*. Toronto: University of Toronto, 1975. While most contributors are inimical to socialism, this work is one of the most complete of its kind in print in English. Chapters deal with all the countries.

Bock, Paul. "Church and State in Czechoslovakia." *Occasional Papers on Religion in Eastern Europe*. Paper No. 2. Edited by Paul Mojzes. Vol. 2, No. 2. Philadelphia: Ecumenical Press, 1982.

Brandon, S. G. F. *Jesus and the Zealots*. New York: Charles Scribner's Sons, 1967.

Christians and Churches in the GDR. Berlin: Panorama DDR, 1980. Sixty-four page official summary of "broad cooperation in public affairs," with many factual details.

Churches and Religions in the People's Republic of Bulgaria. Sofia: Ecumenical Department of the Holy Synod, 1975.

Clarke, O. Fielding. *Christianity and Marxism*. Moscow: Progress, 1977. Anglican minister and vice-president of the British Committee of the Christian Peace Conference compares Christian and communist moralities and favorably describes the role of the Church and religion in the U.S.S.R.

Collins, William Edward, and Alfred Fawkes. "Establishment." *Encyclopedia Brittan- ica*. Vol. 8 Chicago: William Benton, 1959.

Conquest, Robert. *Religion in the U.S.S.R.* New York: Praeger, 1968.

Darby, H. C., R. W. Seton-Watson, Phyllis Auty, R. G. D. Laffan, and Stephen Clis- sold, *A Short History of Yugoslavia from Early Times to 1966*. Edited by Stephen Clissold. Cambridge: Cambridge University Press, 1968. Succint, useful chapters on all republics.

De George, R. T., and J. P. Scanlan, eds. *Marxism and Religion in Eastern Europe*. Dordrecht: Reidel, 1976.

Dimitrov, Georgi. *Selected Works*. Vol. 2. Sofia: Sofia Press, 1972.

Dunn, Dennis. *Detente and Papal-Communist Relations, 1962–1978*. Boulder, Colo.: Westview, 1979.

Fletcher, William C. *Christianity in the Soviet Union: An Annotated Bibliography and List of Works in English*. Los Angeles: University of Southern California, 1963.

———. *Soviet Believers: The Religious Sector of the Population*. Lawrence, Kans.: Regents Press, 1981.

George, Charles H. *Revolution: European Radicals from Hus to Lenin*. Glenview, Ill.: Scott, Foresman, 1971.

Hobsbawn, E. J. *The Age of Capital, 1848–1875*. London: Weidenfeld and Nicolson, 1977.

Hromadka, Josef. *Theology Between Yesterday and Tomorrow*. Philadelphia: Westminster Press, 1957.

Huizinga, J. *The Waning of the Middle Ages*. New York: St. Martin's Press, 1949.

Hutten, Kurt. *Iron Curtain Christians: The Church in Communist Countries Today*. Translated by Walter G. Tillmans. Minneapolis: Augsburg, 1967.

Iaroslavsky, Emelian. *Religion in the USSR*. New York: International, 1934. Translation of work by first and principal leader of antireligious movement in the Soviet Union.

Information (Bulletin of Christian Peace Conference, Prague).

Johansen, Alf. "The Bulgarian Orthodox Church." *Occasional Papers on Religion in Eastern Europe*. Edited by Paul Mojzes. Vol. 1, No. 7, December 1981. Phila- delphia: Ecumenical Press, 1981.

———. *Theological Study in the Rumanian Orthodox Church Under Communist Rule*. London: Faith Press, 1961.

———. *Theological Study in the Russian and Bulgarian Orthodox Churches Under Communist Rule*. London: Faith Press, 1961.

Kidd, B. J. *The Churches of Eastern Christendom. From A. D. 451 to the Present Time*. Milwaukee: Morehouse, 1927. Definitive scholarly work.

Kuczynski, Janusz. *Christian-Marxist Dialogue in Poland*. Warsaw: Interpress, 1979. A Marxist philosopher engaged in friendly and serious discussion with Christians.

Kuroyedov, Vladimir. *Church and Religion in the USSR*. Moscow: Novosti Press Agency Publishing House, 1979. Statement by the Chairman of the Council for Religious Affairs, emphasizing Marxist-Leninist atheism alongside the rights to believe and worship, the loyalty of the Orthodox Church to Motherland in war and peace, and the variety of faiths—Christian, Muslim, Buddhist, Jewish, and so forth.

Laszlo, Leslie. "Religion in a Communist Consumer Society." *Occasional Papers on Religion in Eastern Europe*. Edited by Paul Mojzes. Vol. 1, No. 5. Philadelphia: Ecumenical Press, 1981.

Lenin, V. I. *Religion*. New York: International Publishers, 1933. Collection of major writings, showing changes in point of view.

————. *Collected Works*. Vol. 31. Moscow: Progress Publishers, 1966.

Lochman, Jan M. *Encountering Marx: Bonds and Barriers Between Christians and Marxists*. Translated by Edwin H. Robertson. Philadelphia: Fortress Press, 1977. Creative exploration by Czech theologian at the Comenius Faculty of Theology in Prague.

Lumer, Hyman. *Zionism: Its Role in World Politics*. New York: International, 1973. Marxist analysis of the class nature and roots of Zionism, its historical service to imperialism, and its anti-Soviet ideology.

Mandel, William M. *Soviet But Not Russian. The "Other" Peoples of the Soviet Union*. Palo Alto: University of Alberta Press and Ramparts Press, 1985. Rich with interviews and concrete up-to-date information. See especially the sections on Orthodoxy in the Ukraine and Catholicism in Lithuania, and the chapter on the Jews.

Marcus, Jacob Rader, and Isidore Epstein. "Jews, III. The Modern Period." *Enyclopedia Britannica*. Vol. 13. Chicago: William Benton, 1959, pp. 58–64. A precise and compact history.

Marshall, Richard H., Jr. ed. *Aspects of Religion in the Soviet Union, 1917–1967*. Chicago: University of Chicago Press, 1971. Ample coverage of major and minor religious groups and of social, legal, literary, and historical issues.

Marx, Karl, and Friedrich Engels. *On Religion*. Moscow: Foreign Languages Publishing House, 1958.

Melish, William Howard. *Religion Today in the USSR*. New York: National Council of American-Soviet Friendship, 1945. Work by an Episcopal priest, friendly to socialism and its relations to religion.

Mitrokhin, L. N. "On 'Dialogue' Between Marxists and Christians." *Soviet Studies in Philosophy* 10, No. 4 (Spring 1972): 337–361. One of the few reports on dialogue in the U.S.S.R.

Mojzes, Paul. *Christian-Marxist Dialogue in Eastern Europe*. Minneapolis: Augsburg, 1981. Pioneer work by a major (Christian) leader of Christian-Marxist dialogue in the United States and Eastern Europe.

Ostrogorski, Georgije. *History of the Byzantine State*. Translated by Joan Hussey. Oxford: Blackwell, 1956. Broad survey.

Otetea, Andrei, ed. *The History of the Romanian People*. Translated by Eugenia Farca. Bucharest: Scientific Publishing House, 1970.

Parsons, Howard L. *Christianity in the Soviet Union*. New York: American Institute for Marxist Studies, 1972. Monograph based on 1970 interviews with communists and Christians in the U.S.S.R.

Passant, E. J., et al. *A Short History of Germany, 1815–1945*. London: Cambridge University Press, 1959.

Paul, David W. *The Cultural Limits of Revolutionary Politics: Change and Continuity in Socialist Czechoslovakia*. New York: Columbia University Press, 1979.

The Policy of the Hungarian People's Republic Toward the Churches. Budapest: Budapress, 1977. Government pamphlet giving facts, figures, and a positive picture of state-church relations.

Pope, Earl A. "The Romainan Orthodox Church." *Occasional Papers on Religion in*

Eastern Europe. Edited by Paul Mojzes. Vol. 1, No. 3. Philadelphia: Ecumenical Press, 1981.

Religion in Communist-Dominated Areas. Translation materials in semimonthly publication of National Council of Churches, 1962.

Rukhadze, Avtandil. *Jews in the USSR.* Moscow: Novosti, 1984. A definitive and recent Soviet source of facts and figures.

Samardžić, *Religious Communities in Yugoslavia.* Belgrade: Jugosvlovenska stvarnost, 1981. Up-to-date factual survey, with bibliography, mostly in Serbo-Croatian. 48 pages.

Seton-Watson, R. W. "Serbia." *Encyclopedia Britannica.* Vol. 20. Chicago: William Benton, 1959.

Shenk, N. Gerald. "Some Social Expectations on Christians in Yugoslavia with Primary Emphasis on the Protestant Churches. *Occasional Papers on Religion in Eastern Europe.* Edited by Paul Mojzes. Vol. 1, No. 4. Philadelphia: Ecumenical Press, 1981.

————, and Denton Lotz. "Factors Influencing Baptist Church Growth in Romania." *Occasional Papers on Religion in Eastern Europe.* Edited by Paul Mojzes. Vol. 1, No. 4. Philadelphia: Ecumenical Press, 1981.

Smogorzewski, K. M. "Poland. The People's Republic." *Encyclopedia Britannica.* Vol. 18. Chicago: William Benton, 1959.

Snow, Edgar. *The Pattern of Soviet Power.* New York: Random House, n.d.

Spinka, Matthew. *The Church in Soviet Russia.* New York: Oxford University Press, 1956.

Staat und Kirchen in Ungarn. Vienna: Ungarisches Pressbüro Wien, 1977. Hungarian government publications.

Stackhouse, Max L. "The Religious Situation in the German Democratic Republic." *Occasional Papers on Religion in Eastern Europe.* Edited by Paul Mojzes. Vol. 1, No. 1. Philadelphia: Ecumenical Press, 1981.

Sumner, B. H. *A Short History of Russia.* Rev. ed. New York: Harcourt, Brace and World, 1949. Valuable for its grasp of general features and tendencies and for relevant particulars. Unique is the chapter on the Church. Objective and penetrating.

Tawney, R. H. *Religion and the Rise of Capitalism.* New York: Harcourt Brace, 1926.

Timasheff, N. S. *Religion in Soviet Russia 1917–1942.* New York: Sheed and Ward, 1942. Early account of "the assault on religion" and the "resistance" to it.

Triska, Jan F., ed. *Constitutions of the Communist Party-States.* Stanford, Calif.: Stanford University Hourly Institute on War, 1968.

Werth, Alexander. *Russia: Hopes and Fears.* New York: Simon and Schuster, 1969.

Will, James E. "The Church and Contemporary Social Dynamics in Poland." *Occasional Papers on Religion in Eastern Europe.* Edited by Paul Mojzes. Vol. 1, No. 2. Philadelphia: Ecumenical Press, 1981.

————. *Must Walls Divide: The Creative Witness of the Churches in Europe.* New York: Friendship, 1981.

17

Religion and Politics in the Asian Communist Nations

DAVID YU

This chapter will focus on three points. The first concerns the role and nature of Marxism in contemporary Asia. The fact that Marxism is now the ideology of the Asian communist countries (China, North Korea, Vietnam, Laos, Kampuchea) bespeaks its influence in Asia. According to Max Weber, a new ideology can serve as the surrogate of religion in the transitional period when the traditional religion has lost its effectiveness.[1] Although this Weberian view is kept as a live option in our assessment of Asian Marxism, we also point out that Marxism in these Asian countries is more than just a surrogate of religion; it is in fact a religion—a belief system enforced by these states and followed by their leaders with religious sentiments and dogmatic convictions. It may be called the "official religion" in these countries, as Confucianism was the civil religion of China in the past. Thus speaking realistically, Asian Marxism is the dominant religion against, or competing with, the traditional religions. Moreover, being the ideology of the state, Marxism enjoys a privileged status in these countries; for this reason, the traditional religions are not its equal in terms of resources, power of proselytism, and rewards.

The second point to be stressed is the Asian Marxists' understanding of what religion means. In this regard, two notions are of particular interest. One is that, following the general Marxian caricature that religion is a means by which the ruling class placates the exploited class, they often equate the ruling class with Western imperialists and the exploited class with the colonial nations. Within this interpretive scheme they place the Christian Mission as a partner of Western imperialism. The other notion is that, for some Asian communist scholars, because the classical Marxists associated religion primarily with historical Christianity in the West, they question whether such an understanding of religion would be suitable to the Asian historical context.

The third point concerns the religious policy of the state and its implementations; implementation inevitably involves confrontation between the state and the various religious bodies and their leaders. The relation between the state and religion in these countries is not merely that of the state versus religion; for there is a semi-state agency between them. This is the new national office of the religious body formed specifically to disseminate the government's religious policy to its local groups. This national office is not exactly a state organization, for it does not belong to the state apparatus; nor is it a mere civil association, for it was organized at the state's request and receives its subsidy. It serves as a bridge between the state and the particular religion. Thus, the relation between the state and religion may be conceived in terms of a hierarchy of three levels: state, national religious office, and local groups. The first sets forth the religious policy, the second communicates and interprets it to the local groups, and the third attempts to facilitate it at the grass-roots level.

This chapter deals primarily with China, first, because we have far greater access to materials on China pertaining to this general topic than on the other Asian nations. (For example, no authentic religious information on North Korea is currently available.) Second, because China is the largest and most influential country in Asia, its story of religion may shed light on the religious situation in other Asian communist countries.

MARXISM AS IDEOLOGY OF ASIAN NATIONALISM

The Asian communist countries have a common recent history of colonialism and foreign occupations. Korea was annexed by Japan (1910–1945). Indochina— the collective name of Vietnam, Laos, and Kampuchea—was the colony of France (1860–1940), later occupied by the Japanese forces (1940–1945), still later engaged in the war of liberation against the re-entrance of France (1946– 1954), and, lastly, encountered the American penetrations (1965–1973). At different times in the nineteenth century China was invaded by the leading Western powers. In the twentieth century, China faced Japanese invasions (1931–1945), resulting in Japan's eventual occupation of its entire coastal provinces before the end of World War II. The communist parties in China and Vietnam were founded, respectively, in 1921 and 1930. In both countries, Marxism was conceived as an ideology of national liberation and salvation.

The political situation of North Korea, however, differed from that of China and Vietnam. Soviet troops entered North Korea on the eve of Japan's surrender to the Allied forces. With Soviet backing, Kim Il-sung, who was in Russia during World War II, returned to North Korea to head the Communist Party. Unlike the Communist parties in China and Vietnam, which started as illegitimate groups and gained power only after years of trials and tribulations, the North Korean Communist Party from its very inception was a legitimate party with the blessings of the Soviet troops. But, despite the fact that it did not begin as a people's party, because its birth coincided with the surrender of Japan and its immediate goal was nation-building, it did serve as a rallying point for the North Koreans.

The victory of communism in China, North Korea, and Southeast Asia was in part due to its advantageous use of a common history of colonialism and foreign occupations as a basis for a Marxist interpretation of Asian nationalism.

RELIGION AND POLITICS IN CHINA

Theoretical Considerations of Religion by the State and Marxist Writers

Since the communist takeover of China in 1949, certain conceptions of religion have influenced the government's religious policy. According to the 1954 Constitution, "Every citizen of the People's Republic of China shall have freedom of religious belief." But "freedom of religious belief" must be understood in a particular Marxist context of atheism, which means that whereas freedom not to believe in religion is a right of the majority in a communist country, "freedom of religious belief" is a right of the minority. Thus, when the minority exercises its right to believe, it should not interfere with the right of the majority not to believe. Hence, religious believers have no right to propagate the belief in public, for this might interfere with the right of other people not to believe in religion. Thus, religious freedom is limited to religious activities within the confines of the sanctuary of a private building. In addition, religion is understood strictly in the "pure sense," that is, in doctrines and beliefs that do not have any political import; hence, the prophetic role of religion is automatically ruled out.

In 1963–1965 influential newspapers recorded extensive theoretical debates on the viability of religion. They followed the wake of a recrudescence of religious activities in 1960–62 when Buddhist temples in rural China were allowed to conduct their daily services and urban devotees attended Buddhist festivals in respectable numbers.[2] There were even some Christian revival meetings in the rural areas.[3] These debates were mainly between two groups of writers: the quasi-Marxist group headed by Ya Hanzhang and the Marxist group headed by You Xiang and Liu Junwang.

The quasi-Marxist group held that, because of the peculiar character of Chinese religions, distinctions should be made between (1) religion, (2) feudal superstitions, and (3) animism, even though feudal superstitions and animism have generally been classified under religion. (1) By "religion" is meant a more developed religious system with institutional organization and rules, religious professionals, doctrines, worship, and financial and other obligations from its believers. It was developed in historical times when class conflicts already prevailed, and it was used by the ruling class to keep the oppressed under its control. This is called the "man-made religion" in contradistinction to the "spontaneous religion" of the pre-historical time when there was no class conflict.[4] According to this group, only Buddhism, Taoism, Islam, and Christianity in China can properly be called "religion" in this sense. (The Chinese Marxists, like the Chinese intellectuals of the recent past, consider Confucianism mainly as a political and ethical system.) Hence, only believers of these religions may enjoy the constitutional protection of "freedom of religious belief." (2) Feudal superstitions refer to the shamanic and magical practices traceable to pre-historical China such as divination, exorcism, faith-healing, and geomancy, which are the dominant features of the folk religion of China. Ya Hanzhang wanted to exclude these features from "religion" because they are deficient of organization and of systematic belief. The real reason, however, seems to be that because these "superstitions" were the major obstacle to China's scientific progress in the past, they are incompatible with its present-day modernization programs. Because these "superstitions" are not religion, those who pursue them should not be protected under the constitutional right of religious freedom. (3) Animism (*youshenlun*) refers to the belief in gods, ghosts, and spirits—a prominent feature in Chinese folk religion.[5] Again, Ya excluded such phenomena from "religion" because the animists do not belong to an organized religion, nor do they have a belief-system. If "animism" is to be taken as a religion, then most of the Chinese people today would probably be classified as religious believers. This would give religion too prominent a place in China today. By not considering animism as a religion, those who practice it would not be protected under the religious freedom clause.

Ya made distinctions between these three categories primarily because he wanted to contrast the religious situation in China with that of the West. He argued that because religion for Marx and Engels refers primarily to the monotheism of Christianity and Judaism, it may not be applicable to China where religion mainly involves "superstitions" and "animism." (In this regard, Ya is contradicting his own definition of "religion.")

There is another reason why Ya distinguished "religion" from the other two categories. By doing so he allowed only the more developed religions to exist in China today. Here we detect an ambivalence in his definition of religion: as a Chinese scholar he appears to be empathetic with "superstitions" and "animism"; but as a Marxist he sees all religions as reactionary and exploitative, particularly the "superstitions" and "animism" in Chinese history. Ya's conception of religion is probably politically motivated: because most of the Chinese people believe in these "superstitions" and "animism," and because there are no ways by which they can be regulated, it would be impossible for them to be brought under control. Ya attempted to solve this problem by simply denying their religious nature. On the other hand, because only a small number of the Chinese people believe in the more developed religions which can be directed properly through the national religious associations, the state is in a better position to control them.

The second or the Marxist group faithfully followed Engels's definition of religion: Religion is the individual's fantastic reflection of the actual forces that regulate his or her daily life, through which the actual forces of nature and society are understood to be the appearances of the supernatural beings.[6] This group criticized Ya on two grounds: (1) Ya's distinction between the three categories is unfounded because Engels's definition of religion is inclusive enough to make room for all these three categories. Thus, this group said, "the same principle [of Engels] which explains why the masses believe in the ideals of ghosts and gods, of predestination, and other superstitions can also explain why the Catholics, Protestants, Muslims, Buddhists, and Taoists believe in the ideas of Lord in Heaven, God, Allah, Buddha, and the Immortals."[7] (2) A more severe criticism is that Ya has departed from the Marxist understanding of religion. According to Ya, the more developed religions were derived from animism, which for him existed in a pre-historical time prior to class conflicts. He traced religions to a common source (animism) that did not have an ideological struggle, that is, the conflict between the individual and society/nature. This would contradict the Marxist notion that religion from its very beginning was an ideology, that is, a reflection of conflict between the individual and society/nature. Ya made a similar error when he said that Marx was referring only to the Christianity of Germany when he wrote that "religion is the opium of the people."[8] This would imply that not all religions are necessarily "the opium of the people."

According to the Marxist group, because religious believers generally hold a non-Marxist or "idealistic" world-view, the religious problem in a communist country ultimately is a political one, namely, how to counteract the idealistic world-view of the religious believers which is in basic conflict with Marxism. It would require a far more complex strategy to counteract religion than a mere nationwide educational program to teach atheism, as Ya has recommended.

It may be surmised that these two groups represent two points of view on the meaning of religion: the quasi-Marxists wanted to adopt the Marxian theory of religion to the historical-social context of China, and the Marxists took a doctrinal approach to religion without examining it judiciously within the Chinese context. However, both groups agreed that, whereas religion may be tolerated, it is nevertheless in essential conflict with Marxism in the political sense.

Religious Policy of the State

It is a well-known Marxist litany that religion is a product of uncertain conditions in a class society and when these conditions disappear in a socialistic society, religion will eventually disappear. Thus, a Marxist state can tolerate religion as long as it aims at the elimination of these conditions. This attitude is reflected in Mao's words: "It is the peasants who made the idols, and when the time comes they will cast the idols aside with their own hands; there is no need for anyone else to do it for them prematurely."[9]

But there is a pragmatic reason why religion should be tolerated, based on Lenin's advice that to force people to give up their religious belief not only would hurt their feelings but also would make them adhere to their belief even more "blindly." Following the same line of reasoning, Mao said:

We cannot abolish religion by administrative decrees or force people not to believe in it. We cannot compel people to give up idealism any more than we can force them to believe in Marxism. The only way to settle questions of an ideological nature or controversial issues among the people is by the democratic method, the method of discussion, of persuasion, and not by the method of coercion and repression.[10]

The attitude of the party is that religion is to be tolerated, even though it is unacceptable. Out of this position has come the view that in the transitional stage of the Revolution religious believers can join forces with other civil groups under the leadership of the party for national reconstruction. This point of view is based on the premise that most believers are also the victims of the landlords, the warlords, and foreign imperialism. In this sense, they are also members of the exploited class. This view is called the "United Front" (tongyi zhanxian): the believers may unite with other non-Marxist groups of patriots to form a national front against the enemies of the Revolution. However, this does not imply the acceptance of the believers' religions: the party accepts the believers because of their revolutionary empathy, not because of their religious worldviews. Thus, in dealing with these believers, the party must adopt the principle of "uniting with and struggling against." It must unite with the believers to broaden the revolutionary basis, but it must struggle against their religions through organized efforts: discussion, criticism, atheistic education, and other propaganda methods.

In setting up the religious policy, the party carefully distinguished between "religious worship and belief" and the "counter-religious activities," the latter being activities under the "guise of religion" aimed at subverting the Revolution. As far as this distinction goes, the quasi-Marxist and the Marxist groups are in complete agreement. The general meaning of counter-religious activities was stated by Ya Hanzhang as follows:

As to the utilization of religious superstitions by imperialism in carrying out counter-revolutionary activities, by feudal forces in carrying out activities for a comeback, and by superstitious professionals in swindling money and goods from the people, these are not problems . . . of worship, but problems of contradictions between the enemy and us. In respect of reactionary activities carried out by imperialism and feudal forces by making use of religious superstitions, the method of dictatorship [of the proletariat] must be employed.[11]

In this regard, the party appeared to be particularly sensitive about the historical relations between the Catholic and Protestant Mission and Western imperialism. It accused the Mission of being the tool of imperialism; according to this view, both the Catholic and Protestant churches have engaged in many subversive and reactionary activities "under the cloak of religion." This interpretation of Christian Mission has made Catholicism and Protestantism in Asia particularly vulnerable under communism.

The distinction between "religious worship and belief" and "counter-religious activities" makes one wonder just how much religious freedom there is in China; for any religious activities aimed at criticizing the state may be construed as being reactionary or subversive. Because China still does not have an independent legal system that can judiciously distinguish what is "religious worship and belief" and what is "counter-religious activities," the ultimate arbitrator remains the state.

Reactions of Religious Bodies to the Religious Policy

The first step the new government took after seizing power *vis-à-vis* religion was to establish the Bureau of Religious Affairs (BRA) in 1951 for the implementation of its religious policy. The specific religions under the BRA's control are Catholicism, Protestantism, Buddhism, Taoism, and Islam. Its national office is in the capital, but its branch offices were founded in the provinces, municipalities, and cities. Both the central and branch offices were staffed with cadres of party members: each cadre was assigned to a particular religion.

The following discussion centers on how the government implemented its religious policy and how the different religious bodies responded to it. Three periods are covered: the National Liberation, the Cultural Revolution, and the Post-Cultural Revolution.

Period of the National Liberation, 1949–1966

Catholicism. The Catholic Church was in a particularly vulnerable position in the first decade of communist rule because of the hierarchical and transnational structure of the Church. In the very beginning of this period, two out of three priests and four out of five bishops in China were foreigners.[12] Thus, when the BRA asked the Catholic leaders to organize the Three-Self Movement (self-governing, self-financing, and self-propagating of the Church), it was met with stubborn resistance. From the Catholic point of view, the "Three-Self"—which means the total control of the Catholic Church in China by the Chinese—is diametrically opposite to the tradition of Catholicism. But, as far as the new government was concerned, the continued presence of foreign priests, bishops, and financial subsidies in the Chinese Church was tantamount to the continuing collaboration of the Church with imperialism. Nevertheless, the Church's unequivocal opposition to the "Three-Self" proposition was clearly reflected in the 1951 Catholic statement, made by the bishops in China, which said that this proposition, if followed, would result in the creation of a church separated from Jesus and from the Holy See, and that such a schismatic church was unacceptable to Catholicism.[13]

At the outset, neither the Church nor the government seemed to understand the position of the other. The BRA was having difficulty finding prominent

Catholic priests to head the movement. In 1952 the government intensified its pressures to make the priests follow the directives. It was then that about fifty priests were jailed and another forty were placed under house arrest in Shanghai, with similar imprisonments taking place in other major cities. Only by such harsh means was the state able to win over about a dozen priests who began to take part in the movement, with another hundred who were undecided, out of a total of 3,000 Chinese priests.[14] By mid-1953 an independent Catholic Church was off the ground, but it only represented a tiny fraction of the Catholic population, estimated then at about 3 million.

Because Shanghai was both the most influential Catholic center in China and the last stronghold of Catholic resistance, the government in 1955 took the harshest action against the Shanghai diocese. It arrested their bishop, Kung Pinmei, and jailed about 1,500 Catholics, including about fifty priests. Meanwhile, similar arrests also occurred in other major cities, though on a much smaller scale. The massive persecution in Shanghai was a big blow to Catholic resistance.

By mid-1957 the Catholic Patriotic Association at the national level was inaugurated under the chairmanship of Pi Shushi, Archbishop of Shengyang (Mukden). Since 1958 the Church has elected and ordained its new bishops without Vatican approval. As of 1962, forty-two such bishops were ordained. This number was more than half of the total of seventy Chinese bishops in 1965. (The same report accounted for 2,000 Chinese priests.)[15]

As is well known, in this period practically all the Chinese professionals and intellectuals had to spend a fixed number of hours doing manual labor. Religious personnel in particular had to show their willingness to take part in order to counteract the accusation that they were non-productive. By 1959 all priests and nuns were engaged in manual labor, mostly agricultural.

Protestantism. In comparison with Catholicism, the Protestant leadership in China by 1949 was largely in the hands of the Chinese. In addition, because of the denominational character of Protestantism, there were no uniform doctrines and ecclesiastical structure to which the different church groups had to conform. This made the Protestant Church more amenable to change. Moreover, many Protestant leaders adopted a rather optimistic outlook on the new China; they felt that their religion and Marxism had some ideas in common which might give Christianity some advantage in witnessing in the new age. Thus, these leaders responded positively to the Three-Self Movement. The government also found a person who could be trusted to lead the movement. He was Wu Yaozong (1893-1979), then General Secretary of Literature and Publications, National YMCA.

A group of forty prominent Protestant leaders in 1950 issued a Christian Manifesto, appealing to the churches to rally behind the new government and recognizing that because Christianity in China had been supported by foreign funds and missionaries, it was inextricably tied to imperialism. It said that the first task of the Church was to extirpate its foreign support of any kind. The issuance of this Manifesto signified the formal beginning of the Chinese Christian Three-Self Movement, although it was not actually established until the following year. It was chaired by Wu Yaozong. (According to Wu, there were about 400,000 Protestants in China in 1954 based on the number of signatures collected in support of the Manifesto.) Some debates took place at the executive meeting of the National Council of Christian Churches (NCCC)—the inter-church Protestant body in the pre-communist era—held in 1950 for the endorsement of the Manifesto. But the dissenters were apparently outvoted. By 1951 the Christian Three-Self Movement virtually replaced the NCCC.

But the Three-Self Movement was by no means without opposition. Some fundamentalist church leaders did not support it. Wang Mingdao, pastor of the Christian Assembly in Beijing, refused to join because he believed that the theological position of the Movement did not have a scriptural basis. For this reason he was imprisoned in 1955. A year later, he was released after signing a confession. However, no sooner did he sign the confession than he recanted it, whereupon he was sent back to jail where he remained for twenty-four years before final release. Ni Tuosheng (Watchman Ni), leader of the Little Flock, an indigenous fundamentalist sect, was imprisoned in 1956 for fifteen years for alleged anti-government behavior. Chen Chonggui (Marcus Chen), Vice-Chairman of the Three-Self Movement, made a speech in 1957 mildly criticizing the government for not protecting citizens' freedom of religious belief. As a result, he was the object of severe attack by his Christian colleagues. He was stripped of his positions and accused of being a rightist. But despite these persecutions, the Protestant leaders on the whole suffered much less than their Catholic brothers and sisters.

By 1958, the year of the "Great Leap," Protestant pastors and woman church workers had to work in the fields and factories. Consequently, they had no time to look after their flocks. Meanwhile, the government appropriated hundreds of church buildings for other purposes. During this time many Christians initiated the "house-gatherings" where they met informally in private homes for prayers and scriptural readings. In those days when anti-West sentiments were strong, many Christians felt that it was unwise to continue to worship in the church buildings with their stigma of imperialism. For different reasons, Christians avoided regular church attendance. Hence, there was a large-scale reduction in the number of churches in the cities. For example, 200 churches in Shanghai were reduced or consolidated to 23, and 65 churches in Beijing to 4.[16] The remaining church workers were required to undergo political education. For example, in 1958 over 300 church workers and seminary students in Jiansu province met in Nanjing for almost four months of political study.[17]

Buddhism and Taoism. The fact that Buddhism and Taoism have been on Chinese soil for so long made the government's attitude toward them quite different from the one it had toward Christianity. In the first place, these two religions were unrelated to foreign imperialism. In addition, in terms of size Christianity was very small in comparison with these two religions. Being closely related to the Chinese culture, these two religions could easily be utilized by the reactionary groups to damage the socialization process. Furthermore, what appealed to the Chinese masses about these religions were their "superstitions" and magical rites, aspects the new government could not tolerate. On the other hand, both Buddhism and Taoism built great temples, and produced huge collections of scriptures and numerous artifacts that have become a part of the cultural legacy. Besides, the new government was aware that because Buddhism is Pan-Asian, what the state did to it could be newsworthy to other Buddhist countries. These considerations have compelled the government to move cautiously in implementing its religious policy.

The first step the government took was the publication in 1950 of the monthly, *Modern Buddhism* (*Xiandai Fojiao*), which served as a national organ of communication about directions to be followed by the monasteries and temples. The most urgent task was the political indoctrination of the monks and nuns. The second major step was the creation in 1953 of the Chinese Buddhist Association (CBA) (Zhongguo Fojiao Xiehui), composed of ninety-three members of prominent Buddhists—leading lamas, head-monks of national minorities, notable abbots, and influential devotees. Because they were selected by the state, they were not the representatives of local monasteries and lay Buddhist groups. Their role was advisory at the national level. The real authority was in the hands of three officials: the General Secretary, Zhao Puchu, a lay Buddhist who had close connection with the party, and two Vice-General Secretaries, Ju Jan, a progressive monk and editor of *Modern Buddhism*, and Guo Peng, a party bureaucrat. We may be reminded that in imperial China there was a government bureau for the overseeing of the monasteries.

The CBA's major functions were cultural, diplomatic, and educational. It appropriated funds for the badly needed restorations of the nationally known monasteries. By 1952–1966 it was host to thirty-six Asian Buddhist delegations which visited China and the sponsor of eleven Chinese Buddhist delegations for their journeys abroad.[18] These diplomatic efforts were intended not only to impress the Buddhist countries about China's Buddhist legacy but also to support the Vietnamese monks and nuns in the early 1960s for their protest against the U.S.-supported South Vietnam government. It also established a five-year Buddhist college for the training of monks, which graduated about 200 students in ten years (1956–1966).

The branch offices of the BRA appeared to be the principal agent at the local level for direct contact with the monks and nuns. They made them engage in political study and productive labor. Because the Buddhist clergy were now prohibited from performing religious rituals in the cities for their clients in return for pay, a large portion of monastic income disappeared. Formerly, donations were a major monastic income, but this has been prohibited since 1958. Furthermore, the urban monasteries used to own large plots of agricultural land for the production of income, but this land was now expropriated. The drastic reduction of monastic income resulted in the returning of monks and nuns to secular life *en masse*. The rural monasteries fared better. Although their land now became part of the agricultural cooperatives and was later integrated into the communes, the remaining monks and nuns were allowed to labor in these fields. But because they worked full-time as peasants, they did not have any time left for monastic life. Thus by 1957 about 90 percent of the monks and nuns either died or returned to secular life. (The normative estimation is that there were about 500,000 monks and nuns in 1949.)[19]

Buddhism in Tibet is too complex an issue to be discussed adequately here. Because the Chinese government was aware of the minority nationality problem, it did not push for unilateral reform of Tibetan Buddhism in the first decade. However, it did announce at the outset that there should be a distinction between religion and social reform in Tibet—which implied that because the reform of Tibetan Buddhism was not a religious issue, it was forthcoming. Then in 1959, a Tibetan army insurrection arose. Although it was quickly smashed by the Chinese troops, it resulted in the migration of the Dalai Lama and his followers to north India where he established his government in exile. After the insurrection, the Chinese government stepped up monastic and social reform in Tibet.

With the exception of a few nationally known Taoist temples which were spared as cultural centers, the government generally viewed Taoist religion with contempt, partly because the majority of the Taoist temples were in a very neglected state and partly because the Taoist clergy, poorly educated, were the practitioners of "superstitions" and magical rites. These priests and priestesses were sent to special vocational schools to learn trades. Afterward, they were put to work in the factories. The abandoned temples were then converted for other purposes.

But there was another aspect of this religion which made the government apprehensive: namely, the secret societies historically affiliated with the Taoist religion. As is well known, in times of great social and political unrest, members of these sectarian societies often organized themselves for mutual survival; the leader of such a group often claimed himself as a messianic figure *vis-à-vis* the government. This phenomenon reemerged in the early years of this period. In order to facilitate communication among themselves, these secret societies constructed subterranean chambers and tunnels from Shanxi province in the west to coastal Hebei.[20] In 1955 the government discovered 102 such tunnels in Shanxi alone and arrested over 400 sectarian leaders. In Hebei province, several sectarian leaders were found hiding in the tunnels for over four years. In twelve provinces the "counter-revolutionary activities" of these societies were reported. Their leaders were accused of collaborating with the Nationalist Party of Taiwan and of spying for the United States. By 1955 over 40,000 of these sectarians were executed.

Other than restoring the famous Taoist temples and preserving the Taoist scriptures, the Chinese Taoist Association, founded in 1956, was inactive. This was partly because it did not have the active support of the leaders of the Taoist religion.

Islam. There were about 20 to 30 million Muslims in China in 1949, most of them concentrated in the Northwest and the southwestern province of Yunan; the rest were scattered throughout the country. Five million of these Muslims were Han Chinese.[21] The Muslim minority's languages, customs, diet, and religion were distinctly different from those of the Han Chinese. Partly because most of these people lived in the areas bordering the Soviet Union, which has a vested interest in them, and partly because they were ethnically a minority, the new government was very cautious in its effort to assimilate them into the socialist orbit. The Chinese cadres dispatched to these areas were particularly instructed to honor the Islamic way of life. However, the government viewed Islam primarily as a distinct culture, only secondly as a religion. For example, it considered the Islamic festivals (e.g., the Corban Festival celebrating the end of the Pilgrimage to Mecca) as special days of cultural celebration when the Muslim workers were exempted from work.

Land reform in the Muslim areas was carried out slowly, and it took local conditions into consideration. For example, land owned by the mosques was left intact as late as 1957.[22] However, all *imams* (leaders of the mosques) and *ahungs* (religious teachers) underwent political education and participated in manual labor. They were told to interpret the Qur'an from the Marxist-Leninist perspective.[23]

An important strategy for the modernization of the Muslim youth was through education. All Muslim children had to go to schools where Chinese was the medium of instruction; courses in sciences were emphasized. Special colleges were established in Beijing for the training of the future Muslim leaders. A four-year theological seminary was also established. A new translation of the Qur'an in vernacular Chinese was published in 1952. The government also strove to improve the condition of the Muslim women. Vocational schools were constructed for them to learn technical skills in order to be employed outside homes. These women received an eight-week maternity leave with full pay and had free medical care.

The Chinese Islamic Association was founded in 1953, and its main function was to establish the state in the development of cultural and educational enterprises for the Muslim people. It also played a large role in sponsoring the exchange of Muslim delegations between China and Islamic countries in the Middle East and Africa.

The government's efforts to improve the economic and social conditions of the Muslims notwithstanding, there have been numerous incidents of Muslim resistance and insurrections in this period. Their chief complaint was that the socialist reforms disrupted their religious observances and customs. Another complaint was that the increasing influx of the Han Chinese into their communities infringed on their autonomy.

Period of the Cultural Revolution, 1966–1976

The Cultural Revolution refers mainly to the ideological and power struggle between the radical and the moderate wing of Maoism, which affected all classes of the Chinese. The ascending radical wing, whose leaders were called the "Gang of Four" in the next period, forced the Chinese to accept its own ultra-leftist Marxism-Maoism through mass accusations, thought-reform, and imprisonments. Any ideas not acceptable to it were viewed as either reactionary or revisionist. It inflicted immense suffering on the intellectuals and professionals. The peak of the Cultural Revolution was from 1966 to 1969, after which its power began to diminish.

According to the proponents of the Cultural Revolution, because Western religions supported capitalism and Chinese religions supported idealism and feudalism, the religions of both foreign and Chinese origin should be abandoned. All religious institutions were closed, and formal religious activities ceased in the cities in 1966–1971. Even the semi-official religious associations such as the CBA became inoperative. Islam fared a little better: one mosque in Shanghai and another in Beijing remained open, and the major Islamic festivals were observed publicly in the Northwest.

The religious situation appeared to be better in rural China in this period. One overseas Chinese woman in 1968–1969 visited several well-known Buddhist monasteries in East-Central China; at each place she witnessed the presence of dozens of monks and the burning of incense-sticks. At her request, one monastery conducted a seven-day memorial service for her late husband.[24] A Western couple in 1972 visited a three-monk monastery in rural Xian where they talked to the abbot who was also an herb-doctor. In addition to attending to the sick, he also worked in the fields. These three monks held daily devotions in the mornings and practiced short meditation sessions in the evenings.[25] As for Christianity, there were at least some underground religious activities among both Catholics and Protestants in rural areas.

Although the political situation was still oppressive when China entered the 1970s, the moderate wing headed by Zhou Enlai appeared to recapture power. A number of illustrious monasteries in the cities were restored and reopened in the later part of this period, although no regular worship was witnessed.

Period of the Post-Cultural Revolution, 1976–1982

The death of Mao Zedong (1976) was the immediate cause of the drastic decline of the forces instrumental to the Cultural Revolution. This was a period of general rehabilitation in which a vast number of victims unjustly punished were now redressed materially and reputationally; those who survived regained their posts, and those who perished were publicly exonerated. Economics and proper individual interests, rather than politics, were now deemed necessary for the advance of socialism. And the ban against the pursuit of traditional Chinese learning and against scholarly interests in the capitalist West was now lifted. After a decade of isolation and suppression, the Chinese were now eager to reengage themselves in the various branches of Chinese Studies, as well as learning what was happening in the West. This was the general mood against which the issues of religious restoration must be understood.

In a way, the "revival" of religion in this period was simply a particular instance of the general mood of national relaxation. Hence, in 1979 about 800 religious personalities met in Shanghai to express their grievances: to denounce the religious restrictions and injustices in the past years, and to demand the normalization of religious activities, and the rehabilitation of religious victims. A year earlier, the Chinese People's Political Consultative Conference's religious group, composed of Buddhist, Taoist, Muslim, Catholic, and Protestant representatives, made a study of Article 46 of the 1978 Constitution: "Citizens enjoy the freedom to believe in religion and the freedom not to believe in religion and to propagate atheism." Members of this group felt that inasmuch as the atheists had the right to propagate atheism, the theists should have the same right to propagate theism. Therefore, they petitioned to revise this article by including the right of the theists.[26] It was sent to the forthcoming People's Congress for deliberation. In order to eliminate the abuses of anti-religion by the bureaucrats, the Criminal Code (1979) stipulates that government personnel who unlawfully interfere with the freedom of belief in religion in a serious way "shall be sentenced to imprisonment or detention for not more than two years."[27]

There are indications, as shown below, that the state is now willing to recognize some separation between religion and politics by allowing a degree of autonomy to the religious institutions. Those believers who stayed away from the churches or temples which became too heavily involved in politics in the past years will likely return to them.

In 1980 the Chinese Catholic Church inaugurated two new offices: the Church Affairs Commission designed to look after its internal affairs, and the National Bishops' Conference, composed of both the old bishops appointed by the Vatican and the new ones, designed to oversee doctrinal matters and to maintain relations with the Church outside China. The Catholic Patriotic Association remains. In Beijing in 1978 a company of eighteen priests conducted mass and looked after the spiritual well-being of their diocesan members, although at that time they were not authorized to baptize new members or ordain new priests.[28] The release of Dominic Deng, a Chinese Jesuit, in 1980 after twenty years' imprisonment was welcome news. He was afterward appointed Bishop of Guangzhou by the Catholic Patriotic Association, a post he held before his imprisonment. A year later, while in Rome for a visit, Deng was appointed Archbishop of Guangzhou by Pope John Paul II. The Chinese authorities, however, immediately repudiated the appointment as a subversive act. The Catholic Church is much stronger in rural areas than in the cities today, as was the case before 1949. For example, a group of 150 Catholic families in Long Bow Village, Shanxi, started to hold weekly mass again in 1980 in the home of a carpenter whose father had been a lay officer of the local church.[29]

The Protestant Church, in addition to the Three-Self Movement, founded the China Christian Council (CCC) in 1980 to look after its pastoral needs. Both organizations are now chaired by Ting Guangxun, an Episcopalian Bishop. In order to meet the requests by church members, the CCC printed 135,000 copies of the Bible. Nanjing Theological Seminary reopened in 1981 with an enrollment of fifty-one students—twenty women and twenty-nine men ranging in age from nineteen to thirty-five. About eighty churches are now reopened, ministered to by the surviving pastors. They receive salaries from the funds derived from church property rentals. The informal "house-gatherings" continue to thrive.

The well-known Buddhist monasteries have resumed their religious functions; a few monks reside there, and incense-sticks are offered by lay devotees. Some monasteries closed during the Cultural Revolution have now been reopened. The famous Nanputo Temple at Drum Mountain in Fuzhou is active again with a community of fifty returned monks. In Jiuhua Mountain, Anhui, where there was once the largest concentration of the monastic population, some sixty-seven temples have been reopened. As of 1980, there was a total of 127 Buddhist clergy in these temples—49 monks and 78 nuns. The annual pilgrimage to Jiuhua Mountain has also been revived. It was anticipated that some 750,000 pilgrims would attend the 1980 event. The CBA has also been reactivated. It revived the Buddhist Academy for the training of the clergy; its branch school in Suzhou has an enrollment of twenty students, ranging in age from eighteen to thirty-one.

A few famous Taoist temples have also shared the fortune of religious restoration. The Temple of Goddess of the Dawn (Bi Xia Yuan Jun) at Mount Tai in Northeast China has been fully restored and opened to the public. By 1979 some 400 elderly women from all directions in North China climbed all night to be at the top of Mount Tai to celebrate her birthday. The famous Taoist temple at the Green-Wall Mountain, Sichuan, has also been reopened and is attended by a few resident priests. Some visitors have been seen kneeling in front of the altar in the main hall, where candles were lit and incense-sticks were burning.

RELIGION AND POLITICS IN VIETNAM, LAOS, AND KAMPUCHEA

No sooner did the Japanese troops in Indochina surrender to the allied forces that the Vietnamese Communist Party, led by Ho Chi-ming (1890–1969), declared the independence of Vietnam. A year later, the French returned to reclaim their sovereignty, whereupon the French-Vietnam War began. It ended with French defeat at Dien Bien Phu in 1954. Later in July, the Geneva Conference created the two Vietnams: communist North Vietnam and non-communist South Vietnam. The same conference also guaranteed the independence of Laos and Kampuchea.

Because Vietnam was under French rule for almost a century, Catholic influences were strong. Although the Catholics were a minority—about 10 percent of the population at the time of partition—their influence far exceeded their numbers. The Catholic Church provided the modern educational system which produced graduates who served as civil servants and professionals in colonial Vietnam. These people were among the elite in Vietnamese society. After the partition, about 800,000 refugees from the North migrated to South Vietnam in

1954–1956 among whom 80 percent were Catholic. Ngo Dinh Diem, President of South Vietnam (1954–1963), himself a Catholic, relied heavily on Catholics for the running of his government; they were both efficient and anti-communist.

The largest religious establishment in South Vietnam was Buddhism (predominantly Mahayana, but there were about 1 million Theravadins along the border of Kampuchea). Hoa Hao (pronounced *wah how*), founded in 1937, was a mixture of Buddhism with mediumship, sorcery, and magic. It has about 1.5 million followers in the South. Cao Dai (the "Third Amnesty of God"), founded in 1926, was an eclectic sect which recognized the divinity of Buddha, Confucius, Jesus, and Lao Tzu, and adopted an ecclesiastic hierarchy borrowed from the Catholic Church. It has about 2 million followers in the South. Both Hoa Hao and Cao Dai appealed to the semi-literate Vietnamese; they were intermittently for and against the Vietcong (communists in South Vietnam), depending on the political situations of the local villages where these sectarians resided.[30]

In the early 1960s the Buddhist monks accused Ngo Dinh Diem of giving favor to the Catholics in terms of appointments, refugee benefits, and religious freedom. By then Diem's autocratic and pro-Catholic reputation was widespread. People also resented the inordinate amount of power enjoyed by Diem's family—one brother was government head of Central Vietnam, another, Archbishop of Hué, and another, chief political strategist of the government.[31] The monks' complaints were supported by the Vietnamese masses, whether confessed Buddhists or not. Then, Diem's ban against the Buddhists' carrying their banners at a parade for the celebration of the Buddha's birthday in 1963 incensed them and their sympathizers. This incident precipitated organized demonstrations by the Buddhists against the government's discrimination.

The Buddhist protests were climaxed by the self-immolation of a seventy-five-year-old monk, Quang Duc, in Saigon in June 1963. This was followed by four more self-immolations in August. By now, the aim of the demonstration had shifted from protest against religious discrimination to ousting Diem and his government. A military *coup d'etat* took place in November 1963, which resulted in the death of Diem and the fall of his government.

The overthrow of Diem's government convinced the Buddhist leaders that they possessed the political potential to counteract the other two major forces in South Vietnam: the army and the Vietcong. They successfully overthrew at least two more governments in 1963–1965. Meanwhile, they were able to install Buddhist chaplains in the army. In this period, their political aims included putting more of their people in the strategic government posts, establishment of a civil government on the basis of a constituent assembly, and negotiations with the Vietcong for a peaceful solution for the nation. However, because this was a period of great military build-up with the assistance of the United States *vis-à-vis* North Vietnam and the Vietcong, the amibitions of the monk leaders were badly thwarted.

In the spring of 1965, a new military government was set up headed by Generals Thieu and Ky with the strong backing of the United States, aimed at a military solution for South Vietnam. The bonzes (Buddhist monks) counteracted by organizing a nationwide Struggle Force supported by Buddhist laity, radical student groups, dissident former government officials, and some military personnel. Their immediate goals were the national election of a constituent assembly and the removal of a Thieu-Ky government. At one point of the negotiations between the government and the Buddhist leaders, a 10-point agreement was reached about the election procedures and the resignations of Thieu-Ky. However, a few days later, General Ky revoked the agreement and insisted that his military government was necessary at that time. The Buddhist leaders, headed by Tri Quang and Tam Chau, responded in the spring of 1966 by gathering massive demonstrations in Saigon, Danang, and Hué. Then the government counteracted by putting several thousand Buddhists and dissidents in jail. Through sheer force of military power, the government finally managed to end the resistance of the Struggle Force. The divisiveness within the Buddhist hierarchy also contributed to the final eclipse of the Buddhist resistance.

Laos was besieged with civil war, immediately after its independence, between the government and the Communist Party, called Pathet Lao ("Lao country"). The religion of Laos was principally Theravada Buddhism, which was conservative and disinterested in politics. Kampuchea, bordering along Thailand on its west, has been a Theravada country since the thirteenth century, with about 3,000 Buddhist temples brightening the country. Prince Sihanouk became the ruler of Kampuchea when it gained independence. He advocated "Buddhist socialism" as a national aspiration. Although he declared Kampuchea a neutralist country during the Vietnam War, he also let North Vietnam use his country to transport their ammunitions, supplies, and manpower to South Vietnam. In 1969 U.S. planes bombed the North Vietnamese targets in Kampuchea. The following year, both U.S. and South Vietnamese troops entered Kampuchea to clear out the North Vietnamese supply bases. Meanwhile, civil war broke out in Kampuchea between the government and the Communist Party, called the Khmer Rouge ("Red Khmer"). In 1970 General Lon Nol and Prince Sirik overthrew Sihanouk and attempted political reform. But the new government was unable to stop the growth of the Khmer Rouge.

Immediately after the withdrawal of the U.S. forces in 1973, North Vietnamese troops descended on South Vietnam. In 1975 the two Vietnams were united under the rule of communism. In the same year, the Khmer Rouge gained victory in Kampuchea under the government of Pol Pot, which launched a system of brutality unmatched in history. Then, in 1979 the Vietnamese troops entered Laos and Kampuchea. Since then, the Vietnamese have controlled all of Indochina. Both the Catholic Church and the Buddhist establishment were forced to cooperate with the government in order to survive.

CONCLUSION

Religious freedom is highly restricted in these Asian communist nations. But we must remind ourselves that religious freedom is not an overriding issue in

Asian traditional thought. It can become a meaningful concept only after the doctrine of the separation of church and state is guaranteed in a nation. But this doctrine has never been discussed as part of the intellectual history of the Asian countries. The state in Confucian China took for granted that its authority was total and undivided (no separation between the temporal and spiritual). The Confucian state assumed that it had the right to interfere with religious institutions, an action which a democratic state in the modern West would not take. It should be noted that the Confucian model of the state was the main tradition of the past of these Asian communist countries. The present authorities in these countries can be expected to maintain the same attitude and behavior toward the religious institutions as their ancestors have done in the past. However, the present governments in these nations are more harsh and more hostile toward religious institutions and believers than their counterparts in the Confucian days. This may be due to the particular character of Marxism. The Confucian rulers aspired to benevolence and propriety in dealing with persons and institutions, which might compel them to exercise restraint in matters of religion. In contrast, the communist rulers emphasize struggle and contradiction between the rival groups. If these norms are applied to the religious situation, the result could be suppression and persecution.

As observed in this chapter, Marxism unwittingly functions as a secular religion in these nations. Confucianism as an official institution behaved very much like a religion in the pasts of these countries—that is, it was an ideology enhanced by scriptures, rituals, and myths, and it claimed a total and undivided authority. The present communist states in these countries are a religious continuation of the Confucian states in terms of ethos. Thus, the problem of the state controlling or suppressing religion in these countries can best be understood when it is placed in the perspective of a dominant religion rivaling with or suppressing a less dominant one.

The future of religion in these Asian nations depends on many conditions. The one element crucial in extracting a fair degree of religious tolerance in a communist nation is for that nation to have a relatively open relation with the rest of the world. World opinion and international contact have a certain corrective effect on a country. Hence, a communist country that has contact with other nations, particularly those of the democratic West, would most likely be more sensitive and less authoritarian in dealing with its internal religious problems.[32]

NOTES

1. Max Weber, *Economy and Society*, Vol. 1, p. 486.

2. Union Research Institute, *Zhongguo dalu fojiao ziliao huibian* [Sourcebook on Buddhism in Mainland China: 1949–67], pp. 191–98; hereafter cited as *Sourcebook on Buddhism in Mainland China*.

3. Bush, *Religion in Communist China*, p. 245.

4. Ya Hanzhang, *"Guanyu zongjiao mixin wenti"* [On the Problem of Religious Superstitions], p. 56.

5. In MacInnis's book *Religious Policy and Practice in Communist China*, the term *youshenlun* (animism) is sometimes translated as "theism" and sometimes as "deism"; both translations are misleading. We have translated it as "animism" denoting the belief in ghosts, spirits, and gods. "Theism," a literal translation of *youshenlun*, does not convey what Ya Hanzhang wants *youshenlun* to mean. Ya's meaning of *youshenlun* corresponds roughly to "animism." Bush (*Religion in Communist China*) also translates *youshenlun* as "theism" (p. 26).

6. You Xiang and Liu Junwang, *"Due zongjiao di renshi wenti"* [On Knowing What Religion Is], p. 75.

7. Ibid., p. 77.

8. Ya Hanzhang, *"Ho zichan jieji zongjiaoxue huaqing jiexian* [Drawing a Dividing Line with the Bourgeois "Science of Religion"], p. 83.

9. Sovik, "Religion, Religious Institutions, and Religious Possibilities in China," p. 62.

10. MacInnis, *Religious Policy and Practice in Communist China*, p. 13.

11. Ibid., pp. 41–42. For the original writing, see Ya Hanzhang, *"Guanyu zongjiao mixin wenti,"* p. 65.

12. Bush, *Religion in Communist China*, p. 109.

13. Ibid., pp. 106–107.

14. Ibid., p. 119.

15. Ibid., p. 161.

16. Ibid., p. 231.

17. Ibid., p. 227.

18. Welch, *Buddhism under Mao*, p. 185.

19. Ibid., p. 81.

20. Yang, *Religion in Chinese Society*, p. 400.

21. Bush, *Religion in Communist China*, pp. 264–265.

22. Ibid., p. 270.

23. Ibid., p. 293.

24. Welch, "Buddhism Since the Cultural Revolution," pp. 135–136.

25. Strong, "A Post-Cultural Revolution Look at Buddhism," pp. 325–326.

26. Ting, "A Call for Clarity," p. 146.

27. Zhao, "Buddhism Resurfaces," p. 27.

28. Sovik, "Religion, Religious Institutions, and Religious Possibilities in China," p. 64.

29. "Eased Restrictions Boost China's Religious Revival," *Denver Post*, p. 4BB.

30. Shaplan, *Road from War*, p. 273.

31. Schecter, *New Face of Buddha*, pp. 173, 182–184.

32. In the summer of 1982, after completing the present chapter, I spent five weeks in China. The following report may serve as an appendix: I learned from Chen Zheming, Vice-President of the Nanjing Theological College, that a class of thirty new students would be admitted this fall, that the CCC was sponsoring the second printing of the Bible in 800,000 copies, and that two Catholic missionaries would be inaugurated in 1983. I was graciously received by Chang Ming, Abbot of the Gui Yuan Si (Temple of Returning to the Origin), a prominent Buddhist center in Wuhan. He said that there were twenty resident monks and seven novices in his monastery. In Beijing, I was the guest of two

staff members of the Institute for Research on World Religions, Lin Ying, former Deputy Director, and Gau Wangzhi, Research Associate in Christianity. They said that in comparison with the decade of 1966–1976 today's intellectuals and professionals are more relaxed and have more time to devote to fields of their own interests. On the basis of my associations with relatives and close friends, I have noticed that the Chinese people today have overcome the fears, restrictions, and sufferings that prevailed in 1966–76; they are far more involved in their daily mundane problems than in politics or communism. The intellectuals are very much interested in relating themselves to the cultural history of China as well as current affairs in Western nations. It is my conviction that the problem of religion in China today must be viewed within the context of the general cultural and political trends of post-Mao China.

BIBLIOGRAPHY

Books

Benz, Ernst. *Buddhism Or Communism: Which Holds the Future of Asia?* Translated from the German by Richard and Clara Winston. New York: Doubleday, 1965.

Bush, Richard C., Jr. *Religion in Communist China*. Nashville, Tenn.: Abingdon Press, 1970.

Chu, Theresa. *The Religious Dimension of Mao Zedong's Thought*. Maryknoll, N.Y.: Orbis Books, 1983.

Gheddo, Piero. *The Cross and the Bo-Tree: Catholics and Buddhists in Vietnam*. Translated by Charles U. Quinn. New York: Sheed and Ward, 1970.

Hanson, Eric O. *Catholic Politics in China and Korea*. Maryknoll, N.Y.: Orbis Books, 1980.

MacInnis, Donald E. *Religious Policy and Practice in Communist China*. New York: Macmillan Co., 1972.

Orr, Robert W. *Religion in China*. New York: Friendship Press, 1980.

Schecter, Jerold. *The New Face of Buddha: The Fusion of Religion and Politics in Contemporary Buddhism*. New York: Coward-McCann, 1967.

Shaplan, Robert. *The Road from War: Vietnam 1965–1971*. rev. ed. New York: Harper and Row, 1971.

Smith, Donald Eugene. *Religion, Politics, and Social Change in the Third World: A Sourcebook*. New York: Free Press, 1971.

Union Research Institute. *Zhongguo dalu fojiao ziliao huibian* [Sourcebook on Buddhism in Mainland China]. Hong Kong: Union Press, 1968.

Weber, Max. *Economy and Society*. Vol. 1. Eds. Gunther Roth and Claus Wittich. Berkeley: University of California Press, 1978.

Welch, Holmes. *Buddhism under Mao*. Cambridge, Mass.: Harvard University Press, 1972.

Yang, C. K. *Religion in Chinese Society*. Berkeley: University of California Press, 1961.

Yang, I-fan. *Islam in China*. Hong Kong: Union Press, 1957.

Journal Articles

Bates, M. Searle. "Christianity in the People's Republic: A Time for Study to Understand." *China Notes* 6, No. 2 (April 1968): 6–10.

Chang, Haji Yusuf. "Islam in Modern China." *The Voice of Islam* (Karachi), 14 (September 1966): 689–698.

Chen, Kenneth. "Chinese Communist Attitudes Towards Buddhism in Chinese History." *China Quarterly* 22 (April-June 1965): 14–30.

Claney, M. M. "The Catholic Church in Vietnam." *China Notes* 9, No. 1 (Winter 1970–1971): 7.

Fairbank, John K. "The Chinese Revolution and American Missions." *China Notes* 11, No. 1 (Autumn 1973): 37–41.

Hieu, Pham Quang, "Some Ideas for the Full Development of Democratic Rights of Believers of the Various Religions." *China Notes* 9, No. 1 (Winter 1970–1971): 3–5, transcribed from *Hoc-Tap* (Studies), the theoretical journal of the North Vietnam Workers' Party.

Kramers, Robert S. "The Case Against Confucius in Chinese Universities Today." *China Notes* 12, No. 3 (Summer 1974): 25–29.

MacInnis, Donald E. "Religious Policy and Practice in North Vietnam." *China Notes* 9, No. 1 (Winter 1970–1971): 1–2.

Montvalon, Robert de. "The North Vietnamese Communist Party Speaks of the Rights of Believers." *China Notes* 9, No. 1 (Winter 1970–1971): 2–3.

Needham, Joseph. "Christian Hope and Social Evolution." *China Notes* 12, No. 2 (1974): 13–20.

Shen, Philip. "Toward Understanding China from the Perspective of Hong Kong." *China Notes* 14, No. 3 (Summer 1976): 27–30.

Sovik, Arne. "Religion, Religious Institutions, and Religious Possibilities in China." *China Notes* 17 (Spring 1979): 62.

Strong, John, and Sarah Strong. "A Post-Cultural Revolution Look at Buddhism." *China Quarterly* 54 (April-June 1973): 321–330.

Tang, Edmond. "The Catholic Church in China Today." *China Notes* 19, No. 1 (Winter 1980–1981): 150–153.

Ting, K. H. "A Call for Clarity: Fourteen Points from Christians in the People's Republic of China to Christians Abroad." *China Notes* 19, No. 1 (1980–1981): 145–149.

———. "Facing the Future Or Restoring the Past?" *China Notes* 17, No. 1 (Autumn-Winter 1979–1980): 99–101.

———. "Religious Policy and Theological Reorientation in China." *China Notes* 18, No. 3 (Summer 1980): 121–124.

Wei, Louis Tsing-sing. "China and Vatican." *China Notes* 8, No. 4 (Autumn 1970): 50–54.

Welch, Holmes. "Buddhism Under Communists." *China Quarterly* 6 (April-June 1961): 1–14.

———. "Buddhism Since the Cultural Revoltuion." *China Quarterly* 40 (October-December, 1969): 127–136.

———. "The Buddhists' Return." *Far Eastern Economic Review*, July 16, 1973, pp. 26–30.

———. "The Reinterpretation of Chinese Buddhism." *China Quarterly* 12 (April-June 1965): 143–152.

Whitehead, Raymond L. "The Future Impact of China on the Churches." *China Notes* 14, No. 2 (1976): 17–19.

Young, L. C., and S. R. Ford. "God Is Society: The Religious Dimension of Maoism." *Sociological Inquiry* 47, No. 2 (1977): 89–97.

Yu, David C. "Buddhism in Communist China: Demise or Co-Existence?" *Journal of the American Academy of Religion* 39, No. 1 (1971): 48–61.

———. "Maoism and Buddhism in China." *Journal for the Scientific Study of Religion* 14, No. 3 (1975): 298–301.

Zhao Fushan. "The Chinese Revolution and Foreign Missions Seen Through the May Fourth Movements." *China Notes* 18, No. 3 (Summer 1979): 73–80.

Zhao Puchu. "Buddhism Resurfaces." *US-China Review* 5, No. 1 (January-February 1981): 25–27.

Newspaper Articles

"China's Buddhist Temples Enjoy Religious Revival." *The Denver Post*. November 7, 1980, p. 7BB.

Ching, Frank. "China Experiences Religious Revival." *The Wall Street Journal*, January 6, 1981, p. 35.

"Eased Restrictions Boost China's Religious Revival." *The Denver Post*. July 4, 1980, p. 4BB.

18

Marxism and Religion: The Case of Islam

WILLIAM R. DARROW

Conventional wisdom, with no slight assist from interested parties across the political spectrum, holds to the utter incompatibility of Marxism and Islam. The issues involved in the encounter of these two, at both the theoretical and practical level, are considerably more complicated. This chapter will explore the positions of Marxism and Islam on five theoretical issues as a way of comparing features of the two. These issues are: nationalism, social justice, ownership, class, and the state. Following this theoretical treatment, attention will be given to the roles of Marxism and Islam in the formulation of socialist ideology in the 1950s and 1960s and more recently in the formulations of radical Islamic thinkers. We will then conclude with a brief consideration of the actual encounter of Marxist parties or regimes with Islam in several countries.

INITIAL CAVEATS

First, three caveats are in order. It is in many ways misleading to speak of "Islam." To do so suggests a coherent entity or system that exists somewhere independently of historical and cultural contexts. The Islamic world stretching from Morocco to Indonesia, from the Soviet Union to central Africa, confronts us with a wide variety of political and cultural differences. To attempt to read off from this variety a set of fixed and unchanging characteristics of Islam leads to banality or worse. Focus on the content of Islamic thought may make possible the formulation of certain general features of Islams, but such formulations need filling out in specific contexts if they are to tell us anything. Doing so confronts us once again with the variety of Islams at different times and places. Neither at the cultural nor at the intellectual level is Islam a fixed entity or system. The following discussion on Islam's position must thus be recognized as necessarily incomplete because there is no fixed system that can serve as a point of comparison.

Having issued this caveat, we should recognize that it is in terms of Islam and/or in Islamic terms that political and social issues are addressed by most inhabitants of the contemporary Islamic world. Islam is a major component of the framework in which these issues are discussed. This is because Islam has always addressed all aspects of a believer's life, not just those narrowly defined as religious. In short, Islam is naturally relevant when political and social issues are being discussed. This is not to say that there has not been a sustained critique of Islam and the role of religion in the Islamic world. But such a critique remains peripheral. What is striking is that political debate takes place in Islamic terms, and almost the full range of the political spectrum enunciates its positions in Islamic terms. This means that we in fact have a number of different Islams represented—that of the rulers, that of the opposition, that of the religious establishment, that of the intelligentsia—all competing to give an Islamic coloration to their positions and to define thereby what Islam is. Throughout the Islamic world and in each Muslim country we thus confront a variety of Islamic positions which claim to speak authoritatively about what Islam is.[1]

Our second caveat shares something with the first. If there is no one Islamic system, likewise there is no one Marxist system. Rather, there are a number of aspects of Marxist thought. Muslim thinkers who take Marx and Marxism seriously emphasize different aspects. First, there is Marx the atheistic humanist and critic of religion who usually stands in the Muslim world as a whipping boy for his position dismissing religion. Second, there is Marx the historical materialist whose analysis of the nature of bourgeois capitalism provides a model of specific historicist analysis that has not been thoroughly pursued in the study of the economic history and structure of the Middle East. Marx himself left the student of non-capitalist society comparatively few tools to analyze the traditional economic structures of the Middle East except for his problematic notion of the Asiatic Mode of Production.[2] More fruitful has been the Marxist-Leninist analysis of the capitalist basis of colonialism and imperialism that has become common coin for thinkers in the Third World. Finally, there is the Marxist tradition of revolutionary action. On the ideological level in the Third World, this is closely tied to the Marxist-Leninist diagnosis of imperialism. On the organizational level, it means that the Marxist tradition provides models of revolutionary organization and strategy.

In addition to the potentially separable aspects of the Marxist tradition on the theoretical level, we also need to recognize the variety of organizational structures that have flowed from Marx's thought and to ask what actual form of Marxism has been encountered. Within the Muslim world the histories of individual communist parties have been very different. Communist movements have not been major forces in Islamic countries, with the possible exception of Indonesia and to a lesser extent Iran, Turkey, Syria, and the Sudan.[3] Such organizations have often had a large portion of minority membership in individual countries, thus weakening their appeal to Muslim majorities. In addition, connections with external and international movements have weakened the effectiveness of communist parties in the area, tied as they often were to global strategies of class struggle or national fronts. The parties of North Africa traditionally had close ties to the communist movement in France and a number of French members. The communist movement of Egypt has generally been relatively independent of Soviet control, whereas that of Syria-Lebanon has been more closely tied to the USSR.[4]

Of equal importance is the recognition of what Marxist tradition or Marxist-inspired tradition is encountered by individual Muslims who study abroad. Those who have studied in Western Europe, especially in France, have encountered a Marxism filtered through the existential Marxists, especially Sartre and such marginal Marxists as Frantz Fanon. The work of the critical theorists, especially Herbert Marcuse, is more likely to be encountered by those studying in West Germany and, more recently, the United States. Both existential Marxism and critical theory are forms of what Perry Anderson calls Western Marxism.[5] They are characterized by a major interest in philosophical issues and in aspects of social superstructure rather than in the possibility of real revolutionary change motivated perhaps by a deep pessimism that such change is in fact impossible. Those who study in Eastern Europe encounter "orthodox" Marxism, which is highly dogmatic if less philosophical and more oriented toward revolutionary action.

Our final caveat involves the recognition that the encounter of Islam and Marxism takes place within a political context and is in fact fundamentally political. Marxism is not simply a mode of analysis, a social vision, or a revolutionary strategy; it is also an ideological tradition closely tied to one major set of actors on the geopolitical stage. All discussion of the relation of Marxism and Islam takes place in this political context. It is one where rhetoric is as important as substance, if not more important. Being painted with a "Marxist" label is thus enough to legitimate or discredit a political stance depending on the context. This is illustrated, for example, by the term "Muslim Marxists" which is used to discredit (and sometimes to create) opposition forces. It is also typified by the recent attempt to free the radical Iranian Muslim thinker Ali Shariati from apparent Marxist influences and thus make him acceptable to the more conservative Muslim forces in Iran who wanted to claim his legacy. This chapter attempts to look beyond these very real rhetorical issues to the question of the role of Marxist thought in the recent history of ideological developments in the Muslim world and to the emergence of an Islamic left. We begin with a survey of the five issues which will enable us to pursue these questions: nationalism, social justice, class, ownership, and the state.

NATIONALISM

The idea of nationalism arguably has been the single most potent political idea of this century. The power of the nationalist call in the Islamic world, nuanced and particularized to be sure, underscores this thesis. In the name of Turkish nationalism, Turks renounced the Islamic Ottoman idea and ended the caliphate. The goal of national liberation energized independence movements from Morocco to Indonesia. Persian nationalist aspirations became the ideological underpinnings of the Shah's rule. Arab nationalism, which endeavored to unify all Arabs regardless of country, while in the end an unfulfilled dream, nevertheless inspired a whole generation after World War II to elaborate their identities accenting their Arabness rather than focusing on their more narrow national or religious identities.[6]

Both Islam and Marxism are by definition supranational. Islam posits the unity of the community of Muslims as the most salient bond that gives individual identity and community cohesion. Marxism posits the identity of interest of a particular segment of all advanced societies that should transcend all other interests. Thus, both Islam and Marxism share a problem with nationalism.

Marx himself was ambivalent concerning nationalism, tending to dismiss it as primarily a bourgeois ideology of only temporary significance for the proletariat. The collapse of the Second International in the face of the outbreak of World War I showed the result of that misperception. Conservative Muslim thinkers denounced nationalism as being opposed to Islam and as a foreign ideology that had no place in the Islamic world.[7] Nationalism, they felt, divided the world of Islam that should be united and allowed considerations of power and regional self-interest to destroy the principles under which Muslims should live.

Nevertheless, this very real problem at the theoretical level has not prevented the fusion of Islam or Marxism with specific nationalisms. Stalin's policy of "socialism in one country" enabled the Communist Party to tap the very real nationalist sentiments of the Russian people in order to legitimate the Soviet state. Movements of national independence have enlisted the religious sentiments of the people. For example, al-Bazzaz affirmed the reconcilability of Arab nationalist and Islamic aspirations.[8] Perhaps most striking was the creation of Pakistan in 1947 in which Islam became the basis of national identity. The subsequent history of that country has shown the limits and problems of such a national identity, but it is worthwhile noting that it is still as an Islamic state that the current government of Pakistan seeks to legitimate itself.

History thus shows that what appears theoretically irreconcilable can be reconciled. But we should not just speak of a reconciliation, but of a transformation typical of nationalism in Third World countries in which nationalism is radicalized in a very interesting way.[9] Perhaps the most interesting case is that of Muslim national communism. The period immediately following the Russian Revolution saw the emergence of a number of progressive or radical groups in the different areas of Russian Central Asia. These groups welcomed the revolution and hoped that it would provide the opportunity for winning liberation for the Muslim peoples of Central Asia. The most famous figure in this movement was Said Sultan Galiev, a Tatar from the middle Volga region and a communist theoretician and leader. Galiev attempted in his theory to fuse the nationalist aspirations of his and other peoples of the area, their sense of Islamic identity and communism. Galiev's starting point was in his recognition that the East stood in a fundamentally different relation toward the capitalist West than did the proletariat class in the West. The East as a whole was the victim of the capitalist West. All the East was the proletariat. As such, the East could not necessarily be confident of an amelioration of its situation in the event of a proletarian revolution in the West. The Western proletariat shared many of the elements of colonialist ideology, and an overthrow of the capitalist system did not promise an end to colonialism.

This bifurcation of East and West had one additional implication. As international proletarian revolution became less likely in the West after the end of World War I, it was in the East that revolution that would bring about the end of the capitalist system could be achieved. But revolution in the East was to be achieved differently from revolution in the West. First, revolutionary movements had to respect peculiar national cultures as a whole rather than deny them. This also meant sympathy for larger nationalist movements, above all pan-Turkism, which united particular national cultures. Second, revolutionary movements had to adopt a flexible attitude toward Islam rather than doctrinaire atheism. Galiev was an atheist, but he respected Islam as a young and dynamic religion with a good deal of progressive social principles embodied in its teachings. He held that blanket attempts to destroy Islam would not succeed, especially given the history of earlier Christian missionaries' attacks on Islam. Rather, he suggested an alliance with the progressive elements in the Muslim clergy and among the laity to break the hold of the conservative and reactionary elements in the community. Finally, following on Galiev's analysis of the position and potential of the colonized East, Galiev envisioned a Colonized International that would be the true spearhead of international revolution.

Behind Galiev's formulations one can perhaps see an ideologist of national liberation for his and neighboring peoples in Russian Central Asia. It was certainly for this reason that these movements were ruthlessly suppressed by the Soviets. For our purposes, what is significant is the unique and powerful theoretical synthesis of Marxism, nationalism, and Islam that Galiev achieved. This was achieved by the creative transformation of Marxism to account for a fundamentally different political and social reality experienced by the Muslim peoples of Central Asia. His program did have international significance, sometimes direct, sometimes indirect, long after his movement had been suppressed, and it prefigures a number of trends that became dominant only much later.[10]

SOCIAL JUSTICE

Both Marxism and Islam share a vision of the establishment of a social order in which justice will reign and the alienation of individuals both from themselves and from each other will be overcome. Marxism is inherently optimistic as to the possibility of achieving this goal and clear on the mechanism by which it will be achieved. The abolition of the division of labor and of private property will bring with it the end of human self-alienation and the restoration of the human species-nature. The antagonism of humans toward nature and toward each other is alien to human-nature. A deep humanist confidence in the inherently good nature of human beings breathes throughout Marxist thought. Specific details of the nature of a communist society are lacking in Marx except to say, quite consistently with his dialectical method, that they will be a negation of all those negative characteristics of capitalist society.

The notion of justice is central to understanding the Islamic social vision. The perfected Islamic society is characterized above all by justice. Justice is now manifested in some individuals; in the perfected Islamic society it will be evident in all individuals and in all affairs. Islam, unlike Marxism, does not predicate an inherent goodness to humanity, but it does affirm the inherent potential of human beings to act justly. In addition, the Islamic tradition affirms that such a society did in fact exist once on earth. During the life of the Prophet and his earliest followers such a community was actualized. Thus, Islam is able to describe with some specificity what an Islamic society should look like even if it cannot on the basis of that description suggest how it might be achieved again on earth.

There is thus an apparent ideological complementarity between Islam and Marxism. Marxism provides the guarantee of the coming utopia and a description of the historical mechanism that will bring it about. Islam shares the millenniarian vision and provides content to the description of that utopia. In addition, it can point to an historical example of when such a utopia was achieved. Because we do not know what a perfected communist society will look like, it is difficult to know if the actual features of an ideal communist and Islamic society might differ. In much Islamic literature actual communist society with its emphasis on material rather than spiritual needs, its denial of individual initiative, and its totalitarianism is denounced.[11] But this overlooks the fact that actual communist societies should not be taken as normative expressions of the communist vision. The promise of an end to all forms of alienation and the integration of all aspects of human life, the disappearance of oppression and the universality of justice seem to be a vision shared by both traditions.

There are two areas of potential divergence at the theoretical level. Kenneth Cragg has argued that both Islam and Marxism share a certain myopia when it comes to recognizing the sources of evil in human beings.[12] We have recognized Marx's confidence in human perfectibility arising out of a deep humanism. Does Islam share this confidence? The answer seems to be "yes and no". In the perfected human society, human beings will be perfected. But Islam has always predicated a hierarchy of human perfection. Virtue can be cultivated with different degrees of perfection. In addition, the historical record shows that even perfected communities seem to fail. The age of the early community ended and did so in civil war. This is not to import a doctrine of original sin into Islam, but only to recognize the strong streak of realism in Islam concerning human perfectibility and the need for continual vigilance once a perfected Islamic society is established.

The second question is related to the first. It has to do with the motivation for revolution. Why make revolution? Marxist theory proclaims the inevitability of revolution, though it is not clear whether it is class struggle or a change in the mode of production that guarantees its success. Islam shares no such confidence in the success of revolution, and the historical record clearly seems to suggest that revolutions tend to go wrong. Nevertheless, Islam was born of a revolution, the establishment of the Prophet's community, and it can be argued that much of the history of Islam is the history of a continuing social revolution. In short, revolt and revolution in the name of Islam has a long history, but the promise of success of a revolution does not lie in a scientific theory, but in a vision of justice ordained by divine sanction. Thus, although there is a potential complementarity between Islam and Marxism, the one has no intrinsic need for the other. Each is self-sufficient.

CLASS

With the notion of class we approach the central concept of Marxist sociological analysis. For Marx the emergence of a class is a function of a mode of production and the notion of class predicates the dialectics of a social system. Classes arise as a result of the emergence of modes of production, with the inevitable emergence of different groups in unequal relations to a particular mode of production. The result of this difference is conflict and the inevitable dialectical transformation of a social system. The actual definition of a class in Marx's thought in terms of objective (i.e., modes of production) or subjective (i.e., class-consciousness) criteria is vague. Equally problematic is Marx's recognition of important differences between the proletariat, peasants, petite bourgeoisie, bourgeoisie, land-owners, and intelligentsia that can only partly be related to specific modes of production. This gives Marx's analysis both complexity and incompleteness. What remains central, however, is the concept of class struggle which is endemic to capitalism and finally culminates in the end of capitalism, the dictatorship of the proletariat, and the eventual abolition of all classes. There is thus in Marx a fundamental dialectical contradiction that holds that class struggle is inevitable but can be abolished.

For a variety of reasons, class analysis has remained relatively peripheral and at other points repugnant to Muslim thinkers. As indicated, part of the reason lies in the real ambiguities in the Marxist concept of class in classical capitalism. Is class to be defined simply by an objective criterion, that is, the mode of production, or are these subjective features in terms of ideology that are relevant? These difficulties are exacerbated when one moves out of the classical capitalist system and confronts the economic system of Islamic countries. Brian Turner has suggested that in the pre-colonialist era there existed at least three separate modes of production (feudal, nomadic, and prebendal), thus generating six different classes.[13] In the post-colonial period of capitalist dependency, characterized by labor-intensive agricultural exports, exploitation of raw materials, retarded industrial development, and an expanding petite bourgeoisie dependent on the public sector, an articulated internal class structure is not easily generated. If a more subjective ideological definition of class is assumed, some theorists have considered the ruling elite to be an identifiable class. But such an analysis, while revolutionary in its intent, ceases to be Marxist insofar as the economic base of the group is neglected.[14] From a Marxist perspective, what one confronts in the ruling elite is one portion of the petite bourgeoisie, which shares little ideologically with the remainder of the petite bourgeoisie that is powerless and usually the main source for various opposition trends toward a ruling elite.

More fundamentally, the denial of class and class struggle as a basic category is echoed throughout much Islamic thought. The Islamic emphasis on the independence and responsibility of the individual believer and the unity of the Islamic community as a whole does much to mitigate against the formation of intermediate structures in that community such as class. Here we confront a problem not unlike that of nationalism which in theory seemed to be opposed to Islam. We are thus forewarned against any absolute statements making class consciousness and analysis inconceivable in Islam. Nevertheless, class consciousness and the notion of class struggle are generally denied as fundamental or universal and are specifically inappropriate in a perfected Islamic society.[15] Thus, it would appear that certain features of Islamic thought combine with certain features of the current economic system of Muslim countries to discourage seeing the internal economy in class terms.

OWNERSHIP

It is a mark of the influence of Marxism in the Muslim world that, although class analysis has generally been neglected, discussion of the nature of ownership has become a main feature in the discussion of the foundations of a just Islamic economic order. However, in this discussion some of the features that most sharply distinguish Islam and Marxism come to the fore. The nature of ownership in Marxism is always treated in connection with the notion of modes of production. Particular types of ownership such as communal ownership or private property emerge in particular modes of production. Laws defining and restricting ownership are thus secondary to the production system and in fact merit comparatively little attention in Marxist analysis.

The starting point for the Islamic discussion is theological. God is the creator and absolute owner of the world. Human beings have the world in trust from God and are accountable to Him. Negatively, this means that no human being ever has absolute ownership of his or her possessions. Positively, this means that all human beings are equal because they stand together in the same place with respect to the absolute owner of the world. In addition, God has commanded human beings to work and to use and enjoy the resources of the world. Asceticism is frowned upon, and effort and activity are praised. In the world different individuals, despite their basic equality, will have different levels of success. Thus, God proclaims limits on what human beings can do with the wealth they create and insists that each member of the Islamic community has a responsibility for all the others.

There are both legal-moral limits and structural limits on personal wealth. The legal-moral limits are given in the Islamic legal system. Conspicuous consumption and indulgence in luxury are condemned, and the example of the simple life of Muhammad and the early community is held up as the ideal. Religious charity and care for the needy are required by the law. Strict rules for inheritance prevent an individual from disposing of his wealth in an arbitrary manner against the interests of the family. These legal-moral limits testify to the overarching concern for justice and the social health of the community as a whole and make a clear blueprint of the good society for Muslim thinkers.

More controversial are the structural limits required by an Islamic system. Here there is less unanimity. Some radical thinkers have gone so far as to deny the right to private property at all in Islam. Other thinkers hold that a person has the right to own what is the actual product of his or her labor, a position that is rather close to Marx's labor theory of value. More conservative thinkers reject these positions, but all agree that there are some necessary limitations to the right of private property. A tradition from Muhammad holds that no one can own water, fire, grass, and salt, the basic necessities of life. The categories of communal ownership and state ownership are recognized and for some thinkers provide the basis for the nationalization of means of production. In the mainstream of economic thought communal and state ownership are held to have specific reference to all natural resources, often including land. It is the ownership of these natural resources that leads most easily to some individuals exploiting others. So here the community as a whole must maintain common ownership either directly or through the means of the state.[16]

A discussion of ownership in Islam thus is the area where the nature of an Islamic system is spelled out. The writings of individual Muslims range widely from outright denial of the right to private property to affirmation of it, from the call for the communal ownership of all means of production to state control of natural resources. The plurality of prescriptions is important as a hallmark of the range of views in the Islamic world, but equally important is the common starting point in recognizing God's absolute ownership of the world that informs the full range of the discussion.

STATE

As noted in the previous section, the state has an important role to play in the economic life of the Islamic community, both in ensuring that the Islamic legal-moral rules are enforced and in playing its assigned role as owner of some portion of the community's wealth, although there is disagreement as to what the range of this might be. This continuing role for the state stands in contrast both with Marx's view of the withering away of the state and with his view of the dictatorship of the proletariat which came to be represented in the centralized communist state. For Marx the state, like religion, was an epiphenomenon. In the capitalist system they had important functions to play. The state maintains order and legitimizes the power of the bourgeoisie. Religion does the same and in addition provides comfort for the victims of the system. In a true communist state they would disappear when there was no longer a need for their functions.

Islam does not assume such a functional analysis. Rather, the state has a permanent role to play. In the perfected Islamic society there will continue to be a state. Clearly, a difficulty arises when it becomes necessary to decide whether a particular state is legitimately an Islamic one. When should a state be changed? What will be the characteristics of an Islamic state?[17] Both classical and contemporary Islamic political philosophy address this question in detail. But this problem only underlines the need for an Islamic state and provides some understanding as to why the desire for an Islamic state is pressed with such vigor.

Our comparison of Islam and Marxism has shown that the two have much in common: a strong sense of social justice, a utopian vision, and a nationalist urge somewhat in contradiction to their universalism. In addition, we have seen that Islam and Marxism might complement one another in certain areas. Marxism can provide the conceptual analysis to energize Islamic societies in the actualization of their vision. A Marxist analysis of the structure of Islamic society can nuance the particularized and specific class analysis of Marxism and encourage theoretical advances in the analysis of other social systems. But we have also seen those areas of fundamental disagreement centering around the Islamic claim for certain universal and continuing legal-moral and state forms that are necessary to attain and embody their vision. In the end in this schematic presentation we confront two ideological systems that can stand independent of one another. This picture must now be fleshed out by the contextualization of their encounter in recent intellectual and political history.

FOUR DECADES OF ISLAMIC THOUGHT

Our discussion until now has been deliberately thematic and non-historical. It is now appropriate to sketch briefly the outlines of the history of political and social thought in the Muslim world since 1945. In this brief compass such an outline must be highly generalized inasmuch as it covers such a wide area. Nevertheless, some general characteristics of thought in the last four decades can be seen. The period itself can be divided approximately into decades beginning in 1945.

The first period runs from 1945 until 1956. This period saw the dominance of movements for national independence throughout the Islamic world. As we have seen, these movements often incorporated a successful appeal to Islam as a major base of their ideologies, although it was primarily in the name of the secular ideal of national self-determination that these movements were undertaken. During this period Pakistan, Indonesia, Syria, Iraq, and the Sudan gained independence. A successful nationalist revolution was carried out in Egypt, and an unsuccessful one was carried out in Iran. The model of Western development, and to a lesser extent Western liberalism, remained potent during this time period, though the continuation of colonial and neo-colonialist actions by the West laid the groundwork for the rejection of these values in the next decade.[18] If liberal values, which were a leftover of the pre-war period, came to be shaken during this time, more actively suppressed were the radical fundamentalist movements, above all the Muslim Brotherhood.[19]

The period running from approximately 1956 to 1967 is characterized by the dominance of radical regimes claiming a socialist ideology. These regimes were controlled by ruling elites that had emerged dominant as a result of struggles for national independence. It has been quite cogently argued that such radicalized ideologies were socialist in name only and were really only disguised versions of centralized state capitalism.[20] For our purposes what is important is that the ruling elites in Egypt, Syria, Iraq, Algeria, Sudan, and Indonesia radicalized political discourse in a number of Muslim countries during this period. Even conservative regimes such as that of Iran made gestures toward a reformist agenda.

Two features of this discussion are of special interest. They are, first, the attempt to differentiate the socialist agenda from communism and, second, to identify the goals of socialism and Islam. For example, Nasser's spokesman Muhammad Heikal proposed seven differences between Arab socialism and communism in 1961.[21] (1) Communism, argued Heikal, calls for the elimination of class conflict through the revolutionary triumph of a single class, whereas Arab socialism calls for the elimination of class conflict through the establishment of the framework of national unity within which class barriers will eventually fall. (2) Private property is not itself inherently exploitative according to Arab socialism, though those who do exploit should be dispossessed. (3) Those whose property is expropriated should receive compensation in what is conceived as a just and non-violent process. (4) Arab socialism treats the individual as the central focus of the process of development. The dreams, humanity, and liberty of the individual must never be suppressed. (5) The present generation cannot be called upon to sacrifice everything for the future. (6) Arab socialism is not doctrinally tied to the orthodox communist tradition. It remains faithful to the nation and its heritage and people. (7) Arab socialism rejects the existence of a one-party dictatorship. This description is typical of the attempt to differentiate socialism and communism made by the radical regimes.

The attempt to identify socialism and Islam generated a rich literature during this time period which built on an earlier literature that attempted a firm differentiation of Islam and communism.[22] The result of this earlier discussion was a recognition that there were certain superficial resemblances between Islam and

Marxism and/or socialism, but as a whole these systems stood opposed to one another. Now given the change in political discourse, Islam could be seen as a kind of socialist system. The most significant spokesman for this point of view was Mustafa as-Sibā'ī whose book *The Socialism of Islam* appeared in 1958. as-Sibā'ī was the leader of the Syrian branch of the Muslim Brotherhood. Given the enmity between the Egyptian Muslim Brothers and Nasser, it is somewhat ironic that his work became one of the major theoretical underpinnings of the Arab socialism of Nasser's regime. Nevertheless, his work won approval from both the Nasser regime and some religious scholars.

The primary argument for Islam as socialism rests on the notion of mutual social responsibility central to Islam. The community of Islam is dependent on the notion of the mutual responsibility of each of its members for the other. It involves not only ensuring that each member has the material means necessary for life, but also that the rights of life, freedom, education, dignity, and property are guaranteed. There are limits on the final right which in some cases would allow for the nationalization of property. In addition, mutual social responsibility should inform all areas of the community's life, and the laws of Islam should explicitly direct those actions necessary to help the poor, sick, and handicapped as well as those temporarily in need of kindness, hospitality, and aid.[23] There is perhaps little that is new in as-Sibā'ī, but two points are important. First, there is the implicit apologia for socialism denying that it is simply a materialist heresy or that it automatically means the end of private property. Second, there is the process of equating Islam with an outside ideology. This lends legitimacy to the outside ideology from the Muslim point of view and suggests, at least to conservatives, that somehow Islam was in need of this outside ideology to establish its priorities and identity. Conservative critics were quick to point out this implication and denounce the need to use an outside ideology to interpret Islam.

The period from 1967 until 1977 was a decade of profound crisis for the Islamic world. The debacle of the 1967 war with Israel discredited the self-proclaimed socialist ideologies of the defeated Arab powers, above all Egypt. But the crisis can be seen as more widespread. The disorder of the later years of Sukarno's regime had already led to his de facto overthrow in 1965 and the establishment of a more conservative regime. In 1971 Pakistan was split by civil war, and its identity as an Islamic state was fundamentally questioned. There can be no understanding the depths of despair and disgust that dominated political discourse during this decade.

In this decade several contradictory streams emerged which nevertheless combined to set the range of discourse. One is the significant radicalization of both discourse and action. The promise of socialism was not discredited; rather, only the cynical regimes that proclaimed it while aggrandizing their powers and positions were denounced. The articulation of the radical stance of the Palestinian Liberation Organization (PLO) served as a major stimulus to the general radicalization of discourse throughout the Muslim world.[24] Fundamental and radical critiques of the Arab state structure and Arab culture as a whole were presented. One of the most interesting is that of the American-educated Syrian thinker Sadiq al-Azm who offered a scathing critique of the causes of the defeat of 1967 in several works. The fault, he maintained, lay in the Arab state system which was the predominant political reality. The claims of the progressive Arab states to socialism and revolution had been shown to be empty and were thus no different from the conservative and reactionary regimes. Even the Palestinian movement after its 1970 defeat in Jordan shared the same fatal flaws of the state system. The genesis of these failures was Arab culture itself, including the religious element, Islam. Despite claims to the contrary, Islam in fact stands opposed to science, is informed by outmoded beliefs, looks backward, and hinders needed revolutionary change. While not denying the authenticity of religious feelings, his attack on the religious situation was harsh, direct, and unprecedented. It met with loud protest and never found a major following, but it stands as evidence of the radicalization of political discourse in the decade which continues until now in the more radical quarters of contemporary political thought.[25]

Along with the phenomenon of increased radicalization is that of increased religiosity. Here it is especially important to distinguish between the religion of the rulers and that of the opposition because both have contributed to the increased religiosity, but usually with diametrically opposed intentions. Internationally, the decline of the prestige of the more radical Arab states meant the increasing power of the more conservative states, above all Saudi Arabia which patronized a very conservative form of Islam both within its borders and internationally. In addition, more radical rulers found themselves turning deliberately to the religious sphere for new bases of legitimacy. The most famous case here is, of course, Nasser's post-defeat call for a return to Islam. This increasing patronage of Islam by the rulers then seemed to pay off in the 1973 war with Israel and in the leverage won by the Organization of Petroleum Exporting Countries (OPEC) on the international stage. The success in co-opting the religious was not universal as Bhutto learned in Pakistan, but the phenomenon of increased religiosity of the rulers seemed a general one.

In addition to the rulers' patronage of religiosity, the period saw the re-emergence of the radical fundamentalism that had been discredited and sometimes suppressed during the previous decade. The attractiveness of the message of Islam as the "Third Way" between the two foreign ideologies of capitalism and communism and the vision of the establishment of a just Islamic economic and political order found a new audience in the traditional petite bourgeoisie that had always supported it. This group was now expanded to include the new strata of an educated younger generation who swelled the state bureaucracy and the increasingly large population of displaced rural people that had moved to urban areas in search of employment. It is important to distinguish this source of increased religiosity from that of the rulers, although in practice some rulers such as Qaddafi have successfully tapped this wellspring of religiosity.[26]

The work of Muhammad Jalal Kishk, an Egyptian writer, is typical of the radical fundamentalist critique of contemporary Muslim rulers. This critique shares with the secularist radical critique its diagnosis that there is something seriously wrong with Muslim society. The lack of a coherent ideology and its willy-nilly adoption of Western ideologies that are inappropriate to the Muslim scene mark the beginning of his diagnosis. For him the fundamental fact is the clash of civilizations, East and West. The Muslim East should not turn to the West, but rather into itself to find its authentic ideology. That ideology is Islam. To turn toward either secular nationalism or toward Marxism is to turn toward ideologies imbued with Western values which debilitate the Muslim world.[27]

Kishk's attack on Marxism, contained in several books and tracts, continues familiar themes. But there are several points that are of relevance. Marxism is now being rejected primarily because it is a Western import. Implicit in this attack is an attack on the socialism of the radical Arab regimes in the period before 1967, but of equal importance is recognition that the only sources for generating an authentic society lie within the society itself, specifically in its Islam. Those who turn to Marxism as a basis for criticism put their faith in an exported ideology. That act of putting faith in an exported ideology also gives the lie to a Marxist critique of Muslim religion and culture. How can Marxists criticize religious faith when they must recognize that they themselves have a religious faith? The power of Kishk's attack is symptomatic of the radicalization of political discourse and the increasing appeal of the formulation of an ideology secured firmly in traditional roots typical of this period. It should be clear that it is a position based on a critique of the current scene that shares much with a Marxist critique in approach, even if its diagnosis and prescription would dismiss the usefulness of a Western ideology like Marxism.

The current decade continues the phenomenon of expanded religiosity. The resurgence of Islam is its main hallmark. The success of the Islamic revolution in Iran (1978–1979) lent weight to the radical fundamentalist cause throughout the Islamic world. The subsequent history of the revolution has cooled somewhat the excitement it originally generated, but it has not discredited the vision of the establishment of the Third Way of Islam through revolutionary activity. In regard to the relation of Islam and Marxism in this period, several points are relevant. First, Marxist analysis of imperialism and the nature of the state system has contributed to the articulation of the radical Muslim position. Second, native Marxists have recognized that the Islamic voice is the voice through which the masses speak and are therefore less doctrinally opposed to addressing themselves in that idiom than previously.[28] Third, Marxism and the communist system remains an unacceptable option, an imported ideology no more appropriate to the Islamic world than capitalism. The resurgence of Islam is multifaceted, containing both conservative and radical positions of various shadings. Those of a more radical position have thus set about formulating an Islamic leftist position, fusing a radical agenda with the wellsprings of radical ideology they find in the Islamic tradition.

One interesting figure in the task of formulating an Islamic leftist ideology is

Hassan Hanafi, an Egyptian Islamicist. Hanafi's starting point is that all other ideological alternatives, including Western liberalism, state socialism, classical Marxism, and religious conservatism, have failed. It is now time to formulate and apply an ideology that is authentically Islamic and authentically radical. Both must be there to counterbalance and control each other. Without Islam a radical ideology descends into a Nasserism, dictatorship and a cult of personality. Moreover, without Islam a radical ideology has no appeal to the masses. But without radicalism Islam becomes a retarding and reactionary force.

Hanafi's articulation of a radical theology begins with the recognition that all theology is specific arising out of a particular time and place. It serves the need of particular groups at particular times. The need now is for a theology of revolution. The Islamic theology that he proposes is one that would stress the immanence of God, for stress on God's transcendence leads to the justification of hierarchy and oppression. God has created everything. There is no division in His creation, no hierarchy, no division of spirit and matter. All is God's creation, and the only relevant dichotomy is between those who look forward in history to a better future and those who look backwards. The theology he envisions is one that stresses praxis and is based on a reading of the Qur'an that arises out of reality rather than tradition. There is no room for cult or a sacerdotal class, and Hanafi, like Shari'ati whom we will discuss in a moment, takes Protestantism as his model for a radical Islam. Islam is above all a theology of negation that begins with a NO, a proclamation that there is no god, except God. This model of negation is Islam's starting point, and its message is that of struggle and violence directed against the lack of love and justice in the world. While not predicting the immediate triumph of the Islamic left he envisions, eventually it will be triumphant and enduring.[29]

One other contemporary thinker, 'Ali Shari'ati, is especially significant for our concerns, for his thought represents one of the most interesting and creative encounters with Marxism in the Islamic world. Shari'ati (d. 1977) came from a liberal religious family in eastern Iran. He was trained in France as a sociologist and was a leading ideologue of the Iranian revolution. Dialectic plays a central role in his views of history and society. History unfolds through contradictions, the basis of which is the contadiction of unicity and plurality. This contradiction is manifested in religion in the contradiction of monotheism and polytheism. Socially, it is manifested in the contradiction between oppressor and oppressed. He has an extraordinarily interesting example of this in Cain's murder of Abel, the agriculturalist oppressor destroying the nomadic oppressed. But Shari'ati is also at pains to emphasize that the perception of contradiction, of a dialectic, is not a perception of the fundamental principle of reality, only of appearance in the world. The fundamental principle of reality is unicity, the union of God, nature and man. In this unicity there is no contradiction. The problem is that in the world in which we live unicity is locked in battle with plurality.

Shari'ati's rejection of absolute dialectics has been read as a rejection of Marxism. The world as it is is not the final world. There is a principle underneath it, an essence in which contradiction is impossible. But this is not in fact so different from Marx's vision of a communist society in which history is seen as ended. Shari'ati has in addition a notion of the force of history guaranteeing forward movement that is close to Marx and an epistemology that predicates all knowledge as the result of human activity in the world. Humans are free and autonomous actors who can bring about revolution and change.

Shari'ati stands explicitly in opposition to Marxism in three related areas: in his rejection of simple materialism, in his affirmation of the special character of Shiite Islam, and in his emphasis on the role of the enlightened intelligentsia in making revolution. Marxism, at least in its vulgar form imported from the West, teaches an historical materialism that on the face of it is inconsistent. A consistent materialism must lead to a thorough-going determinism which denies the possibility of human freedom. But Marx does not affirm human freedom and holds that human action is constitutive of change. Humans act responsibly according to values for which materialism cannot account. Therefore, Marxist and other Western schools that predicate materialism are inconsistent. Shari'ati sees his own thought as transcending materialism, as well as simple idealism, and thus being able to give an account of the transcendent sources of value and meaning that are actually encountered in history and are the basis upon which human beings act. But his rejection of materialism should not be read as a full rejection of Marx any more than his embracing of dialectics makes him a Marxist. Such arguments are at the level of polemic rather than constructive thought.[30]

For Shari'ati it is in the specific tradition of Shiism that the clearest expression of historical dialectic and the mode of overcoming it can be found. The community founded by Muhammad was dynamically oriented to the achieving of justice. It was based on the common ownership of property and was classless. Yet the dialectic of history meant the end of that community and the reemergence of oppression, injustice, and the ossification of the religious tradition at the hands of the clergy. But the vision was not lost, and the method for recovering the earlier community through the leadership of the family of the Prophet has always remained a dynamic possibility embodied in the specific actions available to the Shiite, actively awaiting the return of the rightful ruler and struggling to achieve it. This powerful recasting of the basic structure of Shiism was a profoundly important impetus to revolutionary action in Iran, giving deep and new meaning to the young Shiites. Given its strong coloration, it has not been especially exportable to Sunni countries, which comprise the vast majority of Muslims.

According to Shiite doctrine, the rightful rule of the community is vested in a descendant of the Prophet and in his name revolution is to be made. However, the form of Shiism dominant in Iran holds that, while there is a living leader, he is in hiding in the spiritual world and is thus absent from our world. In his absence who is to lead the community? For Shari'ati the masses should be led by the enlightened intelligentsia that understands the dialectic of history. The intelligentsia in fact arises from the masses and is legitimated by them. Shari'ati was suspicious about whether the established clergy could play this role given their history of collaboration with tyrants and their highly scholastic turn of mind. His attitude toward the clergy has been very problematic for the clergy-dominated state that has emerged in post-revolutionary Iran. It is fair to say that Shari'ati did not exclude the notion of a revolutionary clergy, but for our purposes we can lay this issue aside and stress instead that it is a revolutionary intelligentsia of whatever composition that is the agency of revolution.

It can be argued that Shari'ati remains within a Marxist framework, despite these three areas of conscious opposition to Marxism. The crass materialist position he attacks can also be attacked by Marxists. The specificity of his treatment of Shiism can be seen as continuous with Marxist historical specificity. The discussion of the role of the revolutionary elite intelligentsia is also quite close to Marxism. But it is not productive to argue whether they are or are not Marxist positions. What is of more importance is recognizing in Shari'ati a multifaceted and creative encounter with Marxism that enabled him to enunciate a powerful and productive radical Islamic position. The inevitable descending into vulgarization and competition for his legacy should not blind us to a recognition of its power. The lessons we can draw from its self-conscious distancing from Marx and its later vulgarization are also important.

ISLAM AND THE COMMUNIST WORLD

Marxism is the foundation of both a political movement with articulated institutions and an international bloc of diversified nations. We have recognized the importance of contact with Marxist parties or governments at several points in this chapter. In conclusion, it will be useful to make a brief conspectus of recent encounters between Islam and the communist world. In doing so it will be noted that it is the encounter between the Islamic establishment, the religious specialists, and communist governments that we attend to.

Muslims comprise a significant portion of the population of several communist nations. In these countries, Islam has been the object of an anti-religious policy of varying degrees of severity and of state control of the religious establishment. In the most extreme case, in Albania, the only nation in the communist bloc with a nominal majority Muslim population, the practice of religion has been firmly outlawed. Less extreme has been the policy pursued by the Soviet Union and the People's Republic of China, both of which follow a policy dictated in part by international considerations of relations with Muslim countries.

The Muslim population of Soviet Central Asia is non-Slavic, composed of Turks, Iranians, and Ibero-Caucasian peoples. Thus, Soviet relations with Islam mean relations with some of its ethnic minorities in an area that has only been controlled by Russia since the nineteenth century. Soviet policy in the region has been one of radical secularization and control of the surviving religious establishment. This policy has succeeded in achieving a drastic decline in the number of mosques, religious schools, and clerics in the area. Yet religious life, defined by adherence to religious practices in marriage and burial, remains strong even in those areas that were most subject to Soviet policy. The reason for this lies in the survival of some lay forms of religious organizations and in the expanding power of semi-clandestine Sufi mystical orders. In addition, the close interconnection between religious and ethnic identity for the individual peoples comes into play, and the phenomenon of the atheistic Muslim proud of his or her ethnic heritage is not unprecedented as we saw already prefigured in Sultan Galiev's movement. Signs of unrest in Soviet Central Asia have appeared, especially in the wake of the use of Central Asian troops in Afghanistan, and it is clear that the stability of this region is of concern to the Soviet government.[31]

The People's Republic of China has followed the Soviet example of dealing with its Muslim populations primarily as national minorities, even though, in contrast to the Soviet Union, the majority of China's Muslims are linguistically Chinese living throughout China. Officially sanctioned bodies supervise the life of the religiously active Muslim population, including the training of religious leaders and coordination of the Chinese delegation for the pilgrimage to Mecca. Independent control of religious resources seems to have been more successfully eradicated in China than in the Soviet Union. Apparently, organized Muslim dissent movements and rebellions took place in the 1950s and more recently during the Cultural Revolution. On the other hand, the Chinese government seems to have been involved in a propaganda campaign to win over those Muslim peoples that straddle the Sino-Soviet border.[32]

Two states in the Muslim world are avowedly Marxist, the People's Democratic Republic of Yemen (PDRY) and Afghanistan, significantly two of the poorest Muslim countries. The PDRY gained independence from Great Britain in 1967. The successful independence movement came to power and has gradually been radicalized, becoming finally the Yemeni Socialist Party which rules the country. The ideology of the party is Marxist-Leninist, although it prefers the designation "scientific socialism" and the government is firmly allied with the Soviet Union. Despite immense material constraints and little external aid, the period since independence has witnessed a true socialist revolution in which traditional landowners and bourgeoisie have been dispossessed and a centrally planned economy established.

The relationship between the government and the religious establishment has had several facets. Islam is the declared state religion, and Muslim rules of inheritance are maintained. The government has been careful to avoid outright anti-religious positions. Some attempts at transforming the position of women have met with religious resistance and have been modified, but the PDRY has gone further than any other state in the region in ensuring the equality of men and women. The government has appealed to the history of the radical egalitarian Muslim sect of the Qarmathians as its precursor and origin of the south Yemenite people. The religious establishment, which played a relatively small role in the independence movement, unlike the case in a number of other Muslim countries, has clearly lost its traditional bases of power in education and the legal system. In 1970 they were dispossessed of the lands they held as religious endowments.

Nevertheless, until now there has been little evidence of a religiously based opposition movement to the PDRY.[33]

The experience of the Marxist government in Afghanistan has been quite different from that in the PDRY. A Marxist government was established in 1978, and Soviet forces invaded in 1979. Islam has become one of the major galvanizing forces for guerrilla opposition to that invasion. Afghanistan is an ethnically and linguistically fragmented country with a predominantly rural population. As a result of these two factors, no united religious institution has ever existed. Although a number of urban religious leaders played a significant power role in the period before the Marxist regime, rural religious figures connected to specific ethnic and linguistic groups were unorganized and autonomous. The power of these rural figures had begun to decline somewhat as the central government began to expand its influence in education and legal administration. Thus, rural religious figures already were playing an oppositional role. Although the Marxist regime encouraged regional autonomy and tried to win over the support of both the urban and rural religious establishments, they did not succeed. They began an active policy of the repression of religious leaders, at least in the urban areas that marked the limits of their effective control. It is significant that the guerrilla movement has not been centrally organized or had a leadership council emerge to direct it effectively. Although the religious idiom of Islam provides powerful motivation, it is not sufficient to overcome the extreme diversity and fragmentation of the opposition that arises out of the extreme diversity and fragmentation of the country. Even in the unlikely event that the guerrilla opposition were to succeed, there is little likelihood that this situation would change.[34]

This brief survey leads to no simple conclusion. Marxist regimes have both coexisted with and had to struggle against Islam. In general, the dispossession and control of the religious establishment is the primary Marxist policy, with the encouragement of secularization often accompanying it. But control of the religious establishment does not mean full control over the religious life of the community, nor does it prevent the religious idiom from becoming an idiom of opposition, especially when ethnic and nationalist aspirations contribute to popular dissatisfaction.

CONCLUSION

To hold either to the utter incompatibility or to the compatibility of Islam and Marxism is to reify and systematize two fluid and multifaceted poles of comparison. At the level of theoretical comparison, there are areas of deep agreement and of profound disagreement. Individual thinkers will make their way between these. The history of recent Islamic political thought has shown this, with perhaps the one constant that Marxism as an atheistic doctrine tied to a particular superpower cannot be embraced without serious modification, if at all. At the present time the phenomenon of Islamic resurgence has encouraged the formulation of an Islamic left position heavily influenced by Marx in both its analysis of the international economic system and in its vision of a dynamic and revolutionary Islam. But an Islamic leftist position rejects Marx along with all other discredited ideologies in the Islamic world, both domestic and imported. The authentic wellsprings for an egalitarian and revolutionary Islam lie in Islam itself correctly understood and interpreted.

NOTES

1. el-Zain, "Beyond Ideology and Theology," pp. 227–254, and Hudson, "Islam and Political Development," in Esposito, ed., *Islam and Development*, pp. 1–24.

2. Turner, *Marx and the End of Orientalism*, pp. 24–38.

3. Mintz, *Mohammed, Marx and Marhaen*, pp. 126–156, 193–226; Zabin, *Communist Movement in Iran*, pp. 246–259; Confino and Shamir, *U.S.S.R. and the Middle East*, pp. 293–436; and Warburg, *Islam, Nationalism and Communism in a Traditional Society*, pp. 93–168.

4. Laqueur, *Communism and Nationalism in the Middle East*, pp. 52–62, 154–172; Batatu, "Some Preliminary Observations on the Beginning of Communism in the Arab East," in Pennar, ed., *Islam and Communism*, pp. 46–69; Halpren, *Politics of Social Change in the Middle East and North Africa*, pp. 156–195; Pennar, "Arabs, Marxism and Moscow," pp. 156–195; Flores, "Early History of Lebanese Communism Reconsidered"; Flores "Arab CPs and the Palestine Problem"; and Rodinson, *Marxism and the Muslim World*, pp. 185–202.

5. Anderson, *Considerations on Western Marxism*, pp. 49–74.

6. Tibi, *Arab Nationalism*, pp. 173–181.

7. Enayat, *Modern Islamic Political Thought*, pp. 111–124.

8. Haim, *Arab Nationalism*, pp. 172–188.

9. Smith, *Nationalism in the Twentieth Century*, pp. 115–149; and Tibi, *Arab Nationalism*, pp. 13–45.

10. Bennigsen and Wimbush, *Muslim National Communism in the Soviet Union*.

11. Qutb, *Social Justice in Islam*; and Abdul Hakim, *Islam and Communism*.

12. Cragg, "Intellectual Impact of Communism upon Contemporary Islam," pp. 127–138.

13. Turner, *Marx and the End of Orientalism*.

14. Abdel-Malek, *Egypt*.

15. Taleghani, *Society and Economics in Islam*.

16. Rodinson, *Islam and Capitalism*; Cummings, et al., "Islam and Modern Economic Change," in Esposito, ed., *Islam and Development*; Siddiqi, "Muslim Economic Thinking," Ahmad, ed., *Studies in Islamic Economics*; Taleghani, *Society and Economics in Islam*; and Katouzian, "Shi'ism and Islamic Economics," in Keddie, ed., *Religion and Politics in Iran*.

17. Bani Sadr, *Fundamentals and Precepts of Islamic Government*, pp. 67–86.

18. Hourani, *Arabic Thought in the Liberal Ages*.

19. Mitchell, *Society of Muslim Brothers*.

20. Abdel-Malek, *Egypt*; and Enayat, "Islam and Socialism in Egypt," pp. 141–172.

21. Karpat, ed., *Political and Social Thought in the Contemporary Middle East*.

22. Siddiqi, *Marxism or Islam*; and Hakim, *Islam and Communism*.

23. Hanna and Gardner, *Arab Socialism*.

24. Kazziha, *Revolutionary Transformation in the Arab World*; and Ismael, *The Arab Left*.

25. Laroui, *The Crisis of the Arab Intellectual*; Ajami, *Arab Predicament*; Donohue and Esposito, *Islam in Transition*, pp. 113–119.

26. Fischer, "Islam and the Revolt of the Petit Bourgeoisie," pp. 101–125; Dessouki, "Islamic Resurgence," in Dessouki, ed., *Islamic Resurgence in the Arab World*, pp. 3–31; and Ibrahim, "Egypt's Islamic Militants," pp. 5–14.

27. Kedourie, "Anti-Marxism in Egypt," in Confino and Shamir, eds., *The U.S.S.R. and the Middle East*, pp. 321–334; Ajami, *Arab Predicament*.

28. Ahmed, "Interview," pp. 18–23.

29. Hanafi, *Religious Dialogue and Revolution*.

30. 'Ali Shari'ati, *On the Sociology of Islam*; Shari'ati, *Marxism and the Other Western Fallacies*; Shari'ati, *Culture and Ideology*; Amini, "A Critical Assessment of 'Ali Shari'ati's Theory of Revolution," in Jabbari and Olson, eds., *Iran*, pp. 77–103; Abrahamian, " 'Ali Shari'ati," pp. 18–23; and Akhavi, "Shariati's Social Thought," in Keddie, ed., *Religion and Politics in Islam*, pp. 125–144.

31. Bennigsen, "Religion and Atheism Among Soviet Muslims," in Pullapilly, ed., *Islam and the Contemporary World*, pp. 222–238.

32. Pillsbury, "Islam," in Stoddard et al., eds., *Change and the Muslim World*, pp. 107–114.

33. Halliday, "Yemen's Unfinished Revolution," pp. 3–20.

34. Newell, "Islam and the Struggle for Afghan Liberation," in Pullapilly, ed., *Islam and the Contemporary World*, pp. 251–260.

BIBLIOGRAPHY

Abdel-Malek, Anouar. *Egypt: Military Society*. New York: Random House, 1968.
———. *Social Dialectics*. Syracuse, N.Y.: Syracuse University Press, 1982.
Abdul Hakim, Khalifa. *Islam and Communism*. Lahore: Institute of Islamic Culture, 1953.
Abrahamian, Ervand. " 'Ali Shari'ati: Ideologue of the Iranian Revolution." *MERIP Reports* 102 (January 1982): 24–28.
Ahmed, Mohammed Sid. "Interview, 'The Masses Speak the Language of Religion to Express Themselves Politically.' " *MERIP Reports* 102 (January, 1982): 18–23.
Ajami, Fouad. *The Arab Predicament*. Cambridge: Cambridge University Press, 1981.
Akhavi, Shahrough. "Shariati's Social Thought." In Nikki R. Keddi, ed. *Religion and Politics in Iran*. New Haven, Conn.: Yale University Press, 1983, pp. 125–144.
Amini, Soheyl. "A Critical Assessment of 'Ali Shari'ati's Theory of Revolution." In Ahmad Jabbari and Robert Olson, eds., *Iran: Essays on a Revolution in the Making*. Lexington, Ky.: Mazda, 1981, pp. 77–103.
Anderson, Perry. *Considerations on Western Marxism*. London: New Left Books, 1976.
Bani Sadr, A. H. *The Fundamentals and Precepts of Islamic Government*. Translated by M. R. Ghanoonparvar. Lexington, Ky.: Mazda, 1981.
Batutu, John. "Some Preliminary Observations on the Beginnings of Communism in the Arab East." In Jaan Pennar, ed., *Islam and Communism*. New York: Institute for the Study of the USSR, 1960.
Bennigsen, Alexandre A. and S. Enders Wimbush. *Muslim National Communism in the Soviet Union*. Chicago: University of Chicago Press, 1979.

————. "Religion and Atheism Among Soviet Muslims." In Cyriac K. Pullapilly, ed. *Islam in the Contemporary World*. Notre Dame, Ind.: Crossroads Books, 1980, pp. 222–238.

Charnay, Jean-Paul. "Le Marxisme et l'Islam, Essai de bibliographie." *Archives de sociologies des religions* 10 (1960): 133–146.

Confino, Michael, and Shimon Shamir. *The U.S.S.R. and the Middle East*. New York: John Wiley and Jerusalem: Israel Universities Press, 1973.

Craig, Kenneth. "The Intellectual Impact of Communism upon Contemporary Islam." *Middle East Journal* 8, No. 2 (1954): pp. 127–138.

Cummings, John T., et al. "Islam and Modern Economic Change." In John L. Esposito, ed. *Islam and Development: Religion and Sociopolitical Change*. Syracuse, N.Y.: Syracuse University Press, 1980.

Dessouki, Ali E. Hillal. "The Islamic Resurgence: Sources, Dynamics, and Implications." In Ali E. Hillal Dessouki, ed. *Islamic Resurgence in the Arab World*. New York: Praeger, 1982, pp. 3–31.

Donohue, John J., and John L. Esposito. *Islam in Transition: Muslim Perspectives*. New York: Oxford University Press, 1982.

Efrat, Moshe. "The People's Democratic Republic of Yemen: Scientific Socialism on Trial in an Arab Country." In Peter Wiles, ed. *The New Communist Third World: An Essay in Political Economy*. New York: St. Martin's Press, 1982, pp. 165ff.

Enayat, Hamid. "Islam and Socialism in Egypt." *Middle Eastern Studies* 4, No. 2 (January, 1982): 141–172.

————. *Modern Islamic Political Thought*. Austin, Tex.: University of Texas Press, 1982.

Fischer, Michael M. J. "Islam and the Revolt of the Petit Bourgeoisie." *Daedalus* (Winter 1982): 101–125.

Flores, Alexander. "The Arab CPs and the Palestine Problem." *Khamsin* 7 (1980): 21–40.

————. "The Early History of the Lebanese Communism Reconsidered." *Khamsin* 7 (1980): 7–20.

Haddad, Yvonne Yazbeck. *Contemporary Islam and the Challenge of History*. Albany, N.Y.: State University of New York Press, 1981.

Haim, Sylvia. *Arab Nationalism: An Anthology*. Berkeley and Los Angeles: University of California Press, 1962.

Halliday, Fred. "Yemen's Unfinished Revolution: Socialism in the South." *MERIP Reports* 81 (October, 1979): 3–20.

Halpren, Manfred. *The Politics of Social Change in the Middle East and North Africa*. Princeton, N.J.: Princeton University Press, 1963.

Hanafi, Hassan. "The Relevance of the Islamic Alternative in Egypt." *Arab Studies Quarterly* 4, Nos. 1 & 2 (Spring, 1982): 54–72.

————. *Religious Dialogue and Revolution*. Cairo: Anglo-Egyptian Bookshop, 1977.

Hanna, Sami A., and George H. Gardner. *Arab Socialism: A Documentary Survey*. Leiden: E. J. Brill, 1969.

Hourani, Albert. *Arabic Thought in the Liberal Ages*. London: Oxford University Press, 1962.

Hudson, Michael C. "Islam and Political Development." In John L. Esposito, ed. *Islam and Development: Religion and Sociopolitical Change*. Syracuse, N.Y.: Syracuse University Press, 1980.

Ibrahim, Saad Eddin. "Egypt's Islamic Militants." *MERIP Reports* 103 (February 1982): 5–14.

Ismael, Tareq Y. *The Arab Left*. Syracuse, N.Y.: Syracuse University Press, 1976.

Karpat, Kemal H., ed. *Political and Social Thought in the Contemporary Middle East*. New York: Praeger, 1970.

Katouzian, Homa. "Shi'ism and Islamic Economics: Sadr and Bani Sadr." In Nikki R. Keddie, ed. *Religion and Politics in Iran*. New Haven, Conn.: Yale University Press, 1983.

Kazziha, Walid. *Revolutionary Transformation in the Arab World*. New York: St. Martin's Press, 1975.

Kedourie, Ellie. "Anti-Marxism in Egypt." In M. Confino and S. Shamir, eds., *The U.S.S.R. and the Middle East*. New York: John Wiley and Sons; Jerusalem: Israel Universities Press, 1973, pp. 321–334.

Laqueur, Walter Z. *Communism and Nationalism in the Middle East*. London: Routledge and Kegan Paul, 1956.

Laroui, Abdallah. *The Crisis of the Arab Intellectual: Traditionalism or Historicism*. Translated by Diarmid Cammell. Berkeley and Los Angeles: University of California Press, 1976.

Lewis, Bernard. "Communism and Islam." In Walter Z. Laqueur, ed. *The Middle East in Transition*. New York: Praeger, 1958, pp. 311–324.

Mintz, Jeanne S. *Mohammed, Marx and Marhaen: The Roots of Indonesian Socialism*. New York: Praeger, 1965.

Mitchell, Richard P. *The Society of Muslim Brothers*. London: Oxford University Press, 1969.

Newell, Richard S. "Islam and the Struggle for Afghan Liberation." In Cyriac K. Pullapilly, ed. *Islam in the Contemporary World*. Notre Dame, Ind.: Crossroads Books, 1980, pp. 251–260.

Pennar, Jaan. "The Arabs, Marxism and Moscow, an Historical Survey." *Middle East Journal* 22, No. 4 (1968): 433–447.

Pillsbury, Barbara L.K. "Islam: 'Even unto China.' " In Phillip A. Stoddard, David C. Cuthell, and Margaret W. Sullivan, eds., *Change and the Muslim World*. Syracuse, N.Y.: Syracuse University Press, pp. 107–114.

Qutb, Sayyid. *Social Justice in Islam*. Translated by John B. Hardie. Washington, D.C.: American Council of Learned Societies, 1953.

Rodinson, Maxime. *Islam and Capitalism*. Translated by Brian Pearce. New York: Random House, 1973.

———. *Marxism and the Muslim World*. Translated by Jean Matthews. New York: Monthly Review Press, 1981.

Shari'ati, 'Ali. *Culture and Ideology*. Translated by Fatollah Marjani. Houston: Free Islamic Literatures, 1980.

———. *Marxism and Other Western Fallacies*. Translated by R. Campbell. Berkeley, Calif.: Mizan, 1980.

———. *On the Sociology of Islam*. Translated by Hamid Algar. Berkeley, Calif.: Mizan, 1979.

Siddiqi, Muhammad. *Marxism or Islam*. Lahore: Orientalia, 1952.

Siddiqi, Muhammad N. "Muslim Economic Thinking: A Survey of Contemporary Literature." In Khurshid Ahmad, ed. *Studies in Islamic Economics*. Leicester: Islamic Foundation, 1980.

Smith, Anthony D. *Nationalism in the Twentieth Century*. New York: New York University Press, 1979.

Taleghani, Ayatullah, and Sayyid Mahmud. *Society and Economics in Islam*. Translation by R.Campbell. Berkeley, Calif.: Mizan, 1982.

Tibi, Bassam. *Arab Nationalism: A Critical Inquiry*. Translated by Marion Farouk-Sluglett and Peter Sluglett. New York: St. Martin's Press, 1981.

Turner, Brian. *Marx and the End of Orientalism*. London: George Allen and Unwin, 1978.

Warburg, Gabriel. *Islam, Nationalism and Communism in a Traditional Society: The Case of Sudan*. London: Frank Cass, 1978.

Zabin, Sepehr. *The Communist Movement in Iran*. Berkeley and Los Angeles: University of California Press, 1966.

el-Zein, Abdul Hamid. "Beyond Ideology and Theology: The Search for an Anthropology of Islam." *Annual Review of Anthropology* 6 (1977): 227–254.

19

Theravāda Buddhism and Marxism in the Postwar Era

NATHAN KATZ AND STEPHEN D. SOWLE

METHODOLOGICAL APPROACHES

There is disagreement within scholarly literature concerning the nature of Theravāda Buddhist ethics. Modern scholarship can be loosely grouped into two camps: the first claims to find two clearly distinct ethical systems in Theravāda Buddhism, one for those actively seeking enlightenment and another for the (spiritually less advanced) mass of lay Buddhists; the second finds fault with this view and maintains one continuous spectrum of ethical activity with *nibbāna* as its ultimate goal. We will refer to the first as the "two wheels" (of *dhamma*) view and the second as the "one wheel" view.

Most contemporary adherents to the two wheels view have taken their lead from Max Weber, who said of the Buddhist notion of "salvation" that

[it] is not sought through proving one's self by any inner-worldly or extra-worldly action, by "work" of any kind, but, in contrast to this, it is sought in a psychic state remote from activity. This is decisive for the location of the *arhat* ideal with respect to the "world" of rational action. No bridge connects them. Nor is there any bridge to any actively conceptualized "social" conduct. Salvation is an absolutely personal performance of the self-reliant individual. No one, and particularly no social community can help him. The specific asocial character of all genuine mysticism is here carried to its maximum.[1]

Melford Spiro,[2] who quotes this passage approvingly, and Winston King,[3] who also seems to follow Weber (though he does not cite him), have divided the whole of Buddhism into two distinct, even contradictory, ethical fields: "*nibbānic* Buddhism," for those spiritually advanced practitioners seeking enlightenment and escape from rebirth through the cultivation of detachment; and

Note: Select terms used in this chapter are defined in the end-of-chapter glossary.

"*kammic* Buddhism," which is ethically normative for the vast majority of Buddhists and has as its soteriological goal better rebirth in human or heavenly realms. For Spiro and King, this methodological bifurcation corresponds roughly to the division between monastic and lay Buddhism.

The reasoning underlying this position is that the Buddhist doctrine of egolessness (*anattā*), and the extinction of *kamma* necessary for the attainment of this state, implies that no *kammic* action—and hence no social action—can contribute to the cultivation of detachment necessary for liberation. According to Spiro, activity in the world "is more than religiously neutral, it is religiously perilous. Even moral behavior is an obstacle to salvation, since it leads to the accumulation of merit and hence to a continuation of karma and the cycle of rebirth."[4] This is the basis for such claims as (from Spiro): "there is *no* point at which any of the doctrines of *nibbānic* Buddhism articulate with the secular social order, either to give it value, on the one hand, or to provide a fulcrum by which it can be changed, on the other."[5] No consideration is given in this view to the possibility that *kammic* action could constitute a useful, or perhaps even necessary, preparation for the eventual attainment of *nibbāna*.

For those seeking enlightenment, then, the *nibbānic* ethic prescribes complete withdrawal from society into a solitary life of meditation. "The true Buddhist," Spiro says, "is one who abandons all ties and attachments and 'wanders alone like a rhinoceros.' "[6] This opposition between individual salvation and any involvement with society is total, not only for the seeker of *nibbāna*, but also for the fully enlightened *arahant*. King is very clear on this point: *nibbāna* is the "ethic of equanimity (*upekkhā*)," characterized by "emotional non-attachment or neutrality" and "a calm detachment of eternity-mindedness that has little interest [any] longer in the affairs of men."[7] Enlightenment leads to the actual destruction of all emotions, which are superseded and extinguished along with the ego (*atta*). The doctrine of *anattā* is thus interpreted as implying a completely detached neutrality, both to one's own fate and to the fate of others, and complete uninvolvement with and unconcern for affairs in the world.

For the majority of Buddhists who remain in society, on the other hand, accumulation of *kamma* is inevitable, and ethical conduct is thus necessarily organized around the proximate goals of rewards in this life and a better rebirth in the next. Because *kammic* action "cannot be equated with [*dhamma's*] ultimate meaning," a separate wheel of *dhamma*, radically disjunct from the ethic of *nibbāna*, governs the pursuit of these lesser goals.[8]

This has clear implications for any attempt to incorporate Marxism into a Buddhist world-view. The two wheels position would leave room for Marxism, if at all, as a mode of action and belief appropriate only to the *kammic* sphere. Because *nibbānic* Buddhism provides no basis for social commitment, and thus clearly precludes any commitment to social change, a Buddhist social ethic of *any* sort is possible only within the realm of *kammic* Buddhism. The notion of a politically active or Marxist monk is, in this view, simply a contradiction in terms, unless the monk has forsaken *nibbāna* as a goal and has resigned him/herself to further accumulation of *kamma* and continued rebirth.

In response, the one wheel view contends that bifurcating Buddhism in this way misrepresents the true nature of the Theravāda ethical system.[9] Most advocates of the one wheel approach base their arguments on doctrinal and canonical sources, whereas adherents to the two wheels view tend to base their conclusions more on sociological analyses of Buddhist societies. Although it may be an attractive solution to locate the split between the scholarly perspectives in a division between doctrinal Buddhism (seen as supporting a one wheel position) and Buddhism in its actual historical development (where a compromised, doctrinally impure "folk Buddhism" is seen as having arisen for the mass of spiritually unadvanced lay Buddhists), we believe this to be unsatisfactory. For one thing, most supporters of a two wheels position maintain that their sociological findings are consistent with dichotomies found in the Buddhist doctrine (as with Spiro and King); for another, there is evidence supporting a one wheel interpretation from a sociological perspective. Our own position supports a one wheel view not only of Buddhist doctrine, but also of Buddhism as it is actually practiced in Theravāda countries.

Harvey B. Aronson[10] and Nathan Katz,[11] in recent works supporting a one wheel position, have challenged Spiro and King's understanding of Buddhist canonical sources. Both maintain that a detailed reexamination of certain key ethical terms found in Buddhist texts reveals a fundamental continuity, rather than disjunction, within the ethical structure of Theravāda doctrine. Katz has argued that the Buddhist terms *kusala* and *puñña* (roughly parallel to Spiro and King's distinction between *nibbānic* and *kammic* Buddhism) do not refer to two distinct realms of ethical activity, but rather form one continuous spectrum that unites monastic and lay activity in one system. *Puñña*, which refers to meritorious *kammic* activity having pleasing results, is presented in the Pali suttas as the "habituating ground" of *kusala*, which describes the activity of the Buddha or an *arahant* and is activity that has no *kammaphāla* (result of action). The Buddha's notion of spiritual growth is very much a gradualist one, and he never maintained that the proximate goal of higher rebirth and the ultimate goal of a cessation of rebirth were in contradiction. Quite the contrary, the proximate goal can constitute a valuable impetus for the full spiritual realization of the ultimate goal. Ethical activity associated with the term *puñña* is thus said to condition the practitioner for enlightened (activity (*kusala*): "So you see, Ānanda, good conduct leads gradually up to the summit."[12]

It is therefore necessary to "interpret the Buddha's method of teaching heaven to the laity as not postulating a separate, or even proximate, goal as a concession to those of inferior capabilities or situations, but as a stage in a gradual progress towards *nibbāna* or *arahattā*."[13] Passages in the *suttas* that at first glance would seem to support a two wheels interpretation are found, on closer examination, to describe not two contrasting forms of ethical activity (such as *puñña* and *kusala*), but rather two contrasting mental attitudes ("ordinary" as opposed to "noble" right view). The relationship between activity and attitude is complex, but it is clear that the Buddha felt *puññā*, as a type of ethical activity could help Buddhist practitioners develop that attitude which, when habituated, leads to *kusala*, the free and spontaneous activity associated with enlightenment. Spiro and King make the mistake of transferring the radical disjunction between the two attitudes to the forms of ethical activity that stand in complex relation to them.

The rigid distinction between the *saṅgha* and laity stressed by Spiro and King also breaks down in this view. Both monks and lay practitioners tread the same path, and it is not always the case that the monks, because of their more sustained practice of meditation or other techniques, are more spiritually advanced than the lay people. The Pali Canon is replete with accounts of lay *arahants*. This not only exemplifies the unitary nature of *dhamma* and ethical activity, but, insofar as these lay *arahants* continue to live in society, this also casts doubt on the view that the fully enlightened *arahant*, or the person actively seeking *nibbāna*, it necessarily withdrawn from and unconcerned with the world. Indeed, as we will see, the *arahant* has positive motivations for action "in the world."

As Katz explains, and Aronson works out more fully, the equanimity and detachment of the *arahant* is not a neutral, uninvolved, or solitary state. The Buddha (or any *arahant*), the texts say clearly, must and does teach; s/he is both a teacher (*guru*) and spiritual friend (*kalyāpamitta*) to the non-enlightened. The *arahant* teaches because s/he is moved by compassion. The Buddha says at one point: "The fully enlightened one feels love and compassion while teaching others."[14] Aronson, in his analysis of the psychology of meditative states, claims that King and Spiro confuse the "sublime-attitude equanimity" (*brahmavihāra-upekkhā*) which does prescribe the (temporary) cultivation of emotional neutrality and unconcern as a means of helping the practitioner fully overcome the mental defilements preventing the realization of *nibbāna*, with the "limb-of-enlightenment equanimity" (*bojjhaṅga-upekkhā*) and the "six-limbed equanimity" (*chalaṅga-upekkhā*), which the fully enlightened *arahant* possesses.[15] These latter states do not supplant the sublime attitudes of love, compassion, and sympathetic joy, turning the *arahant* into a emotionless shell, but rather provide the balance of mind needed in order for these emotions to be wholly spontaneous and pure. Compassion (*karuṇā*) is not merely a possible emotion for the *arahant*, but one that inevitably moves the *arahant* to teach so that others may benefit:[16] "Gotama . . . was motivated to achieve [*nibbāna*] not merely for his own benefit, but by the wish to exemplify [its] benefits to others and the wish to teach others how to achieve [it]. For Gotama, enlightenment was a means; his own and others' happiness and welfare was the end."[17] This is a far cry indeed from Spiro's emphasis that the fully enlightened individual "wanders alone like a rhinoceros."

Trevor Ling provides a sociological analysis that, at least implicitly, supports a one wheel interpretation of Buddhist culture in Theravāda countries.[18] The traditional two wheels interpretation of "folk Buddhism" (which is often characterized by elaborate mythologies, stories, and even pantheons of gods) stresses the sharp discontinuity between this "compromised" form of Buddhism and the "purer" forms found in the *suttas*. Buddhism, it is argued, was forced to make radical concessions in order to gain mass followings in the countries where it took root, and this resulted in the bifurcation described by those committed to a two wheels view.

Ling maintains that this not only contradicts the Buddha's own style of teaching, but also fails to make sense of the actual development of Buddhism in South and Southeast Asia. Just as the Buddha addressed those whom he taught in ways appropriate to their level of spiritual attainment, Buddhism in its historical development adjusted itself to those forms of popular, naturalistic religions it encountered, transforming these in ways that allowed Buddhist *dhamma* to be communicated in forms appropriate to the mass audiences it sought to set on the path to enlightenment. As Ling says:

If one desires to share the blessings of the Dharma with men who hold animistic beliefs, then one must meet those men where they are, in their situation as animists. One must meet them there—but not leave them there. Rather, such people are to be encouraged and led towards a new and truer perspective, that of the Buddha and his teaching. To do this it is necessary first of all to use the kind of ideas and conceptions which they will be able to grasp, and with which they are familiar.[19]

Ling argues convincingly that this is, in fact, "what historical Buddhism has done: it has, quite *spontaneously*, developed 'bridges' between popular ways of thought and the Dharma."[20]

For example, the Buddhist symbol of Mara, the Evil One, has served as a bridge between traditional animistic beliefs and the Buddhist teaching that the obstacles to be overcome are internal and not external. Lay Buddhists learn how the Buddha overcame evil Mara and how they, too, can defeat Mara through meditation and insight. Although they may not be able to finally defeat Mara and attain enlightenment in this lifetime, they know that it can be done and that they can prepare in this life for eventual liberation in a future life. Through religious forms such as this, says Nyāṇatiloka Mahāthera (quoted by Ling), "Slowly the *puthujjana*, the worldling, is introduced to the truth, and the value of the higher life that alone opens the path to deliverance."[21]

The *saṅgha* in Theravāda societies (especially Burma and Sri Lanka) has actively kept this "frontier" between Buddhist doctrine and popular belief open, though we do not want to deny the existence of some degree of tension between this function of the *saṅgha* as the center of an active, unified Buddhist community and certain counter-tendencies that cause the *saṅgha* to become more insular in its relations with society. We would maintain, however, that writers like Spiro and King have overemphasized these latter tendencies and that Buddhist culture in Theravāda countries remains unified to a remarkable degree.[22]

The implications of a two wheels perspective for the development of a Buddhist social philosophy contrast interestingly with those of a one wheel view. If *kammic* activity is the habituating ground of *nibbāna*, internally related to it within a single ethical structure, then a unitary ethic of social action can be formulated for both the *bhikkhu* and the lay Buddhist. This opens the door for a Marxist social theory which is seen as not simply compatible with one part of the Buddhist system, but as actually speaking to the ultimate values and goals of the Buddhist world-view.

Finally, we should mention at least briefly the more nuanced versions of the two wheels position offered by Frank Reynolds, Gananath Obeyesekere, and Bardwell Smith.[23] For Reynolds and Obeyesekere, the two wheels are seen as more interrelated than in either Spiro's or King's account, with emphasis placed on their "equal and complementary importance."[24] Greater emphasis is placed on the intercourse between *saṅgha* and society, with the *bhikkhus* exemplifying and teaching Buddhist doctrine to the laity, and greater leeway is given for the possibility of lay practitioners achieving *arahattā*.[25] In the end, however, both affirm a dichotomy between *nibbānic* Buddhism and "kammic action which, though it is undertaken in accordance with the Dharma, cannot be equated with its ultimate meaning."[26] They insist there is a "radical difference between the two types of action, and maintain that a social ethic based on the ethic of *nibbāna* is not possible:[27] "salvation involves as its prerequisite an emancipation from the social structure, i.e., emancipation from attachment to the world."[28] Bardwell Smith provides a particularly interesting case, for although he at some points expresses a two wheels position, at others he clearly shows his sympathy with a one wheel interpretation.[29] The positions expressed by these three writers would be compatible with a view that Marxism and Buddhism, while articulating different values and goals, are complementary with one another, and perhaps even imply one another.

STRUCTURES OF PHILOSOPHIC COMPARISONS

Philosophic studies of the relationship between Buddhism and Marxism, whether undertaken by scholars or by those engaged in political activities, tend to understand the complex interrelationship between the two in one of three models: congruency, complementarity, or disjunction. In the first model, Buddhism and Marxism have been viewed as essentially identical or congruent; this position is argued, for example, by philosopher Gunapala Dharmasiri[30] and by U Ba Swe,[31] a member of U Nu's revolutionary government in Burma. Following the second model, many of the advocates of "Buddhist socialism" in Theravāda countries, such as former Sri Lankan Prime Minister S.W.R.D. Bandaranaike,[32] former Burmese Prime Minister U Nu,[33] the influential Thai monk, Bhikkhu Buddhadāsa,[34] as well as the Dalai Lama of Tibet,[35] see Buddhism and Marxism as inherently complementary systems, with each reinforcing and "filling in" those areas of human endeavor that have not been primary foci of the other. For example, it has been contended that Buddhism could "fill in" issues of psychology and epistemology which Marx neglected, while Marx's focus on historical criticism articulates those spheres that are, at most, implicit in the Buddha's thought. Finally, in the third model, others, such as the current President of Sri Lanka, J. R. Jayawardene (in his early writings), see Buddhism and Marxism as disjunct and unrelated.[36] The following subsections of this chapter will attempt a philosophic examination of those themes in the thought of the Buddha and of Marx which have been understood as congruent, complementary, and disjunct respectively, followed by a closer examination of how these relationships have borne on political thinking in Sri Lanka, Burma, and Thailand during the postwar era.

Buddhism and Marxism as Congruent

It has been argued that one area of overlap between Buddhism and Marxism lies in the domain of criticism.[37] Marx is well known for writing that "Religion is the sigh of an oppressed creature, the soul of a heartless world, as it is also the spirit of a spiritless condition. It is the opium of the people."[38] Although for many Buddhists such claims serve as a basis for rejecting Marx, theoretically he is maintaining that any comprehensive criticism of society, philosophy, or ethics must begin with the crticism of religion.

The Buddha made precisely the same point. The very starting point of Buddhism is just such a criticism of religion as it was found in its sixth-century B.C.E. Indian context. The very first text of the Buddhist canon is the *Brahmajāla Sutta* of the *Dīgha Nikāya*, and in it the Buddha is no less thorough in his radical criticism of religion than was Marx.[39]

In this text the Buddha launches essentially two criticisms of religion, one which is identical with Marx's and one which perhaps goes beyond his. The Buddha argues that religion is used to maintain an unjust and irrational caste system, which ordains a certain group of people to think for the masses, who are offered solace in notions such as self (*ātman*), God (*Iśvara*), and hope for a better life the next time around—all of which is insidiously perpetuated by and for the interests of the brahmin caste. Religion, then, is a rationalization of and for class oppression.

But the Buddha does say more, and in this he more closely resembles that other great Jewish patriarch of modernism, Sigmund Freud, than he does Marx. Here the Buddha says, as does Freud in *The Future of an Illusion*, that religion is a projected wish/fantasy/illusion, the concretization of a life-force (eros) which psychological malaise thwarts from authentic expression.[40] So for the Buddha, religion is both a way of reinforcing oppressive class structures and a way of denying human responsibility for our lives. The criticism of religion, we find, is thus the starting point for a general criticism, something that both the Buddha and Marx endeavor to propound.

Another area of congruence between Buddhism and Marxism lies in the analyses of, respectively, dependent co-origination (*paṭicca samuppāda*) and the internal relations these two systems provide. Dependent co-origination forms the basis of Buddhist ontology; it describes for the Buddhist the nature of reality, and it is equated with the highest truth: "He who sees dependent co-arising, sees the Dhamma."[41] Reality is seen as a dynamic organic whole wherein "objects" are dissolved into "relations" and "processes." In other words, there is a rejection of all notions of the self-existence (*svabhāva*) of phenomena, which are instead held to be internally related and mutually constitutive. Each particular phenomenon depends for its nature on its relations with and dependence on all other phenomena. All factors of both our psychic experience and physical reality exist as part of an endless web of mutual causation, with no immutable or autonomous essence subsisting in phenomena. The human psyche, in clinging to and hypostatizing the contingent, transient experiences of existence, produces the suffering (*dukkha*) that characterizes our alienated existence.

Marx's ontology is virtually identical to this, likewise conceiving of social-material reality as an internally related, differentially constituted process. Georg Lukács, one of the earliest Marxists to spell out explicitly the implicit "philosophy of internal relations" that is vital for an adequate understanding of Marx's thought, tells us that "objects" must be dissolved into the "relations" that constitute them: "If change is to be understood at all it is necessary to abandon the view that objects are rigidly opposed to each other; it is necessary to elevate their interrelatedness and the interaction between these 'relations' and the 'objects' to the same plane of reality."[42] All "things," whether they be material objects (the book you now hold in your hands) or social factors (such as capital), "should be shown to be aspects of processes."[43] Friedrich Engels, Marx's frequent collaborator, expresses these thoughts well:

When we reflect on nature, or the history of mankind, or our own intellectual activity, the first picture presented to us is of an endless maze of relations and interactions, in which nothing remains what, where, and as it was, but everything moves, changes, comes into being and passes out of existence.[44]

Thus, for both Marx and the Buddha, general, abstract categories ("Being," "the self," or an economic concept such as "production in general"), which create the illusion of self-identical, self-existent entities, cannot be adequate representations of the world they seek to express. Insofar as abstract categories make the historical, variable, and incomplete appear natural, absolute, and complete, they partake of metaphysics and mystification, the collapsing of difference and relation into identity and self-sufficiency. Humans can understand their place in the world only by seeing themselves as terms in a vast system of relationships that coalesce to form a single organic whole. Relationships, not entities, have "ultimate" reality, and there is thus no such thing as "independent existence."

Within this organic whole, the notions people have of themselves and the world around them are not given in "reality itself," but are, rather, the contingent results of the particular nature of the human species and its interactions with the social-material and natural environment given at any particular moment. Buddhist and Marxist epistemology agree on this point. For Marx, subject and object, mind and material world, are constituted by one another but are irreducible to one another; they are internally related, interdependent structures within which the cognitive process unfolds. There is and can be, Marx maintained, no foundation for cognition independent of particular, historically conditioned configurations of concepts and objects.

This analysis should make it clear that Marx neatly sidesteps the question which Roger Garaudy, the former French communist philosopher, says is the "fundamental" one of all philosophy: "where to begin? With things or the conscience [sic] we have of them?"[45] If the two elements are seen as aspects of one complex process, the question is an illegitimate one; for the "conscience" we have of "things" is the dialectical result of the continuous, mutually conditioning interaction between human action and the social-material world of which we are a part. To give any factor in this process logical or ontological priority over any other would be to commit an unpardonable metaphysical error. This is what enables Marx, in his "Theses on Feuerbach," to refer to the individual as the "ensemble of social relations."[46]

The Buddha similarly rejected the metaphysical notion that the "self" or consciousness has any self-existent basis. Joanna Rogers Macy expresses this idea well:

Possessed of no "I" apart from what it feels, sees, thinks, does, the self does not *have* exprience, it *is* its experience. . . . In *paṭicca samuppāda* [dependent co-origination], however, perception is no passive registering of stimuli. It is a two-way street, a mutual process involving the convergence of sensory signal with attention and sense organ, and the mental constructs imposed by the perceiver. . . . The mutuality is real—the world is neither independent of the viewer nor the viewer independent of his perceptions.[47]

Consciousness and the material world are, as in Marx, seen as interdependent processes, each conditioning the other. Thus, Macy argues that implicit in the concept of dependent co-origination

is the notion that the human being arises co-dependently with its natural and social environment. . . . Within that perception of reality, one is not an autonomous being nor are the institutions of society eternally fixed. They are mutable and they mirror our greed, as does indeed the face of nature itself. Co-arising with our actions, they, like we, can be changed by our actions.[48]

Although they agree up to this point, from here Marx and the Buddha develop their analyses in somewhat different (though not incompatible) directions. Marx's analysis diverges from the Buddha's in emphasizing the predominant role of the mode of material (economic) production in determining the interrelations of the totality and the understanding people have of it. In modern capitalist society,

426 NATHAN KATZ AND STEPHEN D. SOWLE

an individual's class position thus has a major role in determining how one conceives of oneself and one's world. The Buddha, on the other hand, provides us with an extensive analysis of the intrapsychic dynamics that contribute to the understanding people have of themselves and their world, something that Marx largely ignores. We will now turn to a closer examination of these ways in which Marxism and Buddhism complement one another, focusing primarily on their respective analyses of alienation and suffering.

Buddhism and Marxism as Complementary

For Marx, alienation (*Entfremdung*) refers to the condition in which a person finds oneself in opposition to objects, a condition in which one is estranged from even the most intimate of objects, those one produces.[49]

The defining characteristic of being human (*Gattungswesen*, "species being") is that we tend to manipulate our environment such that we are able to combine our labor with matter to produce new and growth-enhancing objects.[50] In capitalist society, however, the inhuman condition of a "labor market," in which we are forced to sell and barter this, the most precious of human characteristics, in a commodity exchange situation, serves to alienate us not only from objects as such, but from our own true natures as free producers as well. Thus, a cruel double movement ensues: alienation from objects reinforces and sustains alienation from our true nature, and vice-versa.

Marx goes on to demonstrate that even the notion of an "object" is itself a reification of experience, that this notion is the product of an alienated consciousness.[51] Looking at a particular "object," one is tempted to call it a "book." However, Marx wants us to see that the term "book" is the name of a commodity, something that participates in this cruel system of capitalist exchange. What is really before one is a combination of various natural and synthetic materials and concretized human labor. But our consciousness has become so alienated by virtue of its participation in a capitalist world that this reflection becomes accepted as though it were natural and self-sufficient. By calling it a "book," we dehumanize it, which is to say that we no longer see it as the product of human effort on nature.

Such reification only serves the interests of that class of society that benefits from the world of commodities. Alienation, then, serves to reinforce and solidify the interests of a given segment of society and enslaves the producing class, who actually produce "objects" but whose full participation in this process is negated by the very way in which we are forced to think and perceive.

The Buddha, of course, did not provide a sustained analysis of the labor market and the conditions of the alienated worker. He couldn't have, as these structures did not exist in his time. His analysis of the human situation, however, does provide analogies to Marx's analysis. He, too, did not see the problem of human suffering as something that was either random or divinely preordained. Rather, suffering could be discussed in purely human terms, resting on the particularity of history (saṃsāra). God does not make us suffer, and suffering is not simply the result of an absurd world. Suffering is a human problem that has human solutions.

In Buddhist parlance, the issue of reification becomes the problems of papañca ("diffuseness of thought") and diṭṭhi ("views" or "opinions").[52] Given a world in which it is convenient to refer by names, we abstract these "convenient designations" (loke vohārā) and take them as referring to things or objects.[53] When our linguistic conventions become deeply rooted, personal convictions, we have reinforced and maintained a system in which a subject is in tension against an object, a condition the Buddha called dukkha, or suffering.

Important to note here are three ideas: (1) that consciousness, explained as alienation by Marx and as intrinsically unsatisfactory (dukkha) by the Buddha, is predicated on an alienated mode of being in the world; (2) that this alienation or suffering is a human problem and construction that could be overcome only by human endeavor; and (3) that the way in which we think, the process of reification or opinionatedness, supports and maintains oppressive structures, and, therefore, any real solution to human suffering involves a radical reversal of thought as well as of action.

The analyses offered by Marx and the Buddha of the problem of alienation/ suffering are complementary in the sense that Marx focuses on its aetiology in the oppressive character of social relations under capitalism, while the Buddha focuses on the psychological and affective roots of suffering. It should be kept in mind, however, that Marx's view did not utterly neglect the psychological and intellectual effects that follow from these empirical relationships, nor did the Buddha ignore how it comes to be that diṭṭhi, while rooted in psychological malaise, was appropriated by certain social classes (e.g., the brahmins) to solidify their socio-economic position to the detriment of other classes.

Buddhism and Marxism as Disjunct

Essentially two perspectives have been employed in arguing for a radical disjunction between Buddhism and Marxism. The first perspective is exemplified in the right-wing nationalism of Bhikkhu Kitthivuḍḍha of Thailand.[54] Bhikkhu Kitthivuḍḍha interprets the three domains of the Buddhist path, sīla or ethical conduct, samādhi or meditation, and paññā or wisdom, in explicit nationalistic and anti-Marxist terms. For example, sīla is taken to mean obedience to law, and the mind is trained not only by meditation but also by conforming it to national values by the practice of loyalty to the government. The bhikkhu has also argued that the fundamental Buddhist precept against taking life is not operative regarding the lives of communist insurrectionists in Thailand; taking their lives would have the effect of preventing them from committing bad kammas, because their goal is understood to be the destruction of that state which provides a source of Buddhist values and disciplines.

A more sophisticated analysis was presented by J. R. Jayawardene, now President of Sri Lanka, when he served as Minister of Finance in D. S. Sennanayake's government.[55] Jayawardene's position is one of a socialist, not of a rightist. He understands Marx as a socialist of a particular variety, a "revolutionary socialist or communist." The distinctions between socialism, which he feels to be utterly compatible with Buddhism, and Marxism are essentially three: the notions of dialectical materialism, economic determinism, and class struggle.

Marx's dialectial materialism, according to Jayawardene, is an extreme view that arose in contradiction to idealism, which dominated continental philosophy at the time and was advocated by Hegel and Feuerbach, among others. The Buddha, he argues, never considered the ideal (mind) and the material (matter) "as quantitatively distinct and separate, but rather as manifestations of the four energies [dhāthus] in different combinations."[56] Buddhism, which he understands as a "scientific" religion, foreshadowed quantum physics in regarding either idealism or materialism as an extreme view, and therefore must eschew Marxism in the particular sense of Marx's being a materialist, dialectical or otherwise.

Jayawardene also rejects Marx's notion of economic determinism, for two reasons. In holding that history determines consciousness, Marx, and especially Engels after him, held that any ethic is of necessity a class ethic. Engels argues that the ethical principle, "thou shalt not steal," merely serves the interests of the owning class. Jayawardene argues that when the Buddhist undertakes the sīla against stealing, s/he does so to preserve ownership only incidentally, and that his or her real motive is the cultivation of detachment and the overcoming of greed. He concludes that Marx and Engels have missed the point of Buddhist ethics, which cannot be reduced to class interest.

Similarly, he argues that holding history to shape consciousness and not the other way around leaves the Marxist unable to account "for men like the Buddha, Christ and various others whom the whole range of history throws up, including Marx himself."[57] Economic determinism, he concludes, violates such Buddhist notions as kamma and the perfectibility of the person and fails to see the uniqueness of human consciousness and endeavor.

Jayawardene's harshest criticisms of Marx revolve around Marx's notion of class struggle, which he sees as teaching a hatred that utterly contradicts the Buddhist principles of the Middle Way and of non-violence (ahimsa). He finds the goal orientation of Marxism utterly inimical to the process-orientation of Buddhism, and he points to the "tragedy of religion in the U.S.S.R." as evidence of Marxism's inability to create adequate values that could serve to cohere, rather than coerce, a society's identity.[58] He therefore opts for a social democracy, embracing Buddhist-socialist values while rejecting those of Marxism.

SRI LANKA

As is the case in many Southeast Asian nations, Sri Lankan politics evidence in large part an admixture of principles drawn from Marxism and Buddhist nationalism. Also similar to other regional countries, 1956 marked a watershed for the commingling of Marxist, Buddhist, and nationalist sentiments, a year known throughout Buddhist Asia as Buddha Jayanti, the 2500th anniversary of the *parinibbāna* (death) of Lord Buddha, which heralded cooperative efforts on diplomatic, economic, and cultural levels throughout the Buddhist world.[59]

To appreciate this 1956 convergence of interests and the nature of religio-political discourses since then, it is necessary to briefly sketch both leftist and Buddhist nationalist movements in Sri Lanka before that time.

Sinhalese Buddhist Nationalism

Sinhalese Buddhist nationalism is not a recent phenomenon. On the contrary, one may easily find its origins in the classical, post-Anurādhapura era as recorded in such ancient chronicles as the *Mahāvaṁsa* (sixth century C.E.).[60] In it, according to Vijaya Samaraweera, one finds that

This ideology was built up around the special destiny claimed for the Sinhalese and the land they inhabited as the chosen guardians of Buddhism, and it brought together—with what proved to be profound consequence—two distinct elements, nation and religion: the unity of Sinhaladīpa (Island of the Sinhalese) and Dhammadīpa (Island of Buddhism) was the fruit.[61]

Also profoundly affecting the self-understanding of many Sinhalese Buddhists is what Donald E. Smith calls the "reconquest myth."[62] Based on *Mahāvaṁsa* accounts, the classical king Dutthagamini (161–137 B.C.E.) embodied the role of the righteous monarch (*cakkavattin*, modeled after the third century B.C.E. Indian emperor, Asoka) by his reconquest of the island from foreign invaders, in this case the Cōḷa Tamils. As Smith recounts,

Dutthagamini to this day is regarded as the greatest national hero of the Sinhalese people, and his story embodies their national myth. . . . In the reconquest myth, the ideal society is not new but ancient. Sacred values cling to a particular territory, but these face extinction when the land is overrun by enemies. The great challenge is to reconquer the land and restore the prominence of the social values.[63]

As Samaraweera argues, this *Mahāvaṁsa* paradigm, and Dutthagamini's reconquest in particular, remained in the background of Sinhalese consciousness to emerge intermittently in times of crisis, usually foreign invasions from south India or, later, from Portugal, Holland, and Great Britain.[64] For example, as the Cōḷas's incursions into the north of the island led to the establishment of a Tamil fiefdom in the thirteenth century, the reconquest myth gained prominence again. Despite the fact that the Sinhalese and Tamil populations of the island generally got along well, this mythology was repeatedly exploited by the Portuguese (1597–1658) and Dutch (1658–1796) imperialists by the usual divide-and-conquer strategy. Nevertheless, the myth remained a bulwark of Sinhalese nationalism and aspirations for independence and self-determination.

One response to these first periods of imperialism was the revitalization of the *saṅgha* under Bhikkhu Valivita Saranakara (b. 1698), who organized the Silvant Samagama ("fraternity of the pious") under the patronage of the Kandyan king, Narendra Sinha. Finding Buddhism in a decadent condition due to Portuguese legislation which undermined the religion's position, the king and the *bhikkhu* turned to Thailand for forces of regeneration and renewal. This organization remains Sri Lanka's largest monastic fraternity, known today as the *Siyam Nikāya*.

Sinahlese Buddhist nationalism became a major political and cultural force in Sri Lanka in response to British imperialism (1796–1948). As is commonly the case, Christian missionaries were the advance forces of imperialism, be it of the Portuguese, Dutch, or British variety. As early as 1828, one sees a reemergent nationalist consciousness in the Buddhist compositions of parodies of Christian missionary writings.[65] While in the early period of British rule the traditional priest-patron relationship between the *saṅgha* and temporal authority was maintained, during the period between 1838 and 1853 "the propriety of a Christian government being the patron of the 'heathen religion' was questioned by Christian missionaries and by Sir James Stephen [the Under-Secretary of State in the Colonial Office during 1840–1847]. This led to a reversal of the earlier policy of the British towards Buddhism,"[66] which itself led to the anti-British insurrection of 1848.

Thus, as the persecution of Buddhism and the experience of colonization became identified, a reemergent Buddhism and the anti-colonial struggle likewise became identified. When the *bhikkhu* Migvettuwatte Gunananda formed the Society for the Propagation of Buddhism in 1862, its missionary techniques—pamphleting, preaching, and debating—closely resembled those of the Christians, developing what could be termed a "defensive mythology" to counter the pervasion of Christian propaganda which both lauded Christian culture (that is, upper-class British mores) and disparaged all things Sinhalese, including Buddhism, the Sinhala language, and all indigenous forms, from clothing to cuisine.

Other major figures in the anti-imperialist Buddhist revival included the Anagarika Dharmapala, whose *Return to Righteousness* became a manifesto for the turn-of-the-century revival.[67] Dharmapala became a close associate of Colonel Henry Steele Olcott,[68] an American who arrived in Sri Lanka in 1880 and proceeded to divide his time between the struggle against Christian missionaries generally and the struggle against their primary mode of indoctrination, their domination in the education of Sri Lanka's youth.[69]

When Olcott arrived in 1880, only three Buddhist educational institutions, most eminently the Vidyodaya Pirivena, which had been chartered in 1873, were recognized by the government as against 811 Christian schools.[70] Olcott's first order of business, after founding the Buddhist Theosophical Society in Colombo, was to inaugurate the National Fund Scheme to promote Buddhist education and culture, establishing Ananda College in Colombo. Traveling around the island in a bullock cart, Olcott, who remains a national hero to this day, also compiled a *Buddhist Catechism* and designed the international Buddhist flag, which is flown in Sri Lanka as often as the national flag today.[71]

This period from 1870 to 1900, starting with the famous Panadura debates (1891), marks the emergence of the modern Buddhist nationalist movement. Its primary locale was the low-country areas where Christianity had made the greatest inroads in subverting Buddhist culture and polity. It was a thoroughly grass-roots movement, drawing support not only from the *sangha* but also from the peasantry, *bhikkhus*, and indigenous educators and physicians following the traditional *Ayurveda* system. In general this was not supported by the indigenous, capitalist elite, who had more to gain from the maintenance of the status quo, and it is not until at least a quarter century later that one finds elite Colombo citizenry embracing the nationalist cause.

The Rise of the Sinhalese Left

An economic depression throughout the British Empire saw a decline in the plantation economy and a steep rise in local inflation rates beginning around 1913. In the early 1920s, the international trade unionist movement reached urban workers in Colombo, culminating in the founding of the Labour Party by A. E. Goonesinghe in 1928. Following the enactment of universal suffrage in 1931, nationalist and leftist sentiments were largely channeled into the electoral process. S.W.R.D. Bandaranaike, later to become Sri Lanka's synthesizer of Buddhist socialism in 1956, founded the Sinhala Maha Sabha, a Buddhist nationalist party, in 1934. Marxists responded by founding three distinct parties: the Lanka Samma Samaja Party (LSSP), with its Trotskyite policies, in 1935 by Dr. N. M. Perera; the Communist Party (CP), which followed Stalinist principles, in 1943; and the Bolshevik Samma Samaja Party (BSSP), also Trotskyite, in 1945. The BSSP and LSSP merged in 1950 and continues as the LSSP to this day.

All of the leftist parties affirmed a Sinhalese nationalist position as part of the anti-imperialist struggle. All ''viewed religion either as inimical or as one of the spheres which needed to be 'reformed' in view of the dominantly land-owning character of the upper echelon of the Buddhist clergy.''[72] It should be noted, however, that among the LSSP leadership of the 1930s and 1940s were ''some of the most politically vociferous *bhikkhus* as its ardent allies.''[73] Similarly, the first President of the CP was an eminent Buddhist monk, Udakandawela Sri Saranankaro Thero.

These *bhikkhus* who assumed leadership roles in the LSSP and the CP gradually congealed into what became known as the Vidyalankara Group, named for the prestigious Vidyalankara Pirivena (now University) in Kelaniya, near Colombo. Among the members of the Vidyalankara Group was Venerable Dr. Walpola Rahula, an eminent monk-scholar, and they began publishing the Sinhala journal,

Kalaya, in 1946. This journal, which was published for only one year, stressed that the notion of "politics" should be extended to all social activities, that traditional monastic discipline (*vinaya*) did not ban monks from participation in the political process, that Marxism and Buddhism were reconcilable philosophies, and that the United National Party (UNP) of D. S. Senanayake served the interests of the capitalist class.[74]

The Vidyalankara Group founded the Lanka Eksath Bhikkhu Mandalaya (LEBM) in 1946, whose program affirmed the role of *bhikkhus* in politics, called for the nationalization of key industries and for the control of foreign exchange, and demanded free education, independence, and prohibition of alcohol in conformity with the five precepts (*pañca sīla*) of Buddhism.[75] While the issues articulated by the LEBM were not reflected in the 1947 general election, their influence continued to be felt.

The 1947 elections saw the UNP organize Sri Lanka's first government, under the leadership of D. S. Senanayake. The focus of leftist and Buddhist nationalist sentiment fell on Senanayake's Minister of Health and Local Government, S.W.R.D. Bandaranaike, who, on behalf of his Sinhala Maha Sabha, demanded state assistance for the revival of Buddhism. The UNP's refusal of this demand led to Bandaranaike's departure from the party in 1951 and to the formation of the Sri Lanka Freedom Party (SLFP) under his leadership.[76]

The 1952 elections saw the UNP returned to power over the SLFP, which now led the opposition. Labor unrest in 1952 forced Senanayake's resignation and the assumption of the prime ministry by Sir John Kotewaia, and the defeat of the UNP was imminent. Organizing for the 1956 general elections, held in the fervor of Buddha Jayanti celebrations, the All-Ceylon Buddhist Congress (ACBC, an organization under lay leadership) and the Eksath Bhikkhu Peramuna (EBP, "United Front of the Bhikkhus") formulated a ten-point program calling for, among other things, the enhancement of Buddhism's position in society, the adoption of Sinhala as the national language, and the implementation of the report of the Buddhist Commission of Enquiry, which called for far-reaching reforms and sustained renewal of Buddhism. This ten-point program was adopted in toto by the SLFP.

The Buddhist Commission of Enquiry had been organized two years earlier to inquire into the state of Buddhism in Sri Lanka and its proper social role. The report issued by the Commission is a condemnation of the state of Buddhism, and it laid the blame for this degeneration squarely on the shoulders of British imperialism and the missionaries' undermining of traditional educational institutions. The British, they argued, in promoting the alien conception of a secular society, had undercut the vital and dynamic role of Buddhism in its relationship to political power (the traditional "priest-patron" relationship). Secularization, the report continues, meant no more than the erosion of Buddhism's role in society, and the vacuum caused by the separation of religion from the state had been filled by capitalistic materialism in the guise of secularism.[77] The report of the committee set the imagination and nationalism of the Sinhalese majority afire. At the same time, an anonymous work by D. C. Wijewardene, *The Revolt in the Temple*, outlined the degradation which had been heaped on the Sinhalese by the imperialists and their missionaries.[78]

In the meantime, the EBP mobilized thousands of its members into "a countryside *bhikkhu* cadre" which effectively urged electoral support for the SLFP.[79] Riding the crest of nationalist and leftist support, the SLFP joined with the LSSP, the CP, and the Sinhala Bhasa Peramuna, a group of nationalists organized by W. Dahanayake around the demand to make Sinhala the national language and to form the Mahajana Eksath Peramuna (MEP), or "People's United Front." The MEP was swept into office as the celebrations of Buddha Jayanti pervaded the country.

Democratic Socialism in Sri Lanka

The 1956 elections led to genuine change not only in the nationalistic aspirations of the Sinhalese, but also in effecting a more egalitarian distribution of wealth and, most specifically, land. Sri Lanka's efforts at land redistribution were undoubtedly made easier by the appropriation of large amounts of fertile land held by foreign tea planters, and they evidence both Sri Lanka's sustained commitment to a egalitarian society as well as its leadership among Third World nations in its execution of socialistic goals.

As explained by Prime Minister Bandaranaike, land redistribution was part of an overall policy of democratic socialism. Speaking for the complete nationalization of paddy (rice-growing) lands, Bandaranaike spoke before Parliament in 1957:

... socialism itself involves a restriction, an inevitable restriction not on the freedoms of democracy but on those illusory freedoms that capitalism evolved for the benefit of capitalists. The two are vastly different from each other. Democratic freedom and capitalist freedom must not be taken as connoting the same thing. . . . [P]rivate property belonging to the landlords must necessarily suffer restrictions under any kind of application of socialist principles. Those freedoms have to be restricted. . . . Democratic freedoms are quite different. Capitalist freedoms are not necessarily democratic freedoms. . . . We are both democratic and socialistic, and in achieving that end there must be a restriction on certain freedoms but those so-called are freedoms of the capitalists.[80]

Such far-reaching reforms, notes W. Howard Wriggins, former American Ambassador to Sri Lanka (1977–1980), are rarely achieved by the electoral process:

The 1956 election was remarkable in that of all the elections held in Ceylon since 1931, and in India and Burma since independence, it alone resulted in marked transfers of political power from one segment of the population to another. The shift in the locus of power was accomplished without bloodshed, mass corruption, or intimidation of the electorate by violence. It was not the elective confirmation of a coup d'etat, but a genuine change in leadership effected by the cumulated choice of hundreds of thousands of individual voters.[81]

Another far-reaching change that grew out of the 1956 election was the reorganization of Sri Lanka's educational system. Prior to 1956, education in Sri Lanka had largely been on a dual track: an elitist, English-medium system administered by various missionaries, and a populist, Sinhala-medium education administered by the state. Because English was the official language of the country, those from elitist schools had clear advantages in seeking employment in government and private sectors. Educational reform was thus wedded to language reform. "As long as English remained the effective language of government administration, business, and higher education," Wriggins writes, "the most energetic and ambitious young people would seek education in English, and in this process they would become half-cosmopolitan, part Christian, and wholly alienated from their cultural and religious roots."[82]

So educational reform, an issue fundamentally connected with language issues, and issues of a privileged Christian population, became a major policy of the MEP government. In 1961 an SLFP government, under the Prime Ministry of Mrs. Sirima Bandaranaike, nationalized Catholic and Protestant missionary schools. Strong resistance to this measure within the Catholic community was in part responsible for an attempted coup d'etat led by right-wing military leaders, many of whom were Catholics. Despite an outcry from Catholics in Sri Lanka and abroad, the SLFP government (and UNP governments since that time) have remained firm in disallowing the use of education for the privilege of certain sectors of society, and Sri Lanka continues to provide free, high-quality education for all its citizens.[83] The current literacy rate is nearly 90 percent, a rate that is unprecedented among poorer countries and that compares well with the literacy rates of the most affluent nations.

In addition to land redistribution and educational reforms, the MEP government also contended with the language issue, around which much nationalist sentiment was focused. As Wriggins observes, "Large numbers of Buddhist laymen and *bhikkhus* came to feel that as long as English was the official language of Ceylon, those who were adept in Sinhal[a]—usually the Buddhists—would not have an equal opportunity to contribute their special qualities to the people of Ceylon."[84] Because official use of English was, effectively, a bar to the Buddhist majority's participation in public life, issues arose as to whether Sinhala only, or a combination of Sinhala and Tamil, should replace English. The ACBC, EBP, Buddhist Commissions on Enquiry, and other nationalist groups were firmly committed to a Sinhala-only program, not simply as an expression of an amorphous nationalistic sentiment, but because mastery of language came to entail economic and political status. Some went as far as to demand that Buddhism be established as the state religion, as in classical times.

S.W.R.D. Bandaranaike aligned himself with these nationalistic forces, but as early as 1951 expressed reservations on the more extreme of these demands. Speaking in Parliament, he said

I make no distinction between one religion and another nor do I want particular favours for one religion against another. . . . I never asked and do not now ask that Buddhism be made the State religion. . . . But I do ask for the vast majority of Buddhists in this country, whose religion has been linked with their lives for two thousand years and is one which has suffered more than any other religion under foreign rule, certain just things which we can expect to be done by the Government of this country.[85]

Thus, he sought to recognize a "special status" for Buddhism but drew the line at making it a state religion or at making Sinhala the official language.

For such a mediating position Bandaranaike was criticized by Sinhala and Tamil partisans. The UNP opposition, branding Bandaranaike's position on the language issue a sellout, gained strength among the *bhikkhus* who had helped Bandaranaike into office. At the same time, the Tamil Federal Party (FP), which had been in the MEP coalition, pressured Bandaranaike for concessions on the language issue. Bandaranaike was forced to break his pact with the FP, and in 1958 communal riots broke out between the Tamils and the Sinhalese, and a state of emergency was declared. The division between the Sinhalese and Tamil communities has continued to frustrate development and any national consensus, and renewed violent confrontations came in 1971 and 1977. Today the opposition party, the Tamil United Liberation Front (TULF, which derives from the FP and other Tamil parties), affirms in its platform the establishment of an independent Tamil state, Eelam.

Bandaranaike was also the architect of Sri Lanka's foreign policy of non-alignment as an expression of the Buddhist principle of "the middle way" (*majjhima patipāda*). As early as 1952 he articulated this principle:

. . . we should in our external affairs follow "the middle way." What exactly is the meaning of the expression "the middle way" in relation to external affairs? It can only mean . . . that we steer clear of power blocs whether they be capitalistic power blocs of the Western world or Communist or other power blocs of other parts of the world, and try to retain reasonably friendly relations with all.[86]

By the time he assumed the Prime Ministry, his notion of non-alignment had become more nuanced, advocating a "dynamic neutralism":

What is this neutralism? It is just that we do not range ourselves with one power bloc or another power bloc to divide the world into two worlds, each hating the other, each fearing the other, which must necessarily lead to war. . . . [I]n the course of time, perhaps the world will banish, let us hope forever, this ever constant and ever present danger of war. This is what I mean by dynamic neutralism, not the kind of neutralism of just remaining on a side, of sitting on a fence . . . it is something much more positive in my view.[87]

This dynamic neutralism, a bulwark of Sri Lanka's foreign policy since 1956, has placed it in a pivotal position of articulating and leading the non-aligned movement. Not only was the Non-Aligned Summit of 1976 held in Colombo, but Sri Lanka has distinguished itself by its contributions to various United Nations peacekeeping operations, such as the present Namibia negotiations, by serving on the World Court, and generally by maintaining a neutralist stance such that it has often contributed to the furtherance of peace through various trans-national organizations.

Bandaranaike's neutralism also led him to seek a middle path between communism and capitalism via his understanding of Buddhist socialism. Ever since his tenure in office, Sri Lanka has remained committed to democratic socialism, non-alignmnet, and social welfare—all as expressions of Buddhist polity in a pluralistic society. Indeed, much of Bandaranaike's Buddhist nationalist-socialist agenda has become the very basis of Sri Lanka's theory of development. As he cogently expressed this middle way principle in 1947, "We must be as equally ready to meet [the threat of big business] ... as to meet ... the opposite danger of Marxism."[88]

The Bandaranaike era came to an abrupt end on September 29, 1959, when he was assassinated. A leading *bhikkhu*, who was a member of the Vidyalankara Group but who seems to have been motivated by personal profit, has been implicated in the assassination. Elections in 1960 saw the SLFP returned to power under Bandaranaike's widow, Mrs. Sirima Bandaranaike. The *bhikkhus* were much less active in this election, as the public outcry surrounding a monk's involvement in Bandaranaike's assassination led to a nationwide reassessment of the proper role for a monk in politics.

The abortive coup d'etat of 1962 led to a furtherance of Buddhist nationalism. After the Catholics tried to seize power, the Governor-General, Sir Oliver Goonetilleke, himself Catholic, was quickly replaced by William Gopallawa, an ardent Buddhist. As Donald Smith reports, "In a ceremony of great symbolic significance the governor-general (later President) placed a tray of jasmine flowers before an image of the Buddha, installed for the first time at Queen's House (the official resident) ... while monks chanted the Buddhist scriptures."[89] Mrs. Bandaranaike's government moved further to the left in its nationalization and currency control programs, which led to an alienation of the more conservative factions within the SLFP. This alienation of the right, along with the aftermath of the coup d'etat attempt, led to the defeat of the SLFP in 1965 by the UNP, now headed by D. S. Senanayake's son, Dudley.

Dudley Senanayake's government moved the UNP leftward, and it now advocated a thoroughly mixed economy in addition to its traditional emphasis on social welfare. However, Buddhist nationalists again entered the electoral fray in 1970 in coalition with Mrs. Bandaranaike's SLFP, the LSSP, and the CP. This new coalition, the United Front (UF), won the 1970 elections and promulgated a republican constitution in 1972 which called for "special recognition'' for Buddhism, but stopped far short of the call of 1956 for its establishment as a state religion.

Perhaps the high point of Mrs. Bandaranaike's government was the Non-Aligned Summit convened at Colombo in 1976. Once again, Sri Lanka found itself in the vortex of the Third World movement, and Mrs. Bandaranaike found herself its spokesperson.

Charges of corruption and nepotism, as well as unacceptable unemployment levels, led to a UNP landslide victory in 1977 under J. R. Jayawardene. Throughout the campaign, Jayawardene stressed the establishment of *Dharmishta*, a society based on Dharma which, as the Ceylon *Daily News* editorialized, ''was more socialist and forward- looking, more pragmatic and development oriented, more realistic and acceptable than the manifesto of [the] Sri Lanka Freedom Party.''[90]

One of Jayawardene's first orders of business was a reorganization of Sri Lanka's government from a parlimentary to a presidential system; Jayawardene occupied the presidential office in early 1978. As was commented in the press, this marked ''a radical change in our system of Government in that for the first time since 1815 when the Kandyan Kingdom ceased to exist as an independent State, we will have a Head of State who is not a mere ceremonial head, but one who is directly vested with executive power by the people themselves.''[91] Indeed, many of the trappings of Kandyan royalty were observed at Jayawardene's inauguration, underscoring the symbolic reliance on the image of the Buddhist monarch drawn from pre-colonial days, as had been done by Bandaranaike some twenty years earlier.

Indeed, Jayawardene's government and the ''new'' UNP saw itself as heir to Bandaranaike's Buddhist socialism, a course which the UNP claimed had been forsaken under Mrs. Bandaranaike. This ''new'' UNP had contributed not only to the development of electoral democracy, but had also been in the forefront of socialistic programs. As journalist Tyronne Fernando commented,

The United National Party Governments' contribution to Socialism is a quiet but solid and practical one: Equality in education ... and free education in the mother tongue; A universal and free health service; Land reform; ... agricultural credit for the farmer, and the Rice Subsidy for the consumer ...; Legislation for labour and industrial welfare ...; Worker ownership and management ...; Rural development; The expansion of the co-operative movement; The pioneering efforts in the field of international trade and aid, e.g., the Colombo Plan conceived by Mr. J. R. Jayawardene (1950), the Rubber Rise Agreement with Communist China (1952), the Colombo Powers' Conference summoned by the then Prime Minister Sir John Kotewala (1954).[92]

At the same time, Jayawardene's consistency as a Buddhist nationalist is stressed. In addition to his notion of *Dharmishta*, a just society, and his use of traditional symbolism at public ceremonies, Jayawardene's commitment to Sinhala as the national language with accommodation for Tamil in Tamil-speaking areas is emphasized, as well as the fact that Jayawardene received his education entirely in Sri Lanka, rather than the obligatory Oxford or Cambridge.[93]

So we see in Jayawardene's government, which was returned to power in October 1982, emphases on socialism within the context of a mixed economy and Buddhist nationalism. These two principles seem to be essential for electoral success in Sri Lanka, which now understands itself as a non- aligned, pluralistic, anti-colonialist, democratic, Buddhist, and socialist society.

BURMA

As in Sri Lanka, Burmese politics since the interwar period have been dominated by an admixture of Buddhist nationalism and Marxism. Burmese nationalism during its early period was largely dominated by Buddhist *phongyis* (monks), who were initially spurred to oppose British rule as a result of the debilitating effects this rule had on the status of the *saṅgha*. This opposition meshed with the broader reaction against the economic and social disruption of British rule in the 1920s and 1930s, and, with the introduction of Marxist ideas in the 1930s, with Marxism as well. Since that time, Burmese politics have been characterized by the attempt to create a new social and economic order based on both Marxist and Buddhist principles, with the Buddhist, however, subordinated from the start to the indigenous forms of Buddhist nationalism. This was undoubtedly necessary in a country that is over 90 percent Buddhist, and where the old saying, "To be Burmese is to be Buddhist," still holds with force. Although the post-World War II era can arguably be said to have seen somewhat of a decline in the direct influence of both Buddhist and Marxist principles, it was still possible in 1956 for a Burmese politician to say, "We are all Marxists now."[94] The importance of Buddhism is demonstrated by the leadership of U Nu, prime minister almost continually from 1947 until the military coup in 1962, who stressed the importance of Buddhism for the guidance of the Burmese state and who saw himself as a protector and propagator of Burmese Buddhism. The term "syncretic socialism" is thus an apt description of postwar Burmese politics and governance, combining as it did Buddhism, democratic socialism, and British-style parliamentary democracy.[95] The military government of Ne Win has elided democracy from this equation, but still sees itself as Marxist and Buddhist in complexion.

As noted above, British colonial rule in Burma (1885–1942) effected a severe disruption of the traditionally symbiotic relationship between the Buddhist *saṅgha* and the state authority (the Burmese kings in pre-colonial days). The British claimed that their policy toward Buddhism in Burma, as in India, was one of strict "neutrality" and "non- interference." It is true that, by and large, they refrained from direct repression of Buddhist institutions, and British rule was not accompanied (as it was in Sri Lanka) by large-scale Christian missionary activity. But in a country where the proper functioning of the Buddhist *saṅgha* depended so heavily on the protection and authority of the state, this neutrality severely fragmented the Buddhist hierarchy and undermined the authority of the *saṅgha*. The attempts by the British to reform the traditional educational system, controlled and run by the *saṅgha*, further weakened the *saṅgha's* standing and authority in Burmese society.

Although the first three decades of colonial rule saw relatively little nationalist opposition, when nationalist sentiment did emerge, it did so strongly and, as might be expected, initially centered around religious issues. The first episode of signifance occurred in 1916, when the Young Men's Buddhist Association (YMBA) protested against the British practice of wearing footwear on pagoda premises, a practice contrary to Buddhist custom. After long and sometimes violent protests, the colonial government, initially intransigent, finally relented and banned the wearing of footwear. The YMBA (later the General Council of Burmese Associations [GCBA] was organized in 1906 as a non-political organization by Western-educated, middle-class Burmans trying to develop ways that Burmese traditions could meet the "challenge of the West." This struggle transformed the YMBA into Burma's first explicitly nationalistic organization, crystallizing the mass outpouring of anti-colonial sentiment sparked by the footwear controversy. Religious issues remained the focal point for nationalist sentiment until the end of the 1920s, and *phongyis* remained the most active organizers of nationalist activity throughout this period.

The next major outbreak of Buddhist nationalist activity came in 1921, when the British jailed for subversive activity an outspoken *phongyi*, U Ottama, who charged the British with undermining Burmese culture and religion and "corrupting the peoples' morals."[96] His arrest led to widespread strikes and mass demonstrations. U Ottama, who would remain in jail almost constantly until his death in 1939, was considered the first martyr to the cause of Burmese nationalism. After U Ottama, the next most significant *phongyi* nationalist was U Wisara, whose death in a British jail after an extended hunger strike undertaken to win the right to wear the traditional *phongyi* yellow robe while a prisoner, sparked another surge of nationalist agitation.

Although all nationalist groups during this period advocated the return to Burma to "indigenous control," they did not call for outright independence, though many nationalists held this as an eventual goal. Some organizations (most prominently the GCBA, supported by U Ottama) called for a total boycott of elections and non-cooperation with the British authorities, while others (such as the Twenty-One Party and the Golden Valley Party) advocated, to varying degrees, more accommodationist stances.

In addition to the religious issues, nationalist sentiment during the 1920s was fed by two other factors: the almost total exclusion of Burmans from governmental affairs (the first Burman was accepted into the British civil service in Burma only in 1923); and the domination of the economy by British and Indian interests. (Burma, during most of its colonial period, was classed as a part of India, and many Indians followed the British to Burma.) The British and Indians controlled foreign trade, the use of land, money-lending and investment, and industry, whereas the Burmese role in the economy was essentially reduced to the cultivation of rice and other crops. Frustration with this state of affairs brought many workers and peasants into the nationalist movement in the 1920s, and even greater numbers in the 1930s when global depression exacerbated the already sorry plight of Burmese laborers.

Burmese nationalism entered an important new phase in the early 1930s with the emergence of a new breed of more militant, leftist-oriented nationalists at Rangoon University. Calling themselves "Thakins," the term used to address the British "masters," these young militants rejected the accommodationist positions of the older nationalists, saying that Burmans must be fully "masters" of their own affairs. This small group, from which would come virtually every major political figure of the post-independence government, found in Marxism (previously unknown in Burma) a strong weapon for analyzing British colonialism and organizing against it. The Thakins, however, were always nationalists first and Marxists second, and they appropriated from Marxism only those elements they found compatible with Burmese traditions and circumstances. They were attracted mainly to the Marxist analysis of imperialism and colonialism and its critique of capitalist materialism, "especially," according to Trevor Ling,

when such materialism was seen masquerading as something else—i.e., putting up a smoke screen of moralistic Christianity to hide its own ugly nature—and when it was characterized as a materialism which allowed the few by their selfish operation of the economy to dominate and exploit the many. What Marx sought, they believed, was a materialism of a different kind, one which was directed and controlled by man for the good of man.[97]

As John Seabury Thomason has said, this was "Marxism with a difference."[98] This difference led most of the Thakins to reject Soviet communism, which they saw as anti-democratic and imperialist, and to reject the blanket condemnation of religion they found in much Marxist literature.[99] They knew that if Marxism was to take root among the Burmese populace, it would have to be made compatible with Buddhist philosophy, and this became a primary focus for them. Thus, during the 1930s,

the Thakins tried to explain the unfamiliar ideology of Marxism with the help of the familiar religious creed of Buddhism. In the ideal Buddhist future, the state and society were to be dissolved into a monastic order with a community of property. With the withering away of the state, therefore, the Buddhist social ideals were expected to find their ultimate fulfillment. But in the transitional phase, statization of the means of production was essential for ensuring economic welfare and alleviating the earthly sufferings of mankind. Statization of private property was to relieve the people of their worldly worries and anxieties, and thereby quicken the process of achieving the highest ideal of Buddhist life, *nirvana*, through the pursuit of meditation in leisure time.[100]

This newly emergent nationalism, therefore, found a ready ally in the older Buddhist nationalist groups, whose influence in the nationalist movement became increasingly indirect as activist *phongyis* allied themselves with the various parties and organizations that grew out of the Thakin movement. "Fully articulate" Burmese nationalism thus included, in Thomson's words, "indigenous nationalism; Buddhism; a background of Western political, economic, and educational institutions; a revulsion against foreign domination ...; and an intellectual bent toward Marxist ideology—the last having been added late and worked into the existing fabric."[101]

The Thakins found the *Dohbama Asiayone* ("We Burmans" Association) in 1935 and began engaging in widespread agitation and organizing among the Burmese people, beginning with the establishment of Marxist study groups and, under the influence of the young U Ba Swe, moving to organize labor and the peasantry. The first major action of the Thakins was the student strike at Rangoon University in 1936, led by U Nu, Aung San, and U Ba Swe. This was followed two years later by a major strike by oil field workers which, under the leadership of the Thakins, quickly moved from its initial focus on wages to nationalist demands. The All- Burma Trade Union Congress (ABTUC), founded in January 1940, was a direct outgrowth of this strike. From this time onward, the labor unions, which previously had been largely inactive and ineffectual, were potent advocates of nationalist and specialist aspirations under the leadership of the Thakins, who rallied the workers around the goal of wresting the country's wealth from the British and Indians and establishing a more egalitarian society.

During the same period, the Thakins organized a mass peasant march on Rangoon, out of which came the All-Burma Peasant's Organization (ABPO). At the conference establishing the organization, they stated their goals as: "(1) national liberation; (2) improvements in the peasants' standard of living and in the general welfare of the impoverished mass of the people; (3) the abolition of landlordism; (4) nationalization of the land; (5) the establishment of a Socialist State under the leadership of the workers and peasants."[102]

By this time, the Thakins had split into two major camps: the socialists (key members were Aung San, Thakin Tin, U Ba Swe, and Kyaw Nyein) and the smaller communists (key members were Thakin Soe, Thein Pe, and Than Tun), as well as a non-aligned grouping (U Nu among them). Thein Pe organized the Communist Party in 1939, which provoked the socialists to organize the People's Revolutionary Party (later the Socialist Party). Although the parties remained largely united at this time around anti-British nationalism and Marxism, the communists were clearly the more militant and more oriented toward the Soviet Union of the two, and were less concerned with effecting an integration of Marxism and Buddhism.

The wartime period was important for the Thakins. Under the Japanese occupation government led by U Ba Maw, the Thakins for the first time held important governmental positions, gaining valuable experience as well as making them better known throughout Burma. Many of the Thakins had originally supported the Japanese occupation, accepting the Japanese promise to free Burma from British rule and declare it independent. When it became clear that the

Japanese had no intention of keeping this promise, the Thakins, both inside and outside the government, worked clandestinely in opposition to Japanese rule. In August 1944 the communists and socialists met to form the Anti-Fascist People's Freedom League (AFPFL), with army general and socialist (though he was not a member of the Socialist Party) Aung San as president and communist Than Tun as secretary-general. This organization was soon expanded to include representatives of other major groups in Burmese society. In March of 1945, the AFPFL rose in open revolt against the Japanese. After negotiating an agreement with the British guaranteeing Burmese independence after the war, Aung San took the Burmese army, organized by the Japanese but controlled by the Thakins, over to the British side.

The several years immediately following the war saw divisive and violent confrontations between the socialists and communists (and at times within each party) as the two groups vied for control of the postwar government. Although both were still avowedly Marxist, the communists espoused the necessity of violence and force in establishing a truly Marxist state and felt that the independence agreement negotiated in 1947 by Aung San betrayed Burmese interests and was a sellout to the imperialist powers.

The first split came in 1946 within the ranks of the Burma Communist Party, when Thakin Soe and his followers withdrew from the Party to form the Communist Party (Burma), which called for immediate insurrection and the overthrow of the governing AFPFL coalition. The "Red Flag" communists, as they came to be known, went underground, while the more moderate "White Flag" communists remained for the time being within the AFPFL.

Later that same year, the second split came when the White Flags, under the leadership of Than Tun, were expelled from the AFPFL after a period of great tension within the coalition, caused by an intense battle for control of the AFPFL between the socialists and the White Flags. In the elections to the Constituent Assembly held in April 1947, the now socialist-controlled AFPFL won an overwhelming victory, winning 248 seats to only 7 for the White Flags.

Three months later, elements from within the Red Flags assassinated Prime Minister Aung San and six members of his Cabinet. Aung San was succeeded by U Nu, who immediately began an intensive effort to reunify all elements of the left. Although this succeeded for a short while with the White Flags, whose cooperation allowed the adoption of the Constitution in September 1947 to be unanimous, relations quickly deteriorated again and, in March 1948, the White Flags went underground and joined the Red Flags in open insurrection. The government, after almost falling to the insurgents in 1949, made steady advances to the point where, by 1952, the communists no longer posed a significant threat.

Burma had thus been firmly established as a democratic-socialist welfare state, built on both Marxist and Buddhist principles and controlled by the AFPFL, which in turn was largely (though not fully) controlled by the socialists. The Marxist and welfare state principles were embodied in the Constitution and the Two-Year Plan of Economic Development for Burma, both adopted in 1947.

The Constitution provided for nationalization of enterprises as might be found to be in the public interest; declared the state to be the ultimate owner of all land and gave the state power to redistribute land; prohibited large landholdings; protected the rights of workers and peasants; and mandated that at least 60 percent of private enterprises must be owned by Burmese citizens. The Two-Year Plan drew on Marxism even more heavily, declaring the goal of "the evolution of a fully Socialist economy in Burma"[103] and stating that "The profit motive and other considerations which usually govern industries in capitalist economies shall not be allowed to determine the development of basic industries in Independent Burma."[104] Along with industrialization and nationalization, the goal of Burma's development was above all "Burmanization"—the wresting of economic power away from foreign interests and the protection of economic independence.

The importance attached to the effort to base these policies on a firm Buddhist foundation can be seen in the statements and actions of the two most important political figures on the Burmese scene during the 1950s: Prime Minister U Nu and socialist leader U Ba Swe. In a speech delivered in December 1951,[105] U Ba Swe stated that Marxism was the guide of Burmese socialism:

Marxism is the guide to action in our revolutionary movement, in our establishment of a Socialist Burmese State for workers and peasants. Our revolution can only be achieved with Marxism as a guiding principle. Only Marxism can pave the way for the attainment of the goal to which we look forward. Our revolution is impossible without Marxism as a guide.[106]

Having said this, he made it clear that Burmese Marxism followed its own path and was not to be equated with Soviet communism:

Only a revolutionary movement which is entirely Burmese, conforming to Burmese methods and principles can achieve any measure of success. . . . The acceptance of Marxism does not necessarily make one a Communist. To be a Communist, you have to observe certain set rules of conduct. Especially the so-called Communists believe that to become a Communist one must unequivocally accept Soviet leadership.[107]

U Ba Swe then made a crucial equation, saying that Marxism was not merely compatible with Buddhism, but that the two were actually "the same in concept," with Marxism providing a guide to material needs and Buddhism dealing with spiritual matters:

Marxist philosophy rejects the theory of creation; but it does not oppose religion. In point of fact, Marxist theory is not antagonistic to Buddhist philosophy. The two are, frankly speaking, not merely similar. In fact, they are the same in concept. But if we want to have the two distinguished one from the other, we can safely assume that Marxist theory occupies the lower plane, while Buddhist philosophy occupies the higher. Marxist theory deals with mundane affairs and seeks to satisfy material needs in life. Buddhist philosophy, however, deals with the solution of spiritual matters with a view to seek spiritual satisfaction in life and liberation from this mundane world.[108]

U Ba Swe then spelled out the five categories comprising the "Burmese Socialist structure": People's Democracy, People's Economy, People's Education, People's Health, and People's Social Security. The principles articulated in these sections were an admixture of Marxist terminology and welfare-state policies; but he again emphasized that:

Marxism cannot provide an answer for spiritual liberation. Neither can Science do. Only Buddhist philosophy can. Only where there is satisfaction of spiritual needs can we find solace in life. Only then can we find our way to the liberation from this mundane world. It must, however, be conceded that material satisfaction of life can be attained only through Marxism.[109]

Burmese socialism was thus to strive for both the material and spiritual uplift of the people, with Marxism and Buddhism working in tandem for the achievement of these goals.

U Nu, more than any other Burmese political figure, undertook to support and propagate Buddhism and was responsible for a wide array of actions in support of Marxism and the Marxist *saṅgha*. Among these actions were: the creation of special courts reestablishing Buddhist control over the affairs of the *saṅgha*; the support and encouragement of traditional Pali studies through the Pali Education Board Act of 1952; the creation of the Buddha Sasana Council in 1950, charged with promoting and propagating Marxism in Burma; the convening of the Sixth Great Buddhist Council in Rangoon in 1954, which lasted for two years, attracted Buddhists from all over Asia, and concluded at the time of the 2500th anniversary of the *parinibbāna* of the Buddha; and the establishment of Buddhism as Burma's offical state religion in 1961, the single act for which U Nu is probably best known.

U Nu's relationship to Marxism is somewhat more complex than U Ba Swe's. Although he continued to espouse Buddhism until 1958, it is fair to say that he was always a Buddhist first and a Marxist second. He was instrumental in implementing the Marxist and social welfare principle embodied in the Constitution and other documents, but often justified these policies on Buddhist rather than Marxist grounds. His support for the Land Nationalization Act of 1950, for example, was based on the conviction that, in Bandyopadhyaya's words,

[T]he peasantry was to be freed from the illusion that land had a value of its own. Land had its value, according to [Nu's] Buddhist ideal, only in the transitional phase as a means of security in the pursuit of *nirvana*. Statization of land, therefore, was to guarantee leisure and security to the people in the transitional phase until the state and society were dissolved into the Buddhist monastic order.[110]

In the early years of his nationalist activity, U Nu had been a much stronger supporter of Marxism and had even translated sections of *Das Kapital* and other Marxist works into Burmese. Even then, however, he expressed his support in terms of his Buddhist convictions. In an article written in the late 1930s entitled

"I Am a Marxist," Nu stated that "to help work for Marxism would be to repay our gratitude to Buddha for his suffering in all his aeons of existence for the benefit of mankind."[111] By the early 1950s, his commitment to Marxism had become much more muted. In parliamentary debate on the Buddha Sasana Council Act of 1950, Nu declared, "It will be our duty to retort in no uncertain terms that the wisdom or knowledge that might be attributed to Karl Marx is less than one-tenth of a particle of dust that lies at the feet of our great Lord Buddha."[112] Finally, in a speech before an AFPFL Congress in 1958, Nu stated:

It is entirely impossible to take the attitude that both Marxism and religion are in the right, and that therefore both can be accepted. . . . When we were younger, we had not studied Marxism in detail or with any exactness. At the same time, more or less on hearsay and cursory reading, we impetuously and loudly claimed that Marxism was the same as Buddhism. We are very remorseful for having made at one time such ill-considered and unfounded claims.[113]

In an article written in 1959 ("What Is Socialism?"), U Nu claimed that socialism was necessary to overcome the pernicious effects of capitalism, but this was explained entirely on Buddhist, not Marxist, grounds: "the reason why an average Buddhist concerns himself not with the final release from *saṁsāra* but with the acquisition of property is to be found in the economic system that prevails in the world."[114] Only a Buddhist socialist state could combat capitalist acquisitiveness and provide the leisure for spiritual pursuits necessary for the attainment of *nibbāna*.

The decade of the 1950s saw a progressive scaling back of the government's ambitious economic and social plans, necessitated in part by a drastic fall in the world price for rice, Burma's major crop, proceeds from which were to fund the development plans. Although social welfare policies remained largely intact, nationalization and collectivization plans were pared back or repealed, decentralization of political and economic decision-making was shelved, and private enterprise and foreign investment were encouraged in many spheres. Accompanying these changes were increasing political tensions between leftist and centrist elements in the governing AFPFL coalition, caused in part by economic stagnation and the consequent reorganization of development policies. In the spring of 1958, the AFPFL split into two factions: the leftist "Stable AFPFL," led by U Ba Swe and Kyaw Nyein, and the more moderate "Clean AFPFL," led by U Nu. Nu's rejection of Marxism in 1958 (quoted above) came in this climate of political discord. The Stable faction, running on a platform that stressed the propagation of Buddhism (including the proposal to make Marxism the official state religion), won the elections of 1960. Two years later, however, the military, under the leadership of General Ne Win, took power in a coup d'etat, thus ending the era of democratic socialism in Burma.

Ne Win's military government, while it has been strongly anti-communist, has nonetheless claimed to be inspired by both socialist and Buddhist principles, thus providing some continuity between the pre- and post-coup periods. The government continues to contain avowed Marxists in many posts, and its statement of program, *The Burmese Way to Socialism*, while it rejects communism as "vulgar materialism," accepts many Marxist principles and stresses the need to advance both the physical and spiritual welfare of the Burmese people.[115] Although the government's rhetoric contains references to both Marxist and Buddhist ideals, its actions have tended to accord more with the Marxist than the Buddhist. On the one hand, it has nationalized banks, commerce, and education, established cooperatives in the agricultural sphere, and suppressed free market mechanisms in favor of the discretion of economic activity by the government. On the other hand, the military government canceled the act making Buddhism the official state religion, abolished the General Council and executive body of the Buddha Sasana Council, and discontinued the practice of closing government offices on the Buddhist sabbath. The government was forced to back down on one decree, which required the registration of all members of the *sangha* and a pledge from the members not to engage in political activity, after loud protests from the *phongyis* (including the self-immolation of one *phongyi*). These and other actions have understandably strained relations between the *sangha* and the government.

Little information is available concerning the development of the government's policies and the status of Buddhism during the last decade because of Burma's self-isolation from world affairs effected by the military regime.

THAILAND

Thailand's modern history has differed in fundamental ways from the histories of Sri Lanka and Burma, and the terms on which Buddhism has encountered Marxist or socialist forms of thought have, accordingly, differed as well. Of primary importance in this regard is the fact that Thailand is the only country in the whole of South and Southeast Asia that was not at any time subject to Western colonial domination. This has meant, on the one hand, that the anti-imperialist struggles which in other countries provided fertile ground for the introduction and profusion of Marxism were absent in Thailand's case, and, on the other hand, that the disruption in the functioning of the Buddhist *sangha* which in other countries led to the politicization of large segments of the *sangha* and lay Buddhist populace were also absent in Thailand. Thus, whatever interaction has taken place between Buddhism and Marxism or socialism in Thailand has been limited to the fringes of the Thai polity and has not been a significant factor in the political development of the modern Thai state.

The absence of a colonial heritage in Thailand has allowed a number of traditional patterns to survive in modern times more or less intact. Changes that did take place as a result of contact with the West were not abrupt, and Thai rulers have successfully introduced reforms in traditional patterns slowly and without major disruptions. The increasing commercialization of agriculture, for example, has proceeded slowly and has not led to large-scale displacement of the peasantry from the land, a not unimportant factor in a country that is still overwhelmingly agriculturally based. Industrialization has likewise proceeded gradually, and thus for a large, discontented urban proletariat has not developed. Politically, the move from monarchy to a more secularly based governmental elite occurred peacefully and in such a way that the traditional symbiotic relationships between the Buddhist hierarchy, the state authority, and the Thai populace, while undergoing changes, have on the whole remained intact and retained their legitimacy and authority. The few leftist parties that emerged on the political scene during the 1950s never garnered more than a small amount of support and, though a couple of them advocated some type of combination of Buddhist and socialist principles, what this would mean in practice was left largely unarticulated. Communist activity has remained almost entirely limited to the minority Chinese and Vietnamese populations.

If these factors explain the lack of appeal of Marxism among the Thai people, they also explain the largely apolitical nature of the Thai *sangha*. All Thai governments in the twentieth century have scrupulously observed their role as protector of the *sangha*, which has accordingly maintained its traditional important role in the Thai polity. In recent years, however, there has been a growing feeling within the *sangha*, particularly among young educated monks, that if Thai Buddhism is to remain fully relevant to the needs and circumstances of an increasingly secularized society the *sangha* must institute certain reforms and broaden the conception of the monk's proper role in society.

In response to these concerns, the two Buddhist universities in Thailand, Mahāmakta and Mahāchulalongkorn, have modernized their curriculum to include training in many "secular" subjects (such as economics, law, sociology, government, and history) that previously had not been a part of monks' training. Phra Srivisuddhimoh, deputy secretary general of Mahāchulalongkorn University, claims that the goal is not "to secularize the Buddhist monk. Rather we are attempting to return him to his traditional place as religious leader and guide of the people."[116] Besides seeking self-enlightenment, he says, "monks are bound with many social obligations to serve their community and to render reasonable services for the benefit of the layman's society."[117] Many monks are now active participants in the government's community development programs and are known as *thammathud* ("missionary monks"). One of the most important of these programs is the Dhammaduta Program, initiated by the government in 1964, which sends monks into the countryside with the dual purpose of promoting dedication to Buddhism and Thai Buddhist institutions and aiding the people through participation in development projects. Although it appears that the program has achieved some impressive results on the development front, one commentator has asserted that respect for the *sangha* has been undermined by the program insofar as the people see the monks as tools of the government, used by the government to prop up its legitimacy.[118]

The most important proponent of some combination of Buddhism and socialism in Thailand is undoubtedly Bhikkhu Buddhadāsa, one of Thailand's most influential and respected monks and a renowned teacher. Buddhadāsa, considered by some to be the greatest living genius within Theravāda Buddhism, heads a forest hermitage outside of Chaiya in southern Thailand. Although Buddhadāsa should not be seen mainly as a political figure, inasmuch as his main concerns involve the presentation of the "essential teachings" of the Buddha, he has in recent years articulated what he terms a "spiritual politics," which involve the application of Buddhist principles and practice in society.[119] He interprets the Buddha's teaching on *nirvāṇa* as implying non-attachment but not non-involvement, and says this should be normative for all members of society and not simply monks: "Those who are hot and bothered need to cool off. For this reason the Buddha meant the teaching about emptiness (*suññatā*) as the basis for the action of ordinary people."[120] The teachings of non-attachment and not-self (*anattā*) would, in a Buddhist socialist society, constitute the foundation for action based on the interests of others, that is, action without a self. Donald K. Swearer, who has studied Buddhadāsa extensively and has visited his forest hermitage, describes his conception this way:

It is a "socialistic" society operating according to mutual restraint (*saṅgama-niyama*) on the one hand, and active other-regardingness on the other, after the model of the *bodhisattva* who sacrifices his own interests on behalf of others. . . . A truly socialistic society, then, is where people work for the good of society, for the benefit of the whole. Or in other terms, acting for the good of others is nothing other than acting for the sake of the act itself, to act non-attached. People in many capitalistic countries, claims Buddhadāsa, are so selfishly motivated that they are completely out of balance. Their work bears no relationship with the real state of things. Material development has superseded mental (*citta*) development. Consequently, mental defilement and grasping continue to increase.[121]

The teaching of dependent co-orgination (*paṭicca-samuppāda*) would in such a socialist society provide a basis for action and social planning rooted in a deep appreciation for and understanding of the interdependence among individuals, specific policies, and the natural environment. Although Buddhadāsa has not explained how such a society could be made to come about (he does reject the use of violence as incompatible with the Buddha's teaching), except through the propagation of Buddhist principles throughout society, he has provided a compelling vision of what a society based on Buddhist principles would look like, a vision that is not wholly dissimilar from Marx's descriptions of a fully communist society.

CONCLUSIONS

Certain general patterns concerning the interaction of Buddhism with Marxism or non-Marxist forms of socialism in South and Southeast Asia emerge from the three case studies we have presented. Most evident among these is the strong impetus given to such an interaction by the struggle against Western colonialism in predominantly Buddhist countries, such as Sri Lanka and Burma. In both of these cases, anti-colonial activists found in Marxism an acute and politically useful analysis of the forces underlying and perpetuating their colonial situation, and in both countries the fight against Western domination was carried out under Marxist banners to some extent. But Marxism was, in many ways, just as foreign to indigenous traditions as the ideology of the colonialists. It was therefore necessary for these activists (many of whom were themselves Buddhists) to blend Marxism with the Buddhist principles that largely define the national ethos of both countries and that, in addition, were the guiding forces of the early nationalist movements in both countries.

The Marxism that evolved in these countries was thus one tailored to the needs and demands of the particular traditions and circumstances in existence. This, combined with the strong desire of the post-independence governments in both countries to remain resolutely non-aligned to international affairs, led in both cases to a rejection of the Soviet version of Marxism. Thus, the guiding philosophies of the postwar Burman and Sri Lankan governments must be described as Buddhist socialist rather than traditionally Marxist in nature.

In Thailand, on the other hand, the absence of a colonial heritage (or any significant disruption from contact with the West at all) meant, as we have seen, that Marxism was unable to attract more than a very small following, and the few attempts that have been made to articulate a Buddhist socialist philosophy have come from figures largely outside the mainstream of Thai society.

If there were forces compelling Marxism to reach out to and incorporate Buddhism in certain South Asian countries, there were equally strong forces compelling Buddhism to address and come to terms with Marxism and other secular influences in these countries. Colonialism in Sri Lanka and Burma not only disrupted the practical, tangible operations of the Buddhist *saṅgha* (e.g., fragmentation of the Buddhist hierarchy, withdrawal of the patronage of the state authority, and interference in the Buddhist education system), but also led to the introduction of secular forms and traditions that threatened to make Buddhism increasingly irrelevant to the circumstances of nations that were more or less forcibly introduced into a world system dominated by Western economic, political, and social patterns. In both of these countries, this forced Buddhists into a sometimes agonizing reappraisal of the proper social and political role of Buddhism that led many Buddhists to embrace Marxism or a non-Marxist socialism. This general tendency is evident in Thailand as well, though in this case the process of coming to terms with secularization evolved in the absence of the severe disruptions present in Burma and Sri Lanka and, for reasons already discussed, has not involved the incorporation of Marxism or socialism. Instead, it has centered more on educational reforms and community development projects.

With the military coup in Burma, Sri Lanka became the most influential country in Asia that can legitimately be termed a Buddhist socialist republic. For those interested in or committed to an integration of Buddhism and Socialism, then, the case of Sri Lanka remains the best example of how such a system can—and does—work in practice.

NOTES

1. Weber, *Religions of India*, p. 213; quoted in Spiro, *Buddhism and Society*, p. 427.
2. Spiro, *Buddhism and Society*.
3. King, *In the Hope of Nibbāna*.
4. Spiro, *Buddhism and Society*, p. 427.
5. Ibid.
6. Ibid.
7. King, *In the Hope of Nibbāna*, p. 162.
8. Reynolds, "Four Modes of Theravāda Action," p. 15.
9. For a strong critique of the two wheels position from a perspective somewhat different from our own, see de Silva, *Value Orientations and Nation Building*, pp 10–17.
10. Aronson, *Love and Sympathy in Theravāda Buddhism*, especially pp. 78–96. See also Aronson, "Motivations to Social Action in Theravāda Buddhism," in Narain, ed., *Studies in the History of Buddhism*, pp. 1–12; and Aronson, "Equanimity (Upekkhā) in Theravāda Buddhism," in Narain, ed., *Studies in Pali and Buddhism*, pp. 1–18.
11. Katz, *Buddhist Images of Human Perfection*, pp. 165–202.
12. Katz, *Buddhist Images of Human Perfection*, p. 180.
13. Ibid., p. 179.
14. Ibid., p. 194.
15. Aronson, "Equanimity (Upekkhā) in Theravāda Buddhism," p. 5.
16. K. N. Jayatilleke agrees: "In other words, far from it being inconsistent for one who has attained Nirvana to minister and preach unto others out of pity and compassion, it would be quite natural for him to do so. He does this not out of earthly consideration of gain or glory or out of a sense of duty . . . but because it would be just what such a person would quite naturally do by virtue of his attainment." Jayatilleke, *Aspects of Buddhist Social Philosophy*, p. 8.
17. Aronson, "Equanimity (Upekkhā) in Theravāda Buddhism," p. 10.
18. Ling, *Buddha, Marx and God*, pp. 27–73.
19. Ibid., p. 42.
20. Ibid.
21. Ibid., p. 40.
22. Gombrich's investigations support this position. See his *Precept and Practice*.
23. See their essays in Smith, ed., *Two Wheels of Dhama*. See also Reynolds, "Four Modes of Theravāda Action."
24. Reynolds, "Two Wheels of Dhamma," in Smith, ed., *Two Wheels of Dhamma*, p. 30.
25. See especially Reynolds, "Four Modes of Theravāda Action," pp. 18–19.
26. Ibid., p. 15.
27. Ibid.
28. Obeyesekere, "Religious Symbolism and Political Change in Ceylon," in Smith,

ed., *Two Wheels of Dhamma*, p. 64. See also Reynolds, "Four Modes of Theravāda Action," pp. 15–16.

29. Smith, "Sinhalese Buddhism and the Dilemmas of Reinterpretation," in Smith, ed., *Two Wheels of Dhamma*. Contrast pp. 56, 82, and 96 with p. 86.

30. Dharmasiri, "Buddhism and Marxism in the Socio-Cultural Context of Sri Lanka," in Katz, ed., *Buddhist and Western Philosophy*, pp. 136–148e.

31. Swe, *Burmese Revolution*.

32. Bandaranaike, *Towards a New Era*.

33. U Nu, *Forward with the People*. See also U Nu, *From Peace to Stability*.

34. Buddhadāsa, *Towards the Truth*.

35. The Dalai Lama, "Spiritual Contributions to Social Progress."

36. Jayawardene, *Buddhism and Marxism*.

37. Katz, "Buddhism and Marxism," pp. 9, 14.

38. Marx, in Easton and Guddat, eds., *Writings of the Young Marx on Philosophy and Society*, p. 28.

39. Bodhi, trans., *All-Embracing Net of Views*.

40. Freud, *Future of an Illusion*.

41. Macy, "Dependent Co-Arising," p. 39.

42. Lukács, "Reification and the Consciousness of the Proletariat," p. 154.

43. Ibid., p. 179.

44. Engels, Preface to *Capital III*; quoted by Ollman, *Alienation*, p. 4.

45. Garaudy, quoted in Ollman, *Alienation*, p. 292 n.12.

46. Marx, "Theses on Feuerbach," in Tucker, ed., *Marx-Engels Reader*, p.145.

47. Macy, "Dependent Co-Arising," pp. 42–43.

48. Ibid., pp. 47, 49.

49. Marx, "Economic and Philosophic Manuscripts (1844)," in Easton and Guddat, eds., *Writings of the Young Marx on Philosophy and Society*, p. 289.

50. Ibid., p. 293.

51. Ibid., pp. 289–290.

52. See Ñāṇānanda, *Concept and Reality in Early Buddhist Thought*.

53. See Katz, "Nāgārjuna and Wittgenstein on Error," in Katz, ed., *Buddhist and Western Philosophy*, pp. 306–327.

54. Swearer, *Buddhism and Society in Southeast Asia*, pp. 56–58.

55. Jayawardene, *Buddhism and Marxism*.

56. Ibid., p. 8.

57. Ibid., p. 10.

58. Ibid., p. 11.

59. Lanka Bauddha Mandalaya (Buddhist Council of Ceylon), *Event of Dual Significance*.

60. *The Mahāvaṁsa*, edited by Wilhelm Geiger; translated by Wilhelm Geiger.

61. Samaraweera, "Evolution of a Plural Society," in de Silva, ed., *Sri Lanka*, pp. 86–87.

62. Smith, "Religion, Politics and the Myth of Reconquest," in Fernando and Kearney, eds., *Modern Sri Lanka*, pp. 84–85.

63. Ibid.

64. Samaraweera, "Evolution of a Plural Society," p. 87.

65. Phadnis, *Religion and Politics in Sri Lanka*, p. 67.

66. Ibid., pp. 48–49.

67. Dharmapala, *Return to Righteousness*.

68. See Karunaratne, *Olcott's Contribution to the Buddhist Renaissance*.

69. Indeed, one point of concord among the diverse Buddhist nationalist and Marxist groups in Sri Lanka has been this tradition of Anti-Christian polemics. From Dharmapala ("A Message to the Buddhist Boys of Ceylon," pp. 345–351) to S.W.R.D. Bandaranaike ("Why I Became a Buddhist," pp. 7–9) to Jayawardene (*Buddhist Essays*), one finds such themes. The left in general, according to Wriggins (*Ceylon*), was able to agree with the Buddhist nationalists during the period just before the pivotal 1956 elections in "identifying the Catholic Church as a creature of Western imperialism," which "satisfied traditional leftist polemic requirements without alienating ardent Buddhists" (p. 332).

70. Phadnis, *Religion and Politics in Sri Lanka*, p. 66.

71. Olcott, *Buddhist Catechism*.

72. Phadnis, *Religion and Politics in Sri Lanka*, pp. 144–145.

73. Ibid., p. 145.

74. Ibid., p. 165.

75. Ibid., pp. 166–167.

76. Bandaranaike, *Towards a New Era*, pp. 3–6.

77. Buddhist Committee of Inquiry, *Betrayal of Buddhism*.

78. Anonymous (D. C. Wijewardene), *Revolt in the Temple*.

79. Phadnis, *Religion and Politics in Sri Lanka*, p. 187.

80. Bandaranaike, *Towards a New Era*, pp. 892–893.

81. Wriggins, *Ceylon*, pp. 326–327.

82. Ibid., p. 197.

83. Thomas, "Ceylon Christians Faced by Crisis," pp. 58–60.

84. Wriggins, *Ceylon*, p. 197.

85. Bandaranaike, *Towards a New Era*, p. 693.

86. Ibid., p. 816.

87. Ibid., p. 849.

88. Ibid., p. 667.

89. Smith, "Religion, Politics and the Myth of Reconquest," p. 97.

90. "Jayawardene Era Has Just Begun," p. 10.

91. Athulathmudali, "Towards a New Era in Sri Lanka," p. 21.

92. Fernando, "Role of UNP in Post-Independence Politics," p. 23.

93. "Jayawardene Era Has Just Begun," p. 10.

94. Thomson, "Marxism in Burma," Trager, ed., *Marxism in Southeast Asia*, pp. 14–57.

95. The term is used by Bandyopadhyaya in "The Evolution of Burmese Socialism," p. 394.

96. Smith, *Religion and Politics in Burma*, p. 96.

97. Ling, *Buddha, Marx, and God*, p. 90.

98. Thomson, "Marxism in Burma," p. 15.

99. Ibid.

100. Bandyopadhyaya, "Evolution of Burmese Socialism," p. 394.

101. Thomson, "Marxism in Burma," p. 19.

102. Rose, *Socialism in Southeast Asia*, p. 97.

103. Quoted in Thomson, "Marxism in Burma," p. 36.

104. Ibid.

105. Later published as *The Burmese Revolution*.

106. Ibid., p. 11.
107. Ibid., pp. 12–13, 14.
108. Ibid., p. 14.
109. Ibid., p. 25.
110. Bandyopadhyaya, "Evolution of Burmese Socialism," pp. 394–395.
111. Quoted in Butwell, *U Nu of Burma*, p. 27.
112. U Nu, *From Peace to Stability*, p. 108.
113. Quoted in Smith, *Religion and Politics in Burma*, p. 130.
114. Quoted in ibid., pp. 132–133.
115. *Burmese Way to Socialism*; discussed by Ling, *Buddha, Marx, and God*, pp. 162–163.
116. Quoted in Swearer, "Recent Developments in Thai Buddhism," in Dumoulin, ed., *Buddhism in the Modern World*, p. 100.
117. Ibid.
118. Somboon Suksamran, *Political Buddhism in Southeast Asia*.
119. *Acting Without Attachment on Behalf of Society* (Bangkok: Society for the Propagation of Buddhism); *The Value of Ethics* (Chaiya: Suan Mokha); and *The Kind of Socialism Which Helps the World* (Bangkok: Sublime Life Mission).
120. Quoted in Swearer, "Bhikkhu Buddhadāsa on Ethics and Society," p. 58.
121. Ibid., pp. 60–61.

GLOSSARY

Shiṁsa (Pali and Skt.): Non-harmfulness, non-violence.

Anattā (Pali; Skt. *anātman*): Non-self, egolessness.

Arahant (Pali; Skt. *arhat*): The "worthy one," a perfected human, equal in spiritual attainment to the Buddha.

Arahattā (Pali): The condition or state of being an *arahant*.

Ayurveda (Sinhala and Skt.): The indigenous medical system of South and Southeast Asia.

Bhikkhu (Pali; Skt. *bhikṣu*; Burmese *phongyi*): A fully ordained Buddhist monk.

Brahmavihāra (Pali and Skt.): "Divine abode," four ethical qualities cultivated through meditation (*bhāvana*).

Buddha Jayanti: The 1956 celebrations throughout Asia commemorating the final release (*parinibbāna*) of the Buddha, 2,500 years prior.

Cakkavattin (Pali; Skt. *Cakravartin*): The "righteous monarch" epithet applied to the Indian emperor, Aśoka (third century BCE), and a paradigm for socio-political leadership.

Dhamma (Pali; Skt. *dharma*): (1) Buddhism; (2) the teachings of the Buddha; (3) religion; (4) irreducible factor of experience; (5) duty, obligation; (6) righteousness.

Dhammadhuta (Thai): A Thai government program, begun in 1964, which involved monks in community development work and in propagating Buddhism.

Dharmishta (Sinhala): J. R. Jayawardene's term for "a just society," the party program of the UNP in 1977.

Diṭṭhi (Pali; Skt. *dṛṣṭi*): "Opinionatedness," given that opinions or "views" preclude real "seeing" (*darsana*).

Dukkha (Pali; Skt. *duḥkha*): suffering or unsatisfactoriness; according to Buddhist doctrine, *dukkha* characterizes all human experience.

Entfremdung (German): "Alienation," a key notion in Marxist thought; compare the Buddhist conception of *dukkha*.

Gattungswesen (German): Marx's "species being," or defining characteristic of the situation of being human.

Guru (Pali and Skt.): A religious teacher or preceptor. See *kalyāṇamitta*.

Kalyāṇamitta (Pali: Skt. *kalyaṇamitra*): "Spiritual friend," preceptor or guide.

Kamma (Pali; Skt. *karma*): An action or volition; that which leads to a "fruition of action" (*kammaphāla*).

Kammaphāla (Pali: Skt. *karmaphala*): Fruition of action; see *kamma*.

Karunā (Pali and Skt.): Compassion.

Kusala (Pali; Skt. *kauśaliya*): "Skill"; the activity of a Buddha or an *arahant*, which is without fruitions (*phala*).

Loke vohārā (Pali): "Speeches in the world," literally; also, "convenient designation" or everyday language.

Mahāvaṁsa: The "great chronicle" of Buddhism in Sri Lanka, a sixth-century CE Pali text.

Majjhima patipāda (Pali; Skt. *madyāma pratipāda*): The "middle way" taught by the Buddha which avoids all extremes in matters of religious practice and philosophizing.

Nibbāna (Pali: Skt. *nirvāna*): The highest goal in Buddhism, the utter resolution of all conflict and anxiety.

Pañca sīla (Pali; Sinhala *pansīl*): The "five precepts" to avoid stealing, lying and gossip, harmfulness, sexual misconduct, and the use of intoxicants, recommended for the Buddhist laity.

Paññā (Pali; Skt. *prajñaā*): The insight or wisdom which is the culmination of the Buddhist path, or *arahattā*. One of the three divisions of the Buddhist path, the others being ethical precepts (*sīla*) and meditation (*samādhi*).

Papañca (Pali; Skt. *prapañca*): "Diffuseness of thought" or reification.

Paṭicca samuppāda (Pali; Skt. *praṭitya samutpāda*): "Dependent co-origination," the Buddhist understanding of causality.

Phongyi (Burmese; Pali *bhikkhu*): A fully ordained Buddhist monk; see *bhikkhu*.

Puñña (Pali; Skt. *puṇya*): "Merit"; those actions (*kamma*) which have pleasant fruitions (*phala*).

Reification: Conversion of experience into concrete entities; ossification. A primary mode of false consciousness for Marx, analogous to the Buddhist notions of *papañca* or *diṭṭhi*.

Samādhi (Pali and Skt.): Meditation generally; concentration of mind specifically. One of the three divisions of the Buddhist path, the others being ethical precepts (*sīla*) and insight (*paññā*).

Saṁsāra (Pali and Skt.): The round of continued death and birth in various states.

Saṅgha (Pali and Skt.): The order of monks and nuns; Buddhism's sense of religious community.

Sīla (Pali; Skt. *śīla*): Ethical precepts; one of the three divisions of the Buddhist paths, the others being meditation (*samādhi*) and insight (*paññā*).

Suññatā (Pali; Skt. *śūnyatā*): "Emptiness" or "no-thing-ness." A proto-Mahāyāna concept which is central to Buddhadāsa's thought.

Sutta (Pali; Skt. *sūtra*): Something "heard" from the mouth of the Buddha; core Buddhist text.

Svabhāva (Pali and Skt.): Literally "own-being"; a term carrying a philosophic sense of essentialism.

Thammathud (Thai): The "missionary monks" of Thailand involved in the community development program of the government.
Upekkhā (Pali; Skt. *upekṣā*): Equanimity; one of the four "divine abodes" (*brāhma-vihāra*) or ethical qualities to be meditatively cultivated (*bhāvana*).
Vinaya (Pali and Skt.): Monastic disciplinary precepts; also, as *Vinaya Piṭaka*, the second collection of the Buddhist canon.

BIBLIOGRAPHY

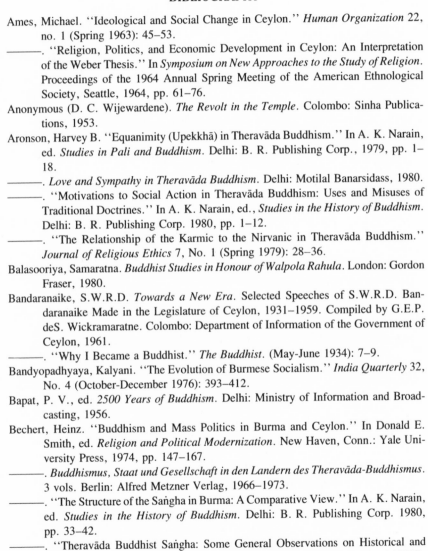

Ames, Michael. "Ideological and Social Change in Ceylon." *Human Organization* 22, no. 1 (Spring 1963): 45–53.

————. "Religion, Politics, and Economic Development in Ceylon: An Interpretation of the Weber Thesis." In *Symposium on New Approaches to the Study of Religion.* Proceedings of the 1964 Annual Spring Meeting of the American Ethnological Society, Seattle, 1964, pp. 61–76.

Anonymous (D. C. Wijewardene). *The Revolt in the Temple.* Colombo: Sinha Publications, 1953.

Aronson, Harvey B. "Equanimity (Upekkhā) in Theravāda Buddhism." In A. K. Narain, ed. *Studies in Pali and Buddhism.* Delhi: B. R. Publishing Corp., 1979, pp. 1–18.

————. *Love and Sympathy in Theravāda Buddhism.* Delhi: Motilal Banarsidass, 1980.

————. "Motivations to Social Action in Theravāda Buddhism: Uses and Misuses of Traditional Doctrines." In A. K. Narain, ed., *Studies in the History of Buddhism.* Delhi: B. R. Publishing Corp. 1980, pp. 1–12.

————. "The Relationship of the Karmic to the Nirvanic in Theravāda Buddhism." *Journal of Religious Ethics* 7, No. 1 (Spring 1979): 28–36.

Balasooriya, Samaratna. *Buddhist Studies in Honour of Walpola Rahula.* London: Gordon Fraser, 1980.

Bandaranaike, S.W.R.D. *Towards a New Era.* Selected Speeches of S.W.R.D. Bandaranaike Made in the Legislature of Ceylon, 1931–1959. Compiled by G.E.P. deS. Wickramaratne. Colombo: Department of Information of the Government of Ceylon, 1961.

————. "Why I Became a Buddhist." *The Buddhist.* (May-June 1934): 7–9.

Bandyopadhyaya, Kalyani. "The Evolution of Burmese Socialism." *India Quarterly* 32, No. 4 (October-December 1976): 393–412.

Bapat, P. V., ed. *2500 Years of Buddhism.* Delhi: Ministry of Information and Broadcasting, 1956.

Bechert, Heinz. "Buddhism and Mass Politics in Burma and Ceylon." In Donald E. Smith, ed. *Religion and Political Modernization.* New Haven, Conn.: Yale University Press, 1974, pp. 147–167.

————. *Buddhismus, Staat und Gesellschaft in den Landern des Theravāda-Buddhismus.* 3 vols. Berlin: Alfred Metzner Verlag, 1966–1973.

————. "The Structure of the Saṅgha in Burma: A Comparative View." In A. K. Narain, ed. *Studies in the History of Buddhism.* Delhi: B. R. Publishing Corp. 1980, pp. 33–42.

————. "Theravāda Buddhist Saṅgha: Some General Observations on Historical and Political Factors in Its Development." *Journal of Asian Studies* 19, No. 4 (1970): 761–778.

Bellah, Robert, ed. *Religion and Progress in Modern Asia*. New York: Free Press, 1965.

Benz, Ernst. *Buddhism or Communism*. Garden City, N.Y.: Doubleday, 1965.

Bharati, Agehananda. "Monastic and Lay Buddhism in the 1971 Sri Lanka Insurgency." *Journal of Asian and African Studies* 11, Nos. 1–2: 102–112.

Bhattacharya, P. K. *Marxism and Buddhism*. Calcutta: Lipi Enterprise, 1976.

Bodhi, Bhikkhu, trans. *The All-Embracing Net of Views: The Brahmajāla Sutta and Its Commentarial Exegesis*. Kandy: Buddhist Publication Society, 1978.

Buddhadāsa, Bhikkhu. *Towards the Truth*. Edited by Donald K. Swearer. Philadelphia: Westminister Press: 1971.

Buddhist Committee of Inquiry. *The Betrayal of Buddhism*. Belangoda: Dharmavijaya Press, 1956.

Burmese Government. *The Burmese Way of Socialism*. Rangoon: Information Department, 1902.

Butr-Indr, Siddhi. *The Social Philosophy of Theravada Buddhism*. Utrecht: n.p., 1953.

Butwell, Richard. *U Nu of Burma*. Stanford, Calif.: Stanford University Press, 1963.

Ceylon *Daily News*. February 4, 1978.

Ceylon Workers Congress. *Manifesto: General Elections—1977*. Colombo: Ceylon Workers Congress, 1977.

Chen, David H.H. "Modern Burma: National Development, Problems and Perspectives." *Asian Profile* 7, No. 1 (February 1979): 37–48.

Dalai Lama, H.H., The. "Spiritual Contributions to Social Progress." *The Wall Street Journal*, October 29, 1981.

de Silva, Colvin R. *Party and Revolution*. Colombo: Lanka Samma Samaj Party, 1974.

de Silva, E. P. *A Short Biography of Dr. N.M. Perera*. Colombo: Ceylon *Daily Mirror*, 1975.

de Silva, K. M. *Sri Lanka: A Survey*. Honolulu: University of Hawaii Press, 1977.

de Silva, Padmasiri. "Basic Needs and the Ethic of Restraint." Ceylon *Daily Mirror*. June 23–24, 1982.

———. "Buddhism and Social Order." *The Young Buddhist* (1981): 155–158.

———. *Value Orientations and Nation Building*. Colombo: Lake House Investments, Ltd., 1976.

Dharmapala, Anagarika. "A Message to the Buddhist Boys of Ceylon." *Maha Bodhi and the United Buddhist World* 29, No. 10 (October 1921): 345–351.

———. *Return to Righteousness*. Edited by Ananda Guruge. Colombo: Government Press, 1965.

Dharmasiri, Gunapala. "Buddhism and Marxism in the Socio-Cultural Context of Sri Lanka." In Nathan Katz, ed. *Buddhist and Western Philosophy*. New Delhi: Sterling Publishers, 1981, pp. 134–148e.

Dissanayake, Piyasena. "Buddhist Perspectives in Socioeconomic Problems." *The Young Buddhist*, 1981, pp. 109–111.

———. *Political Thoughts of the Buddha*. Colombo: Department of Cultural Affairs of the Government of Sri Lanka, 1977.

Dumoulin, Heinrich, ed. *Buddhism in the Modern World*. New York: Collier Books, 1976.

Easton, Lloyd D., and Kurt H. Guddat, eds. *Writings of the Young Marx on Philosophy and Society*. Garden City, N.Y.: Anchor Books, 1967.

Eisenstadt, S. N., ed. *The Protestant Ethic and Modernization: A Comparative View*. New York: Basic Books, 1968.

Ellawala, H. *Social History of Early Ceylon*. Colombo: Department of Cultural Affairs, 1969.

Fernando, Tissa, and Robert N. Kearney, eds. *Modern Sri Lanka: A Society in Transition*. Syracuse, N.Y.: Syracuse University Press, 1979.

Freud, Sigmund. *The Future of an Illusion*. Translated by W. D. Robson-Scott. Garden City, N.Y.: Anchor Books, 1964.

Gard, Richard A. "Buddhism and Political Authority." In *The Ethic of Power: The Interplay of Religion, Philosophy, and Politics*. New York: Conference on Science, Philosophy, and Religion in Their Relation to the Democratic Way of Life, 1962, pp. 39–70.

————. *Buddhist Social Thought*. Washington, D.C.: School of Advanced International Studies, 1952.

Geiger, Wilhelm, ed. *The Mahāvaṁsa*. London: Pali Text Society, 1958.

————, trans. *The Mahāvaṁsa, or the Great Chronicle of Ceylon*. Colombo: Ministry of Information and Broadcasting, 1950.

Ghoshal, U. N. "Principle of the King's Righteousness." *Gautama Buddha 25th Century Volume*. N.p., 1955, pp. 196–204.

Gombrich, Richard. *Precept and Practice: Traditional Buddhism in the Rural Highlands of Ceylon*. Oxford: Clarendon Press, 1971.

Goonetilleke, H.A.I. *A Bibliography of Ceylon*. 3 vols. Zug, Switzerland: Interdocumentation Co., 1970–1976.

Hobbs, Cecil. "The Political Importance of the Buddhist Priesthood in Burma." *Far Eastern Economic Review* 21, No. 4 (1956): 586–596.

Holt, John C. "Sinhalese Sectarianism: Robes, Ploughs, and Revivals." *History of Religions* 20, No. 4 (1980): 368–375.

Houtart, Francois. *Religion and Ideology in Sri Lanka*. Colombo: Hansa Publishers, 1974.

————. "Theravāda Buddhism and Political Power—Construction and Deconstruction of Its Ideological Function." *Social Compass* 24, Nos. 2–3 (1977): 207–246.

Jayasuriya, J. E. *Education in the Third World*. Bombay: Indian Institute of Education, 1981.

Jayatilleke, K. N. *Aspects of Buddhist Social Philosophy*. Kandy: Buddhist Publication Society, 1969.

————. *Facets of Buddhist Thought*. Kandy: Buddhist Publication Society, 1979.

Jayawardene, J. R. *A Better Life for the People*. Colombo: Government of Sri Lanka, n.d.

————. *Buddhism and Marxism*. Tenth Anniversary Lecture Delivered to the Ceylon University Buddhist Brotherhood on 6th March, 1950. Colombo: Times of Ceylon Press, 1950.

————. *Buddhist Essays*. Mount Lavinia, Ceylon: Ola Book Co., 1942.

————. *A New Path*. Colombo: Ministry of Information and Broadcasting of the Government of Sri Lanka, 1978.

————. *Selected Speeches, 1944–1973*. Colombo: H. W. Cave and Co., 1974.

Jayawardene, Visakha Kumari. *The Rise of the Labour Movement in Ceylon*. Durham, N.C.: Duke University Press, 1972.

Jennings, W. Ivor. "Race, Religion and Economic Opportunity in the University of Ceylon." *University of Ceylon Review* 2 (1944): 1–13.

Jones, Ken. *Buddhism and Social Action*. Kandy: Buddhist Publication Society, 1981.

Jupp, James. "Democratic Socialism in Sri Lanka." *Pacific Affairs*, Series 2, 50, No. 4 (Winter 1977–1978): 625–643.

Karunaratne, Saddhamangala, ed. *Olcott's Contribution to the Buddhist Renaissance*. Colombo: Ministry of Cultural Affairs of the Government of Sri Lanka, 1980.

Katz, Nathan. "Buddhism and Marxism." *Vajradhatu Sun* 3, No. 6 (1981): 9, 14.

———. *Buddhist and Western Philosophy*. New Delhi: Sterling Publishers, 1981.

———. *Buddhist Images of Human Perfection: The Arahant of the Sutta Piṭaka Compared with the Bodhissattva and the Mahāsiddha*. Delhi: Motilal Banarsidass, 1982.

———. "Nāgārjuna and Wittgenstein on Error." In Nathan Katz, ed. *Buddhist and Western Philosophy*. New Delhi: Sterling Publishers, 1981, pp. 306–327.

———. "Scholarly Approaches to Buddhism: A Political Analysis." *The Eastern Buddhist* 15, No. 1 (1982): 116–121.

Kearney, Robert N. *The Politics of Ceylon (Sri Lanka)*. Ithaca, N.Y.: Cornell University Press, 1973.

King, Winston L. *In the Hope of Nibbana*. LaSalle, Ill.: Open Court, 1964.

Kitagawa, Joseph M. "Buddhism and Social Change—An Historical Perspective." In Samaratna Balasooriya, et al., eds. *Buddhist Studies in Honour of Walpola Rahula*. London: Gordon Fraser, 1980, pp. 84–102.

Lanka Bauddha Mandalaya (Buddhist Council of Ceylon). *An Event of Dual Significance*. Colombo: Ministry of Home Affairs of the Government of Ceylon, 1956.

Lanka Samma Samaja Party. *The Road to a Socialist Sri Lanka*. Colombo: Lanka Samma Samaja Party, 1978.

Leach, Edmund. "Buddhism in the Post-Colonial Order in Burma and Ceylon." *Daedalus* 102, No. 1: 29–54.

Lewy, Guenter. *Religion and Revolution*. New York: Oxford University Press, 1974.

Ling, Trevor. *Buddha, Marx, and God*. New York: St. Martin's Press, 1966.

———. *Buddhism, Imperialism, and War*. London: George Allen and Unwin, 1979.

———. "Religion and Politics in South and Southeast Asia." *History of Religions* 20, No. 4 (1980): 281–287.

Lukács, Georg. *History and Class Consciousness*. Translated by Rodney Livingstone. Cambridge, Mass.: MIT Press, 1971.

Macy, Joanna Rogers. "Dependent Co-Arising: The Distinctiveness of Buddhist Ethics." *Journal of Religious Ethics* 7, No. 1 (Spring 1979): 38–52.

Malalasekere, G. P., and K. N. Jayatilleke. *Buddhism and the Race Question*. Paris: UNESCO, 1958.

Malalgoda, Kitsiri. *Buddhism in Sinhalese Society, 1750–1900*. Berkeley and Los Angeles: University of California Press, 1976.

Marga Institute. *Religion and Development in Asian Societies*. Colombo: Marga, 1974.

Maung Maung, U. *From Sangha to Laity: Nationalist Movements of Burma, 1920–1940*. Columbia, Mo.: South Asia Books, 1980.

Maw, U Ba. *Breakthrough in Burma: Memories of a Revolution, 1939–1946*. New Haven, Conn.: Yale University Press, 1968.

Mendelson, E. Michael. *Sangha and State in Burma: A Study of Monastic Sectarianism and Leadership*. Ithaca, N.Y.: Cornell University Press, 1975.

Morrell, David, and Susan Morrell. "The Impermanence of Society: Marxism, Buddhism, and the Political Philosophy of Thailand's Pridi Banomyong." *Southeast Asia: An International Quarterly* 2, No. 4 (Fall 1972): 396–424.

Mus, Paul. "Buddhism and the World Order." *Daedalus* 95 (1966): 813–827.

———. "Traditions Asiennes et Bouddhisme Moderne." *Eranos-Jahrbuch 1968*, Band 38. Zurich: Rhein-Verlag, 1970, pp. 161–276.

Ñāṇānanda, Bhikkhu. *Concept and Reality in Early Buddhist Thought*. Kandy: Buddhist Publication Society, 1976.

Narain, A. K., ed. *Studies in the History of Buddhism*. Delhi: B. R. Publishing Corp., 1980.

———. *Studies in Pali and Buddhism*. Delhi: B. R. Publishing Corp., 1979.

Nash, Manning, ed. *Anthropological Studies in Theravāda Buddhism*. New Haven, Conn.: Yale University Press, 1966.

Niehoff, Arthur. "Theravada Buddhism: A Vehicle for Technical Change." *Human Organization* 23, No. 2 (Summer 1964): 108–112.

Nu, U. *Forward with the People*. Rangoon: Ministry of Information of the Government of the Union of Burma, 1955.

———. *From Peace to Stability*. Rangoon: Ministry of Information of the Government of the Union of Burma, 1951.

Obeyesekere, Gananath. "Religious Symbolism and Political Change in Ceylon." *Modern Ceylon Studies* 1, No. 1 (January 1970): 43–63.

Olcott, Henry Steele. *A Buddhist Catechism*. Wheaton, Ill.: Theosophical Publishing House, 1970 (1881).

Ollman, Bertell. *Alienation: Marx's Conception of Man in Capitalist Society*. 2d ed. New York: Cambridge University Press, 1976.

Pardue, Peter A. *Buddhism: A Historical Introduction to Buddhist Values and the Social and Political Forms They Have Assumed in Asia*. New York: Macmillan Co., 1971.

Payutto, Phra Maha Prayudha. "Problems, Status and Duties of the Saṅgha in Modern Society." *Visakha Puja* (BE 2511/1968): 58–73.

Peebles, Patrick. *Sri Lanka: A Handbook of Historical Statistics*. Boston: G. K. Hall and Co., 1982.

Pfanner, David E., and Jasper Ingersoll. "Theravāda Buddhism and Village Economic Behavior: A Burmese and Thai Comparison." *Journal of Asian Studies* 21, No. 3 (May 1962): 345–350.

Phadnis, Urmila. *Religion and Politics in Sri Lanka*. New Delhi: Manohar, 1976.

Pieris, Ralph. *Asian Development Styles*. Columbia, Mo.: South Asia Books, 1976.

———, ed. *Some Aspects of Traditional Sinhalese Culture: A Symposium*. Peradeniya: Ceylon University Conference on Traditional Cultures, 1956.

Puligandla, R., and K. Puhakka. "Buddhism and Revolution." *Philosophy East and West* 20, No. 4 (October 1970): 345–354.

Rahula, Walpola. *History of Buddhism in Ceylon: The Anuradhapura Period, 3rd Century BC–10th Century AC*. Colombo: M.D. Gunasena and Co., Lt., 1956.

Rajavaramuni, Phra. "Foundations of Buddhist Ethics in Contemporary Thailand." No publication data available.

Ramos, Henry A.J. "Problems of Development in Socialist Nations: Material Versus Moral Incentive." *Terra Infirma: The Berkeley Review of Development* 2 (1980): 1–14.

Reynolds, Frank E. "Buddhist Ethics: A Bibliographical Essay." *Religious Studies Review* 5, No. 1 (January 1979): 40–48.

———. "Four Modes of Theravāda Action." *Journal of Religious Ethics* 7, No. 1 (Spring 1979): 12–26.

Rose, Saul. *Socialism in Southern Asia.* London: Oxford University Press, 1959.
Samaraweera, Vijaya. "The Evolution of a Plural Society." In K. M. de Silva, ed. *Sri Lanka: A Survey.* Honolulu: University of Hawaii Press, 1977, pp. 86–107.
Samdong, Rinpoche. "The Social and Political Strata in Buddhist Thought." *The Tibet Journal* 2, No. 1 (1977): 1–9.
Sangharakshita, Bhikshu. *Anagarika Dharmapala: A Bibliographical Sketch.* Colombo: Buddhist Publication Society, 1964.
———. "Buddhism in the Modern World: Cultural and Political Implications." In P. V. Bapat, ed. *2500 Years of Buddhism,* Delhi: Ministry of Information and Broadcasting of the Government of India, 1956, pp. 388–408.
Sanmugathasan, N. *A Short History of the Left Movement in Ceylon.* Colombo: N. Sammugathasan, 1972.
Sarachandra, Ediriweera R. "Traditional Values and the Modernization of a Buddhist Society: The Case of Ceylon." In Robert Bellah, ed. *Religion and Progress in Modern Asia.* New York: Free Press, 1965, pp. 109–123.
Sarkisyanz, Emanuel. *Buddhist Backgrounds of the Burmese Revolution.* The Hague: Martinus Nijhoff, 1965.
Schecter, Jerrold. *The New Face of the Buddha.* New York: Coward-McCann, 1967.
"Seminar on Multinationals and Liberation." *Logos* 15, No. 1 (April 1976).
Senanayake, D. S. "Speech Delivered over the B.B.C. on the 'Middle Path' of Moderation as a Path to Peace, January 1951." *Ceylon Historical Journal* 5: 110–114.
Shaplen, Robert. *A Turning Wheel: Three Decades of the Asian Revolution.* New York: Random House, 1979.
Smith, Bardwell L., ed. *Religion and Legitimation of Power in Sri Lanka.* Chambersburg, Pa.: Anima Books, 1978.
———, ed. *Religion and Legitimation of Power in Thailand, Laos, and Burma.* Chambersburg, Pa.: Anima Books, 1978.
———. "Religious Assimilation in Early Medieval Sinhalese Society." In A. K. Narain, ed. *Studies in Pali and Buddhism.* Delhi: B. R. Publishing Corp. 1979, pp. 347–368.
———. "Sinhalese Buddhism and the Dilemmas of Reinterpretation." *Contributions to Asian Studies* 3 (1973): 1–25.
———. "Toward a Buddhist Anthropology: The Problem of the Secular." *Journal of the American Academy of Religion* 36, No. 3 (September 1968): 203–216.
———, ed. *Tradition and Change in Theravāda Buddhism: Essays on Ceylon and Thailand in the 19th and 20th Centuries.* Leiden: E. J. Brill, 1973.
———, ed. *The Two Wheels of Dhamma: Essays on the Theravāda Tradition in India and Ceylon.* Chambersburg, Pa.: American Academy of Religion, 1972.
Smith, Donald E. "The Political Monks of Burma and Ceylon." *Asia* 10 (Winter 1968): 3–10.
———. *Religion and Politics in Burma.* Princeton, N.J.: Princeton University Press, 1965.
———. "Religion, Politics and the Myth of Reconquest." In Tissa Fernando and Robert N. Kearney, eds. *Modern Sri Lanka: A Society in Transition.* Syracuse, N.Y.: Syracuse University Press, 1979, pp. 83–99.
———. *Religion, Politics, and Social Change in the Third World.* New York: Free Press, 1971.

Somboon Suksamran. *Political Buddhism in Southeast Asia*. London: C. Hurst and Co., 1977.

Spiro, Melford. *Buddhism and Society: A Great Tradition and Its Burmese Vicissitudes*. New York: Harper and Row, 1970.

Sri Lanka Freedom Party. *From Political Freedom to Economic Liberation: Towards a Socialist Society, Election Manifesto—1977*. Colombo: Sri Lanka Freedom Party, 1977.

Stevens, William K. "Election in Sri Lanka: Capitalism Versus Socialism." *New York Times*, October 20, 1982.

Story, Francis. *Buddhism Answers the Marxist Challenge*. Rangoon: Burma Buddhist World Mission, 1952.

Swe, U Ba. *The Burmese Revolution*. Rangoon: Peoples' Literature Committee and House, 1952.

Swearer, Donald K. "Bhikkhu Buddhadāsa on Ethics and Society." *Journal of Religious Ethics* 7, No. 1 (Spring 1979): 54–64.

———. *Buddhism and Society in Southeast Asia*. Chambersburg, Pa.: Anima Books, 1981.

———. *Buddhism in Transition*. Philadelphia: Westminster Press, 1970.

———. "Lay Buddhism and Buddhist Revival in Ceylon." *Journal of the American Academy of Religion* 38 (1970): 255–275.

Tambiah, S. J. "Buddhism and This-Worldly Activity." *Modern Asian Studies* 7, No. 1 (1973): 1–20.

———. *World-Conqueror and World-Renouncer*. New York: Cambridge University Press, 1976.

Thakur, Vijay Kumar. "Socio-Political Relevance of Buddhism in the Modern World: A Historical Analysis." *Maha Bodhi Journal* 86, Nos. 4–5 (1978): 122–125.

Thomas, Winburn T. "Ceylon Christians Faced by Crisis." *Christian Century* 68, No. 2 (1951): 58–60.

Totten, George O. "Buddhism and Socialism in Japan and Burma." *Comparative Studies in Society and History* 2 (1959–1960): 293–304.

Trager, Frank N. *Marxism in Southeast Asia: A Study of Four Countries*. Stanford, Calif.: Stanford University Press, 1959.

Tucker, Robert, ed. *The Marx-Engels Reader*. 2d ed. New York: W. W. Norton, 1976.

United National Party. *The First Year of Freedom: 1949, Souvenir*. Colombo: Ceylon Printers, 1949.

———. *A Programme of Action: To Create a Just and Free Society*. Colombo: United National Party, 1977.

von der Mehden, Fred. "Buddhism and Politics in Burma." *Antioch Review* 21, No. 2 (1961): 166–175.

———. *Religion and Nationalism in Southeast Asia*. Madison: University of Wisconsin Press, 1963.

———. "Secularization and Buddhist Politics: Burma and Thailand." In Donald E. Smith, ed. *Religion and Political Modernization*. New Haven, Conn.: Yale University Press, 1974, pp. 49–66.

Weber, Max. *The Religions of India*. Glencoe, Ill.: Free Press, 1958.

Weeraratne, W. G. *Individual and Society in Buddhism*. Colombo: W. C. Weeraratne, 1977.

Wijeratne, Sir Edwin. "Buddhism and Modern Ceylon." *The Light of the Dhamma* 3, No. 3 (May 1956): 43–46.

Wilson, A. J. *Politics in Sri Lanka, 1947–1973*. New York: St. Martin's Press, 1974.

Wriggins, W. Howard. *Ceylon: Dilemmas of a New Nation*. Princeton, N.J.: Princeton University Press, 1960.

V

THE HOLOCAUST: CHRISTIAN/ JEWISH REFLECTIONS

20

Postwar Reflections on the Holocaust from a Jewish Point of View

NORA LEVIN

The two axial experiences stirring Jewish consciousness in the twentieth century have been the creation of the state of Israel and the Holocaust. They are closely interlocked, as will be discussed later, but two more antipodal historic experiences can scarcely be imagined—the one arousing the deepest emotions of gladness and the culmination of millennial yearning, and the other, deepest anguish, mourning, overwhelming sense of loss, and despair. How does one assimilate both sets of experiences when each drives feelings and intellect to outermost limits? Simply and bluntly, one cannot, and this is especially so in the efforts of Jews to deal with the events surrounding the destruction of two-thirds of European Jewry, generally described as the Holocaust.

For most Jews, almost a half-century of mourning, commemoration, study, and reflection on this dread history have failed to yield a fundamental understanding or comprehensibility. There have been a profusion of survivor accounts, scholarly studies, religious and philosophical works, films, poetry, and fiction, whose authors struggle to pierce the realities of the Jewish experience during the period 1933–1945, but no one altogether understands how mass murder on such a scale, including the murder of over a million children, could have happened or could have been allowed to happen.[1] Indeed, these realities may be incommunicable, as Elie Wiesel has suggested. ''After the war,'' he has said, ''every survivor was asked the same question by the dead: 'Will you be able to tell *our* tale?' Now we know the answer: 'No'. Their tale cannot be told—and never will be. Those who spoke were not heard; the story you hear was not the story they had told.'' The world of Auschwitz was and remains a new and terrifying planet. And yet its incommunicable reality continues to grip many Jews and non-Jews alike, as if by penetrating the universe of Auschwitz we will be able to understand it, or to see into its full horror and perhaps ''learn lessons'' for our future human history. The fast growing literature on the Holocaust in all forms and gradations of quality is indeed phenomenal, revealing its hold on the twentieth-century's imagination and suggesting that by remembering and acquiring more information about what happened we can somehow assuage the failure to understand what happened.

It is often said that the Holocaust has no parallel or precedent in human history, that it shattered long-cherished traditional Western values and taboos against murder without remorse or guilt.[2] In twelve short years the Nazi regime in Germany created a society in which mass murder of a people and the exploitation of human corpses became a civic duty. Their victims had to undergo a wholly new order of experience—not only debasement, depersonalization, and new levels of brutality but also processing into matter while they were still alive. In Hitler-Germany, the state not only devised a rationale and methodology for the physical annihilation of almost six million Jews, coded by the cool phrase "the Final Solution," but perversely refused to characterize it as mass murder. Instead, it was evasively called "special treatment" or "resettlement in the East." The murderers, many of them good family men, ate, played with their children, fed rabbits, listened to sublime German music, and joked at parties after mass killings in the pits and gas chambers. Clearly, the Nazis had devised a new technological objectivity in dealing with human suffering and murder. Jews were their objects, the first people in history to be denatured into matter. This German plunge into a "world without limit" made it possible to create unpersons, out of Jews in twentieth-century Western soiciety, without guilt or remorse, to make the physical annihilation of European Jewry a higher priority than winning the war. All past anti-Semitic savageries in history have been eclipsed by the Nazi execution of "the Final Solution" from 1941 to 1945, beginning with the mass executions of Jews by *Einsatzgruppen* who accompanied the German army that invaded the Soviet Union in June 1941.

From Nazi Germany, the obliteration of Jews, their religious and cultural institutions, creative works, and past history became an obsessive drive, filled with compelling meaning and purpose. For Jews, it was a catastrophe from which they can never recover. Besides the sheer physical losses and the many rich and diverse Jewish cultures, the physical and spiritual heartland of Jewry has been extinguished. Forty-five hundred Jewish communities were destroyed. The minds and gifts of countless Jews and their children are lost for all time. Compounding this bottomless sense of loss is the continuing failure of Jews to find any meaning whatsoever, or solace, in this chapter of their history. The years of the Holocaust are indeed the Kingdom of Night.

Yet many continue to be pulled toward this Kingdom, mostly Jews, but non-Jews as well. It is, as Herbert Butterfield has put it:

. . . when the human race has gone through one of its colossal chapters of experience, men in the after-period have been so appalled by the catastrophe, so obsessed by the memory of it, that they have gone back to the story again and again, finding new angles of research, new aspects of the matter to reflect upon, as one generation succeeds another—

a process of thinking and rethinking which in special cases is capable of continuing for a thousand years or more. As a result of this, there piles up (with the passage of the generations) a tremendous accumulation of commentary on any single great historical theme.[3]

Indeed, the literature of the Holocaust has swelled to immense proportions and continues to increase at a galloping rate. On the level of historical scholarship there has been an outpouring of specialized studies, historical surveys, and monographs as new sources are made accessible.[4] The magnitude of existing documentation is staggering, but much material, particularly in the archives of the Allied powers and the Vatican during World War II, remains inaccessible. This is especially true of the rich store of material in the USSR and countries in Eastern Europe.

Jewish efforts to document the Holocaust actually started during the persecutions when diaries and scraps of all sorts were hidden in walls, cellars, and in the ground, or left with trusted individuals. Despairing of their own survival and determined to leave evidence of the unimaginable, they tried to snatch bits and pieces of their experiences on scraps of paper for posterity, hidden or smuggled for safe-keeping. Some of this material has been uncovered over the years and has been assembled in various centers such as the Centre de Documentation Juive in Paris, YIVO Institute for Jewish Research and the Leo Baeck Center in New York City, the Weiner Library in London (now Tel Aviv University), the War Documentation Center in Amsterdam, Yad Vashem Martyrs' and Heroes' Memorial Authority, and the Institute of Contemporary Jewry (Hebrew University), both in Jerusalem.[5] In the period 1944–1966, Jewish survivors in Poland maintained the Jewish Historical Institute in Warsaw under the direction of Bernard Mark, but when Poland embarked on its anti-Zionist, anti-Jewish course after the Six-Day War in 1967, independent research became untenable and most of the staff emigrated.[6] Moreover, the current anti-Israel and anti-Zionist policies of Eastern bloc communist countries and their persistent refusal to deal with Jews as a people with a distinct history have caused a total disfigurement of the history of the destruction of European Jewry.[7] In the communist view, Jews did not suffer singularly but were victims of fascism—as were millions of others. Thus, because of this view, there is no explicit history, for example, of the annihilation of almost two million Jews in the Soviet Union. Most recently, Soviet hostility toward Zionism and the state of Israel has produced a total falsification of Holocaust history by spreading the propaganda that "international Zionism" helped bring Hitler to power and then assisted Nazis in destroying Jews. It is very difficult to rebut such absurdities in a totalitarian society, but an enormous volume of documentation on the Zionist struggle to save Jews before, during, and after the war exists for those able and willing to read it.[8]

The great increase in Holocaust literature began ten or fifteen years ago, after earlier unwillingness and unreadiness to face the period have been overcome as a result of diminished psychological barriers, the greater distance provided by the passage of time, and the advent of television programs such as "Holocaust" in 1978. Within this period, although much of the output has been superficial, aimed at a mass market,[9] a number of books have appeared based on primary sources and illuminating incompletely understood or unknown segments of Holocaust history.

Among the most important Holocaust studies and monographs have been those in *Yad Vashem Studies on the European Catastrophe* and *Resistance*, published since 1957. To date, fifteen volumes have appeared. Most of the studies have been written by Israeli scholars, but American and German scholars have also been represented. The most important scholarly studies devoted to German Jewry before and during World War II are to be found in the Leo Baeck Yearbooks, published by the Leo Baeck Institute in New York, which also has rich archival material. The YIVO Institute of Jewish Research in New York has valuable archives including *Pinkes* (Book Records) of Jewish communities in Eastern Europe. In Volume 8 (1953) and occasionally in subsequent issues of the YIVO *Annual of Jewish Social Studies*, there are special studies devoted to the Holocaust. The *Weiner Library Bulletin* also contains valuable monographs but stopped publication in 1981. The Tauber Institute, founded in 1980 at Brandeis University, "seeks to set into the context of modern history, the causes, nature and consequences of the crisis of European society in the mid–20th century with a particular focus on the origins of the European Jewish catastrophe."[10] Scholars in several disciplines engage in research and lecture at the institute. Dr. Bernard Wasserstein is director. The Jack Eisner Center for Holocaust Studies has been set up at the Graduate Center of City University of New York, with Dr. Randolph L. Braham as director. Zachor, the Holocaust Resource Center in New York City directed by Dr. Irving Greenberg, co-sponsored *Shoah: A Journal of Resources on the Holocaust* (1978–1984), and has published occasional papers. Its work is being continued by *Dimensions*, as of spring 1985, published by the Center for Holocaust Studies, Anti-Defamation League of B'nai B'rith, New York.

The output of serious works has been very large, but many areas still need to be researched. As Dr. Yehuda Bauer has put it,

"For what is concealed still remains greater than what has been revealed. We have no history as yet of the Jews of Germany during the Holocaust. . . . There are hundreds of Eastern European Jewish communities, hundreds of concentration camps, hundreds of partisan units which included Jews, whose fate remains unknown to us. We have no adequate history of the Jews of France or Belgium, Rumania or Hungary, Yugoslavia or Greece."[11]

There is still the problem of the evolution of Hitler's anti-Jewish obsession from his experiences in Vienna to the decision to physically destroy Europe's Jews.[12] The economic and social constituencies that supported National Socialism are still being researched and argued, but no definitive work has appeared.[13] Nor do we altogether know the extent of popular anti-Semitism within Germany in the early years of the Nazi Regime,[14] or how German passivity or indifference toward the fate of the Jews in the early and middle 1930s escalated to willingness and zeal on the part of many to become mass murderers without remorse or qualms of conscience. We also lack a full-bodied study of the collapse of the Great German Social Democratic movement and the implications of the enmity between it and the Communist Party. Very little is known of the experiences of large numbers of Jews in the Soviet Union during the war. In terms of the placement of Holocaust history, scholars and others disagree about how it should be integrated: within the context of Jewish history, European history, or World War II history. Perhaps it needs to be placed within all three.

For Jews, the Holocaust was quintessentially a Jewish catastrophe. Many other peoples, of course, suffered greatly—Gypsies, Russians, Poles, homosexuals, and anti-Nazi resisters. Many of those groups were murdered in the gas chambers as well as in mass and random executions. But except for the Gypsies, virtually no women or children among them were murdered, and the entire people were not marked, as were the Jews, for annihilation. They were killed for what they did, not for who they were. In the case of the Gypsies, it is estimated that 1.5 million were killed by the Nazis.[15] Most Nazis considered them, like the Jews, to be "sub-human," but there was also some ambivalence. The arch-racist Himmler had a confessed weakness for them and wanted to make sure that two main Gypsy stocks—the Sinte and Lalleri—would be preserved. According to Rudolph Franz Höss, Himmler believed they were direct descendants of the original Indo-Germanic stock.[16] There are few reliable data, including written testimony and documents, but it is believed that most Gypsies were destroyed in German and German-controlled countries, such as Poland, Latvia, Czecho-slovakia, and Yugoslavia. There were no anti-Gypsy programs in Romania or Hungary, which contained large Gypsy populations.

It is estimated that approximately 5 million Gypsies, Poles, Russians, and other despised minorities were killed by the Nazis—a horrendous figure, indeed. What is missing in the documentation about these groups is what dominates, in fact, fills the Nazi universe: the absolute obsession with the Jew, the mobilization of a huge bureaucracy, transport, special killing squads and gas technicians fixated on the goal of killing every Jew in Europe, and, finally, making winning the war secondary to annihilating Jews. This central reality about Nazi ideology has been perverted in some quarters by reference to a Jewish need for ethnic gratification or secularized chosenness, as if the singularity of the Holocaust and the Jewish preoccupation with it constitute a triumph of some kind, another expression of Jewish exclusiveness.

Such debates are fruitless and tend to polarize positions instead of leading to reasoned discourse and clarification. A priori attitudes and intense emotionalism pervade the debates. Similarly, there has been hectic argumentation over the issue of genocide and the Holocaust: whether the Holocaust is another one of a line of historic genocides, which have in common the systematic victimization and destruction of a hated minority, or whether it does indeed constitute a uniquely radical alteration in human history and consciousness, expressed in the term "Planet Auschwitz." Some thinkers have referred to the Holocaust as a turning point in Western civilization. Roy Eckardt speaks of it as "metanoia, the climactic turning around of the entire world," when the history of man and God "comes to a fatal watershed."[17] Others have spoken of it as creating a fatal, irreversible impairment of the universe. Still others argue that there are no basic differences between this and other genocides. No resolution of these matters seems likely in the near future.[18] Sociologists and quantitatively oriented historians tend to look for "models," "uniformities," and statistical tabulations, whereas traditional historians look for social, economic, and political particularities that differentiate historical events.

Three of the more controversial issues in Holocaust history that have troubled Jews relate to Jewish resistance, the role of the Jewish Councils, and the response of American Jews to news of the deportations and mass killings. Each of these questions involves an understanding of the scarcely describable conditions under which Jews struggled to survive and the obligation to grasp a time of raging global warfare when winning the war for the Allies was the only priority. These issues involve complexities that are often glossed over or reduced to simplistic categories of thought. In discussions of resistance, for example, unknowing people have talked about Jews "going like lambs to the slaughter," of not physically resisting the Nazis like other peoples during the war, but such a generalization ignores the numerous instances of Jewish resistance and the unique conditions facing Jews.[19] It is perhaps best to start with a definition, framed by the leading authority on European resistance movements during World War II, Henri Michel. Resistance, according to Michel, is "the fight, waged first clandestinely, later openly, by the peoples whose countries were occupied by the troops of Germany, Italy, and Japan." This fight began after the regular armies had been defeated or destroyed. The Resistance therefore is first of all "a patriotic fight for the liberation of a country." It involves partisan or guerrilla warfare directed at liberation as well as psychological warfare, to weaken the morale of the enemy and increase the strength and numbers of the supporters of the underground. Such resistance includes passive disobedience, propaganda, and various acts of sabotage—refusing or evading the enemy's orders, calling strikes, destroying installations such as railway tracks, warehouses, and bridges.[20] In short, the object of these actions was to frustrate and block the aims of the enemy. Many Jews, of course, participated in the general resistance movements—in France, Greece, Russia, and Holland, for example—but their identity as Jews has not been generally acknowledged or even studied sufficiently.

It should be recalled that the almost six million Jews who perished lived and died in thousands of communities in war-torn Europe. Hundreds of thousands fought and died in the national armies of their homelands—the USSR, Poland, Greece, France, and Yugoslavia—but they were identified not as Jews but as nationals of those countries. These men were armed, had commands and commanders, uniforms, military units, and combat assignments. Many died as soldiers. Those who survived in Nazi-occupied lands generally shared the fate of other Jews: they were stripped of all rights, property, and access to normal work, then reduced to slave-labor in the concentration camps and so-called labor brigades. Jews in the ghettos and camps were diminished by hunger, disease, brutal beatings, random killings, and pyschological maiming. Many of them were gassed. Plans for their physical annihilation were carefully and cunningly concealed from them. Elaborate, paralyzing deceptions were employed to confuse, shock, and starve the victims, thus rendering them helpless to resist. The process was piecemeal but progressively destructive. Starving Jews stumbled toward the trains that would take them "to the East" for "re-settlement" by the lure of a loaf of bread and few ounces of marmalade. Even the entrances to the area of the gas chambers were camouflaged by the presence of special huts for "tailors," "carpenters," "roadbuilders," and other crafts, deceiving Jews into thinking that they were, indeed, being processed for special work units. The gas chambers themselves were camouflaged as showers, but instead, Jews were asphyxiated by the fumes of prussic acid. Hundreds of thousands also died of starvation, brutal beatings, disease, and the bitter cold before the official deportations which began in the summer of 1942.

Moreover, Jews in ghettos and camps were sealed off from each other, and after Pearl Harbor, no mail or parcels or phone contacts were possible. The large Jewish population in the Soviet Union—about three million in 1939—was not even aware of the persecution of Jews in Western Europe under the terms of the Soviet-Nazi Pact of August 1939. Stalin promised Hitler that information about the persecution of Jews elsewhere would be censored in Russia. As a consequence, Soviet Jews had no way of knowing that they would be among the first on the Nazi enemy list, after the German invasion of Russia in June 1941. As the German *Einsatzgruppen*, or special killing squads, moved in with the invading army, they swept into towns and cities, ordered all Jews to report to assembly points, and then marched them to open fields or pits. Those who resisted were beaten with rubber truncheons or whips. They were then forced to remove all of their clothes and lie on the ground on their stomachs. They were then shot in the back of the head. Over a million and a half Jews in Russia—most of them women, children, and old people—died this way during the first few months of the war in Russia. Able-bodied Jewish men under the age of sixty were in the Soviet Army and were thus unable to organize resistance.

When the decisions to resist finally took shape—first in the Nazi ghettos in the Soviet Union (Lachva, Tuchin, Nieswiez, Minsk, Opole, and Mir) and then in the ghettos of Poland and partisan groups in the forests and marshes of Eastern Europe—Jews realized that they were doomed no matter what they did, that they were resisting an official plan for physical annihilation. Thus they could not, as other resistance movements were able to do, weigh the possible gains and losses of every operation, compare the damage inflicted on the persecutor to the losses sustained by the general population, or fight when there was a chance to win specific objectives, to liberate a country, to struggle for freedom. Jews never had that choice or chance. Moreover, non-Jewish resistance movements were completely dependent on outside aid, without which they would have been condemned to disappear or remain powerless. The arms, equipment, and instructions to the various undergrounds came from London or Moscow. They were often armed by the Allied staffs for political or psychological reasons as well as for strictly military reasons. We may now ask the question: Was Jewish resistance also regarded as necessary from the military, political, or psychological point of view? The answer, alas, is no. As early as 1939, the Jews of Palestine asked the British Mandatory Power to allow them to organize a Jewish brigade within the British army and, later, to drop parachutists behind the German lines in the Balkans, but these proposals were put on the shelf year after year until July 1944,[21] by which time the war was almost over and millions of Jews had already perished. Palestine itself was cut off by the British as a place to flee to, and all other places in the world were hostile to the idea of taking in Jewish refugees.[22]

Thus sealed in, some Jews—mostly Zionist and socialist youths—struggled to resist, "to die with honor," as they said. They had no illusions about winning any victories over the Nazis or about escaping death. Besides the well-known uprising in the Warsaw Ghetto in April 1943, there were resistance actions in the ghettos of Bialystok, Vilna, Crakow, Czestochowa, Bendin, Kovno, Riga, and Minsk. Jews also helped to organize revolts in the death camps of Auschwitz, Sobibor, and Treblinka, and conducted guerrilla operations in numerous partisan groups. In recent years, research has also uncovered Jewish resistance activity in France, Bulgaria, Hungary, Slovakia, Greece, Romania, and even in Germany itself.[23]

The complexities surrounding the issue of resistance have also led to a broader definition of the word and a deepened understanding of the deliberate choice of some Jews to meet their fate in the age-old Jewish tradition of Kiddush Ha-Shem, dying for the sake of Sanctification of the Name, with God's name on their lips as they went into the gas chambers. There were other forms of resistance—spiritual and intellectual—at pain of death.[24] When the Nazis forbade religious services, countless numbers prayed clandestinely though they knew they would be killed when discovered. Jewish teachers conducted classes secretly, and both teachers and children were killed for the crime of studying. In many of the ghettos, Zionist youth movements tried to bolster diminishing hope and morale through secretly hectographed bulletins and leaflets. They also organized primitive arts and crafts classes, study groups, poetry readings, and recitals. Often they sacrificed their own meager rations for old and ailing victims in the Nazi ghettos. Indeed, the very survival of Jews beyond Nazi calculations led to the decision to accelerate the killing process. To survive in the Kingdom of Night was the ultimate form of resistance.

The Judenräte, or Jewish Councils, have also provoked contentious discussions and debates among Jews and non-Jews, a great deal of it stirred by the publication of Hannah Arendt's book *Eichmann in Jerusalem: A Report on the Banality of Evil* (New York: Viking, rev. and enlarged, 1965), which did much to create the image of Jewish Councils as willing collaborators and accomplices of the Nazis and the image of Jews as acquiescent and passively resigned to their doom. For her understanding of Jewish behavior Arendt leaned heavily on Raul Hilberg's work, *The Destruction of the European Jews* (Chicago: Quadrangle Books, 1961). Yet in his preface, Hilberg emphasizes the point that "this is not a book about the Jews. It is a book about the people who destroyed the Jews. Not much will be read here about victims." The dilemmas of the victims, including the Council members, most of whom perished, were little appreciated or understood until the publication of Jacob Robinson's *And the Crooked Shall be Made Straight* (Philadelphia: Jewish Publication Society of America, 1965), Leonard Tushnet's *The Pavement of Hell* (New York: St. Martin's Press, 1972), and most particularly, the English translation of Isaiah Trunk's definitive work, *Judenrat: The Jewish Councils in Eastern Europe Under Nazi Occupation* (New York: Macmillan Co., 1972).[25] Up to that time, much of the argumentation was carried on by people with little information or deficient in the kind of imagination required to understand the atmosphere of terror, bafflement, nerve-wracking tension, and fear that gripped the ghettos under Nazi occupation. They oversimplified and overgeneralized. The Councils, Trunk pointed out, varied in all possible ways: in social and political composition, in the relationship to prewar community bodies, in their initiative and energy, in their approach to extreme crisis, and in their attitude toward resistance. The creation of the Councils and their "administration" of the ghettos derived from a plan outlined on September 21, 1939, by Reinhard Heydrich, Nazi chief of Security Police. In this letter, Heydrich outlines preliminary measures to be applied to Jews in conquered Polish territory, "leading to the fulfillment of the ultimate goal," which must remain secret. It is clear that in ordering the setting up of Councils, Heydrich planned to exploit the Jewish tradition of communal autonomy, to delude Jews into thinking they would be safe in the ghettos with their own leaders and institutions, and that ultimately he would use the Councils as Nazi control mechanisms in the implementation of Nazi policies.

Councils were forced on the ghettos. Even though some leaders perceived hidden dangers, in the first stages of ghettoization most believed they could serve the ghettos constructively. Those who hesitated or refused were forced to serve at gun point and threatened with death and/or reprisals against the families. In the early period before any Jews could fathom the Nazi plan of mass destruction, Councils tried to organize the otherwise chaotic conditions in the ghettos, to provide primitive services, and to buffer the brutal Nazi measures. Some were led by saintly men; others by ambitious, power-hungry, if well-intentioned, men. In some ghettos, class and cultural differences were sharp and bitter, and the Nazis exploited these differences to divert Jews from grasping their intentions. Although the ghettos were similar in their repressive framework, they differed greatly in their internal, demographic, and economic structures. These numerous differentiated strands are unraveled with detail and exactitude by Trunk, who refused to generalize or pass judgment. In the early period of the deportations, members were unaware of the fate of the transports. Later their knowledge was mixed with the reflex of unthinkability of extermination—the response of almost all individuals when they first had confirmation of the operation of the gas chambers. At the end, when this knowledge was assimilated, the Councils found themselves, as Trunk has said, "in perhaps the most excruciating moral predicament encountered by a representative body in history." Some Council members committed suicide; others who refused to cooperate in the deportations were themselves deported and killed. A few desperately advocated a "rescue through work" policy; others realized that since not all Jews could be saved, it was better to try and save some. Some secretly supported resistance efforts. Most believed they would bring deadly reprisals and hasten the destruction of the ghetto. Anguished efforts were made to find justification for life and death decisions in the ancient texts or rabbinic decisions. The Rabbi of Kaunas, for example, ruled that "if a Jewish community . . . has been condemned to physical destruction, and there are means of rescuing part of it, the leaders of the community should have the courage to assume the responsibility, to act and rescue what is possible." Others warned of the moral abyss of such a position. Jews had wrestled with all manner of fiendish dilemmas before, but never in a world in which every familiarly human signpost had been so shattered, in which every rational choice and every rational appeal had been obliterated. In the end, virtually all Council members perished in the last deportations.

A third issue that has generated much controversy and concern has been the response of American Jewry to the annihilation of European Jews during the war. The indifference and callousness of the Allies has already been documented.[26] Could American Jews have done more to save the Jews of Europe? The issue has been argued with particular intensity because of the controversy surrounding the creation in 1981 of an American Jewish Commission on the Holocaust to "embark on a searching inquiry into the actions and attitudes of American Jews and others in our country during the Holocaust." The work was to have been funded by a survivor, Jack Eisner, but the commission broke up in dissension after a little more than a year. Eisner withdrew his offer, but commission chairman Arthur Goldberg, former U.S. Supreme Court Justice, reconvened another group "to complete its scholarly study."[27]

There is much evidence that, despite official governmental blockage, indifference, and outright sabotage of efforts, American Jewish leaders and organizations tried to keep the plight of European Jews before the public and achieve practical results, including specific rescue proposals.[28] However, until 1944, when the War Refugee board was created, their pressures and influence had no impact on official American policy. One of their most bitter disappointments was the total exclusion of Jewish organizational representatives from the Bermuda Conference in April 1943, which was allegedly convened to help rescue Jews. (It completely failed to provide any practical rescue or ransom plans.) It has also been pointed out that American Jewry at the time was politically very weak, unassertive, and poorly organized. Moreover, many Jews unquestioningly and uncritically followed Roosevelt's leadership and believed with other Americans that winning the war was the absolute first priority. Even the fight against the British White Paper of 1939, seriously limiting Jewish immigration into Palestine, was not launched until after the Bermuda Conference, in the interest of preserving Jewish unity and not embarrassing the Roosevelt Administration with a global war on its hands and mind.

In the 1980s, it is being argued, American Jewry is stronger, more assertive, and better organized. It reacts to crises affecting world Jewry more aggressively and more independently, thus making it more difficult, if not impossible, to think oneself back to the war period without seeing events through contemporary eyes, insights, tactics, and the huge benefit of fuller knowledge of those events. Judgments are also distorted by a contemporary reading of old ideological conflicts within American Jewry and the desire to settle old political scores. Particularly bitter were those conflicts between Zionists and non-Zionists and those between mainstream Zionist leaders and Revisionist Zionists, including supporters of the Irgun Zevai Leumi in Palestine and Hillel Kook, who took the name of Peter Bergson in America and formed the Committee for a Jewish Army in 1941 and the Hebrew Committee of National Liberation in 1944, and helped found the Herut Party in 1948. In 1977 the head of the Herut Party Menachem Begin, became Prime Minister of Israel. The preparation of the report of the first American Jewish Commission on the Holocaust was entrusted to Samuel Merlin, an Irgunist and co-founder of Herut. Inevitably, that draft revealed the Revisionist Zionist hostility toward "establishment" Zionists and American Jewish organizations and attacked them for not doing enough to save European Jewry. (The film *Who Shall Live and Who Shall Die* carries the same general message.) Stormy disagreements within the first Commission and protests against undocumented charges against American Jewish organizations and leaders resulted in the resignation of Merlin and the dissolution of the group. It is hoped that Goldberg's plan to convene another commission will provide the opportunity for a more balanced, less biased study, with due attention paid to American preoccupation with the war, the state of the war fronts in 1942 and 1943, and the actual political position of American Jewry at the time. Debate and argumentation will undoubtedly continue. Henry L. Feingold has expressed it eloquently: "A simple searing truth emerges from the vast body of research and writing on the Holocaust. It is that European Jewry was ground to dust between the twin millstones of murderous Nazi intent and a callous Allied indifference. It is a truth with which the living seem unable to come to terms."[29] Ultimately, we will be forced to accept the intractable fact that Allied decision-makers scarcely thought about Jews at all during the war and that their rescue was only a sub-item in very few minds.

Although by now one often hears that we have had "too much exposure" to the Holocaust, especially on television, much unpublicized serious study and reflection occur in hundreds of colleges, universities, theological seminaries, and secondary schools throughout the country.[30] Paradoxically, student interest in a study that is grim and depressing, one that raises more questions than it can answer, is very intense. Many students speak of being markedly "changed" after taking such a course, of having a new, heightened awareness of the gift of life. Undoubtedly, there are many more courses and curricula development projects devoted to the Holocaust in the United States than elsewhere. Many non-Jews have pioneered work in this field, and courses are offered in many departments—history, philosophy, political science, theology, sociology, and literature—while some are interdisciplinary.

Jewish students may also take courses on the Holocaust in Jewish settings, where earlier resistance has declined. Coupled with a pervasive Jewish sense that the events of the Holocaust must be studied, made known, and, if possible, "lessons" extracted from such a study, there has been an overhanging anxiety on the part of parents about the dangers of exposing Jewish children to this appalling history. There is fear not only of traumatizing the children, but also of conveying the sense that Jewish history is fundamentally tragic, that Jews are always victims, that they have been targets of centuries-old hatreds that cannot be overcome. Thus, as a result, it is feared, Jewish children may feel helpless, mistrustful, ashamed, and self-hating.[31] There has also been concern over what children undergo spiritually when they have to confront the question, "Where was God during the Holocaust?" Obviously, it requires extremely sensitive and knowledgeable teachers to deal with these loaded questions. If children are to be exposed, adults have to know how to calibrate the quantities and intensities of information. They also have to allow children—especially adolescents—to grope and struggle as they ask their questions and reach for answers. Nor do we need to experiment with role-playing and game-playing gimmicks, such as putting children in dark cellars and depriving them of food and water for several hours, to simulate concentration camp conditions. No experience can duplicate what the victims endured, and it is futile as well as presumptuous to think any vicarious experience can even approximate it. There is also the danger that so-called simulation games rob children of the need to ponder profound questions raised by a study of Holocaust history and the clarification of their own values.

The resistance of Jewish parents was considerable until recent years. There is much less now because of a greater public consciousness of the Holocaust, numerous TV programs, and the growing number of Jewish schools that offer special units on the subject. Many educators have grappled with the serious problems involved in designing curriculum materials, but much more needs to be done in developing carefully thought out approaches, a balanced selection of materials, questions and issues that a study of the Holocaust raises, and the appropriate ways of intergrating Holocaust material in existing courses of study.

Teachers of such courses must also be aware that Christian parents may not want their children to be exposed to Holocaust history and the realities of Christian anti-Semitism, which formed the seed-bed of the widespread receptivity of Hitler and his anti-Jewish persecutions. But these realities, too, must be faced if we are ever to overmaster or at least defuse them sufficiently so as to make them less harmful. There is the problem of dealing with the singular victim— the Jew—a figure already associated with victimization, persecution, hatred, and guilt. Thus, there is the danger of a new caricature, of robbing the Jew of history, of a culture in a given time and place, of all the dimensions of being human— additional problems besetting the teacher.

The adult desire to protect young people from unpleasant facts also prevents youths from confronting hard questions and working their way toward understanding, responsibility, and maturity. Moreover, it has been pointed out that teenagers living after World War II have not exactly been living in cotton batting. *Their* world has been saturated with the barbarities of the Vietnam War, Biafra, Bangladesh, the massacre of the Kurds, the killing madness in Lebanon. The Holocaust may not even strike them as a peculiarly terrible series of horrors in history. They may not even be able to understand that mass murder on the scale perpetrated by the Nazis in the 1940s was then unthinkable. Mass murder on a near genocidal scale is now ideologically and technologically possible, to say nothing of nuclear war. The old taboos have been shattered, and a new radical reality is part of our human consciousness. Old thresholds of restraint have been breached, human sensitivities have been blunted and coarsened. Dulled responses to brutality, violence, and dehumanization have undoubtedly become the chief features of the twentieth century, and the transmission of this dubious legacy to young people constitutes one of the gravest challenges which humanistic educators face.

Students of the Holocaust, as they reflect on the road Germany took to Nazism and the decisions and non-decisions of individual Germans in allowing the Weimar Republic to fall, must give serious thinking to their own values and behavior and those considered desirable in a democratic society. The experiences of Jewish and non-Jewish teenagers during the Hitler period will help American students to identify with their situations and trials and to avoid generalizations and stereotyping. The existence of "the other Germany"—the anti-Nazi Germans, those who were imprisoned in concentration camps, those who had to flee the country, or those who tried to resist Nazism in the last days of the Weimar Republic should also be discussed. On the other hand, the nazification of doctors, lawyers, and the corruption of these disciplines—questions relevant to professional life today—offer another field for fruitful discussion.

Ten years ago, one heard the shocking proposal at a scholars' conference that the teaching of the Holocaust and dissemination of information be somehow restricted to selected, serious individuals and safeguarded from popular discussion. This, of course, has been impossible as well as undesirable. Nevertheless, it must be admitted that the subject of the Holocaust has been vulgarized and trivialized by all the media, especially television, in ways that are embarrassing and offensive. This came about partly because of political events affecting Israel.

The Six-Day War in 1967 and the Yom Kippur War of 1973 aroused the anxiety of many Jews who feared that a new Holocaust threatened the destruction of Israel. By the middle 1970s interest in the Holocaust rose, reflected in and stimulated by the organization of special centers, course curricula, seminars, conferences, new funding sources, numerous novels, and television programs. Survivors felt greater readiness to offer testimony based on their experiences. Holocaust oral history archives and centers were created. In the profusion of material, much was superficial, tasteless, and oversimplified or false to the facts, aimed as it was to a mass market. One can only lament the misuse of a subject that requires the utmost seriousness and soberness, and try to resist the crudities as best one can.

There are other kinds of doubts about the proliferation of material in what some have called a "Holocaust industry." Robert Alter, one of the sharpest critics in this regard, is also deeply concerned about "naturalizing the horror by making it part of the curriculum," through the "academic domestication of murder."[32] He also opposed invoking the Holocaust as "the supreme paradigm" of the Jewish historical experience and "a guide to the Zionist political enterprise." Jacob Neusner is concerned that the television mini-series *Holocaust* has served as the Jewish equivalent of *Roots* for American blacks, a way of experiencing ethnic distinctiveness and finding common cause with other Jews in focusing on the memory of suffering.

For some, focus on the Holocaust has become the substance of Jewish identity, a fiery fixation that has pre-empted all other chapters of Jewish history. This presents the obvious danger of some Jews slipping into morbid preoccupation with the Holocaust, of having it serve as a surrogate for a fuller, more balanced sense of Jewishness. Some rituals of remembrance may also be awkward, inappropriate, or melodramatic. But the pain, at least for middle-aged and older Jews and for survivors and their children, is still very acute. We are still struggling to find ways of dealing with such an appalling history and with memorializing the victims. It is still much too early to speak of a tradition of commemoration, of integration of the Holocaust in prayer, liturgy, or memorial service. We are still groping. Thus, some will be morbidly preoccupied, or obsessed—doubtless many Jews were similarly haunted by the catastrophe of the destruction of the Temple—and may read every Jewish experience, of any dimension, as a threatening new Holocaust. Because of the enormity of the tragedy and the human incapacity to comprehend it, one need not wonder that many Jews are fixated on this particular history. As years pass, new generations will have different feelings, perspectives, and interpretations. But to expect this generation, with survivors and their children still in our midst, to behave "normally," to react to the recent past as if it were already a distant slot in history, is unrealistic. Mental health cautionaries, though well intentioned, cannot deal with the massive psychic and physical wounds which cut deeply into Jewish consciousness.

Even so, most Jews, including survivors, have not been crippled by their deep awareness of the Holocaust. They understand that they must go about their daily lives and that this tragic history must not disfigure the future lives of Jewish children. Both parents and teachers have the somber responsibility of drawing a delicate balance: easing Jewish children into Holocaust history in incremental stages appropriate to their ages, putting this history in the perspective of the long sweep of Jewish history with its richness as well as tragedy, and giving them the necessary psychological armor to bear and withstand anti-Semitism without damaging trustfulness, hope, and faith in a better future. These are very difficult shoals to traverse, but they cannot be avoided. Inevitably, such problems soon touch on the questions: Where was God during the Holocaust? How could He have permitted the near-extinction of European Jewry? But similar questions have been asked throughout Jewish history, and there are no new responses.

The theological reverberations of the Holocaust from the Jewish point of view have been much more muted than among counterpart Christian thinkers. Emil Fackenheim, Elie Wiesel, Richard Rubenstein, and Eliezel Berkovits, among others, have wrestled with the post-Holocaust examination of the Jewish God, but there is not, as yet—if, indeed, there ever will be—a body of thought that provides religious or philosophical answers to the terrible questions posed by the Holocaust.[33] As Elie Wiesel has said, "We can perhaps only keep asking questions. Or remain silent." This incompleteness, this void of incomprehensibility, is consonant with much in Jewish religious tradition. Abraham, Jacob, Moses, Habakkuk, Job, and a long line of rabbis have wrestled with God and have protested His silence in the face of suffering, His fits of injustice, His uncaring. Even the notion that God with averted eyes, God with His back turned, an eclipsed God, an endangered God who needs man more than man needs Him—all of these interpretations have been known to Judaism.[34] Moreover, Jews traditionally do not agonize in their pursuit of the unknowable nature of God. The extent and degree of religious faith cannot be measured, but one has a general impression that the Holocaust has not shattered faith in God among Jews, even among survivors.

Among the Jewish voices responding to the religious implications of the Holocaust, one of the most influential is Emil L. Fackenheim, a survivor, formerly professor of philosophy at the University of Toronto, who recently settled in Israel. Dr. Fackenheim believes that after Auschwitz "everything is shaken, nothing is safe," that to be a Jew after Auschwitz is to have wrested hope from the abyss of despair. "Auschwitz," he writes, "is the scandal of evil for evil's sake, an eruption of demonism without analogy; and the singling out of Jews, ultimately, is an unparalleled expression of what the rabbis call groundless hate. This is the rock on which throughout eternity all rational explanations will crack and break apart." Thus, the search for the purpose in Auschwitz is foredoomed to failure. Yet the Jew must respond. And the response has been "with an unexpected will-to-live . . . an incredible commitment to Jewish group survival." Instead of a redeeming voice, Fackenheim hears a "commanding Voice," commanding the Jewish people to survive as Jews. "Jews are forbidden to grant posthumous victories to Hitler . . . forbidden to despair of the God of Israel lest

Judaism perish." Today it would be sinful for a Jew to respond to Hitler by doing his work, by helping Judaism disappear. The 614th Commandment for the Jew is to survive. Furthermore, the creation of Israel, rising from the ashes of the Holocaust, and Israel's escape from a possible second Holocaust in the Six-Day War have acquired "an inescapable religious dimension" for Fackenheim. The covenant with God endures.[35]

Elie Wiesel has been a compelling voice evoking the Holocaust, the archtypical survivor, witness to the crime of indifference, confronting the outermost limits of human pain and evil, forcing us to stare into the Kingdom of Night, tangling with God, despairing of man, but, in the end, not being overcome by despair, reconstructing a fragile hope in man. Using traditional Jewish forms of story-telling parable and paradox, as teacher and writer Wiesel describes the world that was burned away, the world that keeps on "burning and burning," yet is not past redemption. Not a theologian or philosopher, nor even strictly a novelist, in his work Wiesel explores the unavailing struggle of Jews to break the covenant with God.[36] The relationship has been shattered, but it cannot be severed. In *Legends of Our Time*, Rebbe Pinchas confesses that he fasts on Yom Kippur "not for love of God, but against God,"[37] and in *A Jew Today*, this same defiance is expressed in the prayer of a fifteenth-century Spanish Jew: "In spite of me and in spite of You, I shall shout the Kaddish . . . for You and against You. This song You shall not still, O God of Israel!" In the kabbalistic style, Wiesel writes in paradoxes. An infinite God co-exists with a finite God; an omnipotent God co-exists with a dependent God. From stony silence, for ten years after his liberation, to the searing account of the death of God on the gallows at Auschwitz (as a child slowly dies by hanging) in his autobiographical work *Night*, and in later works, Wiesel suffers along an agonizing spiritual journey: "To be a Jew," he says, "is to have all the reasons in the world not to have faith in language, in singing, in prayers, and in God, but *to go on telling the tale, to go on carrying on the dialogue*, and to have my own silent prayers and quarrels with God." The sign of God upon man is his only possibility of being human. Once this sign is removed, man becomes a Golem, recklessly destructive.[38]

In sharp contrast is the work of Richard Rubenstein, a former rabbi, for whom the Holocaust means the absolute death of God: "We learned in the crisis that we were totally and nakedly alone, that we could expect neither support nor succor from God nor from our fellow creatures. Therefore, the world will forever remain a place of pain, suffering, alienation and ultimate defeat." Secularized culture is harshly condemned: A machinery devoid of both love and hatred was set up and delegated to bureaucrats who overcame the moral barriers that had existed before. We live in a world that is "functionally godless," he believes. "No cold-blooded contemporary David need worry about a modern Nathan the prophet proclaiming the ultimacy of God's law." The modern absolutist state has become the new divinity with the power to decide who shall live and who shall die. Secularization which began by demystifying the power of the sovereign "has dethroned all mystifications of power and morality save its own."[39]

For Rubenstein, the indescribable suffering of the Jews during the Holocaust and God's abandonment of them means the end of any historical understanding of God and reveals instead a "nothingness," which is the Lord of creation. "How can Jews," he asks, "believe in an omnipotent, beneficent God after Auschwitz? To see any purpose in the death camps, the traditional believer is forced to regard the most demonic, antihuman explosion in all history as a meaningful expression of God's purposes." In facing the total meaninglessness of the Holocaust, he can no longer believe in God. Yet he cannot give up being a Jew: "I would like to offer my own confession of faith after Auschwitz. I am a pagan . . . [Yet] paganism does not mean the rejection of one's people's ancestral dance, its distinctive rituals, nor its ancestral story."

Jacob Neusner does not view the Holocaust as the radical evil "from which theologians must draw conclusions radically different from those after other disasters:

Classic Judaic theology was not struck dumb by evil and neither changed its apprehension of divinity, nor claimed in its own behalf a renewed demand on the part of Jews on account of disaster . . . Jewish public discourse is ill-served by Auschwitz . . . we are misled by making a response to Hitler in place of an answer to God, who commands us to be merciful and seek justice. Let the dead lie in peace, and the living honor them in silent reverence. Why should they serve the living as a pretext for belief or unbelief, for a naturalist or supernatural God? . . . The choice is about the future, not the past. Theologians and politicians alike should let the dead rest in peace. We are not well-served by the appeal to the Holocaust, either as rationalization for our Judaism or as a source of slogans for our Jewish activism and self-assertion.[40]

Neusner, however, sees the creation of the state of Israel as a new religious affirmation, for it was Israel that saved the remnant and gave meaning and significance to Jewish survival.

Dr. Eliezer Berkovits, an Orthodox Jewish thinker, faces the problem of *mipnei hataeinu* ("Because of our sins") which pervades Jewish Prayer:

There is suffering because of sins; but that all suffering is due to it is simply not true. The idea that Jewish martyrology through the ages can be explained as divine judgment is obscene. Nor do we for a single moment entertain the thought that what happened to European Jewry in our generation was divine punishment for sins committed by them. It was injustice absolute; injustice countenanced by God. In Biblical terminology we speak of *hester panim*, the hiding of the face, God's hiding of His countenance from the sufferer.[41]

Berkovits then explains that God's hiding during the Holocaust sprang from the wickedness and cruelty of man: "God's hiding himself mysteriously from the cry of the innocent'' is necessary if man is to be free, but man left to his freedom is capable of both goodness and wickedness. But that man may not perish in the tragic destructions of his own making, God must also be present, and because of His presence, evil will not ultimately triumph.

Berkovits believes that the Holocaust was unique, unlike anything the Jewish people experienced in its long history, but that it must not be wrenched out of the totality of Jewish history. Although this perspective does not assuage the pain, it does link Jews to earlier generations of suffering, renewal, and hope and the search for purpose in human life. In our generation, he sees this regeneration in the restoration of the state of Israel: "We must believe because our brother Job believed; and we must question because our brother Job so often could not believe any longer."[42] Berkovits vehemently rejects the neo-Platonic tradition that evil is only the absence of good, as darkness is merely the absence of light. Rather, the evil of the Holocaust was absolute. Thus, Jews must return to the stark faith of the prophets who contend with God, cry out against wickedness, but retain their faith in God.

In 1966 thirty-eight rabbis expressed their beliefs and theological commitments in a book called *The Condition of Jewish Belief*. The editor, Milton Himmelfarb, observed, "There are few new ideas about Judaism. On the whole, therefore, the relative absence of newness was to be expected together with the dominant intellectual, if not emotional calm."[43] This lack of novelty, Seymour Siegel has said, "does not mean a lack of brilliance. The ancient ideas are restated with vigor and beauty, but there is little of the frantic reaching for novelty which to an outsider at least seems to be so much a part of the theological scene within Christianity."[44] Such a statement, however, seems somewhat smug. The Holocaust poses questions of faith which for many cannot be answered. The mere stating of them forecloses answers. If the Jew pushes beyond the biblical framework, his thinking must follow that of Rubenstein. If not, the old rabbis and texts, which have already raised those questions, stand as bulwarks against despair and loss of faith. But it must not be assumed that some Jews have not struggled privately to reach God after Auschwitz.

Yet today as in the past after catastrophes, the affirmation of life and the will to survive, despite the human and divine abandonment of European Jews during the Holocaust, still seem quite strong among Jews. Neither among survivors nor among Jews who were spared have there been large-scale defections from the community, impassioned attacks on the providential God, or manifestations of total despair. The spectrum of outcry against God has already been spanned and stretched. The old texts and rabbis still speak. Only a few Jewish thinkers are preoccupied with the post-Holocaust God-question. Some prefer silence in the face of the incomprehensible. Jews still pray the old or revised prayers in synagogue, or go only at the time of the High Holidays, Rosh Hashanah, and Yom Kippur, which is perhaps as much a demonstration of community solidarity as of faith, and that reaction turns on the extreme vulnerability Jews feel about their own and Israel's survival.

Dreading chaos and the absence of meaning in human existence, Jews continue the struggle to create families and communities and to mend the sense of covenant between God and the Jewish people. But many illusions about the future of Jewish existence in the twentieth century have been shattered. Not only in Israel where many of its people are survivors is there obsessive concern with physical security, but also here in America, Jews feel great anxiety about Israel's security, about the existence of Jews elsewhere, especially in the Soviet Union, and even here under the surface of ostensible security. These fears perhaps explain the quick reflexive reactions to instances of anti-Semitism and general distrust of the non-Jewish world.[45] There is a pervasive feeling that in a crisis Jews can count only on each other, a response, that, at least, for the time, has checked the usually generous support of Jews for large social causes. The universalist face of Judaism has contracted during this age, and the earlier faith in so-called emancipation, human progress, and humanistic values has diminished. There is skepticism about old liberal coalitions, a tendency to close ranks, to draw strength from each other. At the same time, the Jewish habit of self-criticism, even self-chastisement, has not dried up. In some circles there is searching criticism of Israel's policies, indictment of the insularity of contemporary Jewish life, and a call to restore alliances with non-Jews in dealing with Reaganomics, the nuclear threat, and environmental and minority issues.

The broader movement, however, is to huddle together, and this, in turn, has resulted in diminished interest and hope for changed relations through Christian-Jewish dialogue. It is, of course, true that the events of 1933–1945 in Hitler-Europe have compelled some thoughtful Christians to re-examine old anti-Jewish dogmas and doctrines and to confront the destructive consequences of Christian anti-Semitism which prepared the way for the Nazi annihilation of European Jewry. The Holocaust has served as a shocking catalyst in their rethinking of the Christian understanding of Jesus, Judaism, the Jewish people, and the state of Israel. The work of such scholars as A. Roy and Alice Eckardt, Rosemary Ruether, Gerard Sloyan, Eugene J. Fisher, Eva Fleischner, Harry James Cargas, Michael Pawlikowski, Franklin Littell, Leonard Swidler, and Paul van Buren has been, and is, of great constructive value and has resulted in a fuller understanding of Judaism and the creation of greater mutual regard and improved Christian-Jewish relations. On the Jewish side, the Anti-Defamation League of B'nai B'rith under the creative leadership of Rabbi Solomon S. Bernards and individuals such as Benjamin Agus, Marc Tannenbaum, Michael Wyschograd, Pinchas Lapide, Rabbi Leon Klenicki, and Rabbi Irving Greenberg have been responsive to scholarly and collegial contact with Christian counterparts. Many conferences, seminars, retreats, and publications have flowed from these experiences. On a more popular level, some Christian congregations have sponsored lectures and discussions dealing with the Holocaust and the implications for better Christian understanding of Judaism and Jewish history. There have also been Christian Yom Ha-Shoa (Holocaust Remembrance Day) commemorative programs. Undoubtedly, many minds and hearts have been opened in ways that were undreamed of ten or even five years ago. But these voices do not seem to be making any serious impact on most other Christian theologians, and this failure forces us to ask if more theologizing is at all helpful. Can it ever lead to a fuller Christian understanding of what it means to be a Jew? Will it, as in the past, be more contentious, divisive, and even dangerous, than healing? In essentially personal and social Christian-Jewish relations, we seem to be doing better than in the past, exchanging views, sharing knowledge and celebration of holidays and customs, admitting but also trying to respect differences. At this informal level, theological and doctrinal arguments do not seem to impair human relationships. What is much more problematical is the professional hardening of argument into theological constructs, set fast in print, locking thought instead of loosening it, stiffening attitudes instead of liberalizing them. This is, of course, farthest from the intention of the Christian thinkers mentioned here; the ground they have broken is truly fresh and pliant, although not without certain pitfalls. But many others I read are defensive, apologetic, condescending, and still essentially triumphalist.

Christian theological reactions range from those that ignore the Holocaust to those that admit it, only to provide fresh ground for new-old anti-Jewish reaffirmations. Roy Eckardt has recently written that "Most Protestant and Catholic thinking of today remains quite oblivious to the *Shoah*. This is the overall state of affairs in North America."[46] John Pawlikowski has said that "With few exceptions . . . Catholic theologians have done little or no wrestling with the implications of Auschwitz for theological construction within Catholicism." He goes on to say that whatever sensitivity has been expressed "has exercised virtually no impact on the main body of their theology."[47]

Most Jews are frankly skeptical that constructive dialogic efforts, even if they were to be multiplied, can do much more than make a slight dent in centuries-old images, traditions, and mind-sets. We accept anti-Semitism as a given in Christian society and feel that efforts to undo it are too little and too late. The hopes that were aroused by Vatican II have been disappointed, while unceasing, intense Christian missionary activities have defeated the hope that Jews and their faith would be left alone. Most intractable are the anti-Jewish passages of the New Testament, which could be deleted in church services or put into a historical rather than theological context, but which, in the main, are not. Similarly, the reproaches, officially and unofficially, still appear in many services as do the Good Friday prayer and the Eucharistic lections in the period following Easter Sunday. As Gerard Sloyan has said, "It would seem that no amount of critical scholarship is going to meet the pastoral problem caused by the fact that the sacred books of the Christians contain a polemic against a people who, subsequent to the writing, became almost totally other than the community of writers."[48] The evangelists' attacks on "Jews" is heard in a modern context, not in their own setting, and reinforces already built-in anti-Jewish feelings. Much good work in reinterpretation is being done at a number of theological seminaries, especially on the part of younger scholars and their students, but at the level of parish priests and ministers, who meet their parishioners week in and week out, and Sunday school classes, the changes, if any, seem to be glacial.

In Western Europe, the situation is even more discouraging. There, Christian-Jewish dialogue is halting and grudging. Clemens Thoma of the Theological Faculty at Lucerne speaks of "a lot" of activity but "not much" progress in Germany, Austria, and Switzerland, while in France and Belgium, most efforts are overshadowed and displaced by the eruption of rightist and leftist anti-Semitic violence based in part on ultranationalist and anti-Israel feeling, respectively.[49] The continuing tradition of passion plays at Oberammergau and elsewhere in Europe admits no fundamental revisions and underscores the obstacles involved in changing age-old attitudes.[50] Eckardt comments that in Germany, only after "herculean and persisting endeavors over a period of fifteen years, the German church leader and teacher, Professor Heinz Kremers, has at last succeeded, together with Eberhard Bethge, in getting the Synod of the Protestant Church of the Rhineland to acknowledge . . . Christian co-responsibility and guilt for the *Endlösung*."[51] But "hostility to Judaism and Jews continues to pervade much present-day German biblical, and particularly New Testament, scholarship, not excepting the most respected and authoritative figures."

Jewish skepticism and anxiety attend Christian-Jewish theological discussions not only because of the memory of tormenting abuses of traditional theological debates, but also because so many Christians still think of Jews in Biblical, pre-emancipation terms, giving us missions and destinies read from scripture, but wholly at odds with Jewish historical experiences since the time of the French Revolution. Scripture foretells history and history unfolds according to scripture in theological discourse, but the Jew *in* history has no place in this trans-figuration of reality and becomes an abstraction.[52] In the Christian interpretation of scripture the Jew can only be viewed as spiritually deficient, in need of salvation through acceptance of Christ.

Another disappointment, sharply felt by Jews, has been the generally apathetic or negative reaction to efforts to press the American government to accelerate and take seriously its lagging, often sham-prosecution of alleged Nazi criminals still at large in the United States. Individuals such as Beate and Serge Klarsfeld, who were largely responsible for recently tracking down Klaus Barbie, the Gestapo head in Lyon, France, as well as other ex-Nazis; John Loftus, author of *The Belarus Secret* (New York: Knopf, 1982); and Charles R. Allen, Jr., who exposed official neglect over twenty years ago and is considered an expert on Nazis in America, have kept up the pressure to hunt down and prosecute charges against them, but their efforts are exceptional. It is now generally accepted that American officials in the Immigration and Naturalization Service, the State Department, the FBI, and CIA connived at bringing Nazi criminals to the United States in the 1950s, falsified their identities, and used them as agents in the Cold War against the Soviet Union.[53] It is estimated that perhaps as many as 1,000 Nazi criminals are still at large in the United States enjoying freedom, economic prosperity, and citizenship. Simon Wiesenthal, veteran Nazi hunter and head of the Documentation Center in Vienna, estimates that several million former Nazis are still abroad, many in South America. The U.S. State Department has files on 10.7 million Nazi Party members, including many involved in the annihilation of European Jews.

The general public has been either indifferent to or impatient with "digging up the past." At times there has been sympathy for those accused. For example, there have been strong objections to the prosecution of Archbishop Valerian Trifa, head of the Romanian Orthodox Episcopate of America, who was indicted on charges of concealing his ties to the fascist anti-Semitic Romanian Iron Guard when he entered the United States in 1950 and when he gained American citizenship.[54] The Iron Guard attempted a coup against the Romanian government in 1941 and perpetrated numerous anti-Jewish atrocities, including murder. Trifa was sentenced in Romania to life imprisonment, in absentia, inasmuch as he was smuggled out to Germany. The sentence still stands. Yet the National Council of Churches, of which Trifa was a member, never censored or removed him. There have also been angry reactions to the trials of Andrei Artukovic, Feodor Fedorenko, Wolodymir Osidach, and Boleslaus Maikovskis. Some of those charged have instituted libel suits. In several instances, considerable hostility has built up between the local Jewish and Ukrainian communities, even causing confrontations outside courtrooms and creating strained community relations.

For over thirty years, U.S. government agencies did nothing to seek out and prosecute former Nazis living here, most of them from Eastern Europe. Leads were not pursued, and available witnesses were not interviewed. In the middle and late 1970s, prodded largely by Joshua Eilberg, Chairman, and Elizabeth Holtzman, member of the House Judiciary Sub-committee on Immigration, Congress provided funding and full-time staffing and a Special Litigation Unit.[55] It was only in 1979 that loopholes in the immigration laws were closed, permitting the denaturalization and deportation of accused persons and barring their entry in the future. Such persons, however, cannot be tried in this country for crimes committed in the war. As of 1980, files were opened on 480 suspects, but very few have been brought to trial.[56] Open access to all government files is still not possible, and there are strong hints that certain individuals are and have been protected. Those best informed on these matters generally agree that government agencies deliberately blocked or sidestepped war-crimes investigations. There have also been deeply disturbing relationships between some of the alleged Nazis and government officials. Trifa gave the opening prayer in the U.S. Senate in 1955. Vilis Hazners worked for Radio Liberty, which for many years was funded by the CIA. Barbie was not only protected but also financed by our government. Hubertus Strughold, charged with medical atrocities, was brought to the United States after the war and has held prestigious positions in the field of space medicine. A somewhat equivocal inquiry by the General Accounting Office in 1978 nevertheless reported that certain alleged war criminals had been employed or assisted by U.S. government agencies, but the agencies involved did not provide full information. A full story of government complicity awaits full access to all agency files.

The American governmental failure to mete out justice to perpetrators of heinous crimes has been more than matched by the record in West Germany, where a number of men formally charged with crimes not only live freely but have been and are in official positions. Jews have been disappointed and disillusioned by these defaults. The hope for certain reforms in school textbooks related to Jewish history, including the period of the Holocaust, has also faded.

A series of anti-Semitic incidents in Cologne and other cities in the Federal Republic of Germany during the winter of 1959 raised a storm of controversy about the role of German schools in safeguarding the new democracy and the treatment of the Nazi past in history and civics teaching. In 1974 Martin and Eva Kalinsky published an analytical study of the most widely used textbooks from 1960 to 1972 under several headings: the Rise of National Socialism and Anti-Semitism, Anti-Jewish Policies after 1933 and the Annihilation Plan, Knowledge of the Crimes in Germany, War Crimes Trials and Denazification.[57] The authors noted that the ideological orientations of teachers are often closely related to the dominant trends in national political cultures. In Germany, the influence of anti-democratic *völkish* and racist attitudes before and after the First World War was observed. Moreover, some 160,000 teachers were members of the Nazi Party in 1935 and filled the lower ranks of the Nazi hierarchy. Many were dismissed during the denazification period but were re-hired afterward. Nevertheless, the desire to overcome bias and distortion in textbook writing was much discussed in international meetings after the war, and German writers and teachers were affected. Correction of factual errors and neutralization of "the more blatantly offensive material" were achieved, but Martin and Eva Kolinsky felt that "the problem of bias cannot be laid to rest . . . the ensuing reduction of distortion is often limited to the cognitive level . . . the problem of bias, touching on inner cultural and psychological attitudes, remains critical."[58]

These inner cultural and psychological attitudes are identified as "mechanisms of avoidance and evasion" in confronting the Nazi past:

The general principle underlying the presentation and interpretation of the Nazi period, its ideology and policies, is the separation of the Nazis from the German people. . . . By holding Hitler and a narrow elite solely responsible, and by identifying policies with ideology, the books are able to dissociate themselves from past events by merely debunking the ideology and discarding Hitler as politically unbalanced. In this way, the German people emerge unscathed, uninvolved, and absolved. . . . With regard to the treatment of the Holocaust, we noted a partial improvement after 1960. But, apart from Hannah Vogt's text, [*The Jews: A Chronicle for Christian Conscience* (New York: Association Press, 1967] no accounts of Jewish history, and of the social and cultural life of Jewish communities in pre-war Germany and Europe, were to be found.[59]

In a 1980 study by the American Jewish Committee of nine German textbooks in history for students aged ten to sixteen, distributed for the 1978–1979 school year, uncertainty about the goals and methods of teaching history in German schools were aired.[60] The Nazi past, it was said, not only had made "unthinking identification with the national history difficult," but had created "a goodbye to history . . . a retreat into the present." Many young Germans don't want to have to confront the destructive actions of their parents. The roots of modern anti-Semitism, persecutions of Jews during the Middle Ages, and Jewish contributions to German culture were only partially or inadequately treated in the textbooks examined. Seriously undertreated is the development of nineteenth-century anti-Semitism. None of the books examined, however, denies Germany's guilt, and all offer adequate or detailed descriptions of progressive restrictions of Jewish rights, persecution, and murder. But cognitive learning does not necessarily affect attitudes or behavior, and the student's consciousness may be more influenced by parents and teachers, who have apologetic views.

The television production of Gerald Green's *Holocaust* was watched by more than 20 million Germans during the week of January 22, 1979.[61] *Der Spiegel* observed that "a rather shallow American TV series, achieved what hundreds of books, plays, films . . . thousands of documents and all of the war crimes trials of the past three decades had been unable to do: shock millions of Germans with the recognition of the crimes against Jews committed in their name." The television magazine *Medium* called it the "most provocative, effective media event in our television history to date." Numerous newspaper articles and editorials and radio programs were devoted to the series and were particularly aimed at young people. A public opinion survey measuring the effect of the program found that it "deeply touched large segments of the population, changing attitudes and providing a simplified but unique history lesson . . . It led young people to report that they wanted to learn more about the Nazi era and many now say they . . . oppose an end to the prosecution of war criminals."[62] Partly because of the program, the Statute of Limitations on war crimes trials was extended. Yet, what the newspaper *Frankfurter Rundschau* called a "horrifyingly high proportion"— 30 percent—said after seeing the series that "Nazism was a basically good idea that was carried out badly."

The positive impact of such programs, moreover, is transitory, as more powerful influences in the environment overwhelm the individual and diminish or negate the initial compassion. The German failure to prosecute thousands of Nazi war criminals, the persistence of neo-Nazi movements, and the strong national inhibition against a searching examination of the Nazi past reflect some of these forces and the societal drift of feeling toward Jews.

Western historians generally have remained virtually silent on Holocaust history, and their authors, in the words of Gerd Korman,

continue to write in the tradition that prepared no one for the catastrophe, a tradition that still prevents us from attempting to assess and understand what happened; for with precious few exceptions they write of the years before 1945 as if the 1930's and 1940's did not require a reexamination of European history during the nineteenth and twentieth century. . . . Historians today must do something their forbears did not, and perhaps could not, do. They must make room to interlace Gentile-Jewish relations in the mainstream of European history and in contemporary history.[63]

This is, of course, a complex and painful process requiring the overcoming of personal as well as cultural and intellectual prejudices, including the persistent view that the Jew was not a cultural and national presence in history after the establishment of Christianity and up to 1948, and had, in fact, disappeared from history.

Not only is a searching history of anti-Semitism in Christian Europe missing in the textbooks, but there are few references to the fate of Jews in the Hitler-occupied lands of Europe, the concentration camps, or even Auschwitz, the prime annihilation center. Lucy Dawidowitz adduces three reasons for such scanty treatment: the narrow perception of historians, most of whom see Jews as being "outside history"; the historian's "rationalist bias" which cannot cope with the history of mass psychopsychology; and the prevailing view that National Socialism was "an aberration, . . . a deviation from the expected trajectory of German history."[64] Few historians are able to cope with the derangements of anti-Semitism, the obsessions of anti-Semites, the irrational but fundamental truth that there is such a phenomenon as floating, pervasive Jew-hating in much of Western society which cannot be explained through a rational cause-and-effect sequence, an eruptive feeling which the historians themselves may not think important enough to describe or acknowledge and which they may even share.

Some "historians" have been far from silent. These are the so-called revisionist writers who deny the reality of the Nazi annihilation plans and their execution.[65] Spearheaded by books written by H. Elmer Barnes, Arthur R. Butz, Paul Rassinier, and an anonymous book called *The Myth of the Six Million*, seventy people attended the first "Revisionist Convention" in Los Angeles in September 1979 and heard papers denying that the Holocaust ever happened. The papers were then published in *The Journal of Historical Review*, by a so-called Institute for Historical Review with an editorial committee of university professors to give it academic respectability.[66] The only address given has been a Post Office box in Torrance, California, but no editor is named. Rassinier died in 1967 and Barnes a year later, but the literature is still being churned out, given considerable push by Butz's *The Hoax of the Twentieth Century*, published in 1976. Butz, an associate professor of electrical engineering at Northwestern University, was the subject of numerous attacks by scholars, but his tenure at Northwestern has not been questioned. Financial support for many of the publications, including pamphlets, has come from the Liberty Lobby and its subsidiary, Noontide Press.

In France, the chief promoter of the libel that the Holocaust was a lie, created by Jewish propaganda in order to gain support for Israel, has been Robert

Faurisson, who until 1979 was a professor of French literature at the University of Lyon. England has its Richard Verrall, who calls himself Richard E. Harwood, editor of *Spearhead* magazine, a racist publication, and Germany, Udo Walendy, who claims that the photographs of concentration camp survivors and cadavers are faked atrocity pictures. Most disturbing was the June 1980 issue of the *American Historical Review*, the organ of the prestigious American Historical Association, which favorably reviewed a book by Warren B. Morris called *The Revisionist Historians and German War Guilt*, published by the Revisionist Press in Brooklyn, thus giving "academic legitimacy to the outpourings of a variety of neo-Nazis and anti-Semites."[67]

Compounding the harm and danger of this literature and incalculably adding to the pain of survivors is the immense anti-Israel and anti-Semitic output of Soviet communists and Third World nations, including the reprinting of the notorious Protocols of the Elders of Zion. These sources not only deny that Jews were special victims of Nazi mass murder but state, rather, that they were accomplices of the Nazis! The abuse of language and truth can scarcely be more blatant, more cynical, and outrageous.

For Jews, the very effort to undermine incontrovertible evidence of the annihilation of two-thirds of European Jewry is an enraging defamation. At first, survivors and historians were tempted to dismiss it as too preposterous to consider. However, in recent years it has been taken seriously and confronted. People born after World War II view it as ancient history, and it may be susceptible to revisionist lies. This realization has given special importance to the accumulating testimony of survivors in various archival centers, especially at Yad Vashem in Jerusalem, Israel, and the testimony of liberators of camps, many of them non-Jewish.[68] It has also stirred many survivors, who, for many different reasons, were unable to speak about their experiences, to offer their testimony "for the sake of history." Their affirmation as special witnesses to the realities of the Holocaust has been made dramatically manifest in three international gatherings of survivors, the first in Jerusalem in June 1981, the second in Washington, D.C., in April 1983, and the third in Philadelphia in April 1985. These stirring assemblages of thousands of survivors and their children, profoundly bound to each other and sharing a powerful sense of solidarity, also helped to expose "revisionist" frauds. American official recognition of Yom Ha-Shoa and plans for a permanent museum dealing with the Holocaust and Armenian genocide represent impressive acknowledgments of the need for the whole nation to remember these acts of vast, unprecedented annihilation and further repudiation of revisionist lies.[69]

Until recently, survivors have been reluctant to speak of their experiences to their children, largely out of a need to shield them. The psychological traumas they themselves have suffered have created what has been called a "survivor syndrome," resulting in anxiety, depression, guilt, nightmares, feelings of emptiness and meaninglessness in life—behavior patterns that have affected children.[70] Psychologists have been studying and treating some survivors and their children, feeling that there was too much preoccupation with remembering the dead and insufficient attention to the social and mental health of the living. The Second Generation also needed to know what had happened not only to their parents but also to whole families that had been wiped out, depriving them of grandparents, aunts, uncles, and cousins and creating a void in their own identity. Much research was undertaken in Israel soon after the war, and in the United States, most work started in the 1970s. General interest in the problems of children was spurred by the publication of an issue of *Response* in 1975 and Helen Epstein's article, "The Heirs of the Holocaust," in *The New York Times Magazine* in June 1977.[71] Herself a child of survivors, Epstein, other children, and certain psychologists have recognized the children of survivors as a distinct social group struggling to come to terms with their parents' ordeal and with their own identity. "What binds them together," one of the children has said, "is a need to have continuity with the past. It has to do with the process of mourning. They have a need to mourn their grandparents, aunts and uncles." Many have become high achievers, working in "helping" fields such as social work, counseling, and teaching. Some have been able to integrate their parents' suffering; others are still testing themselves, trying to duplicate the suffering of their parents, bearing a vicarious guilt and trying to compensate for what the parents lost. There are about 250,000 children of survivors in this country, and many of them have formed social and political groups to maintain their special identity which range from transmission of survivor testimony to anti-nuclear and other programmatic goals. Some have also organized small counseling groups or "awareness groups" led by one of their own therapists or other professional therapists to deal with the difficult questions, adjustments, stresses, and conflicts which the children faced.

It has been suggested that psychiatrists may have overemphasized the pathological, "using clinical samples that are too small and unrepresentative of the range of adaptations and coping mechanisms that survivors utilize," that psychologists often have little knowledge of the historical background of the Holocaust, and that diagnosis and therapy may be skewed along the lines of a particular school or approach. Jack Porter has pointed to the need for research to examine a possible "socio-political syndrome" among survivors and their children, involving sociological, religious, cultural, political, and economic adaptations of survivors, which stress the positive rather than the pathological adaptations of survivors and their children. Some have been psychically numbed, but most survivors have exhibited remarkable strength considering the shattering experiences they have endured in building new families, struggling to make a living and "Americanize" with little community help, and in making uncounted sacrifices in order for their children to be well educated.[72] They are ardent in their support of Israel and Soviet Jewry, in maintaining survivor organizations, in creating Holocaust centers, memorials, and Yom Ha-Shoa commemorative programs. They and their children do much to keep the history of the Holocaust from deteriorating into a clinical academic discipline or becoming a target of cynical abuse and libelous distortion. Regretfully, neither they nor other Jews have lived to see either better understanding of the Jewish past or present or a more secure Jewish existence—a minimal hope following the Holocaust.[73] Nor can Israel's existence and military power assure that future. Yet the perennial Jewish search for meaning in life and hope in the future persists, as it persisted among Jews during the Holocaust. We do not yet know if our hope is illusory, as was theirs. Meanwhile, new generations will have to re-tell their story, honestly and faithfully carry on research, and integrate Holocaust study and rituals of commemoration. They must especially remember to describe what was lost and, in the telling, be strengthened in the fashion expressed by one survivor: "I have not told you of our experiences to harrow you, but to strengthen you. Now you may decide if you are justified in despairing."

NOTES

1. For some years, silence overwhelmed many writers who pondered the Holocaust and sought a new language to describe it and new forms that would defy its meaninglessness. Some believed that after Auschwitz writing poetry would be impossible. The silence has been broken and a "literature of atrocity" has appeared, but there is no climactic literary masterwork of the Holocaust that transcends that meaninglessness or enhances life, as great art does. The excesses of Holocaust reality exceeded the power of literature and art to transfigure it, perhaps forever, but many have, nonetheless, struggled to render what David Rousset calls a "world . . . impossible to communicate" in language, in *The Other Kingdom*, p. 169. See suggested references in the Bibliography, under "Fiction, Poetry, Literary Criticism."

2. The arguments challenging the uniqueness of the Holocaust continue with accelerating anger and sharpness, often overlaid with references to other holocausts and genocides. See, for example, Helen Fein, *Accounting for Genocide: National Responses and Jewish Victimization During the Holocaust* (New York: Free Press, 1979), pp. 3–30; Irving Louis Horowitz, "Many Genocides, One Holocaust? The Limits of the Rights of States and the Obligations of Individuals," *Modern Judaism* 1 (1981): 74–89; Peter J. Donaldson, "In Cambodia, A Holocaust," *New York Times*, April 22, 1980, p. 17; Uriel Tal, "On the Study of the Holocaust and Genocide," *Yad Vashem Studies* 13 (1979): 7–52; Yehuda Bauer, "Holocaust Questions," *Jerusalem Post*, International ed., March 2–8, 1980, p. 14; "Symposium on Genocides," *Midstream*, April 1984, pp. 19–25. Richard G. Hovannisian, *The Armenian Holocaust: A Bibliography* (Cambridge, Mass.: Armenia Press, 1980); Robert G. Weisbord, *Genocide: Birth Control and the Black American* (Westport, Conn.: Greenwood Press, 1975).

3. Quoted in review of *History: Choice and Commitment* by Felix Gilbert (Cambridge: Harvard University Press, 1977), in *New York Review of Books*, 20 April, 1978.

4. Among the more important studies in the past ten or fifteen years have been the following: Walter Laqueur, *The Terrible Secret: Suppression of the Truth About Hitler's "Final Solution"* (Boston: Little, Brown and Co., 1980); Christopher Browning, *The Final Solution and the German Foreign Office* (New York: Holmes and Meier, 1978); the English translation of Philip Friedman's *Roads to Extinction: Essays on the Holocaust*, edited by Ada J. Friedman (Philadelphia: Jewish Publication Society of America, 1980);

Martin Gilbert, *The Macmillan Atlas of the Holocaust* (New York: Macmillan Co., 1982); Robert Ross, *So It Was True: The American Protestant Press and the Nazi Persecution of the Jews* (Minneapolis: University of Minnesota Press, 1980); George M. Kren and Leon Rappoport, *The Holocaust and the Crisis of Human Behavior* (New York: Holmes and Meier, 1980); Randolph L. Braham, *Genocide and Retribution: The Holocaust in Hungarian-Ruled Transylvania* (Hingham, Mass.: Kluwer Academic Publishers, 1983); Ilya Ehrenburg, ed., *The Black Book: The Ruthless Murder of Jews by German- Fascist Invaders Throughout . . . the Soviet Union* (New York: Holocaust Library, 1980). David Wyman, *The Abandonment of the Jews* (New York: Pantheon Press, 1984); and Lucjan Dobroszycki, *The Chronicle of the Lodz Ghetto* (New Haven, Conn.: Yale University Press, 1984). Lucien Steinberg, *The Jews Against Hitler: Not As a Lamb*, translated by Marion Hunter (New York: Gordon and Cremoresi, 1978). Other important works are fully cited in the Bibliography. The monographs and essays published since 1957 as *Yad Vashem Studies on the European Jewish Catastrophe* should be consulted by every serious student of the Holocaust.

5. Catalogues of the Weiner Library collection, formerly in London, dealing with German and German-Jewish history up to 1945, are available on microfilm at the Leo Baeck Institute in New York. As of 1979, there were five volumes of archival material published jointly by Yad Vashem and the Institute of Contemporary Jewry as *Guide to Unpublished Materials of the Holocaust Period*, edited by Yehuda Bauer. The National Archives in Washington, D.C., is also an important center for Holocaust research, but the material is scattered and requires a comprehensive survey of the holdings and an index. See John Mendelsohn, "The Holocaust: Rescue and Relief Documentation in the National Archives," in Irene G. Shur, ed., *Reflections on the Holocaust*, in *Annals of the American Academy of Political and Social Science* 450 (July 1980): 237–249.

6. As of January 1968, collections in the Archives, Museum, and Library are described in Abraham Wein, "The Jewish Historical Institute in Warsaw," *Yad Vashem Studies* 8 (1970): 203–213. In June 1981 an agreement was signed between Professor Henryk Samsonowicz, rector of the University of Warsaw, and Rabbi Alexander E. Schindler, president of the University of American Hebrew Congregations, giving research scholars access to Jewish archival material currently held by the Polish government, the Catholic Church, and Polish universities. The material includes official Jewish community records, such as the minutes of the Judenrat of Lublin during the Nazi era.

7. Robert Wistrich, "The Anti-Zionist Masquerade," Midstream 29, no. 7 (August/ September 1983): 8–18.

8. See Yehuda Bauer, *The Jewish Emergence from Powerlessness* (Toronto: University of Toronto Press, 1979); William R. Perl, *Operation Action* (New York: Frederick Ungar, 1979); Asher Cohen, "He-Halutz Underground in Hungary: March-August 1944," in *Yad Vashem Studies* 14, (1981): 247–267; Marie Syrkin, *Blessed Is the Match* (Philadelphia: Jewish Publication Society of America, 1976). Bracha Habas, *The Gate-Breakers* (New York: Yoseloff, 1963); Jon Kimche, *The Secret Roads: The "Illegal" Migration of a People, 1938–1948* (London: Secker and Warburg, 1954); and Yehuda Bauer, *Flight and Rescue: Brichah: The Organized Escape of the Jewish Survivors of Eastern Europe, 1944–1948* (New York: Random House, 1970).

9. The abuse and trivialization of Holocaust themes have been widely discussed in recent years. See Paula Hyman, "New Debate on the Holocaust," *New York Times Magazine*, September 14, 1980; Leon A. Jick, "The Holocaust: Its Use and Abuse Within the American Public," *Yad Vashem Studies* 14 (1981): 303–317; Elie Wiesel, "Trivial-

izing the Holocaust: Semi-Fact and Semi-Fiction," *New York Times*, April 16, 1978, Section II, p. 1; Lesley Hazelton, "The Esthetic View of Death," *The Nation*, November 21, 1981, pp. 529–531.

10. Brandeis University, The Tauber Institute, *Annual Report 1982–83* (Waltham, Mass.: 1982–83), p. 2.

11. Yehuda Bauer, "Trends in Holocaust Research," *Yad Vashem Studies* 12 (1977): 7–36. Various research studies in Israeli centers are occasionally listed at the end of *Yad Vashem Studies* volumes.

Although somewhat superseded by subsequent research, Part 3 of Philip Friedman's *Roads to Extinction*, "Methodological Problems" (pp. 467–565), deals with European Jewish and American research on the Holocaust and outstanding problems that remained as of 1950–1957. The need for a world-wide periodical devoted to Holocaust research and for coordination among various centers and a specific research center in the United States still exists. In 1984 the Simon Wiesenthal Center in Los Angeles began publishing a scholarly *Annual*, co-edited by Henry Friedlander and Sybil Milton.

12. Citing Eberhard Jachel and Axel Kuhn, eds., *Hitler, Sämtliche Aufzeichnungen 1905–1924* (Stuttgart: 1980, p. 89), C. C. Aronsfeld refers to a letter by Hitler dated September 16, 1919, in which he condemns the old brand of anti-Semitism which had not brought the "Jewish problem" to a "final solution." His anti-Semitism would be "rational," . . . "ultimately its aim must be, implacably, the elimination of the Jews altogether." See *The Text of the Holocaust, A Study of the Nazis' Extermination Propaganda, 1919–1945* (Marblehead, Mass.: Micah Publications, 1985), p. 1.

13. The social and economic bases of Nazi support have generally been associated with the "lower middle class" (*Mittelstand*), although there has been disagreement over the depth and extent of anti-Semitism in this class. However, a new study by Richard F. Hamilton, *Who Voted for Hitler?* (Princeton, N. J.: Princeton University Press, 1982) shows how the upper and upper-middle classes developed as increasingly dependable sources of support for Hitler. See also David Schoenbaum, *Hitler's Social Revolution: Class and Status in Nazi Germany, 1933–1939* (New York: Doubleday, 1966), reprinted as a Norton paperback in 1980; Geoffrey Pridham, *The Nazi Movement in Bavaria, 1923–1933* (New York: Harper and Row, 1973); and Michael H. Kater, *The Nazi Party: A Social Profile of Members and Leaders, 1919–1945* (Cambridge, Mass.: Harvard University Press, 1985).

14. In her Ph.D. dissertation, "German Opposition to Nazi Anti-Semitic Measures Between 1933 and 1945, with Particular Reference to the Rhine-Ruhr Area" (Buffalo: State University of New York, 1979), revised and published under the title, *Hitler, Germans, and the "Jewish Question"* (Princeton, N. J.: Princeton University Press, 1984), Sarah Ann Gordon notes that "the importance of anti-Semitism for the electorate at large is still an unsettled issue," that only a small proportion of Germans assisted Jews after 1933, but that "We will never fully know how many Germans aided Jews or disagreed with racial persecution."

15. One effort to research this problem is Donald Kenrick and Grattan Puxon, *The Destiny of Europe's Gypsies* (New York: Basic Books, 1972).

16. Rudolph Höss, *Commandant of Auschwitz* (Cleveland: World Publishing Co., n. d.), p. 137.

17. A. Roy Eckardt, *Long Night's Journey into Day: Life and Faith after the Holocaust* (Detroit: Wayne State University Press, 1982), p. 65.

18. One of the most persuasive and impassioned essays in this argument is Henry L.

Feingold, "Determining the Uniqueness of the Holocaust: The Factor of Historical Valence," *Shoah* 2, no. 2 (Spring 1981): 3–11. Irving L. Horowitz, among others, argues otherwise in *Genocide: State Power and Mass Murder* (New Brunswick, N. J.: Transaction Books, 1976). See also Jack Nusan Porter, "What Is Genocide? Notes Toward a Definition," *Humanity and Society* 5, No. 1 (March 1981): 48–74, for a survey of differing interpretations; and Symposium, "Was the Holocaust Unique? Responses to Pierre Papazian." *Midstream* 30, no 4 (April 1984): 19–25.

    19. See Bibliography under "Resistance" and Nora Levin, *The Holocaust: The Destruction of European Jewry*, 1933–45 (New York: Schocken Books, 1973), pp. 317–386. Jacob Robinson rebuts Hannah Arendt's position in his *And the Crooked Shall Be Made Straight* (Philadelphia: Jewish Publication Society of America, 1965), pp. 213–223.

    20. Henri Michel, "Jewish Resistance and the European Resistance Movement," *Yad Vashem Studies* 7, (1968): 8, 8–16. See also Michel, "The Allies and the Resistance," *Yad Vashem Studies* 5 (1963): 317–332.

    21. Levin, *The Holocaust*, pp. 676–677.

    22. Leni Yahil, "Select British Documents on the Illegal Immigration to Palestine (1939–1940)," *Yad Vashem Studies* 10 (1974): 241–42.

    23. See Yuri Suhl, ed., *They Fought Back: The Story of the Jewish Resistance in Nazi Europe* (New York: Schocken Books, 1975) and other references in the Bibliography. The involvement of German Jewish youth and Jewish leftists in anti-Nazi activity is covered in great detail in the monograph by Helmut Eschwege, "Resistance of German Jews Against the Nazi Regime," *Leo Baeck Yearbook*: 15 (London, 1970), pp. 143–180 and in Arnold Paucker, "Some Notes on Resistance," in the same work, pp. 239–247. The problems involved in partisan activity are described in Moshe Kahanowitz, "Why No Separate Jewish Partisan Movement Was Established During World War II," *Yad Vashem Studies*, 1 (1957): 153–168.

    Jewish involvement in resistance in the death camps is described in Józef Garlinski, *Fighting Auschwitz: The Resistance Movement in the Concentration Camp* (Greenwich, Conn.: Fawcett, 1975) and Miriam Novitch, *Sobibor: Martyrdom and Revolt* (New York: Holocaust Library, 1980). See also Konrad Kwiet's valuable essay, "Problems of Jewish Resistance Historiography," *Leo Baeck Yearbook* 24 (1979): 37–57.

    24. The tenacity of religious observance has been documented in Yaffa Eliach, ed., *Hasidic Tales of the Holocaust* (New York: Oxford University Press, 1984); Irving J. Rosenbaum, *The Holocaust and Halakhah* (New York: KTAV, 1976); Peter Schindler, "Responses of Hasidic Leaders and Hasidim During the Holocaust" (Ph. D. Dissertation, New York University, 1972); Eliezer Berkovits, *With God in Hell: Judaism in the Ghettos and Death Camps* (New York: Sanhedrin Press, 1979); and Efroim Oshray, *Response from the Holocaust* (New York: Judaica Press, 1983). Clandestine educational, cultural, and religious activity are described in Isaiah Trunk, *Judenrat: The Jewish Councils in Eastern Europe Under Nazi Occupation* (New York: Macmillan Co., 1972, pp. 186–229); Lucy S. Dawidowicz, *The War Against the Jews* (New York: Behrman House, 1976, pp. 297–338); Shlomo Schmiedt, "Hehalutz in Theresienstadt—Its Influence and Educational Activities," *Yad Vashem Studies* 7 (1968): 107–125; and scattered references in various memoirs and diaries in the Bibliography. The progressive educational ideas and activities of Janusz Korczak, the famous neurologist and head of an orphanage in the Warsaw Ghetto, are described in his *Ghetto Diary* (New York: Holocaust Library, 1978).

496   NORA LEVIN

25. In an analysis of Trunk's *Judenrat*, Hilberg finds that, despite the differences in leadership, demography, economic factors, and internal structure, "the story of all ghettos must be read as one history," that "Polish Jews viewed ghettoization as the culmination of German plans, [failing] to think of a further, more drastic stage in the destruction process," that both communities and leaders were "lulled by the continuation of sheer routines" and failed to grasp the implications that time was running out for them. Raul Hilberg, "An Analysis of Isaiah Trunk's *Judenrat*," in Yehuda Bauer, ed., *The Holocaust as Historical Experience: Essays and Discussion* (New York: Holmes and Meier, 1981), pp. 155–171. Hilberg's views on the Councils have remained essentially unchanged in the revised and enlarged (three volume) edition of his *The Destruction of the European Jews* (New York: Holmes and Meier, 1985). Yehuda Bauer and Henry Feingold in their analyses seem better able to penetrate the atmosphere of fear, anxiety, hunger, and terror that gripped the ghettos at the time and the incapacity of most to think through a strategy beyond the crisis of each day. See pp. 173–192, 223–231. For an extensive bibliography on the Judenraete, see Verena Wahlen, "Select Bibliography on Judenraete Under Nazi Rule," *Yad Vashem Studies* 10, (1974): 277–294. Some insight into the dilemmas and ordeals of the Judenraete can be found in YIVO Colloquium, *Imposed Jewish Governing Bodies Under Nazi Rule*, December 2–5, 1967 (New York: YIVO Institute for Jewish Research). Recent works include Martin Gilbert, *Auschwitz and the Allies* (New York: Holt, Rinehart and Winston, 1983), Monty Penkower, *The Jews Were Expendable* (New York: Harper and Row, 1983); and David S. Wyman, *Abandonment of the Jews* (New York: Pantheon Press, 1984).

26. "Panel on U.S. Jews and Holocaust Dissolved," *New York Times*, January 4, 1983.

27. The report, *American Jewry During the Holocaust*, edited by Seymour M. Finger (New York: Holmes and Meier, 1984), has also aroused a great deal of controversy. See, for example, Yehuda Bauer, "The Goldberg Report," *Midstream* 31, No. 8 (October 1985): 43–48.

28. The relief and rescue efforts and achievements of the American Jewish Joint Distribution Committee, 1939–1945, are described in Yehuda Bauer, *American Jewry and the Holocaust: The American Jewish Joint Distribution Committee, 1939–45* (Detroit: Wayne State University Press, 1981). Reactions and limitations of American Jewry are described in Lucy S. Dawidowicz, "American Jews and the Holocaust," *New York Times Magazine*, April 18, 1982, pp. 47–48, 101–102, 107–114. More detailed analyses can be found in "America and the Holocaust," I and II, *American Jewish History* 68, No. 3 (March 1979) and 70, No. 3 (March 1981). See also Marie Syrkin, "What American Jews Did During the Holocaust," *Midstream* (October 1982): 6–12. Haskel Lookstein, *Were We Our Brothers' Keepers?* (New York: Hartmore House, 1985), examines Jewish responses to six crucial events between 1938 and 1944. Saul Friedman's *No Haven for the Oppressed*, (Detroit: Wayne State University Press, 1973) quite sharply criticizes American Jews and their leaders. A recent biography by Melvin I. Urofsky, *A Voice That Spoke for Justice: The Life and Times of Stephen S. Wise* (Albany: State University of New York Press, 1982) interprets this controversial figure sympathetically.

29. Henry Feingold, "Who Shall Bear Guilt for the Holocaust: The Human Dilemma," *American Jewish History* 63, No. 3 (March 1979): 261.

30. Sixty-five syllabi used at the university level are reproduced in Josephine Knopp, ed., *Course Syllabi*, Vol. 1 (Philadelphia: National Institute of the Holocaust, 1978). Sources for high school curricula are listed in *The Holocaust in Books and Films, A*

Selected, Annotated List (New York: Anti-Defamation League of B'nai B'rith, 1982), p. 58, and *Teaching the Holocaust*, 1986, published by Social Studies School Service, Culver City, California. A good model study guide is *The Holocaust: A Teacher Resource*, rev. 1982, published by the School District of Philadelphia. A special double issue of *Shoah: A Journal of Resources on the Holocaust*, 3, Nos. 2–3 (Fall/Winter 1982–1983), deals with Holocaust education, including the problematic character of teaching the subject, an evaluation of curricula materials, the effects of the Eichmann Trial on Israeli youth, and the evolution of teaching materials in Israel. Sensitively written essays on the difficulties of teaching the subject are John K. Roth, "Difficulties Everywhere: Sober Reflections on Teaching About the Holocaust," *Shoah* 1, No. 2 (Fall 1978): 1–3; and Deborah E. Lipstadt, "We Are Not Job's Children," *Shoah* 1, No. 4 (1979): 12–16. For the perspective of Israeli educators, see Chaim Schatzker, "The Teaching of the Holocaust: Dilemmas and Considerations," and Arye Carmon, "Problems in Coping with the Holocaust in a Multinational Program," in Shur, ed., *Reflections on the Holocaust*, pp. 218–226, 226–236.

31. Rabbi Harold Schulweis has written about the dangers of excessive dwelling on the Holocaust, leading to a "paralyzing pessimism" and "pervasive distrust on the non-Jewish world." He raises serious questions for teachers, parents, and theologians in "The Holocaust Dybbuk," *Moment* (February 1976): 36–41.

32. Robert Alter, "Deformations of the Holocaust," *Commentary* (February 1981): 48–54.

33. In addition to the works cited in the Bibliography, Eugene B. Borowitz's essay, "Confronting the Holocaust" in his *Choices in Modern Jewish Thought: A Partisan Guide* (New York: Behrman House, 1983), pp. 187–217, is a helpful brief summary of the ideas of Rubenstein, Wiesel, Fackenheim, Michael Wyschogrod, and Irving Greenberg.

34. Nora Levin, "Life Over Death," *Congress Bi-Weekly* (May 18, 1973), pp. 22–23.

35. Emil L. Fackenheim, "Jewish Faith and the Holocaust: A Fragment," *Commentary* (August 1968), pp. 31, 32. See also his *God's Presence in History* (New York: New York University Press, 1970) and *The Jewish Return into History* (New York: Schocken Books, 1978).

36. Michael Berenbaum has written a theological treatment of Wiesel's views in *The Vision of the Void* (Middletown, Conn.: Wesleyan University Press, 1979). Byron L. Sherwin, "Elie Wiesel and Jewish Theology," *Judaism* 18, No. 1 (Winter 1969): 39–52; Harry James Cargas, *Responses to Elie Wiesel: Critical Essays by Major Jewish and Christian Scholars* (New York: Persea Books and Anti-Defamation League of B'nai B'rith, 1978); Alvin Rosenfeld, ed., *Confronting the Holocaust: The Impact of Elie Wiesel* (Bloomington: Indiana University Press, 1978).

37. Richard L. Rubenstein, *The Cunning of History: The Holocaust and the American Future* (New York: Harper and Row, 1975), p. 91.

38. Elie Wiesel, *Legends of Our time* (New York: Holt, Rinehart and Winston, 1968), p. 37.

39. Rubenstein, *After Auschwitz: Radical Theology and Contemporary Judaism* (Indianapolis and New York: Bobbs-Merrill Co., 1966), p. 153.

40. Jacob Neusner, *Understanding Jewish Theology* (New York: KTAV, 1973), pp. 188, 193, 195. In his *Stranger at Home: "The Holocaust," Zionism, and American Judaism* (Chicago: University of Chicago Press, 1981), Neusner further develops his

interpretation of the Holocaust and the creation of the state of Israel for American Jews as a religiously felt "myth" imparting a transcendent perspective on historic events.

41. Eliezer Berkovits, *Faith After the Holocaust* (New York: KTAV, 1973), pp. 78, 106–107.

42. Quoted in Zvi Yaron, "Can Faith Survive Hell?" *Jerusalem Post Weekly*, October 2, 1973.

43. Milton Himmelfarb, ed., *The Condition of Jewish Belief* (New York: Macmillan Co., 1966), pp. 4–5.

44. Seymour Siegel, "Contemporary Jewish Theology: Four Major Voices," in James E. Wood, Jr., ed., *Jewish-Christian Relations in Today's World* (Waco, Tex.: Baylor University Press, 1971), p. 77.

45. Earl Raab, "Anti-Semitism in the 1980s," *Midstream* (February 1983), pp. 11–18. See also Nathan Perlmutter, *The Real Anti-Semitism in America* (New York: Arbor House, 1982) for a full analysis of the new dimensions of anti-Semitism and J. L. Talmon, "The New Anti-Semitism," *New Republic* (September 18, 1976), pp. 18–23. A good sampling of Soviet anti-Semitism in *Soviet Antisemitic Propaganda: Evidence from Books, Press and the Radio* (London: Institute of Jewish Affairs, 1978).

46. A. Roy Eckardt, "Contemporary Christian Theology and A Protestant Witness for the Shoah," *Shoah* 2 (Spring 1980): 10.

47. John T. Pawlikowski, "The Holocaust and Catholic Theology: Some Reflections." *Shoah*, 2, No. 1 (Spring/Summer 1980): 6. Some Jewish thinkers express a more measured hopefulness of dialogue in "Nostra Aetate: Twenty Years Later," *Face to Face* (Fall 1985).

48. Gerard Sloyan, "The Jews and the New Roman Lectionary," *Face to Face: An Interreligious Bulletin*, published by the Anti-Defamation League of B'nai B'rith, 2 (Summer/Fall 1976): 7.

49. "Jewish-Christian Relations in Western Europe: Status Reports," in *Face to Face, An Interreligious Bulletin* 7 (Summer 1980): 3–13. Among the very disquieting developments in France was a statement in *Le Monde*, March 14, 1979, declaring that "special continuing commemoration will end up by isolating and entrapping Jews. For the unity of humanity we should put an end to it"; and the explosive anti-Semitic remarks by Darquier de Pellepoix, Commissioner for Jewish Affairs in war-time France, who was interviewed by *L'Express*, October 18, 1978. See also Eva Fleischner, *Judaism in German Christian Theology Since 1945: Christiantiy and Israel Considered in Terms of Mission* (Metuchen, N. J.: Scarecrow Press, 1975).

50. The uphill efforts and largely insignificant changes in anti-Jewish elements in the Oberammergau Passion Play are documented in Saul S. Friedman, *Lance Against Civilization: The Oberammergau Passion Play* (Carbondale, Ill.: Southern Illinois University Press, 1984). I have developed these ideas more fully in "The Limits of Theological Dialogue," *The Jewish Spectator* (Summer 1981): 26–28 and in "Whither Christian-Jewish Dialogue," *Judaism* (Spring 1984): 233–239. More optimistic views are expressed in Geoffrey Wigoder, "Interfaith: An Israeli Perspective," *Sh'ma: A Journal of Jewish Responsibility* (October 28, 1983): 139–141, and in several essays in "Jewish-Christian Relations: Looking to the Twenty-First Century," *Face to Face* (Winter/Spring 1976). There is an excellent review of recent developments and literature in Eugene J. Fisher, "A New Maturity in Christian-Jewish Dialogue: An Annotated Bibliography, 1975–1978," *Shofar* 3, No. 2 (Winter 1985) 1: 5–43.

51. Eckardt, "Contemporary Christian Theology," p. 13.

52. "Possible Cover-up to Shield Nazis Is Focus of Renewed U.S. Inquiry," *New York Times*, May 23, 1982. The government mishandling of charges goes back over ten years. In 1982 charges were made by John Loftus, former prosecutor with the Office of Special Investigations in the Justice Department. In 1984 charges were made by Allan A. Ryan, former OSI director. For earlier charges, see Ralph Blumenthal, "Mixed Reasons for U.S.-Nazi Hunt," *New York Times*, November 28, 1976.

53. "Two Men Work Years to Expose a U.S. Bishop," *Philadelphia Inquirer*, October 24, 1976; and Charles Allen, "Fascist Genocides in Our Midst," *Jewish Currents* 17, No. 2 (February 1963): 8–12. He was finally deported to Portugal in August 1984. See Richard Scheinen, "The Dentist and the Archbishop," *Inside* (Philadelphia), Spring 1985, pp. 73–75 and 92–102 for Dr. Charles Kremer's thirty-seven-year pursuit of Trifa.

54. Elizabeth Holtzman, "Nazi War Criminals in America," *Israel Horizons* (March 1979): 6–12. See also *Alleged Nazi War Criminals—Hearings Before the Subcommittee on Immigration, Citizenship, and International Law of the Committee on the Judiciary, House of Representatives, 95th Congress*, Part 1 (August 3, 1977) and Part 2 (July 19–21, 1978), Washington, D.C., U.S. Government Printing Office.

55. For the status of cases as of April 1985, see Charles R. Allen, Jr., and Rochelle Saidel-Wolk, *Nazi War Criminals in America: Facts . . . Action* (Albany: State University of New York, 1985), pp. 8–24. This book also contains a valuable bibliography of books, periodical and newspaper articles, and television programs dealing with alleged Nazi war criminals, the status of investigations, and suggested actions. The issues of *Martyrdom and Resistance*, a bi-monthly published since 1973 by the American Federation of Jewish Fighters, Camp Inmates and Nazi Victims in New York, regularly publishes current information on the status of investigations and trials.

56. *Report by the Comptroller General of the United States: Widespread Conspiracy to Obstruct Probes of Alleged Nazi War Criminals Not Supported by Available Evidence—Controversy May Continue* (Washington, D.C.: General Accounting Office, May 15, 1978).

57. Martin and Eva Kolinsky, "The Treatment of the Holocaust in West German Textbooks," *Yad Vashem Studies* 10 (1974): 149–216.

58. Ibid., pp. 156–157.

59. Ibid., pp. 213, 215.

60. Wolfgang Bobke, "Jews in West German Textbooks," American Jewish Committee Institute of Human Relations, 1980, pp. 14–15.

61. See Keith Bird, " 'Germany Awakes': The Holocaust—Background and Aftermath," *Shoah* 1, No. 4 (1979), which discusses the problematic effect of the TV program. The Anti-Defamation League of B'nai B'rith and the American Jewish Committee have gathered research on neo-Nazi movements, and articles appear periodically in *Martyrdom and Resistance*, published bi-monthly by the American Federation of Jewish Fighters, Camp Inmates and Nazi Victims in New York City. In 1981 *Stern* reported that a public opinion poll conducted by the sociologist Badi Panahi showed that half the West Germans have negative feelings about Jews and one-third have pronounced anti-Semitic prejudices, mostly among older Germans. For a survey of European extremist organizations, most with a strong anti-Jewish program, see J. F. Pilat, "Euroright Extremism," *Weiner Library Bulletin* 34, new series 53/54 (1981).

62. "Germans Surveyed on TV 'Holocaust,' " *New York Times*, 9 May, 1979.

63. Gerd Korman, "Silence in the American Textbooks," *Yad Vashem Studies* 8 (1970): 183–184, 185–186.

64. Lucy S. Dawidowicz, "The Holocaust as Historical Record," in *Dimensions of the Holocaust: A Series of Lectures Presented at Northwestern University*, (Evanston, Ill.: Anti-Defamation League, 1977). A fuller examination of Holocaust historiography in Britain, the United States, Germany, Poland, and the Soviet Union can be found in Mrs. Dawidowicz's *The Holocaust and the Historians* (Cambridge: Mass.: Harvard University Press, 1981).

65. Among supportive "scholars" are: James J. Martin, Andreas Wesserle, Austen J. App, and John Bennett. See *Spotlight*, September 24, 1979.

66. A letter soliciting subscriptions and urging attendance at the 1982 Convention is signed by Tom Marcellus, Director of the Institute. Mel Mermelstein, a survivor of Auschwitz and Buchenwald, sued the Institute in February 1981, after it refused to pay him the $50,000 reward it had promised for supplying evidence of gassings at Auschwitz. On July 22, 1985, there was a court-approved settlement awarding him $50,000 and an additional $40,000 for the pain and suffering caused. See *New York Times* editorial, July 29, 1985, and "By Bread Alone: The Story of A–4685," *Martyrdom and Resistance* (November-December 1983).

67. Lucy S. Dawidowicz, "Lies About the Holocaust," *Commentary* (December 1980): 36. See also Mark Silverberg, "The Holocaust and the Historical Revisionists," *Journal of Jewish Communal Service* 59 (1982): 16–25.

68. Yaffa Eliach, ed., *The Liberators: Eyewitness Accounts of the Liberation of Concentration Camps* (Brooklyn, N. Y.: Center for Holocaust Studies, Documentation and Research, 1981). The Center for Research in Social Change, Emory University, Atlanta, Georgia, has published three pamphlets, documenting the liberation of camp prisoners, called "Witness to the Holocaust." They include "The Seventy-First Came to Gunskirchen Lager," "Dachau," and "KZ, A Pictorial Report from Five Concentration Camps." This project also includes seven video programs produced in cooperation with WAGA-CBS, Atlanta, containing eye-witness accounts. An account of the international Liberators Conference held in Washington, D.C., in October 1982, organized by the U.S. Holocaust Memorial Council can be found in Annelise Orleck, "International Liberators Conference: When the Political and Historical Merge," *Shoah* 2, No. 3–3, No. 1 (Fall/Winter 1982): 12–13, 22. See also "Hitler Victims Meet Liberators Again," *New York Times*, October 28, 1981; and Robert H. Abzug, *Inside the Vicious Heart: Americans and the Liberation of Nazi Concentration Camps* (New York: Oxford University Press, 1985).

69. See Michael Berenbaum, "On the Politics of Public Commemoration of the Holocaust," *Shoah*, 2, No. 3–3, No. 1 (Fall/Winter 1981–82): 6–9, 37, for a careful evaluation of the risks and gains of "Americanizing" the Holocaust. The survivor gathering in Jerusalem is described in David K. Shipler's "4,000 Survivors of Nazi Horror Gather in Israel," *New York Times*, June 21, 1981, and "Holocaust Survivors Cry Out for Lost Kin," *New York Times*, June 21, 1981, as well as in relevant issues of *Martyrdom and Resistance*. In 1981, at the World Gathering, a National Register of Holocaust Survivors was created, with Yeshiva University as Trustee. Survivors may register at the American Gathering of Jewish Holocaust Survivors, 122 W. 30th Street, New York, New York 10001.

70. There is a large body of psychiatric literature. See, for example, Symposium, Israel Psychoanalytic Society, "Psychiatric Disturbances of Holocaust Survivors," *Israel Annals of Psychiatry* 5 (1967); and "Holocaust Survivors: Psychological and Social Sequelae," a special issue of the *Journal of Contemporary Psychotherapy* 11, No. 1

(Spring/Summer 1980). Jack Nusan Porter, "Is There a Survivor's Syndrome? Psychological and Socio-Political Implications," *Journal of Psychology and Judaism* 6, No. 1 (Fall/Winter 1981) questions the "pathological approach." The first expression of international interest occurred in January 1975 at a meeting of the First International Conference on Psychological Stress and Adjustment in Time of War and Peace in Tel Aviv. See also references in Bibliography.

71. "The Holocaust: Our Generation Looks Back," *Response: A Contemporary Jewish Review*, No. 25 (Spring 1975); Helen Epstein, "The Heirs of the Holocaust," *New York Times Magazine*, June 19, 1977, pp. 12–15, 74–77; and Lucy Y. Steinitz, *Living After the Holocaust: Reflections by the Post-War Generation* (New York: Bloch, 1976). The Jerome Riker International Study of Organized Persecution of Children is devoted to the compilation of the history of child persecution during the Holocaust, directed by Dr. Judith S. Kestenberg, 30 Soundview Lane, Sands Point, New York, 11050.

72. Porter, "Is There a Survivor's Syndrome?" p. 51.

73. Dorothy Rabinowitz, *New Lives: Survivors of the Holocaust Living in America* (New York: Alfred A. Knopf, 1976); Sylvia Rothschild, ed., *Voices from the Holocaust* (New York: New American Library, 1981); Leonard Dinnerstein, *America and the Survivors of the Holocaust* (New York: Columbia University Press, 1982).

BIBLIOGRAPHY

Bibliographies

Cargas, Harry James. *The Holocaust: An Annotated Bibliography*. Haverford, Pa.: Catholic Library Association, 1977.
Friedman, Philip, Jacob Robinson, et al., eds. *Guide to Jewish History Under Nazi Impact*. New York: YIVO Institute for Jewish Research and Jerusalem, Yad Vashem. Joint Documentary Projects, Bibliographic series, no. 1, 1960. Reprinted by KTAV, 1973.
Muffs, Judith Herschlag. *The Holocaust in Books and Films: A Selected Annotated List*. New York: Center for Studies on the Holocaust, Anti-Defamation League, 1982.
Robinson, Jacob, ed. *The Holocaust and After: Sources and Literature in English*. Jerusalem: Israel Universities Press, 1973. Vol. 12 of Yad Vashem and YIVO Bibliographic Series. Of the intervening volumes in the series, four are compilations of works in Yiddish, five are in Hebrew, and one is a bibliography of works on the Holocaust in Hungary.
Szonyi, David M., ed. *The Holocaust: An Annotated Bibliography and Resource Guide*. Hoboken, N. J.: KTAV, 1984.

Special Studies and Monographs—Sources

Leo Baeck Institute. *Yearbook*, Vol. 1 -date. London: Martin Secker and Warburg, 1956-
Yad Vashem Studies on the European Jewish Catastrophe and Resistance, Vol. 1 -date. Jerusalem: Yad Vashem Martyrs' and Heroes' Remembrance Authority, 1957- .
Weiner Library Bulletin. London: Institute of Contemporary History, 1946–1981.

General Works

Bauer, Yehuda. *A History of the Holocaust*. New York: Franklin Watts, 1982.

Dawidowicz, Lucy S. *The War Against the Jews, 1933–1945*. New York: Behrman House, 1976.

Gutman, Yisrael, ed. *The Catastrophe of European Jewry: Antecedents, History, Reflections*. Jereusalem: Yad Vashem, 1976.

Hilberg, Raul. *The Destruction of the European Jews*. Chicago: Quadrangle, 1961. Rev. and enl. ed. published by Holmes and Meier in 3 vols., in 1985.

Levin, Nora. *The Holocaust: The Destruction of European Jewry, 1933–1945*. New York: Schocken Books, 1973.

Poliakov, Leon. *Harvest of Hate: The Nazi Program for the Destruction of the Jews of Europe*. New York: Holocaust Library, 1979.

Reitlinger, Gerald. *The Final Solution: The Attempt to Exterminate the Jews of Europe, 1939–1945*. London: Valentine and Mitchell, 1968.

Roots of Nazi Anti-Semitism

Cohn, Norman. *Warrant for Genocide: The Myth of the Jewish World Conspiracy and the Protocols of the Elders of Zion*. New York: Harper and Row, 1966.

Lane, Barbara Miller, and Leila J. Rupp, eds. *Nazi Ideology Before 1933*. Austin: University of Texas Press, 1978.

Massing, Paul. *Rehearsal for Destruction: A Study of Political Anti-Semitism in Imperial Germany*. New York: Harper and Row, 1946.

Mosse, George L. *The Crisis of German Ideology: Intellectual Origins of the Third Reich*. New York: Grosset and Dunlap, 1964.

————. *Toward the Final Solution: A History of European Racism*. New York: Harper and Row, 1978.

Pulzer, Peter G. J. *The Rise of Political Anti-Semitism in Germany and Austria*. New York: John Wiley, 1964.

Stern, Fritz. *The Politics of Cultural Despair: A Study of the Rise of the Germanic Ideology*. Berkeley: University of California Press, 1961.

Hitler

Bullock, Alan. *Hitler: A Study in Tyranny*. Rev. ed. New York: Harper and Row, 1964.

Heiden, Konrad. *Der Fuehrer: Hitler's Rise to Power*. Boston: Beacon, 1969.

Hitler, Adolf. *Hitler's Secret Conversations, 1941–44*. New York: New American Library, 1961.

————. *Mein Kampf*. Translated by Ralph Manheim. Boston: Houghton Mifflin, 1953.

Jäckel, Eberhard. *Hitler's Weltanschauung: A Blueprint for Power*. Middletown, Conn.: Wesleyan University Press, 1972.

Maser, Werner. *Hitler: Legend, Myth and Reality*. New York: Harper and Row, 1973.

The Nazi State

Allen, William S. *The Nazi Seizure of Power: The Experience of a Single German Town, 1930–1935*. Chicago: Quadrangle, 1965.

Bracher, Karl D. *The German Dictatorship: The Origins, Structure, and Effects of National Socialism*. New York: Praeger, 1971.

Broszat, Martin. *The Hitler State: The Foundation and Development of the Internal Structure of the Third Reich*. Translated by John W. Hiden. London: Longman, 1981.

Crankshaw, Edward. *The Gestapo: Instrument of Tyranny*. New York: Viking Press, 1956.

Dicks, Henry V. *Licensed Mass Murder: A Socio-psychological Study of Some SS Killers*. New York: Basic Books, 1972.

Fest, Joachim C. *The Face of the Third Reich: Portraits of the Nazi Leadership*. New York: Pantheon Books, 1977.

Goebbels, Paul J. *The Goebbels Diaries*. Edited and translated by Louis Lochner. Westport, Conn.: Greenwood Press, reprint of 1948 ed.

Höhne, Heinz. *The Order of the Death's Head: The Story of Hitler's SS*. New York: Coward-Mc Cann, 1970.

Krausnick, Helmut, et al. *Anatomy of the SS State*. New York: Walher and Co., 1965.

Manvell, Roger. *Heinrich Himmler*. New York: Putnam's, 1965.

Mosse, George L., ed. *Nazi Culture: Intellectual, Cultural, and Social Life in the Third Reich*. New York: Grosset and Dunlap, 1966.

Reitlinger, Gerald, *S. S.: Alibi of a Nation*. 1st American ed. Englewood Cliffs, N. J.: Prentice-Hall, 1981.

Shirer, William L. *The Rise and Fall of the Third Reich*. New York: Simon and Schuster, 1960.

Stein, George H. *The Waffen SS*. Ithaca, N. Y.: Cornell University Press, 1966.

Wighton, Charles. *Heydrich: Hitler's Most Evil Henchman*. Philadelphia: Chilton, 1962.

German Jews Under Hitler

Baker, Leonard. *Days of Sorrow and Pain: Leo Baeck and the Berlin Jews*. New York: Macmillan Co., 1978.

Boehm, Eric. *We Survived*. Santa Barbara, Calif.: Clio Press, 1966.

Leo Baeck Yearbook, Vol. 1 -date. London: East and West Library, 1956-   .

Schleunes, Karl L. *The Twisted Road to Auschwitz: Nazi Policy Toward German Jews, 1933–1939*. Urbana: University of Illinois Press, 1970.

Thalmann, Rita. *Crystal Night: 9–10 November 1938*. Translated by Gilles Cremonesi. New York: Coward, McCann and Geoghegan, 1974.

Gross, Leonard. *The Last Jews in Berlin*. New York: Simon and Schuster, 1982.

Emigration Efforts and Failures

Bentwich, Norman. *They Found Refuge: An Account of British Jewry's Work for Victims of Nazi Oppression*. London, Cresset Press, 1956.

Feingold, Henry. *The Politics of Rescue: The Roosevelt Administration and the Holocaust, 1938–45*. New Brunswick, N. J.: Rutgers University Press, 1970.

Friedman, Saul S. *No Haven for the Oppressed*. Detroit: Wayne State University Press, 1973.

Morse, Arthur D. *While Six Million Died: A Chronicle of American Apathy*. New York: Random House, 1968.

Thomas, Gordon. *Voyage of the Damned.* New York: Stein and Day, 1974.

Wasserstein, Bernard. *Britain and the Jews of Europe, 1939–1945.* Oxford: Oxford University Press, 1979.

Wyman, David. *Paper Walls: America and the Refugee Crisis, 1938–41.* Amherst: University of Massachusetts Press, 1968.

Rescue Efforts by Jews and Non-Jews

Avriel, Ehud. *Open the Gates!* New York: Atheneum, 1975.

Bartoszewski, Wladyslaw. *The Samaritans: Heroes of the Holocaust.* New York: Twain, 1970.

Bauer, Yehuda. *Flight and Rescue: Bricha.* New York: Random House, 1971.

Bierman, John. *Righteous Gentile: The Story of Raoul Wallenberg, Missing Hero of the Holocaust.* New York: Viking Press, 1981.

Friedman, Philip. *Their Brothers' Keepers: The Christian Heroes and Heroines Who Helped the Oppressed Escape the Nazi Terror.* New York: Holocaust Library, 1978.

Gutman, Yisrael. *Rescue Attempts During the Holocaust: Proceedings of the Second Yad Vashem International Historical Conference, April, 1974.* Jerusalem: Yad Vashem, 1977.

Hallie, Phillip. *Lest Innocent Blood Be Shed: The Story of the Village of Le Chambon and How Goodness Happened There.* New York: Harper and Row, 1979.

Hirschmann, Ira. *Lifeline to a Promised Land.* New York: Vanguard Press, 1946.

Kranzler, David. *Japanese, Nazis and Jews: The Jewish Refugee Community of Shanghai, 1938–1945.* New York: Yeshiva University Press, 1976.

Kluger, Ruth. *The Last Escape.* Garden City, N. Y.: Doubleday, 1973.

Leboucher, Fernande. *The Incredible Mission of Father Benoit.* Translated by J. F. Bernard. New York: Doubleday, 1969.

Perl, William. *The Four-Front War: From the Holocaust to the Promised Land.* New York: Crown, 1979.

Shepherd, Naomi. *A Refuge from Darkness: Wilfred Israel and the Rescue of the Jews.* New York: Pantheon, 1984.

Yahil, Leni. *The Rescue of Danish Jewry.* Philadelphia: Jewish Publication Society of America, 1969.

Weissberg, Alexander. *Desperate Mission: Joel Brand's Story.* New York: Criterion, 1958.

The Jewish Councils

Patterns of Jewish Leadership in Nazi Europe, 1933–1945. Proceedings of the Third Yad Vashem International Historical Conference, April 1977. Jerusalem: Yad Vashem, 1979.

Trunk, Isaiah. *Judenrat: The Jewish Councils in Eastern Europe Under Nazi Occupation.* New York: Macmillan Co., 1972.

Tushnet, Leonard. *The Pavement of Hell: Three Leaders of the Judenrat.* New York: St. Martin's Press, 1972.

The Warsaw Dairy of Adam Czerniakow: Prelude to Doom. Translated by Stanislaw Staron, edited by Raul Hilberg. New York: Stein and Day, 1979.

The Fate of Jews in Nazi-Occupied Countries—General Surveys

American Jewish Committee. *The Jewish Communities of Nazi-Occupied Europe.* 2 vols. New York: American Jewish Committee, 1944. Reprinted 1982.

The Black Book: The Nazi Crime Against the Jewish People. New York: Duell, Sloan and Pearce, 1946.

Black Book of Localities Whose Jewish Population Was Exterminated by the Nazis. Jerusalem: Yad Vashem, 1965.

Butz, Arthur R. *The Hoax of the Twentieth Century.* Surrey, England: Historical Review Press, 1976.

Fein, Helen. *Accounting for Genocide: National Responses and Jewish Victimization During the Holocaust.* New York: Free Press, 1980.

Institute of Historical Review. *Journal of Historical Review* 1 (1980).

Koehl, Robert L. *RKFDV: German Resettlement and Population Policy, 1939–1945.* Cambridge, Mass.: Harvard University Press, 1957.

Lemkin, Raphael. *Axis Rule in Occupied Europe.* Washington, D.C.: Carnegie Endowment for International Peace, 1944.

Jewish Fate in Nazi-Occupied Countries, By Individual Country

Austria

Carstein, F. L. *Fascist Movements in Austria: From Schönerer to Hitler.* London: Sage, 1977.

Frankel, Josef. *The Jews of Austria.* London: Valentine, Mitchell, 1967.

Bulgaria

Chary, Frederick B. *The Bulgarian Jews and the Final Solution, 1940–1944.* Pittsburgh: University of Pittsburgh Press, 1972.

Oliver, H. D. *We Were Saved: How the Jews in Bulgaria Were Kept from the Death Camps.* Translated by V. Izmirliev. Sophia: Foreign Languages Press, 1967.

Czechoslovakia

The Jews of Czechoslovakia. Vol. 3. Edited by Avigdor Dagan. Philadelphia: Jewish Publication Society of America, 1984.

Lederer, Zdenek. *Ghetto Theresienstadt.* New York: Fertig, 1983.

Terezín. Prague: Council of Jewish Communities in the Czech Lands, 1965.

Denmark

Bertelsen, Aage. *October '43.* New York: G. P. Putnam Sons, 1954.

Flender, Harold. *Rescue in Denmark.* New York: Simon and Schuster, 1963.

Yahil, Leni. *The Rescue of Danish Jewry.* Philadelphia: Jewish Publication Society of America, 1969.

France

Klarsfeld, Serge. *Memorial to the Jews Deported from France 1942–1944.* New York: Beate Klarsfeld Foundation, 1983.

Levy, Claude. *Betrayal at the Vel d'Hiv*. New York: Hill and Wang, 1969.

Marrus, Michael R., and Robert O. Paxton. *Vichy France and the Jews*. New York: Basic Books, 1981.

Paxton, Robert. *Vichy France: Old Guard, New Guard*. New York: Alfred A. Knopf, 1972.

Hungary

Braham, Randolph L. *The Destruction of Hungarian Jewry: A Documentary Account*. 2 vols. New York: Pro Arte for the World Federation of Hungarian Jews, 1963.

————. *Genocide and Retribution: The Holocaust in Hungarian-Ruled Transylvania*. Hingham, Mass.: Kluwer Academic Publishers, 1983.

Levai, Jenö. *The Black Book of the Martyrdom of Hungarian Jewry*. Zurich: Central European Times, 1948.

Sandberg, Moshe. *My Longest Year: In the Hungarian Labor Service*. Jerusalem: Yad Vashem, 1968.

Senesh, Hannah. *Hannah Senesh: Her Life and Diary*. New York, Schocken Books, 1973.

Vago, Bela, ed. *Jews and Non-Jews in Eastern Europe, 1918–1945*. New York: John Wiley and Sons, 1975.

Italy and the Vatican

Friedlander, Saul. *Pius XII and the Third Reich*. New York: Alfred A. Knopf, 1966.

Michaelis, Meir. *Mussolini and the Jews: German-Italian Relations and the Jewish Questions in Italy*. Oxford: Clarendon Press, 1978.

Morley, John Francis. *Vatican Diplomacy and the Jews During the Holocaust 1939–1943*. New York: KTAV, 1980.

Poliakov, Leon, and J. Sabille. *Jews Under the Italian Occupation*. New York: Fertig, 1983.

Latvia

Schneider, Gertrude. *Journey into Terror: Story of the Riga Ghetto*. New York: Irvington Pub., 1981.

The Netherlands

Frank, Anne. *Diary of a Young Girl*. New York: Pocket Books, 1953.

Presser, Jacob. *The Destruction of the Dutch Jews*. New York: E. P. Dutton, 1969.

Warmbrunn, Werner. *The Dutch Under German Occupation 1940–1945*. Stanford, Calif.: Stanford University Press, 1963.

Poland

Apenszlak, Jacob, ed. *The Black Book of Polish Jewry*. New York: Roy Publishers, 1943.

Borzykowski, Tuvia. *Between Tumbling Walls*. Translated by Mendel Kohansky. Tel Aviv: Hakibbutz Hameuchad Publishing House, 1972.

Central Commission for Investigation of German Crimes in Poland. *German Crimes in Poland*, 2 vols. Warsaw: 1946–1947.

Donat, Alexander. *The Holocaust Kingdom*. New York: Holt, Rinehart and Winston, 1965.

Goldstein, Bernard. *The Stars Bear Witness*. New York: Viking Press, 1949.

Gutman, Yisrael. *The Jews of Warsaw*. Translated by Ina Friedman. Bloomington: Indiana University Press, 1982.

Kaplan, Chaim. *Scroll of Agony: The Warsaw Diary of Chaim Kaplan*. Edited and translated by Abraham Katsh. Rev. ed. New York: Macmillan Co., 1981.

Karski, Jan. *The Story of a Secret State*. Cambridge, Mass.: Riverside Press, 1944.

Korczak, Janusz. *Ghetto Diary*. New York: Holocaust Library, 1978.

Meed, Vladka. *On Both Sides of the Wall: Memoirs from the Warsaw Ghetto*. New York: Holocaust Library, 1979.

Ringelblum, Emmanuel. *Notes from the Warsaw Ghetto: The Journal of Emmanuel Ringelblum*. Edited and translated by Jacob Sloan. New York: Schocken Books, 1974.

————. *Polish-Jewish Relations During the Second World War*. New York: Fertig, 1976.

World Jewish Congress. *Extermination of Polish Jewry: Reports Based on Official Documents*. New York: World Jewish Congress, July-August 1943.

Romania

Dorian, Emil. *The Quality of Witness: A Romanian Diary 1937–1944*. Translated by Mara S. Vamos. Philadelphia: Jewish Publication Society of America, 1983.

Fisher, Julius S. *Transnistria: The Forgotten Cemetery*. New York: A. S. Barnes, 1969.

Malaparte, Curzio. *Kaputt*. New York: E. P. Dutton, 1946.

Soviet Union

Dallin, Alexander. *German Rule in Russia, 1941–1945: A Study of Occupation Policies*. New York: Macmillan Co., 1957.

Ehrenburg, Ilya, ed. *The Black Book: The Ruthless Murder of Jews by German-Fascist Invaders Throughout the Temporarily-Occupied Regions of the Soviet Union During the War of 1941–1945*. Translated by John Glad and James S. Levine. New York: Holocaust Publications, 1981.

Meyer, Peter, et al. *The Jews in the Soviet Satellites*. Syracuse, N. Y.: Syracuse University Press, 1953.

Soviet Government Statements on Nazi Atrocities. London, Hutchinson, 1945.

Jewish Resistance

Ainsztein, Reuben. *Jewish Resistance in Nazi-Occupied Europe*. New York, Barnes and Noble, 1975.

Arad, Yitzhak. *The Partisan*. New York: Holocaust Library, 1979.

Barkai, Meyer. *The Fighting Ghettos*. Philadelphia: Lippincott, 1962.

Conference on Manifestations of Jewish Resistance. *Jewish Resistance During the Holocaust: Proceedings*. Jerusalem: Yad Vashem, 1971.

Friedman, Philip, ed. *Martyrs and Fighters: The Epic of the Warsaw Ghetto*. New York: Praeger, 1954.

Kowalski, Isaac, ed. *Anthology on Armed Jewish Resistance*. 2 vols. New York: Jewish Combatants Publishers House, 1984 and 1985.

Krakowski, Shmuel. *The War of the Doomed: Jewish Armed Resistance in Poland, 1942–1944*. New York: Holmes and Meier, 1985.

Laska, Vera. *Women in the Resistance and in the Holocaust: The Voice of Eyewitnesses*. Westport, Conn.: Greenwood Press, 1983.

Latour, Anny. *The Jewish Resistance in France (1940–1944)*. Translated by Irene R. Ilton. New York: Holocaust Library, 1981.

Mark, Bernard. *Uprising in the Warsaw Ghetto*. Translated by Gershon Freidlin. New York: Schocken Books, 1975.

Novitch, Miriam. *Sobibor: Martyrdom and Revolt: Documents and Testimonies*. New York: Holocaust Library, 1980.

Porter, Jack Nusan. *Jewish Partisans: A Documentary of Jewish Resistance in the Soviet Union During World War II*. 2 vols. Translated by the Magal Translation Institute. Washington, D.C.: University Press of America, 1982.

Schoenbrun, David. *Soldiers of the Night*. New York: E. P. Dutton, 1980.

Suhl, Yuri. *They Fought Back: The Story of Jewish Resistance in Nazi Europe*. New York: Schocken Books, 1974.

Syrkin, Marie. *Blessed Is the Match: The Story of Jewish Resistance*. Philadelphia: Jewish Publication Society of America, 1947.

Trunk, Isaiah. *Jewish Responses to Nazi Persecution*. New York: Stein and Day, 1979.

Tushnet, Leonard. *To Die with Honor: The Uprising of the Jews in the Warsaw Ghetto*. New York: Citadel Press, 1956.

Concentration Camps: Human Behavior Under Extreme Stress

Borkin, Joseph. *The Crime and Punishment of I. G. Farben*. New York: Free Press, 1978.

Cohen, Elie A. *Human Behavior in the Concentration Camps*. New York: Universal Library, 1953.

Des Pres, Terrence. *The Survivor: An Anatomy of Life in the Death Camps*. Oxford: Oxford University Press, 1976.

Donat, Alexander, ed. *The Death Camp Treblinka*. New York: Holocaust Publications, 1979.

Eitinger, Leo. *Psychological and Medical Aspects of Concentration Camps: Research Bibliography*. Haifa: University of Haifa, 1982.

Ferencz, Benjamin B. *Less Than Slaves*. Cambridge, Mass.: Harvard University Press, 1979.

Frankl, Viktor. *Man's Search for Meaning: An Introduction to Logotherapy*. Boston: Beacon Press, 1962.

Kogon, Eugen. *The Theory and Practice of Hell: The German Concentration Camps and the System Behind Them*. Translated by Heinz Norden. New York: Farrar, Straus and Cudahy, 1950.

Levi, Primo. *Survival in Auschwitz: The Nazi Assault on Humanity*. New York: Collier Books, 1961.

Mitscherlich, Alexander. *Doctors of Infamy: The Story of the Nazi Medical Crimes*. New York: Henry Schuman, 1949.

Müller, Filip. *Auschwitz Inferno: The Testimony of a Sonderkommando*. Edited and translated by Susanne Flatauer. London: Routledge and Kegan Paul, 1979.

Rashke, Richard. *Escape from Sobibor*. New York: Houghton Mifflin, 1982.

Rousset, David. *The Other Kingdom*. New York: Reynal and Hitchcock, 1947.
Selzer, Michael. *Deliverance Day: The Last Hours at Dachau*. Philadelphia: J. B. Lippincott Co., 1978.
Terezín. Prague: Council of Jewish Communities in the Czech Lands, 1965.
Tillion, Germaine. *Ravensbruck*. Translated by Gerald Satterwhite. Garden City, N. Y.: Doubleday and Co., 1975.
Wells, Leon W. *The Death Brigade (The Janowska Road)*. New York: Holocaust Library, 1978.
Wiesel, Elie. *Night*. Translated by Stella Rodway. New York: Avon Books, 1969.

The Traumas of Survival

Bettelheim, Bruno. *The Informed Heart: Autonomy in a Mass Age*. New York: Free Press, 1960.
Dimsdale, Joel E. *Survivors, Victims, and Perpetrators: Essays on the Nazi Holocaust*. Washington, D.C.: Hemisphere Publishing Co., 1980.
Eitinger, Leo. *Concentration Camp Survivors in Norway and Israel*. London: Allen and Unwin, 1964.
Epstein, Helen. *Children of the Holocaust: Conversations with Sons and Daughters of the Survivors*. New York: G. P. Putnam Sons, 1979.
Frankl, Victor. *From Death Camp to Existentialism*. Boston: Beacon Press, 1959.
Krystal, Henry, ed. *Massive Psychic Trauma*. New York: International Universities Press, 1968.
Rabinowitz, Dorothy. *New Lives: Survivors of the Holocaust Living in America*. New York: Alfred A. Knopf, 1976.
Rothschild, Sylvia, ed. *Voices from the Holocaust*. New York: New American Library, 1981.
Steinitz, Lucy Y., ed. *Living After the Holocaust: Reflections by the Post-War Generation*. New York: Bloch, 1976.

Philosophical, Religious, and Theological Speculation—Jewish Thinkers

Amery, Jean. *At the Mind's Limits: Contemplations by a Survivor on Auschwitz and Its Realities*. Bloomington: Indiana University Press, 1980.
Auschwitz: Beginning of a New Era? Reflections on the Holocaust. Edited by Eva Fleischner. New York: KTAV, Cathedral Church of St. John the Divine and Anti-Defamation League of B'nai B'rith, 1977.
Berkovits, Eliezer. *Faith After the Holocaust*. New York: KTAV, 1973.
Borowitz, Eugene. *A New Jewish Theology in the Making*. Philadelphia: Westminster Press, 1968.
Cohen, Arthur A., ed. *Arguments and Doctrines: A Reader in Jewish Thinking After the Holocaust*. New York: Harper and Row, 1970.
———. *The Tremendum: A Theological Interpretation of the Holocaust*. New York: Crossroad, 1981.
Fackenheim, Emil L. *God's Presence in History: Jewish Affirmation and Philosophical Reflections*. New York: New York University Press, 1970.

510   NORA LEVIN

————. *The Jewish Return into History: Reflections in the Age of Auschwitz and a New Jerusalem.* New York: Schocken Books, 1978.
Neusner, Jacob. *Understanding Jewish Theology.* New York: KTAV and Anti-Defamation League of B'nai B'rith, 1973.
Rubenstein, Richard L. *After Auschwitz: Radical Theology and Contemporary Judaism.* Indianapolis: Bobbs-Merrill, 1966.
Wiesel, Elie. *A Jew Today.* New York: Random House, 1978.
————. *One Generation After.* New York: Random House, 1967.

The Search for Nazi War Criminals

Allen, Charles R., Jr. *Nazi War Criminal in America: Facts . . . Action, The Basic Handbook.* New York: Highgate House, 1985.
Blum, Howard. *Wanted! The Search for Nazis in America.* New York: Quadrangle, 1977.
Klarsfeld, Beate. *Wherever They May Be!* New York: Harper and Row, 1966.
Knoop, Hans. *The Menten Affair.* New York: Macmillan Co., 1978.
Ryan, Allan A., Jr. *Quiet Neighbors: The True Story of Nazi War Criminals in America.* New York: Harcourt Brace Jovanovich, 1984.
Seidel, Rachelle G. *The Outraged Conscience: Seekers of Justice for Nazi War Criminals in America.* Albany: State University Press of New York, 1984.
Wiesenthal, Simon. *The Murderers Among Us: The Wiesenthal Memoirs.* New York: McGraw-Hill, 1967.

War Crimes Trials

Arendt, Hannah. *Eichmann in Jerusalem: A Report on the Banality of Evil.* Rev. and enl. ed. New York: Viking Press, 1964.
Davidson, Eugene. *The Trial of the Germans.* New York: Macmillan Co., 1966.
Gilbert, G. M. *Nuremberg Diary.* New York: Farrar, Straus and Giroux, 1947.
Harris, Whitney R. *Tyranny on Trial: The Evidence at Nuremberg.* Dallas, Tex.: Southern Methodist University Press, 1954.
Hausner, Gideon. *Justice in Jerusalem.* New York: Harper and Row, 1966.
International Military Tribunal. *Trial of the Major War Criminals Before the International Military Tribunal: Official Text.* 42 vols. Nuremberg: 1947–1949. Blue Series.
Nuernberg Military Tribunals. *Trials of War Criminals Before the Nuernberg Military Tribunals Under Control Council Law No. 10.* 15 vols. Washington, D.C.: 1949–1953. Green Series.
Office of the U.S. Chief of Counsel for the Prosecution of Axis Criminality. *Nazi Conspiracy and Aggression.* 11 vols. Washington, D.C.: 1946–1948. Red Series.
Pearlman, Moshe. *The Capture and Trial of Adolf Eichmann.* New York: Simon and Schuster, 1963.
Robinson, Jacob. *And the Crooked Shall Be Made Straight: The Eichmann Trial, the Jewish Catastrophe, and Hannah Arendt's Narrative.* Philadelphia: Jewish Publication Society of America, 1965.
United Nations War Crimes Commission. *Law Reports of Trials of War Criminals: The Belen Trial.* London, 1947.

Holocaust Art

Blatter, Janet, and Sybil Milton. *Art of the Holocaust*. New York: Rutledge Press, 1981.

Costanza, Mary S. *The Living Witness: Art in the Concentration Camps and Ghettos*. New York: Free Press, 1982.

Green, Gerald. *The Artists of Terezín* New York: Hawthorne Books, 1969.

Kantor, Alfred. *The Book of Alfred Kantor*. New York: McGraw-Hill, 1971.

Fiction, Poetry, and Literary Criticism

Alexander, Edward. *The Resonance of Dust: Essays on Holocaust Literature and Jewish Fate*. Columbus, Ohio: Ohio State University Press, 1979.

Becker, Jurek. *Jacob the Liar*. New York: Harcourt Brace Jovanovich, 1975.

Borowski, Tadeusz. *This Way for the Gas, Ladies and Gentlemen*. Translated by Barbara Vedder. New York: Viking Press, 1967.

Celan, Paul. *Paul Celan: Selected Poems*. Harmondsworth, England: Penguin Books, 1972.

Ezrahi, Sidra DeKoven. *By Words Alone: The Holocaust in Literature*. Chicago: University of Chicago Press, 1980.

Fine, Ellen S. *Legacy of Night: The Literary Universe of Elie Wiesel*. Albany: State University of New York Press, 1983.

Halperin, Irving. *Messengers from the Dead*. Philadelphia: Westminster Press, 1970.

Hersey, John. *The Wall*. New York: Alfred A. Knopf, 1950.

Kosinski, Jerzy. *The Painted Bird*. Boston: Houghton Mifflin, 1965.

Kovner, Abba, and Nelly Sachs. *Selected Poems*. London: Penguin Books, 1971.

Kuznetsov, Anatoly. *Babi Yar: A Documentary Novel*. Translated by David Floyd. Uncensored ed. New York: Farrar, Straus and Giroux, 1971.

Langer, Lawrence L. *The Age of Atrocity: Death in Modern Literature*. Boston: Beacon Press, 1978.

————. *The Holocaust and the Literary Imagination*. New Haven, Conn.: Yale University Press, 1975.

————. *Versions of Survival: The Holocaust and the Human Spirit*. Albany: State University of New York Press, 1982.

Lustig, Arnost. *Night and Hope*. Translated by George Theiner. New York: Avon, 1976.

Pinkus, Oscar. *House of Ashes*. Cleveland: World Publishing Co., 1964.

Rosenfeld, Alvin H. *A Double Dying: Reflections on Holocaust Literature*. Bloomington: Indiana University Press, 1980.

Roussett, David. *The Other Kingdom*. Translated by Ramon Guthrie. New York: Reynal and Hitchcock, 1974.

Sachs, Nelly. *O The Chimneys*. New York: Farrar, Straus and Giroux, 1967.

Schwarz-Bart, Andre. *The Last of the Just*. New York: Bantam Books, 1961.

Steiner, Jean-Francois. *Treblinka*. New York: Simon and Schuster, 1967.

Wiesel, Elie. *The Gates of the Forest*. Translated by Frances Frenaye. New York: Holt, Rinehart and Winston, 1966.

Anthologies and Collections of Documents

Dawidowicz, Lucy S. *A Holocaust Reader*. New York: Behrman House, 1976.

Eisenberg, Azriel. *Witness to the Holocaust*. New York: Pilgrim Press, 1981.

Friedlander, Albert H. *Out of the Whirlwind: A Reader of Holocaust Literature*. New York: Doubleday and Co., 1968.

Gilbert, Martin. *Final Journey: The Fate of the Jews in Nazi Europe*. London: George Allen and Unwin Ltd., 1979.

Glatstein, Jacob, ed. *Anthology of Holocaust Literature*. Philadelphia: Jewish Publication Society of America, 1973.

Hilberg, Raul. *Documents of Destruction: Germany and Jewry, 1933–1945*. New York: New Viewpoints, 1971.

Korman, Gerd, ed. *Hunter and Hunted: Human History of the Holocaust*. New York: Delta, 1973.

Noakes, Jeremy, ed. *Documents on Nazism, 1919–1945*. New York: Viking Press, 1975.

Schoenberner, Gerhard. *The Yellow Star: The Persecution of the Jews in Europe 1933–1945*. Translated by Susan Sweet. New York: Bantam Books, 1979.

Szajkowski, Zosa. *An Illustrated Source Book on the Holocaust*. 3 vols. New York: KTAV, 1977, 1979.

Audio-Visual Material

Films and other audio-visual material on the holocaust are of varying quality. A number are listed and reviewed in Judith Muffs, ed., *The Holocaust in Books and Films: A Selected, Annotated List* (New York: Anti-Defamation League of B'nai B'rith, 1982), and "Documenting the Holocaust," in *Medium* (Waltham, Mass.: Jewish Media Service Number 16, Winter 1978). A valuable work describing and evaluating many films dealing with the Holocaust is Annette Insdorf, *Indelible Shadows: Film and the Holocaust* (New York: Random House, 1983). *Archives of the Destruction*, developed by Yad Vashem, contains 15,000 pictures on microfiche (available through Research Publications, Woodbridge, Conn., 06525).

Essays and articles on the Holocaust are too profuse to cite but may be found in all of the major journals of Jewish affairs, such as *Judaism*, *Midstream*, *Commentary*, *Jewish Social Studies*, *Moment*, *Jewish Frontier*, *Sh'ma*, *Jewish Spectator*, *Jewish Currents*, and *American Jewish History*, most of which are Indexed in *Index to Jewish Periodicals*, 1963–   . The major Holocaust research center is Yad Vashem Martyrs' and Heroes' Authority in Jerusalem. Other important centers in Israel are: the Institute of Contemporary Jewry, Division of Holocaust Studies, Jerusalem, the Weiner Library, Tel Aviv University, and the Ghetto Fighters' House near Haifa. In the United States, the most important centers are: Leo Baeck Institute and the YIVO-Yiddish Institute of Scientific Research in New York. The Tauber Institute, Brandeis University, Waltham, Massachusetts, the Eisner Institute for Holocaust Studies, Graduate Center, City College of New York, and the Wiesenthal Center in Los Angeles, have recently been established as centers of Holocaust research and study. In Paris there is the Centre de Documentation Juive Contemporaine; in Milan, Italy, the Centro di Documentazione Ebraica Contemporanea. See also Aryeh Segall, ed., *Guide to Jewish Archives* (Jerusalem and New York: World Council of Jewish Archives, 1981) for valuable information on sixty individual Jewish archives and research institutes in the United States, Canada, Israel, Australia, and Europe (available from the National Foundation for Jewish Culture in New York City).

A number of the Holocaust Resource Centers and oral history archives in the United States are listed in *Shoah* 2, No. 3–3, No. 1 (Fall/Winter 1981–1982): 23. More recent names and locations of centers can be obtained from the Holocaust Catalog Project Institute for Research in History, 1133 Broadway, New York, 10010. Under the direction of Joan Ringelheim, the project is assembling an annotated catalogue of Holocaust oral and video testimonies in archives and Holocaust centers in the United States and Canada.

21

Postwar Reflections on the Holocaust from a Christian Point of View

CLARK WILLIAMSON

When the question is asked, "How have Christians responded to the Holocaust?", one must immediately understand that the question is much larger than it appears on the surface. First, the Holocaust itself is an inexhaustible topic. But responding to the Holocaust itself is only one aspect of Christian reflection on the Holocaust. If there ever were a case, this is one, particularly for Christians, where reflection must be an act of double-reflection—reflection not only on the object of our thinking (the Holocaust), but also on the subject doing the thinking (the Christian). This is the second point: that Christians thinking about the *Endlösung* (Final Solution) attempted by the Nazis must ask questions that call not only Nazism but also Christianity itself before the bar of moral and intellectual judgment.

This is the case primarily for two reasons. The first is the simple fact, as pointed out by Elie Wiesel, that "in Auschwitz all the Jews were victims, all the killers were Christian." Commenting on his own observation, Wiesel adds: "As surely as the victims are a problem for the Jews, the killers are a problem for the Christians."[1] Christians who think about the Holocaust have to do something with all of those Christians among the killers. The other reason actually goes deeper than this moral reason, difficult as it may seem for any matter to be more profound than direct implication in mass murder.

Yet this second reason is more devastating. When we ask how the *Shoah*, the burnt offering of the total victim, was even possible, how Europe in such a few short years could be prepared to accept, to sit by and watch, the systematic, bureaucratic destruction of six million Jews and five million others in factories designed to produce death, then we have gotten at least close to the basic question. What Jules Isaac has called "the teaching of contempt," in a book with that title, has been propagated by the Christian Church for so long that this very teaching and its concomitant practice themselves prepared the ground that made Hitler's attempted "Final Solution" possible.[2]

Rabbi Irving Greenberg tells a story from the Holocaust which more than anything else can help one to see the connection claimed above between traditional Christian teaching and practice and the *Endlösung*:

In 1942, the Nietra Rebbe went to Archbishop Kametko of Nietra to plead for Catholic intervention against the deportation of the Slovakian Jews. Tiso, the head of the Slovakian government, had been Kametko's secretary for many years, and the rebbe hoped that Kametko could persuade Tiso not to allow the deportations. Since the rebbe did not yet know of the gas chambers, he stressed the dangers of hunger and disease, especially for women, old people, and children. The archbishop replied: "It is not just a matter of deportation. You will not die there of hunger and disease. They will slaughter all of you there, old and young alike, women and children, at once—it is the punishment that you deserve for the death of our Lord and Redeemer, Jesus Christ—you have only one solution. Come over to our religion and I will work to annul this decree.[3]

The archbishop's statement—"it is the punishment that you deserve for the death of our Lord and Redeemer, Jesus Christ"—is typical of a tradition of Christian theology that has come to be called the *adversus Judaeos* (against the Jews) theology. This theology takes its name from a long series of tracts or books written by classical Christian theologians and bearing the title *Adversus Judaeos*. The influential St. Augustine of Hippo (ca. 354-ca. 430), for example, wrote a tract with exactly this title. The *adversus Judaeos* theology, however, is not to be thought of as confined to such tracts. It was actually a model for understanding both Christianity and Judaism and tended to permeate all aspects of theology from biblical exegesis to the understanding of the central dogmas of the faith.

Meanwhile, it will be helpful to the reader to have an overview or synopsis of this *adversus Judaeos* theology. As Rosemary Ruether describes it, the themes of the *adversus Judaeos* theology are grouped around two headings: "(a) the rejection of the Jews and the election of the Gentiles, and (b) the inferiority and spiritual fulfillment of the Jewish law, cult, and scriptural interpretation."[4] From my own reading of much of the *adversus Judaeos* literature, I can confirm Ruether's claim that these two themes not only are abundantly present but that they mean exactly what they say: that the price of God's electing the Gentiles in Christ was the abandonment of the Jews and that everything Jewish is inferior to and fulfilled by its Christian counterpart.[5] This theology was joined with the practice implicit in it as soon as Christianity became a licit religion under Constantine. The connection between Christian theology about the Jews and Christian practice toward Jews was made by the church in its own practice.[6] As early as the year 306, for example, a synod at Elvira started the process of legislating relations between Jews and Christians and not only forbade intermarriage of Jews and Christians but banned them from eating with one another, as well as from engaging in interreligious adultery.[7]

We have merely had a *glimpse* of this *adversus Judaeos* theology. What is its relation to the Holocaust? The Holocaust against the Jews of the twentieth century discloses the deep and pervasive impact which this 1,900-year old praxis of Christian anti-Judaism has made on all the cultures of what was once called "Christendom." This praxis of Christian anti-Judaism does not constitute anything like a *sufficient* condition or explanation of the *Shoah* of the Jews, but one would be hard pressed to deny that it is at least a necessary condition of the Holocaust.

THE THEOLOGICAL TASK

Christians thinking about the Holocaust must also think about Christianity. Why is this the case? Because this is precisely what the task of Christian theology requires: that we subject Christian talk and Christian practice to criticism, specifically to two kinds of criticism. We must ask whether any given form of Christian witness (whether talk, action, symbolism, or whatever) actually witnesses to, points to, what it claims to point to (i.e., God, the gospel, the Word of God, Jesus Christ) or whether it points to, declares, something else (e.g., the so-called Aryan race or the American way of life). This is one kind of critical question which theologians simply must ask. This question inquires whether a given form of language or activity is indeed appropriate to that to which Christians claim to witness, whether Christian witness befits or suits that to which it claims to bear witness. In this critical function, theology merely takes the church at its word and says let us take seriously your claim that you are preaching the Word of God and ask if that, indeed, is what you are preaching.

For example, in 1948, the German Evangelical Conference at Darmstadt, meeting in the country whose government had recently carried out an attempted genocide, proclaimed that the terrible suffering undergone by Jews in the Holocaust was a divine visitation on Jews and a call to Jews to cease their rejection of Christ as well as their ongoing crucifixion of Christ.[8] A theologian's first job would be to ask whether this statement is itself befitting the very gospel which those who made it think they are proclaiming. Obviously, the Darmstadt statement is a piece of *adversus Judaeos* theology, a bit of pre-Holocaust theology engaged in after the Holocaust. The more fundamental question, however, is this: is it Christian? That is one of the questions that theology must ask and answer, and for that reason the Holocaust raises the most fundamental of questions for Christian theology.

There is yet another kind of criticism, however, to which the Christian theologian qua theologian must subject all forms of Christian witness. This second critical question has to do with plausibility, the sheer matter of the believability of what is said and done by those making the Christian witness. Awkwardly put, this is the question of the "thinkability" of the things said and done by Christians. Can I think that? Does it make any sense? This is the question of truth. We ask it by saying things like: Is that true? How do you know? Obviously, the criterion for truth cannot be one that is esoteric to the Christian community, but must be one that is publicly available to any interested inquirer. The question of truth cannot be settled by saying, for example, "it's in the Bible." If a statement claims to be true, it must pass muster before the bar of common human experience and reason. Had Christians been somewhat more accustomed to asking this basic question, they may have said many fewer ridiculous things over the course of the last two millennia of *adversus Judaeos* theology.

Of course, this dual critical task of theology carries with it a corollary constructive responsibility. The theologian is also to offer proposals with regard to how the Christian faith ought to be understood if it is articulated in the light of the two criteria of appropriateness to the gospel and of plausibility. Hence, the response of Christian theology to the Holocaust includes, but goes beyond, the task of criticizing the *adversus Judaeos* theology which, in its variegated forms, helped to make the Holocaust possible. Theologians must also offer new, post-Holocaust reinterpretations of what Christianity means. In their respective ways, all Christian theologians who have responded to the Holocaust have done exactly this. They have realized that the Holocaust calls for a re-statement of, that is, a re-conception of the meaning and truth of Christian faith.

Any living tradition, whether religious, scientific, literary, or whatever, must be critically re-appropriated in each new historical context if it is to remain an invigorating source of confidence and hope. "Tradition," as the word itself (*traditio*) indicates, refers to a process or an actual occurrence of "handing over" from one generation to another. The forms of a tradition are to be assessed by reference to their adequacy in the process of handing over: do they help or hinder the actual traditioning which is necessary to a living movement? Our historical situation is ever-changing. Those of us who live a generation after the Holocaust realize how radical the change from one situation to another can be and see that to ask the questions of appropriateness and plausibility of the Christian witness today is to ask different questions from those that would have been asked before the Holocaust. Now when we ask of a given theological proposition, does that statement befit the gospel which it intends to proclaim, we do so in full awareness of that statement's role not only in the *adversus Judaeos* praxis of the church but of its payoff in Hitler's *Endlösung der Judenfrage*.

For example, the ancient theological claim that the covenant with God has passed from the Jewish people to the Gentile church, either that the Jews never had it or that they had it but now, with the coming of Christ, they have lost it and it belongs to us, is certainly one that is up for re-examination today.[9] Whether a Christian ought to make a statement like this, that is, whether this statement is itself "Christian," befitting the gospel which it is the business of Christians to publish, is certainly a question that needs to be raised afresh after the Holocaust. The implication of this doctrine is supersession, the claim that Christians have superseded Jews in God's favor. The term "supersede" comes from two Latin words, *sedere* (to sit) and *super* (on or upon): one thing sits on or upon the place of another, super-seding, dis-placing it. By supersessionist logic, Jews have no theological right to exist, not as Jews. Are such statements and their implication remotely appropriate to the gospel? Should Christians make them? I think not.

By the same token, this statement of theological supersessionism is also clearly incredible, particularly *after* the Holocaust. That God is the kind of God who either could or would act in such a way was sufficiently implausible as to be disbelieved well in advance of the Holocaust. But after the Holocaust we can re-formulate the criterion of credibility as follows: No theological statement should be made that would not be credible in the presence of the burning children.[10]

Armed with this understanding of what theology is and how it is done, we are in a position to reflect critically and constructively on a variety of Christian responses to the Holocaust.

BIBLICAL SCHOLARSHIP

Strikingly, it is within the discipline of critical, historical study of the scriptures that we find the most concentrated and sustained dealing with issues that have been posed by contemplation of the Holocaust. This, of course, is a comparative judgment, and one must remember that even within biblical studies awareness of Holocaust-related issues remains fairly marginal. Students wishing a synopsis of the difference which the dialogue between Jews and Christians has made to biblical studies should see Eugene J. Fisher's article, "The Impact of the Christian-Jewish Dialogue on Biblical Studies."[11]

One can probably best handle these developments in biblical scholarship by dividing them into exegetical and hermeneutical areas of concern. Exegetically, a sweeping change seems, in an unostentatious and hushed way, to be creeping over New Testament studies. New Testament scholars are taking more seriously Jewish sources such as the Tannaim and the Targumim. In two recent works, E. P. Sanders provides striking evidence that many Christian understandings of the Judaism of the first century cannot be sustained on the basis of Jewish sources.[12] Writing half a century after George Foot Moore's classic essay, "Christian Writers on Judaism," Sanders delineates the historical course of the "Weber/Schürer/Bousset description of Judaism" first exposed by Moore.[13] Sanders demonstrates that most of the prominent and influential biblical scholars writing after Moore fail to take note of his criticism of the anti-Judaism in Christian scholarship on Judaism. Sanders's own description of Judaism, drawn from a direct study of Jewish texts, moves him to conclude that: "We must say that the Judaism of before 70 kept grace and works in the right perspective, did not trivialize the commandments of God, and was not especially marked by hypocrisy."[14]

The importance of this comment is that the standard Christian complaint against Judaism "is not that some individual Jews misunderstood, misapplied and abused their religion, but that Judaism necessarily tends toward petty legalism, self-serving and self-deceiving casuistry, and a mixture of arrogance and lack of confidence in God."[15] Such attitudes, attributed to Judaism, cannot be verified by recourse to the original sources. The problem for the Christian interpreter of the New Testament, then, is how to understand the New Testament without using Judaism as a black backdrop against which the white light of the gospel is allowed to shine.

THE PHARISEES AND JESUS

This exegetical change particularly affects our understanding of the Pharisees and consequently of Jesus and Paul. Jesus and Paul are always presented as so bound up with the Pharisees that a revision in the picture of the Pharisees carries with it the necessity of a change in the picture of Jesus and Paul. The portrait of the Pharisees is being redrawn by several scholars.[16] Ordinarily, Christian scholarship pictures them as the "chief heavies" of the New Testament story. Now we recognize that our earliest writer, Paul, never mentions them as his enemies, although the later gospels regularly name them as Jesus's enemies. In addition, scholars increasingly accept that the conflicts between Jesus and the Pharisees in the gospels are the product of the later conflict between the Pharisaic leaders of the synagogue and the church of the late first century. Commenting on this issue in Matthew's gospel, Norman Perrin writes: "So the diatribe against 'the scribes and Pharisees' in Matthew 23 does not reflect a conflict between Jesus and the scribes and Pharisees of his day, but one fifty years later between Matthew and their descendants spreading their influence from Jamnia."[17] The late first century was a time of desperation and conflict for both church and synagogue, each threatened from within and from without by the Roman Empire, and the later New Testament writings reflect one side of this conflict.

The positive point is that in the new scholarship the image of the Pharisees is drastically revamped. Here they are no longer viewed as the one group of official Jews (the others including the Sadducees, the Zealots, the Essenes, and the priesthood) who are sufficiently popular *with the people* to survive the destruction of the Temple. All the other groups disappear, with the exception of the followers of Jesus.

In principle, the problem of reconstructing an historical picture of the Pharisees is much the same as that of retrieving the historical Jesus. We have not only to work backwards from later sources, but also to recognize that these sources did not have historical concerns; they were dealing with their own problems. Nonetheless, with the help of such scholars as Ellis Rivkin and Jacob Neusner and within the confines of historical probability, we can make the following points.

The Pharisaic method of teaching is called the "oral Torah." Oral Torah teaches by the method of interpreting the written Torah; "it is written, but the meaning is. . . . " This method is regularly attributed by Matthew to Jesus: "You have heard it said, but I say unto you." This is a technical Pharisaic expression. Jesus apparently used the teaching method of the Pharisees. The Pharisees also created the role of the rabbi, the one who so teaches and who interprets and specifies religious obligations. The gospels contain numerous references to Jesus as teacher/rabbi, and he teaches not only by oral Torah but also by telling stories, which is also a favorite rabbinic approach. We are frequently told by the synoptics that it was Jesus's custom to go to the synagogue (Luke 4:16), the institution that embodied the Pharisaic type of faith.

As to content, many of the teachings attributed to Jesus are so remarkably parallel to those of the liberal Pharisees, followers of Hillel (the conservative Pharisees at Hillel's time were of the school of Shammai) that Jacob Neusner can declare: "Some of his [Hillel's] teachings are in spirit and even in exact wording close to the teachings of Jesus."[18] For instance, Jesus's proclamation that "the Sabbath was made for man, not man for the Sabbath" (Mark 2:27), reflects the Hillelite saying attributed to Rabbi Jonathan ben Joseph: "Scripture says: 'The Sabbath is holy for *you*' (Exodus 31:14). This means it is given to you (man) not you to the Sabbath."[19]

Jesus's simplification of all the commandments into two is similar to what is found in both Hillel and Philo; his use of the *Shema* ("Hear, O Israel") and his teachings on prayer, particularly the Lord's Prayer, reflect Jewish piety of the home and synagogue. Not incidentally, the Pharisees carried self-criticism to such an extent that the criticism of them attributed to Jesus in the gospels, if authentic, need be no more than Pharisaic self-criticism. In spite of the negative image of them as dry, arid, and lifeless legalists, they laid great stress on the all-present mercy and grace of God.[20]

Jesus's ethical teachings seem clearly continuous with those of the contemporary school of Hillel, and when they differ the method by which the difference is stated is the Pharisaic method. Obviously, there is much else in the sayings attributed to Jesus besides those that have echoes in rabbinic literature. Many of his sayings seem to stand in the tradition of the wisdom literature.[21] He also spoke much of the coming reign of God and may or may not have implied that He himself played some decisive role in that coming. While, like Hillel, He wanted the Torah to be lived and loved, He did not, so far as we know, refer to it in terms of constant study. His exact relations to the Pharisees (in His time, the scribes) defy description.

Nonetheless, several revisionary points have emerged from this discussion: (1) none of the teachings attributed to Jesus falls outside the bounds of the variety of Judaisms of His time; (2) the conflicts portrayed in the gospels between Jesus and the Pharisees are retrojected from the conflictual situation of the later first century church; (3) an *a priori* bias against the "scribes and Pharisees" as such is set aside by honest scholarly reading of Jewish sources and scholarship, thus setting aside at the same time a primary source of anti-Jewish polemic.[22] Ministers of Christian congregations should familiarize themselves with this new scholarship; as they do, they will cease to perpetuate negative images of the forebearers of the synagogue across the street.

PAUL

When we turn from the Pharisees and Jesus to the apostle Paul, we find that a wealth of contemporary scholarship has taken a new look at the apostle to the Gentiles.[23] In spite of this abundance of new scholarship, however, we still find that the traditional, anti-Jewish interpretation of Paul is present in commentaries on his letters. For instance, in his commentary on Romans, Matthew Black comments:

The key to an understanding of Paul's essential thesis is his conviction of the total bankruptcy of contemporary Pharisaic "scholasticism," which seemed to base the whole range of active right relationships within the Covenant ("righteousness") on the meticulous observation of the injunctions of the torah as expanded in the "tradition of the elders." This was "legalistic righteousness," a form of ethics based entirely on a code, external and "written," losing sight entirely of the gracious personal will of a holy and good God, of which it was originally intended to be the divine vehicle of expression.[24]

If the question for Paul indeed was that of Pharisaism *or* the gospel, it is striking that he never once put it that way. Nor does Paul ever juxtapose law and gospel. He never speaks of Pharisaism. In the one passage where he uses the term "Pharisee," he says:

If any other man thinks he has reason for confidence in the flesh, I have more: circumcised on the eighth day, of the people of Israel, of the tribe of Benjamin, a Hebrew born of Hebrews; as to the law a Pharisee, as to zeal a persecutor of the church, as to righteousness under the law blameless (Philippians 3:4–6).

Starting with insights derived from comments such as the above, several contemporary biblical scholars are beginning to reinterpret Paul. As is to be expected, these scholars disagree with each other in significant ways. E. P. Sanders, Markus Barth, J. Christiaan Beker, William D. Davies, and Lloyd Gaston, to name some of the more prominent of Paul's post-Holocaust reinterpreters, are not of one mind on Paul. They do agree, however, that the old way of looking at Paul, which sets him in antithesis to Judaism, is of no avail. They agree with each other more on the questions they ask of Paul than on the answers they find. Yet as every school child knows, it is the questions that are important.

In his *Paul the Apostle: The Triumph of God in Life and Thought*, for example, J. Christiaan Beker argues that the model of Paul as the originator of catholic Christianity was the model of Paul as having liberated Christianity "from its so-called Jewish limitations. Paul the catholic theologian was the 'universalist,' and the key to his achievement was his antipathy to everything Jewish."[25] Beker declares "completely erroneous" this picture of Paul as the originator of catholic dogma and the enemy of Judaism.[26] The traditional anti-Jewish interpretation of Paul dwells much on Paul's so-called conversion, a term that is never used either by Paul or the Book of Acts in describing whatever it was that happened to Paul on the Damascus Road. The term itself is suspect, as it implies a change from one religion to another; yet in Paul's day Christianity was not yet a separate religion from Judaism. In any case, Beker argues that concern with it tells us more about Paul's interpreter than it does about Paul. Paul was actually quite reticent about his "conversion," especially in contrast with his apostleship, about which he was extremely outspoken. His one reference to the Damascus Road event was made in order to support his claim to be an apostle, and that to the Gentiles (Galatians 1:15–17).

It is Beker who points out that Paul never speaks of Christ as having "fulfilled" the promises of God to Israel. In place of such an expression, Paul says that Christ "became a servant to the circumcised to show God's truthfulness, in order to *confirm* the promises given to the patriarchs, and in order that the Gentiles might glorify God for his mercy" (Romans 15:8–9; the emphasis is mine). The verb *bebaiōsai* means "to ratify or confirm."

Beker also points out that Paul maintains a tension between God and Christ, so that Christ is never "fused" with God.[27] For instance, Paul tells the Corinthians "let no one boast of men. For all things are yours . . . , and you are Christ's, and Christ is God's" (I Corinthians 3:23). Paul's is a theocentric, not Christocentric, Christology; it is not a Christolatry. Paul's Christology, furthermore, is affirmed against the prospect or horizon of God's final eschatological reign "that will break into history and transform all creation in accord with the messianic promises."[28] This consummation will only take place with Israel's participation in it (Romans 11:15, 24).

In his "Paul and the Torah," Lloyd Gaston argues that Paul was an apostle to the Gentiles, that he was commissioned by the Jerusalem Council (Acts 15; Galatians 2:1–10) to preach among the Gentiles, that he was not commissioned to preach among Jews and that he apparently never did so. All his letters were sent to congregations overwhelmingly made up of Gentiles. He never wrote to a group of Jews a letter in which he urged them to abandon the Torah. Foremost among the problems faced by those Gentile followers of Jesus to whom Paul wrote was the right of Gentiles *qua* Gentiles to full citizenship in the people of God without adopting the Torah of Israel. Gaston's thesis is that legalism—"the doing of certain works in order to win God's favor and be counted righteous— arose as a gentile problem and was not a Jewish problem at all."[29]

It was the God-fearers *not* under the covenant who "had to establish their righteousness by the performance of certain works, compounded by uncertainty as to what these works should be."[30] The term "works of the law," not found in any Jewish texts, refers to the Gentile habit of adopting certain Jewish practices as a means of self-justification. How else can Paul address the Galatians with the question: "Tell me, you who desire to be under the law, do you not hear the law?" (Galatians 4:21). In this passage, says Gaston, one hears Paul the Pharisee who really knows the Torah replying to amateurs who are only "playing with the idea.''[31] ''When Paul is most negative about the law, he opposes it to—the law, i.e., the Torah! Opposed to 'the other law, the law of sin' is 'the Torah of God' (Romans 7:22).''[32]

One way to re-state Gaston's thesis is to say that in reading Paul one must remember that one is reading letters and that in reading any letter it is of critical importance to know to whom the letter is addressed if the letter is to be understood. Paul's letters are not only all addressed to specific situations of particular communities, as scholars have long insisted; they are also all addressed to specific situations in which Gentile-Christians find themselves, a point insufficiently appreciated heretofore. Hence, Paul spoke as he did to Gentiles, because with them a new way of speaking was necessary. He never spoke to them of repentance, of turning back to the God of the covenant, for example, because ''Paul was interested in gentiles turning *to* him for the first time.''[33] Gaston's views are a helpful corrective of Christian views of Judaism.

In his *Paul Among Jews and Gentiles*, Krister Stendahl sets forth an interpretation of Paul's thinking as having had as a basic concern the relation between Jews and Gentiles with which, he says, the main lines of Pauline interpretation ''have for many centuries been out of touch.''[34] Stendahl seeks to show that Paul's doctrine of justification was worked out in order to defend the rights of Gentile converts to be full and genuine heirs to the promises of God to Israel, and not as a response to the kinds of pangs of conscience which Luther had with the law. In this regard, Stendahl's views are in accord with those of E. P. Sanders; both agree that there is in Paul no criticism of Judaism. For Sanders, the only problem with it, for Paul, is that it is not Christianity; but the usual kinds of problems attested by Christian scholars result from a misunderstanding of Paul's procedure which is to reason from solution to problem and not vice-versa.

Paul's argument about righteousness by faith or by works of Law . . . is viewed as if he were arguing that an individual cannot merit salvation by achieving enough good deeds to present a favorable balance before God. It is believed to be characteristic of Judaism to hold such a position, so that Paul's argument is perceived to be against Judaism. A study of Jewish material does not reveal such a position. More to the point, that is not Paul's argument in any case. The question is . . . whether or not Paul's Gentile converts must accept the Jewish law in order to enter the people of God.[35]

Whatever nuances of interpretation distinguish Stendahl and Sanders from one another they are clearly in fundamental accord with regard to Paul.

Stendahl regards Romans 9–11 as the climax of Paul's most famous letter, that is, Paul's reflections on the relation between the church and the Jewish people. He notes that Paul does not say that ultimately Israel will accept Jesus as the Christ but simply that ''all Israel will be saved'' (11:26), and that Paul writes this whole section of Romans (10:17–11:36) without using the name of Jesus Christ and that the final doxology in the passage is the only one in Paul without a Christological reference. Says Stendahl:

It is tempting to suggest that in important respects Paul's thought here approximates an idea well documented in later Jewish thought from Maimonides to Franz Rosenzweig. Christianity . . . is seen as the conduit of Torah, for the declaration of both monotheism and the moral order to the Gentiles. The differences are obvious, but the similarity should not be missed: Paul's reference to God's mysterious plan is an affirmation of a God-willed coexistence between Judaism and Christianity in which the missionary urge to convert Israel is held in check.[36]

Stendahl's approach to Paul is refreshing: he insists on a simple reading of the text unobscured by what we already think we know. Using this method of addressing Paul's letters, he dismisses the interpretation of Paul's Damascus road experience as a "conversion." Paul was not converted; he was called to the specific task of apostleship to the Gentiles. Of this event, Paul says: "when he who had set me apart before I was born, and had called me through his grace, was pleased to reveal his Son to me, in order that I might preach him among the Gentiles" (Galatians 1:15–16). In this statement are found clear allusions to those calls issued to Isaiah and Jeremiah that they become prophets to the nations (Isaiah 49:1, 6: Jeremiah 1:5). Rather than being a conversion, Paul's experience brought him to a new understanding of the law "which is otherwise an obstacle to the Gentiles."[37] A close reading of the three accounts in Acts yields the same result (Act 9, 22, and 26). Paul did not change his religion; "it is obvious that Paul remains a Jew as he fulfills his role as an Apostle to the Gentiles."[38]

A second major point common to all those who are taking a fresh look at Paul has to do with the question of how to interpret Paul's use of the terms "justify" and "justification." Stendahl notes that the justification vocabulary is pervasive of Paul, whereas forgiveness-language is almost absent. Yet, we usually interpret justification in terms of forgiveness. For Stendahl and for Sanders, this is a mistake: "Paul's doctrine of justification by faith has its theological context in his reflection on the relation between Jews and Gentiles, and not within the problem of how *man* is to be saved, or how man's deeds are to be accounted, or how the free will of individuals is to be asserted or checked."[39] In other words, whenever we find Paul discussing justification, a quick check of the context will disclose, lying near at hand, a specific reference to Jews and Gentiles. For example:

For we hold that a man is justified by faith apart from works of law. Or is God the God of the Jews only? Is he not the God of the Gentiles also? Yes, of Gentiles also, since God is one; and he will justify the circumcised on the ground of their faith and the uncircumcised through their faith. (Romans 3:28–30)

Paul goes on to comment in this passage that to hold this view is to uphold, not to overthrow, the law. This use of the doctrine of justification is continued in Ephesians by a student of Paul: "For by grace you have been saved through faith"; and three verses later: "Therefore remember that at one time you Gentiles in the flesh . . . were separated from Christ, alienated from the commonwealth of Israel, and strangers to the covenants of promise, having no hope and without God in the world'' (Ephesians 2:8; 11–12). The doctrine of justification, then, has not so much to do with the forgiveness of the individual as with the salvation-historical inclusion of the Gentiles in the people of God. Paul, says Stendahl, is "our champion, a Jew who by vicarious penetration gives to us Gentiles the justification for our claims to be God's children in Jesus Christ.''[40]

HERMENEUTICS

Hermeneutically, the question of whether the New Testament is anti-Jewish is now dealt with in a more subtle way. Today scholars tend not to fend off charges of anti-Judaism within the pages of the New Testament. Gregory Baum, in his *Is the New Testament Anti-Semitic* (1965), thought it his duty to "defend the New Testament itself from the accusation of prejudice and falsification.''[41] Almost a decade later, in the introduction of Rosemary Ruether's *Faith and Fratricide*, he states that "my apology for the New Testament led me to a contradiction: for I had to admit in the course of my study that many biblical passages reflected the conflict between Church and Synagogue in the first century.''[42] Indeed, Baum may have gone too far in the other direction (in company with Ruether), in declaring that all efforts of Christian theologians to derive more positive meanings from Paul's views in Romans 9–11 "are grounded in wishful thinking.''[43] Nonetheless, the point here is that, rather than deny anti-Jewish elements in the New Testament, Baum now suggests, indeed demands, that Christian theologians "submit Christian teaching to a radical ideological critique.''[44] The function of an ideological critique is to detect those inclinations in Christian teaching that would legitimate Christian power over others. In a position quite close to that articulated in this chapter, Baum claims that

Christian theologians are able to submit the gospel to a radical critique if they hold that the authentic handing-on of the Christian message in history does not consist in the simple repetition of previous teaching, biblical or ecclesiastical, but rather is a creative process in which Past Christian teaching, in obedience to God's Word in the present, is reinterpreted and reformulated as the good news for the present age.[45]

Similarly, Schubert M. Ogden has argued that, in addition to the hermeneutical procedure of demythologizing and existentialist interpretation, what he calls "an adequate christology of reflection" also requires that we engage in "deideologizing" and "political interpretation.''[46] "Deideologizing" means for Ogden "the method of so interpreting the meaning of the christology of witness as to disengage it from the economic, social, political, and cultural world whose injustices it is used, negatively if not positively, to sanction.''[47]

By the same token, then, we can then admit that there are indeed polemical, anti-Judaic strata embedded in the New Testament traditions. John Townsend, a New Testament scholar, sees in John's gospel discrete layers of development with radically diverse views toward Jews and Judaism. The earlier strata can be as positive ("salvation is from the Jews"—John 4:22) as the later can be hostile ("You are of your father the devil"—John 8:44).

Hence, the question is no longer the overly simple: Is the New Testament anti-Semitic or anti-Jewish, but, rather: are the roots of later anti-Judaism and anti-Semitism in the New Testament?

Although the answer to this latter question is in the affirmative, it allows us to do two things: to isolate how and where anti-Judaism really colors the New Testament, thereby to some extent neutralizing its possibility for harm, and to practice on these anti-Jewish strata a hermeneutics of suspicion, of the sort that Odgen has articulated. Hence, as David Tracy also wants to argue, we could acknowledge the presence of anti-Jewish polemics in the New Testament while relativizing these polemics by showing their historicity and by evaluating them in relation to the norm of appropriateness for Christianity, the gospel. As Tracy claims: "Those anti-Judaic statements of the New Testament bear *no* authoritative status for Christianity. . . . The heart of the New Testament message—the love who is God—should release the demythologizing power of its own prophetic meaning to rid the New Testament and Christianity once and for all of these statements."[48]

This chapter has spent much time on the question of the reinterpretation of the New Testament after the Holocaust. We have done this for three reasons: (1) No normative witness, such as the New Testament, can conceivably function as what it is unless it is constantly reinterpreted in each new context. (2) If any real change is to happen in Christianity after the Holocaust, it will have to take place locally and concretely as Christian pastors and teachers learn to read their normative documents differently. Here is where the real hope lies and why the Roman Catholic Church, behind the hermeneutical clout of *Nostra Aetate* and the Second Vatican Council, provides such a splendid example to all Christians of what an ecclesial response to Auschwitz looks like, in contrast with responses by individual theologians, important as these responses are. (3) As theologians seek to come up with sufficiently radical reinterpretations of Christianity after the *Endlösung*, they are helpless to reinterpret Christianity unless a simultaneous reinterpretation of Christian scripture is taking place. By the same token, scripture would not be undergoing reinterpretation were not radical theological questions being asked. Probably there is some dialectical relation between scriptural reinterpretation and constructive theological work such that the two need each other. In any case, we now turn to some of the more prominent theological efforts at reconstruction.

THEOLOGICAL REINTERPRETATIONS

Rosemary Ruether, toward the conclusion of her magnificent study, *Faith and Fratricide*, contends that the "key issue" in the Christian anti-Judaic myth that needs reconceiving is Christology.[49] In this respect she is surely right, and every post-Holocaust theologian must sooner or later come to grips with Christology. Her by-now-famous way of putting the question is: "Is it possible to say 'Jesus is the Messiah' without, implicitly or explicitly, saying at the same time 'and the Jews be damned'?"[50] The only way to do so, she believes, is to maintain that the Messianic meaning of Jesus's life "is paradigmatic and proleptic in nature, not final and fulfilled." The significance of the resurrection is not that it was the consummation of the eschatological promises of God to Israel but that it was the "proleptic experiencing of the final future."[51] This position rejects the view that Jesus "fulfilled" the Messianic promises; indeed, this is the strongest point in favor of Ruether's position: the observation that the nations have not yet beaten their swords and missiles into plowshares is incontrovertible to any rational person. Other matters are also entailed in Ruether's position: (1) Jesus is interpreted as the one who mediates this hope to us Christians; (2) Jesus's life "does not invalidate the right of those Jews not caught up in this paradigm to go forward on earlier foundations"; (3) the fulfillment of prophetic hope lies in the future of both the church and the Jewish people; and (4) indeed, the final Messianic covenant articulated in Jeremiah 31:31 also "lies as much ahead of the historical reality of Christianity as it does that of Judaism."[52]

Ruether's position is eminently sensible and not one with which this writer wants to quarrel. There are some things to think about with regard to it, however. (1) Its essential point, prolepsis, is not particularly a response to the Holocaust; other theologians, for example, Wolfhart Pannenberg, not thinking about these matters, hold the same view. Yet these other theologians are also quite capable of maintaining that in Jesus there is only a fragmentary and proleptic fulfillment and of holding clearly anti-Jewish views at the same time.[53] How, then, does Ruether's argument secure its desired end, that we can say "Jesus is the Christ" and at the same time avoid saying, "and the Jews be damned?" (2) Ruether apparently assumes that God is the kind of God (particularly having the kind of power required) who is capable of bringing off the final eschaton at some future point. I take it that this is the assumption, at any rate, because otherwise there would be no point in talking of the fulfillment that did occur in Jesus as proleptic. Yet this is apparently an uncriticized assumption in Ruether. Many contemporary theologians, particularly the process theologians, no longer hold this assumption, and even they are hardly alone in this; Paul Tillich long ago argued that " 'der liebe Gott' who is all-powerful does not exist."[54] Part of my point here is that, whereas Christology is the key issue, it is not the *only* issue that needs rethinking. Christian theology needs to be systematically revamped after Auschwitz. This is particularly true with regard to the doctrine of God, which has not only been given quite an anti-Jewish construction through much of Christian history but which also in its classical form is capable of being used to rationalize the very things Ruether rejects. If God is all-powerful and all-knowing and omnibenevolent and the Jews suffer, it would seem reasonable to conclude that God wishes them to do so. This question, too, needs to be answered.

John T. Pawlikowski has written extensively in the Catholic-Jewish dialogue (see the bibliography). In his latest book he, too, tries to restate Christology after the Holocaust.[55] He seeks, however, to erect his Christology on the basis of the historical Jesus, which means, for Pawlikowski, that he must seek to get at "Jesus' *precise* relationship" to the Pharisees, with whom, according to Pawlikowski, Jesus had much in common. Pawlikowski realized the difficulties in reconstructing this historical relationship and admits that his effort is "rather tentative."[56] Consequently, his language throughout makes regular use of such words as "seem to," "appear to," "seems to," and so on, while all the time he is in search of historical precision. Furthermore, he regularly attributes to the historical Jesus feelings and actions that are out of all historical-critical bounds, as in his claim with regard to Pharisaic-type fellowship meals that Jesus instituted "the Christian eucharist at the final one he attended."[57] Pawlikowski also knows things about "Jesus' personal sense of identification with the Father" which are astounding.

Pawlikowski's answer to his own question, "Was Jesus a Pharisee?," is of the "yes, but" variety. In trying to address the precise relationship, Pawlikowski contends that Jesus was a son of the Pharisees, "even though on several key issues . . . he was without doubt his 'own man'."[58] To establish the basis which warrants or grounds his Christology, Pawlikowski isolates seven issues on which he claims that Jesus transcended the Pharisees of his day. These differences "*appear* to be unique dimensions of his teaching" and "*seem* to be important differences at this moment of scholarly inquiry."[59]

(1) Jesus's "Abba experience" involved a "degree of intimacy" with divinity which "no Pharisee of his day would have been willing to grant."[60] (2) He carried the Pharisaic notion of the dignity of each person to its ultimate conclusion to the extent that the Pharisees "gradually began to look upon Jesus' independent stress on the worth of the individual as a potential threat to Jewish communal survival."[61] (3) The difference between Jesus and the Pharisees on their "respective attitudes toward the *am ha aretz* is not readily demonstrable," but nonetheless "there seems to be something in the contrast between Jesus and the Pharisees on this point."[62] This accords with the prior point on the worth of the individual. (4) Whereas, for the Pharisee the source of opposition to divine discipleship was the "evil inclination" (understood as having a sexual base), for Jesus it was wealth. "Thus, for Jesus riches are the antithesis of authentic commitment to God. Riches tend to drive a person away from God because in the process of securing wealth one frequently has to act in a manner that disregards the basic dignity of men and women."[63] Again, Jesus's more extreme stress on individual worth separates him from Pharisaism. (5) Jesus taught love of the enemy; the Pharisees taught that we should not hate the enemy. "Here we have another instance where the dignity of the individual assumes the primacy for Jesus that takes him beyond Pharisaism."[64] Jesus declares that the Kingdom of God was both present (in his own activities) and future, not wholly future as "the Pharisees seemed to imply." This proclamation "alienated him from Pharisaism."[65] (7) Finally, whereas "the Pharisees continued to hold tenaciously to

the traditional view that God alone had the power to forgive sins," "Jesus claims this power for himself."[66] Moreover, "he transfers this power to his disciples."[67] These actions are "revolutionary" and also put stress on the worth of the individual.

The obvious questions for Pawlikowski are: (1) Are these seven statements true? Here he equivocates between phrases like "without doubt" and "appears to" from sentence to sentence, although critical caution fades as the argument progresses. On one page he is aware of the need to be cautious, and on the next he is inside the psyche of the historical Jesus. The results of the attempt to get at the precise relationship of Jesus to the Pharisees are tenuous. (2) After the Holocaust, should Pawlikowski still try to make use of this nineteenth-century form of argument, should he still try to show that Jesus is the Christ because he "went beyond" Pharisaism in these seven ways? How different is this from the approach of Adolf Harnack? For Harnack Jesus was the Christ because he was the perfect knower of God; for Pawlikowski, it is Jesus's "Abba experience" that accomplishes the same thing. Pawlikowski seems hardly less supersessionist in his discussion of Jesus than was Harnack. (3) Should a Christology be based on a set of statements which "seem to" be the case? And (4) is not this Christology based on a "work" accomplished, allegedly, by Jesus, a work of overcoming the Pharisees and their limitations? If so, does not the doctrine of works-righteousness here achieve what Schubert M. Ogden calls "its final and most dangerous triumph"?[68] I think this is a serious problem for Pawlikowski's Christology. It is not accidental that his reconstruction of the historical Jesus leads him to say that Jesus was "a potential threat to Jewish communal survival" in the eyes of the Pharisees, that they regarded His stance as "too dangerous" and His popularity as raising "a threat to national loyalty to Torah."[69] Here we have not moved far, in spite of all of Pawlikowski's best intentions, beyond the conflictual model of Jesus's relationship to Judaism that characterized and still characterizes anti-Jewish Christology.

Along with Ruether and Pawlikowski, A. Roy Eckardt also regards Christology as the key issue in revising Christian theology after the Holocaust. Whereas Ruether, however, would interpret the resurrection experiences of the early church as proleptic, Eckardt's decision is that the resurrection of Jesus Christ must simply be denied. In the *adversus Judaeos* theological tradition, Eckardt rightly notes, the resurrection is God's vindication of an anti-Jewish Jesus against the Jews, it is God's judgment of the Jewish people. Eckardt also sees and again correctly that this way of interpreting the resurrection is continued by modern and contemporary theologians (e.g., Pannenberg).[70] As a result of his analysis, Eckardt concludes that "it is the teaching of a consummated Resurrection which lies at the foundation of Christian hostility to Jews and Judaism, for only with that teaching does Christian triumphalist ideology reach ultimate fulfillment."[71]

With this conclusion and the supplementary argument that as between affirming the resurrection literally and simply denying it there is no coherent third alternative, Eckardt then proceeds to deny the resurrection in order to rid Christianity of its anti-Jewish triumphalism; "there is only one possible ground for denying Pannenberg's vindication—by testifying that Jesus has not yet been raised from the dead."[72] The "not yet" must be noted. Eckardt, like Ruether, places redemption in the future, and his most recent book ends with a powerful statement of faith and hope:

That young Jewish prophet from Galilee sleeps now. He sleeps with the other Jewish dead, with all the disconsolate and scattered ones of the murder camps, and with the unnumbered dead of the human and the nonhuman family. But Jesus of Nazareth shall be raised. So too shall the small Hungarian children of Auschwitz. Once upon a time, they shall again play and they shall laugh. The little one of Terezin shall see another butterfly. We shall all sing and we shall all dance. And we shall love one another.[73]

As a witness to a reformed Christian faith, Eckardt's statement is forceful. As a reflective theological statement, it is open to all the questions that can be raised about Ruether's proposal plus some others. It would be my contention that all modern and post-modern Christologies that seek to ground and warrant the statement "Jesus is the Christ" by reference to the "historical Jesus" in effect dismiss the resurrection. That is, what makes Jesus the Christ is His life, teaching, personal faith, praxis, and so on, to all of which the resurrection is both subsequent and optional. This conclusion cannot be consistently avoided. Yet these modern Christologies (see, e.g., Harnack's *What Is Christianity?*) hardly avoid Christian triumphalism, particularly vis-à-vis Judaism. Eckardt's proposal, then, while dramatic, may finally underestimate the depth of the problem of Christian anti-Judaism.

This last comment is highly ironic. Hardly any Christian has taken the Holocaust more seriously for a longer period of time than has Roy Eckardt. He is one of those, including James Parkes and Franklin Littell, responsible for keeping this concern alive in the Christian community over the past generation. Yet, even he may have underestimated the problem. Indeed, given the limits of what theology can do (how much indeed does theology affect the life of the Christian churches?), a theological response to the Holocaust, no matter how profound, may be totally inadequate, absent from other kinds of ecclesiastical responses. Yet within the limits set for theology, nothing less can be attempted than a total, systematic effort to re-think the nature and meaning of Christian faith in relation to the reality of Judaism. Assertions and denials with respect to this or that key doctrine are inadequate.

Such a re-thinking is what Paul M. van Buren is attempting in his projected four-volume series of books.[74] Van Buren's approach is heavily indebted to Franz Rosenzweig. Says van Buren:

Franz Rosenzweig suggested that the church's special calling is to live in God's plan in a perpetual and creative tension between Israel and the world. For our conversation the consequence is that we are neither as "biblical" as our Jewish beginning demands of us nor as pagan as our origin and context imply.[75]

Van Buren's book is a brilliant unfolding of many of the implications of this statement. Rosenzweig's influence is also seen in van Buren's claim that every further theological point that a Christian wants to make can only be an unfolding of the basic point that the God of whom the church speaks is the God of Israel.[76] So, too, van Buren's view of revelation is close to that of Rosenzweig (as it is to Markus Barth's).[77] But the most important way in which van Buren is influenced by Rosenzweig is shown in a comment such as this:

We [Gentile Christians] are . . . not the first to be called. We are reminded by the Apostolic Writings that our election comes out of and is framed in a specific relationship to that of the Jews. We are called not to be Jews, but to be the historically continuing body of the one Jew, Jesus Christ. Empowered by the Spirit which worked in him and now works also in us, we are to bear witness before the world that we have been sent by the one who sent Jesus, by the one God of Israel. In the name of Israel's God, we are called to be His Gentiles sent to make Him known to other Gentiles.[78]

This is close to Rosenzweig's concern that Christianity and Judaism come to a proper recognition of each other. He expressed Israel's recognition of the church in the terms of a "daughter religion": "The dogma of the Church about its relationship to Judaism calls for a corresponding dogma of Judaism and its relation with the Church. It exists in the theory known to you only from modern liberal Judaism, of the 'daughter religion' which shall gradually prepare the world for Judaism."[79]

Rosenzweig cast a powerful new light on the relationship between Judaism and Christianity. His way of looking at the two preserves the distinctiveness of each, viewing both in a new creative way. The strength of van Buren's proposal is that he takes this Rosenzweig model and runs with it, asking, in effect, how everything looks from this perspective, how every doctrine would be reinterpreted from it. How successful his reinterpretation will be and how adequately he will be seen to have re-visioned Christianity after the Holocaust must, in the nature of the case, remain to be seen. What is really innovating about his work is his engagement in the task of a systematic reinterpretation of Christianity as a whole, and this is the task that is required after the Holocaust.

NOTES

1. Wiesel, *A Jew Today*, pp. 13–14.

2. Isaac, *Teaching of Contempt*.

3. Greenberg, "Cloud of Smoke, Pillar of Fire," in Fleischner, ed., *Auschwitz:*, pp. 11–12.

4. Ruether, *Faith and Fratricide*, p. 123.

5. See Williamson, "The *Adversus Judaeos* Tradition in Christian Theology," pp. 273–296.

6. See, for example, Ruether, *Faith and Fratricide*, pp. 183–225, and Williamson, *Has God Rejected His People?*, pp. 106–122.

7. Williamson, *Has God Rejected His People?*, p. 107.

8. See Greenberg, "Cloud of Smoke, Pillar of Fire," p. 13.

9. For a very early formulation of this claim, see *The Epistle of Barnabas*, *The Ante-Nicene Fathers*, Vol. 1, pp. 137–149.

10. This is a very slight paraphrase of Rabbie Irving Greenberg's "working principle" that "No statement, theological or otherwise, should be made that would not be credible in the presence of the buring children." See Greenberg, "Cloud of Smoke, Pillar of Fire," p. 23.

11. Fisher's article appears in Rousseau, ed., *Christianity and Judaism*, pp. 117–138.

12. See Sanders, *Paul and Palestinian Judaism*, and *Paul, The Law, and the Jewish People*.

13. For Moore's essay, see *Harvard Theological Review* 14, No. 3 (July 1921): 197–254.

14. Sanders, *Paul and Palestinian Judaism*, p. 427.

15. Ibid.

16. See Ellis Rivkin, *A Hidden Revolution* (Nashville, Tenn.: Abingdon Press, 1978); David Flusser, "A New Sensitivity in Judaism and the Christian Message," *Encounter Today* (Autumn 1969): 123–131 and (Winter 1970): 3–12; Jacob Neusner, *From Politics to Piety* (Englewood Cliffs, N. J.: Prentice-Hall, 1963); *First-Century Judaism in Crisis* (Nashville, Tenn.: Abingdon Press, 1975); Jacob Neusner ed., *Understanding Rabbinic Judaism* (New York: KTAV Publishing House, 1974); Leo Baeck, *The Pharisees and Other Essays* (New York: Schocken Books, 1966); John Bowker, *Jesus and the Pharisees* (Cambridge: Cambridge University Press, 1973); John T. Pawlikowski, "On Renewing the Revolution of the Pharisees," *Cross Currents* 20, No. 4 (Fall 1970): 415–434; Michael Cook, "Jesus and the Pharisees—the Problem As It Stands Today," *Journal of Ecumenical Studies* 15, No. 3 (Summer 1978): 441–460.

17. Perrin, *The New Testament*, p. 171.

18. Neusner, *From Politics to Piety*, p. 13.

19. *Yoma*, (Talmudic tractate) 85b.

20. See the section of "Grace" in Montefiore and Loewe, eds., *Rabbinic Anthology*.

21. Sloyan, *Jesus in Focus*, pp. 27–34.

22. Most people learn negative attitudes toward Jews and Judaism from attending church. Where else are Jews likely to be a weekly discussion topic? For sociological confirmation of the point, see: Glock and Stark, *Christian Beliefs and Anti-Semitism*; Stark et al., *Wayward Shepherds*; and Quinley and Glock, *Anti-Semitism in America*.

23. In addition to E. P. Sanders's works cited above, the following are helpful: (1) *The Broken Wall*; *Israel and the Church*; *Ephesians* 2 vols., *The Anchor Bible*; "St. Paul—A Good Jew"; "Jews and Gentiles," pp. 241–267; "Conversion and Conversation", pp. 3–24; "Was Paul an Anti-Semite?" pp. 78–104. (2) J. Christiaan Beker, *Paul the Apostle; Paul's Apocalyptic Gospel*. (3) Davies, *Jewish and Pauline Studies; Paul and Rabbinic Judaism*; "Paul and the People of Israel," pp. 4–39. (4) Stendahl, *Paul Among Jews and Gentiles*. (5) Gaston, "Paul and the Torah," in Davies, ed., *Anti-Semitism and the Foundations of Christianity*, pp. 48–71.

24. Black, *Romans*, pp. 47–48.

25. Beker, *Paul the Apostle*, p. 339.

26. Ibid., p. 340.

27. Ibid., p. 344.

28. Ibid., p. 345.

29. Gaston, "Paul and the Torah," p. 58.
30. Ibid.
31. Ibid., p. 64.
32. Ibid., p. 65.
33. Ibid.
34. Stendahl, *Paul Among Jews and Gentiles*, p. 1.
35. Sanders, *Paul, the Law, and the Jewish People*, p. 20.
36. Stendahl, *Paul Among Jews and Gentiles*, p. 4.
37. Ibid., p. 9.
38. Ibid., p. 11.
39. Ibid., p. 26.
40. Ibid., p. 76.
41. Baum, "Introduction" to Rosemary R. Ruether, *Faith and Fratricide*, p. 3.
42. Baum, "Introduction."
43. Ibid., p. 6.
44. Ibid., p. 7.
45. Ibid., p. 8.
46. Ogden, *The Point of Christology*, pp. 93–94.
47. Ibid., p. 94.
48. Tracy, "Religious Values After the Holocaust: A Catholic View," in Peck, ed., *Jews and Christians After the Holocaust*, pp. 96–97.
49. Ruether, *Faith and Fratricide*, pp. 246–251.
50. Ibid., p. 246.
51. Ibid., p. 249.
52. Ibid., p. 253.
53. Borowitz, *Contemporary Christologies*, pp. 25–49.
54. Tillich, "A Final Conversation with Paul Tillich," in Friedlander, ed., *Out of the Whirlwind*, p. 519.
55. Pawlikowski, *Christ in the Light of the Christian-Jewish Dialogue*.
56. Ibid., p. 92.
57. Ibid., p. 93.
58. Ibid., p. 102.
59. Ibid., p. 103 (emphasis mine).
60. Ibid.
61. Ibid.
62. Ibid., p. 105.
63. Ibid.
64. Ibid., p. 106.
65. Ibid.
66. Ibid.
67. Ibid.
68. Ogden, *Christ Without Myth*, p. 145.
69. Pawlikowski, *Christ in the Light of the Christian-Jewish Dialogue*, pp. 103–104.
70. Eckardt with Alice L. Eckardt, *Long Night's Journey Into Day*, pp. 129–133.
71. Ibid., p. 130.
72. Ibid., p. 133.
73. Ibid., p. 150.
74. van Buren, *Discerning the Way*, and *A Christian Theology of the People of Israel*.

75. Ibid., p. 26.
76. Ibid., p. 33.
77. Ibid., p. 40.
78. Ibid., p. 156–157.
79. Rosenzweig, *Briefe* p. 668.

BIBLIOGRAPHY

Barrett, C. K. *A Commentary on the Epistle to the Romans*. New York: Harper, 1957.
———. *Essays on John*. Philadelphia: Westminster Press, 1982.
———. *Essays on Paul*. Philadelphia: Westminster Press, 1982.
———. *The Gospel According to St. John*. London: S.P.C.K., 1955.
———. *The Gospel of John and Judaism*. Philadelphia: Fortress Press, 1975.
Barth, Markus. *The Broken Wall: A Study of The Epistle to the Ephesians*. Chicago: Judson Press, 1959.
———. "Conversion and Conversation." *Interpretation* 17 (January 1963): 3–24.
———. "Dialogue Is Not Enough." *Journal of Ecumenical Studies* 4 (Winter 1967): 115–120.
———. "Die Einheit der Galater-und Epheserbriefs." *Theologische Zeitschrift* 32 (March/April, 1976): 78–91.
———. "Die Stellung des Paulus zu Gesetz u. Ordnung." *Evangelische Theologie* 33 (1973): 496–526.
———. *Ephesians*. 2 vols. *The Anchor Bible*. Garden City, N. Y.: Doubleday, 1974.
———. *Israel and the Church*. Richmond: John Knox, 1969.
———. *Jesus the Jew*. Atlanta: John Knox, 1978.
———. "Jews and Gentiles: The Social Character of Justification in Paul." *Journal of Ecumenical Studies* 5 (Spring 1968): 78–104.
———. "St. Paul—A Good Jew." *Horizons in Biblical Theology* 1 (1980): 7–45.
———. "Was Paul an Anti-Semite?" *Journal of Ecumenical Studies* 5 (Winter 1968): 78–104.
Baum, Gregory. *Is the New Testament Anti-Semitic?* New York: Paulist Press, 1965.
Beker, J. Christiaan. *Paul the Apostle: The Triumph of God in Life and Thought*. Philadelphia: Fortress Press 1980.
Black, Matthew. *Romans*. London: Marshall, Morgan and Scott, 1973.
Borowitz, Eugene B. *Contemporary Christologies: A Jewish Response*. New York: Paulist Press, 1980.
———. *Paul's Apocalyptic Gospel, The Coming Triumph of God*. Philadelphia: Fortress Press, 1982.
Brown, Raymond Edward. *Biblical Reflections on Crises Facing the Church*. New York: Paulist Press, 1975.
———. *The Community of the Beloved Disciple*. New York: Paulist Press, 1977.
———. *The Epistles of John*. Garden City, N. Y.: Doubleday, 1982. (*The Anchor Bible*.)
———. *The Gospel According to John*. Garden City, N. Y.: Doubleday, 1966, 1970. (*The Anchor Bible*.)
Cargas, Harry James. *A Christian Response to the Holocaust*. Denver: Stonehenge Books, 1982.
———. *In Conversation with Elie Wiesel*. New York: Paulist Press, 1976.

Croner, Helga. *Biblical Studies: Meeting Ground of Jews and Christians.* Ed. with Lawrence Boadt and Leon Klenicki. New York: Paulist Press, 1980.

———. *Christian Mission, Jewish Mission.* Ed. with Martin A. Cohen. New York: Paulist Press, 1982.

———. *Issues in the Jewish-Christian Dialogue: Jewish Perspectives on Covenant.* Ed. with Leon Klenicki. New York: Paulist Press, 1979.

———. *Stepping Stones to Further Jewish-Christian Relations: An Unabridged Collection of Christian Documents.* New York: Stimulus Books. 1977.

Davies, Alan T., ed. *Antisemitism and the Foundations of Christianity.* New York: Paulist Press, 1979.

Davies, William David. *Christian Origins and Judaism.* Philadelphia: Westminster Press, 1962.

———. *The Gospel and the Land: Early Christianity and Jewish Territorial Doctrine.* Berkeley: University of California Press, 1974.

———. *Introduction to Pharisaism.* Philadelphia: Fortress Press, 1967.

———. *Jewish and Pauline Studies.* Philadelphia: Fortress Press, 1983.

———. "Paul and the People of Israel." *New Testament Studies* 24 (1978): 4–39.

———. *Paul and Rabbinic Judaism.* London: S. P. C. K., 1948.

———. *Torah in the Messianic Age and/or the Age to Come.* Philadelphia: S.B.L., 1952.

Eckardt, A. Roy *Christianity and the Children of Israel.* Morningside Heights, N. Y.: King's Crown Press, 1948.

———. "Christian Response to the Endlösung." *Religion In Life* 47 (Spring 1978): 35–45.

———. "Christians and Jews: Along a Theological Frontier." *Encounter* 40 (Spring 1979): 89–127.

———. *Elder and Younger Brother.* New York: Schocken Books, 1967.

———. "Ha'Shoah as Christian Revolution: Toward the Liberation of the Divine Righteousness." *Quarterly Review* 2, No. 4 (Winter 1982): 52–67.

———. "The Holocaust: Christian and Jewish Responses." *Journal of the American Academy of Religion* 42 (1974): 453–469.

———. "How German Thinkers View the Holocaust." *Christian Century* 93 (17 March 1976): 249–252.

———. *Long Night's Journey into Day.* Detroit: Wayne State University Press, 1982.

———. "Recent Literature on Christian-Jewish Relations." *Journal of the American Academy of Religion* 49 (March 1981): 99–111.

———. "Trial of a Presidential Commission Confronting the Enigma of the Holocaust." *Encounter* 42 (Spring 1981): 103–114. With Alice Eckardt.

———. *Your People, My People.* New York: Quadrangle Press, 1974.

Eckardt, A. Roy, and Alice Eckardt. *Encounter with Israel: A Challenge to Conscience.* New York: Association Press, 1970.

Flannery, Edward H. *The Anguish of the Jews.* New York: Macmillan Co., 1965.

Gaston, Lloyd. "Paul and the Torah." In Alan T. Davies, ed., *Anti-Semitism and the Foundations of Christianity.* New York: Paulist Press, 1979, pp. 48–71.

Glock, Charles Y. *The Apathetic Majority: A Study Based on Public Responses to the Eichmann Trial.* With Gertrude J.Selzwick and Joe L. Spaeth. New York: Harper and Row, 1966.

————, with Rodney Stark. *Christian Beliefs and Anti-Semitism*. New York: Harper and Row, 1966.

————, with Bruce D. Foster, Rodney Stark, and Harold E. Quinley. *Wayward Shepherds: Prejudice and the Protestant Clergy*. New York: Harper and Row, 1971.

Greenberg, Irving. "Cloud of Smoke, Pillar of Fire: Judaism, Christianity, and Modernity After The Holocaust." In Eva Fleischner, ed. *Auschwitz: Beginning of a New Era?* New York: KTAV, 1977.

Hamerton-Kelly, Robert, and Robin Scroggs, eds. *Jews, Greeks, and Christians: Religious Cultures in Late Antiquity*. Leiden: E. J. Brill, 1976.

Holmgren, Frederick. *The God Who Cares: A Christian Looks at Judaism*. Atlanta: John Knox Press, 1979.

Isaac, Jules. *The Teaching of Contempt*. New York: Holt, Rinehart and Winston, 1964.

Klein, Charlotte. *Anti-Judaism in Christian Theology*. Translated by Edward Quinn. Philadelphia: Fortress Press, 1978.

Knight, George A. F., ed. *Jews and Christians: Preparation for Dialogue*. Philadelphia: Westminster Press, 1965.

————. *Law and Grace: Must a Christian Keep the Law of Moses?* Philadelphia: Westminster Press, 1962.

Koenig, John. *Jews and Christians in Dialogue: New Testament Foundations*. Philadelphia: Westminster Press, 1978.

Lacoque, Andre. *But As For Me: The Question of Election in the Life of God's People Today*. Atlanta: John Knox Press, 1979

Littell, Franklin H. *The Crucifixion of the Jews*. New York: Harper and Row, 1975.

————, ed., with Hubert H. Locke. *The German Church Struggle and the Holocaust*. Detroit: Wayne State University Press, 1974.

————. *The German Phoenix: Men and Movements in the Church in Germany*. Garden City, N. Y.: Doubleday 1960.

————, ed. with Irene G. Shur and Marvin E. Wolfgang. *Reflections on the Holocaust: Historical, Philosophical, and Educational Dimensions*. Philadelphia: American Academy of Political and Social Science, 1980.

————, ed. "Religious Liberty in the Crossfire of Creeds." *Journal of Ecumenical Studies* 14, No. 4 (Fall 1977).

Moltmann, Jürgen, with Phinn E. Lapide. *Jewish Monotheism and Christian Trinitarian Doctrine: A Dialogue*. Translated by Leonard Swidler. Philadelphia: Fortress Press, 1981.

Montefiore, C. G., and H. Loewe, eds. *A Rabbinic Anthology*. New York: Schocken Books, 1974.

Moore, George Foot. "Christian Writers on Judaism." *Harvard Theological Review* 14, No. 3 (July 1921): 197–254.

Ogden, Schubert M. *Christ Without Myth*. New York: Harper and Brothers, 1961.

————. *The Point of Christology*. San Francisco: Harper and Row, 1982.

Parkes, James William. *Anti-semitism*. Chicago: Quadrangle Books, 1964.

————. *The Conflict of the Church and the Synagogue*. New York: Harmon Press, 1934.

————. *The Foundations of Judaism and Christianity*. Chicago: Quadrangle Books, 1960.

————. *A History of the Palestine from 135 A.D. to Modern Times*. New York: Oxford University Press, 1949.

————. *The Jew and His Neighbour*. London: SCM Press, 1938.

————. *The Jewish Problem in the Modern World*. London: T. Butterworth, Ltd., 1939.

————. *Judaism and Christianity*. Chicago: University of Chicago Press, 1948.

————. *The Story of Jerusalem*. London: Cresset, 1950.

Pawlikowski, John T. "Anti-Zionism – Anti-Semitism: Fact or Fable?" *Worldview* 19 (January/February 1976): 15–19.

————. *Christ in the Light of the Christian-Jewish Dialogue*. New York: Paulist Press, 1982.

————. "The Holocaust: Its Implications for the Church and Society Problematic." *Encounter* 42 (Spring 1981): 143–154.

————. "Martin Luther and Judaism: Paths Toward Theological Reconciliation." *Journal of the American Academy of Religion* 43 (1975): 681–693.

————. *Sinai and Calvary*. Beverly Hills, Calif.: Benziger, 1976.

————. *What Are They Saying About Christian-Jewish Relations*. New York: Paulist Press, 1980.

Perrin, Norman. *The New Testament: An Introduction*. New York: Harcourt Brace Jovanovich, 1974.

Quinley, Harold, and Charles Y. Glock. *Anti-Semitism in America*. New York: Free Press, 1979.

Rosenzweig, Franz. *Briefe*. Berlin, 1935.

Roth, John K. *A Consuming Fire: Encounters with Elie Wiesel and the Holocaust*. Atlanta: John Knox Press, 1979.

Rousseau, Richard W., S. J., ed. *Christianity and Judaism: The Deepening Dialogue*. Montrose, Pa.: Ridge Row Press, 1983.

Ruether, Rosemary Radford. "Anti-semitism and the State of Israel: Some Principles for Christians." *Christianity and Crisis* 33 (1973): 240–244.

————. "Anti-semitism in Christian Theology." *Theology Today* 30 (1974): 365–381.

————. "Christian Anti-semitism and the Dilemma of Zionism." *Christianity and Crisis* 32 (1972): 91–94.

————. *Faith and Fratricide*. New York: Seabury Press, 1974.

————. "Israel and the Land: The Claims of Justice." *Christianity and Crisis* 38 (1978): 147–151.

————. "Judaism and Christianity: Two Fourth-Century Religions." *Studies in Religion, Sciences Religieuses* 2, No. 1 (1972–73): 1–10.

————. "Left Hand of God in the Theology of Karl Barth." *Journal of Religious Thought* 25, No. 1 (1968–69): 3–26.

Sanders, E. P. *Paul, the Law, and the Jewish People*. Philadelphia: Fortress Press, 1983.

————. *Paul and Palestinian Judaism: A Comparison of Patterns of Religion*. Philadelphia: Fortress Press, 1977.

Sloyan, Gerard S. *Jesus in Focus: A Life in Its Setting*. Mystic, Conn.: Twenty-Third Publications, 1983.

Stark, Rodney, et al. *Wayward Shepherds*. New York: Harper and Row, 1971.

————. *Jesus on Trial*. Philadelphia: Fortress Press, 1973.

Stendahl, Krister. *Paul Among Jews and Gentiles*. Philadelphia: Fortress Press, 1976.

————. *The School of St. Matthew and the Use of the Old Testament*. Philadelphia: Fortress Press, 1968.

Thoma, Clemens. *A Christian Theology of Judaism*. Translated by Helga Croner. New York: Paulist Press, 1980.

Tillich, Paul. "A Final Conversation with Paul Tillich." In Albert Friedlander, ed. *Out of the Whirlwind: A Reader of Holocaust Literature*. New York: Schocken Books, 1976.

Tracy, David. "Religious Values After the Holocaust: A Catholic View." In A. Peck, ed. *Jews and Christians After the Holocaust*. Philadelphia: Fortress Press, 1982.

van Buren, Paul M. *The Burden of Freedom: Americans and the God of Israel*. New York: Seabury Press, 1976.

————. *A Christian Theology of the People of Israel*. New York: Seabury Press.

————. *Discerning the Way: A Theology of the Jewish Christian Reality*. New York: Seabury Press, 1980.

Wiesel, Elie. *A Jew Today*. New York: Vintage Books, 1979.

Wilken, Robert L. *Aspects of Wisdom in Judaism and Early Christianity*. Notre Dame, Ind.: University of Notre Dame Press, 1975.

————. *Judaism and the Early Christian Mind*. New Haven, Conn.: Yale University Press, 1971.

————, with Wayne A. Meeks. *Jews and Christians in Antioch in the First Four Centuries of the Common Era*. Missoula, Mont.: Scholars Press, 1978.

Williamson, Clark M. "The *Adversus Judaeos* Tradition in Christian Theology." *Encounter* 39, No. 3 (Summer 1978): 273–296.

————. "Anti-Judaism in Process Christologies?" *Process Studies* 10, Nos. 3–4 (Fall-Winter 1980): 73–92.

————. "Christ Against the Jews: Jon Sobrino's Christology." *Encounter* 40, No. 4 (Autumn 1979): 403–412.

————. *Has God Rejected His People? Anti-Judaism in the Christian Church*. Nashville, Tenn. Abingdon Press, 1982.

————. "Process Hermeneutics and Christianity's Post-Holocaust Re-interpretation of Itself." *Process Studies* 12, No. 2 (Summer 1982): 77–93.

————. "Things Do Go Wrong (and Right)." *Journal of Religion* 63, No. 1 (January 1983): 44–56.

Zabel, James A. *Nazism and the Pastors*. Missoula, Mont.: Scholars Press, 1976.

About the Contributors

LEONARD BARRETT is Professor of Religion and Anthropology in the Department of Religion, Temple University. Among his books are *Soul-Force*: *African Roots in Afro-American Religion*, which was nominated by the American Book Award Association in 1975, *The Rastafarians*, and *The Sun and the Drum*: *African Roots in Jamaican Folk Tradition*. He has also published many articles in the field of religion and anthropology, including a major article in *The American Encyclopedia of Religion* (1986).

CARL BECKER is Assistant Professor of Asian Studies Curriculum Research and Design, University of Hawaii. He has taught at Southern Illinois University, Osaka University (Osaka, Japan), and Tenri University (Nara, Japan). His publications include *Kanji Finder Index, Japan*: *My Teacher, My Love*, and *Christianity*: *History and Philosophy*, as well as articles in *Anabiosis, Journal of Near-Death Studies, The Eastern Buddhist, Soundings, Ming Studies*, and *Journal of the Philosophy of Sport*.

GUSTAVO BENAVIDES is currently associated with the Department of Religion, Villanova University. His areas of research include religion and politics, comparative mysticism, and religions of India. He has contributed chapters for the following books: *Buddhist and Western Philosophy, Buddhist and Western Psychology, Sein und Nichts in der abendländischen Mystik*, and *The Many Faces of Religion and Society*. He is currently working on a book on the study of mysticism, to be published by Greenwood Press.

PATRICK BURKE is Professor of Religion at Temple University. He was previously associated with the University of Iowa, before which he held pastoral positions at the Parish of Maryborough, Queensland, Australia (1958–

61) and at the Parish of Trudering, Munich, W. Germany, as a Catholic priest. His major works include *The Fragile Universe* and *The Reluctant Vision*, in addition to professional articles and books editing. *The Reluctant Vision* was awarded "Best Book of the Year" by the College Theology Society in 1975, and was simultaneously published in German, entitled *Erste Schritte in der Religionsphilosophie*.

WILLIAM R. DARROW is Assistant Professor of Islamic and Middle Eastern Studies at Williams College. His research interests include the religions of pre-Islamic Iran, Islamic intellectual and social history, contemporary thought in the Muslim world, as well as methodology in the study of religions.

JOHN L. ESPOSITO is Professor of Religious Studies in the College of the Holy Cross. He has been a faculty associate of Oxford's St. Anthony's College and Harvard's Center for Middle Eastern Studies. His research has resulted in several books: *Islam and Politics*, *Voices of Resurgent Islam*, *Women in Muslim Family Life*, *Islam in Transition: Muslim Perspectives*, and *Islam and Development: Religion and Sociopolitical Change*.

JANE HURST teaches courses in Comparative Religion, and Religion and Psychology at Gallaudet College, Washington, D.C. She continues her research into new religious movements in America with emphasis on New Age Religions.

T.P. KASULIS is Associate Professor of Philosophy and Religion and head of the humanities division at Northland College in Ashland, Wisconsin. He has been a Japan Foundation Fellow, a Harvard Mellon Faculty Fellow, and an NEH (National Endowment for the Humanities) Fellow. His publications include *Zen Action/Zen Person* and numerous articles and reviews in a variety of major scholarly journals.

NATHAN KATZ is Associate Professor of Religious Studies at the University of South Florida in Tampa. He serves on the editorial boards of *USF Monographs in Religion and Public Policy* and *The Tibet Journal* and on the advisory boards of the AAR Buddhism Group, the International Centre for Ethnic Studies (Sri Lanka), the U.S. Committee for the U.N. Lumbini Development Project, and the Tibet Society, Inc. He previously taught at Williams College, Naropa Institute and the University of Peradeniya (Sri Lanka). He is the author of *Buddhist Images of Human Perfection* in addition to scores of essays, translations, and reviews in scholarly journals.

NORA LEVIN is Associate Professor of Modern Jewish History, and Director of the Holocaust Archive for Gratz College, Philadelphia. She was Visiting Professor at the University of Haifa in 1981. Her books include *The Holocaust: The Destruction of European Jewry, 1933–1945*, *Jewish Socialist Movements*:

1871–1917, and *Endangered Minority: Soviet Jewry Since 1917*. She is Contributing Editor of *Sh'ma*.

FRANKLIN H. LITTELL is Professor Emeritus, in the Department of Religion, Temple University. He is also Adjunct Professor in the Institute of Contemporary Jewry, Hebrew University. He founded the Annual Scholars' Conference on the Church Struggle and the Holocaust. He is Founder and Honorary Chairman of the Anne Frank Institute of Philadelphia, a member of the U.S. Holocaust Memorial Council, and has served as a member of the board of Yad Vashem in Jerusalem. He is author of *An Introduction to Sectarian Protestantism*, *From State Church to Pluralism*, *The Free Church*, *The German Church Struggle and the Holocaust*, *The Crucification of the Jews*, *Reflections on the Holocaust*, and *Religious Liberty in the Crossfire of Creeds*.

PAUL MOJZES is Professor of Religious Studies at Rosemont College. He is also secretary of Christians Associated for Relationships with Eastern Europe and member of The Europe Committee of the Division for Overseas Ministries of N.C.C. He is author of *Christian-Marxist Dialogue in Eastern Europe*, editor of *Occasional Papers on Religion in Eastern Europe* and *Varieties of Christian-Marxist Dialogue*, co-editor of *Society and Original Sin* and *Journal of Ecumenical Studies* and has published many articles in various journals.

JOSEPH MURPHY teaches courses in African and Afro-American religions at Georgetown University. He is author of *Santeria: An African Way of Wisdom*, and has published several articles on the myths and symbols of the Afro-Cuban religion, *santeria*.

HOWARD L. PARSONS is Professor and Chairman, Department of Philosophy, University of Bridgeport. He has taught at University of Southern California, University of Illinois, University of Tennessee, Teachers College of Columbia University, Coe College, Idaho State College, Victoria College (Canada), and Moscow State University. He is a board member of the American Institute for Marxist Studies and of the Foundation for Philosophy of Creativity, and Vice-president of the Society for the Philosophical Study of Marxism. He is author of *Humanism and Marx's Thought*, *Christianity in the Soviet Union*, *Man Today—Problems, Values, and Fulfillment*, *Man East and West—Essays in East-West Philosophy*, *Self, Global Issues, and Ethics*, *Marx and Engels on Ecology*, *Marxism, Christianity, and Human Values*, *Buddhism as Humanism*, and *Man in the Modern World*.

ARVIND SHARMA currently teaches in the Department of Religious Studies at the University of Sidney, Australia. He has also taught at Temple University and McGill University in visiting positions. His books include *The Hindu Scriptural Value System and India's Economic Development* and *Religious Ferment in Modern India.* He is Editor of the *Journal of Studies in the Bhagavad Gita* and *Religious Traditions*, and Associate Editor of the *Journal of South Asian Literature.*

GERARD S. SLOYAN is Professor and Chairman of the Department of Religion at Temple University. He was formerly head of the Department of Religion at the Catholic University of America. He has served as priest of the Diocese of Trenton, N. J. and later parish assistant. He is author of *Jesus on Trial, A Commentary on the New Lectionary*, and *Is Christ the End of the Law?* and has published about two hundred scholarly and popular articles in journals like *The Catholic Bibliographical Quarterly*, *Horizons*, and *Theology Today.*

TAMARA SONN is a faculty member of the Department of Religion, Temple University. She was formerly associated with the School of Religion, University of Iowa. She is author of the forthcoming book *Bandali al-Jawzi's History of Intellectual Movements in Islam*, and a contributor for the second volume of *Postwar Movements and Issues in World Religions.*

STEPHEN D. SOWLE is currently pursuing his doctorate in political theory at the Johns Hopkins University. He has worked as a policy analyst for the Coalition for a New Military and Foreign Policy.

CLARK WILLIAMSON is Professor of Theology at Christian Theological Seminary. He has served as Visiting Professor at the School of Theology in Claremont, California. He has taught at Transylvania University and Downtown Evening Division of the University of Chicago, before joining the faculty of Christian Theological Seminary. He was Interim Minister at University Church of the Disciples of Christ, Chicago, and Assistant Dean at the Disciples Divinity House. He held a student pastorate in Illinois. He served as special editor and advisor for the third volume of Paul Tillich's *Systematic Theology.* In addition to two books, *God is Never Absent* and *Has God Rejected His People?*, he has published numerous articles and critical reviews in *Encounter*, *Criterion*, *The Journal of Religion*, *The Evangelical Review*, *Church History*, *Process Studies*, and *Interpretation.* He is Editor of *Encounter.*

DAVID YU is Professor of Religion and Philosophy at Maryville College, Tennessee. He is author of *Guide to Chinese Religion*, and co-author of *Religions of the World.* He has contributed many articles in the fields of history of religions and Chinese philosophy and religion. Currently, he is working on a book entitled *The Mythical Theme of Chaos in Chinese Thought.*

Index

About the Editors

CHARLES WEI-HSUN FU is Professor of Buddhism and Far Eastern Thought at Temple University. He is the author of numerous books and articles on Eastern and Western thought.

GERHARD E. SPIEGLER is Professor of Religion at Temple University. Formerly Vice-President of Academic Affairs at Temple, Spiegler is a scholar of modern European religious thought and contemporary Christian theology.